The Management of Sport
of Sport
Its Foundation and Application

The Management of Sport
Its Foundation and Application

BONNIE L. PARKHOUSE, Ph.D.
Temple University

EDITOR

With the Endorsement of
The National Association for Sport and Physical Education

St. Louis Baltimore Boston Chicago London Philadelphia Sydney Toronto

Mosby
Year Book
Dedicated to Publishing Excellence

Publisher: Edward F. Murphy
Acquisition editor: Vicki Van Ry
Editorial assistant: Cathy Waller
Project manager: John A. Rogers
Production editor: Catherine M. Vale
Manuscript editor: Joseph P. Lawler
Production: Celeste Clingan
Designer: Liz Fett

Printed in the United States of America

Mosby–Year Book, Inc.
11830 Westline Industrial Drive
St. Louis, MO 63146

Library of Congress Cataloging in Publication Data

The management of sport : its foundation and application / Bonnie L.
  Parkhouse, editor.
       p.   cm.
    Includes bibliographical references and index.
    ISBN 0-8016-3812-7
    1. Sports—Organization and administration—Study and teaching—
United States.   I. Parkhouse, Bonnie L.
GV713.M35   1991
796'.06—dc20
                                                    90-28465
                                                    CIP

GW/RRD 9 8 7 6 5 4 3 2 1

Preface

This book represents a "labor of love" for me personally. When approached by Mosby–Year Book, Inc. and officials of the National Association for Sport and Physical Education (NASPE) to serve as editor of this project, I immediately accepted the challenge. Although it is virtually impossible to exhaustively describe the body of knowledge that constitutes a profession in one volume, *The Management of Sport: Its Foundation and Application* makes a significant contribution to the sport management literature.

In the era of the fitness entrepreneur, sport has become even more significant (especially financially) and pervasive in our society. This multibillion-dollar industry places unique demands on its personnel and increasingly requires specialized training. Jobs in the sport industry involve myriad skills applicable to the sport setting and specific to the increasingly complex and multifaceted areas it represents. As a result, a new breed of specialists has emerged. Sport management is now recognized as a legitimate field of study in colleges and universities throughout the United States, Canada, and other countries. Lacking has been textbooks and related resources in this endeavor. *The Management of Sport: Its Foundation and Application* is the most comprehensive compilation of subject matter published to date for the sport management profession.

AUDIENCE

In increasing numbers, students with a wide variety of backgrounds are choosing a course of study in sport management. Our intention with this book is to cater to this changing and rapidly growing audience.

Also, although this book was primarily written for third- and fourth-year undergraduate and postgraduate students, instructors at other levels are encouraged to review its content for potential use as well. **Practitioners will also find it to be a valuable resource.**

FEATURES
Organization

This book uses a unique approach in addressing the substantive aspects of the profession by presenting the theoretical foundations first and then the subsequent application of these principles.

Content

Topics never before addressed in a text of this nature include research and theory; sport economics; sports law specific to torts, contracts, product liability, employment relations, and trademark licensing; ethics; future trends; and an overview of curricular development. The case study method used in the application chapters is also a unique pedagogical approach.

Pedagogy

This text uses many pedagogical features to aid students' comprehension of many diverse topics.

- Each author has indicated **key terms** with which the student will become familiar while reading the chapter. These terms are located at the beginning of each chapter, as well as in bold face type when they are discussed within the chapter.

- Each major section ends with a **Concept Check** that highlights the main discussion.
- A succinct enumerated **Summary** emphasizes the key points in each chapter.
- Each chapter includes a complete list of **References.** It is recommended that students read these references carefully for suppplemental information.
- **Review Questions and Issues, Case Studies,** and **Exercises** give students further insight as to how to apply the theoretical principles.

ACKNOWLEDGEMENTS

I would like to express my gratitude to all who contributed to *The Management of Sport: Its Foundation and Application.* Vicki Van Ry, the acquisition editor of this text, made an invaluable contribution to this work. Her tireless effort, expertise, and professionalism is greatly appreciated. My gratitude also goes to Katie Vale, production editor of this book. She single-handedly kept all of us on schedule under very challenging circumstances.

The ultimate success of a book is contingent on the quality of subject matter presented. Drawing on the expertise of a "Who's Who" list of authors and contributors, this work—as forementioned—is the most comprehensive compilation of subject matter ever published for the sport management profession. Without question, the authors made a commitment to excellence and set other priorities aside to meet extremely demanding deadlines.

As indicated on the cover of this text, this book is endorsed by the National Association for Sport and Physical Education (NASPE). Furthermore, several members of the NASPE Task Force on Sport Management and the North American Society for Sport Management (NASSM) served as authors or contributors.

The contributing authors and I greatly appreciate the insight provided by reviewers of this text. Their suggestions and comments were extremely helpful. Also, their cooperation in responding to second and third draft manuscripts immediately with little or no advance notice is commendable:

Scott Branvold, University of Oklahoma
Stan Brassie, University of Georgia
Stephen Cone, Keene State College
Gary Gray, Iowa State University
Brad Hatfield, University of Maryland
Peter Thomsen, University of Massachusetts
Suzanne Wingate, State University of New York—Cortland
Rollin Wright, University of Illinois

A special thanks from Glenn Wong goes to Carol Barr, University of Massachusetts—Amherst, for her research and writing assistance. He would also like to thank Margaret Kearney for her editorial assistance and Maureen Kocot for her help in the preparation of Chapters 6 and 13.

I am especially grateful to Scott Branvold, University of Oklahoma, for significant input that enhanced the quality of several individual chapters. Stan Brassie, University of Georgia; Gordon Olafson, University of Windsor; and Rollin Wright, University of Illinois also made major contributions to individual chapters. I would also like to express my appreciation for information provided by Jim Mason, University of Texas—El Paso, and Dan Soucie, University of Ottawa.

Bonnie L. Parkhouse, *Editor*

Editor

BONNIE L. PARKHOUSE
Temple University

Bonnie L. Parkhouse, Professor, received a Ph.D. in Administration from the University of Minnesota. Previous faculty appointments include the University of Southern California and California State University, Fullerton. Over 15 of her studies have been published in distinguished research journals. Numerous articles she has written have appeared in trade and commercial publications, and she is the senior author of two previous books.

Dr. Parkhouse is a member of the editorial boards for the *Journal of Sport Management* and *Quest*. She is also a member of the NASPE Task Force on Sport Management. On invitation, she has served as a consultant in sport management curricular matters at numerous institutions in the United States, as well as in England and Australia. Dr. Parkhouse is recognized as a progenitor of sport management curricula and theory; her publications are frequently cited in related articles by other authors.

Contributing Authors

WILLIAM R. BATTLE, III
The Collegiate Licensing Company

William Battle is President of the Atlanta office of the Collegiate Licensing Company, a company dedicated to the administration, development, and enforcement of several collegiate trademark licensing programs. In a joint venture with International Collegiate Enterprises, Inc., the Collegiate Licensing Company is the exclusive licensing agent for over 120 universities, colleges, bowls, and conferences. The Consortium has become a major force in the trademark licensing industry. Mr. Battle is also President of NASCAR Properties, the licensing arm for the National Association of Stock Car Automobile Racing.

Before developing the collegiate licensing industry, Mr. Battle spent 7 years as the head football coach at the University of Tennessee. Mr. Battle has also served on the board of directors and advisory boards of several corporations.

PATRICIA A. BEITEL
The University of Tennessee—Knoxville

Patricia A. Beitel, Associate Professor, has written many articles on the psychology, pedagogy, and management of sport. She maintains leadership and membership in state, regional, national, and international organizations.

OTHO G. BENDIT
University of Notre Dame

Otho Bendit's experience includes 3 years in public accounting, 7 years in hotel accounting, and 41 years as a member of the Administrative Accounting staff at the University of Notre Dame in Indiana. He is currently the Supervisor of General Accounting at Notre Dame. He is a member of the National Association of Accountants, the Central Association of College and University Business Officers, and the National Association of College and University Business Officers.

MARY DALE BLANTON
The University of Tennessee—Knoxville

Mary Dale Blanton, Assistant Professor, has given workshops in specialty areas of arts/crafts, stress managment, and recreation programming. Her program area includes recreation and leisure studies, and her primary teaching areas are recreation programming, program administration, internship and practicum supervision, and therapeutic recreation.

BARBARA BOTSCH BAILEY
The Collegiate Licensing Company

Barbara B. Bailey accepted her initial position with The Collegiate Licensing Company after receiving her undergraduate degree from Duke University in 1986. As Director of Promotions, Ms. Bailey is responsible for coordinating local, regional, and national promotions with universities and colleges throughout the country. Ms. Bailey is also very active in the development of on-campus consumer awareness campaigns, retailer incentive programs, and internal and external corporate relations.

SCOTT BRANVOLD
University of Oklahoma

Scott Branvold is an Assistant Professor in the Department of Health, Physical Education, and Recreation at the University of Oklahoma, with teaching responsibilities primarily in the university's graduate Sport Management program; his courses include those on legal issues, organizational theory, and sport sociology. He has been involved in sport as an athlete, coach, facility manager, and sports information director. He has taught sport management for the past 5 years at Robert Morris College and at the University of Oklahoma. A charter member of the North American Society for Sport Management (NASSM), he has presented papers at the American Alliance for Health, Physical Education, Recreation, and Dance (AAHPERD); NASSM; and the International Sports Business Conference.

PACKIANATHAN CHELLADURAI
The University of Western Ontario

Packianathan "Chella" Chelladurai holds the degrees of B.Com. and D.P.E. from the University of Madras, India; M.A. in Physical Education from the University of Western Ontario; and M.A.Sc. and Ph.D. in Management Science from the University of Waterloo, Canada. He has taught and coached basketball and volleyball at the university, as well as at provincial and national levels for over 2 decades while in India. A corresponding member of the Academy of Physical Education, Dr. Chelladurai also currently serves as the editor of the *Journal of Sport Management*. Dr. Chelladurai's more than 50 publications include books, chapters in textbooks, and numerous journal articles.

ANNIE CLEMENT
Cleveland State University

Annie Clement, Professor and Director of Sport Management, Cleveland State University, holds a Ph.D. from the University of Iowa and a J.D. from Cleveland State University. She is a member of the Ohio Supreme Court.

Dr. Clement has authored the books *Law in Sport and Physical Activity, The Teaching of Physical Activity,* and *Equity in Physical Education.* A sought-after speaker and writer, she has published works in sport and physical activity literature and in bar reviews.

Dr. Clement is a recipient of both the National Association for Sport and Physical Education Joy of Effort Award and the American Jurisprudence Award for Excellent Achievement in the Study of Business Associations; she was also the 1988-1989 President of the National Association for Sport and Physical Education (NASPE).

LARRY DeBROCK
University of Illinois

Larry DeBrock is currently an Associate Professor of Economics at the University of Illinois in Urbana—Champaign. A member of the American Economic Association, he has won several teaching awards at the University of Illinois. His research is in the area of industrial organization, as well as health economics. He has also published work on economic problems in Major League Baseball.

JOY T. DeSENSI
The University of Tennessee, Knoxville

Joy T. DeSensi is currently an Associate Professor in the department of Human Performance and Sport Studies. She holds an Ed.D. from the University of North Carolina at Greensboro and currently teaches graduate and undergraduate courses in sport sociology and sport management. She has published in the areas of sport management, sport sociology, and sport philosophy and has made numerous presentations at the international, national, district, and state levels. Dr. DeSensi has held major offices in professional organizations and is one of the founders of the North American Society for Sport Management and will serve as the Associate Editor of the *Journal of Sport Management*.

LAWRENCE W. FIELDING
University of Louisville

Larry Fielding received a Ph.D. in Sport History from the University of Maryland. He is Chairman of the Department of Health, Physical Education, and Recreation at the University of Louisville; his research areas include history of the sporting goods industry, history of Civil War sport, and organization theory.

JED FRIEND
U.S. Sports Acrobatics Federation

Jed Friend holds a Ph.D. in Sport Management and Sport Psychology. A former Professor of Sport Management at Rice University, he is the Chief Operating Officer and Executive Director of the U.S. Sports Acrobatics Federation (USSAF) located in Colorado Springs, Colorado. He has served as consultant to both the Houston Astros and the Houston Rockets organizations.

DIANNA P. GRAY
Indiana University

Dianna P. Gray, Assistant Professor, received a Ph.D. from The Ohio State University. Her research focuses on consumer demographics and marketing effectiveness, particularly in college sport organizations. Since 1985 she has taught at the university level and currently is serving as the Coordinator of Sport Marketing and Management at Indiana. In addition to teaching, Dr. Gray has been a consultant to various sport organizations. She has presented papers at a number of national and regional conferences, and her work has been published in various journals.

TERRY R. HAGGERTY
The Pennsylvania State University

Terry R. Haggerty, Associate Professor, holds the degrees of B.A. in Biology and B.P.H.E. (Queen's University), M.A. in Physical Education and a Diploma in Education (The University of Western Ontario), and a Ph.D. in Educational Administration (State University of New York at Buffalo). Dr. Haggerty's experience in sport includes the positions of intercollegiate athlete in football and basketball, high school and university coach, business manager of intercollegiate athletics, a Special Olympics volunteer administrator, and a university professor in both Canada and the United

States. He has served on the Board of Directors of The North American Society for Sport Management and is the author or coauthor of monographs, chapters, and research articles.

STEPHEN P. HOULIHAN
Attorney, The New England

Stephen P. Houlihan received his B.B.A. in Management, cum laude, from the University of Notre Dame and his J.D. from Boston College Law School.

Mr. Houlihan began his professional career in the Tax Department of Coopers & Lybrand in Boston, Massachusetts, where he earned his CPA designation. After leaving Coopers & Lybrand, he served as Assistant Counsel of Estate and Business Planning for State Mutual Life Insurance Company and then as Senior Consultant for New England Financial Advisors, a subsidiary of The New England. Most recently, he was an Assistant Professor of Sport Management at the University of Massachusetts and was also engaged in the private practice of law as a principal in United Sports Advisor's, Inc., a sports representation firm. He rejoined The New England in July of 1990 as an attorney in the Business and Individual Planning Section of the Law Department.

DENNIE R. KELLEY
The University of Tennessee—Knoxville

Dennie R. Kelley, Assistant Professor, is active in state, regional, and national physical education and sport management professional associations. She has written articles in the areas of sport management and sport pedagogy and is co-director of sport management program areas at The University of Tennessee—Knoxville.

LINDA S. KOEHLER
University of the Pacific

Linda S. Koehler is currently an Assistant Professor and the Director of the Sport Management Program at the University of the Pacific in Stockton, California. She is the 1990-1991 President of the North American Society for Sport Management and is a member of the editorial board for the *Journal of Sport Management*. Her professional membership includes the American Alliance for Health, Physical Education, Recreation, and Dance; National Association for Sport and Physical Education; the Association for Fitness in Business; and the Western Society for Physical Education of College Women.

KEITH W. LAMBRECHT
Northern Illinois University

Keith W. Lambrecht received a B.S. in Health and Physical Education and an M.S. in Physical Education with an emphasis in Athletic Administration from the University of Wisconsin—La Crosse. He earned his Ph.D. from Oregon State University with emphasis in Sport Studies and Business Management.

Dr. Lambrecht is currently an Assistant Professor of Sport Management in the Department of Physical Education at Northern Illinois University where he has initiated a master's degree program in sport management. He has authored articles and has made numerous presentations on the competencies required of sport and athletic club managers. He has also held other positions in teaching and coaching at both the secondary and college levels, as well as serving as President of a sport manufacturers' agents firm. Dr. Lambrecht is also engaged part-time in a private sport consulting practice.

BRENDA G. PITTS
University of Louisville

Brenda Pitts received an Ed.D. in Physical Education with a specialization in Sport Administration from the University of Alabama. Director of the Sport Administration program at the University of Louisville, Dr. Pitts has taught many courses in the areas of sport marketing and sport management. Among other career accomplishments, she played professional basketball with the Milwaukee Does and the Minnesota Fillies.

BRUCE B. SIEGAL, Esq.
The Collegiate Licensing Company

Bruce Siegal received a B.A., cum laude, in Pre-Law from the University of Alabama in 1982. He obtained a J.D. from the University of Alabama School of Law in 1986.

Mr. Siegal is an attorney specializing in sports trademark licensing. He is Corporate Counsel for The Collegiate Licensing Company, where he oversees the protection and enforcement of the trademark rights of the colleges, universities, and post-season bowls that are members of the licensing consortium, and he also prepares and negotiates license agreements.

His professional affiliations include the State Bar of Georgia, where he is a member of the Patent, Trademark & Copyright Law Section, Corporate Counsel Committee, Bar Media Conference Committee and Younger Lawyers Section; the United States Trademark Association, where he serves on the Licensing Committee; the Atlanta Bar Association; and the American Bar Association, where he is a member of the Patent, Trademark & Copyright Section.

WILLIAM A. SUTTON
DelWilber and Associates, St. Louis, Missouri

William A. Sutton is currently Vice-President, Properties Division, DelWilber and Associates, and also holds an adjunct faculty appointment in Sports Administration at the University of South Carolina. Before assuming his present position, he served as Coordinator of the Sport Management Program at The Ohio State University and also as an Assistant Professor of Sport Management at Robert Morris College. Dr. Sutton's area of specialization is the marketing of sport, particularly with regard to professional and collegiate programs and subsequent attendance factors and fan attitudes. He has served as a consultant and researcher for a number of colleges, professional basketball and baseball teams, and sport marketing companies. A past president of the North American Society for Sport Management (NASSM), Dr. Sutton has made numerous presentations and his work has been published in leading sport journals. Dr. Sutton is co-author of a sport marketing text published in late 1990.

BETTY VAN DER SMISSEN
Michigan State University

Betty van der Smissen served for 9 years as Director of the School of Health, Physical Education, and Recreation, Bowling Green State University (BGSU). She has given leadership and support to the sport management program, including a major symposium on sport management. She also has taught legal aspects to sport management majors for 10 years. She wrote the chapter on Directions of Sport Management in *Trends in Physical Education.*

Dr. van der Smissen has been involved extensively in future directions and has particular professional insights to the application of data related to societal and professional directions. She has been involved, both at Penn State—where she taught before going to BGSU—and BGSU, with all-university strategic planning and with both the camping movement and recreation and parks curriculum revisions nationally in leadership roles influencing directions for the future. Dr. van der Smissen is presently Chair/Professor, Department of Park and Recreation Resources, Michigan State University.

BRUCE WATKINS
University of Michigan

Bruce Watkins, Associate Professor, received a Ph.D. from the University of Kansas. His research focuses on understanding by children and adolescents about athletic performance and athletic excellence, and on how beliefs are affected by age, sex, and competitive experiences. He also studies the impact of national and international telecommunications policies on televised sports programming.

GLENN M. WONG
University of Massachusetts—Amherst

Glenn M. Wong is the Department Head of the Sport Management Program at the University of Massachusetts at Amherst, where he is an Associate Professor. He also serves as Adjunct Professor in the University of Massachusetts Labor Relations Program. He holds a B.S. from Brandeis University, where he was captain of the basketball team, and a J.D. from Boston College Law School. A member of the Massachusetts Bar and the Labor Arbitration Panel of the American Arbitration Association, Professor Wong specializes in the area of sports law. He is the author of *Essentials of Amateur Sports Law* and co-author of *Law and Business of the Sports Industries.* He has written numerous law review articles and currently authors a monthly column "The Sports Law Report" for *Athletic Business* magazine.

Professor Wong has been an invited speaker at over 50 national and local conferences on sports law and labor relations issues. He is a consultant for various athletic organizations and has served as a salary arbitrator for Major League Baseball.

Contents in Brief

Contents

PART I

Overview of Sport Management

CHAPTER 1

Definition, Evolution, and Curriculum

Bonnie L. Parkhouse

In this chapter, you will become familiar with the following terms:

Sport management	Sport business
Sport administration	Foundation areas
Athletic administration	Applied areas
Sport vs. sports	

Overview

Sport has become a dominant influence in American society. No single aspect of our culture receives the media attention relegated to sport. Although Super Bowl Sunday has been viewed as media hype, it can be argued that it is also a celebration of the masses, rendering it a type of secular religion in our society. The highest television ratings each year are typically associated with such sporting events as the Super Bowl, The NCAA Final Four, golf's Masters tournament, and Wimbledon; the World Series has even preempted news coverage of major world crises. Sport demands its own section in newspapers and is often the political platform for defectors, terrorists, and dissidents. "Sports talk" is common in corporate boardroom negotiations and coffee-break conversation. Sport often provides the visibility for athletes to enter politics or become entertainers or entrepreneurs. Recreational participation in sport also continues to gain popularity each year, because individuals in our society have more time for leisure activities, and more money to spend on their own fitness pursuits.

Sport is big business. The growth of the sport industry in the last half-century has been phenomenal. According to a study done by *The Sporting News* and Wharton Econometric Forecasting Associates Group, if all of the elements of the sport industry were combined—from the manufacturing of sporting goods, to the umpiring of softball games, to the televising of the Super Bowl—sport is a 63.1 billion dollar a year business, making it the twenty-second largest industry in the United

States. When compared to other industrial giants, sport is bigger than the automobile, petroleum, lumber, and air transportation sectors of the U.S. economy (Comte and Stogel, 1990).

As mind boggling as the numbers are today, the estimates for the Gross National Sports Product (GNSP) for the next century are even more amazing. By the year 2000, the GNSP will have increased 141% to 121.1 billion dollars (Rosner, 1989). Furthermore, these figures reflect the business of sport solely in the United States; this market is expanding internationally as well. And, with dynamic changes in Eastern Europe and elsewhere, even greater sums of money will eventually be invested in this industry.

This multibillion-dollar industry also places unique demands on its management personnel. The job requires management as well as marketing, communications, accounting, finance and economics, and legal skills applicable to the sport setting and specific to the increasingly complex and multifaceted areas it represents. Hence a new breed of specialists has emerged from the sport management arena.

SPORT MANAGEMENT: DEFINITION

From an *applied* perspective, sport management has been in existence from at least the time of the ancient Greeks, when combat among gladiators or animals attracted crowds of spectators. Herod, King of Judaea, was Honorary President of the Games during the eleventh-century Olympics. A magnificient ceremony opened the Games, followed by athletic competition where thousands of spectators were entertained lavishly (Frank, 1984). According to Parks and Olafson (1987), given the magnitude of such events, there must have been purveyors of food and drink, promoters, purchasing agents, marketing personnel, and management directors. Today, all of these individuals are known as *practitioners;* this term includes all persons employed in the applied field of sport management.

Although the terms **sport(s) management, sport(s) administration,** and **athletic administration** are often used interchangeably, the first most accurately describes this field from a universal or global perspective. That is, *management* is all-encompassing and represents the myriad sport-related areas identified by DeSensi, et al. (1990),

including facilities, hotels and resorts, public and private fitness and racquet clubs, merchandizing, and collegiate and professional sports. The term *administration* is limiting and suggests a school-related focus, particularly at the interscholastic and collegiate levels. However, Parkhouse (1987) found that a significant number of programs with offerings in such areas as retail sales, fitness and racquet club management, and professional sport management title their curricular programs "Sport Administration" or "Sports Administration." In contrast, those limiting their focus to the study of school-related sports use the term "Sport Management" or "Sports Management."

Obviously, this distinction is not applied universally. Since the labeling of existing programs is inconsistent, too often the title does not accurately describe the curricular focus and content. According to Milewski and Bryant (1985), some programs are titled "Health Promotion and Wellness," "Corporate Recreation," or "Facility Management." This is acceptable only when the content is limited to these specific areas.

The terms *sport* and *sports* are also used interchangeably. According to Parks and Zanger (1990), **sports** is singular in nature, whereas **sport** is a more all-encompassing term. The North American Society for Sport Management (NASSM) has elected to use the collective noun "sport" and encourages its use.

As previously mentioned, *sport* has several definitions (Loy, 1968; Snyder and Spreitzer, 1989; vander Zwaag, 1988); however, a workable definition for our purpose categorizes it as (1) spectator and (2) participant sport. Note that neither category is mutually exclusive. Consumers of participant sports often also want to be entertained, and spectators frequently like the opportunity to demonstrate their physical prowess; however, these are secondary motives. An example of the former is health and fitness clubs that offer members closed-circuit television viewing of special sporting events. An example of the latter includes "audience participation" in which selected fans are invited on the court at halftime to shoot baskets or to return a Chris Evert serve at the end of a celebrity match.

Technically, the term *sport management* is also misleading. Management is limited to subject matter that focuses on the functions of planning, organizing, directing, and controlling. It constitutes only one area of study within business schools. For this reason, business schools have been careful to label themselves as schools of business administration rather than those of business management. Other areas of study in business administration include accounting, marketing, economics, finance, organizational behavior, risk management, and legal studies. These are also legitimate areas of study within quality sport management programs.

Sport business is perhaps a more accurate term to describe both the applied and academic aspects of this industry. Unfortunately, "business" to many, particularly those involved in school-related sports, suggests entrepreneurial, for-profit, and exploitive motives.

Sport management is composed of two basic elements—sport and management. Getting things done with and through other people via planning, organizing, leading (directing), and evaluating (controlling) is the contemporary definition of management. Mullin (1980) defined sport management as including the functions of planning, organizing, leading, and evaluating within the context of an organization with the primary objective of providing sport- or fitness-related activities, products, and/or services. In Chapter 9, Chelladurai defines these four functions and discusses the subsets of each. For example, the subsets of planning include demands and constraints, forecasting, and budgeting. For our purpose, sport is defined as "you watch," or spectator activities primarily at the collegiate and professional levels. Fitness is defined as "you do," or participation activities such as available in health and fitness clubs or corporate fitness programs, or such special events as marathons and 10-kilometer runs. Products are tangible and include such items as fitness equipment, shoes, and clothing. Services are intangible and include installation and repair of fitness equipment, and entertainment, which is the major focus of spectator sport. Practitioners seeking employment in spectator sport will primarily find positions in college and university athletics, professional sport, and arena and stadium management. Opportunities in participant sport can be found in corporations, public and private fitness or racquet clubs, hotels and resorts, retail sales, and the travel and cruise industry (see Chapter 2).

Hardy (1987) described the politics and frustration in attempting to accurately define and label this profession:

> The term *sport management* is not always used to describe the domain, although it has probably become the preferred term. Relatively older programs have undergone several name changes in an effort to match title with curriculum. For instance, Robert Morris College began a management major option in Athletic Administration in 1978. By 1981 the college had a separate department of Sports Management. And in 1984, after many debates with the provost over proper usage, an "s" was dropped, resulting in Sport Management. Colleagues ask which letter will be dropped next. One suspects that many old hands in this field have suffered similar queries of curiosity or disdain.

The department of physical education at a university on the West Coast had recently developed a sport management program. When the course prospectus for a class appropriately titled "Sport Marketing" was sent to the university curriculum committee for review, a territorial-rights "red flag" went up on behalf of the business school. The content of the course was fine, but the word *marketing* had to be replaced by a more innocuous term. As a result, a less-descriptive title for this course, "Sport Consumer Behavior," was reluctantly substituted for the initial title so the course could be approved. Clearly, it is most desirable that names have some discrete and widely understood meaning (Mullin, 1980).

CONCEPT CHECK

From an applied perspective, sport management has been in existence for centuries. Only recently, however, has sport management been acknowledged as an academic pursuit. This field shares two basic elements—sport and business administration or management. The business component includes not only such management functions as planning, organizing, directing, and controlling, but also such areas as accounting, marketing, economics and finance, and law. From a sport management perspective, the term sport includes the spectator sport industry, which focuses on consumer entertainment, and the fitness industry, which concentrates on consumer participation in fitness-related activities. Although the terms sport management, sport administration, and athletic administration are frequently used interchangeably, the first most accurately describes this field from a universal or global perspective.

AN EVOLUTION IN SPORT MANAGEMENT

Although sport management is indeed a relatively new concept in academe, its acceptance as a legitimate area of study is well documented in the literature (Gleason, 1986; Hardy, 1987; Parkhouse, 1987; Parkhouse and Ulrich, 1979; Parks and Zanger, 1990; van der Smissen, 1984). It is also the topic of numerous trade articles and several published textbooks and has been featured in such popular publications as *USA Today* and *Time*.

The first university-sponsored sport management curriculum was established in 1966 at Ohio University. The Sports Administration Program at Ohio University was a master's offering that actually had its roots at the University of Miami in Coral Gables, Florida. James G. Mason, a physical education professor there, prepared a curriculum for a proposed program in sport management at the encouragement of Walter O'Malley, then president of the Brooklyn (soon to become Los Angeles) Dodgers. O'Malley first approached Mason in 1957 with the idea. Although it was never implemented, this curriculum became the basis of the Ohio University program (Mason et al., 1981). A few years later, Biscayne College (now St. Thomas University) and St. John's University became the first institutions granting baccalaureate degrees in sport management. The second master's program was established in 1971 at the University of Massachusetts.

In 1980, 20 colleges and universities in the United States offered graduate programs in sport management (Parkhouse, 1980). By 1985, this number had grown to 83 programs in the United States (40 undergraduate, 32 graduate, and 11 at both levels), as identified by the National Association for Sport and Physical Education (NASPE). The May 23, 1988, issue of *Sports, Inc.* published a compendium of 109 colleges and universities with programs in sport management. Of the 109 institutions identified, 51 offered undergraduate degrees, 33 were master's level, and 25 sponsored both undergraduate and master's programs (Brassie, 1989). Furthermore, three doctoral programs have also recently been identified. Although the first sport management program was established in 1966, the significant proliferation in curricular development was not observed until the mid-1980s. As a result, by 1988 only 10% of the programs had been in existence for more than 5 years.

Unlike the United States, the number of programs in Canada has not changed significantly in the past 10 years. In 1980 Bedecki and Soucie reported that 10 undergraduate, 9 master's, and 2 doctoral programs existed there. Eight years later, Soucie (1988) reported 6 undergraduate, 9 master's and 2 doctoral programs. By 1990 one additional doctoral program had been established.

Present programs in the United States are more applied in nature—focusing on such areas as collegiate and professional sports, facility, and health and fitness club management, whereas those in Canada are more theoretical. That is, the focus is on such subdisciplines as historical and cultural perspectives of sport and physical activity, psychological and sociological dimensions, and physiological and biomechanical aspects. This author believes that as accreditation standards are developed (discussed in the section "Curriculum," as well as in Chapter 22) a balance of applied and theoretical content will occur in programs in both the United States and Canada.

Sport management also has international appeal. In addition to Canada, West Germany, Korea, France, and the United Kingdom have all implemented programs. In 1990 the Bowater Faculty of Business at Victoria College established Australia's first bachelor of business program in sport management. This specialization consists of a core of business courses, a required core of sport studies, and offerings that combine the concepts of sport and management, such as sport marketing and sport law. *The Guidelines for Programs Preparing Undergraduate and Graduate Studies for Careers in Sport Management*, published by NASPE in 1987, were especially instrumental in the development of the Australian model.

The National College of Physical Education and Sports in the Republic of China (Taiwan) has established a curriculum in sport management as well. Beginning in 1992 graduates of this program will be prepared to assume leadership roles in sport management in Taiwan. Again, the United States model was influential in shaping this program, although other Asian models—notably that found in Korea—were also examined. The curriculum in Taiwan includes a business core, a sport studies core, an integrated core, and a variety of field experiences.

Recently the Japanese physical education curriculum has also undergone a significant transformation. The major reason is the decreasing demand for physical education teachers and the increasing need for personnel in the commercial sport sector. Specifically, the demand in the driving range industry is unique to Japan. Unlike the United States and other European countries, Japan has had tremendous growth in this area; over a hundred million people use driving range facilities there each year. These facilities require personnel that have exceptional management skills. Management of spectator sports has also become increasingly important, since this particular industry continues to grow rapidly in Japan as well.

Two professional associations in the United States serve the sport management profession. The North American Society for Sport Management (NASSM) and the National Association for Sport and Physical Education (NASPE) Task Force on Sport Management have monitored the rapid growth in this profession.

In 1985 NASSM was established to promote, stimulate, and encourage study, research, scholarly writing, and professional development in sport management (Zeigler, 1987). NASSM is the successor of the Sport Management Arts and Science Society (SMARTS), which was conceived in the 1970s by faculty at the University of Massachusetts. Like the members of SMARTS, those of NASSM focus on the theory, applications, and practice of management specifically related to sport, exercise (fitness), dance, and play. In addition to an annual conference, NASSM sponsors the *Journal of Sport Management* (JSM). JSM publishes refereed articles relative to the theory and applications of sport management. Published since January 1987, this journal has become the major resource for disseminating significant knowledge in this field.

NASPE approved a Sport Management Task Force in 1986 to meet the needs of its members who were involved in sport management curricula. The NASPE task force included five professors and four practitioners. At its first meeting the Task Force identified three agenda items: (1) curricular guidelines, (2) student guidelines for selecting programs, and (3) a directory of college programs preparing professionals. The Task Force drafted some curricular guidelines and disseminated them to those directors of sport management programs

identified by NASPE for input. Suggestions were then incorporated into the final document. In the fall of 1987, the NASPE Cabinet approved this document as NASPE's official curricular guidelines and published it under the title *Guidelines for Programs Preparing Undergraduate and Graduate Students for Careers in Sport Management*.

In the November/December 1989 issue of the *Journal of Physical Education, Recreation, and Dance* (JOPERD), an article titled "A Student Buyers Guide to Sport Management Programs" appeared. Included in this article were the guidance questions developed for prospective sport management students seeking a suitable program of study.

So that NASSM and NASPE would not overlap in focus or duties, members of both groups met at the American Alliance for Health, Physical Education, Recreation and Dance (AAHPERD) Convention in Cincinnati in 1986. It was agreed that NASSM would hold an annual meeting of professionals and publish JSM. NASPE would deal with curricular needs and offer programs at the annual AAHPERD Convention.

The two associations have continued to work cooperatively for the profession. When NASPE published its guidelines for programs preparing undergraduate and graduate students for careers in sport management, NASSM was invited to endorse the guidelines, and the NASPE Task Force began discussing accreditation of college professional preparation programs.

A NASSM committee was formed to meet with the NASPE Task Force, since many believed the NASPE guidelines were too limited. Hence the cur-

---

CONCEPT CHECK

Although the number of programs in Canada has not changed much in the past 10 years, a significant proliferation in sport management curricula has occurred since the mid-1980s in the United States. Several other countries have also begun offering academic programs in sport management. Members of NASPE's Sport Management Task Force and NASSM's Committee on Curriculum and Accreditation are developing standards for accreditation. Their objective is the development and maintenance of high quality academic environments.

ricular guidelines created by the joint committees (NASPE/NASSM) are much broader in scope than those previously developed. This work has also been praised for its competency-based format, which means that individuals developing a program know exactly what skills and knowledge must be included. It is also useful in course development and in demonstrating a need for new courses, as well as additional faculty. The goal of both committees is for this document to eventually become the officially adopted curriculum in sport management.

CURRICULUM

Curriculum in sport management has changed dramatically over the past 20 years. For example, in 1971 the master's program at the University of Massachusetts included an internship and four required courses in the department of physical education: psychology of sport, sociology of sport, history, and philosophy. No specific sport management courses were offered. Electives were available from the schools of business, journalism, and education, although no prerequisites or prescribed courses were stipulated. Today the University of Massachusetts has a full complement of required and elective courses in sport management and related areas.

Only recently has sport management been acknowledged as an *academic* pursuit (Parks and Quain, 1986). As previously mentioned, curricula in sport management among American colleges and universities have been in existence fewer than 40 years and have escalated at a significant rate since 1985. Research and the attempt to develop a theoretical base in this area are also recent phenomena (see Chapter 3). Individuals involved in the teaching and development of a curriculum, as well as those conducting research and publishing in this area, are referred to as **sport management academicians and/or scholars.**

Historically, sport management has had a strong physical education orientation. This checkered evolution is largely the result of physical education faculty who, when faced with declining enrollments in coaching and teaching, modified traditional curricular offerings to attract students interested in more marketable areas. Unfortunately, many schools merely repackaged an existing curriculum and added some catchy course titles to

cash in on the vogue of sport management (Berg, 1989). Parkhouse (1987) reported that a significant number of sport management programs currently include physical education–related coursework that is questionable in meeting the educational or job-related needs of this industry. Today a handful of programs is sufficiently developed in terms of faculty and curriculum to produce graduates who are competitive in the marketplace (Berg, 1989).

There is a general agreement on the basic components of sport management curriculum today. The components consist of (1) foundation areas of study, (2) application areas of study, and (3) field experiences.

Foundation areas

The **foundation areas** consist of courses typically offered through business schools on college and university campuses. The NASPE Task Force on Sport Management (Brassie, 1989) suggests that the following courses are critical to an undergraduate sport management program: management, marketing, accounting, economics and finance, and computer science. The graduate (master's) courses include more advanced study in these areas. In addition, coursework in research methods and a project or thesis are suggested. Courses in such areas as public relations, advertising, interpersonal communication, and business writing are also suggested for both levels of study and are offered in various departments on campus, especially journalism.

Application areas

The **applied areas** build on foundational subject matter and are specific to sport (Brassie, 1989; Parkhouse, 1984). At the undergraduate level, background content may include such courses as history and philosophy of sport, sport culture, sociology of sport, and sport psychology. Specific applied content should include such courses as sport law, sport marketing, sport administration (management), facility design and management, and sport finance and economics. At the graduate level, advanced application curricular offerings in these areas are suggested. The applied courses should be taught by qualified faculty. That is, rather than being self-taught, these individuals should have taken coursework in the specific subjects that they teach. For example, a faculty member teaching courses in sport marketing should have previous coursework in such areas as basic marketing, consumer and buyer behavior, and marketing research. In addition, the instructor must have the knowledge or field experiences necessary to distinguish between traditional marketing and the unique marketing techniques employed in the sport industry.

Field experiences

This component includes part-time "work" experiences (*practica*) and full-time "work" experiences (*internships*). Students receive academic credit for these experiences. The Task Force (Brassie, 1989) recommends practica and internship experiences at both the undergraduate and master's levels.

Doctoral preparation in sport management has rarely been addressed in the literature. Although there are only three doctoral programs currently in the United States and three in Canada, preparation at this level is becoming increasingly important. This degree (the Ph.D. and Ed.D.) is of particular interest to individuals pursuing an academic career in sport management and administrators seeking tenure-track faculty in this field. There is also a trend toward hiring Ph.D.s with business and sport management orientations as athletic directors at major universities. NASPE and NASSM have jointly developed standards for curricular development at the doctoral level, which include a strong research orientation.*

Sport management curricula vary markedly from one institution to another. Some colleges and universities require coursework and experiences sufficient in scope and magnitude to constitute a full major or a degree program. However, the majority include one to three electives and/or required offerings in foundation and application courses. This is not sufficient to warrant even a minor or a concentration in sport management (Parkhouse, 1987).

---

*NOTE: The purpose of this discussion is to address generally the three basic components of sport management curriculum rather than present a lengthy schema for curricular development or specific course content. Given the focus of this book, such detail is inappropriate. (See Brassie, 1989; Hardy, 1987; Parkhouse, 1987 for more specific information about curricular development. The NASSM/NASPE competency-based accreditation standards can be obtained from NASPE at the AAHPERD headquarters in Reston, Virginia.)

There also appears to be little distinction between undergraduate and graduate offerings in applied courses. Most of those institutions with both undergraduate and graduate curricula in sport management have dual-listed courses that may be counted toward either an undergraduate or graduate degree. This conflicts with the mission of graduate study, in which students build on undergraduate preparation by pursuing a specialized area of study at a higher level of difficulty and sophistication. Doctoral preparation should be even more specialized and advanced (Brassie, 1989; Parkhouse, 1987).

A few years ago Parkhouse (1984) questioned the quality of sport management faculty, indicating that the majority are physical educators using the self-taught method in an attempt to meet current demands in such areas as sport law and sport marketing. This is no longer as major a concern, since a new breed of qualified academicians in sport management are beginning to surface.

Currently the number of full-time faculty in individual sport management programs is a major concern. It is impossible for one or two faculty to have the expertise required to teach the variety of application courses expected in a quality program. Yet, sport management programs with more than two full-time faculty members are very rare. To fill this void, a few institutions are hiring adjunct professors, who are usually active practitioners such as CPAs and lawyers with an interest in sport. The majority are highly qualified to teach these application courses. However, except in rare situations, they do not have the time or experience to advise students in curricular matters. Furthermore, they usually have little interest in or understanding of research methodology and statistics—critical competencies when advising master's and doctoral candidates or serving on their thesis and dissertation committees.

Given its nature, sport management is a multidisciplinary field of study. It requires the cooperation of several disciplines, especially business administration (management) and physical education. The latter is now commonly labeled "sport studies," "exercise and sport sciences," or a similar title that more accurately describes the academic components of physical education. Neither the business school nor the department of physical education can accomplish this task single-handedly, since such an endeavor requires effective application of business concepts to the sport setting.

As noted earlier, three major components of the sport management curriculum include foundation courses, application offerings, and field experiences. A large portion of this book is devoted to the foundation and application components.

CONCEPT CHECK

Historically, sport management has had a strong physical education orientation. Today the focus is on foundation areas of study, with a strong emphasis on business courses, application areas of study that build on foundation subject matter and are specific to the sport industry, and field experiences. Given its nature, sport management is a multidisciplinary field of study. It requires the cooperation of several disciplines, especially business administration (management) and physical education (now commonly referred to as "sport studies," "exercise and sport sciences," or similar titles that more accurately describe the academic components of physical education).

Although the relatively new field of sport management has great potential, its respectability and credibility are major concerns among both academicians and practitioners. Those responsible for its curricular development at both the national and institutional levels must accept much of the responsibility for ensuring quality professional preparation. In this endeavor at the national level, NASPE and NASSM are working collectively to establish accreditation standards comparable to the rigor of those in business administration and communications. At the institutional level, proliferation in the interest of increasing student enrollment must give way to a commitment to excellence. In addition, scholarly efforts in this field must focus on research that tests management theory (see Chapter 3). These efforts are necessary to ensure that sport management acquires the distinction it rightfully deserves in academia.

Whether voluntary or mandatory, accreditation will not become a reality in the near future. Jurisdiction is a major concern (Berg, 1989). Some feel NASPE is the appropriate group; others think NASSM is the logical body. Many believe that a sport management program will carry authority only if it fits into the overall college and university accreditation process. Regardless, guidelines have been developed for those seeking to enhance their programs, since a significant number currently exist more on paper than in practice (Parkhouse, 1987). (See Chapter 22 for further discussion of accreditation.)

SUMMARY

1. Although sport management is relatively new to academia, its acceptance as a legitimate area of study is well documented in the literature.

2. Although the terms *sport management, sport administration,* and *athletic administration* are often used interchangeably, the first most accurately describes this field from a universal or global perspective.

3. There is a general agreement that the basic components of sport management curriculum should include foundation areas of study, application courses, and field experiences. A large portion of this book is devoted to the foundation and application components.

4. The North American Society for Sport Management (NASSM) and the National Association for Sport and Physical Education (NASPE) Task Force on Sport Management corroborate a rapid growth in this profession. NASSM was established to promote, stimulate, and encourage research, scholarly writing, and professional development in the area of sport management. The Task Force focuses on curricular needs. The *Journal of Sport Management* (JSM) is the major resource for disseminating significant knowledge in this field.

5. This relatively new field has great potential, but its destiny is still in question. It is imperative that those responsible for the curricular development of sport management programs at both the national and institutional levels accept this responsibility for ensuring quality professional preparation. At the institutional level, proliferation in the interest of increasing student enrollment must give way to a commitment to excellence.

6. Quality control is currently a major concern of academicians and practitioners in this field. In this endeavor, an accrediting agency comparable to those in business administration and communications is presently being considered in sport management.

REVIEW QUESTIONS AND ISSUES

1. Foundation and application courses, as well as field experiences, are necessary to meet the job-related needs of the sport management industry. What is the difference between a foundation and application offering? Cite an example of a field experience.
2. What is the purpose of accreditation? How can accreditation resolve the quality control problem that currently exists in sport management programs? Why have some academicians been reluctant to support accreditation?
3. Why does the term *sport management* more accurately describe this field than *sport administration* or *athletic administration*?
4. Why is the term *sport management* misleading? Why is *sport business* perhaps a more accurate term to describe both the academic and applied aspects of this industry? Explain why the latter term has not been adopted.
5. How has the sport management curriculum changed over the past 20 years?

REFERENCES

Bedecki, T., and Soucie, D. (1990). Trends in physical education, sport, and athletic administration in Canadian universities and colleges. Paper presented at the 26th Annual Conference of the Canadian Association for Health, Physical Education, and Recreation. St. John's New Foundland.

Berg, R. (1989). The quest for credibility. *Athletic Business*, *13*(11), 44-48.

Brassie, S. (1989). Guidelines for programs preparing undergraduate and graduate students for careers in sport management. *Journal of Sport Management*, *3*(2), 158-164.

Comte, E., and Stogel, C. (1990). Sports: a $63.1 billion industry. *The Sporting News* (January 1), 60-61.

DeSensi, J., Kelley, D., Blanton, M., and Beitel, P. (1990). Sport management curricular evaluation and needs assessment: a multifaceted approach. *Journal of Sport Management*, *4*(1), 31-58.

Frank, R. (1984). Olympic myths and realities. *Arete: The Journal of Sport Literature*, *1*(2), 155-161.

Gleason, T. (1986). Sport administration degrees: growing to fill a need/supply overwhelms demand. *Athletic Administration* (February), 9-10.

Goodwin, M. (1986). When the cash register is the scoreboard. *The New York Times* (June 8), 27-28.

Hardy, S. (1987). Graduate curriculums in sport management: the need for a business orientation. *Quest*, *39*, 207-216.

Loy, J. (1968). The nature of sport: a definitional effort. *Quest*, *10*, 1-15.

Mason, J., Higgins, C., and Owen, J. (1981). Sport administration education 15 years later. *Athletic Purchasing and Facilities* (January), 44, 45.

Milewski, J., and Bryant, J. (1985). A survey of institutions offering sport administration, sport management, or related sport studies programs. Unpublished study, Western Carolina University.

Mullin, B. (1980). Sport management: the nature and utility of the concept. *Arena Review*, *4*(3), 1-11.

Parkhouse, B. (1980). Analysis of graduate professional preparation in sport management. *Athletic Administration*, *14*(2), 11-14.

Parkhouse, B. (1984). Shaping up to climb a new corporate ladder . . . sport management. *Journal of Physical Education, Recreation and Dance*, *55*(6), 12-14.

Parkhouse, B. (1987). Sport management curricula: current status and design implications for future development. *Journal of Sport Management*, *1*(2), 93-115.

Parkhouse, B., and Ulrich, D. (1979). Sport management as a potential cross-discipline: a paradigm for theoretical application. *Quest*, *31*(2), 264-276.

Parks, J., and Olafson, G. (1987). Sport management and a new journal. *Journal of Sport Management*, *1*(1), 1-3.

Parks, J., and Quain, R. (1986). Curriculum perspectives. *Journal of Physical Education, Recreation and Dance*, *57*(4), 22-26.

Parks, J., and Zanger, B. (Eds.) (1990). *Sport and fitness management: career strategies and professional content*. Champaign, Illinois: Human Kinetics Books.

Rosner, D. (1989). The world plays catch-up. *Sports Inc.* (January 2).

Sandomir, R. (1988). The $50 billion sport industry. *Sports Inc.* (November 14).

Snyder, E., and Sprietzer, E. (1989). *Social aspects of sport*. Englewood Cliffs, N.J.: Prentice-Hall, Inc.

Soucie, D. (1988). Promotion of sport management programs in Canada. Paper presented to the North American Society for Sport Management. Champaign, Illinois.

van der Smissen, B. (1984). A process for success: sport management curricula—an idea whose time has come! In B. Zanger and J. Parks (Eds.), *Sport management curricula: the business and education nexus*. Bowling Green, Ohio: Bowling Green State University, School of Health, Physical Education and Recreation, 5-18.

vander Zwaag, H. (1988). *Policy development in sport management*. Indianapolis: Benchmark Press.

Zeigler, E. (1987). Sport management: past, present, future. *Journal of Sport Management*, *1*(1), 4-24.

CHAPTER 2

Career Considerations

Dennie R. Kelley
Patricia A. Beitel
Joy T. DeSensi
Mary Dale Blanton

In this chapter, you will become familiar with the following terms:

Sport
Profit orientation
Nonprofit orientation
Sport management determinants
  Setting
  Focus
  Competency

Clusters of sport management
  Sport for leisure and recreation
  Sport and athletics
  Sporting goods industry
  Hostelries and travel
  Agencies
Sport management
Health and fitness management

Overview

In the first chapter of this book, a definition for sport management, a historical perspective, and a curriculum were presented. This chapter focuses on an understanding of career options in the sport management industry. The first part of this chapter describes some of the general requirements for a career in sport management, while the second half of the chapter explains various career options available to sport management graduates.

According to the Wharton Econometric Forecasting Associates Group, sport has become America's twenty-second largest industry with a 6.1% increase in the gross national sports product (GNSP). In addition, this group has predicted a 4% to 5% increase in the GNSP for 1988 to an estimated 63.1 billion dollars out of the total U.S. GNP of 4.52 trillion dollars (DeSensi, Kelley, Beitel, and Blanton, 1990; Sandomir, 1988). In addition, the health and fitness industry adds 6 billion dollars to the national economy (Pejchar, 1989).

The term **sport** is used in this chapter in a very broad sense that encompasses amateur and professional sport as well as all the activities of the fitness industry. The sport industry also includes, but is not limited to, the production and marketing of sport clothing and other sporting goods. Sport has grown in our society at a phenomenal rate. Such growth can be seen not only by the increase in the number of spectators, but also by the greater number of segments of society that have shown an interest in fitness. This includes increased participation by women, men, youth, and older adults, as well as handicapped persons.

As participation has grown in amateur, professional, and recreational sport as well as in fitness activities, the sport industry has responded with expanded programs and opportunities for individuals and groups. This growth has created an exciting market for sport and a challenge that sport managers must meet. Such growth signifies a trend that should not be overlooked, especially in light of the economic effect of the sport enterprise as a whole. This phenomenal growth brings significant implications about career choices and employment opportunities at the different levels of sport.

As population and society change, new employment options are created (Kjeldsen, 1980). For example, demand has increased for fitness classes and assistance, amateur and professional league play, and sport and fitness clubs. In addition, societal changes such as an increase in leisure time, an increase in expendable income, and a longer life span have improved career opportunities for individuals in sport and fitness management. Sport has changed over the past decades, and these changes have necessitated better management of opportunities and programs in the developing areas of leisure, recreation, fitness, exercise, and sport (DeSensi and Koehler, 1989).

Sport management curricula have grown along with the growth in sport businesses. The field of sport management has developed both as an academic discipline and as a career choice (Parks and Quain, 1986). As sport growth and trends are monitored, it is essential that students of sport management explore their many options in this area of study. The scope of sport management has expanded as this discipline has emerged. The areas of sport, recreation, and health and fitness offer many career opportunities that should be explored in conjunction with the growth trends of the sport industry and the individual's short-term and long-term career objectives (Quain and Parks, 1986). Students of sport management must ask crucial questions as they pursue professional career alternatives in sport management.

CAREER CONSIDERATIONS

Before choosing a career in sport management, some factors should be considered. A candid self-appraisal of the following factors can be very important in the decision-making process and later in planning the professional preparation program. First, it is important that potential sport managers realize that the actual day-to-day operation of sport organizations involves a great deal of hard work, much of which is behind the scenes. Although this field may sound glamorous to some, one of the primary tasks actually is to provide services for other people. Usually the service is ensuring that participants and spectators can participate in or watch the performance in a safe, secure, and attractive environment. To provide this type of setting requires, at minimum, planning and promoting the event, handling all financial considerations, and securing and maintaining the venue. Frequently, sport managers receive very little attention, except when the operation does not run smoothly.

One of the first things that a prospective employee in this field needs to consider is whether he or she is willing to work so that others may enjoy the limelight. At the same time, sport management is a people-centered profession, and unless the person considering this profession is people oriented, the types of positions available are limited. Some positions in large sport organizations lend themselves to the solitary worker, but most sport managers are expected to be able to work with other people in a friendly, outgoing, personable, and enthusiastic manner. The sport manager should be physically fit, have a high degree of work stamina, and be willing to work long hours. Frequently, management responsibilities include working at night and on weekends. It is not atypical for the sport manager's work week to exceed 50 or 60 hours. The number of hours required for the job and the timing of the peak work periods are important considerations. Sport management is not a 9-to-5, Monday through Friday profession.

The sport manager's preferred work location is another important consideration. The self-appraisal should include questions concerning geographical location, including state and region, and—with the growth in the international sports market—whether locating in another country is feasible or desirable. Other geographical considerations are urban vs. rural locales and larger cities vs. smaller towns. Obviously the larger the population of a given area, the greater the potential for employment in sport management. However, many colleges and universities are located in small to mid-size cities and towns and offer sport management positions. Another important factor to consider is job availability and ease of entry into the particular aspect of sport management that is being considered. Two of the most popular settings for positions in sport management are professional sport organizations and college and university athletics. Most professional sport teams are located in larger cities, and the future sport manager may need to compare a position in a desired location, such as a small town, to an opportunity to work in a preferred setting, such as professional sport.

An important factor for most people to acknowledge is the level of remuneration for a particular position in a specific location. There are at least two important aspects of salary to keep in mind. These are the entry-level salaries and the likelihood of salary increases. Unfortunately, salaries in sport management are not competitive with comparable managerial positions in other corporate settings. According to Lewis, in the introduction of the book *Successful Sport Management*, "Sport management in modern times, however, has not developed professionally as rapidly as management in other industries, perhaps reflecting a continuing association in the public mind of sport with play and management with work" (Lewis and Appenzeller, 1985, p. iii).

The student also should decide what is of worth to him or her. Many people seem to feel that sport and therefore sport-related organizations are less important than other corporate enterprises. For some people, sport is a frivolous undertaking, and sport management is a profession lacking in prestige. It is imperative that the novice sport manager acknowlege and deal with these perceptions. How important is it for friends, family, and peers to respect the employment position and the setting? All prospective sport managers should answer this question.

In addition, the workplace environment should be a factor in the self-appraisal process. One consideration is whether the student prefers a large organization or a small setting. Usually, in larger sport management settings there are many more opportunities for interaction, and more contacts are made, which may in turn lead to advancement. In smaller organizations, each employee may be required to be proficient at many different tasks, whereas in larger settings, a few specific competencies may be expected. For example, in a small college setting, an athletic director may be the coach, scout, athletic trainer, sports information director, promotions and marketing director, facilities manager, and director of fund raising and development. In comparison, at a large university there may be a director or manager with assistants and support staff for each of those positions. In general, a greater variety of tasks are required of each sport management employee in smaller settings, and conversely, tasks are more specific in larger settings.

Another workplace factor to acknowlege is the different atmospheres found in **profit-oriented** sport management businesses and **nonprofit** enterprises. Both profit and nonprofit organizations must be operated in a fiscally sound manner, and in many instances the differences between the two settings may be minimal. However, in the nonprofit environment there is always a larger entity—that is, an agency or institution—that serves as an insulator that can provide a cushion in times of financial exigency. In the profit sector the solvency of the sport enterprise may depend on the number of memberships sold, and the enterprise may not have a parent company to absorb some of the financial burden. The prospective sport manager needs to determine whether he or she can handle the pressure of day-to-day economic survival.

Related to the profit vs. nonprofit question is whether a person prefers to be self-employed or to work for someone else. Generally, the opportunities for large, rapid salary increases are reduced when one works for someone else. On the other hand, job security usually is better in a well-established sport business. The sport entrepreneur must compare the risks of self-employment to the potential rewards if this sport venture is successful. There may be less risk of unemployment when working for someone else, although this does not guarantee job security.

Many people are attracted to the field of sport management because it provides, in many cases, a certain amount of freedom. Typically sport managers do not spend all of their work day sitting behind a desk. Some sport management positions, such as grounds managers and some commercial recreation managers, involve work in the outdoors. For some people interested in sport management, this would be a very attractive prospect, whereas others may not care to work in all kinds of weather. Some positions, such as manufacturers' representatives, require extensive travel. Again, each individual must weigh the pros and cons of these types of job expectations and how the job requirements would match the preferred lifestyle.

In summary, it is imperative that each prospective sport manager give serious consideration to these factors. Some may not seem very important at first glance; however, over the course of time all of these in combination determine whether a person is satisfied in his or her position. To an extent,

---

CONCEPT CHECK

It is important for persons considering sport management as a career to remember that sport managers are working in a service-oriented, people-centered occupation. Sport managers should be physically fit and willing to work long hours, often at night or on weekends when many of their friends and family members are off from work. It is important to know that positions in certain geographical locations and in collegiate and professional sport are very difficult to find. Also, sport managers frequently make less money than managers in comparable positions in other businesses.

---

an employee's attitudes toward the job requirements determines that person's success in that particular position. For example, resentment over the number of work hours or time spent traveling can accumulate over time and create a very negative situation for all concerned. Therefore it is wise to spend some time before embarking on a career in sport management trying to determine the type of position and setting best suited for the individual. After embarking on a sport management career, the manager should periodically evaluate his or her interests and career goals.

THREE DETERMINANTS AFFECTING CAREER PLANNING IN SPORT MANAGEMENT

Three **sport management determinants** have been identified that affect career planning in sport management: (1) setting(s), (2) focus, and (3) competencies. The setting where the sport manager is employed, the focus of the sport enterprise, and the specific competencies required by each sport management position all affect the composition of the professional preparation program for each student (Kelley, Beitel, Blanton, and DeSensi, 1990). Consequently, it behooves the sport management student to examine these three determinants.

Settings

The first determinant of the sport management career choice is the **setting** in which the prospective sport manager wishes to work. Five major clusters of sport management settings have been identified (Kelley et al., 1990) as places of potential employment for sport managers (see the box on p. 16). Each of these clusters includes two or more sport management categories that (1) have similar objectives and/or provide similar services, but (2) serve a different clientele and/or occur in slightly different settings.

In addition, settings can be further described as having a profit or nonprofit orientation. The distinctions between the profit and nonprofit organizations are that (1) the objective of the nonprofit organization is to provide excellent services and break even financially, whereas the profit-oriented business enterprise tries to provide excellent services and also make financial gains; and (2) there are differences in the way profit and nonprofit business enterprises promote and justify the relation-

---

Settings for sport management

Settings for sport management fall into five primary clusters, each of which contains two or more categories that have similar objectives and provide similar services but occur in different settings, and/or serve a different clientele (Kelley et al., 1990).

1. **Sport for leisure and recreation** settings include organizations that provide facilities and programs for organized sport or fitness participation of members, such as the following:
   - College and university intramural and sport clubs
   - Corporations and companies with sport or fitness programs
   - Private sport clubs
   - Public sport clubs
2. **Sport and athletic** settings include organizations that provide management of sporting events, athletes, and/or spectator use, such as the following:
   - College and university athletics
   - Professional sport
   - Sport organizations
   - Sport management services
3. **Sporting goods industry** settings include businesses that develop, distribute, and/or promote the sale of sport and fitness equipment or clothing, such as the following:
   - Sport marketing and merchandising
   - Retail sales
4. **Hostelries and travel** settings include businesses that provide lodging and that include recreation or leisure programs and/or facilities for their clientele, such as the following:
   - Hotels
   - Resorts
   - Travel or cruise businesses
5. **Agency** settings include organizations that use nonprofit funding sources to develop, implement, and manage recreation or sport programs, activities, or facilities to meet the needs of the agency members, or populations of governmental districts (e.g., city, county, state), such as the following:
   - Local government agencies
   - Voluntary agencies

---

ship between program offerings and program costs. In most profit-oriented businesses, sport and/or fitness is the primary "commodity," and the owners are in business to make a profit from this commodity. In the nonprofit category, the program is usually one unit within an institution or corporation whose primary objective is not sport or fitness related. For students majoring in sport management, these are important distinctions to note. Although there may be similarities in the types of positions within profit- and nonprofit-oriented businesses, there are several distinctions that might affect the role of the sport manager in those parallel positions (see the box on p. 17).

Focus

Once the student has decided to be a sport manager, he or she next will need to choose the **focus** of his or her career. There are two major foci from which the prospective sport manager may choose: (1) health and fitness management or (2) sport and recreation management (see the box on p. 18). In either case, the key term is management. No matter which focus is chosen, management skill (1) is necessary for success and (2) is the common element that links them professionally as part of sport management. Students interested in the health and fitness management focus are potential managers of wellness centers, spas, health clubs, athletic train-

Benefits and limitations of profit-oriented and nonprofit-oriented sport businesses

Profit-oriented businesses*

Benefits	Limitations
Usually good promotion opportunities	More competitive inter- and intra-business environment than nonprofit
Capital goods and salary benefits tend to be relative to employee responsibility and productivity	In some cluster/categories (see the box on p. 16) many positions are seasonal or part time, and may be minimum wage; thus personnel is unstable
Emphasis is on profit (commission) rather than on salary	May have to start at entry-level or lower-level management
Operations are often more flexible and efficient than in nonprofit, where bureaucracy is prevalent	In some sport business categories, professional management positions are limited mainly to department or general managers, and other positions pay minimum wage
Provides entrepreneural opportunities	
Individuals who are attracted to and retained in the work force tend to be highly motivated; thus it is easier to provide encouragement and to manage personnel	

Nonprofit-oriented businesses*

Benefits	Limitations
Less competitive work environment than profit-oriented businesses	Attaining and maintaining employment depend on who is in political office
Incentives available to managers include tax support and tax breaks	Lower salary ranges in some nonprofit businesses
There is great diversity of types of services and programs among nonprofit organizations; thus personnel have many options of emphasis	Often regulated by government procedures or bureaucracy; thus less efficient and more time consuming than profit oriented businesses
	When finances are tight, services and programs are often the first to be cut
	Some nonprofit organizations may depend on fund raising and development to bring in substantial monies
	Often positions do not provide opportunity for upward mobility
	Sometimes personnel acquire a position and never leave—this job security may be a benefit or a limitation
	Many managerial and administrative positions rely on voluntary or nonprofessional paid personnel to carry out tasks

*NOTE: The terms "profit" and "nonprofit" are nondescriptive terms today. Managers in both must be entrepreneurs—interested in turning a profit to purchase additional equipment or services. Perhaps a better choice of words is mission (nonprofit) vs. motive (profit). In nonprofit the primary goal is to sustain a quality service, whereas for-profit denotes a desire to increase income or make a profit, as well as maintain quality.

ing programs, or sports medicine centers. Therefore, in addition to management skills, they need specific preparation in such fields as nutrition, anatomy, and exercise physiology. In contrast, students who want to work in sport and recreation management positions do not need a science orientation. However, in addition to management, relevant areas of study include, but are not limited to, sport studies such as sociology of sport and/or leisure and recreation, history of sport, philosophy of sport and/or leisure and recreation, and current issues in sport (Kelley et al., 1990) (see Chapter 1).

Competencies

The number and type of tasks in which a sport manager may need to be competent is the third determinant affecting career planning and subsequent career options. Any career option in sport management may require several different **competencies** (see the box on p. 19). However, the specific career option chosen would determine the depth to which one or more of these competencies

would be emphasized. Along with the basic skills needed by all sport managers, the competencies include (1) facility management, (2) fiscal management, (3) marketing and sales ability, (4) program and event management, and (5) personnel management and supervision.

Competencies needed for entry-level positions in sport management settings are quite different from the competencies that are needed for middle- and upper-level management positions in these same settings (DeSensi et al., 1990; Ellard, 1984; Hardy, 1987; Jamieson, 1987; Kelley et al., 1990; Lambrecht, 1987; Whiddon, 1990). Entry-level personnel tend to provide services directly to the consumer, such as sport skill or aerobics instruction, whereas a middle manager would serve as a supervisor of programs and/or personnel and would have limited direct contact with consumers. Entry-level personnel must have specific technical skills (Hardy, 1987), while middle and upper management personnel must be able to see the total picture of the sport operation. Personnel in upper management are responsible for fiscal, personnel, and/or programmatic decisions. Entry-level management positions require only an undergraduate degree, whereas middle- and upper-level management positions usually require a graduate degree (Kelley et al., 1990).

> ## Two categories of focus within the sport managment profession
>
> The specific job of a sport manager might include any combination of skills related to planning, organizing, directing, controlling, budgeting, leading, and/or evaluating in an organization or department whose primary product or service is related to one of two areas of focus.
>
> **Health and fitness focus** could occur in a variety of settings, such as a trainer in professional sport or university athletics, a physical fitness specialist in sport and fitness centers, or in agencies such as YMCAs or YWCAs or local recreation departments.
>
> **Sport and recreation focus** could occur in a variety of settings, such as the athletic director of a university athletic department, the program director for YMCAs or YWCAs, the general manager for a professional sport team, or the manager of the pro shop at a country club or tennis club.

CONCEPT CHECK

The settings, focus, and competencies for sport managers have been identified. There are five clusters of settings: (1) sport for leisure and recreation, (2) sport and athletics, (3) sporting goods industry, (4) hostelries and travel, and (5) agencies. The foci of sport management have two major sections: (1) health and fitness management and (2) sport and recreation management. Six competencies have been identified that are crucial for all sport managers regardless of the setting or focus. These competencies are (1) communication skills, (2) facility management skills, (3) fiscal management skills, (4) marketing and sales skills, (5) program and event management skills, and (6) personnel management and supervision skills. The setting, the size of the organization, and the focus determine the extent to which the sport manager will use any of these competencies.

Facilities management is one competency that may be found within many settings. No matter who owns the facility or where it is located, whether a private business, a municipality, or a university, facilities must be operated cost-effectively. A facilities manager, whether employed by a city or county government, a college/university, or a professional sport team, will be required to have planning and organizational skills, as well as personnel management and communication skills. Depending on the type of setting, the size of the agency, institution, or business determines the extent that facility management is the sport manager's responsibility. For example, a general manager (G.M.) of a major league baseball team or an athletic director (A.D.) at a university may have facilities managers working for them, but the G.M. or A.D. should know what is involved in the facilities management. In contrast, a G.M. in the minor leagues or an A.D. at a small college may be directly responsible for the facilities in addition to a myriad of other duties. This contrast of college or university athletics with professional sport (Beitel, Kelley, DeSensi, and Blanton, 1989) provides a good example of how the focus and the type and size of the setting determine the type and degree of sport management competencies required.

SPORT MANAGEMENT SETTINGS

The purpose of this section is to describe the career options available in the sport management industry by cluster.

Competencies for sport management

The nature of sport management positions in various settings (see the box on p. 16) and across different levels of management determines the degree to which one or more of the **competencies** would be emphasized.

Basic skills needed by all sport managers include oral and written communication skills, computer skills, organizational abilities, and mathematical skills. Leadership skills and a high degree of physical stamina are also necessary.

Communication is the ability to interact in written and oral forms in a clear, concise manner to accomplish a specific purpose. Sport information director, sports promotion director, and media liaison are examples of positions in sport management that require an especially high level of communication skills.

Marketing, merchandizing, and selling includes the ability to promote an idea, advertise the concept or merchandise, and present it to the appropriate consumer to meet the objectives of the specific business or agency. Retail sales of equipment and clothing and promotion of a sports personality or event are some examples in which this particular skill is imperative.

Program event management requires the ability to coordinate the use of time, ideas, and functions to present the program and/or event. Tennis tournaments, racing events such as cycling or skiing, and track and field meets all require people with skills in coordinating short-term sports functions.

Personnel management and supervision is the enhancement of individual and/or group interaction for optimal accomplishment of business, individual, and/or group objectives. Managers such as athletic directors, general managers, and intramural or sport club directors need to be skillful in this competency.

Facility management requires the ability to oversee the total operation of arenas, stadia, business establishments and so forth in such a manner as to help attain the sport business objectives and/or profits. Examples of positions that require facility management skills are concessions manager, golf course manager, director of ticket sales, and field and grounds maintenance manager.

Fiscal management includes the ability to plan, budget, and control all financial aspects of the organization. Such skills are especially important for directors of fund raising and development, vice presidents for finance, assistant or associate athletic directors for finance, and budget directors.

Sport for leisure and recreation cluster

College and university intramural and sport and fitness clubs. College and university intramurals and sport and fitness clubs are two of the nonprofit organizations within this cluster (see the box on p. 16). These are units or departments within a college or university that are involved with the planning, organizing, directing, controlling, budgeting, and staffing of programs associated with competitive sport and noncompetitive activity programs that are participant oriented rather than spectator oriented. These programs require middle managers, that is, sport club directors and intramural directors who supervise lower-level sport managers such as recreation leaders and fitness specialists. The middle managers are also responsible for program implementation and facility supervision. Upper-level administrators such as directors of campus recreation have broader responsibilities, which include policy development and fiscal management.

Corporations and companies. The corporations and companies category within the sport for leisure and recreation cluster (see the box on p. 16) is another nonprofit venture, which companies offer as part of employee benefits. Since chief executive officers and boards of directors of companies have recognized that fit employees work more efficiently, are absent less, and have better morale, more and more companies are giving their employees opportunities for daily health-related activities.

Initially, only the executives of corporations were given access to the corporate gymnasium or weightroom. Recently, many of the more progressive companies have extended some of these privileges to all employees. Depending on the size of the corporation, there may be (1) a mid-level or upper-level sport administrator to coordinate the personnel and facilities for the program of sport and physical activity, (2) a middle-level management exercise physiologist to structure individual exercise programs, and/or (3) an entry-level position fitness leader with American College of Sports Medicine (ACSM) certification to test fitness levels and implement fitness programs for executives (Kelley, DeSensi, Blanton, and Beitel, 1989).

Some programs are very individualized and include fitness assessment and prescription. Others include opportunities for workouts and recreational sports play. In some cases, a full complement of wellness programs (such as smoking cessation and stress reduction) are offered to employees and their family members. All of these programs require people with managerial skills to plan, organize, implement, supervise, and evaluate programs and personnel.

In some instances, particularly in smaller companies, the sport manager may be responsible for the total operation. This one person may have to serve as facilities coordinator, program director, exercise specialist, and general manager. In other settings, there may be several individuals in one or more of the above positions, with a middle- or upper-level sport manager overseeing the total operation (Kelley et al., 1989). Whatever the size or extent of the program, any business that possesses an organized fitness, sport, and/or wellness program for the benefit of its employees is offering another employment opportunity for sport managers to consider. Oil companies, hospitals, insurance companies, department store chains, and banks are some of the organizations that frequently provide such programs.

Public and private sport clubs. Public and private sport clubs (see the box on p. 16) are the next two categories within the sport for leisure and recreation cluster, both of which are profit oriented. The major distinction between these two types of enterprises is that public sport clubs are usually based on *open* memberships, both transient and local, which offer the consumer opportunities in sport and/or fitness. In comparison, private sport clubs are organizations with an *exclusive* membership policy. Private sport clubs may be supported by private memberships or, if part of a large company, by funds from the parent company.

Both of these sport enterprises may have some or all of the following facilities and/or programs: aerobics, weight training, racquet sports, and aquatics. They may have fitness instructors, athletic trainers, personal trainers, nutritionists, exercise physiologists, and strength and conditioning coaches available for members depending on the club's focus. Some clubs focus on racquet sports or weight training, whereas others offer a full complement of services including child care, tanning beds, and fitness assessment and prescription. Marketing and sales specialists, as well as assistant managers and a general manager, are imperative.

Sport and athletic cluster

Four sport business categories are included in the **Sport and athletic cluster** (see the box on p. 16).

College and university athletics. College and university athletics is the first large category of the sport and athletic cluster. It can have a profit orientation in major universities and a nonprofit orientation in other institutions of higher learning. When the athletic department has a profit orientation, the roles are distinctly different from those in a nonprofit situation (see the box on p. 17). College athletics focuses on varsity individual and team performance in intercollegiate competition. Some of the job titles in this setting include athletic director, associate and assistant director, sports information director, promotion or marketing director, academic advising coordinator, ticket manager, and facilities and/or event manager (Kelley et al., 1989). The athletic director is responsible for the overall operation of the collegiate athletic department. Part of that responsibility includes fund raising, as well as substance abuse identification, treatment, and policy development.

In smaller colleges and universities, the athletic director may also be a coach. In some instances, head coaches (usually in men's football or basketball) may also be the director or an associate director. The athletic director is responsible for the total operation and usually answers directly to the chief executive officer of the college or university. By virtue of this relationship, that position is considered upper-level management. Associate and some assistant athletic directorships are middle-management positions. Each of these, especially in larger institutions, has staff support at the entry level.

In the not-so-distant past these entry-level positions were frequently filled by former coaches and ex-athletes. Today, however, more frequently these positions are filled by people who are educated as sport managers (DeSensi et al., 1990; Parkhouse, 1987).

Professional sport. Professional sport is the next category within the sport and athletics cluster, and it has a profit orientation. Professional sport has been defined as an enterprise concerned with management of players and events for spectator consumption, and that uses marketing and promotional activities to sell admissions to events (DeSensi et al., 1990).

Sport management positions in professional sport parallel, yet are different from, the positions found in the athletic department of larger universities (Beitel et al., 1989). Most professional teams have executives with such titles as president, general manager, director of player personnel, budget director, and directors of marketing, promotions, and public relations. The duties of a general manager of a major league professional baseball team have been compared to the duties of an athletic director at a National Collegiate Athletic Association (NCAA) Division I school (Hatfield, Wrenn, and Bretting, 1987). One of the major differences that Hatfield et al. (1987) identified between these two positions was that general managers are responsible for player development, which includes the physical and mental development of the players. In contrast, the collegiate athletic director, in most cases, does not make direct decisions about player recruitment and development. Consequently, the biophysical sciences are more important for a general manager in major league sports than for an athletic director at the collegiate level. Therefore the person planning to be a general manager at the professional level should understand biomechanics, anatomy, kinesiology, and sport psychology, to be better able to evaluate and develop players (Hatfield et al., 1987).

Professional sports teams, depending on the sport and level of play, require some or all of the following positions: (1) lower-level sport management positions, such as equipment manager, computer specialist, traveling secretary, or media liaison, (2) middle-level managers, such as ticket manager, concessions manager, business manager, or marketing director, (3) upper-level management and administrative personnel, such as director of public relations, facilities manager, and budget director. This is not an all-inclusive list, but it does represent a cross-section of the types of positions available in professional sport.

Opportunities for employment in professional sport are expanding as new teams are added to existing leagues. In addition, the international professional sport scene is burgeoning. The World League of American Football, the Goodwill Games, and the World Basketball League are some recent examples of the expansion of sport into international markets. Each of these leagues, teams, and events requires competent managers to ensure that owners and investors do not lose money, that the participants are paid, and that the public receives what has been advertised. In addition to the world market, there are professional teams and leagues for almost every sport from bowling to wrestling in the domestic market.

Sport organizations. One of the sport setting categories, sport organizations, might have either a profit or a nonprofit orientation, depending on the nature of the membership of sport teams and institutions. All sports, whether at the amateur or professional level, require governing organizations that provide an administrative or functional structure and that assist in fulfilling the goals of that particular group. The United States Olympic Committee, the National Collegiate Athletic Association, and the National Basketball Association are examples. Sport organizations are governing bodies that plan, organize, and control events for various levels of sport participation and are responsible for developing and disseminating information and policies germane to that sport. Some of these organizations have a profit motive and share the proceeds with the members of the conference or league, whereas others are designed primarily to serve the membership. Some of the types of positions in sport organizations are executive directors and tournament and competition coordinators. The executive director position is upper-level administrative, whereas the tournament director, director of training for officials, publicity director, and budget director are at the middle-management level.

Sport management services. Sport management services (see the box on p. 16) are another category, perhaps the least known, in the sport and athletic cluster, with job opportunities for sport managers. These are organizations or companies that promote and/or manage athletes and/or sport events. Sport management services include representation of athletes for contract negotiation, personal marketing, financial planning, investment services, and tax planning. Students with an interest in the contract negotiation aspect of sport management services should seriously consider pursuing a jurisprudence degree with specialization in contract law. Personal marketing of an athlete requires expertise in promotion, public relations, marketing, and advertising. Financial planning and investment services require a thor-

ough background in finance. Students interested in becoming a financial planner or investment services representative should pursue certification as a Certified Financial Planner (CFP) from the International Board of Standards and Practices for Certified Financial Planners (IBCFP). Tax planning is a highly specialized field of study and requires advanced study to qualify for positions in this sector of sport management services.

Many sport management services firms market or promote events in a specific sport, whereas other firms represent a variety of events. Firms devoted to event promotion require creative people to design, market, advertise, and sell regional, national, and international sporting events. Some firms serve as consultants for product development and marketing strategy planning for manufacturers of sports equipment, footwear, and apparel. Other firms may secure event sponsor(s), handle press and public relations activities, provide security, and handle leases and contracts.

All sporting events require sport management services for a successful operation. Individuals interested in the sport management services area need expertise in communications, marketing, advertising, sales, promotions, and public relations. Depending on the setting and specific career objectives, additional expertise may be necessary in finance, law, and tax planning.

Sporting goods industry cluster

The sports industry is big business, but few people know just how big it has become. Sports businesses in 1988 accounted for approximately 63 billion dollars of the total economy and ranked twenty-second out of all of the businesses and industries in the United States (Sandomir, 1988). The sporting goods industry alone accounted for approximately 5 billion dollars in the U.S. economy.

Sport marketing and merchandising. The sporting goods industry cluster (see the box on p. 16) includes the sport marketing and merchandising category, which is the marketing and distribution by manufacturers, wholesalers, and retailers of sport-related equipment and clothing to amateur and professional teams and individuals. This includes sales, advertising, promotion, research, and marketing management.

Retail sales. Another facet of the sporting goods industry cluster is the category of retail sales, which is defined as the management, marketing, promotion, and sale of sport equipment and clothing for consumer consumption (DeSensi et al., 1990). Retail sales take place in traditional sporting goods stores, discount stores, department stores, and pro shops, and through mail-order companies. The entry-level position is salesperson, the assistant manager represents the middle-management category, and, in general, the store manager would be considered upper-level management. One exception, however, would be in a large department store where the manager of the sporting goods department would be considered a middle-management position.

Hostelries and travel cluster

Hostelries. Hostelries have been identified as being either resorts or hotels. A resort is a profit-oriented full-service hostelry that provides programs and/or facilities for leisure pursuits and that provides one or more of the following natural attractions: sun, water, mountains, snow, and serenity (DeSensi et al., 1990). In addition, the resort would offer sport, recreational, and/or fitness activities to the clients who are attracted to the setting. Also, many resort areas are expanding their services beyond seasonal activities. For example, areas that are noted for snow skiing in the winter have developed golf or tennis as off-season attractions.

The category of hotels has been defined as profit-oriented full-service hostelries that offer temporary lodging and that provide sport, leisure, and fitness facilities and/or programs. The term full-service hostelry simply means that, in addition to lodging, other facilities are offered, such as food service, bars, and gift or specialty shops. Frequently, the specialty shops will include a pro shop for golf, tennis, skiing, or the resort's particular sport.

Travel and cruise. The travel and cruise category describes a profit-oriented, full-service hostelry offering programs and facilities for the pursuit of sport, fitness, and leisure activities, and providing transportation via water to places of interest. Travel and cruise enterprises hire lower-level sport management personnel such as activity leaders and exercise specialists, middle-level managers such as sport directors, and upper-level managers such as program coordinators.

Agencies cluster

The last of the clusters and one with the most employment opportunities is the **agencies cluster** (see the box on p. 16). The agency may be part of a local government such as a city or county recreation department.

Local government agencies. Local government agencies are created to meet the demand for specific types of recreation and leisure opportunities in cities, counties, and other special districts such as local park and recreation districts. Local government agencies offer entry-level positions such as sports coordinator, recreation supervisor II and III, and aquatics supervisor. Middle-level positions in government agencies have titles such as aquatics manager, recreation center manager, recreation supervisor I, program specialist, and sports or fitness director. Upper-level positions in local government agencies include sports director, club director, director of parks and recreation, and project manager.

Voluntary agencies. Voluntary agencies have been defined as nonprofit organizations supported primarily by membership fees and/or community funds with the focus of developing, implementing, and/or managing recreation or sport programs and/or facilities. Examples of voluntary agencies are youth organizations and churches. Voluntary agencies provide entry-level positions, such as physical director of YMCAs or YWCAs, aquatic director, and physical education or wellness director. Middle-level sport management positions found in voluntary agencies are senior director for each of the aforementioned positions, youth services director, and district director. Upper-management and administrative positions include executive director, associate executive director, branch director,

---

CONCEPT CHECK

All sport management students, no matter which setting or focus they select, should complete a professional core of studies that includes a strong business background. In addition to communication skills, the student must develop computer and leadership skills. Each specific cluster setting requires special areas of study at the undergraduate and/or graduate level.

---

and branch executive (Blanton, Beitel, DeSensi, and Kelley, 1989).

Sport managers, therefore, would serve as program directors, youth sport directors, activities coordinators, and executive directors in both governmental and voluntary agencies (Blanton et al., 1989). In general, the title of executive director denotes an upper-level administrative position. Depending on the size of the organization, program directors and activities coordinators typically are considered middle management, and their staff people would be in entry-level positions.

SPECIAL CONSIDERATIONS FOR THE HEALTH AND FITNESS FOCUS

It is important to differentiate employment (such as exercise technician and instructor) from management opportunities in this industry. Unlike other fields of sport management, the health and fitness field requires a strong science orientation for employment. For example, the exercise technologist, who may or may not have management responsibilities, is responsible for assessment and prescription. This requires study in exercise physiology. To be effective, instructors in such sports as tennis must be able to analyze skill. This requires an understanding of applied kinesiology. Instructors in aerobics must have an understanding of the physiological effects of endurance and the effect of floor stress on human performance. Those in weight training similarly must know about strength development.

Management positions in this field include directors of corporate fitness and rehabilitation centers, as well as managers of health and fitness clubs. Individuals in these positions should have both science and management competencies.

The aforementioned **health and fitness management** focus requires students to have a strong science background, including courses in chemistry, zoology, and human physiology. These prerequisite courses should lead to an in-depth understanding of exercise physiology. Most important, the student with this focus should be able to incorporate applied fitness principles into all fitness activities. Applied kinesiology and applied anatomy are two courses that are necessary for the health and fitness focus. Additional courses of study include nutrition, behavioral psychology, substance abuse, and exercise assessment and prescription.

Health and fitness certification through the American College of Sports Medicine (ACSM) is usually required for entry-level positions in this area. ACSM certification as an exercise technologist or exercise specialist is required for some entry-level and middle-level positions in the health and fitness industry. Program director certification from ACSM is the highest level and would be essential for administrators of hospital and community wellness programs, health promotion directors, and cardiac rehabilitation directors.

Students who choose the health and fitness management focus have employment opportunities in many of the sport management settings discussed previously. For example, strength and conditioning coaches, athletic trainers, and sports medicine personnel are needed at collegiate and professional levels of competition. Many hostelries offer entry-level opportunities for health and fitness management graduates. However, most of the opportunities for people with skills in this area are found in *commercial fitness centers* such as health clubs and wellness centers. Private athletic clubs offer employment opportunities for graduates who have an emphasis in the commercial fitness business. An exercise or fitness specialist working in an athletic club would be expected to have, in addition to fitness leadership skills, those in recreation and wellness programming, aquatics, marketing and promotions, facility operations, business operations, and sales. Entry-level positions in commercial fitness centers include aerobics instructor, fitness leader, front desk manager, pool maintenance person, membership representative, personal coach or trainer, health promotion educator, equipment maintenance person, and tennis, golf, squash, and racquetball instructor. Consultants such as cardiac rehabilitation specialists, nutritionists, and physical therapists may be entry-level or middle-management positions, depending on the size of the organization. Middle-level positions in this area include aerobic or fitness coordinator, aquatic director, general manager or director, sales director, promotions and public relations manager, and health promotion programmer. Regional director, health promotion director, human resources director, corporate sales director, and marketing director are examples of upper-level managerial and administrative positions in commercial fitness ventures.

Corporate and community wellness and health promotion personnel work to provide commercial and/or community clients with medically sound, economically feasible, comprehensive wellness and health programs. The following competencies are needed for employment in this area: nutrition, stress management, CPR, fitness evaluation, health screening, and smoking cessation techniques. In addition, applicants in this area need program planning experience, marketing skills, sales experience, good oral and written communication skills, and public relations skills.

Students with an interest in exercise physiology may want to examine the career opportunities as an *exercise specialist*. Exercise specialists are expected to be proficient in exercise testing and exercise prescription protocols, to serve as fitness counselors (which includes being able to motivate members to achieve their fitness objectives), to organize tournament and league sport activities, and to promote special events. Also, exercise specialists are expected to know the overall business operations of the club or hospital, which includes, but is not limited to, marketing, public relations, sales, human resource development, and management.

CONCEPT CHECK

Students selecting the health and fitness management focus need a strong science background, which includes courses in chemistry, zoology, and physiology. Applied fitness, applied anatomy, applied kinesiology, and courses in nutrition and behavioral psychology are needed for this focus.

SUMMARY

1. Sport management is a relatively new academic area and a newly recognized profession. Today, there are increasing opportunities for employment in the sport management field, partly because of the increased interest in fitness. Although sport is historically a male-dominated domain, and sport management is a reflection of that, there are increasing opportunities for youth, women, older adults, and handicapped persons.

2. Three factors, (1) focus, (2) setting, and (3) competencies, have been identified as important considerations in individual career planning.

3. The focus of sport management includes five clusters or areas for employment in sport management. These five different clusters of settings are classified as profit or nonprofit, depending on the purpose of the organizations and the type of financial support.

4. There are a variety of settings of potential employment for people with a health and fitness management focus. Some employment settings for health and fitness managers are the same as for business or agency managers, that is, the travel and cruise industry, companies, and professional sport. Usually, health and fitness managers are employed in commercial fitness centers, as well as corporate and community wellness and health promotion centers.

REVIEW QUESTIONS AND ISSUES

1. Give examples of personnel with a health or fitness and a sport or recreation focus for the settings identified in the box on p. 18. What competencies (see the box on p. 19) would be emphasized or needed in each instance?

2. What are the three determinants of sport management that affect career planning and subsequent career options? Why are these factors important?

3. Describe one or two sport management positions in the following settings:
   a. Voluntary and/or governmental agencies
   b. College and university athletics
   c. College and university intramurals and sport or fitness clubs
   d. Sport organizations
   e. Facilities management
   f. Professional sport
   g. Travel and cruise industry
   h. Corporations and companies
   i. Sporting goods industry
   j. Sport management services companies
   k. Sport businesses

REFERENCES

*Beitel, P., Kelley, D., DeSensi, J., and Blanton, M. (1989). *Management careers in professional sport and college/university athletics: results of a survey evaluation.* Paper presented at the annual convention of the Southern District of the American Alliance of Health, Physical Education, Recreation, and Dance. Chattanooga, Tenn. February 24-25. ERIC Document Reproduction Service No. ED 314 397.

*Blanton, M., Beitel, P., DeSensi, J., and Kelley, D. (1989). *Needs assessment and curricular evaluation for sport management careers in local government and voluntary agencies.* Paper presented at the Leisure Research Symposium of the annual national convention of the National Recreation and Park Association, Indianapolis, In. October 7. (ERIC Document Reproduction Service No. ED 306 206; Research in Education, No. SP 031 092, September, 1989.)

*DeSensi, J., Kelley, D., Beitel, P., and Blanton, M. (1990). Sport management curricular evaluation and needs assessment: a multifaceted approach. *Journal of Sport Management, 4*(1), 31-58.

DeSensi, J., and Koehler, L. (1989). Sport and fitness management: opportunities for women. *Journal of Physical Education, Recreation, and Dance, 60*(3), 55-57.

Ellard, J.A. (1984). *A competency analysis of managers of commercial recreational sport enterprises.* Unpublished doctoral dissertation, Indiana University.

Hardy, S. (1987). Graduate curriculums in sport management: the need for a business orientation. *Quest, 39*(2), 207-216.

Hatfield, B., Wrenn, J., and Bretting, M. (1987). Comparison of job responsibilities of intercollegiate athletic directors and professional sport general managers. *Journal of Sport Management, 1*(2), 129-145.

Jamieson, L.M. (1987). Competency-based approaches to sport management. *Journal of Sport Management, 1,* 48-56.

*Kelley, D., Beitel, P., Blanton, M., and DeSensi, J. (1990). Undergraduate and graduate sport management curricular models: a research based approach. *Quest* (in review process).

*Kelley, D., DeSensi, J., Blanton, M., and Beitel, P. (1989). *A contrast/comparison of needs assessment and curricular evaluation for management careers in athletics and intramurals.* Paper presented in the Research Consortium of the annual national convention of the American Alliance of Health, Physical Education, Recreation, and Dance, Kansas City, Kan. April 6-10, 1988. (ERIC Document Reproduction Service No. ED 303 451, Research in Education, No. SP 030 877, August 1989.)

Kjeldsen, E. (1980). Sport management: an emerging profession. *Arena Review, 4*(3), i-ii.

Lambrecht, K. (1987). Analysis of the competencies of sports and athletic club managers. *Journal of Sport Management, 1*(2), 116-128.

Lewis, G., and Appenzeller, H. (1985). *Successful sport management.* Charlottesville, Virginia: The Michie Co.

Parkhouse, B. (1987). Sport management curricula: current status and design implications for future development. *Journal of Sport Management, 1*(2), 93-115.

Parks, J., and Quain, R. (1986). Sport management survey: curriculum perspectives. *Journal of Physical Education, Recreation, and Dance, 57*(4), 22-26.

Pejchar, L. (Ed.) (1989). What is the health & fitness industry? *Health and Fitness Career Resources, 1,* 3.

Quain, R., and Parks, J. (1986). April. Sport management survey: employment perspectives. *Journal of Physical Education, Recreation, and Dance, 57*(4), 18-21.

Sandomir, R. (1988). The $50-billion sports industry. *Sports Inc., 1,* November 16, 14-23.

Whiddon, S. (1990). Graduate dual preparation programs in business and sport management. *Journal of Physical Education, Recreation, and Dance, 61,* 96-98.

*Initial funding for the research by the chapter authors was received from the College of Education, The University of Tennessee, Knoxville.

CHAPTER 3

Research, Theory, and Practice

Keith W. Lambrecht

In this chapter, you will become familiar with the following terms:

Foundation

Sport management foundation

Journal of Sport Management

Descriptive research

Theoretical research

Analytical research

Theory

Applied research

Basic research

Practice

Competency

Overview

Sport management, as a field of study, has received much attention in recent years by academicians and practitioners. Although it is generally agreed that the professional preparation of management personnel for sport organizations is an appropriate undertaking for academia, other significant differences remain (Gleason, 1986; Parkhouse and Ulrich, 1979; Parks and Quain, 1986). Current concerns include the lack of quality research studies

Acknowledgement is given to Bonnie L. Parkhouse of Temple University, Philadelphia, Pennsylvania, and Gordon A. Olafson of the University of Windsor, Ontario, Canada, for their contributions in revising this chapter.

that would provide a tenable body of knowledge in the area of sport management, thus creating an area devoid of its own theoretical base (Olafson, 1990; Parkhouse and Ulrich, 1979; Parkhouse, Ulrich, and Soucie, 1982); the inconsistency in curricular development and course offerings among academic programs at both the undergraduate and graduate levels (Parkhouse, 1987); and the ineffectiveness of some current degree programs in meeting the job-related competencies required of practitioners in various sport managerial settings (Lambrecht, 1987; Parks and Quain, 1986).

The purpose of this chapter is to help the reader understand the importance of theory and research in the field of sport management. In addition, the intent is to summarize past and current research efforts and to outline future research needs in order to develop and build a theory of sport management. Another goal is to infer a relationship between research and practice in this field. This concept is demonstrated by profiling the required competencies of sport managers.

THE FOUNDATION OF SPORT MANAGEMENT

To understand the foundation of sport management, it is important to define the meaning of two terms underlying this discussion: *foundation* and *sport management foundation*. The terms *sport* and *management* were defined in Chapter 1.

Foundation

Foundation is a word that has many contextual meanings. In general terms, foundation refers to the basis on which something stands or is supported. However, when considered in an educational context, it refers to a broadly conceived field of study that derives its character and fundamental theories from a number of academic disciplines. This is obviously the case with sport management. The foundation of sport management originates from two primary disciplines: sport studies (physical education) and business administration (Parkhouse, 1987).

Sport management foundation

As stated earlier, the foundation on which sport management is being built comes from two primary disciplines: sport studies and business administration. A traditional concept is depicted in Figure 3-1. Sport studies is composed of such areas of study as the organization and administration of sport programs, sport history, sport philosophy, sport sociology, and sport techniques (skills). Business administration includes such areas as accounting, the analysis of business systems (computers), economics, finance, law, management, public administration, and marketing. If sport management as a field of study is to prosper, university faculties in these two disciplines must cooperate in providing a sport management curriculum that meets the job-related needs of the sport management student.

It has been suggested by several authors (Jamieson, 1987; Lambrecht, 1987; Parkhouse, 1987; Parks and Quain, 1986) that the study of sport management is multi-disciplinary, thus conveying the idea that sport management must draw on theories, concepts, and insights from other related disciplines: communication, computer science, journalism, law, psychology, and sociology, to mention a few. Although this list is not complete, the areas mentioned make up a broad basis on which the field of sport management is being built. Each area adds a knowledge base for sport managers as they prepare for specific careers in the field, such as athletic directors, managers of fitness clubs, and sport consultants (see Chapter 2).

The foundation of sport management is being established with each new piece of research reported. Still, the actual foundation of sport management has yet to be fully determined. More knowledge will develop over the next few years as the field of sport management continues to grow. The foundational areas identified for discussion in this book are accounting and budgeting, business law, communications, economics, management, and marketing. Each will be discussed in later chapters.

CONCEPT CHECK

Sport management is a broadly conceived field of study that has derived its character from two major academic disciplines. The two disciplines are sport studies and business administration. A cooperative effort from these two disciplines is required if the field of sport management is to continue growing. By its nature, the study of sport management is also multi-disciplinary.

RELATED RESEARCH IN SPORT MANAGEMENT

The relatively new field of sport management has developed almost exclusively within departments of physical education (sport studies). Although some management specialists have contributed to the field of sport management, most scholars in the field of business administration have not been particularly interested in examining sport. It is ap-

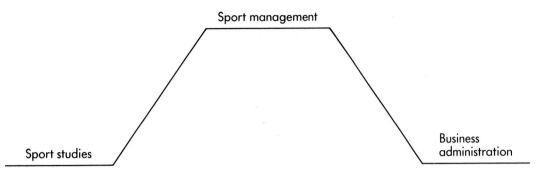

FIGURE 3-1 A traditional concept of the foundations of sport management.

parent that the growth of sport management has been the result of sustained efforts by physical education (sport studies) scholars.

This is evident when one reviews the literature in the field. The field has evolved with three organizational issues: (1) examining the legacy of its past, (2) attempting to cope with the problems of the present, and (3) establishing directions for the future. The nature of sport management in the future will be determined by the research, writings, and practices of those now engaged in the field. Although there has been a tremendous interest in sport management in recent years, research efforts in the field have been lacking in scope and theoretical base (Olafson, 1990; Parkhouse, Ulrich, and Soucie, 1982; Paton, 1987; Spaeth, 1967). Since the advent of the *Journal of Sport Management* in 1987, improvement has been realized; however, much work still lies ahead for the sport management scholar of the future.

Research focus

Early research associated with sport management has dealt primarily with the organization and administration of departments of physical education and athletics. Parkhouse, Ulrich, and Soucie (1982) examined doctoral studies reported in the *Dissertation Abstracts International* that relate to sport management between 1950 and 1980. They concluded that studies that were conducted dealt almost exclusively with physical education and athletics at the collegiate level. Typical topics of study included administrative policies, procedures, and practices;

analysis of program curricular content; administrator job descriptions, responsibilities, and specifications; communications; economic concerns; facility planning; financial and budget considerations; leadership behavior; legal aspects; organizational factors; and philosophy-related matters.

Paton (1987) reviewed 122 sport management–related studies conducted between 1978 and 1984 that were in *Completed Research in Health, Physical Education, and Recreation*. He concluded that 60% of the studies focused on the college or university setting, with the other 40% examining public schools, recreation agencies, and other outside agencies. The primary areas of investigation were leadership behavior and organizational development, with a secondary emphasis on such areas as financing, marketing, legal liability, and the role of women in sport.

In regard to the *Journal of Sport Management*, which publishes articles that focus on management relating to sport, 45 articles had been published since its inception in January 1987 to its issue in July 1990. Of the 45 articles published, approximately 35% focused on college, university, and school issues, examining such topics as academic preparation, job responsibilities and specifications, Title IX, legal liability, marketing, and the role of women in sport. The remaining 65% covered a number of topics, including amateur sports, sport clubs, fitness services, leisure organizations, and professional sports. Yet no single topic was represented more often than the college, university, and school setting.

Research efforts

Past and current research efforts in sport management have been classified as descriptive rather than theoretical (Parkhouse, Ulrich, and Soucie, 1982; Paton, 1987). The nature of **descriptive research** is to characterize the attitudes, conditions, and practices within a set group or population. The most popular form of descriptive research is the questionnaire or survey. Other forms include the interview, the case study, and the job analysis. **Theoretical research**, on the other hand, empirically tests models or theories to predict or identify causal relationships to determine how and why things happen. Theoretical research is more scientific in nature. This concept will be further explored later in this chapter.

In efforts to assess the research base of sport management, several authors have reviewed research literature. In 1967, Spaeth examined the literature within sport and physical education. She found that research in the field lacked theoretical orientation and design (Zeigler and Spaeth, 1975). A further review of related sport management literature reported between 1950 and 1980 was conducted in 1982 by Parkhouse, Ulrich, and Soucie. Of the 336 studies listed in the *Dissertation Abstracts International*, 283 were descriptive and only 53 were based on theory. In 1983, Paris reviewed a list of 48 doctoral studies done between 1972 and 1978. Results indicated that more than 75% of the studies were descriptive. Paton in 1987 examined studies reported in *Completed Research in Health, Physical Education, and Recreation* between 1978 and 1984. Of the 122 studies cited, almost all of them were descriptive.

Current research related to sport management has been reported in the *Journal of Sport Management*, the major research vehicle in the field of sport management. The editorial policy of the *Journal of Sport Management* is to publish manuscripts that focus on the theoretical and applied aspects of management related to sport. As mentioned earlier, as of July 1990, 45 articles had been published since the inaugural issue in 1987; approximately 40% of the articles were descriptive, 35% analytical, and 25% theoretical. **Analytical research** involves an in-depth study and evaluation of available information in a related area to explain complex phenomena. Examples of analytical research include those that are historical or philosophical in nature.

Future research needs

Although the amount of research conducted in sport management is substantial, much work lies ahead for the sport management scholar of the future. Two major concerns have surfaced: the focus of sport management research must be broadened, and more research studies must be based on theory. Olafson (1990) suggests that future research studies in the area of sport management will require more rigorous research designs and analyses.

First, sport management research has focused primarily on educational settings. Future research efforts must also encompass non-educational settings. Examples of these settings include, but are not limited to, amateur sports, sport and fitness centers (public and private), retail sporting stores, sport consulting, and professional sports. Sport is not one dimensional, but multi-dimensional; its research focus should reflect its scope.

Second, research studies conducted in the field of sport management have been descriptive rather than theoretical. This has caused concern for many scholars in the field. While it is true that most scholars feel that theoretical research is "more scientific" than descriptive research, both types are required for the further development of a new discipline such as sport management. Descriptive research provides the basic knowledge that is necessary for conducting further research. Research in the field of sport management could not advance without the accurate identification and description of attitudes, conditions, and practices within the field. There is a need to summarize previous research efforts to determine what has already been learned. From this summary, it may be possible to derive some general principles of sport management that may be useful to academicians developing sport management curricula. An example of this would be a summary of the research completed on the competencies of sport managers. This issue will be discussed later in this chapter.

Once these summaries have been completed and general principles of sport management derived, more theoretical research is necessary. This concept was best expressed by Parkhouse and Ulrich (1979). A schema was developed that depicted the process required in defining a theory of sport management. The schema is shown in Figure 3-2.

Since the development of this schema, sport management research has not changed very much.

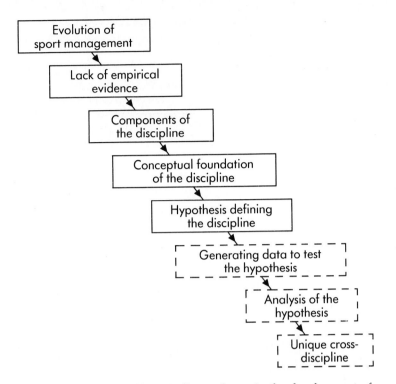

FIGURE 3-2 The schema. Solid lines indicate phases in the development of sport management that have been defined; broken lines represent steps not yet solidified. (From Parkhouse, B., and Ulrich, D. [1979]. A paradigm for theoretical development, scientific inquiry, and professional application. *Quest, 31* [2].)

The field is still in the process of defining the discipline as indicated in Figure 3-2 but is starting to progress to the next step of "generating data to test the hypothesis." The process outlined is not impossible, but years of hard work and quality research are required before the field of sport management will be able to generate its own theory.

Future research attempts in sport management must draw heavily on the theories relating to the foundational base: sport studies and business administration. Yet, given this notion, perhaps there is no need for the field of sport management to develop its own unique theory but to do what related fields such as sport psychology and sport sociology have done. Sport psychology draws theories from the field of psychology, and sport sociology uses those from sociology. Such an approach was outlined by Parkhouse, Ulrich, and Soucie in 1982. They suggested that topics in four

main theoretical areas of business administration be tested in the sport arena. The four categories are represented in the box on p. 32.

Although the box may only partially list appropriate research topics, it is indicative of research needs in the field of sport management today. Sport management is not a mature discipline with a well-defined body of knowledge. As stated earlier, time will be the factor that determines whether this field will eventually be able to generate its own unique theory. Perhaps equally important is to question whether the development of sport management theory per se is necessary. Parkhouse, Ulrich, and Soucie (1982) have demonstrated that it is feasible to borrow existing theory from a related discipline, in this case business administration, to effectively answer relevant research questions in the field of sport management. Whether sport management establishes a unique theoretical

---

Partial inventory of behavioral research opportunities in sport management

Subordinate-related	Organization-related
Role expectations	Organization climate
Job satisfaction	Organization design
Motivation	Communication channels
Career stages	Group development
Stress management	

Superior-related	Environment-related
Goal setting	Efficiency boundary relations
Job design	Ecology studies
Conflict resolution	Market analysis
Socialization	Regulation analysis
Control strategies	
Reward systems	

From Parkhouse, B., Ulrich, D., and Soucie, D. (1982). Research in sport management: a vital rung of this new corporate ladder. *Quest, 34*(2).

---

base or borrows from other disciplines, it is imperative that its research efforts become more theoretical in nature.

CONCEPT CHECK

The field of sport management has developed as a result of the sustained efforts of physical education (sport studies) scholars. This is apparent when one reviews the related literature. The research focus on sport management has dealt primarily with educational settings. Further, past and current research efforts have been analytical and descriptive rather than theoretical in nature. Since the advent of the Journal of Sport Management, research efforts have improved; however, future scholars in the field must address two major issues. First, the focus of sport management research must be broadened, and second, more research studies must be based on theory.

RELATIONSHIP BETWEEN THEORY AND PRACTICE

One of the goals of this chapter is to explain the relationship between theory and practice in sport management and the importance therein. This is a difficult task given the fact that sport manage-

ment is presently devoid of its own theory. However, as aforementioned, theory abounds in related areas. It is vitally important that sport management scholars rely on the theories of these disciplines and understand that theory is needed to develop quality research. In turn, research findings enhance the performance of practitioners. The integration between theory, research, and practice is imperative. To aid in this understanding, a general distinction between theory and practice will be outlined with an ensuing discussion of the importance of theory and practice to the overall development of the field of sport management.

Theory and practice
A **theory** is accepted principles devised to analyze, predict, or explain the nature or behavior of a specified set of phenomena. Theories are tested by research. Research can best be described as a systematic and organized effort to investigate a problem that needs a solution.

When research is done with the intention of applying the results of its findings to solving a specific problem, it is called **applied research**. Most organizations, including those in sport, are interested in applied research and hire researchers and consultants to study a specific problem for the purpose of rectifying the situation. For example, a racquet club is experiencing a high rate of membership turnover. It hires a research consultant who finds that 85% of membership cancellations were from individuals with little skill in tennis who were frustrated because they could find only more advanced opponents with whom to play. The club rectifies the problem by offering tennis lessons and setting up a computerized system to afford individuals the opportunity to play with same-skilled players.

Most research and development departments in various industries, as well as professors in colleges and universities, do basic research to generate knowledge in particular areas of interest to the industries, organizations, and researchers. **Basic research** is conducted to test principles and theories in efforts to produce results that are generalizable to a large number of situations. The main purpose of conducting basic research is to generate more knowledge and understanding of the phenomena that occur and to build theories based on the research results. Such theories are then used in subsequent research as a foundation for further study. This process of building on existing knowledge is the genesis for theory building in the field of sport management.

An example of basic research is a university professor's effort to understand and generate knowledge on how to increase work productivity of white-collar employees in the service industry. Sport organizations are typically part of the service industry. In an effort to accomplish this task the professor might observe workers in various service organizations such as retail sporting good stores, athletic departments, and several types of sport clubs. The professor studies the employees' productivity and factors relating to it, so as to add to the existing body of knowledge to determine how to increase work productivity.

The term **practice** refers to the act of applying or putting something to specific use. In sport management it's the actual performance of one's duties and responsibilities. Good practice relies on appropriate research and theory within a specific area of study. Theoretically based knowledge leads to purposeful actions with direction. Sport management scholars need to develop a tenable body of knowledge to provide adequate guidelines for the direction practitioners in this field should take in the future. As mentioned earlier, "the jury is still out" on whether this body of knowledge should be unique unto itself or borrowed from other disciplines.

Today's sport management practitioners engaged in the daily tasks of their profession tend to focus more on skills than on principles, on ends than on means, on details than on conceptual approaches.

Importance of theory and practice to sport management

The relationship between theory and practice has itself been a subject of debate in the field of sport management. Many view theory and practice as mutually exclusive concepts belonging to separate and different realms. The schism between theory/research and practice must be eliminated. What is needed for the continued growth of theory (knowledge) and practice in this field is an integration of viewpoints and collaboration between sport management scholars, academicians, and practitioners.

Academicians and practitioners need to incorporate into their thinking an appreciation for each other. Academicians must provide the models and theories to explain and predict how and why events happen so that practitioners might be more effective in the actual performance of their job duties and responsibilities.

At the present time the field of sport management does not have a philosophy, foundation, conceptual framework, or theoretical base that is generally accepted by scholars, educators, and practitioners. This is partially due to the fact that sport management is a new field of study. It is probable that during the next decade the field of sport management will continue to reflect a pluralistic society that is made up of many publics each having their own opinions regarding the philosophical and theoretical orientation of this field.

CONCEPT CHECK

At present, the field of sport management is devoid of its own theory but relies on the principles and theories in related disciplines. The integration between theory, research, and practice is imperative. A theory is composed of accepted principles devised to analyze, predict, or explain the nature of a specified set of phenomena; research is a scholarly investigation or inquiry; and practice is the act of applying or putting something to a specific use.

COMPETENCIES FOR SPORT MANAGERS (PRACTITIONERS)

As pointed out previously, completed research in the field of sport management needs to be compiled to determine what has been learned to date. The focus of this section is to summarize research studies related to competencies of sport managers. What are the required competencies of sport managers? Are these competencies generalizable across sport managerial settings? From the results of this summary it may be possible to derive some general competencies useful to academicians as they develop and revise sport management curricula to meet job-related needs.

Competency defined

One of the major problems in identifying competencies in the field is the lack of a consistent definition of the term "competency." A **competency** is a knowledge, skill, or attitude needed to carry out properly an activity to succeed in one's professional life (Butler, 1978). Butler's definition seems logical, since the field of sport management is attempting to understand the functions, roles, and skills required in effectively conducting the business of sport organizations.

Second, an acceptable method of securing job-related competencies from sport practitioners must be determined. A review of competency-based literature in the field of sport management reveals an acceptable descriptive method. This method consists of collecting data from various practitioner groups by using survey instruments, such as questionnaires, to gather descriptions of existing phenomena within the groups in question. Furthermore, the intent is to ascertain job-related skills, practices, and attitudes in order to apply appropriate statistical procedures to determine relationships from data generated. Many social scientists consider this type of research to be an excellent blend of experimental control and situational reality. It is appropriate to survey practitioners in the field, since they have a higher perception of competencies required to perform their job than do educators (Kennedy, 1978).

Competency-based research in sport management

In recent years, four studies have focused on competencies required of managers in sport organizations. In 1980, Jamieson surveyed sport managers in three institutional settings: military, municipal, and institutional. The Jamieson Recreational Sports Competency Analysis (RSCA) instrument included 112 competency statements representing 12 curricular areas. The 12 curricular areas were as listed below:

1. Business procedures
2. Communications
3. Facility and maintenance
4. Governance
5. Legality
6. Management techniques
7. Officiating
8. Philosophy
9. Programming techniques
10. Research
11. Safety and accident prevention
12. Science

Further, three management levels (I—bottom, II—middle, III—top) were investigated to determine differences. All 112 competency statements will not be presented here; however, the top five competencies at each level will be identified. They are significant, because each level relates well with managerial skills outlined by Katz (1974). Katz proposed three main types of skills for management personnel: technical, human, and conceptual. Technical skills involve an understanding and knowledge in a specific activity. Human skills involve interactions with people, and conceptual skills require the ability to view the entire organization. Level I (bottom) reflects technical skills. Level II represents human skills, and level III conceptual skills. See Tables 3-1, 3-2, and 3-3.

TABLE 3-1 *Level* I *(bottom) top five ranked competency statements*

Competency statement	Rank
Recognizes safety hazards that cause injury	1
Knows basic recreational sport terminology	2
Identifies and encourages participants for programs	3
Recognizes various factors that lead to accidents	4
Understands specific risk of sport activities	5

TABLE 3-2 Level II (middle) top five ranked competency statements

Competency statement	Rank
Recognizes safety hazards that cause injury	1
Uses effective decision-making skills	2
Demonstrates ability to schedule tournaments, leagues, and meets	3
Maintains effective communication with the public	4
Identifies and encourages participants for programs	5

TABLE 3-3 Level III (top) top five ranked competency statements

Competency statement	Rank
Uses effective decision-making skills	1
Prepares and defends a budget proposal	2
Examines and analyzes a budget	3
Maintains effective communications with public	4
Maintains effective communications with staff	5

Quain and Parks (1986) surveyed sport practitioners in six careers: physical fitness, sport promotions, sport marketing, sport administration and management, sport directing, and aquatics management. Two hundred questionnaires were mailed to practitioners in each of the six identified career areas. Respondents were presented a list of eight subjectively determined competencies and asked to indicate which of those competencies were required of practitioners in their career area. Table 3-4 shows the eight competencies and the six career rankings of each competency.

This study illustrates the scope of sport management. Sport management is multi-faceted, that is, many career options exist. Parkhouse (1987) emphasized that a one-track curriculum to serve the needs of a variety of sport-related occupations fails to address the unique competencies required of each. This study supports that notion. Sport management programs professing to prepare practitioners in more than one career area should develop specialized tracks accordingly.

Lambrecht (1987) identified several competencies needed to manage sport and athletic clubs and to determine whether differences existed in required competencies for organizations of different size. The population for this study were members of the International Racquet Sports Association (IRSA). Club groups were classified according to membership size and services offered by the club. Group I had 500-999 members; Group II, 1,000-2,000 members; and Group III had more than 2,000

TABLE 3-4 Competencies and ranking per career category

Competency	N =	PFI 55	SP 49	SMKTG 39	SAM 82	SD 81	AQM 59	Total 365
Writing		5	1	1	4	6	7	4
Personnel management		3	6	2.5	2	3	1.7	2
Public speaking		6	2	2	6	7	6	5
Time management		4	4	3.5	5	5	3	3
Finance management		7	2	6	3	4	4	6
Human relations		2	3	5	1	1	1.5	1
Personal fitness		1	8	8	8	8	5	8
Knowledge of sports		8	5	7	7	2	8	7

PFI = Physical fitness industry; SP = Sport promotion; SMKTG = Sport marketing; SAM = Sport administration and management; SD = Sport directing; AQM = Aquatics management

TABLE 3-5 *Rank order of competencies: total sample and club groups*

Competency	Total sample	Mean rankings		
		I	II	III
Communication with clientele	1	1	1	1
Employee motivation	2	3.5	3	2
Handling complaints of customers	3	3.5	2	4
Staff communications	4	2	4	3
Decision-making process	5	5	5	5
Supervision of staff and personnel	6.5	7.5	7	6
Evaluation of club as a business	6.5	7.5	6	7
Time management	8	6	8	9
Strategic planning	9	10	9	10
Budget preparation	10	11	11	8

members. The instrument used in this study was a mailed questionnaire consisting of 33 competency items. Managers responded to the 33 competency items according to a six-point Likert scale rating of importance with a rating of 6 being extremely important. Table 3-5 depicts and compares the top 10 rated competencies for the total sample and the three club group classifications. Note the uniformity of the club group ratings.

In regard to organizational size, 12 competencies were identified as being more complex in larger clubs. This is significant because it suggests that there is a difference between managing larger clubs and smaller ones. This is consistent with literature presented by Daft (1983), which states that managers of larger organizations perform more complex tasks than do managers of small organizations. The following 12 competencies listed were identified in the study as significant, with Group III mean scores greater than those of Groups I and II:

1. Allocation of resources
2. Budget preparation
3. Communication with clientele
4. Decision-making process
5. Employee motivation
6. Employee evaluation
7. Facility development
8. Handling complaints of customers
9. Hiring process of employees
10. Preparing and making public presentations
11. Staff communications
12. Supervision of staff

An international study, conducted by Farmer (1988), utilized the previously discussed compentency instrument designed by Lambrecht. Farmer surveyed official members of the Australian Society of Sport Administrators (ASSA). This body is the accepted and recognized governing body that represents the interests of all sport administrators in Australia. Two hundred forty-three members responded to the survey; the top ten competencies are listed in Table 3-6.

TABLE 3-6 *Rank order of competencies for ASSA*

Competency	Rank
Communication with clientele	1
Decision-making process	2
Budget preparation	3
Writing skills	4
Program preparation and development	5
Strategic planning (long- and short-term)	6
Time management	7
Program goals and objectives	8
Marketing	9
Legal liability and responsibility	10

"Communication with clientele" was the top-rated competency as it was in the Lambrecht study. This is significant, because it suggests that it might be possible to generalize competencies across settings. More research is needed to further document this point. Further, this study demonstrates that the scope of sport management is not a concern just of the United States but is truly a field of interest internationally as well.

In reviewing the four competency studies by Jamieson; Quain and Parks; Lambrecht; and Farmer, it is readily apparent that there are two common themes. First, for the most part, identified required competencies for sport managers are derived from two major disciplines: business administration and communications. This is significant, because most sport management programs in existence today are housed in departments of physical education. Second, all of the authors have suggested that more competency-based studies be conducted in the future to ensure that educators design and implement curricula that reflect the job-related competencies of practitioners.

CONCEPT CHECK

A competency is a knowledge, skill, or attitude needed to properly carry out an activity to succeed in one's professional life (Butler, 1978). Four competency-based studies were reviewed (Farmer, 1988; Jamieson, 1980; Lambrecht, 1987; Quain and Parks, 1986) to determine sport managerial competencies. Competencies, for the most part, are derived from the study of business administration. More competency-based studies should be conducted in the future.

SUMMARY

1. Sport management is a new field of academic preparation and study that has received much attention in recent years; however, it is devoid of its own theoretical base.
2. The foundation on which sport management is being built is sport studies and business administration. Other related areas include communications, computer science, journalism, law, psychology, and sociology.
3. The focus of sport management research has been limited primarily to the educational setting.
4. Past and current research efforts in sport management have been classified as descriptive rather than theoretical.
5. Descriptive research characterizes the attitudes, conditions, and practices within a set group or population. Theoretical research empirically tests models to predict or identify causal relationships to determine why things happen.
6. The *Journal of Sport Management* is the major research vehicle in the field of sport management. The editorial policy is to publish articles that focus on the theoretical and applied aspects of sport-related management.
7. Future scholars in sport management must address two major research concerns. First, the focus of research must be expanded to include more noneducational settings such as amateur sport, sport and fitness centers, retail sporting stores, sport consulting, and professional sports. Second, research in sport management must become more theoretically based.
8. Past and current research studies should be summarized to determine what has been learned to date. This will aid in the development of sport management theory.
9. Academicians and practitioners need to understand the importance of both theory and practice in the development of the field of sport management. Theory is needed to develop quality research, which will enhance theory and result in sound practice.
10. Sport managerial competencies, for the most part, are derived from the discipline of business administration. More competency-based studies should be conducted.

REVIEW QUESTIONS AND ISSUES

1. The foundation of sport management is based on two major disciplines. Identify and outline why each is important to the study of sport management.
2. Why does the field of sport management need to broaden its research focus?
3. Discuss the past, current, and future trends of sport management research.
4. Compare and contrast theory and practice. Discuss their importance to the development of the field of sport management.
5. Why is the *Journal of Sport Management* important to the field of sport management?

6. What competencies are required of sport managers? Can these competencies be generalized across settings? How might this information be put into practice?

REFERENCES

Butler, F. (1978). The concept of competence: an operational definition. *Educational Technology, 18,* 7-18.

Daft, R. (1983). *Organizational theory and design.* New York: West Publishing Co.

Farmer, P. (1988). *Model of curriculum for sport administration at tertiary institutions in Australia.* Unpublished doctoral dissertation. Albuquerque: University of New Mexico.

Gleason, T. (1986). Sport administration degrees: growing to fill a need/supply overwhelms demand. *Athletic Administration.* (February), 9-10.

Jamieson, L. (1980). A competency analysis of recreational sports personnel in selected institutional settings. Unpublished doctoral dissertation. Bloomington: Indiana University.

Jamieson, L. (1987). Competency-based approach to sport management. *Journal of Sport Management, 1*(1), 48-56.

Katz, R. (1974). Skills of an effective administrator. *Harvard Business Review, 52,* 90-112.

Kennedy, D. (1978). *A competency analysis of therapeutic recreation graduates at different educational levels.* Alexandria, Virginia: National Recreation and Park Association.

Lambrecht, K. (1987). An analysis of the competencies of sport and athletic club managers. *Journal of Sport Management, 1*(2), 116-128.

Olafson, G. (1990). Research design in sport management: what's missing, what's needed? *Journal of Sport Management, 4*(2), 102-120.

Paris, R. (1983). A selected listing of doctoral dissertations in administrative theory and practice related to physical education and sport (1972-1978). In E. Zeigler and G. Bowie (Eds.), management competencies development in sport and physical education, pp. 292-295.

Parkhouse, B. (1987). Sport management curricula: current status and design implications for future development. *Journal of Sport Management, 1*(2), 93-115.

Parkhouse, B. and Ulrich, D. (1979). Sport management as a potential cross-discipline: a paradigm of theoretical application. *Quest, 31*(2), 264-276.

Parkhouse, B., Ulrich, D., and Soucie, D. (1982). Research in sport management: a vital rung of this new corporate ladder. *Quest, 34*(2), 176-186.

Parks, J., and Quain, R. (1986). Curriculum perspectives. *Journal of Physical Education, Recreation, and Dance, 57*(4), 22-26.

Paton, G. (1987). Sport management research—what progress has been made? *Journal of Sport Management, 1*(1), 25-31.

Quain, R., and Parks, J. (1986). Sport management survey: employment perspectives. *Journal of Physical Education, Recreation, and Dance, 57*(4), 18-21.

Spaeth, M. (1967). *An analysis of administrative research in physical education and athletics in relation to a research paradigm.* Unpublished doctoral dissertation. Champaign, Illinois: University of Illinois.

Zeigler, E. (1987). Sport management: past, present, future. *Journal of Sport Management, 1*(1), 4-24.

Zeigler, E., and Spaeth, M. (Eds.) (1975). *Administration theory and practice in physical education and athletics.* Englewood Cliffs, New Jersey: Prentice Hall.

SUGGESTED READINGS

Chelladurai, P. (1985). *Sport management: macro perspectives.* London; Ontario: Sports Dynamics.

Jackson, J. (1981). *Sport administration.* Springfield, Illinois: Charles C. Thomas, Publisher.

Jamieson, L. (1987). Competency-based approaches to sport management. *Journal of Sport Management, 1*(1), 48-56.

Lambrecht, K. (1987). An analysis of the competencies of sport and athletic club managers. *Journal of Sport Management, 1*(2), 116-128.

McGuire, J. (1986). Management and research methodology. *Journal of Management, 12*(1), 5-17.

Olafson, G. (1990). Research design in sport management: what's missing, what's needed? *Journal of Sport Management, 4*(2), 102-120.

Parkhouse, B., and Ulrich, D. (1979). Sport management as a potential cross-discipline: a paradigm for theoretical application. *Quest, 31*(2), 264-276.

Parkhouse, B., Ulrich, D., and Soucie, D. (1982). Research in sport management: a vital rung of this new corporate ladder. *Quest, 34*(2), 176-186.

Paton, G. (1973). Administrative theory and graduate physical education. In P. Hunsicker (Ed.), *Administrative theory and practice in athletics and physical education.* Chicago, Illinois: Athletic Institute.

Paton, G. (1987). Sport management research—what progress has been made? *Journal of Sport Management, 1*(1), 25-31.

Zeigler E. (1987). Sport management: past, present, future. *Journal of Sport Management, 1*(1), 4-24.

Zeigler, E. (1985). Understanding the immediate managerial environment in sport and physical education. *Quest, 37*(3), 166-175.

SUGGESTED JOURNALS

Academy of Management Review
Journal of Accountancy
Journal of Business Communications
Journal of Business Research
Journal of Business Strategy
Journal of Management Review
Journal of Management Studies
Journal of Marketing
Journal of Marketing Research
Journal of Sport Management
Quest

PART II

Theoretical Foundations

4

Accounting and Budgeting

Otho G. Bendit
Linda S. Koehler

In this chapter, you will become familiar with the following terms:

Accounting

Separate-entity assumption

Continuity assumption

Unit of measure assumption

Time-period assumption

Cost principle

Revenue principle

Matching principle

Full-disclosure principle

Balance sheet

Profit and loss statement

Depreciation

Cash management

Repurchase agreement

Budgeting

Capital budget

Master budget

Sales budget

Production budget

Department expense budget

Operating expense budget

Line-item budget

Zero-base budgeting

Cash-flow budgeting

Fixed assets

Straight-line method

Sum-of-the-years digits

Double-declining-balance method

Nonprofit organization

Fund accounting

Equity in pooled cash

Statement of changes in fund balance

Corporation

Partnership

Proprietorship

Overview

Sport management should have at its disposal a person or staff that has mastered the fundamentals and principles of accounting. Considering the complexities of today's business environment, no venture, be it profit-oriented or nonprofit, can survive without applying adequate standard accounting procedures to its operation. Sport management is no exception.

The importance of accounting and its resulting financial statements and data, as prepared by responsible accountants, cannot be overemphasized. The need for management to constantly analyze and monitor the growth and trends of its operation is not the only reason for accounting. Outside users of financial data, such as banks, investors, and government agencies, also use financial information and statistics in today's expanding economy.

This chapter addresses the important issues and concepts fundamental to accounting and the sport or fitness manager. Major topics include the definition and role of accounting within the sport or fitness organization, assumptions and principles of accounting, business statements such as balance sheets and profit and loss statements, depreciation, fund accounting, various types of business structures, cash management, the budgeting process, and the use of computers.

DEFINITION AND ROLE OF ACCOUNTING IN THE SPORT AND FITNESS ENTERPRISE

Accounting can be defined as the collection of financial data about an organization (Welsch and Short, 1987). The accounting process includes the gathering, analysis, measurement, recording, and reporting of financial information to the decision makers within the sport or fitness organization. The product of the accounting process appears in the form of financial statements, the most common of which include the balance sheet (assets and liabilities), profit and loss statement (income and expense), and the budget(s).

An effective accounting system can provide information to the sport or fitness manager in a number of ways. The overall process serves to accumulate financial data, aids in planning and controlling financial operations, and is fundamental to problem solving and the decision-making process. Specifically, the accounting process involves the *internal* reporting to managers for routine financial operations and use in making special decisions or long-range plans and the *external* reporting of financial information to stockholders, government, and other outside agencies (Horngren and Sundem, 1987).

ASSUMPTIONS AND PRINCIPLES OF ACCOUNTING

Assumptions

The sport and fitness manager or accountant should be familiar with four basic assumptions. These assumptions are important, because they help to define the boundaries that determine how accounting information is perceived and reported. These assumptions include the ideas of *separate en-*

tity, continuity, unit of measure, and *time period* (Welsch and Short, 1987).

- The **separate-entity assumption** maintains that each sport or fitness business is perceived as an organization in and of itself whose business transactions are not tied to the personal transactions of the owner(s). At the same time, the *personal* transactions of the owner(s) are *not* recorded as transactions of the business.
- The **continuity assumption** suggests that the sport or fitness business has an "indefinite life," and that the business will continue to follow its goals and objectives far into the future.
- The **unit of measure assumption** holds that each sport or fitness business will report its financial statements in terms of the national monetary unit. In the United States, of course, the monetary unit is the dollar.
- The **time-period assumption** maintains that regular, periodic financial information is required by the sport or fitness manager. Although this does not have to be based on the *calendar* year, financial statements customarily cover the financial activity for a full year's time.

Principles

In addition, there are four principles of accounting that should be kept in mind. These serve as further guidelines when measuring and reporting the actual financial data. They are the **cost principle,** the **revenue principle,** the **matching principle,** and the **full-disclosure principle** (Welsch and Short, 1987). According to Welsch and Short, cost is measured as the cash *paid* plus the current value of all non-cash consideration. Revenue, on the other hand, is measured as the cash *received* plus the current dollar value of all noncash consideration received. Further, all expenses incurred in earning revenues within a given period must be *matched* with the revenues of that period. Finally, any periodic financial statement must be *clearly reported*, and all relevant financial information must be fully disclosed (Welsch and Short, 1987).

Accounting is an extremely useful tool in maintaining the financial health and stability of any sport and fitness enterprise. The aforementioned definition, assumptions, and principles should be seriously considered and applied. They provide helpful guidelines when determining what financial information should be gathered and how such information can be reported most effectively.

CONCEPT CHECK

Accounting deals with the financial data of an organization. Such information is organized into financial statements called balance sheets (assets and liabilities), profit and loss statements (income and expense), and budgets. Four assumptions basic to accounting are separate entity, continuity, unit of measure, and time period. Other important principles are the cost, revenue, matching, and full-disclosure principles.

THE ACCOUNTING SYSTEM

The complexity of an accounting system is in direct relation to the complexity and size of an organization or business. A simple system consisting of basic standard balance sheet accounts (assets and liabilities) and profit and loss accounts (income and expense) kept by hand would suffice for a small organization. However, with the availability of today's computer technology, most small operations are choosing to use computers. There are few businesses of any size that do not use such technology.

The **balance sheet** and **profit and loss statement** are the two most important products of accounting. The balance sheet gives a clear picture of the financial condition of a business at the end of each month or year. The profit and loss statement gives management net profit or loss data at the end of the same periods. It is imperative that these two statements be formulated in the simplest accounting terms possible. The purpose of the reports is to give the reader precise and complete financial data that does not contain confusing technical terms.

The box at right shows what is considered to be a standard balance sheet.

Larger and more complex businesses would, of course, require a much more detailed chart of accounts. To the previous balance sheet can be added any number of asset and liability accounts peculiar to a given organization. If a business is on an accrual basis, a number of prepaid and accrued accounts would be needed.

Examples of additional assets:

Petty cash
Notes receivable
Reserve for bad debts
Marketable securities

Balance sheet			
Current assets		**Current liabilities**	
Cash on hand	$13,000	Accounts payable	$ 9,000
Cash in banks	35,000	Notes payable	25,000
Accounts receivable	6,500	Taxes payable	8,000
Inventories	12,000		
Total current assets	$66,500	Total current liabilities	$42,000
Fixed assets		**Net worth**	
Office equipment	$13,000		
Furniture	5,000		
Vehicles	25,000		
Buildings	50,000		
Total fixed assets	$93,000	Surplus (equity)	$117,500
		Total liabilities	
Total assets	$159,500		$159,500

Prepaid advertising
Prepaid insurance
Accrued interest receivable

Examples of additional liabilities:

Mortgage payable
Accrued interest
Deferred income
Accrued payroll
Accrued taxes
Dividends payable

Income and expense accounts may be just as diversified as asset and liability accounts. Income accounts can be opened for each type of sale and revenue once they are determined. Examples are ticket sales, space rental, fees, merchandise sales, and program sales.

Expense accounts generally fall into four major categories: salaries and benefits, supplies and expenses, repairs and maintenance, and depreciation. Common expense accounts used are as follows:

Salaries and benefits	Supplies and expenses
Management salaries	Advertising
Advertising salaries	Cost of goods sold
Publicity salaries	Entertainment
Social security	Insurance
Pensions	Legal fees
Health insurance	Supplies
	Taxes
	Travel
	Utilities

Repairs and maintenance	Depreciation
Building repairs	Building depreciation
Equipment repairs	Equipment depreciation
Furniture repairs	Vehicle depreciation
Vehicle repairs	

Any number of appropriate expense accounts can be added to these. Using some of the typical income and expense accounts mentioned, the following standard profit and loss statement has been constructed:

General health & fitness center
Profit & loss statement
for the calendar year 1991

Income

Fees	$18,000	
Merchandise sales	74,000	
Program sales	5,000	
Space rental	15,000	
Ticket sales	7,000	$119,000

Expenses

Advertising	$ 7,000	
Cost of goods sold	28,000	
Depreciation	6,000	
Entertainment	1,500	
Insurance	13,000	
Interest	4,000	
Legal fees	5,000	
Repairs	2,500	
Supplies	1,500	
Taxes	4,000	
Travel	3,000	
Utilities	1,800	77,300

Net profit	$ 41,700

CONCEPT CHECK

Although the complexity of organizations varies, it is important to report financial data as precisely and completely as possible. The balance sheet and the profit and loss statement are the two most important products of accounting. The standard balance sheet records current assets, fixed assets, current liabilities, and net worth. Profit and loss statements record sales, revenues, and a variety of expense accounts, the most common of which are salaries and benefits, supplies and expenses, repairs and maintenance, and depreciation.

DEPRECIATION

Depreciation is the process of writing off (deducting from taxable income) **fixed asset** items over their determined useful lives by annually recording a portion of the asset as expense. Fixed asset acquisitions, such as furniture, equipment, vehicles, and buildings, are not recorded as expenses at the time of purchase. Rather, they are charged to asset accounts as balance sheet items listed under the heading of fixed assets. This is called the capitalizing of asset purchases.

Depreciation is calculated for each asset according to its useful life, and the depreciated amount is then recorded as expense against income. Fixed assets are generally considered to be those items that cost $300 or more and that have a life of one year or more. These criteria can vary, however. Some organizations capitalize items as low as $100 and others as high as $500. Regardless of the dollar amount used to determine a fixed asset that is subject to depreciation, the amount must be acceptable to the government since all other equipment items are charged directly to expense, thus directly affecting the amount of taxes paid to the government.

A number of methods are used for depreciating fixed assets. The most common are the **straight-line, sum-of-the-years digits,** and **double-declining-balance** methods. Under the straight-line method, fixed assets are depreciated in equal amounts each year for a certain number of years according to the life of the asset. The sum-of-the-years digits method results in more rapid depreciation in the early years of the asset's life. The double-declining-balance method provides for depreciation at twice the rate of the straight-line calculation.

Lives of assets can vary but must be kept within the guidelines of government regulations and depreciation tax laws. Following are examples of three common classifications of fixed assets.

Office furniture	10 years
Office equipment	10 years
Buildings	50 years

In calculating depreciation, the accountant must estimate what the salvage value of each asset will be at the end of its useful life. This is necessary, since each asset will still have some value at the time of its replacement. The box below contains fixed assets data that assumes that a business has decided on estimated lives and also on salvage values for each category. (Land is not depreciated.) Also shown is the computation for the straight-line method of depreciation, which is the simplest and most commonly used.

The $12,140 annual depreciation (see the box below) is charged as an expense against income and credited to a reserve for depreciation account for each category of asset. These reserve accounts, because of their credit balances, are deducted from the debit balance of the fixed asset accounts on the balance sheet to arrive at a net book value of assets.

CONCEPT CHECK

Depreciation is the practice of writing off such fixed assets as furniture, equipment, vehicles, and buildings. Methods of calculating depreciation include straight-line, sum-of-the-years digits, and double-declining. The straight-line method is the most commonly used. Although lives of assets can vary, they must be kept within the guidelines set by government regulations and depreciation tax laws. Factors taken into account when calculating depreciation include the original cost, estimated life in years, estimated salvage value, and the cost to depreciate. Fixed assets are not recorded as expenses at the time of purchase but are charged to asset accounts as balance sheet items.

Example of calculation of depreciation

Fixed assets data

Fixed assets	Original cost	Estimated life (years)	Estimated salvage value	Cost to depreciate
Furniture	$15,000	10	$ 1,200	$13,800
Equipment	25,000	10	3,000	22,000
Vehicles	40,000	5	4,000	36,000
Building	80,000	50	12,000	68,000

Straight-line method of depreciation (using the above data)

Fixed assets	Depreciable cost	Estimated life (years)	Annual depreciation expense
Furniture	$13,800	10	$ 1,380
Equipment	22,000	10	2,200
Vehicles	36,000	5	7,200
Building	68,000	50	1,360
		Total depreciation for first year	$12,140

ACCOUNTING FOR NONPROFIT ORGANIZATIONS

The same accounting principles and theories used to account for profit-oriented businesses can be applied to **nonprofit organizations.** Nonprofit entities are those established under specific regulations and restrictions, by law, to operate on a nonprofit basis and, therefore, they are not subject to income tax laws. Colleges and universities are prime examples of nonprofit institutions. Others include foundations, public hospitals, and municipalities, most of which have sport and fitness programs as an integral part of their operations. Accounting for these institutions is called **fund accounting.**

An accountant familiar with general accounting principles can easily adapt to the system of accounting for nonprofit organizations. Fund accounting differs somewhat from general accounting. The main difference is that fund accounting uses not one balance sheet but a series of balance sheets, depending on the number of funds needed by a particular organization to function. Following are examples of such funds.

Current unrestricted fund
Current restricted fund
Endowment fund
Retirement fund
Plant fund
Trust fund
Agency fund

Each of these funds stands alone as a separate entity, and each has its own separate balance sheet. The balance sheet for each fund is made up of standard balance sheet accounts. However, additional accounts are added that are peculiar to each specific fund. Also, expenses charged to the various funds differ according to the specific purpose of the fund. Expenses for the retirement fund, for example, would be represented as payments to retirees. Trust fund expenses would be the payments to beneficiaries of the various trusts, and plant fund expenses would be the costs of building construction and/or costs of renovating existing buildings. These expenses, along with each fund's investment income and transfers, represent the equity changes of each fund as detailed later in this chapter.

Examples of balance sheets

Current unrestricted fund

Assets			Liabilities		
Cash in banks		$ 2,000	Accounts payable		$ 15,000
Temporary investments		40,000	Notes payable		20,000
Marketable securities		68,000	Accrued salaries		18,000
Accounts receivable	$45,000		Accrued taxes		12,000
Less: Reserve for bad debts	3,500	41,500	Depreciation reserves		16,000
Fixed assets		46,000	Equity in pooled cash—		
			retirement fund		20,000
Land		50,000	Fund equity		146,500
		$247,500			$247,500

Retirement fund

Assets		Liabilities	
Cash in banks	$ 18,000		
Equity in pooled cash	20,000		
Marketable securities	225,000	Fund equity	$263,000
	$263,000		$263,000

The current unrestricted fund is the fund through which flows all regular income and general expenses of the operation, and all of the others act as subsidiary funds outside of the main operation. All funds interact with each other by means of transfers. Each subsidiary fund has an asset account titled **equity in pooled cash,** which corresponds to a liability account in the current unrestricted fund in the same amount. Each time a transfer is made between any of the funds, the equity in pooled cash for each of the funds affected is increased or decreased accordingly.

The box on p. 46 contains examples of the current unrestricted fund interim balance sheet and one subsidiary fund balance sheet. Note that the equity in pooled cash in each fund is in agreement.

At year end, the equity in pooled cash credit in the current unrestricted fund is subtracted from the cash in banks and temporary investments assets, and these two asset categories are combined and listed on the balance sheet as cash and temporary investments. The same is done for the retirement fund, resulting in the year-end balance sheet for the current unrestricted fund shown in the box below, top.

Another important year-end statement is the **statement of changes in fund balance** for each of the funds, which reflects the annual growth of each fund. The box below, bottom, shows the year-end equity changes for each of the two funds. Note again that the transfers between funds are in agreement at the end of the year.

The statements in the box below, bottom, reflect an increase of $49,000 in the current unrestricted fund and $3,000 in the retirement fund.

Finally, a summary statement should be made

Example of year-end balance sheet*

Current unrestricted fund

Assets			Liabilities	
Cash and temporary investments		$ 22,000	Accounts payable	$ 15,000
Marketable securities		68,000	Notes payable	20,000
Accounts receivable	$45,000		Accrued salaries	18,000
Less: Reserve for bad debts	3,500	41,500	Accrued taxes	12,000
Fixed assets		46,000	Depreciation reserves	16,000
Land		50,000	Fund equity	146,500
		$227,500		$227,500

*Computations are based on the figures in the box on p. 46.

Examples of year-end equity changes

Current unrestricted fund		Retirement fund	
Statement of changes in fund balance		**Statement of changes in fund balance**	
Beginning balance	$146,500	Beginning balance	$263,000
Income	$185,000	Investment income	25,000
Expenditures	(126,000)	Payment to retirees	(32,000)
Transfers (out)	(10,000)	Transfers (in)	10,000
Net increase	$ 49,000	Net increase	$ 3,000
Ending balance	$195,500	Ending balance	$266,000

Example of summary statement of growth*

	Beginning of year	End of year	Increase (decrease)
Current unrestricted fund	$ 146,500	$ 195,500	$ 49,000
Current restricted fund	250,600	325,000	74,400
Endowment fund	390,000	450,000	60,000
Retirement fund	263,000	266,000	3,000
Plant fund	625,000	589,000	(36,000)
Trust fund	218,000	230,000	12,000
Agency fund	162,000	169,000	7,000
	$2,055,100	$2,224,500	

Net financial growth for the year $169,400

*Computations are based on the figures in the boxes on p. 47.

that lists each fund's net increase or decrease, which will reflect the financial growth of the entire organization. Using the seven funds mentioned at the beginning of this section, a summary statement shows a net growth for the year in the amount of $169,400 (see the box above).

CONCEPT CHECK

Nonprofit entities are established under special regulations and are not subject to regular income tax laws. The accounting approach for nonprofit institutions is called fund accounting. Endowment, retirement, and trust funds are examples of fund accounting. An account titled "equity in pooled cash" refers to transfers made between any of the funds. Another year-end statement, called the statement of changes in fund balance, reflects the annual growth for each fund reported by an organization. Finally, a summary statement should be made that lists each fund's net increase or decrease, thus reflecting the overall financial growth of the organization.

TYPES OF BUSINESSES
The same accounting principles and theories can be applied to businesses that are established as **corporations, partnerships,** or **proprietorships.**

Corporations
A corporation is formed according to the laws of the state in which it is incorporated. The structure of a corporation provides for officers, that is, president, vice president, treasurer, and secretary, and is governed by an elected board of directors. The entity is authorized to issue stock to outside investors.

The sale of stock to the public is the capital source that enables the company to operate and is a cash source that is not available to partnerships or proprietorships. Corporations need sufficient capital to compete successfully in the marketplace and for research and development to keep pace with the constantly changing business environment.

Investors, both large and small, are attracted to successful corporations. This results in advantages to both the business and the stockholders. The corporation has a source of capital, and the stockholders have no personal liability in the company in which they invest. Also, the liquidity of their investment appeals to investors. They can sell any part or all of their shares on the market at any time.

With today's emphasis on wellness, many corporations are including health and fitness programs in their operating budgets. The operation of these programs is the responsibility of the personnel or human resources department.

Partnerships

Small businesses, which require less capital to operate than larger companies, are often established as partnerships. The partnership usually is the preferred business form of entities promoting recreation, health, fitness, and minor sports.

A partnership is formed by two or more individuals with a common business goal and is governed by bylaws that spell out the rules and financial structure of the organization. The state in which it is formed recognizes the partnership as a business entity.

The source of capital for the partnership is cash investments by each of the partners. If each partner provides cash in the same amount, each shares equally in the net profit from the business. If different amounts are invested by the partners, each would share the net profit according to the proportion of their capital investment to the total cash invested. Following is an example of different amounts of capital contributed.

Capital Contributed		Percent of total contributed
Partner 1	$20,000	30.77%
Partner 2	20,000	30.77
Partner 3	15,000	23.08
Partner 4	10,000	15.38
	$65,000	100.00%

Standard balance sheet and income and expense accounts are used for a partnership. The only change is in the surplus or equity account. A capital account is established for each partner. The net income is credited to each partner's capital account in accordance with the percentage of ownership. By the same token, additional contributions of capital, or withdrawals of funds, are added to or deducted from these capital accounts.

Proprietorships

The sole proprietorship is a one-owner business entity and is the simplest of the three business structures. The individual owner commits his or her own capital and thereby does not depend on outside funds to operate. He or she must, however, separate business capital from capital for personal use outside the business.

A proprietorship is a separate taxable entity, requiring the owner to account for income and expenses separately from other personal income and expenses. The net income is taxable to the proprietorship entity just as net income is taxable to the corporation and to individuals in a partnership.

A proprietorship uses the same standard balance sheet and expense accounts as does a corporation or partnership. The main difference in accounting for the three different entities is in the structure of the capital section on the balance sheet liabilities. The following shows typical capital accounts for each.

Corporation	
Stockholders' equity:	
Preferred stock, $100 par value, authorized	
5,000 shares, outstanding 4,500 shares	$ 450,000
Common stock, $5 value, authorized 300,000 shares, outstanding 200,000 shares	1,000,000
	$1,450,000

Partnership	
Partners' capital:	
Benson capital	$ 65,000
Lloyd capital	30,000
Reynolds capital	30,000
Williams capital	20,000
	$145,000

Proprietorship	
Owners equity:	
Invested capital	$50,000

Each form of business is a taxable entity under the Internal Revenue code. A corporation's taxes are part of the cost of running the business and are charged against income. Dividends are declared on the outstanding stock from net income and paid to stockholders. These dividends are taxable to the investor. The net income from a partnership is prorated to each partner according to each partner's total capital contributed. This net income allocation is taxable to the partners and is included on their personal tax returns. The owner of a proprietorship also includes the net income from the business on his or her personal return.

Advantages and disadvantages of business structures

In establishing a business, the advantages and disadvantages of each type should be considered. Corporations have an advantage in raising capital in their ability to issue shares of stock to the public, which assures a constant source of capital, as long as the new stock issues are considered attractive. The stockholder, in essence, becomes an absentee owner of the corporation, which is another advantage. The death of a stockholder does not disrupt the activity of the business, since the absentee owner is not involved in the day-to-day operations. Another advantage is that stockholders are not personally liable for the debts of the corporation. This is an appealing feature that attracts investors who can purchase ownership in a business and be assured that they are not assuming liabilities of the company.

A disadvantage of corporations is that the control of capital is separated from ownership of capital. The stockholders have no control over capital investment. They can, however, vote their stock in electing members of the board of directors, which manages the capital. Stockholders have one vote for each share of stock owned, and by voting their shares at annual meetings, can have at least some effect on the operations of the corporation.

The partnership form of business has both advantages and disadvantages that neither of the other two have. In a partnership there is no division between management of capital and contributors of capital. Partners share equally in managing the operation of the business. This leads to another advantage. The pooling of the talents of the various partners is an important factor in the success of the venture.

One of the major disadvantages of a partnership is the unlimited liability of the partners. Each is liable for the debts of the partnership. Thus the partner's assets outside the business could be attached to settle partnership debts. Another disadvantage is the need to revise the partnership agreement on the retirement or death of a partner or partners. This interferes with the continuity needed to operate the business successfully. This is especially true of a partnership consisting of only two or three individuals. Those with several partners are not as drastically affected by death or retirement.

A proprietorship is a one-owner business entity that has none of the limitations of corporations or partnerships. The owner does not depend on capital from outsiders and need not consult with other individuals on financial and operational decisions. He or she alone is responsible for the success or failure of the venture.

CONCEPT CHECK

Businesses are established as corporations, partnerships, or proprietorships. They differ from one another in the number of owners, sources of cash for operations, and the issue of liability. The advantages and disadvantages of each type should be considered when establishing a business. Special considerations include issuance of stock, liability for debts, control and management of capital, and the continuation of the organization on the death or disengagement of an owner.

CASH MANAGEMENT

Another important management tool in the operation of a successful sport enterprise is the efficient management and investment of idle cash. **Cash management** is the principle that idle cash should be invested daily to ensure that adequate funds are available to meet specific current expenses. Cash management is also a source of interest income when cash data is made available to the accountant daily.

The person responsible for such investing should receive cash data within an hour after the beginning of each workday to allow time for analysis before investing the funds overnight, or longer, at current interest rates. Investing overnight simply means that cash is invested in a 24-hour security that matures the following day, giving the investor flexibility to properly control cash management. Most banks offer such investment instruments. The most common is a **repurchase agreement** (called a **repo**), which is a simple agreement between the bank and investor to exchange cash for income over a 24-hour period.

A simple method for providing the accountant with cash data can easily be instituted. Following is the information from the previous day that should be available by 9:00 AM each working day.

From the cashier	
Deposits to bank 1	$70,000
Deposits to bank 2	45,000

From accounts payable	
Disbursements from bank 1	$20,000
Disbursements from bank 2	25,000

To illustrate the principle of cash management, information from bank 1 will be used with the assumption that $60,000 cash had been invested overnight the day before. The following gives the amount of cash available, and this table can be used to decide the use and disposition of the available cash.

Cash invested from previous day	$ 60,000
Add previous day's deposit	70,000
	$130,000
Subtract previous day's disbursements	20,000
Cash available for investment	$110,000

At this point, another factor should be considered to earn the most short-term income. Disbursements made the previous day and sent to out-of-town vendors will not clear the bank today. Thus these vendor payments can be added back to the idle cash balance. In view of this factor, the accountant determines that $4,000 in vendor checks sent the previous day can be added to the afore-mentioned available cash figures, giving $114,000 available for investing.

Further, to make sure that adequate cash is available to pay known expenses, some of the cash can be invested for a longer time than overnight. Funds can be invested to mature on peak payment dates such as the due dates for payroll or monthly insurance payments. Therefore the maturity of a portion of the cash invested can be extended a number of days or weeks according to the payment schedule of these expenditures. Certificates of deposits and U.S. Treasury bills are examples of securities that can be purchased for longer maturity dates.

To complete the illustration, begin with the $114,000 cash available figure and invest cash on September 4. It is also known that payrolls, each in the amount of $5,000, are due on the 15th and 30th of the month, and that monthly insurance payments of $2,000 are due on the 18th. With this data, the investment schedule looks like this:

Invest to September 15	$ 5,000
Invest to September 30	5,000
Invest to September 18	2,000
Invest overnight to September 5	102,000
	$114,000

A monthly calendar should be maintained to record the dates of the maturing investments. This gives the cash manager continuing cash invest-

September 1991

Sa	Su	M	T	W	Th	F
	1	2	3	4	5 102,000	6
7	8	9	10	11	12	13
14	15 5,000	16	17	18 2,000	19	20
21	22	23	24	25	26	27
28	29	30 5,000				

FIGURE 4-1 A monthly calendar gives information at a glance.

ment information at a glance. The illustration figures would appear on the calendar as follows (Figure 4-1), showing the various cash investments that mature on September 5 and the other due dates.

Cash management, given adequate time and attention, gives management another advantage in operating a successful business.

CONCEPT CHECK

Cash management involves the daily investing of idle cash. Most banks offer a repurchase agreement that allows customers to exchange cash for income over a 24-hour period. Specific factors to be considered include amounts of deposits, disbursements, possible exchanges with out-of-town vendors, and the possibility of investing for longer times than overnight. A monthly calendar should be maintained to record the date(s) of the maturing investments.

BUDGETING
The budgeting process
Budgeting of income and expense is a useful tool to the sport or fitness manager if done effectively. A budget is a written plan of what the organization expects in sales and expenses in its next calendar or fiscal year. Intelligent budgeting is an important method of controlling expenses and monitoring financial trends. It also aids management in meeting specific objectives in future years.

Some businesses use only a sales budget to forecast sales. This leaves something to be desired. If expenses are not budgeted in direct relation to expected sales, the sales budget would lose its effectiveness.

A budget is, at best, an educated guess. No one can accurately predict the future, which makes budgeting for 1 or 2 years more practical and realistic than doing so for 5 or 6 years.

The budget process should be coordinated by a special committee that includes accountants and management. Various procedures can be used to arrive at an acceptable budget, which is then approved and adopted. The simplest procedure follows three basic steps. The committee's initial objective is to review and predict sales and revenue from various sources, which should result in an estimate of the total for the budget period or periods.

Second, the committee allocates revenue dollars to each of the operating departments within the organization. The department managers or supervisors review the allocations and compare them to their own estimates of funds needed to operate their departments efficiently based on prior years' experience.

Finally, the committee and departmental supervisors should meet to discuss the overall financial forecast. Both revenues and departmental expenses can be adjusted to arrive at an acceptable and realistic budget.

Budgeting serves management in two equally important ways. It aids in controlling expenses, and it provides guidelines for setting specific standards of operation, both of which are essential to the well-run sport or fitness business. Budgeting can be successful only with constant monitoring of both costs and goals by management and department heads.

Types of budgets
Generally, budgets are classified according to the time period they cover. **Capital budgets** are used for long-term planning beyond the current year. The **master budget,** on the other hand, covers shorter time periods of up to a year. Special considerations within the master budget include sales, production costs, and other expenditures such as administrative expenses.

Separate budgets for revenues and expenses can be prepared. For example, a **sales budget** includes revenues generated from such sources as membership fees, dues, ticket sales, sales of merchandise, and facility rentals. A **production budget** lists costs of purchasing and using materials, direct labor, and overhead. This budget is particularly useful to companies within the manufacturing segment of the sport and fitness industry. Also pertinent to the sport and fitness setting is the **department expense budget.** This budget includes expenses specific to different departments and lists such costs as publicity, ticket office operations, pro-shop expenses, equipment purchases and maintenance, and administrative expenses.

When considering expenditures, the budget most fundamental to the budgeting process is the **operating expense budget.** This budget accounts for all of the costs that management anticipates the sport and fitness organization will incur during a particular time period. This time period can be a month, a quarter, or a year. Expense items in this budget include salaries and wages, commissions, insurance, advertising and printing, office supplies, telephone costs, rents, and other miscellaneous costs.

Formats for developing and presenting the budget(s) vary. As in the case of the department expense budget, the sales or expense budget can focus on the different departments (or programs) within the organization. Consequently, the anticipated revenues or costs are listed for each department. Another option for the sport or fitness accountant or manager is the **line-item budget.** When the accountant or manager develops the line-item budget, all expenditures, for example, are grouped into categories and a specific dollar amount is allotted to each category. The following illustrates a monthly operating expense budget presented in the line-item format:

CITY FITNESS CENTER
Operating expense budget
May, 1991

Salaries and wages	$5,000
Workers' compensation	600
Group insurance and benefits	500
Total payroll	**$6,100**
Advertising	200
Supplies	100
Telephone	50
Equipment repairs	100
Utilities	1,800
Subtotal	**$2,250**
Total operating expenses	**$8,350**

Additional types of budgeting include **zero-base budgeting** and **cash-flow budgeting.** Zero-base budgeting means planning the entire budget each time as if for the first time. This approach demands that all activities and related costs be reexamined and justified whenever the budget is prepared and requests are made. Cash-flow budgeting combines concern for the sources of cash, anticipated expenses, and disbursement schedules throughout the stated budget period. It enables the manager to determine the amount of cash an organization needs to pay expenses at predesignated times throughout the month or year.

In summary, a variety of approaches to the budgeting process can be taken. The sport and fitness manager or accountant who has the skill and knowledge to implement the budgeting process

will be much more effective at making decisions that affect both the objectives and the operations of the sport and fitness organization. Specific examples of budgeting problems and solutions and the different types of budgets can be found in Chapter 11 of this text.

CONCEPT CHECK

Intelligent budgeting is an important method of controlling expenses and monitoring financial trends. The budget process should be coordinated by a special committee that is responsible for reviewing sources of sales and revenues, allocating revenue dollars to each operating department, and seeking information from department supervisors about budget needs and financial forecasting. Budgets are classified according to the time period they cover. When considering expenditures, the most useful budget is the operating expense budget, which accounts for all anticipated costs within a particular time period. Line-item budgets, zero-base budgeting, and cash-flow budgeting are important considerations when the accountant or manager develops and presents the budget.

COMPUTER APPLICATION

As stated earlier, there are few businesses—large or small—that do not use today's computer technology. As such, the sport or fitness manager has at his or her disposal any number of computer programs. Generally, these include word processing, data-base management, spreadsheets, graphics, and integrated designs that attempt to combine all software programs into a single package.

There are a variety of programs tailored to the specific needs and expertise of the individual sport or fitness accountant. Electronic spreadsheets, for example, are useful when the accountant wishes to create reports requiring mathematical, financial, or statistical calculations. This option would be particularly useful when creating balance sheets, income and expense statements, or cash management strategies, for example.

Also available are application software packages directed toward accounting in smaller businesses. These include predesigned, structured forms in which the accountant merely plugs figures into existing categories. Such packages are available for the reporting of financial statements, payroll, inventory, and so on.

Finally, there is a host of accounting software packages designed specifically for the sport or fitness business. These include the managing of accounts payable, accounts receivable, payroll, membership tracking and billing, ledgers, cash management, and fund transfer, and any number of financial statements, to mention a few. Information on this software usually is obtainable through the professional organizations within the sport, recreation, and fitness industry.

All available accounting software packages should be explored. Particular consideration should be given to the needs of the sport or fitness enterprise, the expertise of the accountant, and the particular needs of the sport or fitness setting. Only then can the most appropriate application software package be chosen for accounting purposes.

Specific information pertaining to hardware, software packages, and the installation and use of computers within sport and fitness settings can be found in Chapter 20.

SUMMARY

1. Accounting plays a key role in the managing and guiding of a successful sport-oriented enterprise. The financial reports and resulting data provided by accounting are invaluable to management. With this data, management can make intelligent decisions to ensure that the business is, and remains, sound and profitable. Professional sports, intercollegiate athletics, sports clubs, amateur sports, and health and fitness-oriented businesses may have their own individual characteristics and goals, but accounting is an integral part of each.

2. Businesses are not allowed to deduct costly equipment and buildings directly as expenses. These capital assets, as they are called, must be depreciated (written off) over their estimated useful lives. The method of depreciation is not as important as adhering to government guidelines and depreciation tax laws regarding estimated useful lives and cost criteria.

3. No business can function without adequate accounting procedures and records. Nonprofit organizations are no exception. These entities use the same accounting theories as do profit-oriented businesses. Fund accounting, used by nonprofit organizations, differs somewhat from general accounting principles. The differences are relatively slight, and the knowledgeable accountant can easily make the transition to fund accounting.

4. Individuals should consider the different types of business structures before organizing a new business entity. The differences between them and the advantages and disadvantages of each should be studied carefully to make sure that goals can be met and that the financial structure suits the particular business venture.

5. Proper cash management is important to the financial health of a business. The lack of such management can hurt the efforts that management makes to keep the business operating smoothly. Failure to have cash available at peak expenditure times can easily put the business venture in jeopardy.

6. Forecasting revenues and expenditures, to enable management to set up an operating budget, is not an exact science. However, given the past performance of the organization and the current economic trends, management can construct a reasonably accurate budget that will provide guidelines for future operations. Strict adherence to and control of the budget is imperative.

7. Management should take advantage of today's advanced computer technology. Computer programs are available to compile information for management and accounting, regardless of the complexity of the data needed.

REVIEW QUESTIONS AND ISSUES

1. What is accounting and how does the accounting system help the sport or fitness manager?
2. State and distinguish the four assumptions of accounting and the four principles of accounting.
3. What are the basic components in the simplest form of the standard balance sheet? In the income and expense statement?
4. What is straight-line depreciation and how is it calculated?
5. What are the similarities and differences between fund accounting and general accounting?

6. What is the importance of "equity in pooled cash"?

7. Distinguish between corporation, partnership, and proprietorship. List the advantages and disadvantages of each.

8. What are the different strategies available to the accountant for the investment of idle cash?

9. Enumerate the three basic steps important to the budgeting process.

10. What are the different types of budgets and how might each be beneficial depending on the sport or fitness setting?

11. Given the different types of accounting software packages, what should the sport or fitness manager or accountant consider when using a particular approach to accounting?

REFERENCES

Broyles, J. and Hay, R. (1979). *Administration of athletic programs: a managerial approach*. Englewood Cliffs, New Jersey: Prentice-Hall.

Dougherty, N. and Bonanno, D. (1985). *Management principles in sport and leisure services*. Minneapolis, Minnesota: Burgess Publishing Company.

Ellis, T. and Norton, R. (1988). *Commercial recreation*. St. Louis, Missouri: Mosby–Year Book, Inc.

Garrison, R. (1988). *Managerial accounting: concepts for planning, control, decision making* (5th Edition). Homewood, Illinois: Richard D. Irwin, Inc.

Griffin, C., Williams, T., Larson, K., Boatsman, J., and Bill, T. (1985). *Advanced accounting*. Homewood, Illinois: Richard D. Irwin, Inc.

Horngren, C. and Sundem, G. (1987). *Introduction to management accounting*. Englewood Cliffs, New Jersey: Prentice Hall, Inc.

Jensen, C. (1983). *Administrative management of physical education and athletic programs*. Philadelphia, Pennsylvania: Lea & Febiger.

Kieso, D. and Weygandt, J. (1989). *Intermediate accounting* (6th Edition). New York, New York: John Wiley & Sons.

Lewis, G. and Appenzeller, H. (1985). *Successful sport management*. Charlottesville, Virginia: The Michie Company.

Mason, J. and Paul, J. (1988). *Modern sports administration*. Englewood Cliffs, New Jersey: Prentice Hall, Inc.

Meigs, W., Mosich, A., Johnson, C., and Keller, T. (1974). *Intermediate accounting* (3rd Edition). New York: McGraw-Hill Books.

Mikolai, L., Bayley, J., Schroeder, R., and Reynolds, I. (1985). *Intermediate accounting* (3rd Edition). Boston, Massachusetts: Kent Publishing Co.

Railey, J. and Railey, P. (1988). *Managing physical education, fitness, and sports programs*. Mountain View, California: Mayfield Publishing Company.

Solomon, L., Vargo, R., and Walther, L. (1986). *Accounting principles* (2nd Edition). New York: Harper & Row Publishers.

Stallings, W., Hitchinson, S., and Sawyer, S. (1988). *Computers: the user perspective*. St. Louis, Missouri: Mosby–Year Book, Inc.

VanderZwaag, H. (1984). *Sport management: sport management in schools and colleges*. New York: John Wiley & Sons.

Welsch, G. and Short, D. (1987). *Fundamentals of financial accounting*. Homewood, Illinois: Richard D. Irwin, Inc.

CHAPTER 5

Economics

Larry DeBrock

In this chapter, you will become familiar with the following terms:

Equilibrium
Scarcity
Rationing
Opportunity cost
Production possibility frontier
Markets
Demand curve
Substitutes
Complements
Utility
Marginal utility
Law of diminishing marginal utility
Substitution effect
Income effect

Market demand
Price elasticity
Income elasticity
Profits
Competition
Monopoly
Supply curve
Short run
Long run
Law of diminishing marginal returns
Fixed costs
Variable costs
Marginal costs
Surplus
Shortage

Overview

Decisionmakers at every level of society face constraints. The wealthiest individuals in the country are limited in their ability to control resources. Indeed, even the wealthiest nations are still limited in their ability to provide products to their people.

The science called economics is devoted to the analysis of these constraints. Practitioners of this discipline use economic models to help understand, explain, and predict all sorts of allocation decisions. To the lay observer, such models are usually abstract and laden with jargon. However, good economic theories have two common traits: (1) they predict real world phenomena quite well, and (2) they can be explained in simple, understandable terms.

Why should one be interested in such concepts? As just mentioned, all decisionmakers face constraints. Managers of any operation must make allocation decisions each day. The divisions of the operation compete for limited dollars. Likewise, the revenue side of the operation is restricted by the degree of public desire for the product.

The purpose of this chapter is to present an overview of how an economic system works. The framework will be quite general; most examples from the sport arena will be deferred to Chapter 12. However, one must remember that the principles outlined in this chapter relate to the sports industry as much as to the more traditional forms of economic activity.

For now, the goal is to understand how an economic system works, from the viewpoints of producers, as well as consumers of the limited goods available. This chapter will explain how economic phenomena result from equilibrium behavior. **Equilibrium** means that no decisionmaker has better alternatives than those currently available. This is not to say that all decisionmakers are satisfied. It merely says that, given the conditions, all parties are doing the best they can. The concept of equilibrium is extremely powerful and allows one to understand economic principles as logical results of behavior, rather than forcing one to memorize a series of rules.

INTRODUCTION TO ECONOMICS
The economic problem
The classic definition of economics usually is the study of the allocation of scarce goods and services* among competing (indeed, unlimited) wants. This definition is a bit redundant, because the key word, **scarcity**, is sufficient; if goods were not scarce, there would be no economic problem. It is this fact that makes allocation decisions so vital.

Since goods and services are scarce but the desire to have them is virtually unlimited, some method of **rationing** must be devised. Rationing can be considered as the rules used to determine the actual distribution of the scarce goods and services. In essence, there is not enough to go around, and some mechanism must be used to determine who gets how much.

Without scarcity, rationing would be unnecessary; all goods would be free. Economists believe all goods and services are scarce, which is another way of saying that no goods are free. Such a blanket statement, universally supported today, was not common a few decades ago. Indeed, economics textbooks of previous decades often "confessed" that there might be some goods that were not subject to the law of scarcity. Air was the good usually mentioned in these caveats, under the belief that air was "free" and therefore not subject to any rationing. This is, of course, false. Air is a limited and expensive commodity, as confirmed by the extent to which society imposes controls on its use. Pollution control devices, smokestack scrubbers, and the catalytic converters on automobiles are evidence that air is not available in unlimited quantities. Society pays a high price for the air it uses. Today's headlines about the depletion of the world's rain forests are further evidence of the limits on the atmosphere.

The fact that choices are limited leads to the next important concept: **opportunity cost**. The definition of opportunity cost is "the value of the next best alternative." The concept of scarcity implies that each time an individual makes a choice he or she has implicitly ranked a set of alternatives. Electing to consume more of one thing necessarily means the person must get less of others; if this were not true, scarcity would be violated. The person's choice is, presumably, the most attractive of the alternatives. The choice has a cost, the forgone value of the next most attractive path.† This value, opportunity cost, is extremely important in economics. It reflects the true cost of every decision by consumers, producers, and governments. Throughout this brief look at how an economic

---

*Throughout this chapter, the author will conform to standard economics terminology and use the phrase "goods and services" to denote the output of firms; the terms "good" and "product" are synonymous.

†This is the source of the quote often attributed to economists, "There is no such thing as a free lunch." Even if something appears to be "free," by consuming this product one is necessarily forgoing consumption of the next best alternative.

system operates, the concept of opportunity cost will play an important role.

A useful tool for understanding these concepts is the **Production Possibility Frontier** (PPF). Scarcity implies that there are limits on the number or amount of any good or service in an economy. Given the existing level of inputs, there is only so much one can produce of any good, *even if society decided to produce only that good.* The PPF is a way to capture the menu of goods and services available in any economy.

To understand the PPF, an example is in order. While any economy is, of course, made up of a vast number of goods and services, it is useful to divide the goods into two categories.* The classic example in economics is known as the *guns vs. butter* problem. In this case, all possible outputs of an economy are classified as either for consumers (butter) or for the military (guns). For this example, consider investment goods (plant and equipment) vs. consumption goods. Figure 5-1 depicts a PPF for such an economy. The PPF shows the alternatives for this economy. If the economy chooses to have *only* capital goods, it would still be limited to the point A. Likewise, point B depicts the economy's ouput if *all* resources were devoted to the production of consumption goods.

The PPF is a very powerful device. It is a straightforward graphic presentation of the real consequences of scarcity. Decisionmakers must realize that, to obtain one more unit of any good, real opportunity costs must be paid. In the case of Figure 5-1, the movement along the PPF depicts the real cost of an extra unit of one of the goods; in the more formal jargon, the *slope* of the PPF is the opportunity cost of an extra unit of the good. Because of the technological effects of specialization, the PPF will have the characteristic curvature, bowed out from the origin.† As the production of a good continues to increase, the opportunity cost

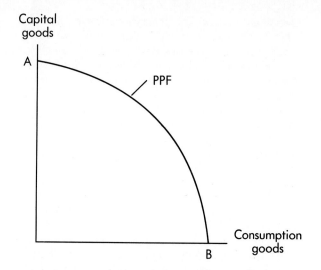

FIGURE 5-1 Production possibilities frontier.

(the forgone units of the other good) gets ever larger.

The PPF is an excellent device to depict the position of sports and leisure in the economy. Suppose all goods could be classified as either "leisure" or "non-leisure" goods. Putting leisure goods on the horizontal axis and non-leisure goods on the vertical axis of Figure 5-1 graphically illustrates the real cost of sports and leisure. *If* the society wishes to increase its consumption of leisure activities, it must reduce its consumption of nonleisure goods. With scarcity, society cannot get more of both. The true cost of leisure is the loss in other types of goods, as shown so well by the PPF.

Economic systems

An economic system is a mechanism for making the allocation decisions just discussed. These de-

---

*It is standard fare in a typical economics lecture to hear the phrase " . . . assume a two-good world . . . " Everyone knows this is hardly a description of the real world. However, the explanatory power of two-dimensional graphs cannot be underestimated. Besides, "assuming" two goods is no different than simply lumping the entire list of goods into two categories. Or, an alternative method to such categorization is to accept that there are *N* goods in the economy, but to treat the decision on goods 1 and 2 as the current problem, holding the other *N-2*

goods as "fixed" for the moment. Either way, the focus of attention is on just two possible products.

†As input resources move from one type of production to another, the resources that are less productive in their current application will intuitively be moved first. However, as more and more resources are switched to the other product, evermore-important resources will be taken away from the original task. Thus the incremental amount or number of the final product forgone will become larger with *each* new unit of the other good.

cisions usually are summarized as three basic questions: *What to produce?*, *How to produce?*, and *For whom to produce?* In any economic system, someone has to decide which products to produce. In addition, the technology to produce these products must be chosen. Finally, some means of distributing (rationing) these scarce goods must be put in place.

One obvious mechanism for handling all these questions is to let some central agency dictate answers. This type of economy is known as a "command system." Unfortunately, the variety and number of decisions that must be made can quickly force such a system into inefficient and myopic responses. The early part of 1990 saw many East European countries move away from command systems for just these reasons.

Another approach to handling these fundamental questions is to use a laissez-faire approach. This system relies on the interaction of buyers and sellers in **markets** to answer the three questions basic to any economic system. Ironically, where a structured bureaucracy fails under the sheer magnitude of decisions that must be made, the market economy thrives on such activity. Individual participants, in a self-interested effort to improve their own positions, will force the economy to an efficient outcome.

This result, known as the "invisible hand," is extremely powerful. Each side of a transaction effectively is the "policeman" of the other side. Sellers cannot force buyers to pay more than a product is worth, and buyers cannot force sellers to part with the product for less than the real costs of producing the product. If sellers cannot sell their product at remunerative prices, they exit. If more people clamor for the good, allowing those currently producing the product to reap comfortable returns, enterprising outsiders will enter and eventually force the price back near costs. Thus individual motives turn out to answer the question of what to produce. The products that society does not desire will be weeded out of the economy without need of some central authority. Likewise, the market system responds quickly to provide the products that consumers desire.

The question of technology is answered by the individual producers. If it is more efficient (that is, fewer scarce resources are used up in the production process) to have a capital-intensive, low-labor

operation, that will be the choice. If the reverse is true, the producers will elect a more labor-intensive form of production.

A market system answers the final question, "For whom to produce," via the rationing device of price. Prices (and, of course, incomes) restrict who can and will purchase different products. Again, the two sides of the transaction are effective constraints on each other. No one forces the buyers to purchase or the sellers to produce. The fact that they voluntarily enter into the transaction is a sign of efficiency.

To better understand how markets operate, look more closely at the two participants. On the buyers' side, a tool known as a *demand curve* must be constructed. On the sellers' side, the tool to be built is called a *supply curve*. After examining their underpinnings, one can put these representatives of the two participants together in a market and describe the *equilibrium* outcome. Equilibrium holds whenever there is no tendency toward change, all other things held constant. As the demand and supply curves are constructed, remember this goal: determining the equilibrium price and quantity in the market.

CONCEPT CHECK

Since all goods and services are scarce, consuming more of one good carries an opportunity cost of forgoing amounts of alternative goods. Economic systems are mechanisms for handling the universal problem of scarcity. These systems answer the fundamental questions of "What," "How," and "For whom" to produce. This chapter focuses on market economies, systems that answer these questions via the decentralized interaction of self-interested buyers and sellers in markets.

CONSUMER THEORY: DEMAND CURVES
A first look at demand

In this section, a **demand curve** will be constructed. This device will reveal the actual quantity of a good that consumers will wish to purchase under different prices. Throughout this process, remember that the focus is not on the "demand curve" per se. Rather, understanding consumer behavior is the objective. This consumer behavior, sometimes called the "Law of Demand," will enable one to

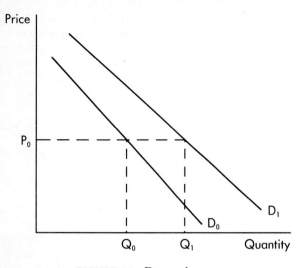

Price

P_0

Q_0 Q_1 Quantity

D_1

D_0

FIGURE 5-2 Demand curves.

originally, but when income goes up consumers can buy more units even if the price does not change.[†] This is depicted on the graph as the point Q_1 at price P_0 in Figure 5-2. Note that this increase in quantity demanded would hold regardless of the initial price. Put differently, for any given price, the new amount demanded is farther to the right (more) than the old amount. Figure 5-2 depicts this effect, known as a change in demand; the new demand curve is labelled D_1.

Such shifts in the demand curve could arise from other sources. For example, changes in taste may cause a shift in the demand curve. In the 1980s, running/basketball shoes became much more popular as casual wear. Regardless of the initial price, more such shoes were demanded. Suppose the quantity of basketball shoes is displayed on the horizontal axis and the price of these shoes is displayed on the vertical axis of a graph, such as in Figure 5-2. The change in tastes would be depicted as a shift to the right by the demand curve.

Finally, such shifts in demand also can be caused by changes in price for other goods. Suppose Figure 5-2 depicted the market for tea and also assume that something caused the price of a different good, coffee, to increase.[‡] Consumers would suddenly desire more tea at any price. To see this, note that tea and coffee are **substitutes**; they fill similar roles in consumers' minds. Thus price changes in one market cause *shifts* in the demand curve for the other good.

Some goods are called **complements**; the use of one good is tied to the use of the other. For example, sugar and coffee are complementary goods. When the price of coffee increased, it is known that *quantity demand* fell for coffee. Since sugar is a complement, the drop in coffee use meant that consumers wanted less sugar *at any price of sugar*. Thus the demand curve for sugar shifted to the left. In the sports realm, the boom in health clubs has increased the demand for complementary goods such as athletic wear and shoes.

summarize buyer behavior with the simple tool known as the demand curve.

Figure 5-2 depicts a standard demand curve, labelled D_0. It clearly shows the inverse relationship between price and quantity. At the price shown, P_0, the total amount demanded is Q_0. The behavior behind such a demand curve is clear. When prices of any commodity are low, consumers will purchase more of the commodity. As the commodity becomes more valued, consumers are forced to cut back on their purchases. Thus this behavior produces the traditional downward sloping demand curve.[*]

First, examine a very important bit of economic jargon. Whenever prices change, consumers will move *along* the demand curve. This is called a "change in quantity demanded." Suppose, however, that the consumer or group of consumers represented by the demand curve in Figure 5-2 become wealthier. This increase in income will enable them to purchase more of the product at any price. That is, at price P_0, Q_0 units are purchased

*The demand curve depicted in Figure 5-2 is drawn as a straight line. Most economists use such linear demand curves for simplicity. In reality, demand will have some curve to its shape. However, the only crucial point is that it is downward sloping.

†The actual size of the increase in quantity is arbitrarily chosen in the example. This amount is unimportant; the key is understanding that quantity demanded has changed.
‡The market for coffee is not depicted here. Just take the announced price increase for granted.

CONCEPT CHECK

Price changes cause movements along a demand curve. This is called "change in quantity demanded." Shifts in the demand curve are called "changes in demand." Such shifts come from changes in income, changes in tastes, or changes in the price of goods that are substitutes for or complements of the good in question.

Consumer motivation and behavior

The brief introduction to the demand curve has confirmed intuition about affordability and purchases. However, to better understand how this curve was actually produced, one needs to investigate consumer behavior in more detail. Consumers buy goods and services because of the **utility** of these products. Economists define utility as the amount of satisfaction or benefit that a consumer derives. Indeed, early economists used to quantify this satisfaction in terms of a theoretical unit of measure called a *util*. Since such utils are not measurable, they can be scaled in a way that makes them the easiest to interpret, that is, make one util equal to one dollar. In other words, one can define the utility a consumer receives as the maximum amount one would pay for the good or service.*

Although the total utility a consumer experiences in a particular period could be quite large, the key to understanding demand theory is merely the addition to utility brought by the next unit purchased. This addition is called **marginal utility**. Each extra unit of a commodity, be it hamburgers, compact disks, or sporting events, has its own marginal effect on the total level of satisfaction the consumer experiences. To understand consumer demand, it is necessary to understand the decision to purchase an individual unit. The total level of utility the consumer has experienced before making the decision is not important; all past purchases are effectively "sunk" and in the past. The decision to purchase or not involves a calculation of the extra utility compared with the cost of acquiring this source of utility. In demand theory, the marginal unit is the focus. The consumer must weigh the costs and benefits of this marginal unit to decide whether to purchase the good. The "cost" to the consumer is the posted price; the consumer must tender cash that has an obvious opportunity cost.† The "value" of the purchase is the marginal utility.

One final observation is needed before the construction of a demand curve. The **law of diminishing marginal utility** says that as a consumer gets more and more of a particular product, the marginal utility of the extra unit of consumption gets progressively lower. This does not say that extra units of the product lower the consumer's utility. What it says is that each incremental unit adds less to the consumer's total utility than the previous unit added.

Consider a simple example. Suppose you were treated to lunch by some generous friend; for the moment, price is not an issue. Your lunch is at a restaurant that specializes in small but delicious hamburgers. Furthermore, you are quite hungry. Finally, suppose (for purposes of our example) we have a device that can actually record your utility, measured in dollars.

When you eat your first hamburger, your utility is quite high. However, you are still hungry and order a second hamburger. This burger is also quite tasty, and you feel much better for having eaten it. The marginal effect on utility, while substantial, is not quite as high as the contribution of the first burger. Now suppose you elect to get a third burger and then a fourth. Both of these are satisfying. However, you are clearly less euphoric with each bite of these burgers than you were on the first or even the second burger. After finishing the fourth hamburger, your friend offers a fifth. At first you decline, but then accept as you do feel a little hun-

---

*In fact, knowledge of the absolute level of utility is not important to demand theory. All consumers need is to be able to judge relative levels of satisfaction. That is to say, all that is needed to produce the results of modern demand theory is an assumption that consumers are able to rank different alternatives, even if they cannot say exactly how much better one alternative is over the other.

---

†Note that a dollar bill has no utility in and of itself. Its value comes from understanding what that dollar bill can get the consumer in terms of some good or service. It is therefore the opportunity cost as it represents the value of the next best (but forgone) alternative.

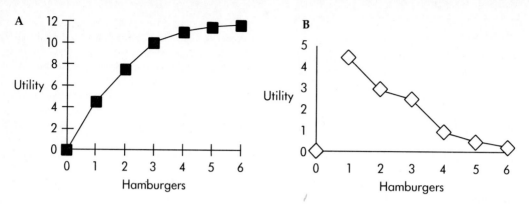

FIGURE 5-3 **A,** Total utility. **B,** Marginal utility.

gry (recall that these are small burgers). This burger is good, but the marginal effect on utility is not great. The friend suggests a sixth. You decline again, but the friend insists, saying it is the least you can do since she is paying. This burger adds very little to your utility. It is quite delicious, but you feel a little uncomfortable because of the size of your meal.

Table 5-1 offers some numbers for both total and marginal utility from this hamburger session. The actual values are arbitrary, but they illustrate a concept. For each additional unit of consumption, the *marginal* increase in utility is smaller.

Figure 5-3 plots the values of total and marginal utility as given in Table 5-1. The vertical axis is scaled in dollars and the horizontal axis in units of the good. Note that while total utility continues to increase, its gain gets smaller as the units increase. The marginal utility graph continues to decline as extra burgers are consumed.*

This concept is quite pervasive, which is why it is called a law. Certainly, some products are much more satisfying or important to individuals than are others. However, *all* products are subject to this same phenomenon. As the consumption of the product in any time period increases, the extra util-

TABLE 5-1 *Hypothetical utility from hamburgers*

Number of hamburgers	Total utility	Marginal utility
0	0	0
1	4.50	4.50
2	7.50	3.00
3	10.00	2.50
4	11.00	1.00
5	11.50	.50
6	11.75	.25

ity gain from each successive unit will be lower. Put differently, although the absolute levels of the curves depicted in Figure 5-3 may be different for different products, the curves of all goods and services have the same general shape.

Returning to the hamburger example, suppose now that your friend no longer offers to pay your expenses; you must pay for each burger. The current price of hamburgers is $2.75 at your restaurant.[†] How many burgers would you purchase? To answer, consider the marginal decision. The first

---

*In fact, if one continued the marginal utility table on to the seventh, eighth, ninth, and tenth burgers, the utility may actually decline below zero. Certainly, there is "x" number of hamburgers that would make one quite sick. In terms of this scenario, the marginal utility of these excess burgers is actually negative!

[†]For now, assume this is the only restaurant in town. Later, the effects of numerous sellers and consumers' obvious power to force sellers to "meet the competition" will be investigated.

burger would return you 4 dollars worth of satisfaction and is therefore quite a deal at only $2.75. Likewise, the second burger is also a good deal; you get back more than you sacrifice in the forgone opportunities implicit in the $2.75 you must pay. However, the third burger is no longer a good purchase. You elect to order two and leave with room in your stomach.

Again, it is important to understand that the third burger is not distasteful. It just does not offer as much to you as the other things you could do with the amount of money you would have to give up. When your friend handled the expenses, you quickly chose to consume a third burger. Its utility contribution, $2.50, was much higher than its cost to you, zero.

Consider the following experiment. Suppose, just as you are deciding how many to purchase, the restaurant announces a "special": All hamburgers are reduced 1 dollar in price. What is your response? Clearly, the third burger's marginal utility of $2.50 is much higher than the $1.75 price, and you increase your purchases. Suppose your waiter informs you that because it is Tuesday, you get yet another dollar off the extra hamburger. Now the fourth burger becomes valuable. Its marginal contribution is only 1 dollar, but it costs only 75 cents.

This "new price experiment" could be continued, but the point should be clear. As the price gets lower, it soon makes economic sense to buy more of the product. While the utility from the hamburger consumption does not change, the lower price means the forgone utility from alternative uses of the money becomes lower than what you can get from hamburgers. Conversely, the logic works the same way for price increases. As prices get higher, you cut back your purchases of hamburgers; you can get more utility out of your money by using it to purchase other commodities.

Return to Figure 5-3, *B*, depicting the values of marginal utility. Suppose horizontal lines were added at the price levels used in the preceding scenario. The consumer will purchase an additional unit of the good as long as the marginal contribution to satisfaction is greater than the expense. As the price line is lowered or raised on the graph, the amount purchased varies, depending on the position of the marginal utility curve. In fact, if you recall the general demand curve depicted in Figure 5-2, you will note the similarities.

The individual consumer's demand curve slopes downward, reflecting the fact that the marginal utility of the product decreases as more of the product is consumed. Any price change, and the resulting movement along the demand curve to a new optimum quantity for the consumer, actually has two effects. On the one hand, the price change causes consumer movement because of the **substitution effect**. This refers to the effect of the fact that the product in question now has a different price relative to all other commodities. If the consumer was happy (in equilibrium) at the early price, and the price increased, this commodity would be less attractive than it was, compared to alternative goods.

The other effect is known as the **income effect** and comes from the fact that any change in price brings a change in one's ability to purchase. If the price of a product goes up, consumers of that product are now implicitly less well off. They can no longer continue to buy *everything* they previously were buying because of the increase in price. Thus income is implicitly reduced. Any time a price changes, the quantity demanded will change. Although it is not apparent how much of the quantity change is due to the substitution effect and how much to the income effect, the distinction should be clear.

Market demand and elasticity

Market demand. The decision-making process of a single consumer was just examined. The goal is to understand how prices are determined in *markets*, and thus the **market demand curve** must be constructed. Put simply, the market demand curve is the sum of the individual demand curves of all participants in the market.

To see this, ask the question "How much quantity would be demanded in the entire market at a price of P_0?" The answer is found simply by adding the quantities demanded by each buyer at this price. This aggregate output would be one point on the market demand curve. One can continue this experiment, calling out other prices. Each consumer will react differently to these prices, just as each consumer's demand curve will have different shapes and positions. However, all that is required is to find the result, the sum of all their purchase decisions. The demand curves depicted in Figure 5-2 represent the general shape of a market demand curve except, of course, there would be a significantly larger scale for the units on the horizontal axis.

Price elasticity. By now, the shape and scenario of the demand curve are familiar. Suppliers can be sure that if they lower the price, more consumers will purchase the product, and price increases will lead to a reduction in quantity demanded. However, it is important to know how responsive quantity demanded is to changes in price. For example, governments routinely tax products. Such taxes are meant to produce revenues for the government. The actual revenue to the government depends on the quantity of the commodity actually purchased at the new, higher price (a price that incorporates the tax). If quantity demanded responds strongly to even slight price changes, the taxing unit should expect to get very little revenue while choking off much of the economic activity. Businesses are just as interested in knowing this responsiveness. If price increases cause very little reduction in quantity demanded, firms may be willing to raise price, lose a few units of sales, but gain significant increases in revenues on the purchases that remain.

The measure of this responsiveness is called the **price elasticity of demand**. It is formally defined as "the ratio of the percentage change in quantity demanded to the percentage change in price." In other words, letting E_d denote price elasticity of demand, the formula can be written as:

$$E_d = \frac{\text{Percentage change in quantity demanded}}{\text{Percentage change in price}} \quad (1)$$

Clearly, the larger this number, the more responsive is demand.*

Economists categorize price elasticity values into the following groups:

Elastic demand: Price elasticity greater than one.
Inelastic demand: Price elasticity less than one.
Unitary elastic demand: Price elasticity equal to one.

---

*Of course, since the change in quantity demanded and the change in price always move in opposite directions, the numerator and denominator of the elasticity term will always have opposite signs, leading to a negative value of elasticity. Fortunately, economists have, by convention, dropped this minus sign when referring to elasticity. Thus they treat equation (1) as if it were calculating the absolute value of the ratio.

Although these cutoffs may seem arbitrary, they actually are important economic categories. As ratios vary about the number one, the numerator becomes greater or smaller than the denominator. This is important, because it tells whether a given percentage price change will lead to a larger or smaller percentage change in quantity demanded.

What is so important about this relationship? Total revenue to a supplier is defined as the price per unit multiplied by the number of units sold. If demand were *unitary elastic*, a 10% price increase would lead to a 10% decrease in quantity purchased. Total revenue to the firm would not change, since the drop in units sold would be exactly offset by the increase in price per unit sold.

Suppose, instead, that the operation manager knows that demand is price inelastic. Now, the 10% price increase will cause quantity demanded to fall by a *smaller percentage*. The net effect on total revenue is attractive to the firm. Although unit sales have declined, the return per sale has increased by a factor that more than offsets the drop in sales.

There have been few attempts at measuring the elasticity of sport and leisure activities, mostly because of the lack of good data. The segment most studied has been Major League Baseball, because good data on prices and quantities has been available over time. Noll (1974) and Scully (1989) both find that the demand for baseball is probably elastic when one considers the full price, that is, the sum of ticket price, parking, transportation, and concessions.

Income elasticity. As previously mentioned, demand curves can shift when income changes. If prices do not change, then the change in income will result in a new optimum quantity demanded. Just as in the case of price changes, it is helpful to measure the responsiveness of demand to this change. Economists have defined **income elasticity** (E_i) as this measure. Similar to the price elasticity formula, this term is defined as the "ratio of the percentage change in quantity demanded to the percentage change in income." That is:

$$E_i = \frac{\text{Percentage change in quantity demanded}}{\text{Percentage change in income}} \quad (2)$$

Recall that in the case of price elasticity the minus sign was "dropped" (that is, the absolute value was used), since the sign was always the same. Now, however, the sign on E_i is important. Some products have positive income elasticity while others have negative income elasticity. Economists again have convenient categories for income elasticity values.

Normal goods: Goods with a positive income elasticity.

Inferior goods: Goods with a negative income elasticity.

Most goods are *normal* goods. Still, studies have found several products with negative income elasticities. Goods such as margarine and bus travel are inferior; consumers purchase *less* of these products as their incomes rise.

CONCEPT CHECK

Demand curves represent buyer behavior in markets. The law of diminishing marginal utility says that incremental units bring less extra satisfaction to consumers. As prices increase, the value of the marginal unit purchased may no longer warrant the outlay. This results in the familiar downward slope of a demand curve. Elasticity measures responsiveness of demand. An elastic demand curve is one that shows a relatively large quantity change for any price change, and inelastic demand curves represent little response in quantity.

THE THEORY OF THE FIRM

The previous section introduced the construction and properties of demand curves as a representation of buyer behavior. Of course, there is a second side to any transaction in a market: the seller. In this section the other side of the market through the supply curve is explored.

The firm

There are many good definitions of *firm*, but perhaps the best is an institution that organizes productive activity. That is, a firm is an entity that pulls together resources to produce a good or service that users desire. A firm need not be profit-oriented; many nonprofit entities perform the same activities as their profit-oriented counterparts.

Regardless of whether the firm is classified as profit-oriented, the goal of those in power at the institution is to maximize *residuals* accruing to the firm. These residuals are the difference between revenues (inflows) and costs (outflows) resulting from the productive activities of the firm. In the case of the profit-oriented firm, these residuals are commonly known as **profits**. Nonprofit organizations still work to maximize these residuals; the residuals simply are not distributed in the same fashion. Regardless, the overriding concern is to produce and market in the most efficient manner possible.

Firms can be organized in one of three forms. The simplest and most common form is the **sole proprietorship**. Businesses such as corner grocery stores, restaurants, and small manufacturing firms are usually organized like this; there is one owner, and he or she makes all the decisions. The advantages of this form are the ease of decisionmaking and the fact that profits are taxed just once, as the income of the owner. The major disadvantage is the *unlimited liability*. All the owner's assets, even those earned long before the birth of the current operation, are at jeopardy.

The next type of business entity is called a **partnership**. It has many of the same characteristics as the sole proprietorship (such as unlimited liability, and the fact that income is taxed only once) except there are multiple owners. This allows risk to be shared to some degree, makes generating funds easier, and enables the joint owners to pool a variety of specialized talents.

The third and final type of ownership is the **corporation**. Although most firms are structured as sole proprietorships, most business, as measured in dollars, is transacted by corporations. A corporation issues ownership shares, and these are owned by many different people. These shares are ownership rights to the firm and all its returns. The owners of a corporation enjoy limited liability; previously earned wealth is not in jeopardy. However, a major disadvantage of incorporation is that the government taxes residuals (profits) twice, first at the corporate level as corporate profits and then at the individual level since dividends paid to owners are treated as income.

Market structure

Before taking a more detailed look at the decisions of an individual firm and the implications of those decisions, the issue of the type of market must be considered. Some markets are supplied by numerous similar rivals. This type of market is known as **competition** or a "competitive market." At the other extreme, some products are supplied by a single producer. This situation is called **monopoly** or a "monopolistic market." Of course, the activities of these markets will be quite different, even if the demand side and the technology were controlled. The reason for this difference is that the monopolist has power over price. The competitive firm is too small *relatively* to have any control over price. Economists call competitive firms "price takers"; they observe the current market price and make their output decisions under the belief that their output will not alter the market price.

For example, consider the individual corn farmer. The farmer makes output decisions assuming the market price for corn is set. The farmer knows that even if he or she doubled or tripled production, there would be no effect on market price; the Chicago Board of Trade would not notice the change in output of a single farmer. Likewise, if the individual farmer decided to cut production by half, market price would remain unchanged.

Contrast this to a market serviced by a sole supplier. When this firm increases production, it knows there will be an effect on price. The demand curve shows that the only way the firm can sell this larger production is by lowering price! Likewise, if the sole supplier were to reduce output, it would see an immediate increase in price.

In the following scenario about firm decision making, assume that the market is competitive. This allows one to ignore the "price effect" of output changes; the individual firm takes price as given and produces accordingly. In the process, many valuable things will be learned about the operation of the firm. Later, monopolistic markets will be considered.

The supply curve in competitive markets

The counterpart to the demand curve, the **supply curve** is a chart that shows how much of the product suppliers are willing to trade at different prices. Figure 5-4 depicts such a curve.

The first thing to notice is the upward slope. As with the demand curve, this should reveal something. Although buyers are discouraged by higher prices, these same higher prices translate to a greater return for the suppliers. Thus, all other things equal, if producers are offered higher prices, they will respond to this inducement with even more output.

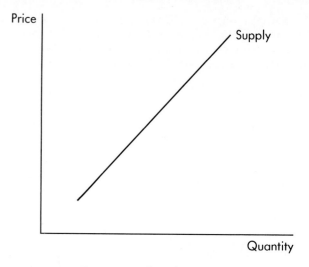

FIGURE 5-4 Supply curve.

The goal is to construct supply curves for individual firms and then aggregate these into a market supply curve. Recall the definition of supply curves: the output sellers would offer at different prices. For individual supply curves, seller responses to a variety of possible prices will be mapped. Therefore prices will, for now, be arbitrarily selected by which to test how firms respond. By mapping responses to all sorts of situations, the market supply curve will be able to be constructed. Finally, combining this supply curve with the buyers' demand curve will enable the determination of the market price.

Firm behavior. What motivates a firm? Firms act to maximize the residual from their productive activity. Again, for profit-oriented institutions, this residual is known as profit. Nonprofit firms have a variety of names for the residual, but it is still the key to understanding their resource decisions.

The residual or profit is simply the excess of total revenue over total cost. Total revenue is straightforward: price per unit multiplied by the number of units sold. Total cost is the sum of all expenses incurred in producing these units. To better understand how these costs arise, consider the production process.

The example of a hypothetical firm producing raquetball and tennis rackets will be used. This firm produces output, rackets, by combining inputs in the most efficient manner. Suppose there are only two types of inputs: capital equipment (the factory) and labor (the workers). At any time the actual size of the capital input is fixed. Changing this input is a long-run proposition, left to the firm's planning experts. The day-to-day decisions about changing the output are therefore affected by the other input, labor. Economists refer to capital as the *fixed input* and labor as the *variable input* although the roles may be reversed.*

For convenience, two different time periods will be used for this analysis of equilibrium. These two periods, the **short run** and the **long run**, are distinguished by whether capital is a fixed input. The term *short run* will refer to the period of time in which capital is fixed. The firm is obligated to use and pay for the given amount of capital regardless of production decisions. The *long run* is the period in which the firm is able to alter capital. That is, the long run is the period of time when both inputs can vary.

As the manager hires more labor to work at the (fixed) racket plant, the output of the firm increases. The exact relationship between specific levels of inputs and the amount of output that results can be described by complex mathematical equations. Every good and service has its own technology and therefore its own equation. Production engineers produce these equations, and they help managers make decisions. For the purpose of this chapter, that much detail is not necessary. All that need be understood is the general process.

This general process—as more inputs are used, the output level changes—has one important characteristic that holds true for all types of production. As the firm continues to add more and more of the variable input, the additional output for each new unit of the input gets smaller and smaller. This fact is known as the **law of diminishing marginal returns**. Just as in the case of utility, the key word in the name is "law"; this means that the concept holds in all productive efforts. As more and more of the variable input continues to be applied, *with the fixed input constant*, the marginal contribution of the variable input becomes smaller.

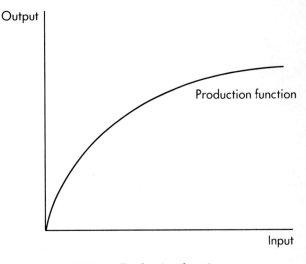

FIGURE 5-5 Production function.

This concept is easily verified with a simple example. Imagine any type of production process at all. Now take the fixed factory, retail outlet, or other form of capital equipment and begin adding more and more units of labor. Eventually, the workers will simply get in the way of each other; production (sales) will grind to a halt. Of course, no firm would ever get to such a ridiculous combination of capital and labor. However, it is an effective way to grasp the law of diminishing marginal returns.

Figure 5-5 depicts the typical shape of the *production function*. The horizontal axis measures the level of the variable input, and the vertical axis measures output. Production increases as the variable input increases; adding input increases output, a result we discussed earlier. Production gets progressively flatter at higher levels of the variable input. This is the graphic depiction of the law of diminishing marginal returns; as the input is increased (the horizontal step), the marginal increase in output (the vertical rise) gets smaller and smaller.

Now a discussion of the actual costs of production is in order. Economists typically break these costs into two categories: **fixed cost** and **variable cost**. For purposes of the definition, the fixed costs do not vary with the level of production. Fixed costs can be considered as the expenses of the fixed inputs. When the time comes to decide production

---

*There are time horizons so short that the manager of the firm has only one input that can be varied, the rest being fixed. For some operations, this variable input may in fact be capital equipment.

levels, these costs are not open to change. Variable costs, costs of the variable inputs, *do* change with changes in outputs. The only way output levels can be changed is by changing the variable input; these changes in input lead directly to changes in cost. For example, as more labor is hired, the total expenses of the institution will increase. This change in cost for a one-unit change in output is known as **marginal cost**.

The marginal cost curve for any operation will slope upward. As the level of output increases, each additional unit of output has higher marginal costs than the previous unit of output. This rule can be proved through rigorous investigation, but such complexities need not be explored here. Simply recall the law of diminishing marginal returns. This concept means that as more units of the input were added, the extra output from each additional input diminished. Put differently, as the firm tries to get more and more output, each additional unit of output will require successively more input. In terms of cost, then, one can see that the marginal costs of production increase with output. As the firm tries to continue *increasing* production, the law of diminishing marginal returns forces the firm to incur ever-increasing costs as the marginal productivity of the variable input drops.

To maximize profits (residuals), the manager must pay close attention to the effect on residuals of the *marginal* unit produced. Just as with consumer theory, the focus of attention is this marginal unit. At *any* level of production, the manager must ask the question, "What happens if we produced one more (or less) unit?" To answer this question, compare this extra unit's contribution to the firm's marginal revenue with the contribution this incremental unit makes to marginal costs. The manager will go ahead with the extra unit of output only if marginal revenue from this unit exceeds marginal cost, that is, what the marginal unit returns is greater than what it costs.

This is a very powerful concept. It says that a firm can be expected to produce to the point at which marginal revenue of production is just equal to marginal cost. No manager would produce past this point, since this would cost the firm more than it would get back. Likewise, no manager would stop short of the output point where marginal revenue just equals marginal cost. To see why, suppose some manager *did* choose to stop at a point

at which marginal revenue is greater than marginal cost. This point *cannot* be optimal since, by definition of marginal revenue and marginal cost, producing the extra unit will increase the firm's revenues by an amount greater than the firm's increase in cost.

Now that some time has been spent on the concept of marginal costs, marginal revenue will be examined. Recall that the individual firm in a competitive market is a *price taker*; that is, the firm treats price as given. Thus the change in revenue for a one-unit increase in output is simply the price per unit. If the price were, say, $5, then each additional unit of production would bring in exactly $5 more to the firm's revenue.

For competitive firms (price takers), marginal revenue is identical to price.

One has already realized that the optimal behavior for an individual firm is to produce at the output level at which marginal revenue is just equal to marginal cost. Figure 5-6 depicts just such a situation. The marginal cost curve is an upward-sloping line. The marginal revenue curve is, for price takers, a horizontal line at P_0, the price in the market.* Optimal behavior would be to select output level Q*.

The optimal output for a firm occurs where marginal revenue just equals marginal cost. If the price changes, the horizontal line in Figure 5-6 would move accordingly. Optimal output still would be the point at which the marginal revenue (horizontal line) located at the new price intersects the upward-sloping marginal cost curve. Thus the firm's marginal cost curve is actually the individual supply curve. It depicts the amount or number of the product the firm would be willing to supply at different prices.

Market supply curve. Just as with demand, the *market supply curve* is found by adding the supply responses of the individual firms in the market. For any price, each firm will maximize profits (residuals) by finding the output at which marginal revenue intersects marginal cost. One could actually calculate these amounts for different prices,

---

*Again, note that it is still not definite where this "market price" originates. The task for now is to consider the behavior of an individual firm under different scenarios. Later aggregation of these individual firms will determine the market equilibrium. The "price" chosen in Figure 5-6 is arbitrary.

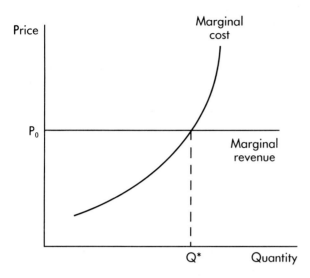

FIGURE 5-6 Profit-maximizing output.

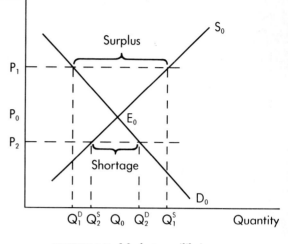

FIGURE 5-7 Market equilibrium.

but it is much easier simply to realize that the market supply curve will be the *horizontal sum of the individual supply curves.* Such a curve was depicted in Figure 5-4.

CONCEPT CHECK

Firms maximize the residuals generated by their production effort. For profit-oriented organizations these residuals are commonly called profits. Marginal cost represents the extra *cost of producing one more unit. Marginal revenue represents the* extra *revenue from selling one more unit. Optimal production occurs at the point at which these two are equal. Producing more or less than this amount would result in lower residuals.*

Market equilibrium in the short run

To review, the goal has been to consider how equilibrium is reached in a market. As previously discussed, no central authority calls out prices and dictates quantities. Rather, independent buyers and sellers enter into voluntary transactions. Now equilibrium price and quantity in such a market will be discussed. Combining buyer behavior and seller behavior will produce a model of a competitive equilibrium.

Return to the racket example; Figure 5-7 depicts a typical market demand and market supply curve. Equilibrium occurs at the intersection of these two curves, the point E_0. Here, market price P_0 guarantees that the quantity supplied (voluntarily) is just the amount that buyers desire.

To illustrate, suppose price happened to be P_1, a price above the equilibrium level.* At this price, only Q^D_1 rackets are demanded, but this higher price will bring out Q^S_1 in supply. This situation is called a **surplus**; more rackets are supplied than demanded. This situation cannot be an equilibrium because unsold goods would put downward pressure on price. As price goes down, two effects simultaneously work to reduce the surplus. First, the lower price increases quantity of rackets demanded as we move down the market demand curve. Second, the lower price restricts output supplied by the firms in the market. Price will continue to drop until the surplus is eliminated.

Price P_2 represents some arbitrary price below the equilibrium. At this price consumers clamor for Q^D_2 rackets, but suppliers are willing to produce a

---

*This price has absolutely no importance other than as an illustration of the current topic. It is simply an arbitrarily higher price than the price known to be the equilibrium.

mere Q^s_2. The result is called a **shortage**. Again, this is no longer an equilibrium because there is internal pressure to change. The shortage will cause prices to climb as buyers scramble for the insufficient allotment of rackets. As price goes up, two effects can again be seen. Some consumers no longer want the product, helping to reduce the shortage. In addition, the higher price makes firms willing to offer more of the product. As long as there is a shortage, that is, as long as the price is below P_0, the price will continue to change.

CONCEPT CHECK

Equilibrium price occurs at the intersection of the market supply curve and the market demand curve. At any other price, the market would experience a shortage or a surplus. Both of these events are out-of-equilibrium situations; there will be pressure on price to change. The only price without such pressure to change is at the intersection, where quantity demanded is exactly met by quantity supplied.

Market equilibrium in the long run

Figure 5-7 depicted the equilibrium in the short run, defined as the period during which capital is fixed. However, firms *can* and do decide to alter capital over time. Of course, until the new capital comes on line, the equilibrium remains as in the short run. As soon as the capital becomes operable, it is again "fixed" at the new level. Labor is still used as the variable input. The cost curve and supply curve shift, and a new equilibrium emerges.

Some changes in capital are responses to technological changes, depreciation, or other factors. However, these are managerial changes and are not very interesting to our study of equilibrium. The more important capital changes come from the acts of *entry* and *exit*. Decisions by firms to leave the market are drastic changes in capital and can therefore occur only in the long run. Likewise, decisions by outsiders to enter an industry are also changes in capital, not unlike the case in which a firm already in the industry decides to double its plant capacity.

Entry and exit are driven by the level of profits. The previous description of optimal output, and the resulting equilibrium, were based on the understanding that maximizing profits required the firm to set output so that marginal cost equaled marginal revenue. Although this output *does* maximize profits, it says nothing about the absolute level of profits. Indeed, it could be that the optimal output actually results in a negative level of profits; setting marginal cost equal to marginal revenue guarantees that the firm earns the maximal available profits but says nothing about the level of those profits.

Negative profits: exit. If profits are negative, firms are in a bind. By definition of *fixed* inputs, the firms cannot get out of the obligations of these resources. Operating at negative profits but still earning some revenues is usually better than earning no revenues (shutting down operations).* However, once the firm is able to alter its capital, in the "long run," it will sell off and exit.

The effect of this exit on industry equilibrium is important. As firms exit, the number of firms in the industry declines. Since the market supply is the sum of the supply curves of all firms in the industry, the result is that the market supply curve shifts to the left. As one can see from Figure 5-7, this would result in a higher equilibrium price for rackets.

How long does this exit continue? As long as price is so low that it gives firms profit levels lower than they could earn elsewhere, they will continue to exit. Economists call the threshold level of profit the *normal* profit. If the industry price generates lower-than-normal profits, firms will continue to exit. Equilibrium will come only when the exit has removed enough supply to make price high enough to generate the normal rate of return.

High profits: entry. Suppose that the price in the industry is so high that it generates profits above the normal level, that is, the average profit opportunity in the economy. In the short run the capital level is fixed. However, in the long run,

---

*Since the firm always will have the fixed obligations regardless of output level, the firm will continue to produce with negative profits as long as the variable input (labor) earns more than its own cost. If this is the case, the firm has at least some money to put against the fixed obligations. If the situation is so bad that the returns from production are less than the variable input costs, the firm will indeed shut its doors and wait to exit the industry when it is finally able to get out of its fixed obligations (that is, in the long run).

outside firms will enter the industry. After all, the "average" firm in the remainder of the economy is only earning normal profits (by definition). The total number of firms in the racket industry expands. As in the exit scenario just discussed, this increase in the number of participants produces a *shift* in supply. Market supply, being the horizontal sum of individual supply curves, moves to the right. As can be seen via Figure 5-7, this new supply curve would force equilibrium price to drop.

As long as price remains high enough to generate supernormal profits, the entry will continue. Long-run equilibrium will be reached when the expanding supply curve forces market price down to a point that produces normal (average) profits.

An example

To close this story of long-run equilibrium, consider this scenario. Suppose the racket industry is currently in long-run equilibrium. Thus it is known that supply equals demand, and the price generated by this equilibrium is just enough to generate normal profits for firms in the industry. No one has an incentive to leave; no one on the outside is trying to get into the industry.

Now suppose consumer tastes change and racket sports become very popular. Of course, the result will be higher prices in the racket industry. However, one now can actually model the effects of this change in tastes.

The consumer taste change is modeled as a shift out (to the right) in the market demand curve; at any price, more rackets are demanded today than yesterday. This increase in demand leads to a shortage at the old price. This out-of-equilibrium situation is corrected quickly. The price rises, choking off some of the excess demand and inducing firms to increase production by using more of the variable input.*

Since profits at the original price were just "normal," the new higher prices are generating attrac-

tive returns to the industry firms. This induces outsiders to enter.[†] This entry, which occurs only in the "long run," will put downward pressure on price, eventually returning it to the original price or near it.

Notice the efficiency of price in the market system. It clears the market of shortage in the short run. It is also used as the market's signal to the economy that consumers value this particular product, rackets, more than the "average" product. The higher prices that result from the growth in demand tell firms to move into this industry, eventually countering the price trend. No central authority was needed to order investment in some industries and not in others. The lure of profits sufficed.

Monopolistic equilibrium

This section considers equilibrium in the monopolistic market. Remember, the monopolist is a sole supplier. Therefore this firm must realize that changes in *its* quantity are identical to changes in *market* quantity. The monopolist still worries about maximizing profits (residuals), but the decision is different.

The actual mechanics of determining the optimal price and quantity are a bit more complicated than need be explored at this point. Just as a firm in a competitive market, the monopolist maximizes profit by choosing output where marginal revenue equals marginal cost. That is, it will find the output such that the cost of the incremental unit just equals the return from that unit. The manager of the firm will consider the effect of increasing the firm's output by one unit. If the extra return (marginal revenue) is greater than the extra cost (marginal cost) of that unit, the manager will go ahead with the production.

Marginal cost for a monopolist is no different than for a competitive firm. Technology and input prices dictate the shape and position of the curve. However, marginal revenue is decidedly different. Remember, the competitive firm was a price taker. That meant that marginal revenue was a constant; no matter the level of production, the firm knew the extra unit would still generate a change in rev-

---

*At this point suppliers are often publicly vilified for their "gouging." For example, in particularly cold winters, home heating fuel suppliers are castigated for "taking advantage of the situation" and raising prices. You now know enough about demand and supply to see that such events as an uncommonly cold winter would bring a shift in demand for heating oil. Thus price *has* to rise to attract more production, restrain some usage, and eventually reach an equilibrium.

[†]Of course, the "entry" could be by insiders. The construction of another plant by a firm already in the industry is the same for the purpose of this discussion as a plant built by an outsider.

enue equal to the (unchanging) market price of that extra unit.

For the monopolist, this is not the case. As the monopolist produces more, the price received for each unit *drops*, since the demand curve slopes downward. In fact, the now lower price for the extra unit cannot even be used as the marginal revenue. To see this, note that the monopolist can only set one price. If it increases output, it lowers price to sell that extra unit of output. However, this means the monopolist must lower price to all buyers. Thus marginal revenue to a monopolist is less than the price earned on the marginal unit by the amount it sacrifices on units it could have sold at the higher price.

Consider this hypothetical example. Suppose a monopolist is selling 60 units at $5 per unit. Assume demand is such that to sell one more unit, the monopolist would have to lower price to $4.95. Thus, it *appears* that the marginal revenue is the $4.95 earned on the marginal unit. However, the monopolist has to realize that it is now sacrificing $.05 on each of the original 60 units it could have sold at $5. Thus, the change in revenue for selling the one extra unit is $4.95 − (60 × $.05), or $1.95. For a monopolist, the marginal revenue curve is always lower than price. Also, for straight-line demand curves, note that at higher output levels the "sacrifice" effect of the price reduction on all other units is even larger. The effect of this is to drive marginal revenue even farther below price at higher outputs. For a linear demand curve, the marginal revenue curve is as depicted in Figure 5-8.

Determining the monopolistic equilibrium is straightforward. The monopolist will choose an output where marginal revenue equals marginal cost, Q_*^M. This optimal output is sold at the highest price the monopolist can get, read off the demand curve above Q_*^M. As can be seen, the price a monopolist receives is significantly above its costs.

What about the long run? In the example of competitive industries, entry resulted from industry conditions that gave firms high profits. In the current case, such entry is impossible. By definition, a monopolist is a sole supplier. The firm has no competitors and hence can continue to earn monopoly returns over time.

As an example of the size of monopoly profits, consider Major League Baseball. The number of

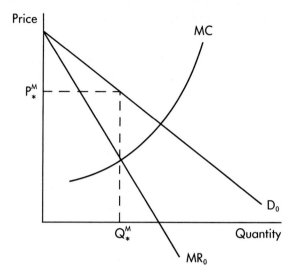

FIGURE 5-8   Monopolistic equilibrium.

franchises (firms) is strictly limited by an organization made up of owners; entry is tightly controlled. Because of outside pressure, the National League chose to add two new teams in 1993. The entrance fee, payable to the other owners, was set at $95 million (Stevenson, 1990). This can be considered as a payment for the reduction in profits each *current* owner will experience because of the entry. It is also a sign of the size of monopoly profits earned by the franchises.

CONCEPT CHECK

In competitive markets, equilibrium occurs at the intersection of supply and demand. In the short run this equilibrium may bring positive profits or negative profits. In the long run the capital stock of the industry can be changed. Negative profits will cause exit and higher prices. Eventually, price will rise high enough to stop the outflow of capital. Conversely, positive profits will attract entry, driving prices down. Then price will fall so low that entry no longer will be attractive. Monopoly markets do not see such entry. Thus monopolists can hold price above costs even in the long run.

SUMMARY

1. The market system generates equilibrium through the interaction of supply and demand in a market. Demand curves are representations of buyer willingness to pay; this willingness is driven by self-interest. Consumers get utility from products and are willing to pay for such satisfaction.
2. Of course, buyers will always try to get a better deal and the sellers will always try to get a higher price. The market disciplines both sides. Price acts as both a rationing device and a signal.
3. In its rationing role, price clears the market by bringing the amount of a product for sale in line with the amount consumers voluntarily wish to purchase.
4. In its signaling role, price is an indicator to the numerous decentralized decisionmakers of society's values. Products that consumers want will generate higher prices as demand grows. Firms will then respond by entering this industry.* Products in which consumers have little (or waning) interest will see falling prices, and firms will exit the industry.
5. The significance of the "invisible hand" should not be missed. Planned economies must decide for the consumers which products and services are available. In a market economy, changes in tastes are quickly and accurately reflected in changes in products offered. Resources are channeled to areas in which consumers have interest without the requirement of a vast bureaucracy or centralized decision making. The sports industry is certainly an example of the diversity of consumer wants and the ability of entrepreneurs to respond to these demands.

REVIEW QUESTIONS AND ISSUES

1. The production Possibilities Frontier (PPF) offers a graphical description of scarcity. If we group all goods into the categories "consumption" and "investment" goods, depict a general PPF. Define opportunity costs and discuss how to read such costs on the PPF diagram. Finally, suppose you are told that the economy is currently operating at a point inside the PPF. What are the implications for the outcome?

2. Some universities offer free "student tickets" to all registered students. If the price is zero, does this imply that the tickets are not scarce? Suppose the success of the school's team leads to greater requests for student tickets than seats available. How will these "scarce" goods be allocated if the university adheres to its policy of not charging students?
3. Recent estimates indicate that the price elasticity of demand for gasoline is approximately .20. Is this elastic, inelastic, or unitary elastic? The 1990 Middle East crisis caused a decrease in gasoline supply and a 50% increase in gasoline prices. Graphically indicate the impact on equilibrium quantity. What happened to revenues received by gasoline producers as a result of this supply shock?
4. Define and discuss the law of diminishing marginal returns. What role does this law play in the shape of the variable cost curve? What does this imply about marginal costs?
5. During the 1980s, many new firms entered the market for athletic footwear, a market that is perfectly competitive. Use graphs depicting equilibria at both the market and firm level to explain this observation. Suppose now that you observe some firms exiting the industry. Offer an explanation, and depict your rationale using graphical analysis.

REFERENCES

Baumol, W., and Blinder, A. (1988). *Economics: principles and policies* (4th Edition). Orlando, Florida: Harcourt Brace Jovanovich.

Noll, R. (1974). Attendance and price setting. In R. Noll (Ed). *Government and the sports business*. Washington, DC: Brookings Institute.

Scully, G. (1989). *The business of major league baseball*. Chicago: University of Chicago Press.

Stevenson, R. (1990). "Pony up $95 million? Sure, for a baseball team. *New York Times*, September 23, 1990.

---

*Of course, such entry is not possible in the case of a monopolist.

CHAPTER 6

Sports Law: The Theoretical Aspects

Glenn M. Wong

In this chapter, you will become familiar with the following terms:

Sports law
Collective bargaining agreements
Federal court system
Trial system
Contract law
Tort liability
Intentional tort
Unintentional tort
Assault and battery
Reckless misconduct
Negligence
Defamation

Libel
Slander
Agency law
Independent contractor
Constitutional law
Due process
Equal protection
Unreasonable search and seizure
Invasion of privacy
Sex discrimination
Title IX of the Education
    Amendments of 1972

Programmatic approach
Institutional approach
Equal Rights Amendment
Equal Pay Act
Title VII of the Civil Rights Act
    of 1964
Criminal law
Antitrust law
Sherman Antitrust Act
Clayton Act
Labor law

Overview

Sports law is a growing component of the sports industry, thus those involved in this industry must be knowledgeable about sports law.

This chapter provides information on how the field of sports law emerged, the issues relative to sports law, and how these issues have an impact on the different factions of the sports industry, such as administrators, coaches, officials, and participants. Key areas of the law and their relation-

ship to the sports industry are identified and defined in this chapter. These key areas are contract law, tort liability, agency law, constitutional law, sex discrimination, criminal law, antitrust law, and labor law.

This chapter also delineates how the different areas of the law affect the sports industry, of what the sport person should be aware regarding these issues, and how the sport person can better deal with potential litigation.

The study of **sports law** is a relatively new field. The first sports law course was offered in 1972 by Professor Robert C. Berry at Boston College Law School. Titled "Regulation of Professional Athletics," the course reflected the fact that most of the sports law issues in 1972 dealt with professional sports. By the end of the 1980s, amateur sports law issues and cases had become as prevalent as professional sports law issues. In the time since Berry's initial sports law course, many law schools and sport management programs have integrated sports law into their curricula. This trend will probably continue into the 1990s, because the increased monetary stakes in the sport industry have propelled all facets of athletics toward a businesslike approach.

Sports law courses differ significantly, with some emphasizing professional sports aspects and others emphasizing amateur sports aspects. Other courses focus on certain substantive areas of the law, such as antitrust law, tort law, or collective bargaining. There is not necessarily a correct syllabus to be followed; rather, student interests and career goals are matched with faculty members' areas of interest and expertise. This chapter presents an overview of the various substantive areas of sports law.

What is sports law? It is the application of various areas of the law to a specific industry—the sports industry. The application of the law to sports has in many instances created new and difficult legal issues for judges, lawyers, and athletic administrators. These legal issues have created the need for—and, in some instances, produced— federal and state legislation specific to athletics. In addition, these unique issues have required the promulgation of rules, regulations, and legal documents pertaining specifically to athletics. An example of federal legislation is Title IX of the Education Amendments of 1972, which governs sex discrimination issues in elementary and secondary schools, colleges, and universities, and is applicable to athletic programs at institutions that receive federal funding. Another example of federal legislation is the Amateur Sports Act, passed in 1978, which governs Olympic sports in the United States. An example of state legislation promulgated for sports is agent legislation, passed in 19 states, which governs the conduct of individuals who represent athletes in contract negotiations with professional teams. In addition, many states have laws pertaining to athletic trainers and/or doctors, requiring their presence at certain high school athletic events. Several states have legislation dealing with fan behavior toward referees and officials, and a number of states have legislation dealing with fitness and exercise facilities. In addition to legislation, some specific rules and regulations governing athletics are listed in the *NCAA Manual*, which is published by the National Collegiate Athletic Association (NCAA). The *NCAA Manual* was first printed in its current format in 1965, although the NCAA bylaws have been printed in other forms since 1913.

Further, all of the professional team sports leagues have had **collective bargaining agreements** governing the terms and conditions of employment for players in their respective leagues. Contracts have also become an important part of the business side of athletics. There are now standard contracts for professional team athletes. Individually-negotiated contracts are the norm for coaches at the college level, for teams that lease facilities and/or broadcast games on television and radio, and for individuals who join health clubs.

Sports law has become increasingly important for sport management personnel. This is evident in that many important leadership positions in athletics are held by professionals who have a legal background. For example, all four current commissioners of professional team sports are attorneys: David Stern in the National Basketball Association, Fay Vincent in Major League Baseball, John Ziegler in the National Hockey League, and Paul Tagliabue in the National Football League. Several general managers of professional sports franchises, college conference commissioners, and athletic directors are also attorneys.

Although many attorneys hold these leadership positions, a law degree is not necessarily a prerequisite to obtaining a key leadership position. Overall, there are certainly more people in key administrative positions in athletics who are not attorneys. However, it certainly helps if the nonattorney is able to recognize and deal with legal issues, simply because legal issues are occurring on a more frequent basis than in previous years. The athletic administrator who has an appreciation and understanding of sports law issues will find it easier to make appropriate administrative decisions to avoid legal difficulties; he or she will also be able to communicate, understand, and question more effectively, as well as instruct the organization's attorney when difficulties do arise.

This chapter provides a starting point for the sport manager who desires to be versed adequately in sports law. The topics for discussion include a review of the court system, contract law, tort law, agency law, constitutional law, sex discrimination law, criminal law, antitrust law, and labor law. The chapter will not focus on legal concerns covered in other chapters, including trademark licensing (see Chapter 15) and product liability law (see Chapters 7 and 14). Chapter 13, Sports Law Case Studies: The Application, which includes a discussion of torts and contracts, can be read in conjunction with this chapter, since it offers several case studies that apply the legal theories discussed in this chapter to actual sports situations.

THE COURT SYSTEM

The sports manager needs a fundamental understanding of the U.S. legal system to deal effectively with the wide variety of legal matters faced today. There are two basic legal systems in the United States: the federal system and the state system.

Federal court system

The **federal court system** in the United States consists of the Supreme Court, 12 courts of appeals, 91 district courts, certain specialized courts, and administrative agencies (Figure 6-1). Federal cases are usually first heard in a district court, although a limited number of cases may be initiated in the higher courts of appeals or in the Supreme Court. Cases that are appealed after being heard in the district courts usually go to a court of appeals—or, in rare cases—will go directly to be heard in the Supreme Court.

The Supreme Court is the highest court in the United States and the ultimate authority on all legal issues. Once the Supreme Court decides an issue, all other federal courts must interpret the law by its lead. Nine justices sit on the U.S. Supreme Court, including a chief justice and eight associate justices. The Supreme Court justices are appointed by the President of the United States and confirmed by the U.S. Senate. Justices serve lifetime tenures.

Supreme Court decisions are made after the justices have heard the oral presentations and reviewed the *briefs*, or written arguments, from both parties. Each justice renders an opinion on why a certain decision should be made, and then the justices vote in order of seniority. After a decision has been reached by majority vote, the justices choose one of their members to write the *opinion of the Court*. A justice who disagrees with the opinion and did not vote with the majority may write a *dissenting opinion*. A justice who agrees with the majority opinion but not with the reasons it was reached may write a *concurring opinion*.

The United States is divided into 11 judicial districts and the District of Columbia. Each of these districts, called *circuits*, has a U.S. Court of Appeals. These 12 appeals courts have only *appellate jurisdiction*, which means that they review cases tried in the federal district courts and cases heard and decided by the federal regulatory commissions (for example, the Internal Revenue Service and the National Labor Relations Board).

The *district courts* are the trial courts of the federal court system. Each state has at least one district court. A total of 91 district courts cover the 50 states, the District of Columbia, and the Commonwealth of Puerto Rico.

Rulings made by such federal agencies as the Federal Trade Commission, the Internal Revenue Service, and the National Labor Relations Board fall into the category of *administrative law*. These agencies are allowed to formulate rules for the administrative area they regulate, to enforce the rules, to hold hearings on any violations, and to issue decisions, including penalties.

State court system

In general, each of the 50 states has a three-tiered court system, with a trial court level, appellate court level, and supreme court level of review (see Figure 6-1). Each state judicial system hears cases and reviews the law based on its state constitution, state statutes, and previous court decisions. In addition, a state court must often interpret the federal constitution and/or federal statutes, based on how they affect state criminal or civil laws that are reviewed under its jurisdiction.

The trial system

For many nonattorneys, a group which includes most athletic administrators, the threat of litigation is a very upsetting proposition. However, with some basic information about how the trial system works, the athletic administrator will realize that

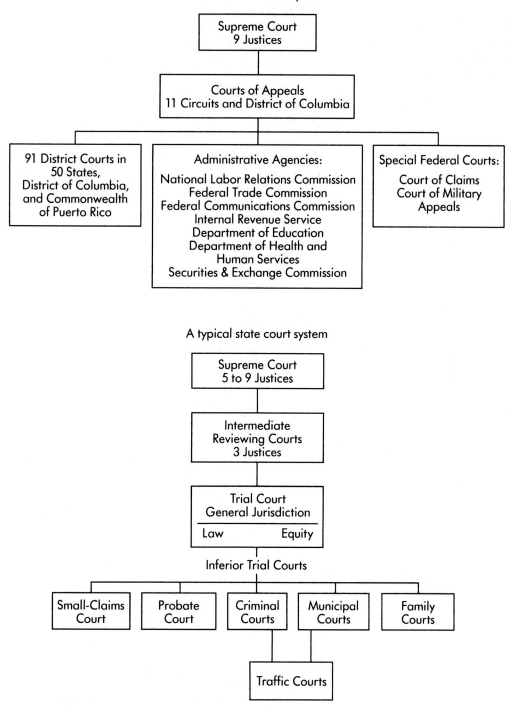

The Federal Court System

Supreme Court
9 Justices

Courts of Appeals
11 Circuits and District of Columbia

91 District Courts in 50 States, District of Columbia, and Commonwealth of Puerto Rico

Administrative Agencies:

National Labor Relations Commission
Federal Trade Commission
Federal Communications Commission
Internal Revenue Service
Department of Education
Department of Health and Human Services
Securities & Exchange Commission

Special Federal Courts:

Court of Claims
Court of Military Appeals

A typical state court system

Supreme Court
5 to 9 Justices

Intermediate Reviewing Courts
3 Justices

Trial Court General Jurisdiction

| Law | Equity |

Inferior Trial Courts

Small-Claims Court

Probate Court

Criminal Courts

Municipal Courts

Family Courts

Traffic Courts

FIGURE 6-1 The federal and state court systems.
(From Wong, G. (1988). *Essentials of amateur sports law*. Dover, Massachusetts: Auburn House Publishing Co.)

dealing with the trial system is not as complicated as it first may seem. The **trial system** can be broken down into the following 10 parts:

1. The *complaint* is the initial pleading in a trial, filed by the plaintiff in a civil case and the prosecutor in a criminal case.
2. The *summons* is the actual serving of notice to the defendant, notifying the defendant of the legal action being instituted and ordering the defendant to "answer" the charge by a certain date.
3. The *answer* is the defendant's initial pleading on the alleged violation of criminal or civil law.
4. Two types of *court jurisdiction* must be satisfied before a court can hear a case: personal and subject matter. *Personal jurisdiction* means that a court must have sufficient contact with the defendant to bring the defendant into its jurisdiction. *Subject matter jurisdiction* means that the court must have authority to hear the subject matter that is being tried.
5. *Discovery* is a pretrial procedure by which each party to a lawsuit obtains facts and information about the case from the other parties in the case to assist all parties with trial preparation.
6. The *parties* are the participants in a legal action. The *plaintiff* is a person or party who initiates a legal action by bringing a lawsuit against another person or party. The *defendant* is the person or party against whom legal action is taken and against whom relief or recovery is sought.
7. The two types of courts in the trial system are the trial court and appeals court. The *trial court* is the court of original jurisdiction in which all issues are brought forth, argued, and decided on by either a judge or jury. The *appeals court* is the court of review in which issues decided at trial are reexamined for error. No new evidence or issues may be presented in appeals courts.
8. The *trial* can involve a jury or can take place without a jury present. Whether a trial will be a jury or a nonjury trial depends on the nature of the trial. A *jury* comprises a certain number of individuals selected according to the law, who are sworn to inquire of certain matters of fact and declare the truth on evidence to be laid before them. The judge oversees the trial but has limited supervision over the decision determined in a jury trial.
9. The *judgment* is the decision given after the closing statements. The judge either instructs the members of the jury on their options in reaching a decision, or the judge—in a trial without a jury—renders the decision.
10. Many judgments by trial courts are *appealed*—that is, the party who lost the case (appellant) requests that the trial proceedings be reviewed by a higher court in the hopes that the decision will be reversed. An appeals court may *reverse* (disagree with) a lower court's ruling either totally or in part, it may *remand* (return) the case back to the lower court for further proceeding, or it may *affirm* (agree with) the lower court's decision.

Case law citations

Cases throughout this chapter and in Chapter 13 are listed according to their case citation. A case law citation consists of a case title and case citation, which includes the court reporter in which the decision can be found, the volume, the court which made the decision, and the page number. For example, *Shelton v. National Collegiate Athletic Association,* 539 F.2d 1179 (9th Cir. 1976) was a case decided in the federal court of appeals (denoted by F.2d, which is the *Federal Reporter*, Second Series), volume 539, page 1179. The case was heard in the Ninth Circuit Court of Appeals and was decided in 1976. In addition to its listing in the federal reporter, a case may be repeated in a state reporter and/or regional reporter.

A citation's case name will reflect the type of case it is—that is, whether it is a civil or a criminal trial. For example, *Jones v. Smith* is a civil case involving one individual suing another, *State v. Smith* is a state criminal law case, and *U.S. v. Jones* is a federal criminal law case.

CONTRACT LAW

Contract law forms the basis for many of the daily activities of an athletic organization. Athletic administrators who have regular dealings with contract law handle contracts in the following areas: games, officiating, personnel, television and radio, membership, facility lease agreements, vendors, suppliers, and scholarships in collegiate athletics. A *contract* is an agreement between two or more parties that is enforceable under the law. A contract can be either written or oral, and it must contain a promise of one or both parties to do something in the future.

Legal concepts

The major legal concepts involved in the formation of a contract are offer, acceptance, consideration, legality, and capacity.

1. An *offer* is a conditional promise made by the offeror to the offeree. An offer usually includes the following essential terms: (1) the parties involved, (2) the subject matter, (3) the time (and place) for the subject matter to be performed, and (4) the price to be paid.
2. An *acceptance* can be made only by the party to whom the offer was made.
3. *Consideration* involves an exchange of value wherein one party agrees through a bargaining process to give up or do something in return for another party's doing the same. Consideration is often viewed as the essential term needed in a contract to make it legally enforceable. Without consideration, there may be a promise to do an act, but it may not be legally enforceable as a contract.
4. *Legality* means that the underlying bargain of the contract must be legal for the contract to be considered valid by the courts. The courts will not enforce illegal contracts, such as gambling contracts, contracts with unlicensed professionals, contracts with "loan sharks," and so forth.
5. *Capacity* is defined as the ability to understand the nature and effects of one's acts. In regard to contracts, the general rule is that anyone who has reached the age of majority (18 in most states) has the capacity to enter into a contract. An exception to this rule is an intoxicated individual, with whom a contract is deemed void.

Breach of contract

Once it has been demonstrated that a contract is formed by establishing these five criteria, another legal issue that is oftentimes raised is whether there has been a breach of contract. A breach of contract is a failure to perform a duty imposed under the contract. Numerous breach of contract cases have arisen in the sports industry. Examples include a lawsuit brought by a coach who argues that a breach of contract occurred when he or she did not receive compensation for aspects of his or her contract after termination from the job [see *Rodgers v.*

Georgia Tech Athletic Association 303 S.E.2d 467 (Ga. Ct. App. 1983)], by a professional athlete against a team for not fulfilling the terms of a contract, by stadium authorities against teams who have moved to another city without fulfilling lease obligations, and by health club members against a health club for failing to provide the services promised in the health club membership.

Remedies for a breach of contract

Remedies for a breach of contract usually entail monetary damages awarded by the court to the aggrieved party. The philosophy of monetary damages is to compensate the injured party for economic losses. The aggrieved party must justify to the court the damages he or she is requesting.

Contract law is an important area of sports law, and the guidelines in the box on p. 80 are offered to assist organizations in reviewing and developing contracts. In addition, the box on p. 81 includes a general checklist of typical clauses that are included in most sports contracts.

CONCEPT CHECK

A contract is an agreement between two or more parties that is enforceable under the law. In the sports industry, lawsuits involving breach of contract have been brought by coaches and athletes against a team for not receiving all that is stipulated in the contract, by stadium owners or managers against teams that have moved from a particular facility to another facility, and by health club members against a health club for not receiving all they were promised in the health club membership.

TORT LIABILITY

A *tort* is a private (or civil) wrong or injury, other than a breach of contract, suffered by an individual as the result of another person's conduct. Civil law provides injured individuals with a cause of action by which they may be compensated, or "made whole," through the recovery of damages. In a tort action the injured party institutes the action as an individual in an effort to recover damages as compensation for the injury received. The law of torts covers the following areas:

Checklist of information to consider when developing contracts

1. If there have been prior dealings between the parties, the lawyer drafting the new contract should be informed of the nature of these dealings in order to decide whether they have any bearing on the new contract.
2. If the contract can only be performed by the original parties to the contract, the lawyer should be informed so as to state in the contract that it will not be assignable.
3. If any party is to be required to furnish a bond or to make a deposit, this information needs to be incorporated into the agreement.
4. If the parties have agreed to any special conditions, the lawyer drafting the contract must know of the conditions in order to include them in the agreement.
5. The consideration for the contract needs to be identified.
6. A description of the subject matter of the contracts should be provided. If property is the subject matter, then a description of the property should be furnished.
7. If there are any circumstances that would excuse either party from performing the contract, these circumstances should be explained in detail and included in the agreement.
8. The lawyer must be informed whether the parties to the agreement need to view each other's books and records.
9. The attorney should know the means of payment agreed to between the parties for the subject matter of the contract, any agreement as to the payment of attorney's fees should a breach occur, and any agreement as to the payment of any resulting taxes.
10. The attorney should have the name, capacity, and residence of each party to the agreement, as well as information about their ability to sign the contract and bind themselves or the organization they represent.
11. The effective date of the contract, the duration of the contract, and how the contract can be terminated before it runs its stated length all need to be incorporated into the agreement.
12. The attorney must be informed of the liabilities of both parties to the agreement and whether the liability of either party is to be limited under the agreement.

From Wong, G. (1988). *Essentials of amateur sports law.* Dover, Massachusetts: Auburn House Publishing Co.

---

1. Intentional harm to the person
2. Intentional harm to tangible property
3. Negligence
4. Nuisance
5. Strict liability
6. Harm to tangible personal interests
7. Harm to tangible property interests

Discussed next are the most common torts arising in an athletic setting.

Intentional vs. unintentional torts

Tort law is divided into intentional torts and nonintentional torts. An **intentional tort**—for example, assault and battery—consists of an intent to commit the act and an intent to harm the plaintiff. An **unintentional tort**, or negligence, involves no intent to commit the act and no intent to harm the plaintiff but a failure to exercise reasonable care. Reckless misconduct, or gross negligence, falls somewhere between an intentional and unintentional tort and consists of intent to commit the act but no intent to harm the plaintiff.

Assault and battery

The torts of **assault and battery** are intentional torts, meaning there was an intent to commit the act and an intent to harm the plaintiff. Such intentional torts as assault and battery are actions characterized by focusing on the defendant's state of mind. Actual injury is not required to recover for the wrong done.

Assault is the apprehension of imminent harmful contact. For an action to constitute assault, three

that was committed. In many cases the plaintiff will be able to establish that an agency—not the individual—was responsible when a teacher, coach, trainer, or a full-time fitness club employee is alleged to be negligent. However, many unique situations arise in the sports industry in which the judicial system has to determine whether the principal is responsible or whether in fact the individual is an independent contractor.

Independent contractor

An **independent contractor** is a person who, although in some way connected to the employer, is not under the employer's control. Thus the employer is not held responsible or liable for the individual's work. The following situations are some in which the issue of whether the person is an independent contractor might be raised.

1. *Physicians hired on a part-time basis by a university athletic department.* As a general rule a physician provided by a school that is hosting an athletic activity is considered an independent contractor. Although paid by the university, the physician is not in any way under the control of the school when making medical decisions. However, the university owes a reasonable standard of care to the participants, coaches, and possibly the fans at the athletic activity. The university, therefore, has a duty to hire a physician who is qualified for the job and has proper training for any medical situations that might normally arise during the course of the athletic activity.

2. *Referees.* Should a referee be held responsible for injury or damages that result during an athletic contest? In some cases the courts have decided that it is the referee's responsibility to ensure that the rules are followed, and an injury that occurs as a result of a violation of these rules should be considered negligent conduct on the part of the referee.

   The courts also need to decide whether there is an employer-employee relationship between the school district and the referee—causing the school district to be responsible for the referee's negligence—or whether the referee is an independent contractor. The current trend is for the courts to find the referee to be an independent contractor.

3. *Part-time instructors at health and fitness clubs.* The court may be asked to decide whether the instructor is an authorized representative of the health and fitness club, thus forming an employer-employee relationship. In addition, the health and fitness club may be held liable if it did not exercise reasonable care in hiring the instructor, ensuring that the instructor had proper skills and qualifications. A key determination for the courts will be whether the club exercised control over the instructor.

Intentional torts

It should be emphasized that where an agency relationship exists, an employer may not be responsible for all the actions of an employee. The employer is responsible for only those actions which are within the scope of the duties and responsibilities of the position. The general rule in agency law cases is that an employer is not responsible for the intentional torts of an employee. An intentional tort involves an intent to commit the act and an intent to harm the plaintiff. So, for example, when a truck driver gets into a fight with another driver and the other driver suffers severe injuries, the company employing the truck driver is not held responsible when sued under agency theory, since fighting is not within the scope of responsibilities for a truck driver.

The sports setting has created some interesting dilemmas for the judicial system. In *Averill v. Luttrell*, 311 S.W. 2d 812 (Tenn. Ct. App. 1957), a pitcher throws a brushback pitch at a batter, and the batter starts toward the mound. The catcher comes up from behind the batter and hits the batter, causing serious injuries. Is the team responsible under an agency theory, since it is the employer of the catcher? Is it within the scope of responsibilities of a catcher to protect a pitcher? In this particular case, the court held that the catcher was liable, but the team was not since fighting is not within the scope of responsibilities. In a case involving basketball, *Tomjanovich v. California Sports Inc.*, No. H-78-243 (S.D. Tex. 1979), the team was held responsible. In a game between the Los Angeles Lakers and the Houston Rockets, a fight broke out, and a Laker player hit and injured a Houston Rocket player. The Lakers were sued, because the Laker player was seen as an "enforcer" in the league and known for "dangerous tendencies." Although fighting is usually seen as outside the scope of responsibility in an employer-employee relationship, this case was decided in favor of the plaintiff, and the Lakers were held responsible as the player's employer. The Lakers were sued on the theory that as the employer of the player they were responsible for curbing his "dangerous tendencies" and that they had failed to do so.

Player representation

Agency law is also important when athletes are represented in contract negotiations and/or financial management by agents (also known as player agents or player representatives). A **player agent** is a person authorized by another person to act in his or her name, and the agent is entrusted with that person's business (*Black's Law Dictionary*). The promise of compensation is not required to establish the relationship, although such compensation is usually presumed.

Some athletes have brought litigation against agents for an alleged breach of a fiduciary relationship (see *Brown v. Woolf*, 554 F.Supp. 1206 [S.D. Ind. 1983], Chapter 13, p. 219). Lawsuits may include the alleged improper negotiation of a contract, or more commonly, the alleged mismanagement of the athlete's money. Unfortunately, the number of cases involving athletes who have been taken advantage of by unscrupulous agents is on the rise.

CONCEPT CHECK

Agency law is applicable in athletics when the athlete/coach is an employee of the team (the employer); subsequently, the team may be held responsible for the actions of the athlete/coach if the actions are determined to be within the scope of responsibility of the team's employment over the athlete/coach. This can also apply to a school, with the school district, principal, and board members all being held responsible for the actions of a coach, trainer, or athlete, if the actions were within the scope of employment responsibilities. An employer is not responsible for the action, though, if it is outside the scope of responsibility, such as an act determined to be an intentional tort.

CONSTITUTIONAL LAW

The Constitution is the basic law of the United States of America, drawn up by the Constitutional Convention in Philadelphia in 1787. The Constitution contains statutory provisions and judicial interpretations concerning important social, economic, and political issues.

Professional sports

Various sections of the U.S. Constitution apply in athletic situations, most of them in amateur athletics. Athletes in professional sports, as indicated in the section on collective bargaining, can surrender constitutional rights in exchange for other benefits. For example, in exchange for benefits accompanying a position in professional sports, athletes in basketball may agree to undergo drug testing. In addition, athletes in all professional team sports give up the right of freedom of expression in terms of what they wear on their uniforms.

Some of the various **constitutional law** arguments that are raised in amateur sports include freedom of expression, due process, equal protection, illegal search and seizure, and invasion of privacy. A chief hurdle for anyone bringing a constitutional law claim is the ability to demonstrate that state action is involved. Any action taken directly or indirectly by state, local, or federal government is defined as *state action* for constitutional purposes. In addition, action by any public school, state college, or state university—or any of their officials—is construed as state action. After state action has been demonstrated, the plaintiff may then argue state and/or federal constitutional law theories.

Due process

Due process is an elusive concept. One definition for the term **due process** is "a course of legal proceedings which have been established in our system of jurisprudence for the protection and enforcement of private rights" (*Pennoyer v. Neff*, 95 U.S. 714 [1877]). The concept of due process may vary, depending on three basic considerations: (1) the seriousness of the infraction, (2) the possible consequences to the institution or individual in question, and (3) the degree of sanction or penalty imposed.

The constitutional guarantee of due process is

found in both the Fifth and Fourteenth Amendments. The Fifth Amendment, enacted in 1791, is applicable to the federal government. It states that "no person . . . shall be deprived of life, liberty, or property without due process of law." In 1886 the Fourteenth Amendment was ratified, reading, "Nor shall any state deprive any person of life, liberty, or property without due process of law . . . ." This amendment extended the applicability of the due process doctrine to the states. Both amendments apply only to federal or state governmental action and not to the conduct of purely private entities.

Although the Constitution extends these liberties to all persons, it is also limiting in that a person must demonstrate deprivation of life, liberty, or property to claim a violation of due process guarantees. Since athletic associations and conferences rarely deprive a person of life, the major interests that trigger the application of a due process clause in the athletic context are deprivations of liberty and property. In collegiate athletics the scholarship has been considered a property right. Unless an athlete or other party can establish that he or she has been deprived of liberty or property, he or she will not be able to establish a deprivation of due process.

Claims of due process protection may be brought based not only on protections guaranteed by state constitutions and by federal and state statutes, but also on the regulations and constitutions of athletic institutions, conferences, and other governing organizations.

Equal protection

Equal protection is the constitutional method of checking on the fairness of the application of law. Through the equal protection clause of the Fourteenth Amendment, student-athletes and coaches are provided with the means to challenge certain rules and regulations that are of a discriminatory nature. The equal protection guarantee of the Fourteenth Amendment reads, "No state shall . . . deny to any person within its jurisdiction the equal protection of the laws." Equal protection requires that no person be singled out from similarly situated people, or have different benefits bestowed or burdens imposed, unless a constitutionally permissible reason exists for doing so.

Different standards of review are used under equal protection analysis. The highest standard of review is that of strict scrutiny. When a rule abridges a fundamental right or makes a distinction based on suspect criteria, the defendant has the burden of proof. The Supreme Court has found three suspect classes: alienage, race, and national origin. Any time a rule has a direct or indirect impact on any of these suspect classifications criteria, the strict scrutiny standard will be applied. The second standard of review under the equal protection guarantee is that of rational basis. This standard requires only that the rule have some rational relationship to a legitimate organizational purpose. The third standard of review imposes an intermediate test, which falls between the strict scrutiny and rational basis tests. It requires that rules classifying certain groups satisfy an "important" but not necessarily a "compelling" interest.

A student-athlete may argue a violation of equal protection because of the existence of two types of classification—student-athletes vs. non-student–athletes—in a drug-testing program. Only student-athletes are tested, whereas non-student–athletes do not have to participate in the school's drug-testing program. In all probability the court would apply a rational basis standard in which the defendant institution has only to establish a rational relationship for the existence of this classification in order to justify the program. If a drug-testing program called for athletes to be tested on the basis of alienage, race, or national origin, a strict scrutiny standard would be employed by the courts. The drug-testing program would be invalidated unless the defendant could demonstrate that the program was supported by a compelling state interest.

Unreasonable search and seizure

The Fourth Amendment provides "[the] right of the people to be secure in their persons, houses, papers, and effects against unreasonable searches and seizures." Applying this protection to a drug-testing program, the act of taking an athlete's urine (or blood) can constitute a **search** within the meaning of the Fourth Amendment. Searches may be deemed reasonable by the courts, however, through the defendant's showing a compelling state interest for the search to occur. While a student-athlete may consent to a search, thus waiving the Fourth Amendment protection, there are limitations on the extent to which a governmental institution may force consent to the search.

Invasion of privacy

An action for **invasion of privacy** is designed to protect a person's mental peace and/or comfort. The laws prohibiting invasion of privacy are intended to protect the purely private matters of a person. In an action for invasion of privacy, the intrusion must be substantial and must be into an area for which there is an expectation of privacy. Challenges to drug-testing programs have involved invasion of privacy arguments. The major concern in terms of the protection of a student-athlete's privacy rights involves the degree of intrusiveness with which the drug-testing program obtains the necessary urine sample. The courts have noted many times that there is a substantial expectation of privacy in connection with the act of urination. This expectation is balanced, however, against the compelling state interest in testing an individual, obtaining the necessary urine sample, and ensuring that the sample obtained is definitely that individual's.

CONCEPT CHECK

Such constitutional law arguments as freedom of expression, due process, equal protection, illegal search and seizure, and invasion of privacy have all been raised in sports. Many of these arguments have been brought in regard to drug-testing programs, with the plaintiff arguing that the drug-testing program is in violation of constitutional rights. Athletes may argue that the collecting of the urine sample is an invasion of privacy and illegal search and seizure. Athletes have also raised equal protection claims due to the fact that they are being tested but the rest of the school student body is not.

SEX DISCRIMINATION

Sex discrimination in high school and intercollegiate athletics has been challenged using a variety of legal arguments, including Title IX of the Education Amendments of 1972, equal protection laws, state equal rights amendments, and the Equal Pay Act, which was passed in 1963 and became effective in 1964. Most challenges have been based on the equal protection laws and/or Title IX, although several claims based on state equal rights amendments have been brought recently. In a sex discrimination case, the plaintiff usually contends that there is a fundamental inequality, regardless of whether a plaintiff employs an equal protection law, equal rights amendment, or a Title IX approach. In attempting to deal with these claims, the court considers three factors. The first is whether the sport from which women are excluded is one involving physical contact. Total exclusion from all sports or from any noncontact sport is usually considered a violation of equal educational opportunity. The second factor is the quality and quantity of opportunities available to each sex. The courts compare the number of athletic opportunities available to each sex, as well as the amount of money spent on equipment, the type of coaches provided, and the access to school-owned facilities. The third factor the courts consider is age and level of competition involved in the dispute. The younger the athletes involved, the fewer the actual physiological differences that exist. Without evident physiological differences, there is little justification for the exclusion of one sex from athletic participation due to biological differences.

The growth of women's sports and the dramatic increase in women's overall participation in athletics have been impressive. Since 1972 the number of women participating in athletics has more than doubled. Athletic budgets for women's athletics have also increased. These indicators, along with the increases in spectators at women's events and local and national media coverage, point to the growth in women's athletics.

Title IX

The development of athletic opportunities for women may, to a large extent, be attributed to Title IX. **Title IX of the Education Amendments of 1972** is a federal statute that prohibits sex discrimination. Section 901(a) of Title IX contains the following language: "No person in the United States shall, on the basis of sex, be excluded from participation in, be denied the benefits of, or be subjected to discrimination under any education program or activity receiving Federal financial assistance." Athletics and athletic programs were not specifically mentioned in Title IX when it first became law in 1972. Congress was generally opposed to placing athletic programs under the realm of Title IX. However, HEW (which was later named the Department of Health, Education, and Welfare) took the position that sports and physical education are an integral part of education and specifically included athletics in Title IX in 1974. Athletic programs, seen as a component of the educational structure, must therefore be in compliance with Title IX legislation.

The key to the Title IX language lies in the last four words: "receiving Federal financial assistance." Only institutions receiving federal financial assistance are required to be in compliance with Title IX. The legal question revolving around this concept was whether Title IX applies to an entire institution or only to those programs within that institution which receive direct federal assistance. This was an important issue for athletic programs, because most do not receive direct federal funding; however, most institutions receive some form of federal financial assistance.

Scope and applicability of Title IX. The case of *Grove City College v. Bell*, 465 U.S. 555 (1984), dealt with the scope and applicability of Title IX. In this case, the Supreme Court ruled that only those programs within an institution which receive direct financial assistance from the federal government should be subject to Title IX legislation. This interpretation is often referred to as the "**programmatic approach**," and it virtually negated the impact of Title IX on athletic programs. It was not until the Civil Rights Restoration Act of 1987, passed by Congress in 1988, that the strength of Title IX and its applicability to athletic programs was restored. The passage of this act restored the "**institutional approach**" of the applicability of Title IX, and as such, athletic departments within institutions receiving federal financial assistance are now subject to the Title IX legislation.

Title IX compliance. Compliance with the dictates of Title IX is monitored by the Office for Civil Rights (OCR), in the Department of Education (formerly part of the Department of Health, Education, and Welfare). The OCR makes random compliance reviews and also investigates complaints submitted by individuals. The OCR conducts a preliminary review to determine an institution's attempted compliance with Title IX. If the OCR determines that a full hearing should be conducted, the OCR becomes the complainant and pursues the claim.

In this situation the individual who initially submitted the complaint does not have the financial burden that a court case would entail.

The policy interpretation of Title IX focuses on three areas that the OCR evaluates to determine whether an institution is in compliance with Title IX regulations with regard to athletics. First, the OCR assesses whether an institution's athletic scholarships are awarded on a "substantially proportional" basis. To determine this, the amount of scholarship money available for each sex is divided by the number of male or female participants in the athletic program, and results are compared. The second area of assessment under the policy interpretation is the degree to which the institution provides equal treatment, benefits, and opportunities in certain program areas. These program areas include equipment, coaching, and facilities. The final area the OCR assesses is the extent to which the institution has met the interests and abilities of male and female students. The policy interpretation requires that the school "equally and effectively" accommodate the athletic interest and abilities of both men and women. This determination requires an examination of the institution's assessment of the athletic interest and abilities of its students, its selection of offered sports, and its available competitive opportunities.

The policy interpretation developed by the OCR contains some strict guidelines for assessing Title IX compliance, including the following:

1. The men's program as a whole must be compared with the women's program as a whole. Comparisons are not made sport by sport.
2. In evaluating overall compliance, there is no exemption from Title IX for revenue-producing sports, as well as football.
3. In evaluating athletic participation opportunities, three factors must be considered: the determination of athletic interests and abilities, the selection of sports, and the levels of competition.
4. Schools must provide "equivalent" (but not necessarily identical) athletic benefits, opportunities, and treatment to female and male athletes. That is, overall athletic programs must be "equal or equal in effect" and the overall effect of any differences must be negligible. Important factors in determining equivalency are availability, quality, types of benefits, opportunities, and treatment.

Equal protection

Equal protection is the constitutional method of checking on the fairness of the application of any law. The equal protection guarantee is found in the Fourteenth Amendment of the U.S. Constitution. It reads: "No state shall . . . deny to any person within its jurisdiction the equal protection of the laws." It is specifically applicable only to the states, but the federal government is held to similar standards under the due process clause of the Fifth Amendment. Equal protection requires that no person be singled out from similarly situated people, or have different benefits bestowed or burdens imposed, unless a constitutionally permissible reason exists for doing so. Historically, sex has been an acceptable category for classifying persons for different benefits and burdens under any given law. The courts have not found sex to be a suspect class, which would elevate it to the status held by race, national origin, and alienage. If sex were considered a suspect class, the highest standard of review—that of strict scrutiny—would be used by the courts. Application of the strict scrutiny standard by the court means that the defendant has the burden of proof and must show that the alleged sex discrimination issue is supported by a compelling state interest. Because sex is not considered a suspect class, the courts use a lesser standard of review.

Historically, challenging sex discrimination based on the equal protection laws has not been totally effective. As long as sex is not considered a suspect class, plaintiffs will have difficulty challenging alleged sex discrimination. Another disadvantage of the equal protection laws is that they constitute a private remedy; therefore the plaintiff must be in a position to absorb the costs of litigation. This reduces the number of complaints filed and encourages settlement before final resolution of a number of equal protection claims.

Equal rights amendment

Although passed in both Houses of Congress in 1972, the federal **Equal Rights Amendment** (ERA) did not receive the necessary 38 votes from the state legislatures by the required ratification date of July 1, 1972. Although a federal ERA has not been ratified, 19 individual states have passed their own equal rights amendments. Thus equal rights amendments have had an impact on athletics at the state level but not at the federal level.

Equal rights amendments at the state level can be very effective and extend greater protection against sex-based classifications than that available under federal equal protection of the Fourteenth Amendment. The state courts, under an equal rights amendment, hold a stricter standard of review regarding the sex-based classification than the lower standard employed by the federal courts under the federal equal protection clause.

Professional sports

There have not been many sex discrimination complaints or cases in the professional sports arena, because relatively few women participate in professional sports. An area in which litigation has occurred involves the barring of media from locker rooms. In *Ludtke v. Kuhn*, 461 F.Supp. 86 (S.D. N.Y. 1978), the plaintiff, a female sports reporter, was excluded from the locker room of the Yankee clubhouse in Yankee Stadium because of a policy instituted by Baseball Commissioner Kuhn. Ludtke alleged a violation of equal protection under the Fourteenth Amendment, because male members of the news media were not similarly restricted. The court ruled in favor of the plaintiff Ludtke, thus allowing her access to the Yankee Stadium locker room.

The issue of access to locker rooms for female reporters has been raised in several instances in the 1990s, with the most celebrated case involving Lisa Olson of the *Boston Herald* and the New England Patriots professional football team.

Sex discrimination in athletic employment

Two separate statutes specifically pertain to discrimination in employment. The **Equal Pay Act**, passed in 1963 (effective date was June 10, 1964), stipulates that an employer must pay equal salaries to men and women holding jobs that require equal skill, effort, and responsibility and that are performed under similar working conditions. Different salaries are permissible, however, when they are based not on the sex of the employees but on a bona fide seniority system or on merit increases.

The other statute available to combat employment discrimination is **Title VII of the Civil Rights Act of 1964.** Title VII focuses on discriminatory hiring and firing practices and advancement policies within companies. It forbids discriminatory employment practices based on the race, color, religion, gender, or national origin of the applicant.

Title VII is applicable only to employers of more than 15 persons, and it specifically covers almost all state and local government employees, as well as employees of most educational institutions.

The basic weakness of these acts is that neither is all-encompassing. They both fail to address the overall problems of sex discrimination that exist outside of the workplace. Thus very few of the problems of discrimination encountered in athletics are addressed by either act. This legislation provides potential relief only in athletic employment. Another major problem in pursuing litigation under these statutes is the cost. Neither statute provides any guaranteed basis for the eventual recovery of attorney's fees and/or damages; therefore cases are seldom pursued.

CONCEPT CHECK

Sex discrimination complaints have been argued using Title IX, equal protection laws, state equal rights amendments, and the Equal Pay Act. The court considers three factors in attempting to deal with these claims: whether or not the sport from which women are excluded is one involving physical contact, the quality and quantity of opportunities available to each sex, and the age of the plaintiff and level of competition involved in the dispute. Title IX and its impact on athletic programs was virtually negated by the Supreme Court's decision in Grove City College v. Bell, *but it regained its effectiveness with the passage of the Civil Rights Restoration Act in 1988. The Office for Civil Rights (in the Department of Health, Education, and Welfare) monitors the compliance of Title IX. Equal rights amendments at the state level can be very effective by extending greater protection against sex discrimination than that available under federal equal protection of the Fourteenth Amendment.*

CRIMINAL LAWS

Criminal laws are statutes, both on the federal and state level, that are designed to protect society. Criminal laws must be **codified**—that is, written in statutory form—so individual members of society know what constitutes a crime. Criminal law is based on society's need to be free from harmful conduct. Criminal law defines criminal conduct

and prescribes the punishment to be imposed on a person convicted of engaging in such conduct. In addition to its broad aim of preventing injury to the health, safety, and welfare of the public, criminal law is also designed to protect society's broader notions of morality. Criminal laws differ from civil laws in that the penalties for criminal acts are a fine and/or imprisonment, as opposed to monetary damages for civil acts. Very few criminal laws have been promulgated specifically for sports; therefore, in most sports settings, the alleged criminal law violation must be based on the general criminal laws. Most alleged criminal law violations involve hockey games during which a player used a stick as a weapon and caused serious injury. For the most part these criminal law violations have not been successfully prosecuted.

Many people consider the punishments given out by the league offices for violent acts during participation in athletic events to be minor when compared with the nature of the conduct. Several well-publicized incidents within the past several years in professional and amateur hockey, football, and basketball illustrate the potential problems of uncontrolled, excessive violence. Most of the incidences of violent conduct have not resulted in any type of criminal prosecution, even though the same events may have resulted in a criminal prosecution if they had not taken place in an athletic contest. Thus the ability of the league offices to control violence with their internal sanctions has been questioned. Many people believe that legislative action is needed, and others believe that specific criminal law sanctions should be invoked.

Crime of battery

The crime of battery is the most likely offense to occur in a sports setting. A criminal **battery** can be defined as an unlawful application of force to the person of another resulting in bodily injury. The elements of a battery are (1) "a guilty state of mind,"(2) an act, (3) a physical touching or harming of a victim, and (4) causation—that is, the act must cause the touching or harm. The key requirement is that a battery be "unlawful." However, determining what is lawful and unlawful in a sport involving contact creates a difficult—and sometimes unpredictable—area for the courts. For example, courts have grappled with the issue of whether a stick-swinging incident in a hockey game should be considered a criminal battery.

Proposed federal legislation

As a result of the difficulty in successfully prosecuting criminal law violations in a sports setting, especially cases of battery, there are some who have suggested that legislation to deal specifically with violence in sports be introduced. In fact, two federal bills were proposed: the Sports Violence Act of 1980 and the Sports Violence Arbitration Act of 1983. Although neither piece of legislation was enacted, some contend that these legislative proposals forced the league offices to act and impose more serious penalties for violent acts. Legislation at the state and local levels has been attempted, but none of these efforts has been successful. Any specific state criminal laws that have been promulgated relate to protecting referees and officials rather than participants. For example, in Oklahoma there is a law that deals with "assault upon a sports officiary."

Sports bribery statutes

In addition to the criminal law cases brought on a battery theory, the criminal law has been applied in cases in which athletes have conspired to "fix" the outcome or point spread in a sporting contest. In the case of *United States v. Burke*, 700 F. 2d 70 (2nd Cir. 1983), a former college basketball player was charged with and convicted of racketeering by conspiring to fix games, sports bribery and violation of the interstate travel and aid to racketeering statutes, more commonly known as RICO. Some states have specific sports bribery statutes in addition to the interstate travel and aid to racketeering statutes, which are general laws also used for nonsports situations.

The federal RICO statutes were also applied in the conviction of Norby Walters and Lloyd Bloom, two player agents, for signing college football and basketball players to representation contracts while the players still had college eligibility remaining. Walters and Bloom gave the athletes money while they were still in college and then threatened the players with physical violence when they attempted to escape from their representation contracts. The use of the RICO statutes against player agents is relatively new and thus quite limited. As a result, many states have passed specific agent regulation legislation.

CONCEPT CHECK

Criminal law is based on society's need to be free from harmful conduct. For the most part, criminal law violations have not been successfully prosecuted in sports. However, the violent nature of some sports makes it difficult for the courts to determine whether the act was a criminal battery or just part of the game. Federal legislation dealing with sports violence has been proposed but has yet to be ratified by Congress.

THE ANTITRUST LAWS

Antitrust laws are designed to promote competition in the business sector through regulation "designed to control the exercise of private economic power" (Gellhorn, 1976). In athletics, antitrust law concerns have primarily involved professional sports leagues, which are composed of private economic entities operated as a business to make a profit. Increasingly, however, amateur athletic organizations have come under the scope of antitrust laws, partly due to the transformation of many areas of amateur athletics into "big business." This situation is particularly true in intercollegiate athletics, primarily football and men's basketball. For example, the NCAA's Football Television Plan for 1982 to 1985 was declared to be in violation of antitrust laws, because it prevented the free flow of the market for televised intercollegiate football. The decision, upheld by the U.S. Supreme Court in 1984, disrupted the entire sports telecasting industry by allowing a glut of televised intercollegiate football to flood the market. The decision caused the financial rights fees for these televised games to drop significantly, and in turn, many institutions experienced a shortfall in their annual budgets.

The two major antitrust laws that form the underlying basis for court decisions are the Sherman Antitrust Act and the Clayton Act.

The Sherman Antitrust Act

The **Sherman Antitrust Act** was passed in 1890 during a period of U.S. history in which business had gained domination over the delivery of goods and services to the detriment of the average citizen. The law was passed to encourage free and open competition in business. The ultimate beneficiary was the consumer, who would not have to pay above-market prices for goods and services.

Federal antitrust laws seek to regulate competitive conduct involving interstate commerce. The Sherman Antitrust Act specifically covers transactions in goods, land, or services. Section 1 of the Sherman Act concerns agreements that restrain trade, such as a group of businesses attempting to fix prices among themselves. Section 2 of the Sherman Act seeks to prevent monopolistic action by a business or businesses: an example of such an action is the attempt to control all televised football to prevent another school's or league's games from being telecast. It is permissible for a monopoly to exist for natural reasons, as long as the monopoly then does not attempt to drive out competition through illegal means.

The Clayton Act

The **Clayton Act** was enacted in 1914 to tighten up some of the generalities of the Sherman Act. It was specifically designed to prevent certain practices in the sale of goods in interstate commerce. Specific sections of the Clayton Act deal with corporate mergers, price discrimination, and the operation of labor unions. The Clayton Act provides that nothing contained in the antitrust laws shall be construed to forbid the existence and operation of labor unions; therefore, under the provisions set forth in this act, player associations in sports leagues can be viewed as labor unions formed to keep the interest of the players in mind when they are negotiating collective bargaining agreements within the league.

Professional team sports applications

The only professional team sports that are governed by and subject to the antitrust laws are basketball, football, and hockey. Baseball is unique and has a special exemption from the antitrust laws as a result of a 1922 decision, *Federal Baseball Club of Baltimore, Inc. v. National League of Professional Baseball Clubs, et al.*, 259 U.S. 200 (1922). The *Federal Baseball* case was most recently affirmed in another Supreme Court decision titled *Flood v. Kuhn*, 407 U.S. 258 (1972). In professional football the key antitrust decision was *Mackey v. National Football League*, 407 F. Supp. 1000 (D. Minn. 1975); in hockey it was *McCourt v. California Sports, Inc.*, 600 P. 2d 1193 (1979); and in basketball, *Robertson v. National Basketball Association*, 556 F.2d 682 (2nd Cir.

1977). All three of these cases were filed by the respective player unions on behalf of the individual players to challenge the restraints that the players felt were in violation of the Sherman and Clayton Acts. These restraints included the college player drafts, the reserve clause, the option clause, and other restrictive terms and conditions of employment. The professional team leagues argued that these player restraints were necessary because of the unique nature of professional team sports. As opposed to a regular business environment, in which one business would like to put a competitor out of business, professional team sports need other teams to have games and a league and therefore survive. Consequently, the argument goes, the teams in a league must cooperate off the field by trying to balance the talent among the various teams so as to ensure interesting and close games during a season. The old adage of "on any given Sunday . . . ." is the philosophy that former commissioner Pete Rozelle espoused for the National Football League. In short, in trying to balance these two arguments, the court has generally applied a standard called the "reasonableness" test, which allows the leagues to explain to a court the reasons for the restraints and demonstrate that the restraints are the least restrictive possible while still meeting the goals of the league.

What transpired after the court decisions in football, hockey, and basketball was that the Players' Associations for each of the sports negotiated collective bargaining agreements with the leagues in which the Players' Association allowed certain restrictive practices to continue (for example, the player draft), in exchange for which the players received concessions and benefits from management. After having become the subject matter of a labor agreement between management and players, the restrictive practices of management became insulated from antitrust scrutiny by the nonstatutory labor exemption. By conceding benefits to players, leagues are able to preserve restraints that they believe are necessary to remain economically viable. For example, in baseball the average minimum salary is $100,000 a year, and although the players have given up some of their freedom to move to other teams, the players are eligible for salary arbitration after 3 years of major league service (except for 17% of the players who have 2 years of major league service), and they are eligible to be free agents after 6 years of major league service.

Major League Baseball, as previously indicated, has a unique legal situation as a result of the *Federal Baseball* decision. Baseball players have been able to obtain tremendous financial rewards and other benefits through their collective bargaining agreement, even though the Players' Association does not have the benefit of the antitrust laws to sue management. The key decision for the players in Major League Baseball was the arbitration case of *Messersmith and McNally v. Major League Baseball,* decided in 1975. This arbitration decision was affirmed in the court case of *Kansas City Royals Baseball Corporation v. Major League Baseball Players' Association,* 409 F. Supp. 233 (W.D. Missouri, 1976). The players challenged the reserve clause and successfully argued that the clause could only be renewed once, rather than perpetually as management argued. Players would therefore become free agents after the expiration of this 1-year renewal. Since this was the period in baseball before the advent of the multi-year contract, this decision resulted in most players in major league baseball becoming potentially free agents in either 1 or 2 years. As a result of this arbitration decision, along with the potential for chaos (that is, every player in the league being a free agent), management agreed to a collective bargaining agreement that greatly increased the salaries and benefits for baseball players. The basis of that agreement has become the framework for the subsequent collective bargaining agreements in baseball.

Antitrust dispute: between team owner and the league

One other area in which the antitrust laws have been relied on in litigation is in disputes between owners and a league. The most celebrated case involves the Oakland/Los Angeles Raiders, in which managing general partner Al Davis challenged the ability of the league to restrict the relocation of the Raiders from Oakland to Los Angeles. Davis was successful in challenging the league on an antitrust theory, and a federal court jury in Los Angeles awarded Davis antitrust damages of 49 million dollars.

Antitrust cases: individual athletes against the league

There have also been antitrust cases brought by individual athletes against the league. Most of these cases have been based on a collective bargaining agreement, which contains the terms and conditions of employment agreed on between the employees (union) and the employer (management). These cases have resulted because the agreement implemented restrictions on individuals who were not part of the bargaining unit. For example, Leon Wood challenged the National Basketball Association because he believed that the salary cap in the National Basketball Association reduced his market value when he was drafted out of college.

The antitrust laws have also been relied on by athletes who were underclassmen and were not eligible for the professional league drafts. In one celebrated case, *Haywood v. National Basketball Association,* 401 U.S. 1204 (1971), Spencer Haywood was successful in arguing that the rule preventing him from being drafted and entering the National Basketball Association restricted his ability to earn a living and was a violation of the antitrust laws. As a result of this case the National Basketball Association, beginning in 1971, has allowed underclass athletes to declare eligibility for the NBA draft. One additional area in which the antitrust laws have been used is where a disciplined player—that is, a player who has been expelled from the league—challenges the league based on antitrust laws because the player does not have any other economic alternatives to playing in the league.

Amateur athletic organizations

In the past, amateur athletic organizations have not been subject to the antitrust litigation faced by the professional sports industry. However, with the increased prominence of amateur athletics and the money now involved, organizations such as the NCAA are increasingly becoming targets for antitrust attack.

Historically, amateur athletic associations, as defendants in antitrust actions, have been successful in arguing that the antitrust laws were inapplicable to them since amateur athletics did not fall into the categories of "trade" or "commerce" as defined by the Sherman Act. Amateur organizations have traditionally argued that since the amateur athletic associations are nonprofit organizations, the primary purpose of which is either educational and/ or noncommercial in nature, they are not involved with trade or commerce and are therefore not subject to the antitrust laws. However, in some recent cases the courts are viewing amateur athletics differently, especially the NCAA. The finding by the courts of the requisite involvement in "trade" or "commerce" thereby subjects certain amateur organizations to the antitrust laws. The most celebrated case in this area has been *NCAA v. Board of Regents of the University of Oklahoma*, 468 U.S. 85 (1984), which went to the U.S. Supreme Court. The Supreme Court decided the lawsuit in favor of the University of Oklahoma and the University of Georgia, in which the schools challenged that the NCAA's national television contract was in violation of the federal antitrust laws. This lawsuit has created an open and free market for college football telecasts, allowing many games—several at the same time—to be on television.

Antitrust law is a very complex area of the law and, when applied to athletics, has resulted in decisions unique to the field of athletics, since the business relationship of professional teams and amateur sports is unlike any others. Successful antitrust litigation has also resulted in some of the most significant structural changes in professional team sports and college athletics.

CONCEPT CHECK

The two major antitrust laws are the Sherman Antitrust Act and the Clayton Act. Violation of antitrust law claims have been filed by athletes against professional teams and leagues regarding the college player drafts, the reserve clause, the option clause, and other restrictive terms and conditions of employment.

LABOR LAW

Labor law dictates the rules and regulations that govern the relationship between labor and management, defining the rights, privileges, duties, and responsibilities of each. A main component of labor law pertinent to professional sports is the area specifically relating to collective bargaining agreements. The National Labor Relations Act of 1935 (NLRA) was the first step that gave government the power to protect the collective bargaining rights of employees. The NLRA also created an independent agency, the National Labor Relations Board (NLRB) to provide the machinery for enforcing the provisions under the NLRA. The NLRB has jurisdiction over labor law issues.

Professional sports

As indicated in the antitrust section of this chapter, labor law is extremely important today in professional team sports. All of the professional leagues have significant labor law issues involved in operating those particular industries. The labor relations of all the major team sports are governed now by collective bargaining agreements that are long (up to 200 pages) and sometimes complex (see the salary cap in the NBA), defining the terms and conditions of employment between the employer, the league and the teams, and the union and its members—the players. The collective bargaining agreements might, for example, address some of the following issues:

1. Minimum salaries
2. Player freedoms, such as the right to be a free agent
3. Salary arbitration (in major league baseball)
4. A grievance arbitration system to decide disputes between players and clubs
5. Pension benefits
6. Health and medical benefits
7. Training camp compensation
8. Meal money
9. Means of transportation and level of transportation (for example, first-class travel and air-flights if the trip is longer than x number of hours)
10. Moving expenses
11. Working conditions
12. When games can be scheduled

Team management personnel may also deal with the labor laws with respect to other nonplayer employees. For example, unionized employees such as the ushers, ticket takers, carpenters, and other trades groups run many stadiums and arenas.

The Professional Golf Association (PGA) and the Association of Tennis Professionals (ATP) are the governing bodies for individual player sports. Each runs its own tours for its players, and each has its own set of rules and regulations to govern memberships, tournaments, and play. The PGA and ATP differ from the professional team sports in that they are more akin to trade associations, and there are no player collective bargaining agreements.

Amateur athletics

None of the athletes involved in amateur athletics is unionized at this point, although some have argued that they should be. Some of the personnel working in an amateur organization such as a college or university may belong to a union and are therefore governed by the union's labor laws and collective bargaining agreements. For example, the faculty at some institutions are unionized, and some of the coaches may be members of that union. Another likely area is the employees on campus, such as the clerical staff or maintenance staff, who may be unionized and governed by a collective bargaining agreement.

Facility management

Many spectator facilities employ various unionized employees, who may belong to as many as 10 to 15 different union groups, all with different collective bargaining agreements. The facility manager must have a working knowledge of all the agreements. Employees of health clubs, however, are for the most part not unionized, so the club manager does not need to be familiar with the labor laws.

CONCEPT CHECK

The collective bargaining agreement is a component of labor law pertinent to professional sports. None of the athletes involved in amateur athletics are unionized at this point and therefore do not have collective bargaining agreements with their schools.

SUMMARY

1. Sports law is a relatively new field. The first sports law course was offered in 1972 by Professor Robert C. Berry at Boston College Law School.
2. Sports law has become an integral part of the curriculum offered by sport management programs in colleges and universities.
3. There are two basic legal systems in the United States: the federal system and the state system.
4. The major legal concepts involved in the formation of a contract are offer, acceptance, consideration, legality, and capacity.
5. A tort is a private (or civil) wrong or injury, other than a breach of contract, suffered by an individual as the result of another person's conduct.
6. Assault and battery are intentional torts that involve an intent to commit the act and an intent to harm the plaintiff.
7. Reckless misconduct is a tort action that is characterized by intent on the part of the defendant to commit the act but no intent to harm the plaintiff by the act.
8. The most common tort actions in athletics result from negligence. Negligence is an unintentional tort that involves no intent to commit the act and no intent to harm the plaintiff but a failure to exercise reasonable care.
9. The purpose of agency law is to hold the principal responsible for the actions of the agent, presuming the agent is acting under the control and direction of the principal. Agency law is important in athletics, particularly in situations that involve tort liability issues.
10. An independent contractor is one who contracts to perform work according to his or her own methods and without being subject to the control of the employer. Thus an employer will not be held responsible for the negligence of an independent contractor.
11. An employer is not held responsible for intentional torts committed by the employee. An intentional tort involves an intent to commit the act and an intent to harm the plaintiff, and this type of tort is seen as outside the scope of the duties and responsibilities of the position.
12. The constitutional law arguments that are raised in sports include freedom of expression, due process, equal protection, illegal search and seizure, and invasion of privacy.
13. Sex discrimination in high school and intercollegiate athletics has been challenged using a variety of legal arguments, including Title IX of the Education Amendments of 1972, equal protection laws, state equal rights amendments, and the Equal Pay Act.
14. The Office of Civil Rights monitors compliance of Title IX.
15. Challenging sex discrimination on the basis of equal protection laws has not been totally effective, due to the fact that sex is not considered a suspect class, a status held by race, na-

tional origin, and alienage. If sex was considered a suspect class, the highest standard of review—that of strict scrutiny—would be used by the courts. Under strict scrutiny the defendant has the burden of proof.

16. Discrimination litigation in employment has occurred under two separate statutes: the Equal Pay Act of 1963 and Title VII of the Civil Rights Act of 1964.

17. Within criminal law statutes, the crime of battery is the offense that is most likely to occur in a sports setting.

18. Federal and state legislation governing criminal law violations in a sports setting have not been successful. The jurisdiction over violent acts has been left to the leagues with the assessment of fines and/or suspensions for such acts.

19. Antitrust law concerns have primarily involved professional sports, although amateur sports have increasingly come under the scrutiny of antitrust laws partly because of the transformation of many areas of amateur athletics into "big business."

20. The professional team sports of basketball, football, and hockey are governed by and subject to the antitrust laws. Baseball is unique and has a special exemption from the antitrust laws.

21. The most celebrated case involving an amateur athletic association and antitrust laws has been the *NCAA v. Board of Regents of the University of Oklahoma.* The Supreme Court ruled that the NCAA's national television contract was a violation of federal antitrust laws. The result of this lawsuit has invoked an open and free market for college football telecasts.

22. Labor law can be defined as the aspect of the law that deals with the rights and privileges due to a laborer.

REVIEW QUESTIONS AND ISSUES

1. List and give a description of the 10 parts to a trial system.
2. List and define the major legal concepts involved in the formation of a contract.
3. Define and give an example of both an assault and a battery.
4. What are the three factors the courts use to determine whether a defendant's action constitutes negligence?
5. List three situations in which an employee may be identified by the courts as an independent contractor, thus resulting in the employer not being held liable for the employee's actions.
6. Define intentional tort. Give an example of a situation in which an intentional tort occurred, and explain why the employer would or would not be held responsible for the intentional tort.
7. Define due process and explain how this concept is used in athletic cases.
8. What three factors are used by the courts in considering a sex discrimination case?
9. What aspect of the Title IX statute initially posed a problem for athletic departments and how has this recently changed?
10. Why hasn't challenging sex discrimination based on the equal protection laws been very successful?
11. What criminal offense is most likely to occur in a sports setting? Define and give the elements needed for this criminal offense.
12. What has historically been the argument regarding amateur athletic associations and their applicability or nonapplicability to the antitrust laws? How has this changed recently?

REFERENCES

Appenzeller, H., and Appenzeller, T. (1979). *Sports and the courts.* Charlottesville, Virginia: The Michie Co.

Appenzeller, H. (1985). *Sports and law: contemporary issues.* Charlottesville, Virginia: The Michie Co.

Averill V. Lutrell, 311 S.W. 2d 812 (Tenn. Ct. App. 1957).

Baley, J. and Matthews, D. (1989). *Law and liability in athletics, physical education, and recreation* (2nd Edition). Dubuque, Iowa: William C. Brown Publishing.

Berry, R., Gould, W., and Staudohar, P. (1986). *Labor relations in professional sports.* Dover, Massachusetts: Auburn House Publishing Co.

Berry, R., and Wong, G. (1986). *Law and business of the sports industries.* Dover, Massachusetts: Auburn House Publishing Co.

Clement, A. (1988). *Law in sport and physical activity.* Indianapolis, Indiana: Benchmark Press, Inc.

Dworkin, J. (1981). *Owners versus players: baseball and collective bargaining.* Dover, Massachusetts: Auburn House Publishing Co.

Federal Baseball Club of Baltimore, Inc. v. National League of Professional Baseball Clubs, et al., 259 U.S. 200 (1922).

Flood v. Kuhn, 407 U.S. 258 (1972).

Gellhorn, E. (1976). *Antitrust law and economics in a nutshell.* St. Paul, Minnesota: West Publishing Co.

Grove City College v. Bell, 465 U.S. 555 (1984).

Harrow, R. (1980). *Sports violence: the interaction between private lawmaking and the criminal law.* Arlington, Virginia: Carrollton Press.

Haywood v. National Basketball Association, 401 U.S. 1204 (1971).

Hochberg, P. and Blackman, M. (1990). *Representing professional athletes and teams.* New York: May 14-16. Practising Law Institute Co-Chairmen.

Kaiser, R. (1986). *Liability & law in recreation, parks, & sports.* Englewood Cliffs, New Jersey: Prentice Hall.

Kansas City Royals Baseball Corporation v. Major League Baseball Players Association, 409 F. Supp. 233 (W.D. Missouri 1976).

Ludtke v. Kuhn, 461 F. Supp. 86 (S.D. N.Y. 1978).

Lupien, T. and Lowenfish, L. (1980). *The imperfect diamond: the story of baseball's reserve system and the men who fought to change it.* New York: Stein & Day.

Mackey v. National Football League, 407 F. Sup. 1000 (D. Minn. 1975).

Maloy, B. (1988). *Law in sport: liability cases in management and administration.* Indianapolis, Indiana: Benchmark Press, Inc.

McCourt v. California Sports, Inc., 600 P. 2d 1193 (1979).

NCAA v. Board of Regents of the University of Oklahoma, 468 U.S. 85 (1984).

Nygaard, G. and Boone, T. (1989). *Law for physical educators and coaches* (2nd Edition). Columbus, Ohio: Publishing Horizons, Inc.

Pennoyer v. Neff, 95 U.S. 714 (1877).

Reed, M. (1989). *IEG legal guide to sponsorship.* Chicago, Illinois: International Events Group, Inc.

Robertson v. National Basketball Association, 556 F.2d 682 (2nd Cir. 1977).

Rodgers v. Georgia Tech Athletic Association, 303 S.E.2d 467 (Ga. Ct. App. 1983).

Ruxin, R. (1989). *An athlete's guide to agents.* Lexington, Massachusetts: The Stephen Greene Press.

Schubert, G., Smith, R., and Trentadue, J. (1986). *Sports law.* St. Paul, Minnesota: West Publishing Co.

Shelton v. National Collegiate Athletic Association, 539 F.2d 1179 (9th Cir. 1976).

Sobel, L. (1981). *Professional sports & the law.* New York: Law-Arts Publishers.

Tokarz, K. (1986). *Women, sports and the law: a comprehensive research guide to sex discrimination in sports.* Buffalo, New York: William S. Hein Co.

Tomjanovich v. California Sports., Inc., No. H-78-243 (S.D. Tex. 1979).

Trope, M. (1987). *Necessary roughness: the other game of football exposed by its most controversial super agent.* Chicago: Contemporary Books.

Uberstine, G. (1985). *Covering all the bases: a comprehensive guide to sports law.* Buffalo, New York: William S. Hein Co.

Uberstine, G. (1988). *Law of professional and amateur sports.* New York: Clark Boardman Co., Ltd.

United States v. Burke, 700 F. 2d 70 (2nd Cir. 1983).

van der Smissen, B. (1990). *Legal liability and risk management for public and private entities.* Cincinnati: Anderson Publishing Co.

Waicukauski, R. (1982). *The law and amateur sport.* Bloomington, Indiana: Indiana University Press.

Weistart, J. and Lowell, C. (1979; 1985 supplement). *The law of sports.* Indianapolis, Indiana: The Bobbs-Merrill Co., Inc.

Wong, G. (1988). *Essentials of amateur sports law.* Dover, Massachusetts: Auburn House Publishing Co.

Wong, G. "Sports Law Report," *Athletic Business.* Madison, Wisconsin (published monthly).

Wong, G. and Wilde, T. (1991). *Sports lawyers guide to legal periodicals.* Buffalo, New York: William S. Hein Co.

Yasser, R. (1985). *Torts and sports: legal liability in professional and amateur athletics.* Westport, Connecticut: Quorum Books.

CHAPTER 7

Sports Law: Product Liability and Employment Relations

Annie Clement

In this chapter, you will become familiar with the following terms:

Liability	Leased employee
Employer	Worker's compensation
Employee	Product liability
"At will"	Strict liability in tort
Labor union	Exculpatory agreements
EEOC	Negligence
Affirmative action	Breach of warranty
Equal opportunity	Merchantability
Procedural due process	Defense
Vicarious liability	Contributory negligence
Respondeat superior	Assumption of risk
Master/Servant	Disclaimers
Principal/Agent	Compensatory damages
Independent contractor	Punitive damages

Overview

Administrators have a number of legal responsibilities that are often neglected until a crisis occurs. These responsibilities occur in employment relationships, from the search for applicants to the termination of employees, and include protection of workers and personal and professional **liability**, or responsibility, for employees.

The use of leased employees and independent contractors is popular in sport management. Each

97

of these relatively new forms of employment requires a fairly sophisticated knowledge of the law. A knowledge of the theory and practice (Chapters 6, 13, and 14) of legal concepts in management gives the entry-level professional an understanding of the complexity of these areas and highlights the need to obtain the advice of an attorney in carrying out specific management functions.

This chapter will give an overview of management legal concerns related to the supervisory role, including employer–employee relationships, vicarious liability, independent contractors, leased employees, and worker's compensation. Sports business is often considered only a service industry. The manufacture and sale of equipment, however, play a primary role in generating profits in the sports business. For this reason the legal theory of product liability is provided to guide the manager who is also a manufacturer, retailer, or wholesaler.

General tort liability will be presented separately from the legal concerns of management in this chapter. General tort liability affects teachers, coaches, and those supervising physical activity and/or activity facilities; employment liability affects employers, including manufacturers and retailers, in the sport industry.

EMPLOYER–EMPLOYEE RELATIONSHIPS

Employers and administrators have a number of well-defined responsibilities for and to their **employees**. Among them are ensuring an equitable hiring process, a safe working environment, and an evaluation system based on the job description.

Equitable hiring process

Hiring systems differ among industries. For years the most popular employer–employee relationship was known as **"at will."** The employer had a task to be done, sought out a person believed capable of carrying out the task, and offered the job and a wage; both agreed to the arrangement with a handshake. When the employer no longer wanted or needed the employee, the employee was asked to leave. If the employee no longer enjoyed the work environment or had a better offer, he or she was free to leave. "Two weeks notice" grew to be a popular termination notice in this work relationship.

Another characteristic of "at will" employment

was that the reason for termination was seldom public knowledge and, on occasion, was unclear to one of the parties to the agreement. Many people continue to be employed in this manner today. Also, most part-time employment is "at will."

Labor unions have brought drastic changes in the "at will" employment pattern in the past 50 to 75 years. Labor unions are private associations formed to represent groups of workers with common needs and a common desire to obtain the best wages possible for the entire group. They also negotiate contracts with entire industries.

Employment contracts are another form of employer–employee work relationship. They are written agreements that identify tasks to be accomplished, length of employment time, and salary. Such contracts are specific agreements between one employee and a particular business.

Contract, labor union, and "at will" are the employer–employee relationships most often used in business and industry in the United States.

Today's employment environment is subject to federal laws, such as laws created to remedy race, color, sex, age, religion, national origin, and handicap discrimination. The Equal Pay Act of 1963 and a number of executive orders of the 1950s and 1960s paved the way for legislation on employment discrimination. Title VII of the Civil Rights Act of 1964, the Age Discrimination in Employment Act of 1967, and the Rehabilitation Act of 1973 are the framework of most civil rights legislation. Title VII prohibits discrimination in the work environment based on race, color, sex, religion, or national origin. Affirmative action and equal opportunity employment are the results of Title VII. The age discrimination act protects people 40 to 65 years of age; the rehabilitative acts accomplished the same goal for the handicapped. Although these acts refer to government contractors only, the Supreme Court has extended the requirements for race discrimination to private employees.

The **Equal Employment Opportunity Commission** (EEOC) is the federal government agency responsible for administering the discrimination acts. Under the equal opportunity act, when a vacancy occurs in a company, all qualified individuals are to be made aware of the vacancy and allowed to submit papers for review; and the position is to be given to the best qualified individual.

Affirmative action is a special program designed

to remedy past discriminatory practices in hiring from minority groups. It is used when discrimination has been found. The program enables the protected group to receive special attention in employment until their numbers in that organization are proportionate to their percentage of the overall population. If 60% of the population available for a certain job is black, the affirmative action program will continue until the particular organization has 60% black membership. Affirmative action programs are influenced by availability of skill and talent and the organization's record of discrimination. Employers may volunteer to create an affirmative action program or be required by the court or an administrative agency to establish one in response to a finding of discrimination.

Safe work environment

Employers are responsible for providing a safe work environment for their employees. When the nature of the work prohibits an assurance of safety, the employer is expected to warn the employees of risks. In situations where the work is hazardous, employers are responsible for informing employees of the dangers and for providing as safe an environment as possible. Warnings about hazardous or unsafe conditions must be comprehensive and must be understood.

When special safety equipment is mandated by law, it must be provided. If protective equipment is available for purchase but is not mandated by law, such equipment is recommended. Employees should be made aware of the protective equipment. Employers may or may not pay for safety equipment not required by law. Even if employees are expected to purchase this equipment, employers should make employees aware of it.

The primary goal is to make employees aware of all risks before they accept a position. Before accepting a position they should also be told about the state of the art in protective equipment and whether such equipment will be provided.

In recent years the psychological environment, in addition to the physical environment, has been considered a factor in a safe work environment.

Evaluation

Employees are to be evaluated in a fair and equitable manner. The evaluation is to be based on the job description. The job description should include the position description and the day-to-day tasks of the jobs. *Griggs v. Duke Power Company* 401 U.S. 424 (1971) was the court decision that has played the most important role in establishing the need for job requirements that are directly related to job performance for both hiring and evaluation. If certain requirements, such as a college degree or specific inservice training, are given a high priority in evaluation, then evidence must show that the requirement is essential to successful job performance.

The results of evaluations are to be discussed with and available to employees. Where serious deficits in work habits are identified, there must be a **due process system** to enable employees to present their side of the situation. Employees also must be given the opportunity to overcome the deficits, and the employer must monitor the progress of the employee's rehabilitation program.

Policies on termination are to be established and, if possible, be in writing. A system of warnings preceding termination is to be in effect and is to include rehabilitation. These systems are to be related to job opportunities and are to be executed in such a way that the rights of the employee are paramount.

CONCEPT CHECK

Employment relationships are either "at will," labor union, or contract. Whatever the relationship, the burden is on the employer to follow federal rules on discrimination. In situations where the court or administrative agency has found the employer in violation of a federal or state equity employment law, the employer is required to conduct business under an affirmative action plan. Employees should know the status of their employment and whether they are working under a court-ordered or voluntary affirmative action program.

The employer is also responsible for the safety of the employees in the workplace. The employer must tell employees the risks involved, provide protective equipment when mandated by law, and inform workers of problems and methods of protection.

VICARIOUS LIABILITY

Vicarious liability means that one is responsible or liable for the torts of another. Liability means responsibility. Legal liability is that "liability which courts recognize and enforce as between parties litigant" (Black's Law Dictionary). Tort is a "private or civil wrong or injury . . . for which the court will provide a remedy in the form of an action for damages. A violation of a duty imposed by general law or otherwise upon all persons occupying the relation to each other which is involved in a given transaction" (Black's Law Dictionary). Vicarious liability is the responsibility that a manager carries for the torts of his or her employees even though the employer was not present and not aware that the tort was committed. Under the theory of **respondeat superior**, administrators become liable for the torts of their employees merely by virtue of being an administrator. It should be noted that the same administrator can also be held personally liable for hiring an incompetent person.

For an administrator to be liable for the tort of an employee, the tort must occur within the scope of the worker's employment and while the worker was under the supervision of the administrator. (Scope of employment is the set of job responsibilities of the position.) Torts occurring outside these parameters are not considered to be under vicarious liability. The administrator's right to control the employee and to direct the work is the test of vicarious liability or the respondeat superior theory.

This relationship between employer and employee is called either a **master–servant** or a **principal–agent** relationship. The master is the employer, and the servant is the employee; the principal is the employer, and the agent is the employee. Master–servant and principal–agent relationships are similar in many ways. They differ in that the master has the right to control the physical conduct of the servant, whereas a principal's right to control is restricted to business matters and does not include physical concerns. An agent acts on behalf of the principal. Among an agent's duties is the creation of legal relationships between the principal and third parties.

When the employee's torts go beyond the scope of employment, that is, the agreed-on job description, the employer's liability ceases. An employee's intentional torts, such as a worker hitting a fellow worker or a coach telling an athlete to beat up an opponent, are beyond the responsibilities of the employer.

Volunteers working in administrative roles take the same risks of vicarious liability as salaried employees. The expertise of the volunteer, rather than the wage, determines the level of liability.

INDEPENDENT CONTRACTORS

An **independent contractor** is one employed, by contract, to provide a service or complete a project without restrictions imposed by the hiring party as to the means to be used, selection of workers, training of staff, or supplies and materials to be used. The employer has a contract right only to the results; the employer has no control over how the tasks are accomplished. Another difference is that the independent contractor is usually paid in one or two lump sums; regular employees are paid wages and fringe benefits and are given supplies and equipment.

Employers are usually not liable for independent contractors or for the employees of independent contractors. Independent contractors, in turn, are responsible for themselves and for anyone they employ. They must carry insurance, pay wages and benefits, and withhold taxes. Independent contractors are responsible for their actions on the job; the employer is responsible only if the work environment becomes hazardous or if the employer takes control of the way the task will be accomplished. If the employer takes away the independent contractor's freedom, the liability also moves to the employer.

Even though an employer sets out to create an independent contractor relationship, the employer can, by accident, assume control sufficient to end the status. To avoid this situation, the parties should identify in writing the party who will be responsible for providing worker's compensation; withholding taxes; adhering to civil rights legislation, including age discrimination, wage, and labor law; and ensuring employee safety. Employers should also know that, even though their employees have met the requirements of independent contractor status, the employer may be held liable for an employee under other legal theories. Employers may be personally liable for the following:

1. Selecting a contractor with a history of carelessness.
2. Allowing a hazardous situation to exist.
3. Failing to perform a duty that they cannot delegate by law.

4. Allowing the party to do inherently dangerous work.

The differences between regular employment and independent contractor status determine the party responsible for the legal, financial, and social obligations.

LEASED EMPLOYEES

Leased employees are a combination of the regular employee and the independent contractor. The leasing firm serves as the independent contractor to the employer. The employee becomes an employee of the leasing firm and is given salary, fringe benefits, and liability coverage by the leasing firm. Leasing firms also hire, fire, and evaluate the employees. The employer merely creates a contract for a specific task to be accomplished, and the leasing company provides the service.

Regular employee and independent contractor relationships have been used for many years, but the leasing of employees originated in the early 1980s. Redeker and Castagnera (1985) reported only six leasing firms with 4,000 employees in 1981, and more than 200 companies employing more than 60,000 people in 1984. Leasing firms have been valuable to small companies by providing personnel when needed, while at the same time giving employees fringe benefits far superior to what the small business could have provided to the same employee. As a result of the great number of people they employ, leasing firms have been able to profit from participating in massive employee benefit packages and have been willing to pass that profit on to employees.

Leasing firms also provide the same services to major corporations. In fact, many large corporations lease some or all of their fitness and recreation employees.

CONCEPT CHECK

Vicarious liability is an automatic liability assumed by an administrator by virtue of being an administrator. The legal theory is respondeat superior, and the relationship between the employee and employer is master/servant or principal/agent.

Workers may be regular employees, independent contractors, or leased employees. An independent contractor is a person who contracts with the employer

to produce a specific product or to do a task. The employer has no control over how that task is accomplished. Payment usually is in the form of a lump-sum fee at the completion of the task.

A leasing firm is a combination of an independent contractor and a regular employee. The leasing firm is an independent contractor in its relationship with the employer and a regular employer in its relationship with the employee or worker. The leasing firm contracts to provide a specific service or product just as an independent contractor does. The leasing firm is responsible for employee wages, fringe benefits, and insurance and withholding taxes.

WORKER'S COMPENSATION

Worker's compensation is a statute varying by state, that provides benefits and medical care to employees and their families, for injuries the workers suffer in the course of employment. Proof of negligence is not required for compensation. Compensation is provided once proof of injury in employment has been established.

Worker's compensation was created to assist workers when they are injured without requiring workers to resort to the courts for a determination of liability. Support for an injured employee is automatic.

PRODUCT LIABILITY

Sport managers may be manufacturers, wholesalers, retailers, or owners of sport organizations or sport-related products. Even if they are none of the above they will be users of sport equipment. The manufacture and sale of sport equipment is big business. Those who invest considerable money in sport equipment expect a product that will be safe and will meet their needs.

Whether the sport administrator is the chief executive officer of a large sporting goods manufacturer, purchasing agent for a National Football League team, or merely someone about to purchase a set of golf clubs for personal use, product liability is important. **Product liability** becomes an issue when a product is defective. For the product to be considered defective, the defect must have existed when the product left the manufacturer's or retailer's (defendant's) contact, and the defect must have caused the injury. Product liability may be strict or automatic liability in tort, negligence, misrepresentation, breach of warranty, or violation of a Consumer Product Safety Commission rule. **Strict liability in tort** is imposed by a court of law when the product is dangerous and the defective condition has caused an injury. Strict liability in tort makes a seller liable for all defects or hazards that threaten the user's safety. Negligence occurs when the manufacturer, wholesaler, or retailer, who has a duty of care, violates the "reasonable standard of care" in placing a faulty product on the market. Breach of warranty occurs when the product fails to operate according to its written specifications, advertising brochures, or public announcements. Defenses against product liability include contributory negligence, assumption of risk, misuse, and Uniform Commercial Code disclaimers. Both state and federal laws govern product liability. States may differ in their laws, and state courts may differ in the interpretation of similar laws. Our interpretation of these concepts will be general and acceptable in most situations.

Strict liability in tort

United States courts apply the definition of strict liability as stated in the Restatement of the Law of Torts (Second) 402 A:

> One who sells any product in a defective condition unreasonably dangerous to the user or consumer or to his property is subject to liability for physical harm thereby caused to the ultimate user or consumer or to his property if: a) the seller is engaged in the business of selling such a product, and b) it is expected to and does reach the user or consumer without substantial change in the condition in which it was sold (American Law Institute, 1965; pp. 347-348).

Strict liability applies to anyone in the selling process or anyone who holds out himself or herself as a seller. They must sell the product. It does not apply to users of the product.

To determine strict liability, an objective test is used: Was the product's danger beyond what an ordinary person would understand? Was its danger so sophisticated or so obscure an ordinary person would fail to recognize it? Physical harm is usually required. Under strict liability the seller is liable even though the seller has used ultimate care in the design and preparation of the product. This liability will be imposed even if the victim has released the responsibility through **exculpatory**

agreements, often called waivers or releases. The nature of this responsibility is such that the consumer cannot "contract away" the responsibility of the manufacturer.

The product defect must be proved, and evidence must substantiate that the product is unreasonably dangerous. Strict liability usually focuses on the defect in the product rather than the behavior of the manufacturer or retailer. The three primary types of product defects are defective manufacturing, defective design, and lack of proper instruction or warnings.

Manufacturer's defect means that the product does not perform or was not built as the manufacturer planned, that an unsafe product has been created in the construction process. A defective design means that the product, built according to the manufacturer's plans, contains a design flaw or fault that will expose the user to unreasonable harm. The manufacturer is held to the status of design expert.

"Proper instruction" means that the manufacturer, wholesaler, and retailer have a duty to provide instructions on the proper use of the product and a duty to warn of any risk or danger. They should provide instructions in such a way that the purchaser will pass on the instructions and warnings to the users of the product.

Duty to warn

One has a duty to warn another when the danger is not apparent to the user of the product. Many courts have ruled that there is no duty to warn if the danger is obvious. Some courts have said that, even though the danger might be considered obvious to some people, the manufacturer retains a duty to warn. When the user, as a result of expertise and experience, knows of the product's danger, there is no duty to warn. When a product's dangers are generally known to a profession, there is no duty to warn.

The manufacturer is to give the product user information and directions about the characteristics and use of the product. This information is to be written in such a way that, if caution is essential, a reasonable person would recognize the need to exercise caution. The objective is to avoid injuries that could result from ignorant misuse of the product.

Failure to inspect or test

The manufacturer is expected to inspect the manufacturing process regularly and to inspect and test the finished product. The manufacturer is to have the skills and knowledge adequate to conduct such an inspection and/or test. If the manufacturer does not possess such skills, he or she is to contract for appropriate advice. When a significant defect is identified before the product is released, the defect is corrected or the production must be stopped. When a significant defect is identified after the product has been released, the sale of the product must be halted or purchasers clearly warned of the defect.

Manufacturers are required to test products to ensure their safety. They are not, however, required to ensure that the product is perfect. The magnitude of the harm that would be caused by the defect is considered in evaluating the manufacturer's diligence in uncovering defects. "The greater the likelihood of substantial harm resulting from a product defect, the higher the degree of preventive care" (Wittenberg, 1989; p. 1.02). Also, the greater the suspicion of a hidden defect, the more diligent the search must be. Reports of defects from current owners are to be checked by the manufacturer and should influence future inspection and testing.

The manufacturer's duty to inspect and test is high. Wholesalers and retailers (sellers) depend on the manufacturer to identify problems. As a result, the seller's liability is decreased. If sellers perform functions such as installing, repairing, or assembling as part of readying the product, they assume added responsibility for inspecting in general and testing the functions in which they have participated.

Negligence

Negligence in product cases is similar to negligence in general: A duty must exist, it must have been breached, the breach must relate directly to the injury, and the injury must be substantial. Negligence may be found for the manufacturer, the wholesaler, the retailer or seller, and the people supervising the use of the product. Negligence in product cases most often involves failure to warn adequately of foreseeable dangers or failure to pass on the seller's warnings. These dangers include the dangers resulting from the foreseeable use and misuse of the product. Failure to inspect or to test a product may also result in negligence. Products failing to conform with industry standards or with standards imposed by law will also be treated under negligence. In both negligence and strict liability, the probability and magnitude of the risk is balanced against the use of the product. Is the product easy to handle and inexpensive? Would a change so increase the cost of the product that it would prohibit its use?

Misrepresentation

Misrepresentation is an untrue statement of fact that leads a person to believe something that is not true. The statement may be incorrect or intentionally false. The Restatement (Second) of Torts 402 B states:

> One engaged in the business of selling chattels, who, by advertising, labels, or otherwise, makes to the public a misrepresentation of a material fact concerning the character or quality of a chattel sold by him is subject to liability for physical harm to a consumer of the chattel caused by justifiable reliance upon the misrepresentation, even though (a) it is not made fraudulently or negligently, and (b) the consumer has not bought the chattel from or entered into any contractual relationship with the seller (American Law Institute, 1965; p. 358).

When facts about the product or statements as to its use have been misrepresented by the seller, an injured plaintiff may sue for misrepresentation. The product need not be defective or unreasonably dangerous; however, a physical injury is required for a claim to be brought.

Advertisements, brochures, and salespeople's comments should be examined to ensure that they do not contain misrepresentation. In the sporting goods industry the comments of the salespeople should be carefully monitored to ensure that the purchaser is aware of potential hazards and risks of using the equipment.

Breach of warranty

Breach of warranty is the failure of the industry, manufacturer, retailer, or wholesaler to honor the warranty established at the time of the sale. Liability in warranty exists regardless of fault. A warranty, also covered by the Uniform Commercial Code, may be express or implied.

An express warranty is any verbal statement or printed document that contains promises about or descriptions of the goods.

Implied warranties begin when a person buys an article of goods. These warranties need not appear in writing, nor need they be mentioned. Implied warranties include merchantability and fitness.

Fitness involves the purchaser's assumptions that the product will be what it is purported to be and that it will be fit for its intended use. It is assumed a tennis racquet will be used to hit balls back and forth across a net and that a golf cart will be used only on a golf course and not as a vehicle for commuting to one's job.

Merchantability means that the goods are suitable for the purposes for which they were created. The level of suitability is to be average or reasonable; it need not be perfect. Fitness means that the product has been made for a particular purpose.

Consumer product safety act

In 1968 Congress established the National Commission on Product Safety to explore the need for federal regulation of consumer products. Congress found many unacceptable products, including ones from which people were unable to protect themselves (15 USCA 2051[a]). The commission proposed the Consumer Product Safety Act (CPSA) (15 USCA 2051) to reduce the unreasonable risks of injury and death that come with the use of products available to the public. The legislation helps consumers evaluate products, helps develop safety standards, promotes research, and supports investigations into the causes of injuries and death (15 USCA 2051[b]). The CPSA also requires manufacturers to inform the commission of substantial product hazards that can cause serious harm to users.

An individual injured by a product whose manufacturer is in violation of a consumer product safety rule may bring an action in federal court. They are required to prove the following:

1. A manufacturer has distributed
2. A consumer product
3. Which presents a hazard
4. Without giving notice to the CPSA of the hazard;
5. That the failure to give notice was knowing or willful; and
6. That the failure to give notice was a proximate cause of the plaintiff's injury (Epstein, 1986; p. 70).

Sample of product liability state legislation

On occasion, state law may be quite specific on elements of product liability. Ohio's "Tort Reform Act of 1987" says that a product is defective in design if either:

1. The foreseeable risks associated with its design exceed the benefits of that design, or;
2. It is more dangerous than an ordinary consumer would expect when used in an intended or reasonably foreseeable manner, thus retaining the consumer expectation standard upon which prior law defined defect, and which was based upon Section 402 (A) of the Restatement, Second, of Torts (Page's Ohio Revised Code 2307.75[a]).

Foreseeable risk is defined as:

A risk of harm that satisfies both of the following:
1. It is associated with an intended or reasonably foreseeable use, modification, or alteration of a production question;
2. It is a risk that the manufacturer in question should recognize while exercising both of the following:
   a. The attention, perception, memory, knowledge, and intelligence that a reasonable manufacturer should possess;
   b. Any superior attention, perception, memory, knowledge, or intelligence that the manufacturer in question possesses (Page's Ohio Revised Code 2307.71[f]).

When a person brings a product liability suit to state court they use a state law similar to the one just mentioned.

Defenses

Defenses to product liability are contributory negligence, assumption of risk, misuse, and disclaimers. Comparative negligence statutes, which are becoming popular throughout the United States, allocate liability by percentages to each of the parties involved in a case. A further discussion can be found in several sources (Kaiser, 1986; Clement, 1988).

Contributory negligence occurs when the user is negligent in his or her use of the equipment. A user who fails to read the manual, who assembles the equipment incorrectly, or who chooses to use the product in a way never anticipated by the manufacturer or the retailer has acted with contributory negligence. **Assumption of risk,** another defense, requires that the plaintiff knew of the danger or was given facts sufficient to enable a reasonable person to comprehend the danger involved. The user must be aware of the danger, recognize and appreciate the risk involved in using the product, and voluntarily take the risk.

A major defense in breach of warranty is the **disclaimer.** This is a statement in which the manufacturer and retailer explain how the product is to be used and state that they will not be responsible if the product is used in ways other than that recommended. Merchantability and fitness, mentioned earlier, cannot be disclaimed.

Damages

Damages in product liability are usually compensatory and sometimes punitive. **Compensatory damages** are payments for the direct expenses of the injury and rehabilitation. **Punitive damages** are damages assessed against the party responsible for the harm and awarded to the injured party in an effort to stop the responsible party from continuing to create the harm.

The severity of the damage and the amount of damages necessary to force the industry to reconsider continuing to manufacture and sell the defective product are two important factors in the assessment of punitive damages.

CONCEPT CHECK

Breach of warranty may be express or implied. Implied warranties are merchantability and fitness. To prove breach of express or implied warranty, certain conditions must be met.

The Consumer Product Safety Act was created to reduce the amount of injury and death resulting from the use of products. Most states have also instituted their own product liability laws to reduce the danger that results from the use of products. A person may file a claim under either federal or state law in the court of their choice.

SUMMARY

1. "At will" is and has been the most popular form of employment relationship. Labor union and individual contracts are other forms of employment used today.
2. Employers are to adhere to federal discrimination laws in hiring, evaluating, and termi-

nating employees. The laws include the Equal Pay Act, Title VII of the Civil Rights Act, and the Age Discrimination Act.

3. Affirmative action programs are special programs designed to remedy past discrimination. They may be court ordered or voluntary.
4. Employers are responsible for providing a safe work environment and, when unable to provide a safe environment, are responsible for warning employees of unsafe conditions.
5. Employees are to be evaluated according to predetermined criteria based on job description and the tasks associated with the position. The evaluation is to be fair and equitable.
6. Vicarious liability is one's responsibility for the torts of another even though one was not present. Administrators are vicariously liable or responsible for the torts of their employees under the legal theory of respondeat superior.
7. There are three types of employment: regular, independent contractor, and leased.
8. Independent contractors are responsible for wages, insurance, benefits, compensation, and the withholding of taxes for themselves and those they employ. Employers of independent contractors contract only for the result. They do not control or supervise the process.
9. Leased employees have a regular employment relationship with the leasing firm, whereas the leasing firm has an independent contractor relationship with the organization for whom the work is provided.
10. Worker's compensation is a state statute that provides benefits and medical care to employees injured in the course of employment. Proof of negligence is not required.
11. Managers who are manufacturers, wholesalers, retailers, or owners of sport products play a role in product liability.
12. Product liability may be strict liability in tort, negligence, misrepresentation, breach of warranty, or violation of a Consumer Product Safety Commission statute.
13. The three primary types of product defects are manufacturing defects, design defects, and lack of proper instruction or warning.
14. Negligence in product liability is the same as negligence in general. That is, a duty must exist, it must be breached, the breach must directly relate to the duty, and substantial damages must occur.

15. Breach of warranty may be a breach of an express or implied warranty. Implied warranties include merchantability and fitness.
16. Consumer Product Safety Commission statutes have been created to reduce society's risk of injury and death from the use of products.
17. Defenses against product liability are contributory negligence, assumption of risk, misuse, and disclaimers. Damages are compensatory and sometimes punitive.

REVIEW QUESTIONS AND ISSUES

1. Tort liability differs from vicarious liability. Explain the differences and their significance to the role of the administrator.
2. Describe an environment in which you have been employed. Pretend that you have been named supervisor of that organization. Identify the hazards in the work environment. Create a system for alerting personnel to those hazards.
3. Name the hiring and evaluation requirements that arose from *Griggs v. Duke Power Company* and explain how you would incorporate them into your employee evaluation system.
4. Product liability may be found in strict liability in tort, negligence, misrepresentation, warranty, or violation of consumer product safety standards. Which legal theories affect manufacturers, retailers, and sellers in general? Name the theories most important to people who supervise the use of products.
5. The duty to warn includes a duty to inform the purchaser about the proper use of the product and to warn of potential dangers in the use of the product. Using a product you know, write a warning statement for that product that satisfies both the duty to inform and the duty to warn.
6. Identify the product liability statute in your state. This can be found in the state code, which is available in all county and local law libraries, public libraries, and some college and university libraries. Access to a law school library is not needed for this assignment.

REFERENCES

American Law Institute. (1965). *Restatement of the law of torts, 2d* (Student Edition). St. Paul, Minnesota: American Law Institute.

Black, H. (1979). *Black's law dictionary*. St. Paul, Minnesota: West Publishing Co.

Clement, A. (1988). *Law in sport and physical activity*. Indianapolis: Benchmark Press, Inc.

Epstein, J. (April, 1986). Failure to warn, the Consumer Product Safety Act provides a new wrinkle. *Trial*, pp. 67-70.

Griggs v. Duke Power Company, 401 U.S. 424, 91 St. Ct. 849 (1971).

Kaiser, R. (1986). *Liability and law in recreation, parks and sports*. Englewood Cliffs, New Jersey: Prentice Hall.

McGuire, E. (November, 1988). Foreseeable misuse of products. *Trial*, p. 43.

Page's Ohio Revised Code (1989 Supplement). 2307.71 to 2307.80, Product liability. Cincinnati, Ohio: Anderson Publishing Co.

Redeker, J., and Castagnera, J. (February, 1985). Labor relations, the legal nightmare of employee leasing. *Personnel Journal*, pp. 58-62.

Title 15, *United States Code Annotated*. (1982, update 1990). Consumer Product Safety, Section 2051 to 2083. St. Paul, Minnesota: West Publishing Co., pp. 209-294.

White, J., and Summer, R. (1980). *Uniform Commercial Code*. St. Paul, Minnesota: West Publishing Co.

Wittenberg, J. (1989). *Product liability*. New York: Law Journal Seminar Press.

SUGGESTED READINGS

Berry, R., and Wong, G. (1986). *Law and business of the sports industries*. Volumes I and II. Dover, Massachusetts: Auburn House Publishing Co.

Clement, A. (1988). *Law in sport and physical activity*. Indianapolis: Benchmark Press, Inc.

Kaiser, R. (1986). *Liability and law in recreation, parks and sport*. Englewood Cliffs, New Jersey: Prentice Hall.

Riffer, J. (Updated to June 1, 1989) *Sports and recreational injuries*. Colorado Springs, Colorado: Shephard's McGraw-Hill Book Co.

Seton Hall Sport Law Review. Newark, New Jersey: Seton Hall University.

15:1 *Thurgood Marshall Law Review*. Houston, Texas: Texas Southern University.

Weistart, J., and Lowell, C. (1979). *The law of sports*. New York: Bobbs Merrill Co., Inc.

Wittenberg, J. (updated through 1989). *Product liability: recreation and sports equipment*. New York: Law Journal Seminars Press.

Yasser, R. (1985). *Torts and sports*. Westport, Connecticut: Quorum Books.

CHAPTER 8

Communications

Bruce Watkins

In this chapter, you will become familiar with the following terms:

Interpersonal communication	Task and socioemotional interactions	Public interest
Mass communication	Task process activity	Deregulation
Dyad	Relational activity	Owned-and-operated television station
Small group	Topical activity	Affiliated station
Organization	Downward/upward/inward/ outward communication	Independent station
Content and relationship dimensions	Macronetworks	Superstation
Self-disclosure	Bridge and liaison	Basic tier cable
Group communication network	Mass and specialized appeal periodicals	Premium cable
Distance and centrality of communication		Pay-per-view cable
		Overnight and sweeps television ratings

Overview

Communication is the exchange and sharing of messages. It is the cornerstone of human society. Without communication, a society could not function on a daily basis, nor could it change or pass on its heritage to future generations.

Communication can occur at an **interpersonal** level—when two people talk, they share their ideas, beliefs, emotions, and attitudes. Interper-

sonal communication also occurs when people interact in small groups or in large organizations. This communication is often more complex than that involving only two people. Communication may also occur when one or a few people send messages to hundreds, thousands, even millions of recipients. This process is called **mass communication.**

Not all communication is successful, however.

Often messages are distorted, and sometimes the message received is opposite from that intended. These failures occur in both interpersonal and mass communication. This chapter presents fundamental theories about effective interpersonal and mass communication. The discussion of interpersonal theory focuses particularly on principles of communication in groups and organizations. The discussion of mass communication centers primarily on the institutional practices under which mass media operate in our society. Several examples of how these theories relate to sport management contexts will be examined, although this chapter presents primarily theory, reserving specific applications for Chapter 16.

INTERPERSONAL AND MASS COMMUNICATION

In 1948, political scientist Harold Lasswell proposed that a convenient way to understand communication was to analyze "who says what in which channel to whom with what effect." Theory and research in communication have centered on these elements: communicator characteristics ("who"), audience composition ("to whom"), the content of the communications ("what"), and especially, the impact ("effect"). However, Lasswell's identification of the "channel" was especially important, because it focused attention on several important differences between interpersonal and mass communication.

Communication at the interpersonal level may be tailored to the individual. Interactions are affected by the knowledge and experiences of those involved in the communication process. Most important, interpersonal communication involves feedback. The rich array of verbal and nonverbal feedback—questions, laughter, facial expressions, "body language"—provides information about communication successes and failures.

Mass communication is characterized by a few individuals communicating to many. There are attempts to tailor mass communications to the recipients, but the targets are inexact, based on broad demographic categories, such as women between the ages of 18 and 34 who live in households with more than $50,000 in annual income. Of course others will receive the media communications as well, even though they may not be the targeted audience. Feedback is also different. Imprecise

feedback may be provided by circulation figures (in the case of newspapers and magazines) and by listenership and viewership ratings (in the case of radio and television). Readers, viewers, or listeners may also write letters to the editor or to a station or network as a way of providing feedback. However, recipients of mass communication are not able to affect or alter the message when they are reading, watching, or listening.

These differences contributed to separate research approaches and theory development for interpersonal and mass communication during the formative years of 1930 and beyond, but especially post–World War II years. Researchers studied a few topics in both areas (such as persuasion), but generally research and theory development overlapped very little. Some have reasoned that interpersonal and mass communication share more than they differ, and therefore theories should be better integrated (see "Symposium on Mass and Interpersonal Communication," 1988). However, the two areas will be considered separately here for a rather simple reason. Several of the well-developed mass communication theories that share the most with interpersonal concerns are those that examine effects of the mass media. In what way do the media set agendas for public concerns and discussion? What effect do media presentations have on our behavior or that of our children? How do these presentations contribute to social perceptions or to socialization?

These are worthy areas of study, but in the context of sport management, the nature of mass media as industries is the topic now at hand. Indeed, many mass media exist to turn a profit for owners and managers. Decisions about what to communicate, to whom to direct the communication, and even who communicates, are often made with financial considerations paramount. Of less interest are the effects as opposed to the business and economic aspects of media industries. How are audiences selected and targeted? How are advertising decisions made? What are some of the unique aspects of programming for television? What issues are important in sport journalism? Therefore this chapter will focus on mass communication industry structures, relevant regulations, and decision-making processes in media industries.

In the interpersonal area, theories in dyadic, small group, and organizational communication will be examined. These theories describe how people communicate in various relationships, and what factors facilitate and inhibit relational communication.

Importance of interpersonal and mass communication to sport management

Knowledge of both mass and interpersonal communication is important for sport managers. Managers of sport organizations—whether community recreation programs, health clubs, sport arenas, university athletic departments, professional sports teams, or corporations involved in sporting goods or sport marketing—need to be skilled in communicating with their employees and with those outside the organization. The ability to speak and to write clearly is paramount, as is skill and sensitivity in interacting face-to-face with individuals or with groups. Finally, knowing how best to facilitate communication in an organization—from writing memos, to providing proper grievance channels, to ensuring that employees feel free to challenge ideas or to suggest alternatives—will do much to guarantee that the organization functions smoothly.

Sport managers also need a solid understanding of the institutions of mass communication. Reporters, columnists, and broadcasters who cover sports for the print and electronic media must understand journalistic principles. Similarly, directors of college, university, and professional sports information divisions must understand the special circumstances and pressures under which journalists operate. Individuals who are charged with marketing a sport or a sports team, or with using sport as a marketing tool for their sporting goods company, must have a solid grasp of how the mass media industries are structured, how they operate, and how people use and are influenced by the mass media.

CONCEPT CHECK

Interpersonal and mass communication differ in several important ways that affect theories about each. Interpersonal communication may be tailored to individuals and to the knowledge and experiences of those who are communicating. Feedback from interpersonal communication is usually immediate and precise, and informs the communicators about their successes and failures. Mass communication involves a single individual or a few communicators sending messages to many recipients. Feedback is imprecise, and there is often little control over who receives mass media messages. Many communication-related decisions in mass media industries, such as targeting an audience or setting a program schedule, are based on economic aspects.

THEORETICAL FOUNDATIONS OF INTERPERSONAL COMMUNICATION

There are four major areas of interpersonal communication study. The first is specific communication skills, and the teaching of these skills, designed to make messages easier to understand or perhaps more persuasive. Communication educators often focus on skills used in writing or public speaking. The other three areas embody the study of how people relate to and interact with each other. Scholars in these areas study interpersonal interaction in **dyads** (such as two strangers; a manager and a subordinate; or a married couple), **small groups** (such as a team or a committee), and small to large **organizations** (such as a local health club or a multi-national corporation). In these contexts scholars study both verbal and nonverbal behaviors.

Theoretical foundations of communication skills

Of the major interpersonal areas, this one is most lacking in theory. The primary reason is that university speech departments based their growth on the teaching of communication skills. They saw their purpose as just that—teaching. Delia (1987) has noted that "the basic pedagogic areas included public speaking, persuasion, group discussion, business and professional communication . . . Instruction in most areas was utilitarian." (pp. 78-79). A good theoretical foundation is a product of research. Variables are identified and measures are specified. Hypotheses about the relationships between these variables are formulated and tested, leading some theories to be supported and others to be discarded. Speech and writing teachers often saw the research process as irrelevant to the "real world," because it isolated only a single variable for examination. Their conception of research was more holistic, historical, and interpretive, such as examining especially important and effective speeches (Delia, 1987).

When the speech field finally incorporated empirical research approaches around 1960, research tended to focus on persuasive communication, drawing on other social sciences and moving beyond the rhetorical tradition. This does not mean that there are no guidelines for effective speaking and writing. There are a number of good "prescriptions" for effective communication, some that deal specifically with business communication skills (Andrews and Baird, 1989; Lewis, 1987; and Munter, 1987). The knowledge has been developed in a tradition different from that in the other interpersonal areas, however. For the most part, this means that the procedures have not been formally tied to an overall theory of effective communication. Rather, they seem to be based on common sense and anecdotal evidence rather than on a set of formal tests of their effectiveness. Nevertheless, clear oral and written communication skills are important to the sport manager.

Theoretical foundations of dyadic communication

There are more interesting theories and issues in the study of interpersonal interaction than there is space to cover them in this chapter. The discussion of the theoretical foundations will be limited to those areas that are related to behavior in groups and organizations. Other sources are available that more fully outline theory and research in interpersonal communication (Littlejohn, 1989, Trenholm, 1986).

Theory in dyadic communication deals with the formation of relationships. It focuses on the interactive processes by which people come to evaluate, understand, and relate to each other. Some researchers study factors that contribute to interpersonal attraction (such as physical proximity, physical attractiveness, interpersonal similarity, and status), the ability to influence and persuade others (such as competence, status, and ethos), and the dimensions of creating and managing impressions (such as ingratiation, intimidation, self-promotion, and supplication).

This research has identified individuals' behaviors that occur on single dimensions of an interaction. However, interactions occur on more than a single dimension. A representative of a sport marketing firm, in trying to sign a famous athlete to a contract, might be exerting influence and pressure while at the same time attempting to create an impression of helplessness or indecision so that the athlete feels he or she is in control. Anthropologist Gregory Bateson was among the first to recognize this. His approach to communication, termed relational communication, asserted that each interpersonal exchange really has two messages. Bateson called these a report and a command. Later, Bateson followers (known as the Palo Alto group) called these content and relationship dimensions (Watzlawick, Beavin, and Jackson, 1967).

The **content** dimension contains the actual substance of a communication, whereas the **relationship** dimension is a "metastatement" about the relationship of the communicators. Woody Allen fans will recall the rooftop scene in the movie *Annie Hall* when Allen's character is getting to know Annie Hall (Diane Keaton). Each content statement (such as "I would like to take a serious photography course" or "The medium enters in as a condition of the art form itself") is accompanied by a subtitled relationship statement (such as "He probably thinks I'm a yo-yo" and "I don't know what I'm saying . . . she senses I'm shallow"). Interactions between coaches and athletes often carry both content ("Maybe you should try passing the ball to your teammates more often") and relationship communications ("I'm the coach here and we'll do what I say!").

Relational theory proposes that interactional communication patterns are characterized by relationship statements that show complementarity (such as dominant to submissive) or symmetry (such as dominant to dominant, or submissive to submissive). The coach-player relationship just cited is a clear example of complementarity—as long as the player is willing to submit. But baseball fans might recall the classic confrontation between New York Yankees coach Billy Martin and Reggie Jackson, when Martin yanked Jackson from his left field post mid-inning for failing to run for a fly ball. Jackson tried to shift from complementarity to symmetry by physically confronting Martin in the dugout. Appropriately, Watzlawick, Beavin, and Jackson noted that relational messages often are given nonverbally, whereas content messages are primarily verbal.

Relationships change over time. Partners in dyads change their perceptions of themselves and of the relationship. An approach favored by Miller and Steinberg (1975) views interpersonal communication and the development of relationships as evolutionary processes. According to their theory, relationships become increasingly intimate over time, and, as relationships move toward greater intimacy, changes occur in three dimensions.

Rules governing the relationship change, becoming increasingly personal and unique to a particular relationship. Miller and Steinberg referred to cultural, sociological, and psychological levels of communication rules. Cultural rules are those shared by all members of a particular culture (such as those governing use of language or sanctioning behaviors). Sociological rules operate at the level of subcultures, such as ethnic groups or professional societies. They establish a "unique set of agreements about appropriate communicative behaviors" (Trenholm, 1986), such as saluting in the military or exchanging "high fives" on the field of athletic competition. Psychological rules are those that are unique to and created by individuals in specific relationships; they are not common to other relationships at the sociological or cultural level.

Changes also occur in the level of information that is shared as people seek to "reduce the uncertainty of the relationship" (a major function of interpersonal communication, according to Berger and Calabrese [1975]). Information at the cultural and sociological levels is replaced by that at the psychological level (such as beliefs or values).

Finally, changes occur in the level of knowing, moving from a descriptive level through a predictive level (that is, knowing what a person will do in a given situation), and finally to an explanatory level (understanding the cause or rationale for a person's behaviors). For example, consider how the communication changes between a club golf pro and a member taking lessons. The longer they work together, the more acceptable it becomes for the pro to criticize (constructively, of course) the member's approach, stance, and swing. With time the member will also feel more comfortable talking not only about mechanics, but about more personal information, such as how difficult the changes seem or how she feels about not accomplishing her goals. These represent changes in rules and in levels of information.

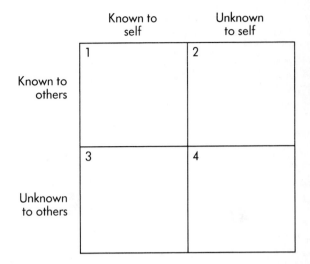

FIGURE 8-1 Levels of interpersonal information. (From Luft, J. [1969]. *Of human interaction.* The National Press.)

An important interpersonal process is **self-disclosure.** This refers to the revealing of attitudes and feelings to others. The goal of self-disclosure is to reduce uncertainty and increase intimacy of a relationship. Littlejohn (1989) has summarized a number of review articles on self-disclosure research. The following are some interesting findings:

- Disclosure increases with increased intimacy and with an increased need to reduce relational uncertainty.
- Women tend to disclose more often than do men.
- Disclosure tends to be reciprocal.
- The relationship between disclosure and satisfaction is curvilinear. Low satisfaction with a relationship is related to both very low and very high self-disclosure behaviors. Satisfaction is highest when disclosure is moderate.

Another approach to self-disclosure was offered by Luft (1969), who developed the "Johari Window"* illustrated in Figure 8-1.

The window contains four quadrants that represent four types of information about every person. Quadrant 1 (*open*) is most transparent. It con-

---

*Joseph Luft created the window with Harrington Ingham— thus the term Johari.

tains information that is known both to an individual and to others, such as feelings toward others or attitudes about work and leisure. Quadrant 2 *(blind)* contains information that is known to others but not to the person. Perhaps a particular person is seen by others as too arrogant or too demanding, even though he or she does not see himself or herself that way. Quadrant 3 *(hidden)* is composed of information available to a person but not to others. Maybe a person pretends to like his or her tennis doubles partner, but really would rather play with almost anyone else. Luft also proposed a fourth quandrant *(unknown)* that contains information with which neither a person nor others are familiar. An example might be a deep-seated fear of failing that hinders performance, even though he or she is not aware of this fear and may appear supremely confident to others.

The function of good interpersonal communication is to increase the amount of information in the open quadrant. That is, as individuals feel more free to disclose information about themselves, the contents of the hidden quadrant move to the open quadrant. As others feel more free to share their perceptions about a particular person, information should also move from the blind quadrant to the open quadrant. The good sport manager should look for ways to enhance self-disclosure in both face-to-face and organizational contexts.

CONCEPT CHECK

Interpersonal exchanges in relational communication carry several messages simultaneously (Watzlawick, Beavin, and Jackson, 1967). Relationship messages carry meaning about the kind of affiliation or association between the communicators. Content messages contain the actual substance of the communication. Relationships change over time as participants act to reduce relational uncertainty. The rules about the relationship and level of information shared become increasingly personal and unique to the particular relationship. Moderate self-disclosure enhances the growth of interpersonal relationships.

Theoretical foundations of small group communication

Many interpersonal interactions, especially from a management perspective, take place in groups. A group is a collection of people small enough (3 to 20) that each will be aware of and react to others, whose goals are mutual and interdependent. It is also characterized by people who have a sense of belonging and whose behavior is based on a set of agreed-on norms, values, and procedures (Brilhart, 1978).

Think for a moment about the number and variety of groups to which people belong. There are business-related groups (such as university department, management team, office committee, or newspaper sports department), recreation-related groups (such as softball team, weekly tennis doubles partners, barbershop quartet, ski club, or Little League parents), neighborhood groups (such as neighborhood watch program), and public service groups (such as Rotary Club or ecology center). A good deal of communication takes place in groups, especially in sport-related endeavors.

Theory in the study of small groups has centered on group structure and membership (Why do people join groups? What type of group is joined? What is the most desirable group structure?), group processes, especially decisionmaking (What inhibits or facilitates group work? How do people behave in groups?), and leadership (What makes a good leader? What is the relationship between leader style and group satisfaction and effectiveness?). Although there are models in each of these areas, there is no overarching theory that integrates them.

Recognizing this fractionalized state of theory in small group study, Shaw (1981) instead has summarized many of the important research findings in the following eight categories of hypotheses: (1) those about individuals and groups (for example, groups usually produce more and better solutions than do individuals), (2) those about group formation and development (for example, individuals affiliate with others who have abilities equal to or greater than their own), (3) those about physical environment of groups (for example, seating arrangement influences communication patterns and quality of interaction), (4) those about characteristics of members (for example, women talk more than men in groups and are more likely to conform to majority opinion than are men), (5) those about group composition (for example, members of high-cohesive groups communicate to a greater extent than those in a low-cohesive group), (6) those about group structure (for ex-

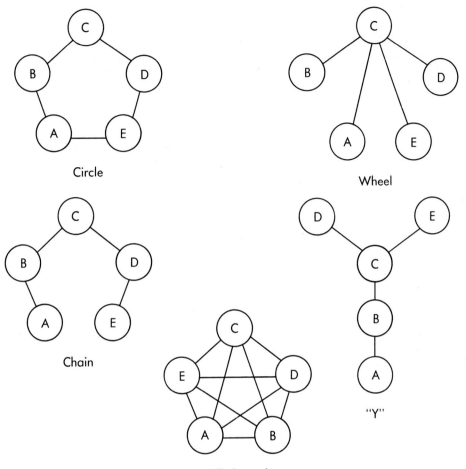

FIGURE 8-2 Common communication networks in five-person groups.
(From Fisher, B. [1980]. *Small-group decision-making* [2nd Edition]. New York: McGraw-Hill Book Co.)

ample, communication that is directed upward in a status hierarchy is likely to be biased toward positive information rather than negative), (7) those about leadership (for example, member satisfaction is greater with democratic leadership than autocratic leadership), and (8) those about group tasks and group goals (for example, group success leads to a choice of a more difficult task, whereas failure leads to choice of an easier task). Shaw's hypotheses serve as excellent summaries of the research findings, and some are good beginning points for further study in small group communication.

Study of small group communication focuses

specifically on message transmission and reception processes. Who speaks with whom? What are the patterns of communication "links" between group members? Group communication is studied by examining the **communication networks** that guide message exchanges. Fisher (1980) outlined the major network patterns; several of these are diagrammed in Figure 8-2.

For example, a *wheel* refers to a pattern in which most communications are directed at or through a single individual. According to historians, communication in the National Collegiate Athletic Association under the autocratic Walter Byers, who considered the organization to be "the alpha and omega of his life" (Spence, 1989, p. 128), could be characterized as having this structure. All decisions went through him, and most communications were directed at him.

In contrast, an *all-channel* structure describes a pattern in which participants communicate equally well with each member of the group. Communication is open, and subsequent decisionmaking is shared and is based on everyone possessing adequate information.

Communication networks are characterized by distance and centrality. **Distance** refers to the number of links necessary for a message to be transmitted and received by two participants. For example, Figure 8-2 shows that four links are necessary for A to communicate with E in the chain model. It might represent a high school basketball team in which each player gets along with only one or two teammates. In contrast, A and E communicate directly in the all-channel model, as do A and C, A and B, and A and D. Each additional link may distort the message, increasing communication difficulty.

Centrality is an index representing how many links are needed for a given individual to communicate with every other group member. In the wheel structure, for example, only four links would be needed for individual C to communicate with all other members. C is clearly in charge of all communication in this centralized network. C would require six links in the circle and the chain structures, and five in the Y structure. A communication network is centralized to the extent that one member needs fewer links than others to communicate. These members may be considered gatekeepers of information. In Figure 8-2, the wheel, chain, and Y structures are centralized. Often, the more centralized the network, the less satisfactory is the communication.

Communication is very important to group process, especially decisionmaking. In this regard communication theory has been strongly influenced by the interaction process analysis of Robert Bales (1976), which centers on "communication acts" and "interacts." Bales' theory divides group communication behaviors into four types: *questions* (asking for information, asking for opinion, asking for suggestions), *attempted answers* (giving suggestions, giving opinion, giving information),

positive—or mixed—actions (acting friendly, agreeing, dramatizing), and *negative*—or mixed—actions (disagreeing, showing tension, acting unfriendly). Bales argued that two group leaders typically emerge. One facilitates the **task interactions** (questions and attempted answers) and makes sure that information is disseminated and discussed. A second leader facilitates the **socioemotional interactions** (positive and negative actions) and makes sure that members feel good about their efforts and the outcomes. Efforts of both are necesary for group success. Littlejohn (1989) presents a more complete analysis of Bales' approach, as well as criticisms of it.

As in dyads, natural transitions and phases occur over time in most small groups. Moreland and Levine (1982) argued that the roles of group members, rather than remain stable, continually change as individuals redefine themselves, and the group members redefine each other's contributions. Certainly, individual behavior in groups will vary. Some persons are more talkative than others; some value consensus and accord, whereas others prefer to explore alternatives.

According to Moreland and Levine, the process of group socialization ensures that members either conform with the group goals or isolate themselves and eventually leave the group. During an evaluative phase the group defines its goals and appropriate behavior to achieve these goals. Members determine the rewards of membership and any tradeoffs they must make. Based on these determinations, members commit to the group, accept group goals and values, develop positive affect for other members, and express willingness to accept and work toward group goals. Because both evaluation and commitment may continually change, roles change throughout the life of the group.

Readers who have been members of an athletic team, whether a university team or one formed at a local squash club, will recognize that these processes that hold true in the management conference room also hold true for competitive teams. Usually, the seniors on a college baseball team are much more group- or team-oriented than they were during their freshman season. Their athletic skills have changed, but more important, their commitment and especially, the roles they have played on the team, have changed over the collegiate years. Maybe the highly-recruited freshman was a disruptive force and was removed from the team. Maybe a first-year walk-on became a team leader and senior captain. Stories about or by noted collegiate coaches (Feinstein, 1986; Schembechler and Albom, 1989) reveal how these naturally-occurring group processes are used to mold teams.

Some group scholars believe that an important reason for joining groups is to search for people with similar values, opinions, or abilities, against whom one might compare oneself. Most theories about group process see movement toward agreement and uniformity as positive outcomes. Irving Janis (1983) instead warned about the dangers of *groupthink,* a decision-making process that can lead to high group satisfaction but unsatisfactory solutions. Because of escalating pressures to reach a decision and natural pressures to be cohesive and to conform to group norms, a variety of negative results might occur. The number of alternatives considered by the group might be limited. Although each position is scrutinized, once a position is a clear favorite it is never reanalyzed for less obvious flaws. Alternatives that the majority of members originally discount are not examined. Opinions from outside the group are not sought. Because some alternatives are favored and others are not, the process of gathering and considering information is highly selective. Group members develop illusions of invulnerability and unanimity. Finally, there is even greater pressure on dissidents to conform to group opinions (Littlejohn, 1989).

Many theories about group functioning assume a finite life for each small group. However, there are many examples of small groups that operate for years, focusing on a variety of tasks and problems. For example, in many communities the recreation department is staffed by the same people for many years. Scott Poole's parallel activity model (Poole, 1983; Poole, Seibold, and McPhee, 1985) recognized the long-term nature of many groups. Poole noted that *group process* is really a number of parallel, simultaneous processes. There are **task process activities,** such as member orientation or establishment of guidelines for problem definition or problem solution. In the case of community recreation departments, new staff members or volunteers may join, new state guidelines must be considered, or perhaps decisions must be made about beginning community coeducational teams at younger ages.

There are also **relational activities**—interactions between members may be ambiguous or focused; positions may be criticized or praised. Perhaps the director and assistant director have never agreed on anything, or perhaps a new member is too shy to speak up or to confront the others. There are also **topical activities** that occur during group interactions—topic A (or solution A) might be discussed for a while, then topics B and C, then topic A again.* Poole's approach to group process argues that conflict or resolution may be occurring on one dimension, but not on the others. Development and unification therefore proceed haltingly and sometimes not at all. Showing the need to pay attention to communication on all three levels is a major contribution of Poole's approach.

CONCEPT CHECK

Communication is central to successful group activity. Network analysis is used to describe group communication patterns. Groups may be categorized according to the distance between members or the number of links necessary for a message to be transmitted by one member and received by another. Groups may also be categorized by their centrality, or the extent to which some members need fewer links than others to communicate with all members. Group communication takes place at the task level and at the socio-emotional or relational level. Group functioning and communication patterns change as members adjust and perhaps assume different roles. Attention to facilitating communication at all levels usually distinguishes good group communication from bad.

Theoretical foundations of organizational communication

For sport management, organizational theory is especially important. Much of what we do—both at work and at play—takes place in organizational contexts. Athletic administrators, facility managers, coaches and athletes, health club owners, journalists, and broadcasters all operate in organizations.

---

*Littlejohn (1989) attributed this erratic focus to the intense nature of group interaction that requires intermittent breaks from task work.

Communication serves several functions in organizations. First, it is used to exchange ideas and information. Second, communication makes it possible to persuade others, to get them to adopt ideas or attitudes. Third, it is through communication that evaluation occurs; feedback about expectations and performance occurs through written and oral communication. Finally, communication is central to the decision-making process. The more responsibility one has in an organization, the greater percentage of one's time is spent communicating (Andrews and Baird, 1989). It is impossible to imagine organizations functioning without communication. The role of theory, and of theory-based research, is to describe the conditions under which communication is encouraged and successfully implemented in organizations.

What sets an organization apart from other social groups? Foremost is the stable and hierarchical structure, which results in a variety of separate and discrete functions for organizational units and members. For the most part these units and individuals act in cooperative relationships toward some common and collective goals. Usually, organizational size also prohibits close personal relationships among all members, although some strong relationships often develop among smaller groups within the organization.

Because of their size, hierarchical structure, and need to achieve common goals, organizations need effective communication to function properly. Communication in organizations occurs in a **downward** fashion—from management to employees. For example, a manager of a sporting goods company might decree that the company's products will no longer be sold through university bookstores. Through downward communication, management implements new policies, clarifies objectives of the organization, seeks to persuade or inform employees, or tries to clear up misunderstandings. However, predominantly downward communication, and its one-way route, may spell trouble for organizational effectiveness.

Communication also occurs in an **upward** fashion—employees communicate to management. Members of the sporting goods sales force may question management's decision or seek a fuller explanation, especially if they were not consulted. Through upward communication, employees inform management about an ineffective policy or a grievance, or simply let management know about their beliefs and opinions.

Distortions may occur in both downward and upward communications. Management and employees may withhold, screen, or manipulate information for various purposes. Managers distort to maintain power and authority; employees distort when complete disclosure would threaten their position or goal attainment. This is more likely to occur in an organization that maintains an arbitrary and inflexible authority structure (Lewis, 1987).

Communication within the organization occurs in a horizontal fashion—when employees consult or argue with one another, or simply talk with each other during a coffee break. Two other types of organization-related communication also occur. These are outward communication and inward communication.* **Outward** communication occurs when the organization communicates to those outside, such as its clients. For example, a health club mails a monthly newsletter to its members, perhaps listing upcoming events or highlighting a member-of-the-month. **Inward** communication occurs when those outside the organization communicate to it. For example, health club members request an early-morning aerobics class or a once-a-week nutrition lecture; of course, complaints about increases in monthly fees also qualify as inward communication. Organizational theories have emerged that propose ways of fostering these types of communication.

There are three general classes of organizational theories, but not all three attach equal importance to communication. Classical theories focus on organizational structure. These theories view most organizational members within the confines of a bureaucratic hierarchy and ask, given this hierarchy, how work is divided, how many levels of authority and control exist, what specific jobs are performed at each level, and so on. Communication questions per se are seldom examined using classical theories.

Human relations theories focus on organizational structures and functions in the context of their effects on the attitudes, values, and need sat-

---

*In both collegiate and professional sports, outward and inward communications are the province of the sports information or public relations departments. Their roles will be discussed in Chapter 16.

isfaction of organization members. These theories examine issues such as assumption of roles, status relationships, and employee attitudes and morale (Littlejohn, 1989).

The prototypical theory in this approach is that of Rensis Likert (1967), who was interested in classifying organizations in terms of their productivity and achievement as well as their "internal states," such as employee satisfaction. He outlined four systems. System 1, *exploitative–authoritative*, is characterized by rule-by-authority. Organizational goals supersede individual goals, and decisions are centralized at the top. Communication in this type of structure is top-down, which leads to decisions based on incomplete information, as well as a general atmosphere of distrust. System 2 is *benevolent–authoritative*. It is characterized by a somewhat more diffuse decision-making structure and by management that is more sensitive to employee needs. Communication patterns flow from the bottom up, as well as from the top down. However, considerable filtering of the communication still occurs, and decision making remains at the top.

Likert's System 3 is *consultative.* Although final decisions are still made by upper management, this organization is characterized by a high level of interaction and consultation between management and employees, and therefore by frequent communication. Not only are decisions in such a system based on more and better information, but the atmosphere is characterized by trust and cohesiveness—and therefore—employee and employer satisfaction. Likert's System 4 is termed *participative.* Communication flows from the top down, from the bottom up, and from position to position across the organization. Goal setting and decision making in such organizations are participatory, and of course the atmosphere is positive. Likert said that productivity was highest in a participative organization.

There are also social systems theories that guide the study of organizations. Because these systems theories tend to focus on processes—decision making, problem solving—communication is central in theory development. Systems theories emphasize that each part of an organization is important but depends on the healthy functioning of the other parts (this approach is owed to similar theories in biology, economics, and sociology). Therefore special attention is paid to the processes that facilitate interdependent relations between key organizational parts. Communication plays a central role by facilitating this interdependence.

The seminal work in the systems theory approach was that of Katz and Kahn (1978). They proposed that organizations are social in nature—small societies. One must analyze the social processes that contribute to organizational stability, change, and goal attainment: rule enforcement, role behavior, norms, and value imposition. Analysis of communication was not central to their models, however.

A more recent systems approach that centers on communication is the structural–functional orientation of Farace, Monge, and Russell (1977). This approach asserts that information is among the most important organizational resources. It seeks to determine what information is known, who knows it, and especially, what the patterns of information diffusion are. Three dimensions are important: the *level* of the system (individual, dyad, group, or organization), the *function* of communication at any particular level (for producing and coordinating activity, for innovation and change, or for maintaining values and interpersonal relationships), and *structure* (communication structure, power structure, or leadership structure).

Questions of power and leadership structure deal with patterns of hierarchy and the ways that various group roles are distributed. Who in the local department of education is responsible for upkeep of the athletic fields? To whom does he or she report? What is the chain of command or responsibility for action?

Questions of communication structure deal with patterns of interactions within groups (the micronetwork) but especially between groups. Does the president of the sport marketing firm consult equally with the heads of each division, or is the head of the celebrity-endorsement division heard most often? Is there smooth communication between the divisions? Do people in the celebrity-endorsement division communicate with those in the corporate sponsorship division? Recall Fisher's models of within-group communication patterns. Farace, Monge, and Russell (1977) asserted that there are characteristic patterns of communication between groups as well. This between-group information transmission—the **macronetwork**—is a key to understanding organizational communica-

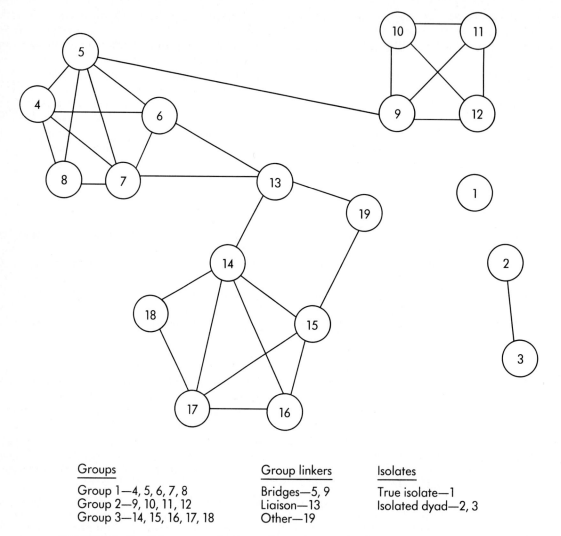

Groups

Group 1—4, 5, 6, 7, 8
Group 2—9, 10, 11, 12
Group 3—14, 15, 16, 17, 18

Group linkers

Bridges—5, 9
Liaison—13
Other—19

Isolates

True isolate—1
Isolated dyad—2, 3

FIGURE 8-3 Possible communication patterns in organizations.
(From Farace, R., Monge, P., and Russell, H. [1977]. *Communicating and organizing.* New York:
McGraw-Hill Book Co.)

tion. A sample macronetwork is illustrated in Figure 8-3.

For example, an organization might actually consist of three smaller groups of four, five, and seven members each (see Figure 8-3); one person who is isolated from all groups; and two persons in an isolated dyad. Persons in the isolated dyad do not communicate with the other groups nor with the isolate, who similarly does not commu-

nicate with the others. One person in one group (5) communicates with one person in another (9); they are **bridges.** Further, one person in one group (13) communicates with two persons in others (6,7); he is a **liaison.** There are no direct communications between two of the groups. Bridges and liaisons may function either to improve communication in organizations or to impede the sharing of information.

Clearly this communication structure is more useful in understanding an organization and its functioning than is a simple supervisory structure. By identifying bridges and liaisons, management may simplify information transmission within the organization. Further, management may wish to explore ways of creating new bridges and liaisons between groups to improve communication within the organization. Certainly, to the extent that many problems in organizational functioning may be traced to improper communication, a framework for studying communication processes is quite valuable. Monge (1987) has provided a good summary of the various approaches to communication network analysis.

Important foundations in interpersonal communication have been reviewed. In Chapter 16 some of these principles will be applied to sport management. This discussion now turns to theoretical foundations in mass communication.

CONCEPT CHECK

Because of size, hierarchical structure, and emphasis on goal achievement, sound organizational functioning depends on good communication. Downward organizational communication occurs when management communicates to employees. Upward communication occurs when employees communicate to management. Outward communication—or organizations communicating to clients—and inward communication—or clients communicating to organizations—also occur. Of Likert's four systems (exploitative–authoritative, benevolent–authoritative, consultative, and participative), unrestricted communication takes place only in the participative organization. It is also the one that has highest productivity. Patterns of organizational communication may best be understood by analyzing communication macronetworks and identifying intraorganizational groups, isolates, bridges, and liaisons.

THEORETICAL FOUNDATIONS OF MASS COMMUNICATION AND MASS MEDIA INDUSTRIES

Although professional training in print journalism or in the operation of radio and television stations is a major part of mass communications, the education includes very little theory or research in the social-scientific sense. Theory from related social sciences, such as sociology and economics, has illuminated the study of large mass media organizations (such as newspapers, commercial television networks, or major advertising firms), or the interaction of these organizations and other social institutions (such as the Federal Communications Commission or Congress). Psychological theories, especially social learning and cognitive theories, have contributed to the study of how media affect "consumers" (such as newspapers' effects on political knowledge, television's effects on children's behavior, or the persuasive effect of advertising).

Studying mass media organizations

Structural functional theory (DeFleur and Ball-Rokeach, 1982) has explored how organizational structure (size, activity patterns, manager–subordinate relationships, communication flow) and function (goals, norms, rules) combine to affect behaviors such as gatekeeping and agenda setting in media organizations. Structural functional theory has identified several functions that mass media serve for modern society. In the context of sport management, this section will focus primarily on the entertainment function of mass media, but media serve other important social functions. They contribute to the formation of public opinion by helping to identify and analyze key issues, and by providing a forum in which the public can debate these issues. The media allow members of society to keep informed on events that are both important (such as governmental actions) and relatively unimportant (such as the winner of the Michigan–Notre Dame football game). This has been termed a *surveillance* function. To the extent that the media focus only on selected items, they also "set the agenda"—contributing substantially to what people think about and discuss. Mass media also help to transmit our social heritage, allowing for the passing of knowledge and values from generation to generation. Finally, as used in our society, mass media serve important functions for our economic system by both providing an avenue for advertisers to reach large numbers of people and creating similar tastes and product desires in segments of the population.

Mass media have effects on other large social institutions even as they perform their other functions. Some of these effects may be traced to the media's ability to focus attention on issues, events, and people, making some seem important and others less so. For example, by making "superstars" out of a few professional athletes, the media themselves have contributed to skyrocketing salaries among professionals. Subsequently, so that owners may pay these salaries, owners have increased event ticket prices (affecting sport consumers) and have greatly increased the broadcast rights fees paid by local and network broadcasters. As a result, income from the media has surpassed income from ticket sales. Lately sports have changed in a variety of ways to make them more attractive to television: television timeouts, 2-minute warnings, tie-breaks and yellow balls in tennis, tournament play in golf, the NBA's 24-second clock, and playoff and World Series baseball games held during evening prime-time viewing hours (Klatell and Marcus, 1988). Thus the mass media—and television in particular—have had important effects on sport institutions. This has happened without mass media expressly setting out to affect sports, although certainly a number of major sports would disappear without media interest and support.

Some theory in the study of mass media organizations also outlines ways in which the media organizations regulate and constrain behavior of people in their organizations, and the effect of this constraint on media performance (see review by Ettema, Whitney, and Wackman, 1987). For example, news media organizations use certain processes that determine what is selected as important and what is ignored. Individuals in organizations function as *gatekeepers;* they control and select what information will be read, heard, or seen. That is, not every piece of news is published or broadcast. In broadcasting, many ideas for programs that might be interesting or informative are never selected. Decisions about which stories should be written, which idea is promising, or which collegiate basketball game will be showcased are continually made by those at one end of the mass communication processs. The decision chain involves reporters, editors, and publishers in print media, and reporters, writers, editors, directors, producers, programmers, advertisers, and executives in broadcast media. Information is managed and controlled within the communication industries by a hierarchy of gatekeepers.

Studying mass media effects

Theories about the effects of mass media focus on intended functions, as well as some unintended effects of the media. Theories of persuasion examine characteristics of messages and communicators that most effectively change attitudes and behaviors (see Miller and Burgoon, 1978 and Smith, 1982 for reviews of persuasion literature). These theories are especially important to media advertisers, who spend millions of dollars to create ads that affect only a small percentage of persons who see or hear them.

Other theories focus on the way by which mass media is used to "construct" social realities. How are people socialized into work roles? Into relationships with others? Into patterns of consumption? How do media presentations affect what people believe about themselves and others? Advances in cognitive psychology and social cognition (Fiske and Taylor, 1984; Sypher and Applegate, 1984) have been applied to the way communication affects humans' cognitive schemata, that is, knowledge, expectations, and attitudes. The most interesting aspect of communicated reality is its ability to replace direct experience, yet have almost the same effect. For example, it is known what the surface of the moon and the depths of the ocean look like, even though the vast majority of people have never actually been to either place. Similarly, television viewers see the same extraordinary plays in the World Series as do the people who are sitting in the stands. Media realities often replace experiences.

Behavioral theories focus on the relationship between mass media presentations and individual behavior. Much of this focus has been on negative effects of media—television's effects on antisocial behavior, for example. Social learning theory (Bandura, 1977) has guided effects research. Social learning theory assumes that media give people models for behaviors. Individuals are most likely to attend to and learn from models with certain desirable characteristics (power, status, attractiveness, nurturance). Individuals will reproduce these behaviors, provided they are not physically difficult or impossible, if given the motivation, opportunity, and reward. This theory is useful, for example, in examining the process by which children choose athletes as role models and learn from their behavior. Although this theory is tailored to the processes by which younger viewers learn from media, it does have implications for adult learning as well.

This discussion now turns to an examination and analysis of some important principles in mass media industries.

CONCEPT CHECK

Theories about the mass media deal with the structure and function of media industries and with media effects. Organizational theories have identified various social functions that media serve: to entertain, to form public opinion, to provide surveillance, to set agendas, to transmit a heritage, to play an economic role, and to provide popular culture. Effects theories have examined both intended and unintended media effects. Media portrayals affect both the construction of social reality, which often substitutes for direct experience, and the modeling of media behavior by print and electronic media consumers.

THE PRINT MEDIA: NEWSPAPERS AND MAGAZINES

As leisure pursuits have become increasingly important to postindustrial society, so has the amount of space that newspapers devote to sport and leisure increased. Significant coverage of sport began in U.S. papers around 1830, as industry's adoption of mechanical power shortened the work week and increased leisure time (McChesney, 1989; Stevens, 1987). At the same time more Americans were learning to read. Eventually most daily newspapers created separate sport sections to cover leisure pursuits. Now, reporters are assigned to the sport beat in the same way assignments are made to other beats. As an index of interest, consider that *The National*, a daily newspaper devoted solely to sport, began publication in January of 1990.

Almost all adults read a daily newspaper. About 6 billion consumer magazines are sold annually in the United States; most adults (90%) read about seven magazines per month (Gropp, 1987). Publishers do not want to put out periodicals that will be hoarded. They want their newspapers and magazines to be passed from reader to reader, thus increasing total readership. On average, about four people read each magazine (Gropp, 1987); five or six is a desirable target. Because magazines that are received by health-and fitness-related organizations, such as clubs, community recreation programs, arenas and stadiums, and industrial or corporate sport and fitness programs, obtain higher reader-per-copy numbers, they provide excellent outlets for advertisers for whom mass appeal periodicals would be poor investments.

Daily newspapers and weekly and monthly magazines have **mass** or **specialized** appeal. Mass appeal periodicals include *Time, Newsweek, People, USA Today*, the *Los Angeles Times*, the *Washington Post*, and *Sports Illustrated*. Specialized periodicals are aimed at a fairly narrow group of readers, defined either demographically, professionally, or by leisure pursuits. An index covering international newspapers and magazines devotes 60 pages, with about 50 entries per page, to sport-related periodicals. Most entries are highly specialized (*Hog Call Fanletter*: circulation 510; *Australian Table Tennis*: 3,000; *Sumo World*: 5,000), but a few are widely circulated (*Sporting News*: 725,000; *Sports Illustrated*: 2.9 million). There are also a number of specialized monthly or weekly trade publications devoted to sport management areas, especially health and fitness. The box below provides a list of just a few of these.

Selected mass appeal and specialized sport management magazines*

Athletic Administration (3,800)
Athletic Business (45,000)
Business and Health (8,500)
Club Industry (30,000)
Fitness Industry Magazine (24,000)
Fitness Management (21,000)
Health World (50,000)
Management Review (90,000)
Sport (931,517)
Sport Inc. (2,500)†
Sports Business (9,700)
Sports Illustrated (2,875,000)
The Sporting News (725,000)
Total Health (77,000)
Triathlete (105,000)
Women's Sports and Fitness (300,000)

*Circulation figures from *Ulrich's International Periodicals Index 1988-1989* in parentheses after magazine title.
†Ceased publication in early 1989.

Specialized publications have a major advantage over mass appeal periodicals in that they can present material for a narrow audience. A reader profile for a specialized magazine or newspaper is based not only on demographics, but on lifestyle information as well (leisure activities, interests, or social attitudes).

A very specialized category of trade periodicals is academic research journals. Several academic journals publish useful findings and interpretations of research in the sport, health, and fitness areas. Academic and research journals reach an audience composed mostly of college and university researchers, although others active in scientific applications, such as science writers or sport psychologists, also read them. Circulation is generally smaller for these publications than for other specialized magazines. A few are listed in the box below.

Economic basis: readership and ad revenue

Accurate circulation figures—how many people read the periodical—are very important because advertising accounts for close to 75% of newspaper and magazine revenue. Potential advertisers need access to recent circulation figures when choosing the best periodical for ads. *Gale Directory of Publications* provides up-to-date circulation figures and detailed advertising costs (such as per line or per

page) for major magazines and periodicals. *Ulrich's International Periodicals Directory* provides circulation figures for newspapers and some magazines as well. Figures are based on multiple sources, including the publishers themselves, the Chicago-based Audit Bureau of Circulation (ABC), and the U.S. Postal Service. Sample entries from *Ulrich's* and *Gale* are presented in Figure 8-4.

Many newspapers and magazines also collect demographic information about their readership or commission researchers to collect it for them. Data on the sex, educational level, and household income of the "average" reader enables advertisers to better target potential consumers. This data, along with detailed reader characteristic information, is available from specialized services such as the New York-based Simmons Market Research Bureau.

Advertising rates are determined primarily by a publication's overall number of readers, but the purchasing power of this group and the type of products advertised also influence rates. In fact, subscription figures are often supplemented by reader-per-copy figures when advertising rates are determined. Such a move has helped the print media hold its own in its competition for advertisers with radio, television, and direct mail. Both newspapers and magazines are read by "upscale" adults—better educated, professional, aged 18 to 49 (magazines only), and more affluent. Both newspaper and magazine audiences may be targeted by market, advertisement size, and cost. Both are associated with and read for information on consumer products and services. This is particularly true for magazines—people who are heavy magazine readers own twice as many appliances as light magazine readers (Gropp, 1987).

Most newspapers and some magazines have two rate structures, one for local businesses and one for national advertisers.* Most will also discount for volume business over a particular span of time (such as 6 months or a year). Of course the size of an ad affects cost, with larger and full-page ads costing considerably more. The wisdom of paying for full-page ads has been challenged by a number of readership studies that demonstrate that full-

---

Selected research journals relevant to sport management*

American Demographics (30,000)
American Journal of Public Health (35,000)
Health Education (10,000)
Journal of Physical Education, Recreation, and Dance (40,000)
Journal of Sport Behavior (240)
Journal of Sport Management (Not available)
Journal of Sport and Exercise Psychology (1,600)
New England Journal of Medicine (226,000)
Research Quarterly for Exercise and Sport (11,000)
The Sport Psychologist (Not available)

*Circulation figures from *Ulrich's International Periodicals Index 1988-1989* in parentheses after journal title.

---

*Major national magazines have regional editions that allow local or regional advertising on certain pages.

796   US   ISSN 0038-805X
SPORTING NEWS: the nation's oldest and finest sports
    publication. 1886. w $59.95 Sporting News Publishing
    Co. (Subsidiary of: Times Mirror Company) 1212 N.
    Lindbergh Blvd. Box 56, St. Louis, MO 63132 Tel
    314-997-7111. Ed. Tom Barnidge. adv. bk. rev. illus.
    stat. circ. 725,000. (tabloid format: also avail. in
    microfilm (from UM): reprint service avail. from UMI)
    Indexed: Access. Mag. Ind. Sports Per.Ind.
    Sportsearch.

11593   THE SPORTING NEWS
1212 N. Lindbergh Blvd.
St. Louis, MO 63132
Sports news tabloid: **Estab.:** March 17, 1886. **Frequency:** Weekly. **Printing
Method:** Offset. **Trim Size:** 11 1/2 x 14. **No. of Cols. Per Page: 5. Col. Width: 23 nonpareils. Col.
Depth: 185 agate lines. Contacts: Tom Barnidge, Editor; Richard Waters, Publisher; Arnie Green,
Advertising Manager. ISSN: 0038-805X.**
Subscription: $59.95 $2.25 per issue.
Ad Rate: BW: $14,080.00   **Circulation:** *725,000
             4C: $17,730.00
The Sporting News is a wholly-owned subsidiary of Times Mirror.

FIGURE 8-4   Sample entries from Ulrich's International Periodicals Directory 1988-1989,
and Gale Directory of Publications, 1989.

page ads attract only a few more (10% to 15%) readers than do smaller ads (Bergendorff, Smith, and Webster, 1983). Ad buyers seek to place their ads near a section of the periodical that their targeted audience is likely to read.

Certainly the newspaper and magazine industries are important to sport management. Specialized publications enable managers to keep up with the latest ideas and practices in their fields. In addition, the success and development of competitive sport and sport teams has often been linked to coverage in the American press. Indeed, until *New York Clipper* sportswriter Henry Chadwick published his guidelines for baseball following the Civil War, there was considerable disagreement over the rules of baseball, including the dimensions of the field and the number of participants (Stevens, 1987). Newspapers and magazines seek to stimulate interest in community, local collegiate, or professional sports teams, and to help fans identify with the teams.

Early in this century, however, radio began to compete with print media to be the primary source of information about competitive sport, and in the last several decades, television has become of paramount importance to sport. It has contributed to a "sport explosion" at the professional and collegiate levels, increased interest in many minor sports, and heightened the awareness of the average sport consumer. This discussion now turns to the electronic media.

CONCEPT CHECK

Print media may be categorized as mass appeal or specialized appeal. Specialized publications present material for a narrowly targeted audience. Targeting is based on certain demographic variables (such as age and sex) and on related interests and professional or leisure pursuits. This information is used in deciding the content of the newspaper or magazine and in attracting advertisers. Advertising usually accounts for 75% of print media income, with subscriptions and sales accounting for the remainder.

THE ELECTRONIC MEDIA

Most people tend to think of electronic media as being national. The big television networks (American Broadcasting Company, Columbia Broadcasting System, National Broadcasting Company) are especially well known. But the legal philosophy that guides regulation of broadcasters focuses instead on the important role played by the local broadcaster—to serve the public by providing important news and information, by keeping the people in touch with their government, and by providing an arena where important issues may be discussed and debated. The entertainment function has not been viewed as a responsibility, but rather has emerged as a strategy for economic competition.

Commercial broadcasters

Because they use the public airwaves, commercial radio and television stations are required to compensate the public for use of this resource. Stations are granted *free and exclusive use* of a particular broadcast frequency for a fixed time, currently 7 years for radio and 5 for television. In return a broadcaster is required to serve in the "**public interest,** convenience, and necessity." The meaning of serving in the public interest changes with the regulatory philosophies of Congresses, presidential administrations, and the Federal Communications Commission (FCC), the governmental agency charged with broadcast oversight.

Providing information during emergencies (such as a flood or tornado), broadcasting news, and serving as a forum for the discussion and analysis of important issues are all seen as public interest services. In 1946 and again in 1961 the FCC tried to specify guidelines for broadcasters to use to fulfill their public interest obligation. In fact, the 1961 policy statement listed 14 types of programming usually necessary for television stations to

meet the public interest; sports programs were one of these requirements.*

Over the past dozen or so years, radio and television broadcasters have been **deregulated.** That is, a number of longstanding rules, regulations, and assumptions about broadcaster service were discarded by the FCC during the 1970s and 1980s. Broadcaster service prompted by regulation was replaced by broadcaster service stimulated by competition in the marketplace (Fowler and Brenner, 1987). Under this philosophy the public, through its listening and viewing decisions, decides what is or is not serving its best interests. By listening or not listening, watching or not watching, the public is assumed to define its interest. The modern FCC sees its role as encouraging healthy competition between broadcasters. As will be seen, several of these deregulatory moves had major effects on viewers' access to televised sport content.

Radio. Radio became an important and indispensable mass medium during the 1920s. In contrast to print, radio could deliver news and entertainment programming, including sports, instantly, and its popularity grew rapidly. Its growth was accelerated by the formation of three national radio networks that provided programming for affiliated stations: NBC Red, NBC Blue, and CBS.[†] From newspapers, the fledgling radio industry adopted a business-oriented, advertiser-supported philosophy.

With the growth of television during the middle part of this century, network-originated and national radio programming declined. Radio became

---

*Indeed, members of Congress have been particularly interested in making sure that American television viewers have adequate sport content available through commercial broadcasting. A number of hearings addressing this were held during the 1950s and 1960s, a time when it seemed as if pay and pay-per-view television might "siphon" most of the sports programming from the commercial broadcasters. Congress firmly expressed its view that sport content should always be available to viewers of "free" commercial television. Recent developments might threaten this free sport programming, and Congress has renewed its concern—a Senate hearing on "siphoning" was held in early 1990.
†RCA created and owned both NBC networks. In 1943 the FCC forced RCA to give up one of its networks. NBC Blue was bought and became ABC. For an excellent discussion of the history of radio and television, see Erik Barnouw's *Tube of Plenty* (New York: Oxford University Press, 1977).

a local medium. There are now many more radio stations that are independent—not affiliated with any programming network—than network affiliated. This has increased radio's attention to local news, public affairs, and sports coverage. It has also helped radio retain its importance as a medium for local advertising.

Commercial television OAOs and affiliates. Commercial television stations are usually one of three types: network owned and operated **(OAO)**, network **affiliate,** and **independent.** OAOs are stations, generally in the larger markets such as New York and Los Angeles, that are owned by a major network. An organization may own up to 12 stations provided that the combined audience reached by these stations is less than 25% of the nation's viewers. Network affiliates are not owned by the networks—they are often owned by local investors—but have chosen to affiliate with one of the commercial networks.

Both OAOs and affiliates have access to a network's programs (such as news, prime-time shows, and sports) and are compensated by the network for carrying its programs. The more affiliates a network has, the larger its potential audience, and therefore the more it may charge for advertising time during its programs. Although the numbers fluctuate somewhat, each network has about 200 affiliates (*Broadcasting/Cablecasting Yearbook,* 1988). There are about 480 stations that are either independent or affiliated with a smaller network (such as Fox Broadcasting).

Commercial independent television stations and superstations. Television stations that are not owned by or affiliated with a network are independent. Their programming generally comes from their own productions, those of private production companies, older films, or syndicated offerings. Syndicated programs include reruns of programs initially aired on the networks (such as the Cosby Show) or first-run game or talk shows (such as *Wheel of Fortune, Oprah Winfrey,* or *Entertainment Tonight*). Syndicated sports offerings include Super Sports Follies, This Week in Sports, Wrestling Network, and World Wrestling Federation.

Several well-known independents are also **superstations** (WWOR, New York; WTBS, Atlanta; and WGN, Chicago). A superstation is a commercial station, usually an independent, whose signal is picked up by a common carrier company* and retransmitted by microwave to a satellite, which makes it available to cable systems around the country. The stations receive no compensation from the cable systems, but the common carrier does. Sports, especially baseball and basketball, have been a common offering of the national superstations.

There are risks and benefits associated with being a superstation. Because it is transmitted nationally, the station may charge advertisers more than what is paid to reach a local audience. However, with penetration of distant markets comes the potential for increased licensing costs. Corporations that hold the rights to the movies or syndicated series that the station carries may want more money for those rights. Sport teams whose games are carried nationally may justifiably want more for broadcast rights than they would if the station's signal were transmitted only locally.

Commercial broadcasting programming considerations. Milton Berle has been credited with saying that television is called a medium because nothing on it is ever well done. Certainly with a mass medium, the common strategy is to program to the widest possible audience. This philosophy governs decisions at both the network and local affiliate levels. A station programmer must consider many factors. What kind of station is it? Network affiliates and OAOs have access to network programs, but independent stations must buy or produce all their own programs. Which costs more: buying syndicated shows or producing your own? What shows are currently available through syndication? Who is the audience at various times of the day? Will enough advertisers sign on as sponsors to cover the costs? What is the competition showing—will we be able to pull in more viewers than other stations? Eastman, Head, and Klein (1985) have provided an excellent and detailed analysis of the different programming strategies for each type of broadcaster (and cablecaster).

---

*Communication law distinguishes a common carrier, which is a delivery medium only (such as telephone, telegraph, or satellites), from a mass medium (such as radio or television), which creates and delivers messages. In at least one superstation the common carrier company and the station are owned by the same entity (Ted Turner's Southern Satellite Systems and TBS).

Cable

Because cablecasters do not use the public airwaves but rather send signals through wires, cable channels are not obligated to serve in the public interest. Different standards apply in a variety of areas (such as obscenity or program requirements). In contrast to broadcasters, cable channels are *narrowcasters*. They provide heterogeneous programming that appeals to a narrow segment of the viewing audience. There are channels devoted to children's fare, news, and music, and several are devoted partially or fully to sport. Local cable systems (there are currently about 9,500; *Broadcasting*, Feb. 26, 1990) typically offer **basic tier** channels, **premium** channels, and **pay-per-view** (PPV) channels. The basic tier includes the major commerical network and independent stations, local public broadcast stations, and some cable channels (such as CNN and MTV). Premium channels (such as Disney, HBO, and Showtime) carry an additional monthly fee, usually around $10 to $20. Pay-per-view channels carry a fee, from $15 to $35, each time a PPV program is selected.

National and regional cable networks. Cable networks are sources of programming for local cable systems. A cable network transmits its signal through a communication satellite. Cable systems have the option of receiving this signal and dedicating one of their system channels to it. If a system chooses to carry a cable network, it then pays a fee to the network based on its number of subscribers. Some networks are offered on a national basis (such as MTV, Nickelodeon, HBO, Disney, and ESPN), and others, because their appeal is to a specific geographical area, are offered on a regional basis. Most of the content of regional cable channels is sport related.

National cable networks are a rather recent phenomenon. They became possible when restrictions on cable telecasting were eased during the mid-1970s. For example, 1972 FCC rules limited the number of distant signals that cable systems could import and air. These rules also limited the distance over which cable companies could import independent stations' (that is, superstations') signals. The goal of most of these rules was to shield local broadcasters from cable competition. In early 1976 the commission dropped its distance requirements, allowing reception of satellite-transmitted signals

from anywhere. In 1980 the FCC revoked its limit on how many distant signals could be imported. A cable system now may program any number of cable channels for its customers, limited only by how many channels its wiring can deliver to customers. Around that time the FCC also reduced the minimum size requirements for satellite reception dishes. Until late 1976 the requirements were so strict that each dish cost about $100,000.

Pay-per-view. A pay-per-view cable channel is a channel dedicated to delivery of a few special programs. Recipients may view a program on this channel only by specifically requesting it and by paying a fee for the program. The advent of addressable cable technology—enabling a cable system to send programming to selected homes—has accelerated the development of pay-per-view channels, but pay cable penetration is still relatively low, available in less than 30% of television households.

CONCEPT CHECK

As are the print media, organizations in the electronic media are profit-oriented ventures. Because they use the public airwaves, however, commercial radio and television stations are mandated to serve in the public interest. Providing sport programming has been one requirement of television broadcasters. Radio stations are primarily locally owned and programmed. Some commercial television stations are also independent, but most are either owned by or affiliated with a network. Superstations are independent stations whose signal is also transmitted to satellites and subsequently received and carried by local cable franchises. Over the past 15 years, cable has become a significant competitor to commercial television. Some cable networks transmit nationally, others regionally. Cable franchises carry these signals on the basic tier, premium tier, or pay-per-view basis.

Economic basis of broadcasting and cable: advertising and audiences

Broadcasters and cablecasters are in the audience delivery business. They promise advertisers that they will deliver a certain kind of audience (such as females over 18 or males 25 to 34) to the advertiser through their programming. They then charge the advertisers a rate based on the number of people they deliver. An advertiser prefers to pay for a group of homogeneous people (that is, people who will be most interested in their product) than an equal number of heterogeneous ones. Sport programs are coveted by television executives because of their ability to deliver a specific audience to advertisers.

Ratings. Audience information is based on viewership (or listenership) ratings, which are estimates of the size and type of audience based on a very small sample of the viewing population. Television ratings are provided by the A.C. Nielsen Co. and Arbitron, Inc.; radio ratings are provided by Arbitron and the Birch Co.

Television ratings are collected overnight or during one of the national "sweeps" periods. Nielsen **overnights** are collected daily from metered households in 23 markets,* and Arbitron overnights are collected from households in 14 of these markets. Overnights provide estimates of how many viewing households were tuned to particular programs in each market. They are used mostly by network programmers and ad departments to assess how well network programming compares with that of the competition, although local programmers may also use the findings.

Sweeps information is provided for commercial stations in about 210 or 212 markets, ranging from New York (the largest: 6.9 million television households) to Glendive, Montana (the smallest: 5,100 television households). The viewing figures are based on data collected several times a year from a combination of metered households and those maintaining television viewing diaries. Findings are reported for viewership among certain demographic groups (such as teens 12 to 17, women 18 to 24, or men 18 to 49), and are reported for each 15-minute block of daily programming. This information is used primarily to set advertising rates for the local stations, and to help local programmers schedule their programming day.

---

*The markets are New York, Los Angeles, Chicago, Philadelphia, San Francisco–Oakland, Washington, D.C., Detroit, Boston, Dallas–Fort Worth, Houston, Miami–Fort Lauderdale, Denver, Atlanta, St. Louis, Seattle–Tacoma, Phoenix, Hartford–New Haven, Indianapolis, Sacramento–Stockton, Cincinnati, Minneapolis–St. Paul, Tampa–St. Petersburg, Milwaukee, and Portland.

Ratings from a station's immediate broadcast area, called *area of dominant influence* (ADI) by Arbitron and *designated market area* (DMA) by Nielsen, are the most useful to local advertisers. Each county in the United States belongs to only one ADI/DMA. As noted, reporting of ADI/DMA information is by demographic category (such as women aged 18 to 34) and by "daypart" (such as Monday through Friday 7 to 9 AM, 9 AM to 4:30 PM, and 9 AM to noon) so that both advertisers and programmers may compare how well stations in a particular market attract viewers at all times of the day.

For television stations, early morning (7 to 9 AM), early fringe (4:30 to 6 PM), and prime-time (7:30 to 11 PM) daypart information is especially informative. Ratings services estimate the number of viewing households in each of the 210 to 212 markets. Then, based on viewing patterns from sample households in each of these markets, they collect and publish information on estimated program and station ratings and shares. Figure 8-5 presents sample pages from an Arbitron ratings book. Beville (1988) has written an excellent text on television and cable ratings.

Birch and Arbitron ratings information for radio listenership is quite similar to that provided during the television sweeps. Station-by-station listenership is reported by demographic category and by specific daypart. Ratings for morning and afternoon "drive time" (6 to 10 AM and 3 to 7 PM) are especially important to local station programmers and advertising staff.

Ratings methodology. There are four methods for collecting ratings information: telephone coincidentals, viewing diaries, audimeters, and people meters. Telephone coincidentals are calls made during a specified time asking which program is currently being viewed and by whom. They are used mostly by and for local stations.

Household viewing diaries were once the principal source of ratings information. Family members are given a small diary booklet that covers one week (Wednesday to Wednesday). Each family member writes down his or her viewing in 15-minute blocks. Therefore at the end of the week the diary will show what was viewed, as well as which family members were viewing at any particular time. The diary method has always had its meth-

Daypart Estimates

DAYPART AND STATION	ADI TV HH RTG	SHR	F89	N88	My88	Mr88	Metro RTG	SHR	2+	18+	12-24	12-34	18-34	21-49	25-49	25-54	W18+	W12-24	W18-34	W18-49	W21-49	W25-49	W25-54	WW	M18+	M18-34	M21-49	M25-49	M25-54	M	TN 12-17	C 2-11	C 6-11	METRO	HM ADI	ADJ#1	ADJ#2	ADJ#3	RTG#1	RTG#2	RTG#3
col	5	6	59	60	61	62	8	9	11	12	13	14	15	16	17	18	22	23	24	25	26	27	28	29	30	31	32	33	34	35	36	37	38	63	66	67	68	69	70	71	72
MON-FRI 8:00P-11:00P																																									
WCBS	9	15	16	14	16	18	9	15	6	7	4	4	5	5	5	6	7	4	5	6	6	6	6	6	4	5	5	5	5	4	2		3	82	98		1	1			1
WNBC	14	22	21	20	21	22	14	22	9	10	7	8	7	8	9	9	11	8	9	10	10	10	10	10	8	6	7	7	8	8	9	6	8	81	97	2	1		3		
WNYW	6	9	9	13	11	10	6	10	3	4	1	2	3	3	3	3	4	1	3	3	3	4	4	4	2	3	3	3	3	3	1	1	1	83	94	2	2		1		
WABC	15	23	22	22	20	21	15	23	9	9	9	10	9	10	10	10	11	11	11	11	11	11	11	10	8	7	8	9	9	8	12	7	9	83	98	2	1		1		
WWOR	4	7	5	6	8	6	4	7	2	2	2	2	2	2	2	2	3	1	1	2	2	2	2	2	3	2	2	2	2	2	1	2	2	76	87	2	4		1	1	
WPIX	4	6	9	9	9	7	4	7	2	2	2	2	2	2	2	2	2	2	2	2	2	2	2	1	3	2	2	2	2	2	1	1	1	81	90		2	1			3
WXTV	2	3	3	3	2	2	2	4	1	1	1	1	1	1	1	1	1	1	3	2	2	2	2	1	1	1	1	1	1	1				99	99						
WNJU	3	5	4	2	2	3	3	5	1	1		1	1	2	2	2	1		2	2	2	2	2	1	1	1	1	1	1	1				98	99						
WNET	3	4	5	4	4	5	3	5	2	2		1	1	1	1	1	2		1	1	1	1	1	2	2	1	1	1	1	1				85	97		2	1			
WLIW			1	1																														95	99						
WNYC																																		99	99						
VHBO	2	4	**	**	**	**	3	4	1	2	2	2	2	2	2	2	2	1	2	2	2	2	2	2	2	2	2	2	2	1	1			83	96		1	1			
H/P/T	64		67	65	61	60	63		42	46	32	37	37	40	42	43	49	35	41	44	45	46	47	45	42	32	37	38	39	40	36	24	29	83	96		1	1			
11:00P-11:30P																																									
WCBS	8	16	19	18	19	19	8	16	5	6	2	2	3	4	4	4	6	1	3	4	4	4	4	4	5	3	3	4	4	4	1	1	1	84	99		1	1			
WNBC	10	21	21	20	19	19	10	21	6	7	2	3	4	5	5	6	7	3	4	5	5	6	6	6	7	3	4	5	5	5	2	1	1	89	99		1	1			1
WNYW	5	10	9	9	12	11	5	10	2	3	1	2	3	3	3	3	3	1	3	3	3	3	3	3	3	3	3	3	3	3				85	97		1	1			1
WABC	10	20	19	21	20	21	10	21	5	7	3	5	6	6	6	7	7	4	7	7	8	8	8	7	6	5	5	5	6	6	2			86	98	1	1	1			1
WWOR	3	7	7	6	9	6	4	8	2	2	2	2	2	2	2	2	1	1	1	1	1	1	1	1	3	2	2	2	2	2	2			84	93	1	2	4			1
WPIX	5	10	11	10	7	6	5	11	3	3	4	4	4	4	4	4	3	3	3	3	4	4	4	3	3	4	4	4	4	4			1	76	88	2	3	3			
WXTV	1	2	2	2	2	1	1	3																										99	99						
WNJU	1	3	3	1	2	2	2	3			1	1	1								1	1	1				1	1	1					99	99						
WNET	1	2	2	2	3	3	1	2																										94	98			2			
WLIW																																		86	99						
WNYC																																		99	99						
VHBO	2	4	**	**	**	**	2	4	1	1	1	1	1	1	1	1	1		1	1	1	1	1	1	1	1	1	1	1	1				86	97		1	1			
H/P/T	47		51	48	47	44	48		28	34	18	23	26	30	31	33	34	16	27	31	32	33	33	30	33	26	29	30	31	32	14	3	4	86	97		1	1			
11:30P-12:30A																																									
WCBS	3	10	12	16	14	15	3	10	2	2	1	1	1	1	1	1	2	1	1	1	1	1	1	1	2	1	1	1	1	1				80	97	2	1				1
WNBC	6	19	19	18	18	16	6	19	3	4	1	2	3	3	3	4	4	1	3	3	4	4	4	3	3	3	3	3	3	3	1			86	98	2	1				1
WNYW	5	15	13	9	8	7	5	16	2	3	2	2	2	2	2	2	3	2	2	2	2	2	2	2	3	2	2	2	2	2	1			86	94	1	1				
WABC	5	15	16	17	17	18	5	15	2	3	1	2	3	3	3	3	3	1	2	3	3	3	3	3	3	2	2	2	3	1	1			84	98	1	1				4
WWOR	3	8	9	8	13	8	3	9	1	2	1	1	1	1	1	1	1		1	1	1	1	1	1	2	1	1	1	1	2				84	94						
WPIX	4	13	13	13	13	13	4	13	2	3	4	4	4	3	3	3	2	3	3	3	3	3	3	2	3	4	4	4	3	3	3	1	1	80	92	1	2	3	1	1	
WXTV	1	2	2	2	2			1	2																									99	99						
WNJU					2	1	1	2																										99	99						
WNET	1	3	3	3	3	3	1	3																										92	99			1			
WLIW																																		72	99						
* WNYC																																		99	99						
VHBO	2	5	**	**	**	**	2	6	1	1	1	1	1	1	1	1	1		1	1	1	1	1	1	1	1	1	1	1	1				85	96		1	1			
H/P/T	33		36	34	32	31	33		18	21	14	16	18	20	21	21	21	12	17	20	20	21	21	17	22	20	21	21	20	21	10	3	4	85	96		1	1			
11:30P-1:00A																																									
WCBS	3	10	11	16	14	15	3	10	1	2	1	1	1	1	1	1	2	1	1	1	1	1	1	1	1	1	1	1	1	1				81	97	2	1				
WNBC	5	18	18	17	17	15	5	18	3	3	1	2	3	3	3	4	4	1	3	3	3	3	3	3	3	3	3	3	3	3	1			84	97	2	1				1
WNYW	5	16	14	9	8	8	5	17	2	3	2	2	2	2	2	2	3	2	2	2	2	2	2	2	3	2	2	2	2	1	1			84	98	1	2				
WABC	4	14	15	17	16	18	4	14	2	2	1	1	2	2	2	2	3	1	2	2	2	2	2	2	2	2	2	2	2	1	1			86	95	1	1				3
WWOR	3	10	11	7	13	8	3	11	1	2	1	1	1	1	1	2	1		1	1	1	1	2	1	2	1	1	1	1	2	1			80	92	1	2	3			1
WPIX	4	13	13	13	13	13	4	13	2	2	3	3	3	3	3	3	2	2	2	3	3	3	3	2	3	4	4	4	3	3	3	1	2	80	92	1	2	3	1	1	
* WXTV	1	2	2	2	2			1	2																									99	99						
WNJU																																		99	99						
WNET	1	3	3	3	3	4	1	3																										93	99			1			
WLIW																																		75	99						
* WNYC																																		99	99						
VHBO	2	5	**	**	**	**	2	6	1	1	1	1	1	1	1	1		1	1	1		1	1	1	1	1	1							84	96		1	2			
H/P/T	30		32	31	29	28	30		16	19	13	15	17	18	18	18	19	11	16	18	19	18	18	16	19	19	19	19	19	19	9	3	4	84	96		1	2			
SATURDAY 8:00A-1:00P																																									
WCBS	3	12	11	12	12	13	3	12	2	1	1	1	1	1	1	1	1	1	1	1	1	1	1	1	1	1	1	1	1	1	2	8	9	77	96		3	1			1
WNBC	4	14	12	13	14	15	4	15	2	1	2	1	1	1	1	1	1	3	2	1	1	1	1	1	4	2	9	7	85	99								
WNYW	3	12	12	10	12	13	3	13	2	1	2	2	1	1	1	1	1	1	1	1	1	1	1	2	2	2	2	2	2	3	2	8	85	96		1	1			
WABC	5	17	18	16	14	12	5	18	3	1	3	2	2	2	1	1	1	3	2	2	2	2	2	2	1	1	1	1	1	4	12	9	85	98		1	1			
WWOR	2	7	7	10	11	10	2	7	1		1	1	1	1	1	1	1		1						1	1	1	1	1	4	2	2	64	83	1	2	3			
WPIX	3	12	12	12	11	11	4	14	2	2	3	2	2	2	2	2	2	3	2	2	2	2	2	2	1	1	1	1	1	4	4	3	82	90	1	2	4	1		
WXTV																																	99	99						
WNJU																																	99	99						
WNET	2	6	7	7	7	7	2	7	1	1				1	1										1	1	1	1	1	2			82	99		1	1			
WLIW																																	99	99						
WNYC											1	1						1												1			99	99						
VHBO	1	4	**	**	**	**	1	4																						1	1		82	95		1	1			
H/P/T	28		29	28	25	27	27		17	12	17	15	12	12	12	12	12	17	12	12	12	12	12	12	11	12	11	12	12	12	24	42	40	82	95		1	1			
col	5	6	59	60	61	62	8	9	11	12	13	14	15	16	17	18	22	23	24	25	26	27	28	29	30	31	32	33	34	35	36	37	38	63	66	67	68	69	70	71	72

* ESTIMATES EXCLUDE QTR-HRS STATION WAS NOT ON AIR
** SHARE/HUT TRENDS NOT AVAILABLE
+ COMBINED PARENT/SATELLITE

FIGURE 8-5 Sample pages from the Arbitron ratings book.

Time Period Estimates

	ADI RTG				PERSONS			WOMEN						MEN					TNS	CHILD			TIME			TSA IN 000's		
DAY AND TIME	TN	CHILD		TV																				ADI	MET				
				HH																			TV	TV	TV	WOM	MEN
STATION PROGRAM	12-17	2-11	6-11		18+	12-34	18+	18-34	18-49	25-49	25-54	WKG WOM	18+	18-34	18-49	25-49	25-54	12-17	2-11	6-11	HH RTG	HH RTG	HH	18+	18+			
	36	37	38	39	42	41	45	46	47	48	49	50	51	52	53	54	55	56	57	58	5	8	39	45	51			
RELATIVE STD-ERR 25% △ THRESHOLDS (1σ) 50%	7 2	7 1	9 2	109 27	101 25	103 25	79 19	77 19	75 19	69 17	70 17	73 18	76 19	86 21	76 19	70 17	71 17	119 30	150 38	128 33	2 –	2 –	109 27	79 19	76 19			

SUNDAY

NOON-12:30P

STATION	PROGRAM	TN 12-17	CH 2-11	CH 6-11	TVHH	P18+	P12-34	W18+	W18-34	W18-49	W25-49	W25-54	WKGWOM	M18+	M18-34	M18-49	M25-49	M25-54	TNS12-17	CH2-11	CH6-11	ADIrtg	METrtg	TVHH	WOM18+	MEN18+
WCBS	NCAA BSKTBLL	2			268	327	115	96	3	29	29	29	43	231	69	116	79	101	44	4						
	NBA BSKTBALL	1			180	189	79							189	62	87	87	106	17							
	NCAA PRE GME				157	179	72	21		21	21	21		158	72	119	97	97			6	6				
	NCAA PLAYOFF		1	1	243	275	119	34		19	19	19		240	119	193	151	151		13	13				
	CBS SPTS SUN		1		179	304	61	167	6	76	76	87	59	137	55	75	54	78		13					
	--4 WK AVG--	1			207	262	88	73	2	31	31	34	25	189	70	108	86	102	15	7	2	2	2	161	50	120
WNBC	HDLNES TRIAL				99	35	5	12	2	2	2	8	10	23	4	4		8				2	2	114	33	39
WNYW	WWF CHALLNGE	9	5	7	432	488	295	228	59	125	103	118	39	260	105	162	105	119	131	138	111	4	4	289	141	154
WABC	D BRNKLEY SP				412	536	103	268	15	47	33	91	68	268	88	141	141	141							
	DAV BRINKLEY				304	400	44	164	9	30	26	41	30	236	35	90	84	114				5	4	350	194	259
	--4 WK AVG--				331	434	59	190	10	34	28	53	40	244	48	103	98	121							
WWOR	SUN AFT MOV1	10	7	5	434	467	279	378	99	118	113	175	55	89	32	32	32	34	148	170	65				
	OUT THS WRLD	6	10	8	404	280	201	184	66	125	84	90	112	96	33	92	92	92	102	244	123				
	--4 WK AVG--	7	9	7	412	327	221	233	75	123	91	111	98	95	33	77	77	78	113	225	108	6	6	405	191	71
WPIX	ESTR SEAL TL				48	33	8	8	8	8	8	8	17	7											
	SUN MOVIE 2		1		224	202	54	113	37	52	46	68	17	90	17	49	44	55	25	3					
	SMITHSN TRES	4			117	115	56	33		24	24	24	24	81		55	55	62	56						
	--4 WK AVG--	1			153	138	43	71	21	34	31	42	19	67	9	38	35	43	14	13	2	3	3	201	95	80
WXTV	NUESTRO CINE				78	31	14	14	14	14	14	14		17		17	17	17							
	3RD BPTST CH				25																				
	--4 WK AVG--				64	23	10	10	10	10	10	10		13		13	13	13			1	1	65	3	4
																							5	7	
WNJU	VISION ASIA				3																	1	1	53	10	12
WNET	PTV				36	25	13	10	3	7	7	7	3	15	10	15	12	12							
WLIW	PTV				2																				
WNYC	PTV																								
	H/P/T	19	16	17	1739	1732	734	827	182	366	303	383	234	906	279	520	426	496	273	383	223	30	29	1643	724	743

12:30P-1:00P

STATION	PROGRAM	TN 12-17	CH 2-11	CH 6-11	TVHH	P18+	P12-34	W18+	W18-34	W18-49	W25-49	W25-54	WKGWOM	M18+	M18-34	M18-49	M25-49	M25-54	TNS12-17	CH2-11	CH6-11	ADIrtg	METrtg	TVHH	WOM18+	MEN18+
WCBS	NCAA BSKTBLL	4			321	383	160	108	4	61	61	61	42	274	87	165	112	142	69	9						
	NBA BSKTBALL	3			225	239	96							239	49	89	59	77	47							
	NCAA PLAYOFF		1	1	340	405	136	95		68	68	68	22	310	136	205	159	177		16	16				
	CBS SPTS SUN	1			301	532	118	284	5	88	88	97	107	249	103	124	98	129	10	11					
	--4 WK AVG--	2			297	390	128	122	2	54	54	57	42	268	94	146	107	131	32	9	4	4	3	247	94	223
WNBC	GRANDSTAND				97	57	20	24	9	9	9	24	24	34	12	15	3	9			1	2	100	18	27
WNYW	WWF CHALLNGE	10	7	9	515	582	342	270	84	151	133	146	50	312	107	191	138	157	151	167	134	6	7	485	263	290
WABC	EYWT NW CONF				212	247	40	133	6	21	14	37	25	114	28	38	33	33	5			4	4	279	161	179
WWOR	SUN AFT MOV1	11	8	5	573	609	330	463	122	142	132	212	100	146	41	55	55	61	167	204	86				
	TRPLE THREAT	3	2	2	208	142	92	95	16	37	29	35	32	49	11	24	24	42	65	54	34				
	--4 WK AVG--	5	4	3	299	259	151	187	43	64	55	79	49	71	18	32	32	47	90	91	47	5	5	360	206	87
WPIX	ESTR SEAL TL				65	31	11	27	11	11	11	11	23	3											
	SUN MOVIE 2		1		270	206	53	111	32	65	62	93	19	95	21	64	51	59		16	3				
	SMITHSN TRES	4			142	131	58	31		27	27	27	19	99		70	70	73	58						
	--4 WK AVG--	1			187	143	44	70	19	42	40	56	22	73	11	49	43	48	14	8	2	2	2	158	66	67
WXTV	NUESTRO CINE				71	21	9	9	9	15	15	15		11		11	11	11							
	AYR HY MNANA				70	15		15		15	15	15													
	--4 WK AVG--				70	17	7	11	7	11	11	11		9		9	9	9			1	1	71	14	13
																							5		
WNJU	SH NL GRIEGO				6																	1	1	24	12	10
WNET	PTV				25	25	1	13				3	3	12	1	6	6	10				1	1	11	5	2
WLIW	PTV				24	19	13	14	9	11	7	7	5	5		5	5	5	2	2					
WNYC	PTV																								
	H/P/T	20	14	15	1732	1741	746	844	179	363	323	420	220	898	272	491	376	449	294	277	187	31	29	1740	839	898

1:00P-1:30P

STATION	PROGRAM	TN 12-17	CH 2-11	CH 6-11	TVHH	P18+	P12-34	W18+	W18-34	W18-49	W25-49	W25-54	WKGWOM	M18+	M18-34	M18-49	M25-49	M25-54	TNS12-17	CH2-11	CH6-11	ADIrtg	METrtg	TVHH	WOM18+	MEN18+
WCBS	NCAA BSKTBLL	6			385	439	230	120	5	65	65	65	40	319	122	208	133	164	103	5						
	NBA BSKTBALL				192	211	36	10		10	10	10		201	36	110	90	90		5	5				
	NCAA PLAYOFF	2	1	1	404	459	115	122		102	102	102	46	337	89	233	202	231	26	19	19				
	CBS SPTS SUN	3			431	773	273	381	68	196	196	207	102	393	167	219	182	225	38	9					
	--4 WK AVG--	3			353	471	164	158	18	94	94	96	47	312	104	192	152	178	42	9	6	5	5	331	139	294
WNBC	NBC CL BK-SU	1			154	176	105	60		14	14	14		116	95	109	90	90	9						
	ACC BKBL CHP	1			180	265	74	119	25	65	57	57	65	146	38	84	84	84	12						
	BORN FAMOUS	3	1	2	526	46	63	23						23	17	17			46	32	32				
	PUB PEO PVLV				117	106	112	34			34	34	72	72	72			40							
	--4 WK AVG--	2			154	148	89	59	6	20	18	26	25	89	56	71	44	44	27	8	8	2	2	124	38	59
WNYW	5 STAR MOVIE	4	7	9	434	510	199	362	108	227	210	222	95	148	28	69	55	79	63	177	130	7	7	485	322	236
WABC	LIKE IT IS			1	165	174	34	53	4	18	17	20	9	121	30	48	30	37	1	10	7	3	3	178	88	118
WWOR	SUN AFT MOV1		6		391	353	107	252	82	137	130	133	108	101	25	53	53	57		153					
	METS EXHIBTN	2	1	1	398	464	174	203	58	120	109	119	60	261	64	106	95	107	52	34	18				
	--4 WK AVG--	1	4	1	395	408	141	227	70	129	120	126	84	181	45	80	74	82	26	93	9	4	4	334	206	119
WPIX	SUN MOVIE 3	9	4	5	321	209	222	85	39	78	68	68	55	124	50	87	64	60	132	160	110				
	SUN MOVIE 2				380	311	100	104	67	86	86	86	41	207	33	157	135	156		31	3				
	--4 WK AVG--	4	3	2	351	260	161	95	53	82	77	77	48	166	41	122	91	108	66	96	57	3	3	260	81	116
WXTV	NUESTRO CINE				67																				
	PRA GNT GRND				18																1	1	67	3	4
	--4 WK AVG--				55																		10		
WNJU	SH NL GRIEGO				18																1	1	53	44	22
WNET	PTV				83	103		74		6	6	6		30		4	4	8						32	17	7
WLIW	PTV				28	23	8	16	5	5		2		7	3	7	7	7		4			1	4	2	2
WNYC	PTV				9	9		4				4		5				2								
	H/P/T	25	16	17	2045	2106	796	1048	264	581	542	579	308	1059	307	593	457	545	225	397	217	33	31	1878	940	977

| | 36 | 37 | 38 | 39 | 42 | 41 | 45 | 46 | 47 | 48 | 49 | 50 | 51 | 52 | 53 | 54 | 55 | 56 | 57 | 58 | 5 | 8 | 39 | 45 | 51 |

FIGURE 8-5, cont'd Sample pages from the Arbitron ratings book.

Program Average Estimates

TIME AND STATION / DAY	PROGRAM	ADI RTGS TN 12-17	ADI RTGS CHILD 2-11	ADI RTGS CHILD 6-11	TOTAL SURVEY AREA IN THOUSANDS: TV HH	PERSONS 2+	PERSONS 18+	PERSONS 12-34	PERSONS 18-34	PERSONS 18-49	WOMEN 18+	WOMEN 18-34	WOMEN 18-49	WOMEN 25-49	WOMEN 25-54	WOMEN WKG WOM	MEN 18+	MEN 18-34	MEN 18-49	MEN 25-49	MEN 25-54	TNS 12-17	CHILD 2-11	CHILD 6-11
		36	37	38	39	40	42	41	43	44	45	46	47	48	49	50	51	52	53	54	55	56	57	58
▲ RELATIVE STD-ERR THRESHOLDS (1σ)	25%	7	7	9	109	156	101	103	90	87	79	77	75	69	70	73	76	86	76	70	71	119	150	128
	50%	2	1	2	27	39	25	25	22	22	19	19	19	17	17	18	19	21	19	17	17	30	38	33
8:00P																								
	WPIX																							
WKD	YANKE EXHBTN	3	1	1	437	575	505	183	134	253	175	34	81	65	67	76	330	99	172	135	146	49	21	21
WKD	8 OCLOCK MOV	2	3	4	364	559	447	166	129	243	231	71	124	102	122	68	217	59	119	104	119	37	75	57
SAT	MRS WRLD PGT	3	4	6	256	459	309	120	73	146	179	47	83	83	83	27	131	25	63	63	75	47	102	79
	^8 OCLOCK MOV	1	1	1	226	363	308	112	92	177	190	62	109	92	115	75	118	30	68	64	78	20	35	20
SUN	WAR OF WRLDS	1	2	2	180	316	210	138	78	142	108	29	70	70	73	34	102	49	72	41	52	61	46	34
TYP	8 OCLOCK MOV	2	3	3	340	524	423	157	123	231	224	69	121	100	121	69	199	54	110	97	112	34	68	51
	WXTV																							
MON	AMANDOTE	1	1		168	245	213	152	141	203	155	125	147	124	124	76	59	16	56	56	56	12	20	
TUE	AMANDOTE	2	1	2	153	249	195	160	131	183	139	108	131	102	102	55	56	23	52	41	41	29	25	25
WED	AMANDOTE				135	77	77	71	71	71	71	71	71	71	71	43	6							
	NCHE CARNAVL	1	2		219	242	186	72	54	81	169	39	65	59	110	44	17	15	15	15	15	18	38	
	PRIMAVERA		2	3	188	336	295	127	127	250	233	127	188	146	146	86	62		62	62	62		40	40
THU	AMANDOTE	5	1		164	246	150	188	107	143	136	101	136	100	100	38	14	6	6	6	6	80	16	
	PRIMAVERA		1	1	150	263	245	103	103	188	195	103	145	131	131	90	50		43	43	43		18	18
FRI	AMANDOTE	4			158	149	89	117	56	83	83	56	83	61	61	14	6					61		
	PRIMAVERA				242	245	245	103	103	214	221	103	190	139	139	103	24		24	24	24			
WKD	AMANDOTE	2	1		157	207	156	144	107	148	123	97	119	95	95	48	33	11	28	25	25	37	14	6
WKD	PRIMAVERA		1	1	193	281	262	111	111	217	216	111	174	139	139	93	45		43	43	43		20	20
	WNJU																							
MON	ABIGAIL				190	116	116	41	41	53	40		12	12	12		75	41	41	29	29			
	ANGELICA	1	1	1	176	196	155	53	39	109	87	19	69	58	76	27	68	21	40	30	37	13	28	20
TUE	ABIGAIL				128	55	55	9	9	13	13		4	4	4		42	9	9	9	9			
	ANGELICA	1			177	231	202	52	30	99	141	17	68	60	109	59	61	13	32	24	31	22	6	6
WED	ANGELICA	2			164	185	154	78	53	84	88	30	54	43	74	27	66	23	30	20	29	25	6	6
THU	ANGELICA			1	180	176	162	50	44	102	93	28	71	60	81	28	69	16	31	21	27	6	7	7
FRI	ANGELICA				134	156	148	54	52	102	90	29	65	61	77	12	58	23	37	28	32	2	6	6
WKD	ABIGAIL				159	85	85	25	25	33	27		8	8	8		59	25	25	19	19			
WKD	ANGELICA	1		1	165	186	163	58	45	99	98	25	65	56	82	29	64	20	34	24	31	13	10	9
SUN	CINE MUNDO		1	1	180	200	181	35	35	181	93	9	93	93	93	51	89	26	89	78	78		19	19
	MINISERIES				99	53	53	13	13	30	13	13	13	13	13	13	39		17	17	17			
ALL	MINISERIES				137	100	96	33	29	59	40	21	38	38	38	12	56	7	21	15	15	4		
8:15P																								
	WCBS																							
THU	NCAA PLAYOFF	2	2	3	355	520	456	159	134	287	151	42	69	63	90	49	305	92	218	175	190	25	39	38
FRI	NCAA PLAYOFF	3	2	1	428	576	488	164	120	301	200	34	107	107	138	80	288	87	193	150	183	43	45	17
WKD	NCAA PLAYOFF	2	2	2	392	548	472	161	127	294	175	38	88	85	114	65	297	90	206	162	186	34	42	27
ALL	NCAA PLAYOFF	2	2	2	369	522	457	158	133	273	141	30	77	66	82	51	317	102	196	164	206	25	40	30
8:30P																								
	WCBS																							
MON	HEARTLAND	6	3	3	702	981	815	284	197	407	500	117	236	215	255	177	314	80	171	171	185	87	79	46
	KATE-ALLIE	3	3	4	746	1202	1094	289	245	529	718	169	332	300	333	242	376	77	198	184	185	43	65	52
FRI	MARVIN	2	5	6	230	366	233	97	73	189	152	45	120	120	127	87	81	29	69	61	61	24	109	84
ALL	KATE-ALLIE	4	2	2	704	1062	957	308	245	506	641	178	336	308	333	224	316	67	170	153	165	63	42	35
	WNBC																							
MON	HOGAN FAMILY	21	18	23	1084	2097	1295	916	581	953	804	351	569	468	516	258	491	230	384	311	339	336	467	346
THU	DIFFRNT WRLD	29	18	22	1629	3057	2166	1194	734	1476	1359	452	892	755	838	495	807	282	584	482	504	460	431	315
	DY BY DAY	27	13	14	1361	2551	1845	987	585	1044	1208	361	654	530	599	348	637	224	390	312	378	403	303	194
SAT	AMEN	14	10	13	1248	2330	1844	655	443	899	1224	312	585	484	568	313	620	131	315	278	294	212	273	198
SUN	DY BY DAY	9	5	6	572	1017	767	359	220	537	477	128	318	283	311	199	289	92	219	172	188	139	111	82
	NBC SUN MOV	8	3	5	852	1290	1066	546	404	770	447	169	310	277	299	160	619	235	460	427	474	142	82	70
ALL	NBC SUN MOV	8	4	6	876	1506	1286	506	380	779	618	176	369	323	369	181	667	204	410	360	401	126	94	78
	WNYW																							
SUN	MARRIED CHLD	21	10	16	1262	2608	1996	1250	918	1516	1018	425	731	612	686	349	978	493	785	628	679	332	280	249
	WABC																							
TUE	WONDER YEARS	31	23	31	1532	2934	1906	1270	793	1478	1186	517	892	725	774	379	720	276	586	511	553	477	551	448
WED	HEAD OF CLSS	23	17	25	1339	2357	1543	1041	644	1089	980	404	667	533	579	360	563	240	423	364	398	397	418	367
FRI	FULL HOUSE	19	19	22	1112	2183	1439	885	592	1004	894	366	591	463	499	263	545	227	413	351	367	293	451	324
	WWOR																							
FRI	KNICKS BKBL	2	4	4	362	561	430	222	183	254	163	85	110	62	66	66	267	98	144	122	122	39	92	52
ALL	KNICKS BKBL	1	3	3	293	451	371	150	131	203	145	58	79	60	85	45	226	73	123	105	131	19	61	47
9:00P																								
	WCBS																							
MON	MURPHY BROWN	5	2	3	839	1269	1119	431	335	688	711	210	411	375	415	271	408	125	277	227	240	96	55	44
TUE	CBS TUE MOV	4	2	3	482	774	668	218	162	309	380	94	173	151	185	81	288	68	136	95	119	56	50	45
WED	JAKE-FATMAN	2	1	2	1069	1632	1567	258	226	493	922	125	273	230	304	210	645	101	220	196	239	32	34	32
	THE EQUALIZR	5	2	2	857	1355	1227	301	221	478	712	109	268	245	296	172	516	113	210	190	241	80	48	33
THU	PARADISE	1	2	1	444	728	668	132	113	206	365	68	123	73	101	87	303	45	83	73	85	19	40	8
FRI	DALLAS	1	2	3	854	1338	1241	300	262	553	845	179	364	324	374	242	396	83	188	173	206	38	59	42
SAT	TV 101	6	2	2	249	495	362	206	119	203	214	67	123	93	95	38	148	52	79	62	68	87	46	36
SUN	CBS SUN MOV		2	1	677	1112	1062	192	187	313	679	106	176	137	204	157	382	81	137	109	115	6	44	14
	PEO CHCE AWD	9	1	2	1288	2194	2034	449	312	825	1354	216	537	459	550	438	680	95	288	263	291	137	22	22
ALL	CBS SUN MOV	4	8	6	1064	1765	1509	454	392	707	862	220	412	354	408	269	647	171	295	263	325	62	194	92
ALL	CBS TUE MOV	5	2	4	537	876	742	262	187	374	395	105	194	166	205	93	347	83	180	130	153	74	59	56
	WNBC																							
MON	NBC MON MOV	9	5	7	1022	1690	1419	509	364	760	941	276	526	439	503	260	478	88	234	220	264	145	126	96
TUE	HEAT OF NGHT	4	1	2	961	1627	1533	292	226	521	948	120	325	295	364	284	585	106	197	160	212	65	29	27
WED	NIGHT COURT	13	3	4	.902	1451	1172	665	462	801	664	249	425	344	386	260	508	212	376	330	360	204	75	62
THU	CHEERS	19	8	12	1556	2721	2220	1060	760	1572	1284	437	881	788	852	520	935	323	691	595	657	299	202	172
FRI	MIAMI VICE	2	1		744	1061	1006	349	312	576	568	146	306	275	322	166	438	166	270	216	238	36	18	6
SAT	GOLDEN GIRLS	15	10	14	1697	3059	2561	749	520	1093	1675	353	685	617	759	489	886	167	408	369	392	229	269	215
SUN	NBC SUN MOV	8	4	6	885	1589	1370	490	371	783	684	179	392	341	396	189	686	192	391	334	373	119	99	82
ALL	MIAMI VICE	4	2	3	738	1110	1000	390	330	620	530	149	321	266	303	140	470	181	299	237	263	60	50	42
ALL	NBC SUN MOV	8	4	6	876	1506	1286	506	380	779	618	176	369	323	369	181	667	204	410	360	401	126	94	78
	WNYW																							
FRI	DRUG FREE KD		1	1	156	311	276	92	87	221	125	62	99	95	99	52	150	24	122	105	105	5	30	17
SAT	BEYOND TMRRW	8	1	2	396	688	539	331	214	417	241	155	175	175	196	108	298	60	242	208	218	117	33	33
	COPS	10	8	11	556	1117	763	414	257	523	388	114	267	258	301	121	374	143	257	211	246	157	197	169
SUN	G SHANDLING	12	3	5	611	995	727	600	419	646	344	198	299	250	265	156	383	222	347	296	300	181	87	76
ALL	BEYOND TMRRW	9	2	3	423	763	568	356	217	385	243	97	142	140	178	81	324	120	243	173	185	139	57	40
		36	37	38	39	40	42	41	43	44	45	46	47	48	49	50	51	52	53	54	55	56	57	58

Program Averages

FIGURE 8-5, cont'd Sample pages from the Arbitron ratings book.

odological problems.* However, it was reasonably suited to measuring viewing when there were only a handful of channels. Now, as cable has multiplied the number of viewing options, it is almost impossible for diaries to measure viewer behavior accurately.

Audimeters are devices attached to a family's television set or sets. They automatically record when the television set is on and to which channel it is tuned. Currently, most ratings information is based on information collected by audimeters and supplemented with diaries.

Recently, Arbitron and Nielsen have begun to use people meters, which are more precise audimeters. Each meter has a set of buttons, one for each member of the viewing family. A viewer presses her particular button when she starts viewing and again when she leaves the viewing area. In this way the people meter records what is being watched during each moment, as well as which family members are watching at the time. One of the weaknesses of the people meter is fatigue—viewers become tired of button-pushing. The ratings services are now working to develop a passive people meter, one that stores and later "recognizes" a viewer's facial features and records viewing starts and stops automatically for those it recognizes. There are strengths and weaknesses with each method, but the people meter probably provides the most precise information, especially for viewers with cable.

---

*For example: (1) The sample may not be representative. Historically blacks and Hispanics are less willing to be involved, and their diary response rate is lower than it is for whites. (2) VCR viewing is not correctly recorded. (3) Those who view away from home—in college dorms, hotels, and bars—are not counted. (Sport viewership is significantly affected by this under-representation. A recent ABC-initiated study showed that viewership of Monday Night Football was underestimated by about 10%. Regular ratings figures gave MNF of October 24, 1988, a total of 26.7 million adult viewers per average minute. Supplementary data collected from a sample of bars, college campuses, and hotels added 1.6 million; 800,000; and 400,000 projected viewers, respectively. A separate ABC-sponsored study showed that overall the unmeasured viewers tend to be better educated, younger, and more affluent.) (4) Cable has increased viewing options and in some cases changed viewing behavior, and may not be recorded correctly. Viewers with remote control change the channels more frequently, selectively watching only a few minutes of each program, and are more likely to change channels (or "zap") when commercials come on the air.

Advertising rates. Advertising rates vary depending on daypart, estimated total viewership, and demographic composition of the viewers. Ads during prime time cost more than those in early morning or late evening times. A station that can promise advertisers exposure to twice as many viewers between 8 and 10 PM as its competition may charge more than the competing station for ads during this period. Advertisements might be scheduled vertically (that is, as many commercials as possible throughout the course of a viewing day) or horizontally (that is, during the same daily time spot across the course of the week). Bergendorff, Smith, and Webster (1983) noted that in contrast to advertising rates in periodicals or even radio, television rates fluctuate continually. Prices are based on volume, spot supply and demand, competitive factors, and changing ratings, and thus stations (and networks) often negotiate rates each time ads are bought.

Because each station in a particular market might charge a different amount each time, ad buyers need a way to compute the best investment. Ratings figures are used to determine the cost to reach a targeted audience that might be viewing one of a number of competing programs. This process will be covered in detail in Chapter 16.

CONCEPT CHECK

Broadcasters and cablecasters deliver specified audiences to advertisers. Broadcasters' fees to advertisers are based on the absolute number of listeners or viewers delivered, as well as the demographic composition of the audiences. The A.C. Nielsen Co. and Arbitron, Inc. provide television ratings information to networks and individual stations. Arbitron and the Birch Co. supply ratings information to radio. Nielsen and Arbitron collect information on household viewing of national programming using overnight samples from major markets. Arbitron and Nielsen also collect information on household and individual viewing in 210 to 212 local markets. Sweeps figures are collected several times during the year. Ratings information is based primarily on viewer diaries, audimeters, and people meters. Advertising rates are based mostly on these listenership and viewership ratings, which are used to compute the cost to reach a targeted audience.

SUMMARY

1. Although interpersonal and mass communication processes share several common elements, each has developed a separate tradition of research and theory. Theories in interpersonal communication deal with communication skills (such as speaking and writing) and interpersonal communication behaviors in dyads, small groups, and organizations. Theories in mass communication deal with research in mass media effects and in the institutional practices of mass media.

2. Important theories in interpersonal communication treat the interpersonal relationship—whether in dyads, small groups, or organizations—as evolutionary. These theories focus on how communication behavior changes over time.

3. Relational theory proposed that communication occurs in both a content dimension and a relationship dimension. Scholars and practitioners are interested both in what is said and in how it is said—the metastatements about the relationship of the communicators.

4. Study and understanding of communication behaviors in groups and organizations are improved by analyzing communication networks. Several common patterns of communication have been identified, ranging from a *wheel* (all communications are directed through a single individual) to an *all-channel* (each member communicates equally well, unimpeded, with all others). These patterns differ in their distance and centrality.

5. Communication in organizations occurs in multiple directions: downward (from management to employees), upward (from employees to management), horizontally (from employee to employee), inward (from clients to the organization), and outward (from the organization to clients). Within the organization, communication may be analyzed by studying both communication micronetworks, or within-group patterns, and communication macronetworks, or between-group patterns. Network analysis helps identify communication bridges and liaisons.

6. Success in print or broadcast media usually requires an ability to identify and target an audience of consumers, and to attract advertisers who wish to reach the target audience. Print media of both mass and specialized appeal therefore collect information on overall number of readers, as well as on the demographics and lifestyle characteristics of these readers.

7. Commercial television and radio stations are regulated by the Communications Act of 1934 and the Federal Communications Commission. Because they use the public airwaves, broadcast stations are required to serve in the public interest. Nevertheless, most programming decisions are based on economics, and in particular on a need to deliver an attractive and affluent audience to advertisers.

8. Commercial television (and radio) stations are categorized as owned and operated (OAO) by a major network (such as ABC, CBS, or NBC), affiliated with a network, or independent. Network OAOs and affiliates receive much of their programming from network feeds. Independents produce their own programs and purchase programming from syndicators. A superstation is a commercial broadcast station whose signal is received by a common carrier and delivered via satellite to cable franchises; it therefore has both a local and a national audience.

9. Cablecasters do not use public airwaves and are regulated differently from commercial broadcasters. Local cable franchises may offer channels on basic tier (for a fixed monthly price), a premium tier (channels such as HBO or Disney), and a pay-per-view basis. National cable networks (such as ESPN or MTV) are delivered to local cable franchises by satellite and receive compensation from each franchise based on number of system subscribers. Recently, a number of regional cable channels have been developed; the majority of programming for these regionals is sport related.

10. The foundation of broadcast economics is ratings. Television ratings are provided by the A.C. Nielsen Co. and Arbitron, Inc. Ratings are collected overnight in a number of major metropolitan areas, and during several sweeps periods each year in 210 national markets. Overnights are especially useful for national programmers and advertisers; sweeps information is especially informative for local programmers and advertisers. Ratings are col-

lected using a combination of viewer diaries, audimeters, and people meters. Subsequent advertising rates are based on estimated total viewership, viewer demographics, and program daypart.

REVIEW QUESTIONS AND ISSUES

1. Discuss the relationship between distance and centrality in small group communication. Which is most related to information control? Which is most related to information distortion?
2. There is usually a fine line between the need for consensus and pressure toward conformity in small groups. Discuss ways a leader might handle both.
3. What are the advantages of bridges and liaisons in organizations? What are the disadvantages of relying on bridges and liaisons to communicate in organizations?
4. Imagine that Figure 8-3 represents a sport marketing firm. Assign some divisional responsibilities to each of the smaller groups (such as client recruitment, contracts, corporate sponsorship, or television relations). Discuss what communication might be like in this firm.
5. What are the differences between mass and specialized print media?
6. What readership demographics would be most important to magazine advertising decisions?
7. What is your ADI? How many commercial broadcast stations compete for the audience in your ADI? List them and tell what type of station each is.
8. Discuss the strengths and weaknesses of each method for gathering viewership ratings.

REFERENCES

Andrews, P., and Baird, J. (1989). *Communication for business and the professions.* Dubuque, Iowa: W.C. Brown Group.

Bales, R. (1976). *Interaction process analysis: a method for the study of small groups.* Reading, Massachusetts: Addison-Wesley Publishing Co., Inc.

Bandura, A. (1977). *Social learning theory,* Englewood Cliffs, New Jersey: Prentice Hall.

Bergendorff, F., Smith, C., and Webster, L. (1983). *Broadcast advertising & promotion!* New York: Hastings House Publishers.

Berger, C., and Calabrese, R. (1975). Some explorations in initial interaction and beyond: toward a developmental theory of interpersonal communication. *Human Communication Research, 1,* 99-112.

Beville, H. (1988). *Audience ratings: radio, television, and cable,* Hillsdale, New Jersey: Lawrence Erlbaum Associates, Inc.

Brilhart, J. (1978). *Effective group discussion,* (3rd Edition). Dubuque, Iowa: W.C. Brown Group.

Broadcasting / Cablecasting Yearbook. (1988). Washington D.C.: Broadcasting Publications, Inc.

DeFleur, M., and Ball-Rokeach, S. (1982). *Theories of mass communication* (4th Edition). New York: Longman, Inc.

Delia, J. (1987). Communication research: a history. In C. Berger and S. Chaffee (Eds.), *Handbook of Communication Science.* Beverly Hills, California: Sage Publications, Inc., 20-98.

Eastman, S., Head, S., and Klein, L. (1985). *Broadcast / cable programming: strategies and practices* (2nd Edition). Belmont, California: Wadsworth, Inc.

Ettema, J., Whitney, D., and Wackman, D. (1987). Professional mass communicators. In C. Berger and S. Chaffee (Eds.), *Handbook of Communication Science.* Beverly Hills, California: Sage Publications, Inc., 747-780.

Farace, R., Monge, P., and Russell, H. (1977). *Communicating and organizing,* Reading, Massachusetts: Addison-Wesley Publishing Co., Inc.

Feinstein J. (1986). *A season on the brink.* New York: Simon and Schuster, Inc.

Fisher, B. (1980). *Small-group decision-making* (2nd Edition). New York: McGraw-Hill Book Co.

Fiske, S., and Taylor, S. (1984). *Social cognition,* Menlo Park, California: Addison-Wesley Publishing Co., Inc.

Fowler, M., and Brenner, D. (1987). A marketplace approach to broadcast regulation. *Texas Law Review, 60,* 207-257.

Gropp, M. (1987). Magazine advertising. In G. Selnow and W. Crano (Eds.), *Planning, implementing, and evaluating targeted communication programs: a manual for business communicators.* New York: Quorum Books.

Janis, I. (1983). *Groupthink: psychological studies of policy decisions and fiascoes.* Boston: Houghton Mifflin Co.

Katz, D., and Kahn, R. (1978). *The social psychology of organizations* (2nd Edition). New York: John Wiley & Sons, Inc.

Klatell, D., and Marcus, N. (1988). *Sports for sale: television, money, and the fans.* New York: Oxford University Press.

Lasswell, H. (1948). The structure and function of communication in society. In L. Bryson (Ed.), *The communication of ideas.* New York: Harper and Row Publishers, Inc., 37-51.

Lewis, P. (1987). *Organizational communication: the essence of effective management.* New York: John Wiley & Sons, Inc.

Likert, R. (1967). *The human organization: its management and value.* New York: McGraw-Hill Book Co.

Littlejohn S. (1989). *Theories of human communication* (3rd Edition). Belmont, California: Wadsworth, Inc.

Luft, J. (1969). *Of human interaction.* Palo Alto, California: National Press, Inc.

McChesney, R. (1989). Media made sport: a history of sports coverage in the United States. In L. Wenner (Ed.), *Media, sports, & society.* Newbury Park, California: Sage Publications, Inc., 49-69.

Miller, G., and Burgoon, M. (1978). Persuasion research: review and commentary, In B. Rubin (Ed.), *Communication Yearbook 2*, New Brunswick, New Jersey: Transaction Books, 29-47.

Miller, G., and Steinberg, M. (1975). *Between people: a new analysis of interpersonal communication*. Palo Alto, California: Science Research Associates.

Monge P. (1987). The network level of analysis. In C. Berger and S. Chaffee (Eds.), *Handbook of Communication Science*. Beverly Hills, California: Sage Publications, Inc., 239-270.

Moreland, R., and Levine, J. (1982). Socialization in small groups: temporal changes in individual–group relations. In L. Berkowitz (Ed.), *Advances in experimental social psychology*. New York: Academic Press, Inc.

Munter, M. (1987). *Guide to managerial communication* (2nd Edition). Englewood Cliffs, New Jersey: Prentice Hall.

Poole, M. (1983). Decision development in small groups, III: A multiple sequence model of group decision development. *Communication Monographs, 50*, 206-232.

Poole, M., Seibold, D., and McPhee, R. (1985). Group decision-making as a structurational process. *The Quarterly Journal of Speech, 71*, 74-102.

Schembechler, G., and Albom, M. (1989). *BO*. New York: Warner Books, Inc.

Shaw, M. (1981). *Group dynamics: the psychology of small group behavior*. New York: McGraw-Hill Book Co.

Smith, M. (1982). *Persuasion and human action: a review and critique of social influence theories*. Belmont, California: Wadsworth, Inc.

Spence, J. (with Diles, D.) (1989). *Up close and personal: the inside story of network television sports*. New York: Atheneum Publishers.

Stevens, J. (1987). The rise of the sports page. *Gannett Center Journal, 1*, 1-11.

"Symposium on mass and interpersonal communication." (1988). Special issue of *Human Communication Research, 15*, 236-318.

Sypher, H., and Applegate, J. (1984). *Communication by children and adults: social cognitive and strategic processes*. Beverly Hills, California: Sage Publications, Inc.

Trenholm S. (1986). *Human communication theory*. Englewood Cliffs, New Jersey: Prentice Hall.

Watzlawick, P., Beavin, J., and Jackson, D. (1967). *Pragmatics of human communication*. New York: W.W. Norton & Co., Inc.

CHAPTER 9

Management

P. Chelladurai

In this chapter, you will become familiar with the following terms:

Planning	Budgeting	Organizational effectiveness
Organizing	Staffing	Performance appraisal
Leading	Job analysis	Contingency approach
Directing	Job description	Outer environment
Evaluating	Job specification	Objectives
Controlling	Departmentation	Technology
Stakeholder	Hierarchy of authority	Structure
Forecasting	Individual differences	Personnel
		Management approach

Overview

Most of us have an elementary knowledge of management, because we have been managed from the time we were born. Our parents, brothers, sisters, teachers, coaches, and others close to us influenced our behaviors and had a hand in the management of our lives. From a different perspective, we ourselves have been managers in one way or another. Think of the times you have organized an intramural team or a weekend party, or the times you have tried to influence your group of friends, classmates, or teammates. In all these instances you

have been a manager, effective at times and in some projects, and not so effective in others. So it should not be surprising that all of us have an inkling of what management means. But this understanding of management is limited, since it pertains only to individual operations in informal settings. Also, such information gleaned from personal experiences is likely to be piecemeal and fragmented.

In reality, management is a complex field of study, drawing its subject matter from such diverse fields as psychology, sociology, anthropology, and economics. In fact, university education in business management/administration takes 4 years to complete. Therefore it is not possible to do full justice to the field in one chapter. However, this chapter attempts to present the basic elements of management in a comprehensive and coherent manner.

Because management is integrally linked to organizations, it would be useful to begin with a definition of organizations. Sofer (1977) defined organizations as "purposive bodies which get a pay off from multiple contributions by coordinating them toward a common end" (p. 6). This definition includes the concepts of (1) the coordination of the efforts of (2) more than one person in order to achieve (3) a previously specified goal. Thus all organizations consist of people who have been purposely brought together into a social system striving toward certain goals.

The previously mentioned coordination of the efforts of different people is not a random phenomenon. It is a result of the conscious thought and effort of one set of people who are assigned the task of (1) setting and clarifying the goals, (2) selecting appropriate activities to achieve those goals, (3) assigning specific tasks to specific people in the organization, (4) motivating and directing them to carry out the tasks assigned to them, (5) coordinating their activities, (6) evaluating individual and organizational performance, and (7) taking corrective action as necessary. This group of people is the managers, and they and their actions collectively represent management. Thus "management is getting things done through other people" (McFarland, 1985a; p. 487), and a manager "is best defined as a member of an organization whose tasks, duties, and responsibilities require the supervision of others" (McFarland, 1985b; p. 518).

CONCEPT CHECK

Management is concerned with directing the resources of an organization toward the attainment of its goals. The major responsibility of management lies in setting goals, motivating members of the organization toward those goals, and coordinating their activities.

MANAGERIAL SKILLS

Theorists have used different approaches in defining and describing management. For instance, Katz (1974) described management in terms of three skills required of the managers: technical, human, and conceptual skills. Later, Zeigler (1979) added two more skills to this list: conjoined and personal. These authors emphasize the need for the managers to be skilled in certain ways to be effective in management. These five skills are defined in Table 9-1.

MANAGERIAL ROLES

From an extensive observation of the activities of chief executive officers Mintzberg (1975) concluded

---

TABLE 9-1 *Managerial skills*

Skill variety	Description
Technical (Katz)	Skill involving methods, procedures, or techniques associated with the tasks of the organization
Human (Katz)	Skill in understanding human perceptions, attitudes, and behaviors, and adjusting one's own behaviors accordingly
Conceptual (Katz)	Understanding the organization as a whole, how its own parts fit together, how the total organization meshes with the economic, social, and political realities
Conjoined (Zeigler)	A combination of technical, human, and conceptual skills, reflecting the need to be minimally proficient in all three skills
Personal (Zeigler)	Skill in managing personal time efficiently, articulating well-organized thoughts, and keeping abreast of information and events

From Katz (1974) and Zeigler (1979).

that all of these activities fall under 10 managerial roles. He further grouped the 10 roles into three broader sets: **interpersonal roles, informational roles,** and **decisional roles.** These 10 roles are outlined in Table 9-2.

MANAGEMENT FUNCTIONS

A more enduring approach in describing management has been to outline the functions (or activities) managers must perform. Traditionally, these functions have been labelled **planning, organizing,**

leading (directing), and **evaluating (controlling).** In the author's view, this functional approach encompasses the thrust of the other perspectives. As Carroll and Gillen (1987) point out: "The classical functions still represent the most useful way of conceptualizing the manager's job, especially for management education, and perhaps this is why it is still the most favored description of managerial work in current management textbooks" (p. 48).

Accordingly, the four functions of **planning, organizing, leading (directing),** and **evaluating (controlling)** are illustrated in Table 9-3 and explored in the following sections.

Planning

Planning is the process of "selecting objectives and means of accomplishing them" (Koontz, 1980; p. 183). While this definition is simple and direct, it does not do justice to the complexity of the process. Embedded within this simple definition is the notion of a multitude of objectives an organization may pursue, and also a multitude of means to achieve each of those objectives. For instance, Chelladurai, Inglis, and Danylchuk (1984) have

TABLE 9-2 *Managerial roles*

Roles	Description
Interpersonal roles	
Figurehead	Performing ceremonial duties in public functions
Leader	Supervising and motivating subordinates
Liaison	Establishing and maintaining contacts outside the organization
Informational roles	
Monitor	Seeking pertinent information from inside and outside the organization
Disseminator	Passing on the information to relevant individuals
Spokesperson	Justifying the organization and its activities, and lobbying for it
Decisional roles	
Entrepreneur	Initiating innovative projects
Disturbance handler	Reacting to changes and pressures beyond the manager's control
Resource allocator	Distributing resources to different units or members
Negotiator	Settling issues with outsiders, as well as internal conflicts

From Mintzberg (1975).

TABLE 9-3 *Managerial functions*

Functions	Description
Planning	Setting objectives, selecting activities to achieve those objectives, and allocating resources to each set of activities
Organizing	Breaking down the total work into specific jobs, assigning these jobs to qualified personnel, and establishing coordination through departmentation and hierarchy of authority
Leading	Motivating and directing members of the organization
Evaluating	Assessing organizational effectiveness and member performance to ensure that everything goes according to plan, and taking corrective action if necessary

TABLE 9-4 *Goals of intercollegiate athletics*

1. Entertainment	To provide a source of entertainment for the student body, faculty/staff, alumni, and community
2. National sport development	To contribute to the national sport development and performance in the international realm
3. Financial	To generate revenue for the university
4. Transmission of culture	To transmit the culture and tradition of the university and community
5. Career opportunities	To provide athletic experiences that increase career opportunities for the athletes
6. Public relations	To enhance the university–community relations
7. Athletes' personal growth	To promote the athletes' personal growth and health (physical, mental, and emotional)
8. Prestige	To enhance the prestige of the university
9. Achieved excellence	To support those athletes performing at a high level of excellence (relative to athletes in other universities)

From Chelladurai, Inglis, and Danylchuk (1984).

identified nine goals that could be pursued in intercollegiate athletics. These are described in Table 9-4.

Selecting one set of objectives from among these is the first critical step in planning, and athletic departments may differ in the relative emphasis they place on the various goals. Further, the athletic departments may also differ in the means they adopt to attain the selected objectives. In general, however, specific goals entail specific means. For example, in the Canadian context, Chelladurai and Danylchuk (1984) have shown that athletic administrators who emphasized public relations, prestige, entertainment, and/or financial objectives tended to favor athletic scholarships and unrestricted recruitment.

Demands and constraints. The selection of one set of objectives and the appropriate programs of activities to achieve those objectives is influenced by the available resources (material and human), the restrictions imposed by governments, and the values and expectations of society in general. These forces constitute one set of demands and constraints. Further, the choice of goals and associated programs of activities will also be influenced by people and/or organizations closely associated with and interested in the focal organization. These **stakeholders** (so called because they have a stake in the organization and its activities) could be in-

ternal (such as the employees of a city recreation department) or external to the organization (such as the parents and community groups). These stakeholders impose another set of demands and constraints. Effective planning is the art and science of selecting the goals and activities that would satisfy most of the demands and would be within the constraints.

Forecasting. Because planning is future oriented (that is, attainment of a desired state in the future), a significant component of the process is **forecasting** of future events. In the case of a fitness club, for example, the future demands for types of programs and/or facilities has to be carefully forecasted. The current demand for an activity and/or facility may turn out to be a fad after all. To the extent the future environment of the selected goals and/or activities is not properly forecasted (or cannot be forecasted), the developed plan may require several revisions as new information becomes available.

Budgeting. The planning process also entails the allocation of available funds to various activities or programs. That is, planners consider the total available funds and the cost of each activity before selecting one set of activities in pursuit of specified goals. Then, when a final set of activities is selected, specific amounts of funds will be allocated to each activity. A city recreation department may decide to promote participation and competition in several sports, and accordingly allocate different amounts of money to each sport. This is known as **budgeting.**

Some authors have treated budgeting as a separate function of management because of its importance. In fact, some approaches to planning have emphasized the budgeting aspects of planning more than the other aspects. For example, the Planning, Programming, Budgeting System (PPBS) is in fact the process of planning as just described. However, the scheme is often called a budgeting system (as by Haggerty and Paton, 1984). Whether budgeting is considered a separate function or not, it is important to realize that planning and budgeting are integrally linked.

Two different sets of documents will issue from the planning process. The first document is the organizational plan, which in essence specifies the goals and the policies and procedures to be adopted in carrying out specific activities in pursuit of those goals. The second document is the budget, which specifies the exact number of dollars allocated to the units or departments of the organization for carrying out specific activities assigned to them.

CONCEPT CHECK

A critical task of management is to identify and specify the goals for the organization, and to select the activities or programs that will efficiently achieve the specified goals. Thus the planning process sets the domain and direction for organizational activities.

Organizing

Once the goals have been set, the program of activities has been identified, and dollars have been allocated, management must ensure that these programs of activities are carried out by qualified people, and that their activities are coordinated toward organizational goals. These operations come under the title organizing, which is defined as the process of "developing a structure or framework which relates all personnel, work assignments, and physical resources to each other and to the enterprise objective" (Flippo and Munsinger, 1978; p. 12).

The first responsibility is to break down the program of activities into specific jobs. Consider, for example, the case where the local YMCA wishes to offer a program of fitness activities for seniors. First, the manager needs to break down this total program into specific jobs such as scheduling of activities, reserving the required facilities, leading the fitness classes, conducting medical check-ups and supervision, arranging and supervising locker-room and shower facilities, and so on. Once these tasks are clearly spelled out, these individual tasks must be assigned to the right people. As one can see, these various tasks require different kinds of knowledge and abilities (for example, contrast medical supervision with locker-room supervision). It is also possible to combine some of the tasks into one job and assign it to one person (such as scheduling activities and leading fitness classes).

Staffing

If there are not sufficient workers to carry out the new set of activities, or if qualified persons are not available to carry out specific tasks (such as medical supervision), it would be necessary to recruit new workers, which is a very significant part of management. The recruiting and training of workers is so significant that several theorists designate it as a separate function called **staffing.**

The major responsibilities within the staffing functions are **job analysis, job description,** and **job specification.** Job analysis is the study of the duties, equipment, and materials used to perform the job. It is also the analysis of the supervisory and other interpersonal relationships with other jobs. All of this information is stated in the form of a job description. Then it is necessary to specify the qualities, skills, education, and experience that are required of an individual to carry out the job effectively. Thus the two statements—job description and job specification—form the basis for further staffing activities. These further activities may include advertising the position, calling for applications, conducting psychological and physical tests, screening and interviewing the applicants, and finally selecting the appropriate individual(s). The thought and effort that go into the staffing activities are critical to the success of the organization, since it depends on its employees for attaining its purposes.

Departmentation and hierarchy of authority. Defining the jobs clearly and assigning appropriate personnel to these jobs becomes complex as the organization and its activities grow. For instance, staffing is relatively simple in a small fitness club with two or three aerobics instructors. As the club expands to offer squash, tennis, weight training, aquatics, and other fitness and sporting activities, it will have to hire more people with different abilities and talents. As the number and variety of employees increase, coordination and supervision of their activities becomes more complex. When the owner and/or top executive find this task to be too complex to handle by themselves, they may group similar jobs into operational units (such as the tennis section, the squash section, and the aerobic section) and place each unit under the jurisdiction of a supervisor or coordinator. At the next higher level, some of these work units may be grouped into larger units (such as racket sports, aquatics, and fitness departments), and higher ranking officers put in charge of them. Depending on the extent and variety of its operations, there may still be a need to group the departments into larger units and to appoint still higher ranking supervisors (such as a vice president).

The grouping of jobs and people into work units is known as **departmentation.** The number of departments and the size of these departments depend on the type of organization. For instance, in a high school the athletic program may consist of just two departments—boys and girls. In contrast, a professional sports organization may have several departments (such as player personnel, coaching, media and public relations, and marketing) with several employees in each.

The vertical arrangement of officers with progressively increasing supervisory authority is known as the **hierarchy of authority.** Again, the number of levels in the hierarchy depends on the organization. In the previous example the high school physical education department may have just two levels (head of the department and the teachers/coaches), whereas the professional sports club may have several hierarchical levels as illustrated in Figure 9-1.

CONCEPT CHECK

The coordination of the activities of the members is achieved by clearly describing the tasks and grouping the tasks and those who perform those tasks into units

or departments under positions with specific supervisory authority. Thus the organizing process establishes the authority relationships and channels of communication.

Leading

⚹The primary goal of the leading function is to influence the workers to carry out their jobs effectively to attain the organizational goals. Thus leading has been defined as "interpersonal influence which occurs when one person is able to gain compliance from another in the direction of organizationally desired goals" (Tosi, Rizzo, and Carroll, 1986; p. 550).

The emphasis on channelling member efforts toward goal attainment has led some theorists to label this function as directing. For instance, Fiedler and Garcia (1987) stated: "Leadership, as we use the term, refers to that part of organizational management that deals with the direction and supervision of subordinates rather than, for example, inventory control, fiscal management, or customer relations" (p. 3). ⚸

House and Dessler (1974) described four forms of leadership behaviors that a manager may use in discharging his or her leadership duties. **Instrumental leader behavior** is aimed at controlling and coordinating members' activities and facilitating their performance. **Achievement-oriented behavior** is setting challenging goals for the subordinates and expressing confidence in them. Through **supportive behavior,** the leader expresses concern for the members and the group. Finally, in **participative behavior** the leader permits members to participate in decision making.

In Chelladurai's (Chelladurai, 1978, 1985; Chelladurai and Carron, 1978) multidimensional model of leadership, the leader is expected to vary the previously mentioned behaviors according to two sets of equally potent, and at times conflicting, forces—situational demands and member preferences.

Situational demands. The first set of forces acting on the leader are the situational characteristics. As servants of the organization, the leaders are required to achieve the goals of the organization. Thus goals constitute one set of demands for the leaders. The leaders also need to consider the nature of the task assigned to their groups. Although

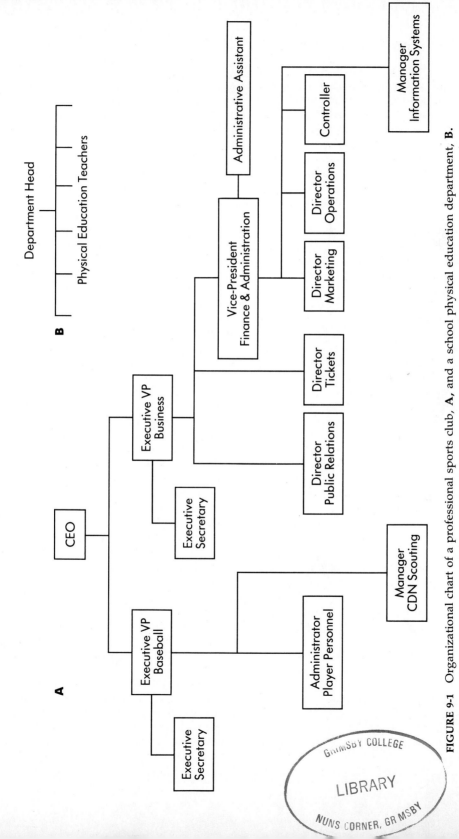

FIGURE 9-1 Organizational chart of a professional sports club, **A**, and a school physical education department, **B**.

the leaders are governed by organizational rules, they must also be concerned with the constraints imposed by government and legal regulations and requirements, and societal and cultural norms and expectations. For instance, the law may prohibit a coach from prescribing performance-enhancing drugs, and a physical education teacher from administering corporal punishment. Similarly, societal norms permit the coach to be "tough" with the athletes but expect the physical education teacher to be "soft" with the students. These situational demands and constraints affect not only the leader, but also the group and individual members.

Member preferences. Within the broad requirements and constraints placed by the situation, the leader has some discretionary control over how he or she behaves and reacts to the members' needs and dispositions. Workers may also differ considerably in their abilities, knowledge, and attitudes. These **individual differences** of members will be reflected in their preferences for one or more of the leader behaviors previously described. The effectiveness of leadership depends on the degree to which the leader can channel the efforts of the members toward organizational goals while helping members reach their personal goals (Chelladurai, 1985; Chelladurai and Carron, 1978; House, 1971; Osborn and Hunt, 1975).

Leader characteristics. Like members, leaders also differ in their personality, knowledge, and abilities. These individual differences would affect how leaders perceive the situational and member characteristics, what actions they take, and how they react to members. In fact, Fiedler (1967) proposed the extreme view that leadership style is solely a function of one's personality, and that it is not alterable. But such a view is not strongly supported. Instead, it is generally accepted that leaders can adapt their leadership style to suit the particular mix of situational and member characteristics.

CONCEPT CHECK

While the goals of the organization and its organizational structure give direction to the employees, the leadership provided by the managers is most critical in motivating the members of the organization. Managers need to adapt their leadership to the situational and task differences, and more important to the individual differences.

Evaluating

Evaluating is the process of assessing (1) the performance of the total organization in relation to the goals set in the planning stage, and (2) the performance of the members in the jobs assigned to them. The former is concerned with **organizational effectiveness,** and the latter is commonly known as **performance appraisal.**

Organizational effectiveness. Three interrelated approaches have been adopted in the study and measurement of organizational effectiveness. The goals model views organizational effectiveness as the degree to which the organization has achieved its previously specified goals (Etzioni, 1964; Price, 1972). Although this approach is the most direct and logical method of evaluating organizational effectiveness, its application to all organizations is limited because of a lack of clearly defined goals and the difficulty of measuring goal attainment. For instance, physical education in schools is purported to promote health and an active lifestyle among the students. Because there is debate about what constitutes health and an active lifestyle and because those two concepts cannot be easily measured, the goals model of organizational effectiveness becomes irrelevant.

In view of this, Yuchtman and Seashore (1967) proposed the system resources model, in which organizational effectiveness is measured by the ability of an organization to secure necessary resources. The model views the organization as an open system that depends on the environment for its inputs (resources) and the acceptance of its outputs (products). "Thus, a measure of the degree to which the system is able to obtain its resources is, in fact, a measure of the acceptability and utility of its outputs" (Chelladurai, 1985; p. 176).

However, the system resources model loses its potency when applied to organizations whose resources are guaranteed by legislative action and/or tax revenues. Consider a school physical education department in the following setting. The school system is almost totally funded by the government, everybody under age 16 in that locality is required by law to go to that school, and the school system has made physical education a compulsory subject for all grades. Under these circumstances the physical education department cannot claim effectiveness using the system resources model, since it gets the needed human and monetary resources by mandate.

Finally, the internal process model views organizational effectiveness as the degree to which the internal processes are logical and consistent with each other (Pfeffer, 1977; Steers, 1977). From a systems perspective, the internal processes (the throughput) are the means by which the inputs are converted into desired outputs, and therefore they constitute a valid point in the cycle for the measurement of effectiveness of the total system. However, if the goals are ambiguous and their attainment is not easily measured, determining what processes are appropriate becomes subjective to some extent.

All three approaches to organizational effectiveness have strengths and weaknesses, and a prudent manager will capitalize on the strengths of each. That is, criteria of effectiveness can be drawn from each model, thus using all three models simultaneously. Thus the manager of a fitness club may refer to (1) the actual profits made (that is, the goals model), (2) the number of new members recruited (that is, the system resources model), and/ or (3) the smoothness of its operations, the satisfaction of its employees, and the lack of conflict among the employees and customers (that is, the internal processes model) as indicators of organizational effectiveness.

Performance appraisal. According to Steers (1984), management can employ performance appraisals to (1) give employees feedback on their performance, (2) tell them their strengths and weaknesses, (3) assess performance to determine compensation, (4) help make decisions on promotions, transfers, and other personnel matters, and (5) evaluate its own hiring and placement decisions and its training and development programs. These purposes of performance evaluation reflect the perspectives of the organization, as well as the members. An effective performance appraisal system would attempt to combine the goals of assessing individual performance for organizational purposes with assisting individual employees in their career aspirations and growth. Such an appraisal would consist of (1) periodic consultations between the employee and the supervisor, (2) setting of challenging goals, and (3) the providing of timely and objective feedback.

While the two sets of evaluations (organizational effectiveness and individual performances) are expected to be similar to each other, there may be instances when the two may differ. That is, in-

dividual members may perform adequately, but the organization may not achieve its purpose, or vice versa. Such a situation would arise, for example, when the employees of a commercial fitness club are performing better than adequately, but the firm is not making a profit because the planners did not choose the appropriate location, facility, or activities when they set up the business.

These two types of evaluations should be carried out periodically and continuously. Managers may have to take some corrective actions when the total organization or the employees are not performing up to the standards. These corrections may be changing the activities, the people engaged in the activities, or the goals themselves if they are perceived to be too high or too low. For instance, a sport governing body that finds that it has not achieved its goal of winning a medal in the Olympics may decide to embark on a different set of training programs, or change the coaches in charge of their teams, or in fact lower their expectations by changing their goal to placing in the top 10 in the next Olympics.

The notion that evaluations are used mainly to control the movement of the organization and its members and guide them in the predetermined direction has led several authors to label this function as the **controlling** function. For example, Flippo and Munsinger (1978) describe the function as follows:

> The final function of management is that of controlling, or regulating whatever business action results from direction. The objective of control is to assure proper performance in accordance with plans. . . . Thus, the control function closes the system loop by providing information feedback to the manager so that he (she) may replan, reorganize, and redirect the enterprise (p. 12).

CONCEPT CHECK

In any endeavor, particularly within organizations, it is important to verify whether such effort has resulted in the attainment of the goals. The ongoing evaluative process would help in identifying whether and which organizational activities are failing, and whether the goals themselves are unattainable.

Concurrent nature of managerial functions

The sequence in which the four managerial functions (planning, organizing, leading, and evaluating) have been examined is logical and convenient. In practice, however, such sequential treatment may be appropriate only in one-shot projects (such as a community staging the national championships of a specific sport) or in the initial stages of a regular operation (such as the start-up of a tennis club). In ongoing concerns, managers may find themselves going back and forth among the four managerial functions. For example, it is not uncommon for managers to realize in the middle of the plan period that their original goals were too high, or that their organization of work was faulty, or that they have not assigned the work to appropriate personnel. This scenario suggests that there is constant evaluation of the organizational performance, which is followed by corrective actions that may involve planning, organizing, and/or leading.

CONTINGENCY VIEW OF MANAGEMENT
As Robbins (1976) noted:

Administration is a universal process in all organized activities. Even though there are factors that constrain administrators from having full and complete transferability, we believe it is possible to isolate these constraints, or contingency variables, and make it possible to discuss administrative skills as being transferable between organizations and cultures. Once we can control for the constraining factors, the concepts of planning, organizing, leading, and evaluating are applicable and equally valid when employed in political, educational, military, religious, social, and athletic groups, as well as in profit-making firms (p. 23).

However, this is not to suggest that there is one best way of managing all organizations. Since organizations differ in many significant ways, the importance and complexity of each function, and the manner in which each is carried out would vary considerably from organization to organization, depending on the nature of the organization and the context in which it operates. On a global level, the emergence of separate fields of management such as business administration, hospital administration, educational administration, and sport management illustrates the differences between the organizations in their goals, the publics or clients they serve, and the types of service or goods they produce.

Further, each specialized field of management still has to deal with a variety of organizations that cannot be managed the same way. That is, the contingency or situational factors mentioned by Robbins may operate even within one specialized field of management such as sport management. For instance, the management of a high school athletic department is obviously quite different from that of a professional sports club because of the differences in their goals (educational service vs. profit through providing entertainment), their clients (young students vs. adult spectators), the levels of skill and competition, the laws and cultural and social norms surrounding them, and several other factors that affect these organizations.

Contingency factors
In the **contingency approach** to management, these various factors are reduced by focusing on the more critical situational elements. According to Flippo and Munsinger (1978):

The unlimited number of specific factors in any managerial situation may be reduced to six general ones that have major impact. Not only must the manager determine the nature of these factors, but he or she must also interrelate them and *align* them if the best results are to be forthcoming. The contingency-oriented manager must constantly be aware of the configuration of major situational elements (p. 24).

These six contingency factors—**outer environment, objectives, technology, structure, personnel,** and **management approach**—are briefly discussed in the following sections.

Outer environment. The outer environment of an organization consists of elements external to the organization that impinge on organizational activities. The larger society; the governments; and the legal, political, and economic systems constrain the organization in a general way. In addition, the local interest groups that have a stake in the organizational activities would also influence the organization. For example, parents are vitally interested in the operation of any youth sport league in which their children participate. Similarly, the professional team owners and managers have a stake in the operation of the university athletic programs, since they produce future professional athletes.

Organizational environments may be characterized as relatively stable or unstable based on changes in the environment (such as, are the technology and equipment for fitness testing and training changing?), the rates of such change, the predictability of such change, the frequency of feedback, and the number and heterogeneity of external groups (such as, how many commercial fitness clubs, schools and colleges, and nonprofit organizations are competing with the focal organization?).

Objectives. It was mentioned earlier that the selection of organizational goals is influenced by factors inside and outside the organization. Because organizations depend on the environment for their inputs and for the absorption of their outputs, organizational goals tend to reflect the nature of the external environment. That is, to the extent the external environment is turbulent and unpredictable, the goals tend to be more global and flexible. Such flexibility would allow the organization to face new constraints and/or seize new opportunities. On the other hand, specific and clear goals would be advantageous when the environment is stable and predictable.

Technology. Another factor that affects the organization is the organization's technology, which refers to the skills, knowledge, methods, and equipment used to produce organizational outputs, be they services or goods. "The technology for manufacturing a serviceable automobile is better worked out than that for teaching college students. In turn, the technology for teaching is better developed than the technology for curing mental illness" (Flippo and Munsinger, 1978; p. 27).

The more developed technologies may be characterized as routine, as in the assembly line production of goods. In contrast, the technology used in educating a child, treating a mentally disturbed individual, or prescribing exercise for a cardiac patient is sufficiently complex and problematic that it cannot be routinized. Similarly, the technology of organizing tournaments is relatively more developed and routinized than coaching athletes.

These technologies depend more on the human performers than on machines and assembly lines. However, the advances made in computer technology are converting several complex activities into routine activities. For instance, the training equipment and the computerization of training programs and exercise evaluations are enabling commercial fitness clubs to dispense with the services of professionals qualified in exercise physiology.

Structure. Structure is the outcome of the organizing process that was described earlier. It consists of job descriptions, number and types of departments created, the organizational chart (which outlines the hierarchy of authority and the vertical and lateral relationships among individuals and units), and the policies, procedures, and standards that govern the activities of the organization and its members. The structure could be either very formalized, where the activities are completely and clearly specified for the members, or it could be less formalized, as when member activities are not very rigidly codified. As one can readily see, the degree of formalization parallels the environmental stability and/or routineness of technology. That is, the higher the environmental stability or the more routine the technology, the higher the formalization.

Another component of structure is the extent to which major decisions are made at the top or lower levels of the hierarchy. Centralized decisions (that is, those made at the top) would make sense in the context of stable environments, specific objectives, and routine technology. In contrast, uncertain environments, loose and flexible objectives, and complex technologies would call for more decentralized decision making.

Personnel. The foregoing contingency factors clearly show that the personnel employed in different organizations should also be different depending on the particular configuration of the environment, organizational goals, technology, and structure. Lorsch and Morse (1974) suggested that people can be distinguished, for example, on the basis of (1) their tolerance of ambiguity, (2) their attitude toward authority, (3) their attitude toward individualism, and (4) their preference for simple decision making. They found that members developed a sense of competence and performed better when their personal talents and dispositions were congruent with organizational factors. Thus members with low tolerance for ambiguity, high regard for authority, and preference to work alone and make simple decisions would be more comfortable in organizational settings marked by stable environments, specific objectives, routine technologies, and rigid structures.

Management approaches. For the purposes of description and discussion, management may be dichotomized as either classical—which emphasizes the more autocratic and mechanistic approach to management—or behavioral—which emphasizes the participative, humanistic, and organic approach to management. In the contingency view of management, each of these management approaches is legitimate and acceptable provided it matches the other factors described earlier.

Alignment of the contingency factors

The basic premise of contingency theory is that there is an optimal mix of these two management approaches that fits the various configurations of the other contingency factors previously described.

The critical element of the contingency approach is that all of the major situational factors must be in alignment if the organization is to be effective in terms of output. It is the configuration of factors, rather than any one factor, that is significant. (Flippo and Munsinger, 1978; p. 29)

Consider, for example, a city recreation department and a physical education research unit concerned with exercise for cardiac patients. The city recreation department's environment is more stable, and its mandate to make recreational facilities available to the citizenry and to organize tournaments is specific and clear-cut. The technology of maintaining the facilities and organizing tournaments is rather well developed and therefore is routinized. This permits the specification of formal rules and procedures for the conduct of the department's affairs. Also most of the decisions can be centralized.

In contrast, the cardiac research unit faces more uncertainty, because of the knowledge explosion in its field and the uniqueness of each client. Thus its technology is not routinized. Instead of laying down specific rules and procedures to govern the operations of the researchers, the unit has to rely on its members to make the best decisions given the changing technology and variation among clients. That is, decision making is considerably decentralized. Consistent with this, the members of these units would be expected to be capable of handling ambiguity in their challenging and complex tasks, and making decisions independently.

CONCEPT CHECK

Although the general principles and functions of management are transferable across organizations, effective management would ensure that the critical con-

tingency factors are consistent with each other. The environment, including resource contributors and stakeholders, has great influence on the organization. The objectives of the organization, the technology used, the organizational structure, the personnel, and the management styles need to be consistent with each other and also aligned with the environmental demands.

MANAGEMENT IS PEOPLE BUSINESS

For the purpose of clarity and conciseness, we have outlined and described management from the perspectives of both the functions to be carried out and the contingency factors that affect organizational processes. But, one must remember that the effectiveness of management and the organization is ultimately judged by the extent to which the members of the organization contribute to goal attainment. In other words, all of the functions and the alignment of the contingency factors would improve organizational effectiveness only through their effects on the people, their attitudes, and their motivation to work toward organizational goals. This point is stressed by the definition "Management is the art of getting other people to do all the work" (Anonymous, quoted in Vecchio, 1988, p. 4).

The emphasis on people in organizations is highlighted by the emergence of specialized fields of management research and education such as organizational behavior, human resource management, and personnel management. These specialized fields study individual and group behaviors within organizations. They provide some insights into how all of the functions, the alignment of the contingency factors, and other organizational practices affect employee attitudes, motivation, and productivity.

In the final analysis, it is important that the people in the organization are treated well and used properly. This need stems from two different but related sources. First, organizational effectiveness greatly depends on attracting and retaining talented individuals. Their commitment to the organization and their involvement in their jobs are critical factors that improve productivity. The second reason is grounded in humanism and social responsibility and focuses on the individuals in the organization. Organizations as instruments of the society have a responsibility to foster the growth of their employees and to ensure their happiness and satisfaction. It is readily apparent that the focus on individual growth and development would, in turn, contribute to organizational welfare.

SUMMARY

1. Management is defined and described in terms of the skills required of a manager and the roles played by a manager. The four functions of management are planning, organizing, leading, and evaluating.

2. Planning involves the specification of the goals and the identification of the activities to achieve those goals. This process is carried out with due consideration of the constraints and forecast facing the organization.

3. The organizing function is concerned with arranging the tasks and the people into meaningful work units and establishing mechanisms to coordinate these work units. A significant component of this function is the hiring and training of appropriate personnel, which is properly labeled the staffing function.

4. Since the success of the organization depends on its employees, influencing and motivating them toward organizational goals (that is, leading) is a critical function of management. The type and extent of leadership provided depends on the nature of the task, as well as the abilities and personalities of the concerned employees.

5. The final function mentioned in the chapter is evaluating, which consists of assessing the effectiveness of the total organization and appraising the performance of individuals and groups. Evaluation is carried out on a regular basis so corrective action may be taken if necessary.

6. The contingency view of management holds that the factors of environmental conditions, organizational objectives, technologies used in the production of goods or services, organizational structure, personnel, and management styles need to be aligned and consistent with each other. Finally, management is fundamentally a people business.

REVIEW QUESTIONS AND ISSUES

1. Identify the "stakeholders" of the intercollegiate athletic department in your college or university. Suggest what goals each set of stakeholders is likely to hold for the athletic program.

2. Discuss how the employees and their jobs ought to be organized in a fitness (or tennis) club.

3. Discuss how the situational differences would affect leadership in coaching a professional sports team and leadership in managing a city recreation department.

4. What criteria would you use in evaluating the effectiveness of a city recreation department? Group these criteria under the three models of effectiveness outlined in the chapter.

REFERENCES

Carroll, S., and Gillen, D. (1987). Are the classical management functions useful in describing managerial work? *The Academy of Management Review*, 12(1), 38-51.

Chelladurai, P. (1978). *A contingency model of leadership in athletics*. Unpublished doctoral dissertation. University of Waterloo, Canada.

Chelladurai, P. (1985). *Sport management: macro perspectives*. London, Canada: Sports Dynamics.

Chelladurai, P., and Carron, A. (1978). *Leadership*. Ottawa: Canadian Association for Health, Physical Education, and Recreation.

Chelladurai, P., and Danylchuk, K. (1984). Operative goals of intercollegiate athletics: perceptions of athletic administrators. *Canadian Journal of Applied Sport Sciences*, 9, 33-41.

Chelladurai, P., Inglis, S., and Danylchuk, K. (1984). Priorities in intercollegiate athletics: development of a scale. *Research Quarterly for Exercise and Sport*, 55, 74-79.

Etzioni, A. (1964). *Modern organizations*. Englewood Cliffs, New Jersey: Prentice Hall, Inc.

Fiedler, F. (1967). *A theory of leadership effectiveness*. New York: McGraw-Hill Book Co.

Fiedler, F., and Garcia, J. (1987). *New approaches to effective leadership: cognitive resources and organizational performance*. New York: John Wiley & Sons, Inc.

Flippo, E., and Munsinger, G. (1978). *Management*. Boston: Allyn and Bacon, Inc.

Haggerty, T., and Paton, G. (1984). *Financial management of sport-related organizations*. Champaign, Illinois: Stipes Publishing.

House, R. (1971). A path-goal theory of leader effectiveness. *Administrative Science Quarterly*, 16, 321-338.

House, R., and Dessler, G. (1974). Path-goal theory of leadership: some post hoc and a priori tests. In J. Hunt and L. Larson (Eds.), *Contingency approaches to leadership*. Carbondale, Illinois: Southern Illinois University Press.

Katz, R. (1974). Skills of an effective administrator. *Harvard Business Review*, 52, 90-102.

Koontz, H. (1980). The management theory jungle revisited. *Academy of Management Review*, 5(2), 175-187.

Lorsch, J., and Morse, J. (1974). *Organizations and their members*. New York: Harper & Row Publishers, Inc.

McFarland, D. (1985a). Management, definitions of. In L. Bittel and J. Ramsey (Eds.), *Handbook of professional managers*. New York: McGraw-Hill Book Co., 487-488.

McFarland, D. (1985b). Management, definitions of. In L. Bittel and J. Ramsey (Eds.), *Handbook of professional managers*. New York: McGraw-Hill Book Co., 518-519.

Mintzberg, H. (1975). The manager's job: folklore and fact. *Harvard Business Review*, 53, 49-61.

Osborn, R., and Hunt, J. (1975). An adaptive-reactive theory of leadership: the role of macro variables in leadership research. In J. Hunt and L. Larson (Eds.), *Leadership frontiers*. Kent, Ohio: Kent State University Press.

Pfeffer, J. (1977). Usefulness of the concept. In P. Goodman and J. Pennings (Eds.), *New perspectives on organizational effectiveness*. San Francisco: Jossey-Bass Inc., Publishers.

Price, J. (1972). The study of organizational effectiveness. *Sociological Quarterly*, 13, 3-15.

Robbins, S. (1976). *The administrative process: integrating theory and practice*. Englewood Cliffs, New Jersey: Prentice Hall, Inc.

Sofer, C. (1977). *Organizations in theory and practice*. New York: Basic Books Inc., Publishers.

Steers, R. (1977). *Organizational effectiveness: a behavioral view*. Santa Monica, California: Goodyear Publishing Co., Inc.

Steers, R. (1984). *Introduction to organizational behavior*. Glenview, Illinois: Scott, Foresman and Co.

Tosi, H., Rizzo, J., and Carroll, S. (1986). *Managing organizational behavior*. Marshfield, Massachusetts: Pitman Publishing Inc.

Vecchio, R. (1988). *Organizational behavior*. Chicago: The Dryden Press.

Yuchtman, E., and Seashore, S. (1967). A system resource approach to organizational effectiveness. *American Sociological Review*, 32, 891-903.

Zeigler, E. (1979). Elements of a competency based approach to management development: a preliminary analysis. Paper read at the Convention of the Canadian Association for Health, Physical Education and Recreation. Winnipeg, Canada.

CHAPTER 10

Sport Marketing

William A. Sutton

In this chapter, you will become familiar with the following terms:

Intangibility
Product mix
Locus of control
Target market
Bundle
Product life cycle
Segment
Elasticity

Promotion
Advertising
Telemarketing
Publicity
Pride in place
Positioning
Perception
Frequency

Overview

The purpose of this chapter is to introduce some new thoughts and interpretations about sport marketing, as well as applying concepts from traditional or mainstream marketing to sport marketing. This goal will be achieved by building a definition of sport marketing by illustrating the differences between marketing products and marketing sport; illustrating the evolution and development of sport marketing through the exploits and theories of individuals who have had a significant effect on that

evolution and development; and analyzing the process of product formulation, presentation, and exchange by examining eight key marketing concepts and their relation to sport.

Only by understanding the difference between marketing sport and other products and how this distinction came into being can the student appreciate the unique marketing properties and problems of sport and how the traditional marketing approaches can be applied, given their limitations in relation to the product.

What is Sport Marketing?

A definition of sport marketing must be preceded by a definition and examination of marketing. McCarthy (1975) defines marketing as the performance of activities that direct the flow of goods and services from producer to user to satisfy the customer and accomplish the organization's objectives. Kotler (1976) defines marketing as the human activity directed at satisfying needs and wants through exchange processes.

These activities or processes require a communication network established on the basis of inquiry, needs, and fulfillment of needs through product development, delivery, and exchange.

More closely related to sport is a concept defined as life-styled marketing. Hanan (1980) defines life-styled marketing as a strategy for seizing the concept of a market according to its most meaningful, recurrent patterns of attitudes and activities and then tailoring products and their promotional strategies to fit these patterns. Sport attendance and participation studies (Miller Lite Report, 1983; Sports Poll '86, 1986. NOTE: A description of these studies is found later in this section) document not only the patterns of sport-related attitudes and activities, but also their frequencies and intensities. The essential question is whether sport as a product differs significantly from other goods and services. Mullin (1983, 1985) maintains that sport has certain characteristics in its core, extensions, and presentation that make the sport product unique, requiring an approach that may, at times, lay beyond the concerns and approaches of "mainstream" business marketing. We will briefly examine those unique qualities of sport that will alter traditional marketing approaches and dictate the "locus of control" of the sport marketer.

Intangibility and subjectivity

Simply put, the consumer takes nothing away from attending a sporting event but impressions and memories. The wide variety of possible impressions and interpretations of that event pose a challenge for the sports marketer, namely to achieve a probability of consumer satisfaction. For example, consider a group of five people attending a professional baseball game. One member of the group might remember that parking was difficult and expensive; another might have been disappointed with the outcome of the game. A third may have

been impressed by the quality of the "pitching matchups," while the fourth member of the group was disappointed in the lack of scoring. The fifth and final member of the group may remember enjoying the event because of the reactions of, and social interaction with, the other members of the group. Each member of the group had an opinion that, although not necessarily related to the "core," or game itself, will influence future purchasing decisions regarding that product. In describing baseball, Veeck illustrates the **intangibility** of the sport product by stating, "The customer comes out to the park with nothing except the illusion that he is going to have a good time. He leaves with nothing except a memory" (Veeck and Linn, 1965; p. 20).

Inconsistency/unpredictability

One of the great attractions of sport, for participants or spectators, is the belief that on any given day any team or individual, regardless of past performance, can win. Many factors can affect the outcome of a game or contest. Such factors include injuries to players, player trades, momentum, motivation, and environmental conditions such as weather and time of year. These factors and the "lack of script" interact to guarantee that each game, event, or contest will be unique and the outcome will not be "guaranteed."

Product perishability

The sport product can be sold no later than the day of the event. In reality, it should be sold well before the date to help ensure franchise stability, consumer interest, and product credibility. There is no consumer market for yesterday's boxing match or basketball game. In professional sport, as well as basketball and football at "major" schools, tickets should be presold to guarantee stable revenue and to generate profits. If tickets are not presold, fluctuations in attendance and subsequently revenue will depend on performance, and if performance is poor or not up to expectations, revenue will suffer.

Emotional attachment and identification

In the mid 1980s, two studies were conducted to measure the attitudes and behavior patterns of Americans regarding sport participation and attendance, as well as the effect of sport on the lives of

Americans. The Miller Lite study of 1983 revealed, among other findings, the tremendous effect sport has on the daily lives of Americans, not only in sport participation, but also in attendance, and in reading and viewing habits. The *Sports Illustrated* Study, Sports Poll '86, established the most popular sports activities in terms of participation and the types of activities in which Americans are participating. Both studies also surveyed the attitudes of Americans toward sport. According to the Miller Lite study (1983) and Sports Poll '86 (1986), 95% of American society is affected by sport (reading, discussing, watching, listening, or participating) each day.

This effect has recently received a great deal of credibility through the establishment of a gross national sports product (GNSP), a statistic comparable to the gross national product. The GNSP includes gate receipts, sporting goods, broadcast rights, advertising, legal gambling, magazine subscriptions and more. In 1987, the GNSP for 1986 was calculated at 47.2 billion dollars, making it the twenty-fifth largest industry in the United States (Sandomir, 1987).

Development of merchandising departments in all professional and major collegiate athletic programs has given interested fans an opportunity to identify with a particular sports team (or individual) by purchasing uniform replicas or related team apparel. For example, wearing boxer shorts as shorts, a trend on college campuses, has been transformed by sports marketers into a licensed logo item that generates more than 5 million dollars per year for the Green and Dickerson Company (Sandomir, 1987).

Public consumption and social facilitation role

Studies (Department of Economics, University of Pittsburgh, 1977; Rudman and Sutton, 1989) have shown that more than 94% of those people attending professional sporting events attend with at least one other person, and their enjoyment of that activity often depends on the enjoyment of others. In recent years sport marketing personnel have recognized this trend and have developed various "product niches" to position their product to capitalize on this social consumption. Such product niches include family seating sections, no-alcohol seating sections, group discounts, and special promotional dates earmarked for large groups of co-workers, civic clubs, or organizations.

Focus and "locus" of control

In mainstream business marketing, marketers play a critical role in determining the composition of their organization's **product mix,** (how the eight *P*'s will be blended and used) and positioning (how the consumer views the product). In sport marketing (marketing of spectator sports and events), the marketer's input is inappropriate and thus is not allowed. Players are acquired, traded, platooned, and used with no input from the marketer, whose responsibility is to market the tickets for the game. Although the trade or acquisition of a particular player may help or hurt attendance, these decisions are not the functions of a sport marketer. Scheduling or determining the opposition is another factor that is outside the scope of a sport marketer, yet has a significant effect on attendance in team sports (Rudman and Sutton, 1989). Similarly, in participant sports crucial ingredients such as weather or road construction are outside the **locus of control** of sport marketers but have significant effects on demand at golf, tennis, and ski facilities. Thus the focus of the marketer is on prod-

The game itself, the "core product," is an element completely beyond the control of the sport marketer. (Photo from *Focus on Sports.*)

uct extensions that are within (the locus of) his or her control.

With these limitations in mind, sport marketing, for the purpose of discussion in this chapter, will be defined as *the identification of organizational and product-related structural limitations, and the incorporation of these limitations in the development, presentation, and positioning of the sports product through promotional strategies to facilitate a delivery of goods or services to the selected consumer target market(s).*

CONCEPT CHECK

Sport marketing, although based on the principles of "mainstream marketing," is a unique area with limitations and considerations not found in most areas using mainstream marketing techniques. Intangibility, subjectivity, inconsistency, unpredictability, perishability, emotional attachment and identification, social facilitation, public consumption, and focus and locus of control all interact to form a series of challenges for the sport marketer.

HISTORICAL DEVELOPMENT OF SPORT MARKETING IN THE UNITED STATES

In the last 150 years of American history, certain entrepreneurs and businesspeople have made significant contributions to the philosophies and practices that now are part of the field we call sport marketing. Beginning with legendary showman P.T. Barnum and continuing through the late Bill Veeck, each of these individuals initiated or refined a marketing-related concept or practice in sport or entertainment in general. A biographical overview of these individuals will help illustrate how certain practices and approaches evolved in common sport marketing practices.

P.T. Barnum (1810-1891)

The name P.T. Barnum is most frequently associated with the circus, but it must be remembered that Barnum did not become involved with the circus until 1871, when he was over 60 years old. Barnum's contributions to sport marketing came in the areas of media use, event promotion, creation of scenarios to use "word of mouth" advertising, and product presentation. Throughout his life,

Barnum was involved in publicity campaigns for many acts, shows, and exhibits that he presented. Barnum's exhibits, some of which were hoaxes and fabrications, capitalized on Americans' curiosity and penchant to believe that anything was possible. In fact, many of Barnum's promotions were successful, because of attendance by people who knew of Barnum's reputation for illusion and trickery but still thought this event could be authentic. However, the one event that epitomizes Barnum's talents for using the media, generating publicity, and presenting the product was the Jenny Lind concert tour of 1850-1851.

The Jenny Lind concert tour was an attempt by Barnum to cultivate an image for himself as a patron of the arts. To that end he wanted to produce a concert tour by Jenny Lind, who at that time was the premier singing attraction on the European continent. Terms of the contract included payment of $1,000 per concert for a concert tour of 150 dates, all expenses paid for herself and her entourage, and the right to sing for charity whenever she wished. More important the entire guaranteed sum of $187,500 was to be deposited at a bank in England before she sailed for the United States. Although this in itself was staggering, even more staggering was the fact that Barnum had never seen or met Jenny Lind and based his evaluation and interest on secondary reports and European media coverage. Even more discouraging was that after signing the agreement, Barnum discovered that his premier attraction was virtually unknown in the United States, and awareness was limited to those who had traveled to Europe.

Barnum's significant marketing task was not only to create awareness and consumer demand, but to do so throughout all of the cities on the tour. That Barnum was not just successful in accomplishing this feat, but highly successful, is a tribute to his promotional talents. Jenny Lind's core product was her singing talent, but since awareness of this talent was limited, Barnum capitalized on what we call product extensions, namely, her personality, characteristics, and values to help create the awareness level needed to stimulate consumer demand. By examining her career and character, Barnum found something that would appeal to the temper of the times—her virtue and her dedication and benevolence to a variety of charities (Wallace, 1959). Press releases emphasizing the character and virtue of Jenny Lind, as well as her charitable inclinations, were printed in every major newspaper in the U.S. tour cities. Barnum capitalized on this initial interest by launching a monthly magazine devoted to Jenny Lind and by sponsoring a contest to write lyrics for a song to be titled "Greeting to America," which would be sung by Jenny Lind as the finale of her opening concert in New York. Barnum created additional publicity and accentuated consumer demand for tickets by auctioning them to the opening concert.

The result of the publicity campaign was best described by Joel Benton in 1891 when he said, "Never, in the history of entertainment in America, has the advent of a foreign artist been hailed with so much enthusiasm. A large share of this public interest was natural and genuine, and would, in any event, have been accorded to Miss Lind. But a considerable portion of it was due to the shrewd and energetic advertising of Mr. Barnum. Under any auspices the great singer's tour in America would have been successful, but under no other management would it have approximated to what it was under Barnum" (Wallace, 1959; pp. 131-132). The concert tour proved to be a highly profitable enterprise for all parties concerned. In all, Miss Lind performed 93 concerts and received $176,675, and Mr. Barnum amassed $535,486 in gross receipts.

Albert G. Spalding (1850-1915)

Although Spalding is famous for his exploits as a professional baseball player with the Boston Red Stockings and Chicago White Stockings, and as the founder and later president of the National Baseball League, his most significant accomplishments may be those he made as a businessman in the development, expansion, and modernization of the sporting goods industry.

Spalding's awareness of societal and industrial changes played a key role in his presentation of sport, for both participants and spectators, as a stabilizing factor to counteract the changes in American lifestyle. Sport could serve as a valuable outlet for the needs of groups and individuals in a rapidly changing society. Initially, in his sporting goods endeavors, Spalding capitalized on his status as the best pitcher in baseball (Levine, 1985). His later status and influence as a league founder and president gave him the opportunity to have

his products adopted as "official" by the professional leagues and to launch a campaign to market his baseball to consumers as the "official baseball" of the major leagues.

Spalding's most significant contributions to the development of sport marketing were his use of endorsements, "official" recognition, advertising sponsorships from companies associated with baseball support activities (such as hotels and restaurants near ballparks), different product quality levels designed to make sporting goods affordable to all classes, and the creation of instructional materials designed to increase the public's game knowledge and skill development, which would help product sales and distribution. These marketing innovations were presented and positioned through the use of *Spalding's Official Baseball Guide,* a contract to be the official supplier of baseballs to the National League, and the establishment of *Spalding's Athletic Library,* which contained more than 300 instructional manuals ranging in price from 10 to 25 cents (Levine, 1985).

William "Bill" Veeck Jr. (1914-1986)

Veeck would best be described as "Everyfan." In other words, Veeck's approach was to market and promote baseball and its product extensions in a manner that would be accepted by common fans, whose tastes varied and whose motivation to attend baseball games was to be entertained and to escape from their normal daily activities. Veeck acknowledged that the most reliable method of attracting customers was to give them a winning team (the all-time record for baseball attendance in Cleveland was set during the Veeck regime in the pennant-winning season of 1948—2,620,627 [Veeck and Linn, 1962]). But Veeck also realized that a winning team is not always possible, and that tickets must be sold during noncontending seasons as well. The best way to sell tickets for a noncontending team, according to Veeck, was through promotional stunts and events designed to create a festive atmosphere that helps entertain.

Veeck's promotional repertoire included a variety of circus acts, nights of recognition and appreciation for groups such as ladies, "A" students, and Boy Scouts; giveaway items; and Grand Stand Manager's night (for a more complete description of Veeck's promotional philosophies and activities see Veeck and Linn, 1962: *Veeck—As in Wreck*). The most famous of all Veeck promotional stunts involved a midget named Eddie Gaedel and the role he played in an actual major league baseball game. On August 19, 1951, the last-place St. Louis Browns were scheduled to play a doubleheader against the Detroit Tigers. Veeck's *announced* promotional ploy was a birthday celebration commemorating the fiftieth "birthday" of the American League. The role of Eddie Gaedel was not announced, in keeping with Veeck's philosophy of never divulging the nature of a gag or stunt unless the situation demanded it. Gaedel, at 3 feet 7 inches tall, had been signed by Veeck to an official league contract. He was the first hitter in the second game of the doubleheader and walked to the delight of the 20,000 (18,369 paid, the largest crowd in 4 years) fans in attendance. Gaedel walked on four consecutive pitches and ensured his place and that of Veeck in baseball history. (NOTE: It has often been alleged that this was not an original idea but borrowed from Ring Lardner's fictional work *You Could Look It Up* [Eskenazi, 1988]).

Veeck's trademark was his ability to take an ordinary activity and transform it into something that would attract attention and word-of-mouth publicity, as well as some media reports. For example, Veeck would prefer to deliver 10,000 cupcakes to one fan rather than present a cupcake to each of the first 10,000 fans. In Veeck's own words, "It isn't enough for a promotion to be entertaining or even amusing; it must create conversation. When the fan goes home and talks about what he has seen, he is getting an additional kick about being able to say that he was there. Do not deny him that simple pleasure, especially since he is giving you invaluable word-of-mouth advertising to add to the newspaper reports" (Veeck and Linn, 1965; p. 13).

Veeck also made significant contributions to the development of sport marketing through his use of effective public relations strategies, such as player caravans, speaking engagements throughout the team's potential reach areas, and the first serious attempts at hospitality management, a concept now linked with the management practices of Disney World. Veeck's hospitality management philosophy emphasized comfort, cleanliness, and communication. Veeck's comfort philosophy can be seen through such innovations as his giving fans free plastic rain capes, his adding a nursery/day care facility to his operations in St. Louis, and his

remodeling of restrooms at all of his parks. No example better illustrates his attention to cleanliness (and its promotional benefits) than his activities in his first stint as a club owner in Milwaukee in 1941. On arriving in Milwaukee in June, seeing the condition of the stadium, and seeing the 22 fans at the game, Veeck employed 100 scrubwomen, a painting crew, and a remodeling crew to begin work after the game and work all night (with the stadium lights on all night to attract attention) refurbishing the run-down Borchert Field. The attention the media gave the activity and the word of mouth brought a crowd of 4,800 to the next game (Veeck and Linn, 1962).

Public relations, and specifically, being accessible, was a Veeck trademark. An "open-door" policy for Veeck was literally an open door (he had his office door removed in St. Louis and Chicago), and his mingling with the crowds before, during, and after baseball games was copied with great success by Mayor Ed Koch of New York City.

One of the more important public relations gestures Veeck developed was something he called *safaris*. Designed to let the small towns know that club ownership considered them important, safaris consisted of banquets and press conferences with Veeck and high-ranking members of his staff (such as front office personnel, the manager, and coaches). While in St. Louis Veeck explained the rationale by saying that, as the population (at that time) of St. Louis was only 850,000, and two ball clubs were competing for the entertainment dollar, attracting fans from out of town was essential for success (Veeck and Linn, 1962).

Veeck understood that performance on the field could not be controlled or guaranteed and that he must satisfy the fans' need for entertainment and excitement by using any and all means available. Veeck attempted to do this by maintaining a philosophy that "every day was Mardi Gras and every fan was king."

Charles O. Finley (1918-)

A contemporary and rival of the late Bill Veeck, Finley attempted to make his mark on sport marketing through the activities on the playing field itself. Finley began by altering the image of ballplayers by changing uniform styles and adding color. His Kansas City and Oakland teams did not wear the traditional home "whites" and visitor "grays" but shades of green, gold, and white called "wedding gown" white, "Fort Knox" gold, "Kelly" green, and "Pacific Ocean misty" green (Michelson, 1975). More color was added through the use of mascots and ball girls. Finley was also responsible in part for World Series games and the All-Star game being played at night, and he played a role in the adoption of the designated hitter in the American League.

The designated hitter rule is one of the most significant actions in sport marketing, because it demonstrated the willingness of league ownership to alter the core product (the rules and traditions of the game itself) to increase financial return through attendance and/or media revenue. The rule actually resulted in part from a decline in attendance at American League baseball parks, where attendance had fallen by more than 500,000 in 1972, and that, since 1962, had attracted almost 30 million fewer fans than their National League counterparts (Schlossberg, 1980).

As has been previously stated, the sport marketer is relegated to marketing product extensions and peripheral elements of the game rather than the game itself. The league, however, acting as a single entity, has the power to alter rules and playing conditions for reasons it determines to be in its best interests. Similar changes have been made in basketball (three-point shot, shooting clocks), and have even resulted in new products: indoor soccer and arena football.

Finley suggested a variety of other core innovations, such as the designated runner, a three-ball base on balls rather than four, and even platoon baseball, whereby certain players would be used only defensively and others offensively. None of these suggestions received any significant support, and they were discarded. Finley's suggestion to adopt orange baseballs instead of the traditional white also failed to gain support, even though scientific tests have documented the increased visibility of orange balls, and orange balls are used in tennis and golf. (NOTE: In the fall of 1989, Charlie Finley introduced a high-visibility football for experimental use in Indiana high schools.)

Most of Finley's suggestions were based on his belief that they would increase scoring and that increased scoring would bring higher attendance and television ratings. Although most of the ideas and innovations Finley advocated were not origi-

nal, he should be credited for taking the lead in bringing these ideas to the forefront.

Gary L. Davidson (1934-)

Davidson is an entrepreneur who founded or played a role in founding the American Basketball Association (ABA), the World Hockey League (WHL), and the World Football League (WFL). Inspired in part by the success of the American Football League (AFL) and that league's ultimate merger with the National Football League (NFL), Davidson set out to change the face of professional sports on the North American continent.

Davidson believed that leagues could be formed based on the theory that markets without franchises or markets with the potential to support multiple franchises had a demand for the sports product. He also assumed that these markets would be able to support these franchises, guaranteeing league success or possibly forcing a merger with the "established" older league. History supported Davidson's premise because at that time the Cleveland Browns and San Francisco 49er's of the NFL, the American League of Baseball Clubs, and the New York Mets and Houston Astros were all products of competing leagues that were merged into established leagues to eliminate possible competition from a new league. According to Davidson (1974), "People call new leagues 'rebel leagues' and term their leaders 'invaders' who are trying to tap into a good thing . . . but this is a normal business practice. If there is a gas station profiting on a busy corner, a rival opens up across the street. . . ." (p. 29).

Davidson's strategy had a type of "marketing warfare" approach. Ries and Trout (1986), authorities on marketing strategy and marketing warfare in particular, advocate finding a weakness in the leader and attacking that point. Davidson's analysis of that weakness was that the other leagues (NBA, NFL, and NHL) were so well established they were no longer innovative in their product format and presentation and were not aggressive in expanding. In addition, Davidson thought that the leagues would not be prepared to engage in prolonged "warfare" in the "battles" to sign players and so would "surrender" by merging or letting the new league survive on a limited competitive basis, meaning that the leagues would not be direct competitors for players and so on, but would compete at a lower level. Davidson's warfare was successful in both basketball and hockey as he drove up the cost of doing business through litigation and bidding wars to such a point that limited mergers took place between the NBA and ABA, and the NHL and WHL.

However, in the WFL/NFL competition, he was unsuccessful for several reasons. First, he underestimated the market saturation with football by not examining the effect of high school and collegiate football. Second, he erred in his estimate of demand for the product. Although there was interest in professional football, his product was not in demand because the consumer perception was that the product lacked the prestige and quality of its NFL counterpart (a perception that would plague the United States Football League a decade later) (Byrne, 1986).

What then were Davidson's contributions to sport marketing? Simply put, he reexamined the content and presentation of the sports product. His reexamination resulted in rule changes (three-point shot in basketball, kickoff changes in football) that Davidson's league introduced and were later adopted by the established league; marketing of professional games in cities without professional teams to measure demand for possible expansion or merely as a way to ensure capacity crowds for meaningless exhibitions while using expansion as a "carrot"; and an aggressive, competitive attitude toward assembling players to create a competitive sport product. Although the ABA and WHL efforts were at least partly successful, the World Football League's marketing efforts were crippled by a lack of credibility and insufficient operating capital. Nonetheless, through the dramatic effect of Davidson's efforts, professional sport learned that it must stay in tune with the times and must be aware of the changing needs and interests of its consumers.

CONCEPT CHECK

Sport marketing of today has been shaped by people with little or no involvement in sport (Barnum), by manufacturers (Spalding), promoters (Veeck and Finley), and entrepreneurs (Davidson). In addition, other individuals currently refining and developing sport marketing are Ted Turner (founder of CNN, TBS, and TNT cable television networks), David Stern (Commissioner of the National Basketball Association), Don Canham (former athletic director of the University of Michigan), and the International Racquet Sports Association (IRSA), which acts as a source and catalyst for many of the changes in private club marketing throughout the United States.

FACTORS INVOLVED IN THE MARKETING OF SPORT: THE EIGHT *P*'s.

As has previously been defined, marketing is a complex process and its success (to culminate in an exchange) requires the formulation of a methodology to attract and reach the potential consumer. That formula is composed of eight distinct yet interdependent facets that vary with the nature of the product or service and also with the **target market.** An examination of these eight facets will aid in understanding the complexities of developing the *marketing mix* (Figure 10-1).

Product

As has previously been discussed, the sport product is unique and possesses qualities or limitations that dictate that it cannot be marketed as traditional products or services are marketed. A product, according to Luck and Ferrell (1985), is a **bundle** of satisfaction that buyers perceive that they will obtain if they enter into a transaction. The bundle includes everything, favorable and unfavorable, that a buyer receives in the exchange. Lazer and Culley (1983) interpret a product as containing three elements: **attributes, benefits,** and a **support system** (Figure 10-2). *Attributes* are associated with the core product itself and include such elements as ingredients, quality, style, brand, color, packaging, and manufacturing style and preparation. Attributes are observable, concrete, measurable, and intrinsic to the core product. Product *benefits* are defined as what the consumer perceives as meeting his or her needs such as taste, warmth, or durability. The third element, called the marketing *support system*, includes any (if any) and all services provided in addition to the core product.

Does this definition and concept of product apply to the sport product? The answer to this question will be found by examining the purchase of a ticket to a sporting event.

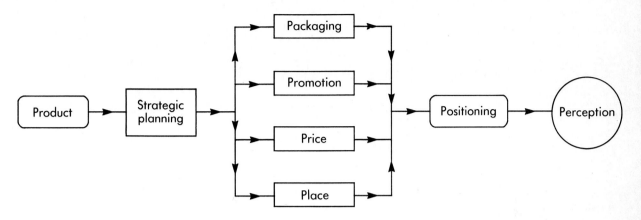

FIGURE 10-1 The eight *P*'s: marketing mix.

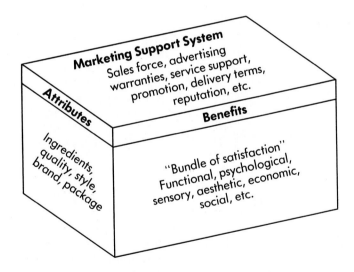

FIGURE 10-2 Basic product dimensions.
(From Lazer, W., and Culley, J. (1983). *Marketing management.* Boston: Houghton Mifflin Co.)

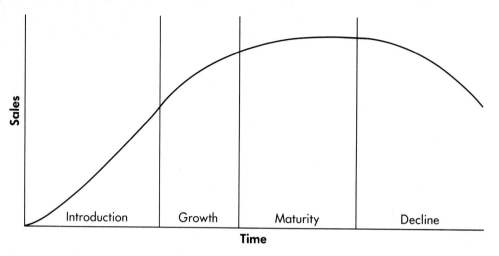

FIGURE 10-3 Product life cycle.

Baseball game ticket

Attributes	Benefits	Marketing support system
Style of play	Expected	"Rainout
Presence of	enjoyment	Guarantee"
superstars	Social	Ticketing
Location of	interaction	services
seat	Identification	"Customer
Quality of	with team	Satisfaction
opponent		Guarantee"
Presence or		
absence of a		
promotional		
event or		
giveaway		

Yes, the application seems plausible, but the nature of the sport product, especially its unpredictability and intangible nature, dictates its differences. Attributes can change because of injuries, trades, weather, and so on. Benefits can change because of the result of the contest, other activities that occur with large crowds at sporting events, traffic congestion, parking, crowd behavior, and so on. Marketing support systems are recent refinements in the sport product. Certain teams have fan satisfaction guarantee programs (Cleveland Indians), most now have family seating sections and sections where no alcohol is sold or consumed, and most also have sales departments specializing in

types of tickets sales (such as group, season, or corporate).

A product is generally seen as having a life cycle (Figure 10-3). A **product life cycle** is the story of the product's sales. The four stages of the product life cycle, **introduction, growth, maturity,** and **decline,** are accompanied by the formulation and implementation of strategies and procedures designed to ensure profitability and growth and minimize profit loss and product decline.

An excellent example of a sport-related product life cycle is the case of the Air Jordan basketball shoe. During its introductory stage the Air Jordan basketball shoe was accompanied by an expensive advertising campaign and aided by an NBA ruling that the shoes, initially available in only black with red and white trim, solid red, or white with black and red trim, could not be worn in official NBA games. Jordan's on-court performance also aided the product's introduction and helped the product gain momentum through the growth stage. The growth stage was characterized by heavy demand and increased production and distribution outlets. As the sales of the shoe skyrocketed, market imitators began producing shoes of similar style, color, and quality, as well as shoes of lesser quality and similar appearance. During the maturity stage, the price of the shoe declined to meet market challenges, as well as to counteract declining growth.

As sales began to decline, Nike launched a new

market offensive by introducing basic white and team color Air Jordan shoes, thus opening a new market by offering a product that high school and collegiate teams could wear, because the colors no longer were limited. Later strategies included the use of exotic leather, further technological modifications, the introduction of a clothing line, and the offering of the product for youth, toddlers, and babies.

Another question to be answered is the motivation for the purchase of the sport product. Is the need being satisfied an identification need, a social interaction need, an entertainment need, an image need, or something else? This purchasing rationale will be explored later in this section.

Strategic planning

Every sport organization should review its marketing policies and procedures annually. As a result of this review, a strategic marketing plan should be constructed. The purpose of the strategic plan is to govern and direct the organization's marketing efforts, strategies, and product positioning. A marketing plan depends on the development of research and planning processes that enable an administrator to examine past performance, present status, and future trends and implications (Sutton, 1987).

One of the most basic steps in the strategic marketing planning process is the identification of the target market. Market targeting consists of the decision processes and activities conducted to find a market to serve (Luck and Ferrell, 1985). Market research should identify unsatisfied or partially satisfied needs. However, since there are an almost infinite number of differences in the population, and because not all needs are universal, it is highly unlikely that a marketer will be able to satisfy all needs. The marketer needs a method to divide or **segment** the population in some manner and then to target the respective segments. Market segmentation is an attempt to identify and then classify potential consumers into a homogeneous group (similar age, sex, education, preferences, and so on). Once the target market is identified, the marketer can then plan the methodology to reach the targeted segment (a selected portion of the entire available market) and initiate the exchange process.

To segment the market, research must be conducted to identify the population according to

traits, interests, and desires that relate to the proposed product or service. The research can begin by examining the organization's own consumers or those of the competition. With a health and fitness club as a case study, the types of research and inquiry required to segment the market will be examined.

Phase I

Who are the clients or customers who are members of your club?

Who are the clients or customers using your club through programs and so forth who are not members?

Where do the members of these groups work? Live?

How many of each of these groups are there?

How often do they use the club? (You may wish to break this down into classes, weight room, tennis, and so on.) This will define members and participants as light, medium, and heavy users.

When does this use occur (weekday, weekend, day, evening, late night, and so on)?

Phase II

Analyze the information generated in phase I and examine it in terms of demographics. Consider the following variables:

Age
Education
Gender
Occupation
Marital status
Ethnicity (In some cases nationality may be important.)
Geographic proximity (home and work ZIP codes)

Phase III

The marketer may be able to complete phases I and II solely from organizational records (membership lists, program rosters, and so on). Phase III, however, will require a questionnaire with the purpose of assessing preferences, attitudes, and opinions about the club and its facilities, personnel, service, appearance, and value, as well as collecting psychographic information about the individual completing the survey.

After the information has been collected and analyzed, a consumer profile can be constructed, which provides information about the types of individuals who use the club and its amenities, as well as why they use and participate. This profile will then be generalized, and a target market (those sharing the same characteristics or a percentage of the characteristics of the customer profile) of potential members will be constructed. A target market of the types most likely to participate in classes but not join the club can also be constructed. This information also enables the club to position its product to appeal to certain targets and to direct advertising to those selected groups. For example, a direct mail campaign could be targeted on the basis of ZIP code (residence or work) or on income. Effective targeting results in more efficient use of resources and increases the likelihood of success in marketing efforts.

A key component of the strategic planning process is conducting an environmental analysis (Sutton and Migliore, 1988). An environmental analysis is an assessment of the "climate," including internal and external factors, that may or may not affect marketing efforts. For example, in intercollegiate athletics the environment would include the university itself, the athletic department, the local community, alumni, state government, media, boosters and corporate sponsors, and in this particular case, the federal government. How can the federal government affect the operations of an intercollegiate athletic program? It can enact legislation altering the tax-exempt status of gifts to the college athletic program, particularly contributions made to ensure "priority seating," a product requiring a donation for the "right to purchase" tickets. Such legislation could devastate athletic departments throughout the country and would affect not only the importance of marketing efforts, but also the scope and direction of those efforts. Figure 10-4 illustrates the steps and progression of the strategic planning process.

It is important that the marketer conduct an environmental analysis of the historical market, as well as the present market climate and future market assumptions. In considering a city as a possible expansion site for a professional sports team, the league office would wish to understand the sports attendance history of that city, as well as sports and entertainment competition for the entertainment dollars of that city's populace. For example, if the city of Pittsburgh was being considered for a possible NBA expansion franchise, an environmental analysis would provide the following information:

Past professional basketball franchises

> Pittsburgh Rens (ABL)
> Pittsburgh Pipers (ABA)
> Pittsburgh Condors (ABA)

It would also reveal that the Philadelphia 76ers played a limited schedule in Pittsburgh in the late 1960s.

Current sports competition

Pittsburgh Steelers (NFL)—some seasonal overlap

Pittsburgh Pirates (MLB)—some seasonal overlap

Pittsburgh Penguins (NHL)—direct competition; arena managed by hockey ownership

Pittsburgh Bulls (lacrosse)—some seasonal overlap, and also a tenant

University of Pittsburgh—Division I college basketball

Duquesne University—Division I college basketball

Robert Morris College—Division I college basketball

In addition to these competitors, there are college basketball programs at the Division III, NAIA, and junior college levels. Also, as in all areas of the country, there are high school sport programs in basketball, hockey, and wrestling.

This type of research in the planning process provides a realistic assessment of the market and should also reveal past practices that were successful and those that failed. This process basically is part of a strengths and weaknesses assessment that is used to illustrate the strong and weak points of strategies, concepts, plans, and focal points.

The strategic market planning process justifies resource allocation, personnel decisions, media use, and ultimately organizational direction by defining organizational objectives. The strategic market planning process then enables the marketer to consider strategies that may or may not be used in the organizational marketing efforts to achieve those objectives. Such strategies may be related to price, promotions, distribution, packaging, and positioning.

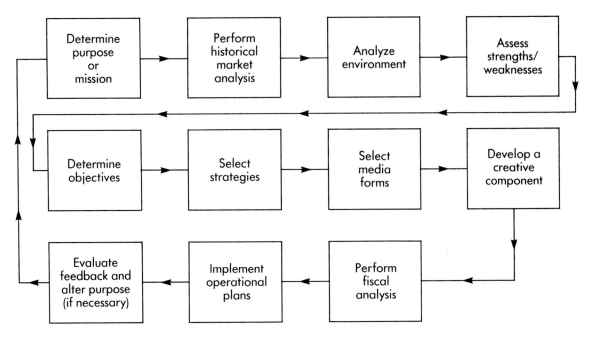

FIGURE 10-4 Strategic market planning process chart.

Price

Price functions as a very visible variable, and because of discounts, rebates, coupons, promotional incentives, and so forth, it is considered controllable and flexible. Price involves the determination of goods and services and the calculation of value of the exchange that can be used by all parties involved in the transaction (Luck and Ferrell, 1985). In mainstream marketing, price tends to be a key strategic consideration and, in some cases, the most important component of the marketing mix. Sport, and in particular spectator sport, does not give price the same strategic importance as does mainstream business. In a 1989 study of 3,009 fan responses in two selected National Basketball Association cities, Rudman and Sutton (1989) found that cost of tickets ranked fourth in importance in one city and fifth in another city, behind such considerations as opponent, team record, presence of superstars, and effect of the game on league standings.

Consumers equate price with value. A product that is deeply discounted or even free may be perceived as having little or no value. Bill Veeck, a sport marketer whose exploits were briefly examined earlier in this chapter, would never give away tickets, no matter how poorly his teams were performing. According to Veeck, "Tickets are the one thing I have to sell. To give them away is to cheapen the product I am selling" (Veeck and Linn, 1962; pp. 127-128). Similarly, when new sports leagues launch franchises in cities with existing professional sports teams, the new product usually is priced nearly the same as the existing product. To offer the new sports ticket at a lower price would tell the public that, in some way or another, the new product must be inferior to the existing product (Mullin, 1983).

How then are prices determined for products and, in particular, for the sport product? Prices are determined via a four step process composed of the following analysis and determination:

Step one: Conducting a "break-even" analysis, illustrating the costs involved in the production, distribution, promotion, presentation, and packaging of the product. This is done by identifying and calculating fixed costs and variable costs. Fixed costs include rent, taxes, equipment, loan payments, and more. Variable costs include factors associated with output levels such as wages, materials, utilities, and repairs. A break-even analysis will also illustrate the levels of production necessary to decrease the cost per product.

Step two: Determining the conditions of the market. Where is the competition in similar industries? How is the competition faring? How are the marketing climate, receptivity to the product, tax incentives, local economy, and so on?

Step three: Evaluating the pricing structure and product offerings of direct competitors, as well as competitors vying for the same type of consumer dollars.

Step four: Determining the amount of profit the enterprise hopes to achieve. This uses a cost-plus approach. In other words, if a cost analysis shows that the cost for a pair of basketball shoes is $10, the competition is selling shoes for $16, and you wish to achieve a profit of 50% per pair, you could price the shoes at a minimum of $15 per pair.

The University of Kansas attempted to stimulate attendance at its 1989 football games by offering season tickets at two prices. Seats between the 10-yard lines were the higher priced at $90 each. The 7,000 seats located outside the 10-yard lines were priced at $65. This area would be called the "Hawk's Nest," and since this area was sparsely populated in the past, all revenue would be "new" revenue. According to Doug Vance of the University of Kansas athletic department, "The reduced rate is intended to make it more affordable for fans to become season ticket buyers" (Jayhawks . . . , 1989; p. 8).

The key to successful pricing strategies is to react to market demand and the **elasticity** or inelasticity (how price changes affect or do not affect the consumer and hence demand for the product) of that

consumer demand. In other words, does a price increase or decrease affect demand? In most cases, pricing strategies do not stand alone at all times. Promotional strategies and product positioning may alter perceived value and in some cases, actual price (for a time). Such strategies combined with pricing usually increase consumer demand for the product.

Promotion

The term **promotion,** as defined by Govoni, Eng, and Galper (1986, p. 12), includes "all those means by which marketers communicate to their target market." This communication is primarily one way (directed to the potential consumer), and its primary function is to send a message. Promotion usually follows the AIDA formula, in that it attempts to persuade the receiver of the message to alter behavioral patterns or practices.

AIDA formula

create Attention
maintain Interest
arouse Desire
initiate Action

Advertising, publicity, sales promotion, and personal selling are all forms of promotion used extensively in the marketing of sport. A key to the effective use of promotional strategies and activities is determining what you wish to accomplish and designing a specific "promotional activity" to reach this identified outcome (Successful Promotion, 1985). Using spectator sport as an example and having a goal of increasing attendance, the marketer would need to know who attends and who does not attend, what promotional efforts have been used in the past, and how successful they were. Similarly, the marketer needs to identify variables that attract fans or affect a fan's decision to attend or not attend a game. Marcum and Greenstein (1985) in a season-long analysis of selected professional baseball teams, identified day of the week, opponent, and type of promotion as factors affecting attendance. Hansen and Gauthier (1989) through a small cross-section of marketing personnel from a variety of professional sports, found that team quality, price, entertainment, competition, and convenience were factors affecting attendance. Table 10-1 ranks 11 attendance factors identified by Rudman and Sutton in a 1989 study

TABLE 10-1 *NBA attendance factors*

	Cleveland		Indiana	
Factor	Average score	Rank	Rank	Average score
Opponent	3.28	1	1	3.51
Superstar	3.10	2	2	3.45
Standings	3.08	3	5	2.54
Record	2.99	4	6	2.46
Price/Cost	2.73	5	4	2.63
Game day	2.56	6	3	2.75
Weather	2.50	7	7	2.28
Arena access	2.30	8	9	2.09
Game time	2.27	9	8	2.24
Television	2.26	10	10	1.96
Event/Promotion	1.83	11	11	1.82

NOTE: Survey results are composed of the responses of 3,009 people. Means reflect Likert scale, ranging from 1 (never) to 5 (always).

of 3,009 fans who attended professional (NBA) basketball games in two selected cities.

In sport marketing, most promotional strategies are in the form of sales promotion. Sales promotion is defined as any activity that cannot be defined as advertising, personal selling, or publicity, but actually may use all three. For example, Northwestern State University of Louisiana was experiencing low student attendance at home football games during the 1982 and 1983 seasons. The football team had a losing record during both seasons, and research showed that most students went home on weekends, including football weekends. The goal or focus of the promotional campaign for the 1984 season then was to persuade students to remain on campus and attend football games. Promotional strategies and efforts before and during the 1984 season included pep rallies, special intramural contests, miscellaneous activities in the student union on Thursdays and Fridays, gifts, food, and "tailgate" parties. The result of these well-targeted promotional strategies was an average increase in attendance of 3,000 per game, and two attendance records were set (Successful Promotion, 1985).

Using a "theme" as part of a promotional strategy can also be very effective. The University of Iowa used as a promotional theme an attempt to set an NCAA attendance record and drew an NCAA-record crowd of 22,157 to a 1985 women's basketball game (White, 1985). A theme, sometimes called a *creative component*, can be used throughout a season. The theme, which should be present in all functions of the marketing effort, will cause the greatest interaction with potential audiences and the media.

The marketing theme should enable the intended audience to form a mental image, impression, or association with the product (Sutton and Duff, 1987). Such was the case with the very successful promotion of the Oakland A's (now Athletics) entitled "Year of the Uniform" held in 1981. This promotion was targeted at youth 14 years of age and under and was designed to "guarantee" that the youth attended multiple games, because an individual needed to attend at least six games to receive the entire clothing set, and an additional two games for gifts such as balls and mugs. According to Andy Dolich of the A's, attendance at "Year of the Uniform" games, which were strategically scheduled against quality opponents to maximize attendance and related nongate revenues, was 40% to 60% higher than on other days.

Advertising, a form of promotion, can be defined as any identified (has a sponsor), ***paid*** form of nonpersonal presentation or message transmitted through the mass media. It is directed to a mass

Selling corporate advertising in the form of signage is a popular source of revenue used in most arenas and stadiums.

audience to inform or persuade targeted publics. Advertising in sport is present in many media. Sport advertising uses traditional media such as newspapers, radio, and television but also uses scoreboards, in-arena signage, outfield fences (baseball), schedule cards and calendars, giveaway items, game programs and media guides, and announcements during games or contests.

One of the most popular forms of advertising used in sport marketing is endorsements. Endorsements feature a well-known or noteworthy athlete who endorses the benefits of a particular product or service. Miller Brewing Company has used former athletes to endorse the qualities of its Miller Lite beer, namely taste and low calories. Nike has used athletes to introduce and endorse two of its "flagship" products, the "Air Jordan" basketball shoe and the Cross Training Shoe, made famous by two-sport star Bo Jackson. Endorsement contracts sometimes contain performance and morality clauses to protect the sponsor from damages resulting from association with a "tainted" athlete. Such contracts may require drug testing, restrict the athlete's lifestyle, and require that the athlete use the product.

Personal selling is another form of promotion that can be very successful if the marketer capitalizes on its unique strengths and uses it in the right situations. Personal selling is direct interpersonal communication to inform and persuade. The advantage of personal selling in persuading and informing is that it enables the salesperson to interact with the prospect by explaining, questioning, and refuting objections. A common form of sport-related personal selling takes place in the health and fitness club industry. The personal selling usually takes place after the prospect samples the product through a free visit. At the conclusion of the visit the prospect is briefed about the benefits of membership and may or may not be offered a financial incentive to join the club immediately. If the prospect has objections or reservations, the salesman has a list of responses to refute the objection and break down resistance. Although the methodology of personal selling does not include coercion, in some cases it is used in the hope of closing the sale.

Personal selling can take place face to face or through **telemarketing**, a form of personal selling using the telephone to inform and persuade and to offer the consumer an opportunity to purchase goods or services. Telemarketing has been a very effective sales tool for spectator sports. Telemarketing companies that specialize in the management of telemarketing campaigns and that train salespeople often contract to sell season tickets, group tickets, game plans, or selected individual tickets for professional teams, as well as for colleges and universities that face difficult marketing tasks or limited resources. The team or organization usually contracts to pay the telemarketing company's expenses and a percentage of income generated. The contract may or may not include a minimum payment regardless of success.

Publicity differs from advertising in that it is *nonpaid*, nonpersonal communication about a prod-

uct or organization. Usually the sponsor is not identified, and the message reaches the public because of its newsworthiness. Nonprofit agencies involved in recreation, such as the YMCA, YWCA, or YMHA usually depend on publicity as a primary tool to communicate with the public. A great deal of publicity comes through news releases. A news release tells about an event or activity that is newsworthy and that merits publicity through the appropriate media. A news release should tell the who, what, where, when, why, and how in a concise and timely format and should be given to the appropriate media personnel by the agency or organization. Most nonprofit agencies and organizations depend on publicity as the prime way of generating awareness of their missions and programs. To assist local YMCAs, the National YMCA office issues press kits for specific programs. For example, a press kit for youth soccer may provide a release containing information about soccer participation in the United States, and quotes from physicians or soccer players about the benefits of play and competition. Often the local program director merely inserts the information about registration, place, and time for the local program.

A unique form of publicity in professional sport involves the United Way and the National Football League. Television messages, paid for by the National Football League, promote and publicize various United Way agencies and services within the home cities of each National Football League franchise. These publicity spots are unique in that they also serve as advertisements for the National Football League by promoting the activities of its players and the charitable activities and functions of the league.

Place

The term *place*, in a marketing context, is multifaceted. In a historical examination we find the concept of "pride in place," defined by sports geographer John Rooney as a unifying factor that promotes civic or regional pride and identification. **Pride in place** in a marketing analysis would be seen in resource allocation, preferential treatment for the home team, media coverage, and overall "product support" (of tickets, merchandising, and so on). An excellent example of pride in place is seen in the fact that a 1984 World Series game between the San Diego Padres and the Detroit Tigers was not televised in San Francisco so that a regular season game featuring the hometown 49ers could be televised (Nelson, 1989).

For the purposes of marketing *place* will refer to the geographic location of the target market and also to the targeting point or point of distribution, as well as being a tool in the marketing mix to attract potential consumers.

Distribution of the product involves activities related to the *transfer* of products, goods, and services from the producer or originator to the buyer or consumer. This transfer may be direct or may require wholesalers, retailers, and assorted "middlemen." Probably the most unique aspect of this distribution process in the case of spectator sports is that the product does not move from the production site to a consumer outlet. The production and consumption occur at the same site—the stadium or arena. Thus the "consumption site" in sport is perceived to be more critical than the distribution channels of traditional marketing. This same perception accounts for the emphasis on color and product extensions such as juice bars, lounges, and child care facilities in the construction of new comprehensive health and fitness clubs. Several factors associated with the location may affect the success of the enterprise. Among these factors are accessibility, attractiveness, and the actual location.

Accessibility has been described as a variable that affects fan attendance at professional sport (Marcum and Greenstein, 1985). Accessibility, or the relationship between the location of the product presentation and the location of the target market or consumer, is a key aspect of sport marketing. Accessibility is a convenience factor, and the consumer's perception of this convenience may significantly affect the success of the enterprise. Access factors such as highways, public transportation, transportation costs, "route" (direct or indirect) and length of time required all can significantly affect consumer traffic and success in reaching the target market.

Another function of the place concept is attractiveness. Is the "place" (area, facility, and so on) attractive (both interior and exterior)? How does the attractiveness element function in attracting potential consumers? Do all of the qualities of the "place" combine to form a pleasing attraction, or do some elements conflict with other aspects, weakening the total attractiveness? For example,

consider Candlestick Park, home to both the San Francisco 49ers (football) and San Francisco Giants (baseball). A location at the mouth of the bay sounds very attractive, but when the location brings fog, wind, and cold (weather in October and November is often better than the summer months) the picturesque location is overcome by combined meteorological effects that make the "place" unattractive (Nelson, 1989). The construction of a new facility, especially a unique facility, as is the Toronto Sky Dome, can serve as an attraction and can become a marketing tool in itself. After the opening of the Sky Dome in June of 1989 the Blue Jays enjoyed 15 consecutive sellouts, and as of August 26, 15 of the final 22 games were also listed as sellouts (Waddell, 1989).

Although the technological innovations of the Sky Dome (such as the retractable roof) are greatly appreciated and do ensure fan comfort, the new trend in facility design, especially in baseball, is to "take the nostalgia and intimacy of old ball parks and marry it to modern amenities. . . . . [It produces] a stadium that becomes a permanent marketing tool which helps bring people into the ballpark" (Murphy, 1988; pp. 1 and 23). The success and attractiveness of Pilot Field in Buffalo (set minor league attendance record in 1988 and led the league without breaking a record in 1989) supports this type of facility design and construction.

The issue of location is also complicated by the location's appropriateness for the activity. The prestige of the facility or the public's opinion of the facility also affect its success. At Ohio State University, soccer and lacrosse are played in Ohio Stadium, a facility that seats about 90,000 spectators. Although the matches in these sports rarely attract more than a few hundred spectators, the prestige of playing in the stadium helps recruit athletes and also implies the sport is more important than it would be if it were played on a field in another part of the campus.

The arena may also affect marketing efforts because of past uses, former tenants, other uses, and proximity to desirable or undesirable activities or regions. The marketing plan for the Columbus Horizon (Continental Basketball Association) calls for the team to play its games in the Ohio State Fairgrounds Coliseum. The Coliseum is traditionally used for livestock shows at state fairs and has been the home of several unsuccessful sports franchises. However, annually it is the home of the state basketball championships, which draw sell-out crowds. Concerned about the perception of the arena, the Horizon marketing team plans to publicize the interior and exterior improvements made to the arena to help provide a more positive image (Behm, 1989). Research conducted by the Pittsburgh Pirates (Moore, 1989) showed that although facility appearance and security were high-ranking factors, the proximity of restaurants was rated low as a possible factor in attendance. The mention of restaurant proximity as a factor might show that the consumer perceives attending a ball game as part of an evening's entertainment package and that complimentary attractions such as restaurants, taverns, and shops, add to the enjoyment and increase the likelihood the consumer will attend a baseball game.

Packaging

Packaging, or product presentation, is a key factor in successful marketing. The importance of packaging in traditional marketing is underscored by the following quote, "Packaging as a medium of persuasion is an island of neglect" (Heller, 1989; p. 207). In other words, too much is assumed about the consumer's point of purchase decision. Heller states that the package should function as an advertisement and should make its promise loud and clear. Obviously, this philosophy has a great deal of merit for traditional products, but what does it mean for the sport product? Is there an effective packaging methodology for the sport product? With sporting goods and related sports products, the package can explain benefits, such as Nike's "air system" or Asics "gel system." Packaging also can explain the benefits of a "larger sweet spot" on a tennis racket or the strength and control of a "graphite" ski. Is there a similar package for spectator sport?

The factors that make packaging spectator sport different are the same factors that make spectator sport different from more traditional products. That is, the intangibility of the spectator sport product requires the packaging to be composed mainly of expectations. Second, the packaging, because of the nature of the spectator sport product, is not used at the point of purchase, but must be informational and is used before the actual event. Brochures, pamphlets, and "imagery-related" advertising are the essential packaging forms used for spectator sports. Highlight films, depicting the

high points of the past season, are also integral to the packaging function, in that they illustrate the "ingredients" contained in the product.

Some packaging techniques used in professional sports are selling groups of tickets called weekend packages, which include only tickets for games held on weekends; "Super Saturdays," a variation of the weekend package containing only Saturdays; or mini-plans, a group of games from the entire season combining strong and weak attractions. Other offers include promotional events, weekend and weekday games, limited game packages such as the Six Pack or Baker's Dozen, whereby the fan or the organization selects specific games. The benefits are the low initial cost of a limited number of games, the fact that seats are guaranteed, and usually a "free" or bonus game, that is, 13 games for the price of 12.

Finally, the newest form of tiering is the flex book. The flex book is a series of coupons that may be redeemed at the box office for games of the customer's choice. The flex book is attractive by enabling the consumer to choose any games with no date restriction, and it usually offers the benefit of one "free" or bonus game. The limitation of the flex book from the consumer's perspective is that the seats are limited by availability, and consumers are cautioned to redeem their coupons as soon as possible to guarantee a seat for the games of their choice. In most cases, flex coupons are not redeemable at the gate on game day, forcing some planning by the consumer. On the other hand, the consumer may use all coupons for one game or elect to attend a variety of games, giving the consumer a degree of discretion. Tiering, and especially the packaging of flex books, usually is used in cases where ticket demand is less than supply. In cases where demand exceeds supply, packaging is limited and often is confined to season tickets and "mini" season tickets.

Another technique is packaging the primary product with product extensions. An excellent example was devised by the Peoria Chiefs, a baseball club of the Class A Midwest League. The Chiefs have designed packages for groups that include game tickets and concession or souvenir items for a discounted price. For example, a $5.50 group ticket (available to groups of 20 or more) includes a general admission ticket, popcorn or peanuts, a 22-ounce soda in a souvenir plastic cup, and a team yearbook (purchased separately the items would

Product extensions, such as mascots, contests, half-time shows, and events, add to the "sport package" by providing entertainment in addition to the "core" or the game itself.

cost $6.50). According to Mark Vonachen, Chiefs' director of group sales, "The packages have been effective in luring groups to the park for the first time because it makes it easy for people who haven't been here before" (New Packages . . . ; 1989 p. 4).

Positioning

According to Ries and Trout (1986) **positioning** "starts with a product, a piece of merchandise, a service, an institution, a company or even a person. But positioning is not what you do to a product. Positioning is what you do to the mind of the prospect. That is, you position the product in the mind of the prospect" (p. 2). McDonald's, arguably America's premier franchise restaurant, provides an excellent example of positioning. In the early 1970s, McDonald's was positioned, through advertising, as a "benevolent institution—a place that had an uncanny understanding of new con-

sumer needs and offered a 'happy experience' to boot" (Love, 1986; p. 307).

Positioning can use factors such as price, age, distribution, use, size, time, and technology to communicate its message (Ries and Trout, 1986). A classic example of the use of a positioning strategy in sport involved the Stowe, Vermont, ski resort area. A column in *Harper's Bazaar* by travel writer Abby Rand listed what she perceived to be the top 10 ski resorts in the world. Stowe was one of the top 10. The complete list was Stowe; Aspen, Colorado; Courcheval, France; Jackson Hole, Wyoming; Kitzbuhel, Austria; Portillo, Chile; St. Christophe, Austria; St. Moritz, Switzerland; Sun Valley, Idaho; and Vail, Colorado. Seizing the opportunity to position itself as simultaneously elite and accessible, Stowe developed advertisements that showed the shoulder patches of the "top 10" ski resorts, with the caption, "Of the world's top ten ski resorts, only one is in the East. You don't have to go to the Alps or the Andes or even the Rockies to experience the ski vacation of a lifetime. You need only head for the Ski Capital of the East: Stowe, Vermont" (Ries and Trout, 1986; pp. 173-174). By mentioning the top 10 ski resorts in the world, the advertisement created a list of elites in the consumer's mind, forming the basis for comparison of all resorts not on the list. Professional sports have been positioned as having the most talented athletes in the world, and this positioning has been the downfall of new sport leagues as they have attempted to compete with the established leagues.

A popular form of positioning used in spectator sports is to position a sporting event as more than the activity itself. This is done primarily through such promotions as "fireworks night," appearances by the Famous Chicken (formerly known as the San Diego Chicken), and so on. The positioning is that you are receiving something more for your money, a bonus. Family nights are a promotion and a pricing strategy that helps position the sporting event as a "family affair," something wholesome and traditional that gives the family an opportunity to share an event. As mentioned previously, time of day is a positioning factor, and time of day has been used effectively to market a sport event as a "businessperson's special." A businessperson's special is a game (usually baseball) scheduled for early to midafternoon on a weekday. It is positioned as a way for a businessperson to entertain clients, reward employees, and so on. Taking the businessperson positioning a step further, professional basketball and hockey teams have created a ticket package aimed at the businessperson who may work late, have clients to entertain, and so on. The businessperson's special package usually contains all weeknight games and is positioned as being tax deductible (as an entertainment expense) and an effective way to impress clients and sponsors. The package may also be developed to combine private club accommodations (if available), giving the businessperson additional reason to purchase the product.

An interesting sport marketing example of positioning is seen in the competition for teams and vacationers between Florida's Grapefruit League and Arizona's Cactus League. (NOTE: The Grapefruit League and Cactus League are nicknames for the exhibition leagues composed of Major League Baseball teams using Florida and Arizona, respectively, for spring training.) The cactus league has attempted to position itself as the leader in certain factors that are weaknesses of the grapefruit league. For example, the cactus league emphasizes as its strengths dry heat for player conditioning, the number of playing dates available without inclement weather, the short travel distance between cities, and the proximity to the hometown. This positioning capitalizes on the grapefruit league's weaknesses of high humidity, frequent rain, and longer travel distances between locations (Governor's Special Task Force on Cactus League Baseball, 1988). The key to this positioning is that very little can be done to reposition the Florida league regarding the first two factors, which are natural conditions. Thus the cactus league enjoys a natural geographic advantage and can concentrate other positioning efforts on facilities, community and corporate support, governmental involvement, and even attracting Japanese professional baseball teams.

Marketing research, and in particular consumer feedback and reactions, is the key to successful positioning. Marketing research is the key because your marketing solution is not inside the product or even inside your own mind, but inside the mind of the prospective consumer (Ries and Trout, 1986). If poor attendance is a problem, find out from consumers why they attend and also research nonat-

tenders to determine why they are not attending. The problem could be lack of awareness, product presentation, quality, price, or a legitimate disinterest in the product. Positioning can only truly become effective when the receiver's reaction to the message is analyzed. A 1987 marketing study conducted by the Pittsburgh Penguins (NHL) was designed and administered with the following goals in mind (Schnurr, 1987):

1. To examine behavior (attendance) patterns, motivational factors, and attitude toward the Penguins and the Civic Arena
2. To measure the intentions of fans to purchase either season or partial season tickets for the 1987-88 season
3. To determine whether home hockey games on television affected attendance at the arena
4. To measure radio listening and television viewing habits of fans at specific programming times
5. To explore the purchase behavior and attitudes toward the Penguins' magazine *Goal*
6. To profile the Penguin fan both demographically and geographically.

The findings of the study were used to determine future positioning not only for the ticket portion of the sports product, but also advertising, magazine sales, media use, and the future direction of organizational marketing efforts.

Perception

Perception can be defined as consciousness or awareness. In marketing, perception is the reception of the marketing message and the feelings about that message. Feelings can range from strong receptivity to no interest in the message at all. Marketers may use strategies aimed at altering initial perceptions or increasing the receptivity initially expressed by the receiver of the message. For example, an individual who has attended several basketball games has received the message and his or her perception of the message can be considered favorable. Additional messages may be directed to that individual (as well as a target audience composed of similar individuals) to attempt to alter his or her perception regarding the **frequency** with which basketball games are attended. Perception can be directly linked to other factors such as place and price. For example, most health and fitness clubs offer a free trial visit to prospective members. This initial visit includes a tour, individual attention, and instruction. The club is trying to create a perception that its staff is attentive, well informed, courteous, and concerned.

Perception is the step in the marketing process that will be translated into activity or inactivity. Favorable perception will usually result in some movement toward the actual exchange, which culminates the marketing process.

CONCEPT CHECK

The eight P's (product, strategic planning, packaging, promotion, price, place, positioning, and perception) are a formula that helps the producer reach the potential consumer. These facets may be manipulated, emphasized, combined, and integrated to help achieve the correct formula.

SUMMARY

1. The area referred to as sport marketing has roots in traditional marketing but is also distinct in a variety of ways.
2. Entrepreneurs have shaped sport marketing and contributed distinct methods of operation, especially in the use of publicity and public curiosity.
3. Sports are consumed for a variety of reasons, some of which may have little or no relation to the intent of the producer of the product. The sport marketer must be aware of these motivations for consumption of the product.
4. Sport marketing concepts act as a formula (the eight P's) and function in an interrelated manner to produce the effect that the marketer planned to achieve. Each of these factors can be manipulated to reach a target market, create awareness, provide information, or force a reaction.
5. The key to a successful formula is the amount of knowledge the sport marketer has about not only the product and the potential consumer, but also about the environmental factors both within and beyond his or her control.

6. The sport marketing process should be strategically and systematically planned. Research, monitoring, and feedback are essential in the development of a successful sport marketing plan and the achievement of organizational goals.

REVIEW QUESTIONS AND ISSUES

1. Define the term **target market.** Discuss the steps in identifying a target market when marketing "official clothing" of a professional sports team. How might this target market differ (if at all) from that of a target market for "official clothing" of a college or university?
2. What does the term **product** mean? Describe the attributes of a sport-related product of your choice.
3. In your opinion, of those who contributed to the development of sport marketing mentioned in this chapter, who do you feel made the most significant contribution and why?
4. What does the term **positioning** mean? How would you attempt to position a Christmas basketball tournament to be held for the first time on your campus to students? To alumni? To the community?
5. The benefits of telemarketing as a form of personal selling have been previously discussed. What are some of the limitations of telemarketing as a form of personal selling?
6. Discuss how the marketing of sport differs from that of "traditional" products.
7. What are the differences between core product and product extensions? Which of these concepts is more important to the sport marketer and why?
8. What does the term **market segmentation** mean? What are the types of segmentation that are commonly used, and how does segmentation help the sport marketer identify the target market?
9. Using an example of your choice, illustrate the process necessary to determine an effective price for your product.

REFERENCES

Barnum, P. (1869). *Struggles and triumphs; or forty years' recollections of P.T. Barnum written by himself.* New York: American News Company.

Behm, G. (1989). Personal interview, May 14, Columbus, Ohio.

Benton, J. (1891). *Life of honorable Phineas T. Barnum.* Philadelphia: Edgewood.

Byrne, J. (1986). *The $1 league: the rise and fall of the USFL.* Englewood Cliffs, New Jersey: Prentice Hall.

Davidson, G. (1974). *Breaking the game wide open.* New York: Atheneum Publishers.

Department of Economics, University of Pittsburgh, (1977). *An Economic impact study of the Pittsburgh Pirates Baseball Club on the city of Pittsburgh.* Pittsburgh: The University.

Eskenazi, G. (1988). *Bill Veeck: a baseball legend.* New York: McGraw-Hill Book Co.

Governor's Special Task Force on Cactus League Baseball (1988). Office of the Governor, State of Arizona, Dwight Patterson, Chairman.

Govoni, N., Eng, R., and Galper, M. (1986). *Promotional management.* Englewood Cliffs, New Jersey: Prentice Hall.

Hanan, M. (1980). *Life-styled marketing: how to position products for premium profits.* New York: AMACOM Book Division.

Hansen, H., and Gauthier, R. (1989). Factors affecting attendance at professional sport events. *Journal of Sport Management 3*(1), 15-32.

Heller, R. (1989). *The supermarketers.* New York: E.P. Dutton

Jayhawks hope pricing change will attract fans (1989). *Team Marketing Report, 1*(9), 8.

Kotler, P. (1976). *Marketing management: analysis, planning and control* (3rd Edition). Englewood Cliffs, New Jersey: Prentice Hall.

Lazer, W., and Culley, J. (1983). *Marketing management.* Boston: Houghton Mifflin Co.

Levine, P. (1985). *A.G. Spalding and the rise of baseball: the promise of American sport.* New York: Oxford University Press, Inc.

Lieberman Research Inc. (1986). *Sports Illustrated, Sports Poll '86.* New York.

Love, J. (1986). *McDonald's: behind the golden arches.* New York: Bantam Books.

Luck, D., and Ferrell, O. (1985). *Marketing strategy and plans.* Englewood Cliffs, New Jersey: Prentice Hall.

Marcum, J., and Greenstein, T. (1985). Factors affecting attendance at major league baseball. Part II. A within-season analysis. *Sociology of Sport Journal, 2*, 314-322.

McCarthy, E. (1975). *Basic marketing* (5th Edition). Homewood, Illinois: Richard D. Irwin, Inc.

Michelson, H. (1975). *Charlie O.* Indianapolis: Bobbs-Merrill Co.

Moore, M. (1989). *The Pittsburgh Pirates Baseball Club: market research report, 1988 fan surveys.* (Unpublished study).

Mullin, B. (1983). *Sport marketing, promotion and public relations.* Amherst, Massachusetts: National Sport Management, Inc.

Mullin, B. (1985). Characteristics of sport marketing. In G. Lewis and H. Appenzeller (Eds.), *Successful sport management.* Charlottesville, Virginia: The Michie Co.

Murphy, B. (1988). Stadiums: back to the future. *Sports Marketing News 3*(13).

Nelson, K. (1989). San Francisco. *Sport Magazine, 80*(10).

New packages boost Chiefs' group sales (1989). *Team Marketing Report 1*(8), 4.

Research and Forecasts, Inc. (1983). *Miller Lite Report on American Attitudes Toward Sports.* New York.

Ries, A., and Trout, J. (1986). *Marketing Warfare.* New York: McGraw-Hill Book Co.

Ries, A., and Trout, J. (1986). *Positioning: The battle for your mind.* New York: McGraw-Hill Book Co.

Rudman, W., and Sutton, W. (1989). The selling of the NBA: market characteristics and sport consumption. Presentation at the National Basketball Association's Annual meeting. Palm Springs, California: September.

Sandomir, R. (1987). The gross national sports product, *Sports, Inc. 1*(1), 14-18.

Schlossberg, D. (1980). *The baseball catalog.* New York: Jonathan David Publisher, Inc.

Schnurr, N. (1987). *Pittsburgh Penguin fan survey.* (Unpublished consultant report).

Sutton, W. (1987). Developing an initial marketing plan for intercollegiate athletic programs. *Journal of Sport Management, 1*(2), 146-158.

Sutton, W., and Duff, R. (1987). Creating themes to market your athletic programs. *Athletic Administration, 22*(5), 17-18.

Sutton, W., and Migliore, R. (1988). Strategic long range planning for intercollegiate athletic programs. *Journal of Applied Research in Coaching and Athletics, 3*(4), 233-261.

Successful promotion: identify the problem before trying to solve it (1985). Athletic Business, March, 22-23.

Veeck, W., and Linn, E. (1962). *Veeck—as in wreck:* New York: The Putnam Publishing Group.

Veeck, W., and Linn, E. (1965). *The hustler's handbook.* New York: The Putnam Publishing Group.

Waddell, R. (1989). Attendance ups & downs for major league baseball teams. *Amusement Business, 101*(34), 18 and 31.

Wallace, I. (1959). *The fabulous showman: the life and times of P.T. Barnum.* New York: Alfred A. Knopf, Inc.

White, J. (1985). Presentation at the NCAA marketing and promotions seminar, Cincinnati.

SUGGESTED READINGS

Govoni, N., Eng, R., and Galper, M. (1986). Promotional management. Englewood Cliffs, New Jersey: Prentice Hall.

Hanan, M. (1980). Life-styled marketing: how to position products for premium profits. New York: AMACOM Book Division.

Hansen, H., and Gauthier, R. (1989). Factors affecting attendance at professional sport events. *Journal of Sport Management, 3*(1), 15-32.

Kotler, P. (1976). *Marketing management: analysis, planning and control,* (3rd Edition). Englewood Cliffs, New Jersey: Prentice Hall.

Lewis, G., and Appenzeller, H. (1985). *Successful sport management.* Charlottesville, Virginia: The Michie Co.

Lieberman Research Inc. (1986). *Sports Illustrated, Sports Poll '86.* New York.

Luck, D., and Ferrell O. (1985). *Marketing stategy and plans.* Englewood Cliffs, New Jersey: Prentice Hall.

Research and Forecasts, Inc. (1983). *Miller Lite Report on American Attitudes Towards Sports.* Milwaukee.

Ries, A., and Trout, J. (1986). *Positioning: the Battle for your mind.* New York: McGraw-Hill Book Co.

Sutton, W. (1987). Developing an initial marketing plan for intercollegiate athletic programs. *Journal of Sport Management, 1*(2), 146-158.

Sutton, W., and Migliore, R. (1988). Strategic long range planning for intercollegiate athletic programs. *The Journal of Applied Research in Coaching and Athletics, 3*(4), 233-261.

Veeck, W., and Linn, E. (1962). *Veeck—as in wreck.* New York: The Putnam Publishing Group.

PART III

Applied Areas

11

Accounting and Budgeting

Otho G. Bendit
Linda S. Koehler

In this chapter, you will become familiar with the following terms:

American Institute of Certified
  Public Accountants
American Accounting
  Association
Financial Accounting Standards
  Board
Forecasting
Financial-planning model
"What if" questions

Overview

This chapter discusses the field of accounting for different kinds of sport and fitness organizations. Since the same accounting principles can be applied to any size or type of business entity, only the accounts differ when one constructs balance sheets, income and expense statements, and related statistical reports for the different entities.

Financial statements are uniform throughout the accounting profession because professional ac-counting organizations have published standard accounting procedures and principles. Among the most important of these organizations are the **American Institute of Certified Public Accountants** (AICPA), the **American Accounting Association** (AAA), and the **Financial Accounting Standards Board** (FASB). All sports and fitness entities, regardless of size and complexity, including college and university athletic departments, adhere to the standard accounting procedures as determined by the professional accounting institutions and associations. One can only imagine the chaos there would be in the accounting profession if these common procedures were not used by all businesses and organizations.

Businesses range from small individually owned sport and fitness clubs to large corporations such as professional sports entities and universities. Annual volume can vary from several thousand dollars to many millions. Once an individual has mastered the fundamentals and principles of accounting, however, it is not difficult to adapt these principles to any size or type of business organization.

Accounting for a small business can generally be done by a single accountant. Because of the complexity of large sport or educational entities, they may require several accountants to manage their financial departments, such as payroll, accounts payable, accounts receivable, and general accounting.

This chapter explores the standard accounting procedures and principles as they apply to sport management. Included are problems and their solutions based on accounting principles as they would apply to several different sport or fitness enterprises.

COLLEGE AND UNIVERSITY ATHLETICS

Athletic departments vary in complexity according to the size of the college or university. Institutions range from small colleges with a few hundred students to large universities with tens of thousands. They can be privately owned or state supported. Thus accounting for athletic departments can vary somewhat among institutions.

The departments in large universities are often considered separate entities and therefore must produce enough revenue to be self-sufficient. At other colleges the athletic department is considered an integral part of the organization and is treated the same as any other administrative or academic department. In both cases, the accounting procedure for the department is the same.

The following example focuses on a university whose varsity teams participate in intercollegiate competition; the university has several nonvarsity sport teams, and it does not consider the athletic department a separate entity. The university recognizes that not all sports produce revenue. Such

intercollegiate sports as track, fencing, wrestling, swimming, and tennis generally do not produce revenue. However, this too varies from college to college. Following are typical income accounts needed for each athletic team/event that *does* produce revenue:

Game income	Concessions income
Radio broadcast income	Parking income
Television income	Program income

These accounts would be set up for football, men's basketball, women's basketball, hockey, volleyball, baseball, and any other sport that produces income.

In addition to the special income accounts for athletics, there are expense categories that are peculiar to the athletic department. These are used in addition to other general expense accounts used by all departments. The following are some of these special expense accounts:

Film	Scholarships
Medical services	Security
Dental expenses	Recruiting
Officials' fees	Scouting
Food and lodging	Team travel
Ushers	

A separate income and expense statement for the athletic department is included in the university's annual financial report. All direct expenses of each sport are deducted from the sport's income to arrive at a gross profit amount before indirect expenses. All *indirect (overhead) expenses* are then deducted from gross income. The result is the net income from the operation before depreciation. This is the true net income, since depreciation is not a cash outlay.

Overhead expenses are those not directly attributable to a specific sport and that are prorated to each sport based on their percentage of the total direct expenses. Examples of departments whose expenses are considered overhead are the following:

Administrative offices	Athletic buildings
Ticket office	Publicity
Trainers' facilities	Stadiums
Sports information	Stadium grounds

Figure 11-1 is a completed income and expense statement as it would appear in the university's

General University

Statement of income and expense

For the calendar year ending December 31, 1991

Income	Total income	Football	Men's basketball	Women's basketball	Hockey	Other sports
Game	$3,600,000	$2,800,000	$700,000	$30,000	$45,000	$25,000
Radio	150,000	135,000	15,000			
Television	1,300,000	1,050,000	250,000			
Parking	80,000	70,000	10,000			
Programs	60,000	54,000	6,000			
	$5,190,000	$4,109,000	$981,000	$30,000	$45,000	$25,000
Direct expense						
Food and lodging	$ 215,000	$ 143,000	$ 21,000	$ 6,000	$ 7,000	$ 38,000
Medical service	136,000	86,000	8,000	7,000	8,000	27,000
Officials' fees	68,000	17,000	23,000	3,000	5,000	20,000
Recruiting	250,000	163,000	28,000	18,000	7,000	34,000
Salaries	1,500,000	813,000	195,000	105,000	48,000	339,000
Scholarships	1,075,000	638,000	140,000	128,000	86,000	83,000
Scouting	66,000	31,000	14,000	8,000	2,000	11,000
Team travel	390,000	190,000	85,000	36,000	19,000	60,000
Total Direct Expense	$3,700,000	$2,081,000	$514,000	$311,000	$182,000	$612,000
Percent to total Direct expense	100.00%	56.24%	13.89%	8.41%	4.92%	16.54%
Gross income (loss) before overhead expense	$1,490,000	$2,028,000	$467,000	(281,000)	(137,000)	(587,000)
Overhead expense						
Administrative expense	$ 440,000					
Ticket office	142,000					
Sports information	192,000					
Trainers quarters	86,000					
Stadium grounds	79,000					
Other	193,000					
Total overhead	$1,132,000					
O.H. distribution to sports		$636,637	$157,235	$95,201	$55,694	$187,233
Net income (loss)						
Before depreciation	$ 358,000	$1,391,363	$309,765	(376,201)	(192,694)	(774,233)
Depreciation	82,000	26,000	18,000	8,000	4,000	26,000
Net income (loss)	$ 276,000	$1,365,363	$291,765	(384,201)	(196,694)	(800,233)

FIGURE 11-1 A university's income and expense statement.

annual report. For the sake of simplification, only a few sports and their corresponding expenses are used in this example.

Colleges and universities have excellent facilities that employees and students can use when teams are not using them. Employees can schedule their own fitness programs within the times the facilities are available. Students can participate in intramural sport programs organized by the athletic department. Following are examples of facilities and programs that institutions can offer to students and employees:

For students	For employees
Intramural football	Tennis courts
Intramural soccer	Swimming pool
Intramural basketball	Fitness equipment
Athletic fields	Golf course
Tennis courts	Handball courts
Swimming pool	Fitness classes
Gymnasium	

CONCEPT CHECK

Athletic departments vary in complexity, depending on the size of the college or university. Regardless of whether the athletic department is considered a separate entity or an integral part of the organization, the accounting for the department is the same. Typical income accounts needed for each athletic team are game income, radio and television income, concessions, and parking income. The expense categories peculiar to the athletic department include medical services, officials' fees, security, and team travel. The income and expense statement for the athletic department is included in the university's annual financial report, and it reports income, direct expense, gross income before overhead expense, overhead expense, and net income. Programs in addition to varsity teams, such as intramurals and fitness programs for faculty, may also require income and expense accounts within the athletic department.

HOTELS AND RESORTS

Many hotels and resorts offer fitness programs to guests and local residents. These programs are set up as a separate regular department of the hotel or resort and have their own separate income and expense accounts.

Typical income and expense accounts for such an operation are:

Income	Expenses
Local membership	Advertising
Guest income	Entertainment
Massage income	Guest supplies
Other income	Linen
	Office supplies
	Payroll taxes
	Printing
	Salaries and wages
	Travel
	Uniforms

Figure 11-2 is an annual statement of income and expense for a hotel/resort fitness operation.

CORPORATE FITNESS PROGRAMS

Corporate fitness and health programs typically are administered by personnel or human resources departments within larger corporations. Management must consider several aspects of such programs before beginning operations. Following are several of those.

Who will participate?

Employees
Spouses or partners
Children
Retirees

Who shares the cost if not fully paid by the corporation?

Employees
Spouses or partners
Retirees

What facilities are available?

Fitness room (in-house)
Administrative office space (in-house)
Swimming pool (city, school)
Track (in-house, city, school)
Gymnasium (school)

What are the anticipated expenses?

Program director
Class instructors
Support staff
Liability insurance
Promotional expense
Equipment purchase
Equipment maintenance
Supplies

Hotels/Resorts

Statement of income and expense

Fitness department

For the calendar year ending December 31, 1991

Income
Local memberships	$ 33,000
Guest income	66,000
Massage income	22,000
Miscellaneous income	3,000
	$124,000

Expenses
Advertising	$ 5,000	
Entertainment	3,000	
Guest supplies	6,000	
Linen	4,000	
Office supplies	2,000	
Payroll taxes	4,000	
Printing	1,000	
Salaries and wages	68,000	
Travel	8,000	
Uniforms	5,000	$106,000

Net profit $ 18,000

FIGURE 11-2 An annual statement of income and expense.

Following is an example of a corporation that has decided to launch a fitness program. After considering the previously mentioned aspects of such a program, the XYZ Corporation's management made several decisions. First, employees and their spouses and retirees would be eligible to participate. Second, since the program would be considered an additional employee and retiree benefit, there would be no charge to participate.

The corporation provided an in-house fitness room and purchased exercise equipment. A human resources department employee was assigned to coordinate the program, and a fitness specialist was hired to supervise the fitness room.

The corporation arranged with a local high school to rent a swimming pool and gymnasium once a week for a small rental fee. A pool and gymnasium attendant was hired to be on hand during the employee and retiree night at the pool.

At the end of the program's first year, the corporation included the department in its income and expense statement under the title of "Fitness and Health Program," with expenses totaling $94,000. A breakdown of the expenses showed the following:

Fitness and health program

Expenses

Human resources employee salary	$38,000
Fitness specialist	25,000
Pool and gymnasium attendant	12,200
Equipment depreciation	2,500
Equipment repairs	500
Liability insurance	10,000
Rental of pool and gymnasium	5,200
Supplies	600
Total expenses	**$94,000**

Properly planned and administered corporate fitness and health programs are gaining popularity and are playing a vital part in today's corporations. Supporting the mental and physical health of employees is an important way to reduce absenteeism and to increase productivity.

FITNESS AND HEALTH CLUBS

Fitness and health clubs are a fast growing segment of the sport and fitness industry. Ranging from small, individually owned clubs to national chains of fitness and health spas, these entities provide equipment, services, and an environment to help people reach their fitness and health objectives. Members are properly supervised, use excellent facilities and equipment, and are guaranteed the best possible programs to help reach their particular goals.

To account for fitness and health clubs, the accountant must determine the income accounts to be used. Typical income accounts for an average-size club are the following:

Membership fees—monthly
Membership fees—annual
Diet food sales
Gift certificate sales
Juice bar sales

Standard expense accounts can be used for fitness and health clubs. Other accounts peculiar to these clubs, such as swimming pool supplies and maintenance, and fitness equipment repairs and maintenance, should be included with the standard accounts.

Expense accounts

Advertising	Pool supplies and
Building depreciation	maintenance
Building repairs	Postage
Equipment depreciation	Printing
Fitness equipment repairs	Salaries and wages
and maintenance	Telephone
Insurance	Taxes
Office supplies	

The year-end statement of income and expense would appear in a club's annual report as shown in the box on p. 181.

CONCEPT CHECK

Hotels, resorts, corporations, and independent clubs are launching an increasing number of sport and fitness programs. Each of these types of organizations has particular concerns with its sport or fitness program and must use specific accounts to construct its financial statements. Management within these settings must base financial decisions on typical income and expense categories regardless of whether the program is set up as an additional regular department with its own separate accounts, and on those responsible for administering the program within the larger organization.

Fitness and health club		
Statement of income and expense		
For the calendar year ending December 31, 1991		
Income		
Memberships—monthly	$20,000	
Memberships—annual	62,000	
Diet food sales	17,000	
Gift certificates	3,000	
Juice bar sales	6,000	$108,000
Expenses		
Advertising	$ 3,000	
Building depreciation	2,000	
Building repairs	1,500	
Equipment depreciation	8,000	
Fitness equipment repairs and maintenance	900	
Insurance	4,000	
Office supplies	500	
Pool supplies and maintenance	2,000	
Postage	400	
Printing	1,300	
Salaries and wages	58,000	
Telephone	2,000	
Taxes	4,200	87,800
Net income		$ 20,200

THE BUDGETING PROCESS

A budget is a written plan of the organization's sales and expenses for its next calendar or fiscal year. Although the budget appears static on paper, it reflects a very serious process of detailed planning and systematic analysis of the organization's financial operations. This process addresses factors such as the financial performance of the organization, its projected financial performance, and information and financial data from a variety of sources.

Several procedures can be used to generate an acceptable budget. Ideally the budget process should be coordinated by a special committee that includes accountants and management. This committee is responsible for reviewing all sources of sales and revenues, allocating dollars to each department, and seeking information from department supervisors about their budget needs.

The first step of this procedure is to review and determine all sources of sales and revenues. There is a wide gamut of possible revenue sources among different types of sport or fitness enterprises. Typical income accounts for collegiate athletics, for example, are game income, radio and television income, concessions, programs, and parking. Resort managers on the other hand, need to consider such elements as memberships and guest fees and massage income. The operations of the sport or fitness business must be examined carefully to ensure that *all* sources of income have been included.

Second, the budget committee allocates dollars to each of the operating departments. As in the case of revenues, all expenses must be examined. As an extension of this step, the department managers or supervisors should review their allocations and compare them to their own estimates of dollars needed to operate their departments efficiently. These estimates can be based on prior years' experience and financial performance and on anticipated expenses resulting from any changes in their programs. This stage also helps to guarantee that the managers directly affected give their analysis and opinion, and that this is analyzed and factored into the resulting budget. Budget request forms often are distributed to make this part of the process easier.

Finally, the budget committee and department managers should meet to discuss the overall financial forecast for the organization. Revenue and expense items can be adjusted at this time to help generate an acceptable and realistic budget.

As basic guidelines in planning and preparing the budget, Jensen (1983; p. 129) suggests that the budget:

1. Accurately present what the program or business needs to meet its objectives
2. Reflect honesty in its preparation and avoid padding and exaggeration
3. Balance anticipated income from all sources with anticipated expenditures including possible emergencies
4. Be rigid enough to provide structure yet flexible enough to accommodate changes
5. Be prepared with ample time for analysis, evaluation, and review
6. Involve everyone within the organization who should be consulted

Two more techniques that will help the sport or fitness manager develop the budget are **forecasting** and **financial-planning models** which can answer **"what if" questions**. According to Horngren and Sundem (1987), a sales forecast, for example, is a prediction of sales (and therefore an estimate of revenue) assuming a certain set of conditions. The sales budget, then, is the result of the decision by management to assume those conditions will be in effect. Some conditions to consider are past patterns of sales, changes in prices or fees, conditions predicted by marketing research studies, the continuation of or any change in advertising and promotion strategies, and the general economic and competitive environment of the specific sport or fitness product or service.

Finally, although quantitative methods using statistical analysis can be used for forecasting, often the experience and insight of the department managers or supervisors proves most valuable.

Forecasting can be applied when considering both sales and expenses. The following illustrates forecasting by analyzing an organization's past financial performance. Figure 11-3 shows the financial activity of a hotel fitness club in its first year of operation. Both sales and expense items have been recorded in actual dollar amounts and percentages for the month of June. With this basic information, the manager can predict the financial activity for the month of July, for example. Assuming operations are similar in June and July, the manager could expect financial performance to be similar as well. However, any expected changes in such conditions as membership lists, fees, advertising expenses, or salaries would have to be considered from a monetary and percentage standpoint. Once such records are available for each month, forecasts can be made for a longer time, usually up to a year. This information becomes valuable in preparing the budget, as well as identifying sales patterns such as seasonal peaks and slow periods.

The sport or fitness manager also may use financial-planning models. Financial-planning models help predict the effect of alternatives that management may be considering in the financial operations of the organization (Horngren and Sundem, 1987). For example, a racquetball club manager may want to learn the consequences of increasing membership fees by 5% each year over the next 3 years and compare this to the consequences of raising the cost of guest passes by 10% each year over the next 2 years. The financial-planning model can help predict the effect of each option, thus helping the manager choose between the two.

This process is often called asking "what if" questions. Examples of "what if" questions are the following:

1. What if membership drops 15% below projections?
2. What if the cost of employee group insurance is increased by 5%?
3. What if attendance at women's basketball games increases by 20% over the next two seasons?

Usually the product of the financial-planning model is a mathematical expression in which all factors are considered. Computer-based programs can be tailored to any organization, can make any number of assumptions, and can answer any "what if" questions. These programs should be made available to sport and fitness managers.

CONCEPT CHECK

The budget is the product of a process that includes detailed planning and systematic analysis of the financial operations of the sport or fitness organization. The budgeting process includes a detailed examination of all sources of revenue, all expenditures, the needs of all departments, and information and analysis from individuals directly affected by the allocations to departments. Also needed in budget planning are an accurate estimate of the financial needs of the organization, honesty, structure yet flexibility, and ample planning time. Forecasting and using financial-planning models for asking "what if" questions are also useful techniques.

Description	June, 1991	%	July, 1991 Forecast
Local memberships	$ 7,000	68.0%	_____
Guest income	2,000	19.4	_____
Massage income	1,000	9.7	_____
Misc. income	300	2.9	_____
Net sales	$10,300	100.0%	_____
Salaries and wages	$6,000	72.4%	_____
Bonuses	200	2.4	_____
Sick pay	200	2.4	_____
Group insurance/work compensation	800	9.7	_____
Employee meals	300	3.6	_____
Uniforms	200	2.4	_____
Office supplies	175	2.1	_____
Telephone	60	.7	_____
Advertising	200	2.4	_____
Repairs/maintenance	100	1.2	_____
Misc.	50	.6	_____
Total expenses	$8,285	99.9%	_____
Department profit (loss)	$2,015		

FIGURE 11-3 The financial activity for a hotel fitness club in its first year of operation.

PROBLEMS AND SOLUTIONS

The following problems and solutions will help illustrate the financial statements and accounts that a sport and fitness enterprise might use. The first problem and solution concern the balance sheet and profit and loss statement (income and expense statement) for a professional team. This problem demonstrates that, although the accounts a professional sport team uses may vary from those used in other sport and fitness settings, the accounting procedures remain the same. Refer to both this chapter and Chapter 4 in solving the problems.

PROBLEM 1: BALANCE SHEET AND INCOME AND EXPENSE STATEMENT

The ABC professional football team's fiscal year ended March 31, 1991. The accountant's trial balance showed the following accounts and amounts as of that date. Prepare a balance sheet and statement of income and expense for ABC, placing these accounts in the correct categories. When the statements are completed correctly, the asset category and the liability category on the balance sheet each will total $1,365,000. The net profit on the income and expense statement will be $570,000.

Notes payable	$ 35,000	Mortgage payable	$ 75,000
Equipment repairs	35,000	Fixed assets—building	1,220,000
Security	56,000	Salaries and wages	2,160,000
Prepaid advertising	10,000	Cash in banks	100,000
Entertainment	120,000	Accrued salaries	22,000
Game income	3,200,000	Administrative travel	82,000
Advertising	68,000	Depreciation expense	32,000
Accrued taxes	16,000	Shareholders' equity	1,198,000
Supplies	52,000	Prepaid insurance	36,000
Taxes	140,000	Team travel	1,361,000
Reserve for equipment depreciation	20,000	Television income	1,400,000
Accounts receivable	32,000	Reserve for building depreciation	116,000
Medical insurance	160,000	Accounts payable	19,000
Radio income	260,000	Program income	36,000
Cash on hand	5,000	Fixed assets—equipment	80,000
Parking income	120,000	Liability insurance	180,000
Inventories	18,000		

SOLUTION
PROBLEM 1: BALANCE SHEET AND INCOME AND EXPENSE STATEMENT

To produce the balance sheet and income and expense statement for ABC, the preceding accounts must be placed on the proper statement as an asset, liability, income item, or expense item. The following shows the accounts in the proper statements:

Assets (Debits)		Liabilities (Credits)	
Prepaid advertising	$10,000	Notes payable	$35,000
Accounts receivable	32,000	Accrued taxes	16,000
Cash on hand	5,000	Reserve for equipment depreciation	20,000
Inventories	18,000	Mortgage payable	75,000
Building	1,220,000	Accrued salaries	22,000
Cash in banks	100,000	Shareholders' equity	1,198,000
Prepaid insurance	36,000	Reserve for building depreciation	116,000
Equipment	80,000	Accounts payable	19,000
	$1,501,000		$1,501,000

	Income (Credits)		Expense (Debits)	
Games	$3,200,000	Equipment repairs		$35,000
Radio	260,000	Security		56,000
Parking	120,000	Entertainment		120,000
Television	1,400,000	Advertising		68,000
Programs	36,000	Supplies		52,000
	$5,016,000	Taxes		140,000
		Medical insurance		160,000
Less: Expenses	4,446,000	Salaries and wages		2,160,000
Net profit	570,000	Administrative travel		82,000
		Depreciation		32,000
		Team travel		1,361,000
		Liability insurance		180,000
				$4,446,000

At this point the assets and liabilities do not equal the $1,365,000 as shown in the problem presentation. This is because the building and equipment depreciation reserves should be reclassified to the asset side of the balance sheet as a reduction of the building and equipment fixed assets, thus showing the net book values of these assets. The following reconciles the assets and liabilities to the $1,365,000 figure, which also will be on the completed balance sheet.

	Assets	Liabilities
Total before depreciation reclassification	$1,501,000	$1,501,000
Less: Building depreciation	(116,000)	(116,000)
Less: Equipment depreciation	(20,000)	(20,000)
	$1,365,000	$1,365,000

In reviewing the completed balance sheet, note that the asset and liability accounts are listed and placed on the statement according to the customs of a standard balance sheet. That is, the cash items are listed first in the assets, and fixed assets are listed last. Likewise, accounts payable is the first item in the liabilities, and shareholders' equity is listed last.

On the income and expense statement, the expense accounts typically are listed in alphabetical order as can be seen on the completed statement.

SOLUTION
PROBLEM 1: BALANCE SHEET AND INCOME AND EXPENSE STATEMENT

ABC professional football team
Balance Sheet
March 31, 1991

Assets			Liabilities	
Cash on hand		$5,000	Accounts payable	$19,000
Cash in banks		100,000	Notes payable	35,000
Accounts receivable		32,000	Mortgage payable	75,000
Inventories		18,000	Accrued salaries	22,000
Prepaid insurance		36,000	Accrued taxes	16,000
Prepaid advertising		10,000	Shareholder equity	1,198,000
Fixed assets—equipment	80,000			
Less: Reserve for equipment depreciation	20,000	60,000		
Fixed assets—building	1,220,000			
Less: Reserve for building depreciation	116,000	1,104,000		
Total Assets		**$1,365,000**	**Total Liabilities**	**$1,365,000**

ABC professional football team
Statement of income and expense
For the fiscal year ended March 31, 1991

Income		
Games		$3,200,000
Television		1,400,000
Radio		260,000
Parking		120,000
Programs		36,000
	Total Income	$5,016,000
Expenses		
Administrative travel	$ 82,000	
Advertising	68,000	
Entertainment	120,000	
Equipment repairs	35,000	
Depreciation	32,000	
Liability insurance	180,000	
Medical insurance	160,000	
Salaries and wages	2,160,000	
Security	56,000	
Supplies	52,000	
Taxes	140,000	
Team travel	1,361,000	4,446,000
Net Profit		$ 570,000

PROBLEM 2: DEPRECIATION

The First Fitness Club purchased land, constructed a new building, and purchased new equipment before commencing operations. The club estimated life and salvage values of these assets as shown. Set up a depreciation schedule to arrive at the amount of depreciation expense to be taken in the first year of operation.

	Original cost	Estimated Life (years)	Estimated Salvage value
Office Furniture	$ 18,000	10	$ 2,000
Office Equipment	22,000	10	3,000
Computer Equipment	30,000	5	2,000
Exercise Equipment	52,000	15	5,000
Vehicles	20,000	4	1,000
Building	200,000	40	15,000
Land	70,000	—	—

SOLUTION
PROBLEM 2: DEPRECIATION

The first step in setting up a depreciation schedule is to deduct the salvage value from the original cost to arrive at the amount of cost to be depreciated. The second step is to divide the total cost to be depreciated of each asset by the estimated life of the particular asset. The resulting figures are added to determine the total depreciation expense for the year. The following steps illustrate the depreciation for office furniture.

Step 1.

$$\text{Amount of cost to be depreciated} = \begin{array}{r} \$18,000.00 \quad \text{(original cost)} \\ - \quad 2,000.00 \quad \text{(salvage value)} \\ \hline \$16,000.00 \end{array}$$

Step 2.

$$\frac{\$16,000 \text{ (cost to be depreciated)}}{10 \text{ years (estimated life)}} =$$
$1,600.00 (first year depreciation expense for office furniture)

Solution continued on p. 188.

First fitness club asset depreciation schedule
for the fiscal year ending March 31, 1991

Fixed assets	Original cost	Estimated life (years)	Estimated salvage value	Cost to depreciate
Furniture	$ 18,000	10	$ 2,000	$ 16,000
Equipment	22,000	10	3,000	19,000
Computers	30,000	5	2,000	28,000
Exercise equipment	52,000	15	5,000	47,000
Vehicles	20,000	4	1,000	19,000
Building	200,000	40	15,000	185,000

Asset	Depreciation cost	Estimated life (years)	First-year depreciation expense
Furniture	$ 16,000	10	$ 1,600
Equipment	19,000	10	1,900
Computers	28,000	5	5,600
Exercise equipment	47,000	15	3,133
Vehicles	19,000	4	4,750
Building	185,000	40	4,625
	$314,000		$21,608

PROBLEM 3: NONPROFIT ORGANIZATION BALANCE SHEET—UNRESTRICTED FUND

The General University had the following assets and liabilities in its unrestricted fund at the end of its fiscal year. Prepare a balance sheet for this fund. The assets and liabilities each will total $347,000.

Notes payable	$ 82,000	Depreciation reserves	$20,000
Reserve for bad debts	10,000	Accrued salaries	16,000
Land	50,000	Fixed assets	80,000
Accrued taxes	22,000	Accounts payable	18,000
Cash on hand	10,000	Equity in pooled cash—trust fund	35,000
Accounts receivable	52,000	Marketable securities	65,000
Equity	209,000	Cash in banks	80,000
Temporary investments	75,000		

SOLUTION
PROBLEM 3: NONPROFIT ORGANIZATION BALANCE SHEET—UNRESTRICTED FUND

As in Problem 1, the assets and liabilities first must be placed on either the asset or liability side of the balance sheet as follows:

Assets (debits)		Liabilities (credits)	
Land	$ 50,000	Notes payable	$ 82,000
Cash on hand	10,000	Reserve for bad debts	10,000
Accounts receivable	52,000	Accrued taxes	22,000
Temporary investments	75,000	Equity	209,000
Fixed assets	80,000	Depreciation reserves	20,000
Marketable securities	65,000	Accrued salaries	16,000
Cash in banks	80,000	Accounts payable	18,000
	$412,000	Equity in pooled cash—trust fund	35,000
			$412,000

Again, as in Problem 1, the totals do not yet agree with the total of $347,000 mentioned when the problem was presented. After moving specific liability accounts to the asset side, the accounts will correctly total $347,000. The reserve for bad debts of $10,000 and the depreciation reserves of $20,000 must be deducted from accounts receivable and fixed assets respectively on the asset side as shown on the completed balance sheet. Also, the equity in the pooled cash—trust fund liability account in the amount of $35,000 must be deducted from cash and temporary investments on the asset side as follows:

Cash on hand	$10,000
Cash in banks	80,000
Temporary investments	75,000
	$165,000
Less: Equity in pooled cash-trust fund	(35,000)
Cash and temporary investments	$130,000 (Balance sheet figure)

The above assets and liabilities are then placed on the balance sheet in their proper sequence as shown on the following completed statement.

General University
Balance sheet
Unrestricted fund
June 30, 1991

Assets			Liabilities	
Cash and temporary investments		$130,000	Accounts payable	$18,000
Marketable securities		65,000	Notes payable	82,000
Accounts receivable	52,000		Accrued salaries	16,000
Less: Reserve for			Accrued taxes	22,000
bad debts	(10,000)	42,000	Equity	209,000
Fixed assets	80,000			
Less: Depreciation				
reserves	(20,000)	60,000		
Land		50,000		
Total Assets		$347,000	Total Liabilities	$347,000

NOTE: On this year-end balance sheet, the category titled "Cash and temporary investments" includes cash on hand, cash in banks, temporary investments, and equity in pooled cash—trust fund.

PROBLEM 4: PARTNERSHIP EQUITY

The "Over 50" Fitness Center was formed as a partnership with eight partners. The partnership agreement stated that the partners would share the net profit according to each partner's percentage of the total capital contributed. Using the following, prepare the liability equity account for the partnership, showing the amounts contributed and each partner's percentage contributed.

Barry capital	$80,000	Kelly capital	50,000
Clark capital	20,000	Long capital	40,000
Dane capital	100,000	Moore capital	15,000
Foster capital	60,000	Shaw capital	35,000

The Fitness Center had a net profit of $160,000 after its first year of operations. Distribute this net profit after completing the liability equity account.

SOLUTION
PROBLEM 4: PARTNERSHIP EQUITY

In preparing a liability equity account for a partnership, the custom is to list the partners according to amount of capital contributed, from highest to lowest. This gives a clear picture at a glance of how each partner's dollar contribution and percentage contribution relate to the total dollars contributed.

Next, each partner's contribution must be divided by the total amount contributed, $400,000, to arrive at the percentage for each partner. For example:

$$\text{Dane capital} = \$100,000 \text{ divided by}$$
$$\$400,000 = 25\%$$
$$\text{Barry capital} = \$80,000 \text{ divided by}$$
$$\$400,000 = 20\%$$

The percentages should total 100%. The partners' capital contributed and percentage of the total would look like the following:

Partnership capital		Percentage of total
Dane capital	$100,000	25.00%
Barry capital	80,000	20.00
Foster capital	60,000	15.00
Kelly capital	50,000	12.50
Long capital	40,000	10.00
Shaw capital	35,000	8.75
Clark capital	20,000	5.00
Moore capital	15,000	3.75
Total capital	$400,000	100.00%

Following these percentages, the net profit of $160,000 would be distributed as follows:

Partner	Percentage of total contributed	Distribution of net income
Dane	25.00%	$ 40,000
Barry	20.00	32,000
Foster	15.00	24,000
Kelly	12.50	20,000
Long	10.00	16,000
Shaw	8.75	14,000
Clark	5.00	8,000
Moore	3.75	$ 6,000
	100.00%	$160,000

PROBLEM 5: CASH MANAGEMENT

The Skyview Ski Resort uses only one checking account for all general cash transactions. The accountant receives at 9 AM on Friday, March 30, the following cash information:

March 29 cash receipts—deposited at 8:30 AM on March 30	$460,000
Vendor checks written and sent on March 29	205,000
Idle cash invested on March 29 overnight to March 30	4,745,000
Payroll due April 13	1,000,000
Payroll due April 30	1,000,000
Mortgage payment due April 12	200,000
Construction payments due April 26	500,000

From these figures, determine how much cash may be invested on March 30 and how much of that amount may be invested for the 3 days over the weekend to April 2. Also, make up the April calendar showing the funds invested to specific dates by the accountant.

SOLUTION
PROBLEM 5: CASH MANAGEMENT

To determine the cash available for investment, the accountant adds the cash deposit of $460,000 on March 30 to the $4,745,000 that had been invested overnight the previous day. From this figure, the accountant subtracts the vendor checks mailed the previous day and arrives at $5,000,000 available for investment.

Invested overnight to March 30	$4,745,000
Cash deposited March 30	460,000
	$5,205,000
Less: Vendor checks sent March 29	(205,000)
Amount available for investment on March 30	$5,000,000

Solution continued on p. 192.

The next step is to consider the due dates of upcoming payments and invest in securities that mature on those particular dates. The amount not needed for established payments is invested for three days to April 2.

Total cash available		$5,000,000
Less: Payroll due April 13	$1,000,000	
Payroll due April 30	1,000,000	
Mortgage due April 12	200,000	
Construction due April 26	500,000	(2,700,000)
Amount to invest three days to April 2		$2,300,000

Sunday	Monday	Tuesday	Wednesday	Thursday	Friday	Saturday
1	2 $2,300,000 (Invested 3 days over weekend)	3	4	5	6	7
8	9	10	11	12 $200,000	13 $1,000,000	14
15	16	17	18	19	20	21
22	23	24	25	26 $500,000	27	28
29	30 $1,000,000					

April 1991

PROBLEM 6: BUDGET FORECASTING

The following represents the financial operations for August for the fitness center in the Hotel Deluxe. August is a very strong month for revenues. However, in September, revenue from some sources declines. Last year's records show that in September, local membership revenue dropped 30% from August, guest passes dropped 35%, and revenue from massage and miscellaneous income remained relatively constant. As the accountant, you know that some expense items will not change in September. However, the advertising, printing, and group insurance expenses will all increase by 10%, and guest supplies and employee bonuses will be reduced to $200 each. Based on this information, what is the projected net profit (loss) for the month of September?

Hotel Deluxe
Fitness center
August, 1991

Description	August amount	Percentage
SALES		
Local memberships	$8,000	74.8
Guest income	1,500	14.0
Massage income	1,000	9.3
Misc. income	200	1.9
Total Sales	$10,700	100.0%
EXPENSES		
Payroll		
Salaries/wages	$5,000	62.2
Payroll taxes	600	7.4
Worker's compensation	650	8.1
Employee bonuses	250	3.1
Group Insurance	500	6.2
Total Payroll	$7,000	87.0%
Other Expenses		
Linen (staff uniforms, towels)	$200	2.4
Guest supplies	250	3.1
Advertising	150	1.9
Printing	200	2.4
Office supplies	70	.9
Telephone	50	.6
Equipment (maintenance/repair)	90	1.1
Misc. expenses	50	.6
Total other expenses	$1,060	13.0%
Total Expense	$8,060	100.0%
Department profit (loss)	$2,640	

SOLUTION
PROBLEM 6: BUDGET FORECASTING

The September forecast is determined according to the figures from August of the current year and the trends from September of the previous year. Projected sales are obtained by calculating the percentage of change in September of last year compared to August and applying this percentage to August figures for this year. For example, local memberships for September would be 30% less than those in August ($8000 − $2400 = $5600).

Forecasting expenses for the month of September requires adjustments in the figures for five categories. The August costs for advertising, printing, and group insurance each must be increased by 10% (that is, advertising expenses will increase from $150 to $165 for the month of September). The employee bonuses and guest supplies line items each should be recorded as $200.

In this particular example, the manager of the fitness center in the Hotel Deluxe would anticipate a net loss of about $270.

Hotel Deluxe
Fitness center
Forecast: September, 1991

	Description	August amount	Percentage	Percentage of increase (decrease) over 1989	September amount	Percentage
SALES						
	Local memberships	$8,000.00	74.8	(30)%	$5,600.00	72.0%
	Guest income	1,500.00	14.0	(35)	975.00	12.5
	Massage income	1,000.00	9.3	–	1,000.00	12.9
	Misc. income	200.00	1.9	–	200.00	2.6
	Total Sales	$10,700.00	100.0%		$7,775.00	100.0%
EXPENSES						
	Payroll					
	Salaries/wages	$5,000.00	62.2	–%	$5,000.00	62.2%
	Payroll taxes	600.00	7.4	–	600.00	7.5
	Worker's compensation	650.00	8.1	–	650.00	8.1
	Employee bonuses	250.00	3.1	(20)	200.00	2.5
	Group insurance	500.00	6.2	10	550.00	6.8
	Total Payroll	$7,000.00	87.0%		$7,000.00	87.1%
	Other Expenses					
	Linen (staff uniforms, towels)	$200.00	2.4	–%	$200.00	2.5%
	Guest supplies	250.00	3.1	(20)	$200.00	2.5
	Advertising	150.00	1.9	10	$165.00	2.0
	Printing	200.00	2.4	10	$220.00	2.7
	Office supplies	70.00	.9	–	$70.00	.9
	Telephone	50.00	.6	–	$70.00	.6
	Equipment (maintenance/ repair)	50.00	.6	–	50.00	.6
	Misc. expenses	90.00	1.1	–	$90.00	1.1
	Total other expenses	$1,060.00	13.0%		$1,045.00	12.9%
	Total Expense	$8,060.00	100.0%		$8,045.00	100.0%
	Department profit (loss)	$2,640.00			($270.00)	

SUMMARY

1. The same accounting principles are applied to professional sport organizations, college, athletics, hotel fitness programs, sport clubs, and to any other type of sport or fitness business. However, the *specific* accounts within the organization must be considered when constructing the financial statements. Accounting procedures have been standardized by such organizations as the American Institute of Certified Public Accountants, the American Accounting Association, and the Financial Accounting Standards Board.
2. Accounting for athletic departments varies depending on factors such as the size of the college or university, whether the university is private or state supported, and whether the athletic department is considered a separate entity and must produce enough revenue to be self-sufficient.
3. Hotels, resorts, corporations, and independent clubs are launching an increasing number of sport and fitness programs. Important accounting factors include the organization's particular income and expense items and the designation of individuals to be responsible for administering the program.
4. Managers and accountants of any sport or fitness organization should be familiar with several important procedures and financial statements. These are balance sheets, income and expense statements, depreciation schedules, unrestricted funds for nonprofit organizations, partnership equity, cash management, the budget, and the budgeting process.
5. Developing the budget is a detailed and systematic process. Factors to consider include the objectives and needs of the organization, sources of revenue, expenditures, and information from individuals directly involved. Ideally, this process is directed by a committee of individuals responsible for gathering and reviewing information about budgetary needs and the allocation of the funds.

REVIEW QUESTIONS AND ISSUES

1. Name at least three university varsity sports that typically do not produce income.
2. Name at least four departments within university athletics whose expenses are considered to be indirect (overhead) expenses.
3. What are the four questions to be answered before launching a corporate fitness program?
4. What department is usually responsible for administering a corporate fitness program?
5. Why is it helpful to list partners' equity accounts according to the size of their capital contribution?
6. Which liability accounts are moved to the asset side of the balance sheet to arrive at net assets and liabilities?
7. What four accounts make up the "Cash and temporary investments" amount on a nonprofit unrestricted fund balance sheet?
8. What are the accepted useful lives for office furniture and computer equipment for depreciation purposes?
9. What three items of information does an accountant need to determine the amount of cash available for short-term investing?
10. How is sales forecasting useful when preparing a budget?

CASE STUDY 1: PREPARING THE INCOME AND EXPENSE STATEMENT

The statement of income and expense (profit and loss statement) covering the past fiscal year for the athletic department must be submitted to the university accounting office in one month. As the director of athletics, you are responsible for several programs. One is varsity sports, which include football, women's basketball, men's basketball, women's volleyball, and men's baseball as revenue-producing sports. Non–revenue-producing sports in your program are track, wrestling, swimming, tennis, and field hockey. In addition, there are several club sports under your direction. These are soccer, rugby, lacrosse, water polo, and crew. Finally, your department oversees a fitness program offered to faculty, their partners, retirees, and students.

1. *What are some typical accounts you would use for each program?*

2. *What special income and expense accounts are you likely to encounter for each program?*
3. *Into what major categories would the income and expense statement be divided?*
4. *What types of indirect overhead would you have for each program?*
5. *How would indirect overhead expenses affect your figures?*

CASE STUDY 2: PREPARING THE BUDGET

As manager of a corporate fitness program, it is your responsibility to submit a budget for the next fiscal year to the director of human resources and development. The fitness program, which employs two fitness specialists and you, has operated for 3 years and has consistently lost money. The director of human resources and development has agreed to subsidize the program with an additional $2,000 with the understanding that a portion of the funds will be allocated to a marketing and advertising campaign.

1. *What steps would you take in planning and preparing your budget?*
2. *From whom would you solicit information?*
3. *What options do you have when allocating funds?*
4. *What changes in the budget would you propose?*
5. *Would the process of forecasting be helpful to you? If so, how?*
6. *How might asking "what if" questions be useful?*

CASE STUDY 3: INVESTING IDLE CASH

You have been an accountant for a local fitness and health club for 2 years. During that time you have closely watched the flow of general cash. You believe that the available funds for each month could be put to better use by investing them on a short-term basis. You are eager to try a cash management approach using weekend investing.

You are writing a proposal to the manager/owner of the club covering your plan for idle cash.

1. *What information do you need to determine the amount of cash available for short-term investing?*
2. *How will you justify your proposal?*
3. *What written materials, such as graphs, charts, or dates, do you need to support your plan?*
4. *What specific strategies will you include in your proposal?*

REFERENCES

Broyles, J., and Hay, R. (1979). *Administration of athletic programs: a managerial approach*. Englewood Cliffs, New Jersey: Prentice Hall.

Dougherty, N., and Bonanno, D. (1985). *Management principles in sport and leisure services*. Minneapolis, Minnesota: Burgess Publishing Co.

Ellis, T., and Norton, R. (1988). *Commercial recreation*. St. Louis, Missouri: Mosby–Year Book, Inc.

Horngren, C., and Sundem, G. (1987). *Introduction to management accounting*. Englewood Cliffs, New Jersey: Prentice Hall.

Jensen, C. (1983). *Administrative management of physical education and athletic programs*. Philadelphia, Pennsylvania: Lea & Febiger.

Lewis, G., and Appenzeller, H. (1985) *Successful sport management*. Charlottesville, Virginia: The Michie Co.

Mason, J., and Paul, J. (1988). *Modern sports administration*. Englewood Cliffs, New Jersey: Prentice Hall.

Railey, J., and Railey, P. (1988). *Managing physical education, fitness, and sports programs*. Mountain View, California: Mayfield Publishing Co.

VanderZwaag, H. (1984). *Sport management: sport management in schools and colleges*. New York: John Wiley & Sons.

SUGGESTED READINGS

Broyles, J., and Hay, R. (1979). *Administration of athletic programs: a managerial approach*. Englewood Cliffs, New Jersey: Prentice Hall.

Lewis, G., and Appenzeller, H. (1985) *Successful sport management*. Charlottesville, Virginia: The Michie Co.

Mason, J., and Paul, J. (1988). *Modern sports administration*. Englewood Cliffs, New Jersey: Prentice Hall.

VanderZwaag, H. (1984). *Sport management: sport management in schools and colleges*. New York: John Wiley & Sons.

12

Economics in Sport

Steve Houlihan
Larry DeBrock

In this chapter, you will become familiar with the following terms:

Allocation
Residual returns
Sports unions
Compensation
Opportunity cost
Broadcast television
Cable television
Free agency
Gross National Product

Gross National Sports Product
Licensing agreements
Demographics
Input
Output
Risk
Disposable income
Sponsorship

Overview

You have been hired as an assistant to the athletic director (A.D.) at Big State University. Big State, which has a reputation for successful athletic teams, has an athletic budget of 10 million dollars and strong alumni support.

In recent years Big State has added several women's programs, which have been successful on the field but bring in very little revenue. An athletic facility was recently built and intramural programs

have expanded, since there is now a facility to meet the demand.

The A.D. is responsible for providing all sport programs—varsity, club, and intramural—on the 10-million-dollar budget. Whatever revenue comes in is used to offset the money budgeted. The stated goal is to operate on a balanced budget (expenditures equal revenue). However, Big State has usually operated in the "red." Until recently, nobody seemed to care. Recent events have changed that attitude.

Two years ago Big State was investigated by the NCAA, and its football program received significant sanctions. Certain faculty on campus have questioned the value of the sport programs. Also, the state economy is in severe financial difficulty, and the legislature is threatening to cut the athletic budget.

The A.D. has asked you to do an economic and financial analysis of the entire athletic program. Your jobs depend on bringing the budget under control. He has asked you to prepare a preliminary memo discussing the problems you expect to encounter when doing the analysis. He would also like you to make suggestions to improve the position of revenues vs. expenditures.

The aforementioned material represents some typical problems faced by A.D.s at universities involved in intercollegiate athletics. The various decisions involve **allocation** of scarce resources among many competing "needs." These problems are faced by all sport and leisure industry operations, not just collegiate athletics. This chapter will explore these problems in more detail.

One disclaimer: this chapter is not a primer on how to start a business, nor is it a rulebook for operating a current business. Rather, this chapter attempts to introduce the economic status of the sport industry and its components. A central theme will become obvious. All segments of the industry face the same economic decisions. These decisions may be couched in different jargon, but the problems will be the same. As pointed out in Chapter 5, some concerns expressly maximize "profits"; these are the commercial operations. Others, officially designated as not-for-profit organizations, will endeavor to maximize the **residual returns** over expenditures on their lines of operation. The focus of all concerns will be to select and use inputs in the most efficient manner, to price the resulting product optimally, and to maintain an awareness of consumer (or fan) trends.

THE SPORT SEGMENT OF THE AMERICAN ECONOMY

What is the "Sport Industry"? Is it fair to call it an "industry" in the same way that term is used to describe the manufacturing sector of the economy? In Chapter 5, basic principles of economics were presented. Once a person understands those basic principles, it should be possible to apply them to

sport settings to assist the managerial decision-making process. However, practical problems may arise in applying economic and financial theory to such settings due to the unique role sport plays in our society.

This section begins with a discussion of how the attitudes toward sports have affected economic and financial behavior and what the role of the sport industry is in our economy. Also discussed will be some of the problems that may be encountered when making an economic analysis of a specific component of the sport industry. For illustrative purposes, intercollegiate athletics and the role of the athletic administrator will be evaluated. The discussion will then focus on a variety of the components of the sport industry to illustrate the application of the principles learned in Chapter 5. Case studies will be used to assist the student to understand the principles and to apply them to specific situations. An integrated approach will be emphasized.

The status of sports in the economy

Predicting economic and financial behavior depends in part on assumptions of how people are motivated or will act. The attitude towards sport, its values, and whether it should be considered "big business" has changed dramatically in the last 30 years. Many people say that all the money spent in health and fitness clubs and on leisure and participant sports is a waste. Many sports fans and sportswriters long for the day when athletes played for "the love of the game." People in academia claim that colleges and universities should not spend significant sums of money on sport; the money spent on them diverts funds from more worthy academic programs.

These attitudes are important in understanding the traditional economic and financial approach to sport. Since sport was not considered business by most people, little attention was paid to their economic and financial aspects. This attitude is changing. In some cases the value of a sport-related enterprise may now be overstated. Legitimate economic and financial concerns need to be addressed by the possible overzealous promotion of sports. For example, the state of Maryland recently issued 200 million dollars in bonds to finance a new football stadium in Baltimore, despite the fact that Baltimore has no football team (*The Economist*, 1989).

A similar technique was used in St. Petersburg to finance a baseball stadium in hopes of luring a professional baseball team to the area. Some cities build new stadiums in an effort to retain teams. The "new" Comiskey Park in Chicago is part of a deal to keep the White Sox baseball club in the city. The justification is that sport franchises attracted by a stadium will bring a variety of economic benefits to an area. However, there is considerable disagreement regarding what the real economic return will be, and few studies have addressed both sides of the issue.

Based on what has happened in recent years and what is projected to happen in the future, those people who are sport promoters are likely to prevail. Although certain Americans have always been concerned with fitness (for health considerations or for a perceived edge on the competition), the "fitness boom" is a recent phenomenon (Green, 1986). The number of health clubs and related facilities has grown from 1,200 to 10,000 in the past 2 decades. Americans spend over 5 billion dollars annually to keep fit; the majority is spent at health clubs (Crossley and Jamieson, 1988). In some areas of the country, the average annual cost of belonging to a club is in excess of 1,000 dollars per year (*The Economist*, 1987).

Many of the related fitness products, such as footwear and athletic equipment, have gone through a transformation in the way they are sold and marketed. The emphasis is on "high tech" and status. Some old firms that have not adapted to the demands of a different market and have not adjusted their choice and use of inputs in the production process have been forced out of business. This provides opportunities for young people with economic and financial, as well as sport management and marketing, backgrounds to make their impact in this growing area of the economy.

Similarly, the traditional attitudes about spectator sports are important in understanding the application of economic principles to this segment of the sports industry. Traditionally, professional sports teams have been owned by wealthy individuals for a variety of reasons, including the attractiveness of the lifestyle, the glamour of being around professional athletes, and in many cases the opportunity for "income tax write-offs"—the ability to reduce taxable income by tax losses generated by the team (Kovat, 1977). Generating prof-

its has not always been the major focus, and in many cases, neither was fielding a winning team. Perhaps one of the most notorious illustrations of that attitude occurred in 1920, when Harry Frazee, the owner of the Boston Red Sox, sold Babe Ruth to the New York Yankees. Frazee wanted the cash to finance his "real business," producing Broadway plays. Mr. Frazee's action changed the course of baseball history.

The athlete, the most significant commodity in the production process of professional sports, has been historically underpaid. Many people feel that athletes are adults playing children's games. However, a myriad of causes including television, the advent of **sports unions,** and the effect of legal decisions have changed the relationship between the team owner and the players dramatically. Athletes now receive considerably more **compensation.** This is one of the reasons greater attention is being given to economic and financial considerations in running a professional sport team.

At one time the only business opportunities in professional sports were for members of the owner's family or for former athletes and coaches. Now there are opportunities for those educated in the economic and financial aspects of sport to be involved in the operation of professional teams.

At the college and university level, spending on sports programs has increased over the years. Traditionally, studies of college life have focused on certain "intangibles" such as the personal, cultural, and academic experience of the student (Cady, 1978). Many people always considered sports an integral part of that experience. The "bottom line" may not have been important or even relevant.

At many institutions, sport is no longer an extracurricular activity but a business with a perceived effect on status, influence, and public support. Often, athletic directors will refer to their sports programs as "our product" in public statements. The ineligibility or unavailability of an individual athlete can result in a large financial loss to the institution (Berry and Wong, 1986). It is estimated that Patrick Ewing and Doug Flutie were responsible personally for bringing in millions of dollars in additional revenue to Georgetown University and Boston College, respectively.

With increased spending and exposure comes a greater need for justification and therefore greater attention to economic and financial matters. The need for individuals with a sport management background has increased. The role of an A.D. is more complex and difficult in the real world than it might appear in the idealized world of the average sports fan (Singer, 1989). The A.D. and his or her staff need to have training in economics and finance, as well as marketing, law, and other business-related subjects.

CONCEPT CHECK

Traditional economic and financial attitudes toward sport have been changing in recent years. With the increased recognition that sport is big business and significant sums of money being spent on sports-related products, there has been a corresponding demand for utilizing sound economic principles when evaluating a sport enterprise. This has lead to employment opportunities for individuals with economic-management backgrounds.

Historical and current descriptive statistics

The function of an economic system is to allocate scarce resources and to provide certain products and services at the sacrifice of others. For every service-related job created by the construction of a new athletic facility, the **opportunity cost** might be a reduction in manufacturing-related jobs. For every dollar that is spent in an athletic department of a college or university, the opportunity cost might be a reduction in dollars spent in the English department. To quantify such sacrifices, consider how significant a role the sport industry plays in our economic system.

The natural questions are: Is sport big business? Does the sport industry play a significant role in our economy? Based on what has been learned thus far, the answers to these questions appear to be yes. However, sport is perhaps not as big a business nor does the sport industry play as significant a role as some people claim; also, success is not guaranteed. In other words, individuals, companies, and colleges and universities will likely fail if they simply acknowledge the seemingly insatiable appetite for sports-related products and services (demand) without using sound economic and financial analyses when supplying these products and services (supply).

The industry in aggregate. First, the actual size of the sport industry should be analyzed. Most publicity and academic studies about the economic and financial aspects of sports are about professional and collegiate spectator sports and the role of television. Why? At the professional level, the National Football League's (NFL) television contract signed in 1990 was for 3.6 billion dollars, a 92% increase from the contract signed just 3 years earlier in 1987 (Zoglin, 1990). Five different **broadcast and cable television** networks are part of the pact. The National Basketball Association's (NBA) 1989 contract with NBC was for 875 million dollars, a 250% increase from the contract amount of 1986. The escalation in television deals began in 1988 when CBS won the rights to broadcast major league baseball for 4 years for 1.08 billion dollars, and ESPN agreed to pay 400 million dollars to broadcast games on cable stations (Zoglin, 1990). These numbers are significantly higher than the 1.59 billion dollars spent on network sports coverage in 1987 (Hoffman and Greenberg, 1988).

Along with these large television packages has come criticism that the television packages do not make economic or financial sense. The issue is whether the total costs—which include the rights fees, the production and promotion of the event, and the impact of displacing other television programs—can be justified by the total return, which includes advertising revenue, promotion benefits, public image, and good will (Klatell and Marcus, 1988). Some industry experts do not believe so and feel that network television will become a depressed industry (Klatell and Marcus, 1988). Why then were the deals made? Certain network executives believe there is a guaranteed audience for sports that will carry over to other programming, thereby providing the economic justifications for making the deals. Profit maximization involves long-run decision making.

A likely result or by-product of the television deals, and reinforcement of the perception that professional sport is big business, will be further increases in players' salaries. Although many factors, such as **free agency** (the ability of an athlete to play for whom he or she wishes), affect the ultimate salaries of all players, the increase in television revenues will make more money available for everyone. Average salaries in basketball are approaching 1 million dollars per year, and baseball salary averages are approaching three quarters of a million dollars per year. Football salaries averaged around 300,000 dollars in 1989, but television contracts could lead to a salary explosion in that sport.

At the collegiate level, CBS and the NCAA made an agreement in 1987 in which CBS would pay 166.5 million dollars for the exclusive rights to broadcast college basketball games (Simpson, 1988). How important is this money? The dollars generated by the broadcast of the Division I basketball championship is the NCAA's most significant source of revenue and is distributed to its member institutions (Berry and Wong, 1986).

In 1990 the Collegiate Football Association (CFA) negotiated a 5-year deal with ABC for 210 million dollars. Subsequently, the University of Notre Dame, a member of the CFA, signed its own deal with NBC for 30 million dollars.

These numbers sound impressive and to most people seem larger than life. But just how "big" are professional and collegiate sports? Total professional and collegiate sport expenditures, including television and radio rights fees, account for less than ½ of 1% of the **Gross National Product** (GNP) of the United States (Koch, 1986). To put things in perspective, Gulf & Western Corporation owns Madison Square Garden, which in turn owns the New York Knicks and the New York Rangers. Gulf & Western's profit has been as high as three times the combined gross revenue of all professional sport leagues (Berry and Wong, 1986). Professional athletes, although hardly impoverished, earn far less money than many entertainers and less than many executives and business owners. The University of Michigan has an annual athletic budget of approximately 20 million dollars and has over 100,000 people attend each of its home football games. However, the combined annual athletic budgets of the members of the Big Ten Athletic Conference are less than 25% of the budget of the smallest Fortune 500 company (Koch, 1986).

Although professional and "big-time" collegiate sports are the most visible and generate the most media attention, they account for only a small percentage of the sport economy. According to a study by the Wharton Econometric Forecasting Association (WEFA) and *Sports Inc.* magazine, the **Gross National Sports Product** (GNSP), which is the sum of the output and services generated by the sports industry, totaled 50.2 billion dollars in 1987 and

was on the rise (Sandomir, 1988). This represented 1.1% of the GNP, the sum of output and services generated by all industries. According to the WEFA study, the sport industry was the twenty-third largest industry in America and likely to become larger. As of 1990, sport was a 63.1 billion-dollar a year business, making it the twenty-second largest industry in the United States (Comte and Stogel, 1990).

The largest single component of the sport industry, accounting for over 16 billion dollars in revenue and over 30% of the GNSP, is leisure and participant sports. This includes golfing green fees and memberships, bowling, ski rentals and lift tickets, and health club memberships (Sandomir, 1988).

The next largest component of the GNSP is sporting goods, accounting for over 15 billion dollars in revenue, including footwear, equipment, and clothing sales. The sporting goods industry is capitalizing on the increased popularity of spectator sports by entering into **licensing agreements** with various athletic organizations. The sale of licensed sport properties represents an increasing share of the total sporting goods market.

Other significant components of the sport industry include advertising (3.6 billion dollars), spectator sports receipts (3.3 billion dollars), concessions and souvenirs (2.1 billion dollars), television and radio rights fees (1.2 billion dollars), and corporate sponsorships (1 billion dollars).

Less significant in total revenues generated but representing areas of opportunity are sport magazines and books, stadium and arena construction, sport insurance, and sport organizations (for example, the United States Olympic Committee and the various sport halls of fame).

What does the future hold?

Two factors will play an important role in the future growth of the sport industry. First, **demographics** show that an increasing number of Americans will be "retired." However, these people will remain active and, with the increase in leisure time brought on by retirement, will increase the demand for sport activities. Second, the future will see shorter average "work weeks." Again, this increase in leisure time should lead to a growth in demand for sport activities.

One study suggests that the GNSP will more

than double by the year 2000, that sport advertising will more than triple, and that there will be tremendous growth in the foreign markets (Rosner, 1989). Opportunities exist for those individuals with appropriate backgrounds in economics and finance.

CONCEPT CHECK

Recent television deals in professional and collegiate sport has created considerable interest in the role the sport industry plays in our economy. While these deals have received significant media attention, they account for only a small percentage of the GNSP. On the whole, the sport industry accounts for approximately 1.1% of the GNP. The major components include leisure and participant sports, sporting goods, advertising, spectator sports, television, and corporate sponsorships of sporting events.

AN OVERVIEW OF THE ECONOMIC PROBLEMS IN SPORT MANAGEMENT

One can expect problems making economic analyses of the sport industry that are similar to those encountered in analyzing more traditional industries. These problems are compounded by the diverse components that make up the sport industry. Given the historical and unique role of sport in our society, one may encounter additional problems when doing analyses.

A basic task of an economic system is to combine certain input to produce output. To illustrate some of the economic problems in sport management, apply them to intercollegiate athletic programs. Intercollegiate athletics is an industry component that can be viewed as a collection of firms (colleges and universities), each providing products (athletic entertainment) that have considerable substitutability to the potential buyers (fans) (Koch, 1986).

Input to the process includes athletic facilities, equipment, and, most importantly, people. These people are the players, coaches, and athletic administrators. The **output** is athletic entertainment.

One of an athletic administrator's functions is to oversee sport programs a college or university offers. The A.D. must be concerned with budgets, revenues, expenses, and the cost effectiveness of the programs. Because of cost restraints, a decision

whether to continue a specific athletic program may have to be made.

The A.D. is likely to face problems making any economic or financial analysis regarding which athletic programs should be continued. For example, when the University of Oklahoma announced in 1989 that it was going to discontinue the women's basketball program, the decision was greeted with nearly unanimous criticism from the national media. This media attention could have distorted other variables besides the impact on revenues and costs. Oklahoma's decision to discontinue the program was subsequently reversed. However, when the University of Massachusetts, facing substantial cost issues, discontinued its athletically successful women's lacrosse program, few protests were made. The variable being tested, the direct costs associated with a certain program, was similar. However, the underlying conditions, the relative size of the remaining programs, were different.

Suppose a college or university temporarily cancels an athletic program, as Tulane University and the University of San Francisco did with their men's basketball programs in the 1980s. An analysis of the financial impact of such a decision should consider the effect on contributions made to the college or university. To conclude without analysis that contributions decreased (or increased) because of the decision to cancel the athletic program may be incorrect. Several studies of the hypothesis that athletic success has a direct impact on contributions have been undertaken. The results are inconclusive (Telander, 1989). Cancelling a basketball program at one school could have a long-term beneficial effect on that school's financial well-being; the opposite might be true at another institution.

As previously mentioned, the most important input for the college or university producing athletic entertainment is people, particularly the student–athlete. The A.D. is in part responsible for "acquiring" the input. In a pure market economy the college or university would compete for the best athletes and rely on the principles of supply and demand. The outcome would be similar to that of professional sport leagues. However, colleges and universities do not operate in a pure market system. A governing body, in most cases the NCAA, operates like a cartel. It sets regulations to promote elements of fairness and efficiency. More significantly, these rules and regulations limit the competition for the student–athlete. The ingenuity of the schemes to circumvent NCAA rules in compensating athletes is evidence of the great value of these athlete inputs, as well as the pressure on the program to do well. The A.D. must know these rules and be able to factor in their effect when making any economic or financial analysis of the athletic department.

Another input used in providing athletic entertainment is athletic equipment. Recall that the A.D.'s goal in financial management is profit maximization (or for not-for-profit entities, maximization of the residuals). Thus the A.D.'s focus should be to obtain the necessary equipment at the lowest available cost. The factor of **risk** must also be considered. Risk factors might include the possibility of the supplier going out of business or of a student–athlete being injured due to inferior equipment.

A facility is another input used to provide the product. If an A.D. proposes a new facility, knowledge of the tax system would be helpful in making decisions about the facility's use. For example, colleges and universities are tax-exempt institutions. This is because Congress, as a matter of social policy, encourages provisions for educational services. However, it is possible to be taxed on income unrelated to the basis for the tax exemption. Athletic programs have been considered an integral part of the educational process, but issues can arise regarding income from (1) fees for use of a facility for profit-making entertainment presented primarily for the general public (football games, basketball games, concerts), (2) income from fees for the use of the facility by the general public, and (3) income from fees charged to private companies, such as health clubs, that operate under the auspices of the athletic department (Wong, 1988).

Finally, the A.D. needs to make financial forecasts to plan and make capital budgeting decisions. Consideration of cultural, political, demographic, and technological trends may be important. For example, one of the crucial issues in intercollegiate athletics is women's programs. The increased pressure for women's programs has put a strain on athletic budgets. Congress, with the passage of Title IX and the Civil Rights Restoration Act, has made it clear that equal opportunities need to be provided. Before the passage of Title IX in 1972,

only 294,000 girls participated in high school sports, as compared to 3.7 million boys. By 1986, 1.8 million girls and 3.4 million boys participated (Sage, 1990). If demographic information indicates that more women will be entering college and participating in athletics in the future, this combination of factors requires appropriate current planning to meet the demand in the most cost-efficient manner.

CONCEPT CHECK

The sport industry faces many of the same problems in conducting economic and financial analyses as do other large industries. The economic problems include allocating inputs to produce outputs, testing variables, and recognizing the effect of outside influences. The financial management problems include appropriate choice of risk levels, careful consideration of capital contributions, the effect of the income tax system, and understanding cultural, political, demographic, and technological trends.

CASE STUDY

Return to the opening section of this chapter. There you were presented with a hypothetical task faced by an athletic director. You are now better equipped to discuss the problem issues. Prepare your report, making sure you discuss the pros and cons of any suggestions you make.

MAJOR COMPONENTS OF THE SPORT INDUSTRY

Thus far, the ways by which attitudes toward sports have affected economic and financial behavior and the role of sports in our economy, as well as fundamental problems faced in making economic and financial analyses, have been discussed.

Now the focus turns to four specific components of the sport industry and some of the issues that might arise in managerial decision making. The components are as follows:

- Leisure and participant sports
- Sporting goods
- Professional sports
- Sponsorships

A brief overview of each component will be presented, followed by a case study. These studies are designed to test a student's ability to recognize and address multiple economic and financial issues and to apply the principles learned in Chapter 5.

Leisure and participant sports

According to the study conducted by *Sports Inc.* and the Wharton Econometric Forecasting Association, the largest component of the sport industry, leisure and participant sports (which includes health club memberships, golf, bowling, skiing, and related activities) is the most mature (Sandomir, 1988). In other words, significant future growth in demand is not expected. It is imperative for individuals involved in this sport industry component to compete effectively with other suppliers and be financially efficient.

A large segment of the leisure and participant sport component is health club memberships, accounting for over 5 billion dollars (Sandomir, 1988). As discussed earlier, there has been tremendous growth in this area in recent years. However, some studies indicate the boom may be over. One contributing factor is based on demographic information. "Baby boomers" born between 1945 and 1965 compose about one third of the United States population, and they are aging (Wendell, 1989). Health clubs might be adversely affected by that aging factor. According to this study, 10% of the population under age 35 is likely to use a health club facility. This percentage drops as the sample gets older, with 5% between the ages of 45 and 55 and only 2% of those over 55.

Many of the baby boomers are now two-income families with high **disposable income;** those in high income brackets spend more money on fitness-related activities. However, many also have children. While disposable income is high, the availability of leisure time is expected to be an issue. Participation in activities where the whole family is involved is increasing. The health club industry must work to meet the changing demand. Health clubs require a variety of facilities and equipment. Studies indicate that a club needs a support population of 50,000 to 70,000 people within a several-mile radius (Crossley and Jamieson, 1988). This population should produce a membership of sufficient size to be profitable (Crossley and Jamieson, 1988).

The largest segment of the leisure and participant sport component is golfing greens fees and memberships, accounting for almost 6 billion dollars in revenue. In 1986, there were over 12,000 golf courses, either public, private, or municipal, and 18 million golfers in the United States (Crossley and Jamieson, 1988). Most golfers are male with above average incomes. Forty percent of all golfers are senior citizens. What does this demographic information mean to the golfing industry? Golf is adversely affected by time constraints and lack of facilities. Golf courses are expensive, costing as much as a quarter of a million dollars per hole in construction expenditures. However, golf will benefit from the aging of the population, as well as that population's growing wealth.

CASE STUDY

You have been hired by ABC Health and Fitness, a racquetball and tennis club. ABC also operates a bar and nightclub on the premises. An additional line of business is the sale of tennis and racquetball equipment and clothing.

The owner of ABC has hired you as an economic consultant as she plans for next year's operations. She informs you that the club has many competitors in the area, and thus she must price her memberships according to the local "market" price. Using the concepts introduced in Chapter 5, depict the market demand and supply curves for memberships in health clubs. The owner has recently received a report by a national association representing health clubs indicating that demand for health club memberships is very price elastic. Provide a thorough explanation of this, using a graph as an aid. Also, be sure to alert the owner about the implications of this elasticity and market price changes.

The owner of the ABC club disputes this finding of elasticity, pointing out that while prices have risen 20% over the past year, memberships at the ABC club have grown by 30%. The owner conjectures that she has found a market with upward sloping demand curves. Using your knowledge of economics, as well as the information that the local population has grown significantly, convince the owner that she has not found an exception to the law of demand.

Finally, this growth in demand and the resulting price increases have contributed to a very profitable year for the ABC club. In the owner's plans for the coming year, she has forecast that profits will continue their path, growing even higher. Using the supply and demand analysis from Chapter 5, show her why she should not expect such high profits to continue. All other things being equal, what would you predict to happen to market price over the coming months?

Sporting goods

The second largest component of the GNSP is sporting goods. According to the National Sporting Goods Association, Americans spent 9.6 billion dollars on athletic equipment in 1989 (Samuelson, 1989). Add to that the revenues generated on related athletic footwear and clothing and the amount spent on this industry approaches 20 billion dollars. In the late 1980s the amount of sporting goods manufactured in the United States and exported to foreign countries rose dramatically, creating even more opportunities.

Those involved in the sporting goods industry must meet the demands of a variety of sports at a variety of levels. New products and improvements on old products are constantly introduced. Marketing, quality control, and pricing are important. For example, in the early 1980s Wilson Sporting Goods lost 54 million dollars over a 2-year period and considerable market share in two of its strongest lines, golf and tennis (Goulian, 1988). Industry experts attributed the blame to Pepsico, manufacturer of Pepsi, Wilson's parent company. Products that had been traditionally sold in pro shops and specialty stores were being distributed to discount sporting goods chains and then sold at discount prices. Wilson subsequently lost that traditional market.

Currently, one of the most lucrative areas of the sporting goods component is athletic footwear. Another successful area is the sale of licensed sport properties. Major League Baseball and the National Football League each have exceeded 500 million dollars in annual licensed merchandise sales. Colleges have also seen tremendous growth and profit in sales of their licensed goods. Big-time college athletic programs have licensing revenues from 450,000 to 650,000 dollars annually (Sage, 1990).

CASE STUDY

You have been hired by a major manufacturer of athletic footwear and clothing. You are on a team

that is to introduce and market a new basketball sneaker to be priced at the upper end of the scale. You've been asked to begin a market analysis on the potential demand for the new sneaker, what amount your company should supply, and at what price, using the concepts presented in Chapter 5.

What are some of the factors to consider in determining the expected demand for the sneaker? What are the effects of the status of the sport of basketball? What is your competition doing? What are some of the factors to be considered in determining how many sneakers should be supplied?

Once you have discussed the relevant factors, assume the following demand and supply information:

Demand schedule for basketball sneakers

Price/pair	Quantity/million
200	10
180	20
160	30
140	40
120	50

Supply schedule for basketball sneakers

Price/pair	Quantity/million
200	50
180	40
160	30
140	20
120	10

Using the tools from Chapter 5, illustrate the demand and supply schedules by drawing a demand curve and a supply curve. Next illustrate the equilibrium price. Finally, what are some of the factors that could cause a shift in either the demand curve or the supply curve?

Professional sport

Professional sport is an interesting paradox. It receives an inordinate amount of attention in relation to its economic impact on society. While its strong position in American day-to-day life cannot be questioned, total revenues generated and total employment created are relatively small. Professional sport, however, presents some of the most interesting economic and financial issues, particularly in its close relationship to the mass media.

The four major team sports—football, baseball, basketball, and hockey—obtain their revenue primarily from two sources: broadcast contracts and gate receipts (Berry and Wong, 1986). Over 93 million people will attend a game from these sports, and the networks broadcast as many as 25 hours of these sports per week (Sage, 1990). A third and rapidly growing source of revenue is concessions and souvenirs.

In all sports, player salaries are the single most important team expense. Other expenses include the cost of staging games, managing the business affairs of the team, and in some cases, supporting minor leagues (Noll, 1988). Recently, with the sales of certain sport franchises for record prices, the interest expense on money borrowed to finance the purchase has become an increasingly important expense.

The economic performance of individual teams within a league will vary, but in some cases not as much as might be expected. This is primarily due to the fact that each professional league has revenue sharing arrangements. For example, in football, television rights and merchandise sales are shared equally among all the NFL teams. In baseball, each team shares national television rights equally but can sell its own local television rights (Noll, 1988). Teams like the New York Yankees, located in a large media center, have the opportunity to make considerably more on the sale of local rights than a team like the Milwaukee Brewers.

As for gate receipts, football generally divides the net gate 60-40, with the home team receiving the larger share. Baseball gives the visiting team somewhere between 10% and 20%, and there is no split in basketball and hockey (Noll, 1988).

Another factor that affects the economic performance of a team is competition for players. Since players salaries are the most significant expense, to the extent competition can be suppressed, salaries will be lower and profits greater for the owners. Football, through its draft and restrictive free agency policies, has been the most successful in keeping salaries down. Free agency in baseball and basketball has increased salaries tremendously.

To analyze the financial health of a professional team, the sport manager not only has to be able to interpret the financial data, but also needs to be aware of the peculiar structure of professional teams. Most teams are partnerships or closely held corporations owned by one or two families (Noll, 1988). They are generally able to control reported profits through legal accounting and tax techniques. Owners of teams may have an interest in the stadium in which the team plays or the media outlet that reports the games. Funds are often transferred between these entities to produce the best overall financial picture for the owners.

CASE STUDY

You are part of a group interested in purchasing a baseball team, either an existing franchise or one authorized by Major League Baseball as part of its expansion program. One issue you are responsible for researching is the type of legal entity your group should form to purchase and operate the team. Discuss the choices and the advantages and disadvantages of each, using the ideas presented in Chapter 5.

If you are to purchase an existing franchise, what are some facts you should know about the financial records of the current owners? If you are to purchase a new franchise, what are some of the economic and financial issues about the selected city and its facilities that you should know?

You will also be responsible for helping to set the price of tickets to the games. What are some of the factors that will determine the ticket price? Explain what is meant by "price elasticity of demand" and give examples.

Sponsorships

Corporate **sponsorship** of athletic events is a growing area in terms of revenue generated: over 2 billion dollars. Once an area dominated by the beer industry, it now includes the auto industry, financial services companies, oil companies, computer companies, and others. Corporate sponsorship is also an area that traditionally witnessed goals other than company profits being introduced into the decision-making process. Frequently, the chief executive officer (CEO) or chairman of the board was a fan of the particular sport and made the decision to act as a sponsor. In effect, such decisions were made to maximize the *CEO's private utility*, rather than the corporation's profit.

Sponsorships gained in popularity as an alternative to television advertising and individual player endorsements of the product. The belief was that it was more cost effective than television ads and had fewer potential problems than individual endorsements. Only now have studies begun to measure the effectiveness of sponsoring an event.

John Hancock Financial Services Company, the

sponsor of the Boston Marathon and the Sun Bowl, uses the "equivalent advertising dollar" method to measure the effectiveness of sponsoring an event. Hancock evaluates the amount of exposure they receive in sponsoring an event, such as print and television publicity, and assigns it a length or time span. Then they assign a dollar value that would be the cost of equivalent television advertising to gain the same amount of exposure. They computed a value of 8.2 million dollars in the first year of its 10-year, 10-million-dollar investment in the Boston Marathon. They found the return sponsoring the Sun Bowl to be approximately the same in dollar value as the cost of a 1-year rights fee (Klatell and Marcus, 1988).

Although the use of economic principles to measure the cost effectiveness of sponsorships is in the infant stage, most experts believe it will become more sophisticated as the demand for accountability increases.

CASE STUDY

Your company, a manufacturer of athletic equipment, is considering sponsoring an athletic event to increase its name recognition and goodwill. You have been asked to evaluate how such a sponsorship might increase the market demand for your company's products. Explain what market demand is and how a corporate sponsorship might increase it. What other methods could your company adopt to increase market demand? Compare corporate sponsorships to those methods and discuss the advantages and disadvantages of each.

Assuming you are successful at increasing market demand, what are some of the problems your company might have meeting the demand? Discuss the concepts of production function, diminishing returns, marginal product, and fixed and variable costs introduced earlier in Chapter 5.

SUMMARY

1. Chapter 5 presented the basics of economic analysis as it relates to the sport industry. The overriding concern of that chapter was to present a clear and intuitive picture of "the economic problem": allocation of scarce resources. Much attention was devoted to the workings of a market economy when making resource allocation decisions. Throughout, the focus of Chapter 5

was kept in mind and the reader was reminded that the sport industry is subject to the same constraints as traditional lines of commerce, such as manufacturing and transportation.

2. The present chapter has presented the economic problems faced by the sport industry in more detail. This has not been a "cookbook" or "how-to" approach. The authors have tried to show how the problems previously outlined impact segments of the sport and leisure industry.

3. For many, the concept of sport as an industry is foreign. These people consider sports, especially as represented by the highly-visible team sports, to be "games" and therefore different from normal lines of commerce. The historical exemption from antitrust statutes that many professional sports have enjoyed at various times is a manifestation of that position.

4. The sport industry, as a percent of economic activity, is not a dominant segment. Spending on sport and leisure accounts for less than 2% of all economic activity, yet considerable attention is devoted to sports in our daily lives.

5. The last section of this chapter offered details about the size and structure of some of the prominent segments of the sport industry. The average person may perceive team sports as representative of the sport industry; this is not reflected in the level of economic activity. Despite the media attention devoted to professional and collegiate team sports, the largest segment of the sport industry is the leisure and participant sport portion.

6. The sport industry is not different from other industries in terms of economic analysis. The consumer of the products offered by the sport industry may view these as enjoyable contests or exercises, but the decision to spend hard-earned money on the consumption of sports is just as economic as decisions on weekly food purchases, transportation, or shelter. Products offered by the sport industry are in competition for scarce consumer dollars. Consumer spending decisions are captured by the same laws of demand present in all segments of the economy. On the supply side, it is clear that managers in the sport industry face the same economic decisions faced by managers in nonsport industries.

REVIEW QUESTIONS AND ISSUES

1. Define and distinguish between the Gross National Product (GNP) and the Gross National Sports Product (GNSP). What do these numbers imply about the size and importance of the sports industry?
2. Speculate what effect the projected change in the demographic profile of Americans will have on the sports industry. Regardless of the "total" impact, would you expect to see any differences across areas inside the sports industry? Explain.
3. Define the term *firm*, and discuss the motivation behind such an entity's behavior.
4. Using supply and demand analysis, depict a situation of growing interest in a certain sport. What does your analysis say about the predicted prices in this industry?

REFERENCES

Berry, R., and Wong, G. (1986). *Law and business of the sports industries* (Volumes 1 and 2). Dover, Massachusetts: Auburn House Publishing Co.

Blackman, M., and Hochberg, P. (1988). *Representing professional athletes and teams.* New York: Practicing Law Institute.

Cady, E. (1978). *The big game: college sports and American life.* Knoxville, Tennessee: University of Tennessee.

Comte, E., and Stogel, C. (1990). Sports: a $63.1 billion industry. *The Sporting News* (January 1), 60-61.

Coughlin, C., and Erikson, O. (1984). An examination of contributions to support intercollegiate athletics. *Southern Economic Journal, 51*:180-195.

Crossley, J., and Jamieson, L. (1988). *Introduction to commercial and entrepreneurial recreation.* Champaign, Illinois: Sagamore Publishing.

The Economist. (1987). *303;* 66, May 30.

The Economist. (1989). *315;* 89, April 14.

Goulian, L. (1988). Wilson's rebirth. *Sports, Inc.,* July 18, 25-29.

Green, H. (1986). *Fit For America, health, fitness, sport and American society.* New York: Pantheon Books.

Hoffman, D., and Greenberg, M. (1988). *Sport$biz.* Champaign, Illinois: Sagamore Publishing.

Lodging & Hospitality. (1989). *45,* 84, November.

Klatell, D., and Marcus, N. (1988). *Sports for sale.* New York: Oxford University Press.

Koch, J. (1986). The economic reality of amateur sports organizations. *Indiana Law Journal 61* (9).

Kovat, D. (1977). *The rich who own sports.* New York: Random House, Inc.

Noll, R. (1988). Economics of sports leagues. In G. Uberstine (Ed.), *Law of professional and amateur sports.* New York: Clark Boardman Co., Ltd.

Quirk, J. (1973). An economic analysis of team movement in professional sports. *Law and Contemporary Problems 38,* 42.

Rosner, D. (1989). The world plays catch up. *Sports, Inc.,* January 2, 6-13.

Sage, G. (1990). *Power and ideology in American sport.* Champaign, Illinois: Human Kinetics Publishers, Inc.

Samuelson, R. (1989). The American sports mania, *Newsweek,* September.

Sandomir, R. (1988). The $50 billion sports industry, *Sports Inc.,* November 14, 14-23.

Simpson, K. (1988). The power in college basketball. *Sports, Inc.,* March 28, 20-23.

Singer, D. (1989). Role of director of athletics in restoring integrity to intercollegiate athletics. In R. Lapchick (Ed)., *The rules of the game: ethics in college sports.* New York: Collier McMillan.

Telander, R. (1989). The big lie. *Sports Illustrated,* October 2.

Waltrop, J. (1989). Feeling good. *American Demographics,* May.

Wendell, T. (1989). Time: the incessant foe. *Sports, Inc.,* January 2, 49-51.

Wong, G. (1988). *Essentials of amateur sports law.* Dover, Massachusetts: Auburn House Publishing Co.

Zoglin, R. (1990). The great TV takeover. *Time,* March 26.

13

Sports Law Case Studies: The Application

Glenn M. Wong

In this chapter, you will become familiar with the following terms:

Case study	Slander
Precedent	Public figure
Temporary restraining order	State action
Diversity of citizenship	Diminished responsibility theory
Defamatory communication	Stare decisis
Libel	

Overview

The basic legal principles of sports law were introduced and defined in Chapter 6. This chapter applies those legal principles to actual sports law cases. Using the case study method and applying the legal principles to the facts of actual cases will enable the reader to better understand principles of sports law. The facts of a case, if changed even slightly, can affect the outcome of the case.

The sport manager will benefit from understanding sports law and its application. This understanding may help the sport administrator to

manage more effectively and possibly to avoid litigation by foreseeing and preventing problems.

This chapter discusses several court decisions that illustrate how the law affects sports. This chapter is best read with Chapter 6, which examined some of the basic legal principles on which the courts based their decisions. The cases in this chapter illustrate the legal principles that were introduced in Chapter 6, applying the legal principles to actual cases.

The study method of reading a case and applying legal principles to the facts of the case is called the **case study** method. The case study method is extremely helpful in showing how the courts interpreted the facts of a case and the legal reasoning behind the decision. The case study method helps the reader not only to learn the substance of the law, but also to think like a lawyer. One of the interesting aspects of studying law, which can be seen when using the case study approach, is that, if a fact or group of facts are different, the result of the case can change. For instance, in a tort case involving a spectator injured by a ball or bat that left the field, the courts employ the assumption-of-risk theory, reasoning that the spectator assumed the risk involved. However, if the spectator had been a minor, he or she might not have known the danger involved and therefore should not have been asked to assume the risk. A minor is held to the "reasonable child" standard, which states that the child should act reasonably according to children of like age, intelligence, and experience. Thus changing one fact in the case—the age of the injured spectator—could change the outcome of the case.

Another concept to remember when reading and analyzing legal cases is **precedent.** Courts are required to follow previous decisions by other courts within their jurisdiction. However, they are not obligated to follow decisions rendered in other jurisdictions. For example, the high school drug-testing case *Schaill by Cross v. Tippecanoe County School Corp.*, which is discussed later in this chapter, would serve as precedent in its home state of Indiana but would not bind the courts in Texas if a high school drug-testing program were challenged there. In addition, the state laws of Indiana and Texas may differ. The Texas state constitutional laws regarding invasion of privacy, illegal search and seizure, and due process may differ or be interpreted differently from the Indiana state laws. Therefore the outcome of identical cases could vary, depending on the state constitutional laws under which they are argued.

For each area of sports law (such as tort law or contract law) discussed in Chapter 6, one or more cases are studied in this chapter. In addition, at the end of each section, several more cases are presented with short summaries, to illustrate different situations, other areas of the sport industry, and other unique cases. Students who are interested in any of these cases can research and read the entire case.

THE COURT SYSTEM

There are two basic legal systems in the United States: the federal system and the state system. Each state has at least one federal district court. To be in federal court, the case must involve a possible violation of federal law, or parties involved in the litigation must be from different states. Each state's judicial system hears cases and bases decisions on its state constitution, state statutes, and previous court decisions. In addition, a state court must interpret how the federal constitution and/or federal statutes affect state criminal or civil laws that are under its jurisdiction.

Sport managers should have a general understanding of the court system in case they or their organization becomes involved in a sports law complaint. The court system can be confusing, and the sport manager may not always understand how a case is argued or decided in court. A prime example of this potential confusion and the importance of knowing how the court system operates is the *Rose v. Giamatti* case.

CASE: *Pete Rose v. Bart Giamatti,* 721 F.Supp. 906 (S.D. Ohio 1989)

ISSUE: In what court, state or federal, should this case be tried?

Pete Rose, the manager of the Cincinnati Reds baseball team, was being investigated by Major League Baseball Commissioner Bart Giamatti on allegations of gambling. On May 11, 1989, after receiving a 225-page report from a Washington, D.C. lawyer named John Dowd, who investigated the allegations against Rose, Commissioner Giamatti scheduled a hearing for May 25 for Rose. Rose's lawyers asked for, and were granted by Giamatti, a 30-day postponement to prepare for the hearing.

On June 19, Rose filed suit against Giamatti in state court, the Hamilton County Common Pleas Court in Ohio, to prevent Giamatti from deciding the case. Rose argued in his suit that (1) Giamatti "prejudged" the case and therefore could not rule impartially, (2) the methods of investigation violated the rules of baseball, and (3) the investigation failed to "comport with natural justice and fair play." On June 25, Judge Norbert Nadel granted a temporary restraining order postponing Giamatti's hearing. A **temporary restraining order** is an order that forbids the defendant to do the threatened act until a hearing on the application for an injunction can be heard. (An injunction forbids the defendant to perform an act against the plaintiff.) In this case the temporary restraining order prevented Giamatti from taking any action against Rose for 2 weeks, when the injunction case could be heard. The injunction would prohibit Giamatti from investigating and taking action against Rose for the gambling allegations. Major League Baseball, on Giamatti's behalf, appealed Nadel's decision to the state appellate court, the Ohio Court of Appeals, which rejected the appeal.

On July 3, Major League Baseball filed to move the case to U.S. District Court, arguing "diversity of citizenship" among the principals. **Diversity of citizenship** means that the parties involved in the case are from different states, thus the case needs to be heard in federal court instead of state court. For the case to be moved to federal court, Giamatti's lawyers needed to convince the federal judge that neither the Cincinnati Reds nor Major League Baseball was a proper defendant in the case, but that instead the case was between Rose and Giamatti. The lawyers could then establish diversity (Rose being from Ohio and Giamatti from New York) to justify the case being moved to federal court. Giamatti wanted the case to be moved to federal court to fight the injunction so he could conduct a hearing against Rose. Rose, of course, wanted the case to stay in the state courts of Ohio, where he was more likely to receive a favorable final judgment, especially after he was already granted a temporary injunction.

On July 31, Judge John D. Holschuh, of the Southern District of Ohio federal court, ruled in favor of Major League Baseball, saying that a diversity of citizenship did exist, and therefore the case should be heard in federal court. This ruling, in effect, extinguished the temporary restraining order issued by the state court. Rose appealed Holschuh's ruling to the 6th U.S. Circuit Court of Appeals, but his petition was denied. Judge Holschuh set an August 28 date for a preliminary injunction hearing. At this point, Rose's alternatives were to appeal to the U.S. Supreme Court or allow the case to proceed in federal district court. Most legal experts believed that Rose's chances of winning in the Supreme Court were very slim, as was his chance of winning a temporary restraining order in the federal district court. Because

Rose thought he was unlikely to win in the courts, he entered into an agreement with Giamatti on August 24. The agreement stated that Rose would not pursue legal action against Giamatti, and it suspended Rose from baseball.

At question in this situation was whether or not the case contained the elements necessary to move it from state court to federal court. The lawyers for Commissioner Giamatti believed they had the elements required for the move—a move they thought was necessary to increase their chances of success. After moving the case from state court to federal court, Giamatti increased his chances of getting Rose to testify at a hearing. With the hearing procedure pending, it was in Rose's best interest to settle the case, which he did through the agreement.

The key to Rose's strategy in this case was to have the case tried in state rather than federal court. If the case had stayed in the state court, Rose might have allowed the case to go to trial. But when the case was moved to the federal court level, Rose realized his chance of success had greatly diminished, thus he changed his strategy and instead signed an agreement. In this agreement Rose agreed not to pursue the case in court and agreed to be banned from baseball, although the agreement allowed him to file for reinstatement after 1 year (from August 23, 1989).

COMMENTS: The court in which a case will be heard can be extremely important, particularly because the court's jurisdiction, the case law, and the applicable statutes can vary. Court selection is also important when, for example, filing sex discrimination litigation because some states have equal rights amendments, meaning that the case might be heard in state court, relying on the state's constitution for support. Some states do not have equal rights amendments, meaning a sex discrimination case must be argued under the federal laws of equal protection and Title IX legislation. Much preliminary maneuvering in a case may be done to determine the court in which the case will be heard.

CASE NOTES:

1. In *Eckles v. Sharman*, 548 F.2d 905 (10th Cir. 1977), Mountain State Sports, owner of the Utah Stars (Utah) of the American Basketball Association (ABA), brought a breach of contract action against Bill Sharman, their former coach. The plaintiff also filed suit against California

Sports, Inc., owner of the National Basketball Association (NBA) team, the Los Angeles Lakers, for tortious interference with the plaintiff's contract with Sharman. The trial court in Utah directed a verdict against the defendants and returned an award for the plaintiff of $250,000 against Sharman and $175,000 against California Sports.

The defendants appealed the decision, and the court of appeals stated that the trial court had erred and criticized the trial court judge for showing a strong personal bias and prejudice toward the plaintiff. One sign of the judge's bias was the size of the damage award, a total of $425,000, which exceeded the original $345,000 purchase price of the franchise. The court of appeals reversed the trial court decision and remanded the case to a judge from outside the state of Utah for a new trial.

2. The following is an example of a case that was heard in an administrative agency, the Internal Revenue Service's tax courts. On appeal, the case was heard in the federal court of appeals. Professional athletes travel frequently and may own a house in one state while playing and living in another state. In *Wills v. Commissioner of Internal Revenue*, 411 F.2d 537 (9th Cir. 1969), the court held that Maury Wills' deductions for travel, meals, and lodging in the Los Angeles area were not allowable as business expenses. The court needed to determine Wills' "tax home," since Wills maintained a residence in Spokane, Washington, and rented in Los Angeles while playing for the Dodgers. The court found that since Los Angeles was his principal place of business, and his reasons for the Spokane residence were purely personal, Los Angeles was his home according to the Internal Revenue Code definition. The court ruled that the expenses he incurred while living in Los Angeles were not deductible.

3. In *Hill v. NCAA*, No. 619209 (Ca. Super. Ct. 1987), the court enjoined the NCAA from enforcing its drug-testing program and its requirement that all Stanford athletes sign consent forms before participating in athletics (see Case Note 1 in the section on constitutional law). This case was a state court decision based on state law, therefore the NCAA cannot carry out its drug-testing program at Stanford. Stanford is the only school exempt from the NCAA drug-testing program.

This case was appealed by the NCAA; however, the Sixth District Court of Appeals in California affirmed in 1990 the lower court's decision by declaring that the drug-testing program violated the right to privacy in the California constitution. The NCAA has appealed this decision to the California Supreme Court.

CONCEPT CHECK

The selection of the court in which a case will be heard can be extremely important, particularly because the court's jurisdiction, the case law, the interpretations, and the applicable statutes may vary. When the Rose *case was moved from state to federal court, Rose felt his chances of success had decreased and thus, rather than pursue the case in court, he entered into an agreement with then Major League Baseball Commissioner Bart Giamatti.*

CONTRACT LAW

A contract is an agreement between two or more parties that is enforceable under the law. Contracts shape many of the daily activities of athletic organizations. Contract law is an area of increasing concern for athletic administrators, who may be responsible for game contracts, officiating contracts, television and radio contracts, facility lease agreements, athletic scholarships, and personnel (coaches, trainers, doctors, and so on) contracts.

Coaches at all levels are under tremendous pressure to win, and as a result coaches are judged on their ability to produce a winning team. A coach who does not produce a winning program is often a candidate for termination. The termination of a coaching contract, if not handled in accordance with the contract terms, the applicable collective bargaining agreement, and state law, could constitute a breach for which an institution could be held liable for damages. Schools often have eliminated this potential liability by paying the coach the dollar value of the salary for the remaining years of the contract. However, a 1983 decision by the Georgia Court of Appeals in *Rodgers v. Georgia Tech Athletic Association* shows that an institution may be liable for more than the salary of a coach's contract.

CASE: *Rodgers v. Georgia Tech Athletic Association,* 303 S.E.2d 467 (Ga. Ct. App. 1983)

ISSUE: Is a coach entitled to damages for a loss of perquisites as a result of being terminated?

Franklin C. "Pepper" Rodgers filed a breach of contract suit against the Georgia Tech Athletic Association to recover the value of certain perquisites that were part of his contract as the head football coach at the Georgia Institute of Technology. In April 1977, Rodgers had accepted the position of head football coach and had signed a written contract, effective through December 1981, that provided an annual salary, various insurance and pension benefits, and perquisites. Some of these perquisites were profits from television and radio shows, tickets to local professional sporting events, dues and cost of membership at local country clubs, and spending money at home and away football games.

On December 18, 1979, the Georgia Tech Athletic Association's Board of Trustees voted to remove Rodgers from his coaching position. The association voluntarily continued Rodger's base salary, health insurance, and pension plan benefits through the end of his contract in December 1981. In settling Rodgers' contract, however, the association did not include any compensation for the perquisites listed in the contract. Thus Rodgers brought suit seeking to recover the value of these perquisites.

The Georgia Court of Appeals ruled that the inclusion of the word "perquisite" in Rodgers' contract might permit a jury to award Rodgers some of the damages he was claiming. Certain perquisites were seen as a direct result of Rodgers holding the position of head football coach and thus were lost when he was terminated from this position. As such, these perquisites could be viewed as the basis for compensation to Rodgers for the remainder of his contract. The parties settled out of court before trial on the issue.

COMMENTS: This case illustrates how important it is that the athletic administrator pay close attention to the wording of contracts and employ expert legal counsel when drawing up a contract of any form. An institution may encounter problems in terminating a coach before the end of his or her contract. An institution not only must be careful with monetary settlements when terminating a coach, but also must avoid liability for defamation

by appropriately announcing the termination and the reasons for it. These issues all need to be addressed and included, if possible, in the written contract. The box on p. 81 in Chapter 6 is a list of typical clauses included in sports contracts.

Athletic administrators should consider using legal counsel when drawing up contracts. Many athletic departments employ their own attorneys. If not, the athletic administrator may be able to use the university counsel or an outside counsel when negotiating and drawing up contracts. The athletic department advisory board also can be useful when legal assistance is needed. Athletic administrators may find, however, that they need to work closely with the attorney, especially when working with an outside counsel who may not be familiar with athletics, to ensure that applicable NCAA rules and regulations are followed in the contract. Many coaches now have their own attorneys or agents, and these representatives may be very experienced in negotiating contracts.

There has been a tremendous increase recently in cases involving contracts. Coaches are pursuing legal recourse for salary and/or other benefits when termination occurs before the end of their contract. Termination clauses for coaches' contracts increasingly are specifying goals for the coach, including a won/loss record, a level of teaching ability, and even a graduation rate of those student–athletes in the program.

Universities also have sued coaches for leaving the institution before the end of the coach's contract. In 1978 Warren Powers had 2 years remaining on his Washington State contract when he left to become head football coach at Missouri. Washington State University filed suit for breach of contract and won a $55,000 settlement for allowing Powers to make the move. As a result, some universities and coaches now include buyout clauses when negotiating contracts. In addition, athletes increasingly are suing schools, alleging violations of scholarship contracts.

CASE NOTE:
1. In *Yukica v. Leland,* No. 85-E-191 (N.H. Super. Ct. 1985), the plaintiff sought declaratory judgment prohibiting the defendant, Dartmouth College's athletic director, from terminating the plaintiff's employment. The plaintiff was the head football coach at Dartmouth College and

had a contract through June 30, 1987. A paragraph in his contract stated that head coaches who, in the opinion of the Dartmouth College Athletic Council, should not continue in their coaching positions should be given notice of their termination of at least 12 months. The defendant sent a letter to the plaintiff dated November 29, 1985, stating that he was being terminated as head football coach and that another position would be offered to him immediately. The Superior Court of New Hampshire found that the plaintiff had a reasonable expectation of no less than 12 months' advance notice of actual termination by the Dartmouth College Athletic Council and that any attempt on the part of the defendant to give less than 12 months' advance notice of such termination constitutes a breach of the terms of the employment agreement between the parties. The Superior Court therefore found for the plaintiff, granting an order enjoining the defendant college from terminating the coach and restraining the college from interfering with the plaintiff's duties as head coach and from taking any steps to replace him.

CONCEPT CHECK

Athletic administrators should consider using legal assistance when entering into a contract. Institutions may be liable for damages resulting from a breach of contract if an administrator or coach is not terminated according to the terms of the contract.

TORT LAW

Tort law involves a private (or civil) wrong or injury, other than a breach of contract, suffered by an individual as the result of another person's conduct. Tort law gives an injured individual the opportunity to be compensated for the negligent act of another party.

Tort law applies in many sport activities; therefore sport managers must know how tort law applies to their particular situations. For instance, a school can be held vicariously liable for the negligent acts of its employees if an agent relationship exists. The need for sport managers to know potential liability areas, such as the use of facilities, sufficient medical care, equipment use, the activities of coaches and instructors, and proper instruction, cannot be overemphasized.

When a tort complaint is filed involving a high school or college, typically several defendants are listed. The reason is that usually the coach or instructor is alleged to be liable, and, because the school and coach have an employer-employee relationship, the school principal, athletic director, and school district also can be named as defendants in the complaint. The complaint usually alleges that the coach or instructor performed a negligent act; the school principal, athletic director, and school administrators are alleged to be liable because they hired, supervised, and/or assumed vicarious liability for the coach or instructor. *Gasper v. Friedel*, which follows shortly, illustrates a multidefendant complaint.

Tort law also is important and liability may arise in the use of waiver and release forms. These forms are used frequently, not only in high school and college sports, but also in the health club industry. *Brown v. Racquetball Centers, Inc.*, the second case, is a complaint argued on the legality of a waiver.

CASE: *Gasper v. Friedel*, 450 N.W.2d 226 (S.D. Sup. Ct. 1990)

ISSUE: When a tort is committed at a school or college, who should be liable—the coach, teacher, principal, athletic director, or school district?

In *Gasper v. Friedel*, a student injured during a summer weight-training program filed a complaint against his coaches, the superintendent of the school, and the school board. In June 1985, Gasper was participating in a summer weight-training program under the supervision of two high school coaches. Gasper tried to lift 335 pounds at the squat rack without using spotters and without warming up properly, although he had been taught to do both in a clinic before the program started. He lost his balance and fell backward, landing on the floor in a jackknife position with the weight on his shoulders. Gasper filed suit, alleging that the defendants permitted an unauthorized and unlawful conditioning program without proper supervision at the school's facilities. The trial court ruled for the defendants based on the grounds of sovereign immunity. That is, the court ruled that the coaches were working within the scope of their responsibility, were qualified to run such a program, and did not commit an intentional tort, thus they were protected by sovereign immunity. The superintendent was employed by the school board and was directed to organize such a program, therefore he was protected under sovereign immunity. The school board is a state agency, and the members knew about the program's existence and the use of facilities. They also were protected under sovereign immunity.

COMMENTS: In this type of case, the coaches are sued for negligence, and the superintendent, school board, and any other school officials are alleged to be vicariously liable for the actions of the coaches. Therefore the school administrator must know of potential areas of liability in sport programs and activities the school offers.

Another issue in the Gasper case was sovereign immunity. Sovereign immunity protects against tort liability based on the status or position of the defendant. Governmental entities, such as federal, state, or local governments, are immune to tort liability actions. This immunity results from the belief that public agencies have limited funds and should use them only for public purposes, the idea that the state can do no wrong, the idea that the public cannot be held responsible for the torts of its government employees, and the idea that government bodies themselves have no authority to commit torts. State universities, public high schools, and quasi-public associations such as high school athletic associations can be classified as governmental entities, thus protecting the employees from tort actions under sovereign immunity. The status of sovereign immunity varies from state to state.

CASE: *Brown v. Racquetball Centers, Inc.*, 534 A.2d 842 (Pa. Sup. Ct. 1987)

ISSUE: Does a waiver or release-of-liability form release the fitness center from all liability?

In *Brown v. Racquetball Centers, Inc.*, a fitness club member sued his club to recover for injuries caused by slipping on a wet tile floor. The plaintiff slipped while exiting the shower and hit his head. The plaintiff claimed that the accident was a result of the club's negligent maintenance of the shower room. The club said that the release Brown signed when he became a member released the club from liability for Brown's injuries. The Superior Court of Pennsylvania, in ruling for the plaintiff, held that the release he signed, which stated that the fitness club member assumed all risks of injury sustained

in connection with activities in and about the premises, did not absolve the fitness center of liability for its own negligent acts. The court ruled that the release did not spell out the intention of the parties with the necessary clarity and specificity. The court also ruled that the language in the release did not say in an unambiguous manner that the releasor, in signing the agreement, absolves the releasee of liability for the releasee's own negligence.

COMMENTS: Waiver and release-of-liability forms do not always release the facility owner from liability for negligence because the courts have taken the stance that the individual (facility owner) responsible for the negligent act should be held accountable for the act. If the fitness club owner in this case did not take reasonable care in managing the facilities and this mismanagement caused the incident, the owner can be held liable for the incident and deemed negligent. To prevent a club member from using the facilities unless he or she signs a release does not free the club from the responsibility to take reasonable care in the day-to-day running of the club. The club owner is still responsible for the activities provided and the use of the facilities by the club members.

Waiver forms may be upheld by the courts if the fitness club owner could not have prevented the incident through reasonable care in the management of the facility. In such cases, the courts usually rule that the club member assumed the risks involved by signing the waiver and thus cannot hold the facility owner responsible for the incident. Courts usually do not uphold waiver forms that are unclear and ambiguous, that a minor signs, that violate public policy, or that use legal language that the readers do not understand. A waiver cannot release the facility owner from the legal responsibility of taking reasonable care in managing the club facilities.

Whether a waiver form will be upheld in court is uncertain, but athletic administrators and facility owners should still use waiver forms whenever appropriate but not rely on them to be enforced. Administrators should take care to make sure the waiver pertains to the specific situation and is readable and understandable.

CASE NOTES:

1. In *Gauvin v. Clark*, 404 Mass. 450 (Mass. Sup. Jud. Ct. 1989), two college hockey players were involved in an incident. After a face-off between

the two players, Gauvin felt a stick in his abdomen and looked down to see Clark pulling the "butt-end" of his stick away from Gauvin's abdomen. Gauvin sued Clark, Clark's team's coach, and Clark's college for injuries sustained in the incident. On appeal, the Massachusetts Supreme Judicial Court held that participants in an athletic event owe a duty to other participants to refrain from reckless misconduct and that a player may be liable for causing injuries by breaching that duty. However, because the jury determined that Clark did not act with reckless disregard of safety, the decision of the lower court in favor of Clark was affirmed.

2. Tort actions also have been brought by plaintiffs alleging negligence by the defendant, facility owners, or operators of the game, because of projectiles leaving the playing field and causing injury. In *Iervolino v. Pittsburgh Athletic Co.*, 243 A.2d 490 (Pa. Super. Ct. 1968), the plaintiff–spectator sought recovery for an injury sustained by being struck by a foul ball. The superior court ruled that the operator of the game had not deviated from ordinary standards in erecting or maintaining the ballpark and thus was not liable for this injury. In cases such as this, the courts consider the assumption-of-risk concept, which says that the spectator, by purchasing a ticket and attending the event, assumes the risk of injury from events arising from the game. As long as the event is conducted under ordinary standards, the facility owner or event coordinator will not be held liable for injury caused by unforeseen events.

3. In *Witherspoon v. Haft*, 106 N.E. 2d 296 (Ohio Sup. Ct. 1952), a spectator at a football game sued for injuries sustained by falling from the last row of temporary bleachers, which the defendant installer had fastened negligently. The Ohio Supreme Court held that reasonable minds could conclude that failure of defendants to fasten the top plank seat securely could result in a serious hazard to the plaintiff. The defendant was deemed negligent and liable for the incident because reasonable care was not taken and because the spectator should not have to assume the risk of a bleacher that has not been erected correctly.

4. Defamation is another important area of tort law. As mentioned in Chapter 6, the *Restatement (Second) of Torts*, section 559, defines a **defam-atory communication** as one that "tends to harm the reputation of another as to lower him in the estimation of the community or to deter third persons from associating or dealing with him." Libel and slander are the two types of defamation. **Libel** is the publication of defamatory matter, and **slander** is the utterance of defamatory matter. In *Parks v. Steinbrenner*, 520 N.Y.S.2d 374 (New York App. Div. 1987), plaintiff Parks, a baseball umpire, filed a libel and slander suit against New York Yankees owner George Steinbrenner. Steinbrenner had issued a press release that criticized Parks' abilities as an umpire and accused him of "having it out" for the Yankees. The court found that construing the statements as defamatory was questionable, since "razzing the umpire" is done to inspire baseball fans and players.

Most athletes and coaches and many administrators are considered public figures. A **public figure** is a person who chooses to engage in a profession that is of public interest or who assumes a role of special prominence in the affairs of society (*Black's Law Dictionary*). For a public figure to prove defamation, the plaintiff must prove that the defendant made a statement with actual malice—that is, knowing that the material was false or in reckless disregard, whether it was false or not. Proving actual malice is very difficult; thus it is difficult to win a case alleging defamation of a public figure.

5. In *Wagenblast v. Odessa School District*, 758 P.2d 968 (Wash. Sup. Ct. 1988), a plaintiff–student and parents sought declaratory and injunctive relief, seeking to enjoin the school district's use of release forms. This complaint sought to prohibit a public school district from requiring students and their parents to sign forms that released the school district from liability for all future school district negligence resulting from a student's participation in high school athletics. The Supreme Court of Washington ruled that the exculpatory releases, relieving the school district from blame or fault for any future school district negligence, were invalid because they violated public policy. The court ruled that interscholastic sports in public schools are a matter of public importance, thus the party (school district in this case) performing a service of great importance to the public cannot seek exculpation. This decision severely limits the use of re-

leases by public schools in the state of Washington.

CONCEPT CHECK

Schools can be held liable for the negligent acts of their employees if there is an agency relationship. Waiver and release-of-liability forms do not always release the facility owner from liability for negligence, especially if the owner did not take reasonable care in managing the facilities. Waiver forms may be upheld by the courts if the fitness club owner could not have prevented the incident through reasonable care in managing the facility.

AGENCY LAW

Agency law applies to athletics in the way the principal or employer is held responsible for the actions of an athlete, coach, physician, trainer, or other employee. The purpose of agency law is to hold the principal (or employer) responsible for the actions of the agent (or employee), presuming the agent is acting under the control and direction of the principal. Teams, leagues, school districts, and others, in their role as employers, may be responsible for injuries caused by the negligence of their employees if they either encourage or do not discourage improper action(s) by their employees. Such improper actions can occur often in sport settings. Thus teams, leagues, school districts, and any other employers may find themselves liable for the negligent actions of their coaches, trainers, physicians, and referees.

Courts have found agency relationships between a school and a coach employed by the school. In instances of negligence by the coach, the school can be held responsible by being vicariously liable as the employer of the coach (see *Morris v. Union High School District A, King County*). Courts also have found agency relationships when a player has committed a violent act. Is the player an employee of the team, thus making the team liable for the actions of the player? Is the team responsible for intentional torts committed by the player? (See *Tomjanovich v. California Sports, Inc.* and *Averill v. Luttrell.*)

CASE: *Morris v. Union High School District A, King County*, 294 P. 998 (Wash. Sup. Ct. 1931)
ISSUE: Is a school responsible for the negligent

actions of a coach employed by the school?

The plaintiff, Morris, was a student and member of the football team at Union High School. On September 7, 1928, Morris received injuries to his back and spine while practicing with the team. On September 21, 1928, Morris was still suffering from these injuries, but his coach "permitted, persuaded, and coerced" him to play in a regular game. As a result of participating in the game, he suffered serious injuries to his back and spine. Morris filed suit against the school district, stating that the school district was liable for the negligence of its coach. The Washington Supreme Court held that a school district is liable for the negligent acts or omissions of its officers and agents acting within the scope of their authority. Therefore, the court held that if a school district organized and maintained a football team and used one of its teachers as a coach, and the coach knew that a student was physically unable to play football but nevertheless permitted, persuaded, and coerced the student to play, which resulted in injury to the student, the district would be liable.

COMMENTS: The general rule for coaches, trainers, and administrators is that they are considered employees of the school. Only in situations in which the liability-causing activity is beyond the scope of responsibility will the school (employer) *not* be held liable under the doctrine of vicarious liability.

CASE: *Tomjanovich v. California Sports, Inc.*, No. H-78-243 (S.D. Tex. 1979)
ISSUE: Is there an agent relationship between a team and a player on the team? And, if there is such a relationship, is a violent act outside the player's responsibility, thus releasing the employer (team) from any liability?

In *Tomjanovich v. California Sports, Inc.*, a game between the Los Angeles Lakers and the Houston Rockets involved a fight between several players. During the scuffle, Lakers player Kermit Washington saw Rockets forward Rudy Tomjanovich's red jersey out of the corner of his eye and pivoted, throwing a right-handed punch that crashed into Tomjanovich's face. Tomjanovich suffered fractures of the nose, jaw, and skull; facial lacerations; a brain concussion; and leakage of spinal fluid from the brain cavity. Tomjanovich and the Rockets sued the Los Angeles Lakers but not Washington personally. Although fighting is usually considered to be outside an employee's responsibility in an employer–employee relationship, a jury found the Lakers negligent and awarded damages of $3.3 million to Tomjanovich. The Lakers were sued on the theory that as Washingon's employer, they knew of his dangerous tendencies, since he was known as an "enforcer" in the league, and therefore the Lakers were responsible for these actions because they fell under Washington's responsibilities, as defined by the employer–employee relationship.

The Lakers appealed the decision, and in 1981 California Sports, Inc., the Lakers parent company, and Tomjanovich settled out of court for an undisclosed amount. The Rockets also sued the Lakers for the loss of Tomjanovich's services. After the Tomjanovich–Lakers settlement, the Rockets and Lakers also settled out of court for an undisclosed amount.

CASE: *Averill v. Luttrell*, 311 S.W.2d 812 (Tenn. Ct. App. 1957)

ISSUE: Is there an agency relationship between a team and a player, and is the team responsible for an intentional tort committed by the player, or is this act considered outside the player's responsibility?

In the Tomjanovich case, a player intentionally committed a tort, and the team was held responsible. Teams generally, however, are not held responsible for intentional torts committed by their employees. In *Averill v. Luttrell*, Luttrell was struck by a pitch while batting against the Nashville Vols. Considering himself intentionally struck, Luttrell threw his bat at the pitcher, whereupon Nashville's catcher, Averill, stepped up behind Luttrell and struck him hard on the head with his fist. The blow rendered Luttrell unconscious, and falling face first to the ground, he fractured his jaw. Luttrell sued Averill and his employer, Nashville Baseball Club. The jury trial resulted in a verdict for Luttrell against both defendants, Averill and Nashville Baseball Club. On appeal, the judgment against Nashville Baseball Club was reversed, because no proof was given that the assault was other than a willful, independent act by Averill, entirely outside his duties. As a result, Nashville Baseball Club was not held liable for the actions of its employee, Averill.

COMMENTS: Both of these cases concern a violent act inflicting an injury. The court in *Tomjanovich v. California Sports, Inc.* found the employer responsible for its employee's act, and in *Averill v. Luttrell* the court found the employer not liable for its employee's act. To learn why the results of these cases differ, we must look closely at the facts of each case. In *Tomjanovich v. California Sports, Inc.*, the court learned that the Lakers player, Kermit Washington, was known around the league as an "enforcer." The Lakers knew of his playing style and may have even employed him because of this style. As a result the Lakers were held liable for Washington's actions, because they were aware of his "dangerous tendencies" and therefore had the responsibility of controlling Washington's actions. The court found that the Lakers did nothing to control Washington's dangerous tendencies; therefore the Lakers were judged responsible for his actions. In *Averill v. Luttrell*, on the other hand, Averill's action against Luttrell was determined to be outside the scope of his employment, and thus the employer, Nashville Baseball Club, was not held liable for Averill's action. Averill was not known to commit violent acts nor was he instructed to do so by his employer; therefore there was no agency relationship in this act. Usually an intentional tort, such as assault and battery, is not found to be within an employee's responsibilities, thus the employer is not held liable for such actions by an employee.

CASE NOTE:
1. Agency law also applies in situations involving a professional athlete and the athlete's agent who represents the athlete when negotiating contracts and other obligations. In *Brown v. Woolf*, 554 F.Supp. 1206 (S.D. Ind. 1983), the plaintiff, a professional hockey player, sued his agent. Woolf helped negotiate a 5-year contract in 1974 between the Indianapolis Racers, a new team in a new league, and Brown for $800,000. Thereafter, the Racers began having financial difficulties; ultimately, the Racers' assets were seized, and the organizers defaulted on their obligations to the plaintiff. Brown stated that he received only $185,000 of the total $800,000 compensation due under the Racers contract, but that Woolf received his full $40,000 fee (5% of the contract) from the Racers. Brown brought action for constructive fraud and breach of fiduciary duty against Woolf. Woolf's motion for a summary judgment was denied, and the parties settled out of court before the trial.

CONCEPT CHECK

The purpose of agency law is to hold the employer responsible for the actions of the employee if the employee is acting under the control and direction of the employer. Only in situations in which the action is beyond the responsibility of the employee will the employer not be held liable. Agency law applies in college and high school sports when a school district or university is held liable for the actions of its employee (such as a coach, trainer, or administrator).

CONSTITUTIONAL LAW

Constitutional law is federal and state statutes written to protect the constitutional rights of the individual. The constitution's guarantees of due process—including equal protection, freedom from illegal search and seizure, and freedom from invasion of privacy—have been argued in athletic situations. These include cases in which the athlete has been forced to do something that he or she does not want to do (such as submit to drug testing) or when the athlete is denied something (such as eligibility). The constitutional safeguards of the Fifth and Fourteenth Amendments apply only when state action is present. The plaintiff in constitutional law claims must first demonstrate that **state action** is involved before the claim can go to court. An action by any public school, state college, state university, or their officials is construed as state action. State action is present because the state or federal government provides aid to that institution. Once state action is proved, the plaintiff must show that the defendant has infringed on a constitutional right, using either federal or state constitutional law or both.

CASE: *Schaill by Cross v. Tippecanoe County School Corp.*, 679 F.Supp. 833 (N.D. Ind. 1988)

ISSUE: Is a drug-testing program legal and permissible or can such a program be found unconstitutional as an invasion of privacy, with failure to provide due process, and as an illegal search and seizure?

In *Schaill by Cross v. Tippecanoe County School Corporation*, two plaintiffs, Darcy Schaill and Shelley Johnson, challenged the drug-testing program of the Tippecanoe County School Corporation. The program was designed to test all student–athletes, defined as all participants in interscholastic sports. As part of the rationale, the program stated that student–athletes are especially respected by the student body and are expected to be "good examples of conduct, sportsmanship, and training, which includes avoiding drug and alcohol usage."

The program called for random mandatory testing by urinalysis, with no limits set on the number of individuals to be tested or the number of times that tests were to be conducted. Collection of the urine sample was not to be observed. In addition, a student–athlete could be tested when there was a reasonable suspicion that he or she was abusing drugs or alcohol.

The drug-testing program policy statement said its purposes were educational, diagnostic, and preventive, as opposed to punitive or disciplinary. The program specifically said that no student–athletes who tested positive would be disciplined academically. Instead, testing positive one or more times during a year would result in penalties. The first positive test for alcohol would result in suspension from 20% of the athletic contests in the student–athlete's particular sport. A first positive test for other drugs would bring suspension from 30% of the athletic contests. The second positive test for drugs or alcohol would result in a 50% suspension. The third positive test would result in a full calendar year of athletic suspension, and the fourth would result in the student's being barred from all interscholastic athletic competitions during the remainder of his or her high school career.

The plaintiffs alleged that the following actions were violations of several federal constitutional rights: requiring them to submit to an unreasonable search and seizure in violation of the Fourth Amendment to the U.S. Constitution, interfering with legitimate expectations of privacy, violation of the due process clause of the Fourteenth Amendment, violation of the equal protection clause of the Fourteenth Amendment (by testing student–athletes only, and not all students), and limiting participation in interscholastic sports to students who waive their constitutional rights.

The district court relied on the U.S. Supreme Court decision in *New Jersey v. T.L.O.* in making its decision. The court stated that as in the *T.L.O.* case, the *Schaill* case involved a balancing of needs—primarily, the public school's need to search balanced against the students' right to privacy. The court reasoned that the random testing procedure, or testing conducted based on reasonable suspicion, was reasonable and not a violation of the students' rights. In negating the due process and equal protection claims, the court said that the policy statement allowed student–athletes to explain a positive drug test, and due process rights were protected. The court cited the policy statements, which said that the program was designed primarily for the health and safety of participants, the fact that the testing program was in writing, the fact that due process rights were protected, the fact that student–athletes were given the opportunity to explain a positive test, the fact that the collection of the urine sample was not observed, the fact that the program was not punitive, and the fact that no academic penalties were contemplated.

In *Schaill by Cross v. Tippecanoe County School Corp.*, 864 F.2d 1309 (7th Cir. 1988), the Seventh Circuit Court of Appeals affirmed the district court ruling, stating that the Tippecanoe County School Corporation had chosen a reasonable and limited response to a serious evil. The Appeals Court went on to say that the school district had been sensitive to the privacy rights of its students and was therefore not acting inconsistently with the mandates of the U.S. Constitution.

COMMENTS: The *Schaill* case upheld drug testing in Indiana high schools, but whether it allows random mandatory drug testing at high schools in other states is hard to predict. In addition, the *Schaill* case will probably have little to no effect on intercollegiate drug testing issues, as the court in *Schaill* considered colleges to be distinct from high schools. Thus drug-testing programs in other states will gain approval only when these programs go to court, and college drug-testing programs will be clarified only by court decisions involving college drug-testing programs.

Drug testing is a new issue for sports and society and as such will probably see a lot of litigation before the issue is finally decided. All drug-testing cases involving federal constitutional law have been decided in favor of the testing program. The only exception was a Caifornia case, *Hill v. NCAA* No. 619209 (Ca. Super. Ct. 1987), which was argued and decided on California constitutional law. The court enjoined the NCAA from enforcing its

drug-testing program and requirement that Stanford athletes sign consent forms before participating in sports.

CASE NOTES:

1. In *Hill v. NCAA*, a California court relied on the state statute governing invasion of privacy in deciding for the plaintiff. The court enjoined the NCAA from enforcing its requirement that Stanford obtain signed drug-testing consent forms from its athletes and from requiring Stanford athletes to sign such forms before participating in NCAA activities. The court also held that the NCAA may not declare any athlete ineligible or take punitive action against an athlete for failing to comply with or participate in the NCAA drug-testing program. On appeal, the Sixth District Court of Appeals upheld the decision of the lower court.

2. In *O'Halloran v. University of Washington*, 679 F.Supp. 997 (W.D. Wash. 1988), the plaintiff sought a preliminary injunction against the University of Washington and the National Collegiate Athletic Association forbidding them from barring her from competition while waiting for a decision on the action she brought challenging enforcement of the NCAA drug-testing program. O'Halloran claimed the NCAA drug-testing program was an invasion of privacy, because urination is monitored and because private facts about the student–athlete's activities in addition to the use of drugs may be revealed. O'Halloran also claimed the drug-testing program was an unreasonable search and seizure through the collection of urine. The District Court held that the drug-testing program was a "search" for purposes of the Fourth Amendment, but there was a reasonable basis for the testing. In addition, the NCAA's use of monitored urine testing to enforce its drug-testing program did not unreasonably infringe on the student–athlete's expectation of privacy. O'Halloran's motion for a preliminary injunction was denied.

CONCEPT CHECK

Constitutional law guarantees due process, equal protection, freedom from illegal search and seizure, and privacy. Arguments often are based on constitutional law in drug-testing litigation, with the plaintiff alleging an unreasonable search and invasion of privacy through the collection of a urine sample. Courts have upheld drug-testing programs using a balancing-of-needs test, stating that the importance of the test outweighs the unreasonable search and invasion of privacy claims by the plaintiff. The courts have also negated constitutional law claims, saying the drug-testing program is reasonable for its objectives.

SEX DISCRIMINATION

Sex discrimination complaints have been made in athletic settings, when a plaintiff contends that treatment is fundamentally unequal. Sex discrimination litigation has been brought over females being prohibited from joining a male team, lack of a female team while a male team is offered, inequality of employment of coaches and athletic personnel, inequality in the amount of money made available to females and males in team budgets and scholarships, use and maintenance of facilities, and amount of publicity given to female and male sports and athletes. Males also have filed sex discrimination suits, contending they should be allowed to participate on female teams when no team is offered for males. Sex discrimination complaints have been argued under federal equal protection laws, Title IX, and state equal rights amendments. The plaintiff must prove that the alleged sex discrimination action is a violation of individual rights under federal and/or state law.

CASE: *Wing and the Gateway Regional High School v. The Massachusetts Interscholastic Athletic Association,* No. 89E0033G1 (Mass. P. & Fam. Ct. 1989)

ISSUE: Can the exclusion of a high school soccer team from a boys' tournament because the team has a girl on it be deemed sex discrimination and a violation of the team's rights under federal and/or state law?

One of the more frequently litigated sex discrimination issues is the constitutionality of prohibiting female participation on all-male teams. Gateway Regional High School in Massachusetts operated a boys' interscholastic soccer program but not a similar program for girls. In 1989 Nicole Wing tried out for and made the Gateway boys' soccer team. Because Wing was on the team, the Massachusetts Interscholastic Athletic Association

(MIAA) ruled that the Gateway team was a "mixed-gender" team and was ineligible for postseason play in the boys' division.

When it became likely that Gateway would finish the season with a sufficient record to qualify for the boys' tournament, school officials asked the MIAA to reverse the ruling. All requests were denied. At the end of the season, when Gateway finished with a record sufficient to qualify for the MIAA Western Massachusetts Boys Division III tournament, the Gateway principal made a written request for reconsideration of the disqualification from the boys' tournament, but the MIAA again denied the request. Having exhausted the administrative remedies, Wing and Gateway applied for a preliminary and permanent injunction in Massachusetts Probate and Family Court to restrain the MIAA from disqualifying Gateway from the boys' postseason tournament.

For a preliminary injunction to be granted, Wing and Gateway had to prove the following:

- That they would suffer irreparable harm if the injunction were not granted
- That the threatened harm to them outweighed the harm that granting an injunction might do to the MIAA
- That there was a substantial likelihood that they would win at a full hearing

The court had little difficulty in affirming the first two points for the plaintiffs. The third point was more difficult to prove. Wing and Gateway argued that the MIAA rule denied females the equal opportunity to participate athletically with males and therefore violated the Massachusetts Constitution and state equal rights amendment.

The court reasoned that the objective of the rule was to discourage male participation on female athletic teams and thereby promote female opportunities. The court found, however, that the rule had the opposite effect of discouraging female participation on male athletic teams. The court concluded that no compelling interest had been identified to justify excluding from boys' postseason competition a boys' team with a girl member when their school sponsored only one team. A preliminary injunction was granted. The MIAA appealed the decision, and the appeal was denied by the appeals court. Gateway participated in the 1989 boys' tournament and lost in the championship final.

COMMENTS: The most effective way for plaintiffs to pursue sex discrimination complaints is through a state equal rights amendment, if the particular state has one. A total of 19 states have enacted their own equal rights amendments. Otherwise, plaintiffs must allege a violation of federal equal protection law or Title IX. Title IX has become a much better grounds for arguing sex discrimination cases against athletic departments since the Civil Rights Restoration Act was passed in 1988. Before this act, the courts took a "programmatic" approach to Title IX issues, meaning that only specific programs that received direct federal funding needed to adhere to Title IX legislation. Since most athletic departments do not receive direct federal funding, they could not be held in violation of Title IX. The Civil Rights Restoration Act, however, established the "institutional" approach, meaning that if any program of the college or university received federal funding, all programs at that college or university needed to adhere to Title IX. This legislation restored the strength of Title IX as grounds for college sex discrimination cases.

In addition, the Office for Civil Rights, under the Department of Education, is also organized to pursue sex discrimination complaints, and the Equal Employment Opportunity Commission investigates employment sex discrimination complaints under the Equal Pay Act and Title VII.

CASE NOTES:
1. In *Blair v. Washington State University*, 740 P.2d 1379 (Wash. Sup. Ct. 1987), the trial court concluded that the university had discriminated against the plaintiffs on the basis of sex and awarded damages, injunctive relief, attorney fees, and costs. The plaintiffs appealed the decision, however, on the basis that the award was too low because football was excluded when the court calculated the amount of money spent on sports and athletic scholarships. The state equal rights amendment prohibited such an exclusion; therefore the appeals court ruled that the trial court erred when it excluded football in calculating the amount spent on sports and athletic scholarships. Including football would give higher amounts for sports and athletic scholarships for males, creating a greater deficiency in the totals for female sports and athletic scholarships. This helps female sports receive greater compensation, to make up the difference.

2. Males also have filed sex discrimination complaints, claiming that they were denied their constitutional rights by being barred from participating on female teams when no male team was offered. The courts have taken different stances on this issue.
a. In *Gomes v. Rhode Island Interscholastic League*, 469 F.Supp. 659 (D.R.I. 1979), vacated as moot, 604 F.2d 733 (1st Cir. 1979), the plaintiff brought this action under the federal civil rights statute, seeking preliminary injunctive relief enjoining school officials from barring him from the female volleyball team. The school offered no separate male team in this sport. Gomes alleged that the rule against male participation in volleyball competition violated both the Fourteenth Amendment and Title IX. The district court ruled in the plaintiff's favor, granted the preliminary injunction, and ordered the league to allow Gomes to compete on the volleyball team.
b. In *Clark v. Arizona Interscholastic Assn.*, 695 F.2d 1126 (9th Cir. 1982), cert. den., 464 U.S. 818 (1983), plaintiffs brought suit after being prohibited from participating on the female volleyball team. No male team was offered. The court ruled for the defendant, stating that the physiological differences between males and females would affect the game of volleyball. The court found that the rules and regulations of the Arizona Interscholastic Association, which prohibited males from participating on the female team, did not violate the equal protection clause of the Fourteenth Amendment. The court held that maintaining a girls-only volleyball team "is substantially related to and serves the achievement of the important government objective" of (1) promoting equal athletic opportunities for females in interscholastic sports and (2) redressing the effects of past discrimination.

3. In *Ludtke v. Kuhn*, 461 F.Supp. 86 (S.D.N.Y. 1978), the plaintiff sought an injunction against the enforcement of a policy set by Baseball Commissioner Kuhn, requiring that accredited female sports reporters be excluded from the locker room of the Yankee Clubhouse in Yankee Stadium. Ludtke alleged that her equal protection and due process rights were violated. The court ruled there was a violation of equal protection because the plaintiff, while in pursuit of her profession as a sports reporter, was treated

differently from her male counterparts solely because she was a woman. The court also ruled that Ludtke's due process rights were violated because the right to pursue one's profession is a fundamental "liberty" within the meaning of the Fourteenth Amendment's due process guarantee. The court ruled that the Kuhn policy substantially and directly interfered with the right of plaintiff Ludtke to pursue her profession as a sports reporter.

The issue of access to locker rooms for female reporters has been raised in several instances in the 1990s, with the most celebrated case involving Lisa Olson of the *Boston Herald* and the New England Patriots professional football team.

CONCEPT CHECK

Sex discrimination complaints have been argued under federal equal protection laws, Title IX, and state equal rights amendments. The courts are divided on allowing males to compete on female teams. Courts that do not allow males to participate cite physiological differences and see all female teams as an attempt to redress the effects of past discrimination. Courts that allow males to participate cite equality of opportunity for males and females. The most effective way for plaintiffs to pursue sex discrimination complaints is through a state equal rights amendment if that particular state has one. Title IX has become a more effective grounds for a sex discrimination complaint since the Civil Rights Restoration Act was passed in 1988.

CRIMINAL LAW

Criminal laws are statutes that are designed to protect society from harmful conduct. Sports violence presents the difficult issue of determining whether an act is conduct within the rules of the game, conduct that results from the heat of the game, accidental conduct, and criminal conduct. The problem is that certain sports are extremely physical, and violent physical contact is condoned under the rules. In addition, the key in criminal law prosecutions is showing criminal intent, which is difficult to do in a sport setting. Most criminal law charges allege that a hockey player used his stick as a weapon. For the most part, criminal law prosecutions in sports have not been successful.

Certain factors can relieve a defendant of responsibility for a crime, even though they are not true "defenses." Thus, even though the prosecution proves every element of the crime charged, the defendant can escape punishment by showing that he acted in the heat of passion or was intoxicated. A person who acts as the result of an involuntary action may not have the mental judgment that is required under the definition of the crime.

The **diminished responsibility theory** has been used to defend athletes in criminal cases alleging sports violence. Defendants have argued that players are trained in the skills and the mental attitude necessary to be a successful athlete. Because of this training, defendants argue, their actions were not voluntary but merely instinctual responses or reflex actions.

CASE: *State v. Forbes*, No. 63280 (Minn. Dist. Ct. 1975)

ISSUE: Should a stick-swinging incident that caused serious injury during a hockey game be considered a criminal act?

In *State v. Forbes*, a hockey player hit another player with his stick and was charged with aggravated assault. The defense argued that the player performed the act because the sport required aggressive behavior and because of how he was taught to play the sport. In December 1974, the Minnesota North Stars and the Boston Bruins played an NHL hockey game in Minnesota. Early in the first period, Henry Boucha, a member of the North Stars, chased a loose puck against the boards. David Forbes of the Bruins proceeded to check Boucha using his elbows as offensive weapons, which is commonly done by hockey players. After being elbowed, Boucha turned and knocked Forbes down. The referee penalized both players and sent them to their respective penalty boxes. While in the penalty boxes, the players exchanged threats.

After both players returned to the ice, Boucha started to skate toward his team bench when Forbes said, "Okay, let's go now" and swung at Boucha. Forbes missed with his hand but connected with his stick just above Boucha's right eye. Boucha dropped to the ice, covering his injured face. Forbes then discarded his stick and gloves, jumped on top of Boucha, and proceeded to bang Boucha's head on the ice until he was forcibly removed. Boucha was taken to the hospital and received 25 stitches to close the cut above his right eye. Five days later, when a patch was removed from his eye, Boucha complained of double vision and underwent surgery to repair a small fracture in the floor of the right eye socket.

After hearing evidence about the incident, NHL Commissioner Clarence Campbell suspended Forbes for 10 games. On January 15, 1975, Forbes was indicted by a Minnesota grand jury and charged with aggravated assault. At trial the prosecution argued that Forbes had committed aggravated assault, which was a crime whether it was carried out in public or during a game. The defense argued a variation of the temporary insanity defense, based on the theory that from the age of 4, hockey players are taught not to let other players intimidate them. Coaches emphasize the need for physical violence against other players, and crowds cheer the sight of fighting and blood. The defense argued that given these circumstances, hockey, and not David Forbes, should be on trial. The trial ended in a 9-to-3 hung jury in favor of the assault conviction. In this type of trial, the jury needs to determine guilt beyond a reasonable doubt and reach a 12-0 decision to convict a defendant. The prosecution could have had the case retried but decided against it because the initial split decision would have made the required unanimous verdict virtually unreachable.

COMMENTS: The courts have a difficult time in sport cases deciding what is a criminal act and what is just a part of the game. Some leagues have been under pressure to control the violence in their sports, such as ice hockey. If the leagues are successful, they may slow the intervention of the courts and criminal law prosecutions, but some sports will always have an aggressive overtone to them, stimulating athletes to lose control and commit violent acts. League commissioners have the power to suspend a player for such an act, but the public may believe the commissioner's penalties are inadequate. After all, these players serve as role models for children, and a suspension may not be harsh enough to convey a condemnation of violence to young fans. In addition, the injured party may pursue a private remedy, but this case may be heard in a courtroom, and the complaint would be based on a tort theory and not a criminal law theory.

The *Forbes* case shows the difficulty of winning a criminal prosecution for violent acts committed during a sporting event. In *State v. Forbes*, after the

criminal suit ended in a hung jury, the civil case was settled out of court.

Another method for deterring violence in sports that has been investigated is legislation. The Sports Violence Act was proposed in 1980 and 1981, but the bill never reached the floor of the House of Representatives. The act would have made it a criminal offense for professional athletes to engage in excessive violence. Another bill, the Sports Violence Arbitration Act, was introduced in 1983. Instead of setting a federal criminal statute, as the Sports Violence Act proposed, the Sports Violence Arbitration Act would have required each professional league to establish an arbitration panel with the power to punish teams and players for conduct found to be inconsistent with the goals of the sport. This act also was not passed by Congress.

CASE NOTES:

1. A growing area of criminal law in sports is ticket scalping, that is, reselling tickets at prices greater than the face value price. In *State v. Spann*, 623 S.W.2d 272 (Tenn. Sup. Ct. 1981), Spann argued that the scalping legislation violated both Tennessee's and the U.S. Constitution's due process clauses. Although he acknowledged that the state can exercise its police power to ensure a reasonable resale of tickets, Spann contested the state's total prohibition on the scalping of tickets. In rejecting Spann's arguments and affirming the lower court's decision, the Tennessee Supreme Court stated that the "statute in question does not prohibit the resale of a ticket at all. It does, however, prohibit such resale for a premium or a profit, and we believe that this is a regulation which is entirely reasonable and within the police power of the General Assembly."

2. In *Carroll v. State of Oklahoma*, 620 P. 2d 416 (Okla. Crim. App. 1980), Carroll, the assistant coach of the losing team at a baseball tournament, was convicted of "assault upon a sports officiary" under Oklahoma laws after hitting the umpire in the jaw after the game. Carroll challenged the statute on the grounds that it was unconstitutionally vague. The Oklahoma Court of Criminal Appeals, however, held that the statute clearly said who was covered and also what particular conduct was punishable.

3. In *Regina v. Ciccarelli*, (Ontario Prov. Ct. 1988), Minnesota North Star Dino Ciccarelli was con-

victed of assault for his actions in an incident on January 6, 1988, in a National Hockey League game in Toronto, Ontario, between the North Stars and the Toronto Maple Leafs. During the game Ciccarelli hit Maple Leaf defenseman Luke Richardson twice over the head with his stick and punched him once in the mouth. Ciccarelli was immediately ejected from the game, and later the NHL suspended him for 10 games. After finding Ciccarelli guilty of assault, Ontario Provincial Court Judge Sidney Harris said, "It is time now that a message go out from the court that violence in a hockey game or in any other circumstances is not acceptable in our society." Ciccarelli was sentenced to 1 day in jail and ordered to pay a $1,000 fine. This is the first known case of an athlete going to jail for an offense committed during a game.

CONCEPT CHECK

Criminal convictions are difficult to obtain in sport situations, because certain sports are extremely physical and physical contact is condoned under the rules. Criminal intent also is difficult to prove in sports settings. One defense used in criminal law cases is that the defendant was taught to play "rough" to intimidate the other team. Federal legislation to discourage violence in sports has not yet been passed.

ANTITRUST LAW

Federal antitrust laws regulate competitive conduct in interstate commerce. Congress first moved against concentrated power in the commercial world in 1890 by adopting the Sherman Act, which is intended to prevent monopolistic practices and unfair restraints of trade, at least as they affected interstate commerce. The Clayton Act of 1914 added more legislative restrictions. Sections of the Clayton Act deal with corporate mergers, price discrimination, and labor unions. Professional sports also are covered and are subject to antitrust laws, although baseball has an exemption as a result of a 1922 decision, *Federal Baseball Club of Baltimore, Inc. v. National League of Professional Baseball Clubs, et al.,* 259 U.S. 200 (1922). Amateur athletics historically were not affected much by antitrust laws until the court's decision in *NCAA v. Board of Regents of University of Oklahoma and University of*

Georgia Athletic Association (see Case Note #2 on p. 227). In addition, because of the recent growth in the amateur sports industry, amateur athletic organizations may find courts applying antitrust laws to them.

Free agency has long been a topic of conversation at the bargaining table between the National Football League and National Football League Players Association (NFLPA). In the 1976 case *Mackey v. NFL,* 543 F.2d 606 (8th Cir. 1976), the court decided that the Rozelle rule, which allowed the NFL commissioner discretion to award players or draft choices to a team losing a player to free agency, violated antitrust laws. As a result, management decided it was in its best interests to negotiate a collective bargaining agreement with the union that would give management a labor exemption, that is, an exemption from antitrust laws for practices that otherwise would violate the antitrust laws. The NFLPA agreed in 1977 to this modification of the Rozelle rule, provided that a team could retain a free agent by matching another club's offer (first refusal), or choose not to match the offer and receive compensation in the form of draft choices.

In 1982 a new collective bargaining agreement was reached that included this first refusal/compensation system of free agency and this labor exemption for management. This agreement expired in August 1987, and a new collective bargaining agreement could not be reached. The players began collective bargaining negotiations with management but were unable to make satisfactory progress, especially on the issue of free agency. The players decided to go on strike during the 1987 season. However, the strike was unsuccessful, and the players returned after missing four games. The players later filed suit in federal district court; the *Powell* suit challenged the legality of the league's adherence to the expired 1982 agreement and argued that the labor exemption expired in 1987 when the collective bargaining agreement ended.

CASE: *Powell v. National Football League,* 888 F.2d 559 (8th Cir. 1989)

ISSUE: Does the NFL antitrust exemption regarding NFL restrictions on player movement between teams continue after the collective bargaining agreement expires?

In January 1988 the district court, in what is

commonly called "Powell I" 678 F.Supp. 777 (D. Minn. 1988), held that the exemption survives the expiration of a collective bargaining agreement but ends when the employer and the union reach a bargaining impasse on the issue. Therefore, even though no collective bargaining agreement is in place, the first refusal/compensation system of free agency remains in effect and is not considered a violation of antitrust laws. In April 1988 the NFLPA renewed its motion for an injunction against the NFL on the first refusal/compensation system (that is, to prevent the use of the restrictive first refusal/compensation system). In June 1988 the district court in "Powell II," 690 F. Supp. 812 (D. Minn. 1988), held that the parties had reached an impasse on free agency but declined to issue the injunction for reason of jurisdiction. Still, the ruling opened the door for a trial on whether the league's free agency policy violated antitrust laws. The NFL appealed this decision.

The 8th Circuit Court of Appeals ruled in "Powell III," 888 F.2d 559 (8th Cir. 1989), that the parties had not yet reached a point at which the labor exemption would terminate. The court said that the exemption would survive at least until the union had exhausted its available remedies, including collective bargaining, economic force (union strike), or proceedings before the National Labor Relations Board. The NFLPA appealed this decision to the U.S. Supreme Court. The Supreme Court rejected the appeal.

COMMENTS: The "Powell III" decision is a victory for management, since it preserves the labor exemption for management. A further complication for the union is that the "Powell III" decision does not tell when the labor exemption does expire. Before it will decide whether to hear this case on appeal, the U.S. Supreme Court wants the Justice Department to comment on "Powell III," and the court is unlikely to decide whether to hear the players' appeal until the government files this brief.

In addition to filing the appeal, the NFLPA has decertified itself as the union representing the players. The legal strategy behind this decertification is to take away the labor exemption from management—if there is no union, there can be no labor exemption. The union believes this would strengthen the antitrust argument individual players use in their lawsuits against management, because management could no longer use the labor

exemption as a defense. Management has disputed the union's decertification, and the status of the NFLPA as a bargaining unit for NFL players is uncertain.

CASE NOTES:

1. In *Flood v. Kuhn*, 407 U.S. 258 (1972), baseball's exemption from the antitrust laws was affirmed by the Supreme Court. In 1969, after playing for 12 seasons with the St. Louis Cardinals, Flood was traded to the Philadelphia Phillies in a multi-player transaction. Flood was not consulted about the trade, was informed by telephone, and received formal notice only after the deal had been consummated. In December 1969 Flood complained to the commissioner of baseball and asked that he be made a free agent and be allowed to strike his own bargain with any other major league team. His request was denied. Flood then filed this antitrust suit in January 1970 in federal court against the commissioner of baseball, the president of the two major leagues, and the 24 major league clubs.

The Supreme Court affirmed the court of appeals and district court rulings for the defendants, saying that this exemption has been upheld for over half a century and is fully entitled to the benefit of **stare decisis,** a doctrine stating that once a court has laid down a principle of law applying to a certain set of facts, the courts will adhere to that principle, and apply it to all future cases where the facts are substantially the same (*Black's Law Dictionary*).

2. In *National Collegiate Athletic Association v. Board of Regents of University of Oklahoma and University of Georgia Athletic Association*, 104 S. Ct. 2948 (1984), the universities brought suit against the NCAA, alleging that the NCAA's football television contract violated the Sherman Antitrust Act. The NCAA controlled the televising of intercollegiate football. The NCAA television plan paid the member institutions a minimum sum for a televised game and limited the number of times the school could appear on television. The district court held that the controls the NCAA exercised over the televising of college football games violated the Sherman Act. The court of appeals affirmed the district court decision and held that the NCAA television plan constituted illegal price fixing. The court of appeals also

stated that the NCAA practices constituted a "restraint of trade" in the sense that they limit members' freedom to negotiate and enter into their own television contracts. The Supreme Court affirmed the decision of the court of appeals.

CONCEPT CHECK

Professional sports are governed by and subject to the antitrust laws, although baseball has an exemption. The players' associations serve as unions for their sports and represent the players in negotiations between the owners and the players.

LABOR LAW

Labor law applies to the relationship between labor (the players) and management (the owners). Labor law is used to define the rights, privileges, and duties of both labor and management. The main component of labor law applying to professional sports is the area that governs collective bargaining agreements. Players' associations are a principal force in professional sports, and they negotiate, on behalf of their members, collective bargaining agreements that resolve employment issues affecting their members. The players' associations rely on labor laws to protect the collective bargaining rights of their employees.

CASE: *Kansas City Royals Baseball Corporation v. Major League Baseball Players Association*, 409 F.Supp. 233 (W.D. Miss. 1976)

ISSUE: Are the owners of baseball clubs exempt from a collective bargaining agreement's grievance and arbitration clause issues because they are exempt from antitrust laws?

This case involves the Major League Baseball player contracts of Andy Messersmith of the Los Angeles Dodgers and David McNally of the Montreal Expos. The players filed grievances about the reserve clause of their contracts, each saying that the club did not own the rights to the player after the player finished his renewal year (last contract year), thus the player should be considered a free agent. The case went to arbitration, and the arbitrators found in favor of the players. The club owners filed suit, saying that the issue should not be decided by an arbitrator. The court held for the defendant, stating that the grievances the two play-

ers filed were within the duties and powers of the arbitration panel to arbitrate as stated in the collective bargaining agreement.

COMMENTS: In the *Kansas City Royals Baseball Corporation* case, the reserve clause and right to arbitration, as parts of the collective bargaining agreement, required the owners to comply with the aforementioned clauses according to labor law. This case stated that the "fact that owners of major league baseball clubs were exempt from antitrust laws did not mean that they or their employees were exempt from other federal law applicable to industries which affect commerce, including national labor laws."

The court's decision upheld the arbitration award, and as a result gave the players' association tremendous leverage in negotiating a new collective bargaining agreement. This power came from the fact that the players then were under 1-year contracts, and all the players would be free agents in either 1 or 2 years. The teams did not want to face this possibility and therefore negotiated a collective bargaining agreement that gave the players many rights and benefits, including free agency after 6 years.

NOTES:
1. Major League Baseball, in its collective bargaining agreement, gives certain players the right to file for salary arbitration, in which an arbitrator will select either the figure the player submits or the figure the team submits. The arbitrator cannot select a figure between the two. This system is called "last best offer arbitration."
2. Most collective bargaining agreements involving employees at facilities have a "grievance arbitration clause." This allows an employee who has a dispute with management to take the case before a neutral third party. The dispute could be over working conditions, overtime pay, a promotion, discipline, or any other issue. This clause is extremely important for both the employer and the employee.

CONCEPT CHECK

Labor law applies to the relationship between management (the owners in professional sports) and labor (the players). Collective bargaining agreements are used to resolve employment issues affecting players.

SUMMARY

1. The case study method is the one that involves reading a case and applying legal principles to the facts of the case.
2. Courts are required to follow previous decisions by other courts within their jurisdiction (the concept of *precedent)*, but they are not obligated to follow decisions rendered in other jurisdictions.
3. When the *Pete Rose* case moved from state court to federal court, Rose's chances of success in court decreased; thus he reached an agreement with Commissioner Giamatti.
4. The termination of a coaching contract, if not handled in accordance with the contract terms, applicable collective bargaining agreements, and state law, could constitute a breach of contract, for which an institution could be held liable in damages.
5. A waiver form may not be upheld by the court if the court determines that the form is unclear or ambiguous, that a minor signed the form, that the form uses legal language that is unclear to the reader, or that the waiver violates public policy.
6. As a general rule, referees and physicians are not considered employees of the school and thus the school district is not held liable for their actions. However, coaches, trainers, and administrators are considered employees, and the school district is potentially responsible for their actions under agency law.
7. Plaintiffs in athletic drug-testing litigation use constitutional law arguments citing due process, equal protection, illegal search and seizure, and invasion of privacy.
8. All drug-testing cases that have been argued on federal constitutional law have been decided in favor of the testing programs.
9. In allowing females to participate on all-male teams and barring males from participating on female teams, the courts have reasoned that this helps achieve the important governmental objectives of (1) promoting equal athletic opportunities for females in interscholastic sports, and (2) redressing the effects of past discrimination.
10. Criminal law violations are difficult to prove in a sports setting because showing criminal intent is difficult.
11. The collective bargaining agreement in professional football expired in August 1987. The courts, however, have ruled in the *Powell* case that an antitrust exemption survives the expiration of a collective bargaining agreement. This preserves the labor exemption for management; otherwise some of their practices would violate antitrust laws.
12. The main component of labor law applying to professional sports is collective bargaining agreement law.

REVIEW QUESTIONS AND ISSUES

1. Define the case study method and list ways it can help the reader.
2. In *Pete Rose v. Bart Giamatti,* why did Rose decide not to pursue the case in court?
3. What was the argument by the plaintiff, Yukica, about his coaching contract in the case *Yukica v. Leland?*
4. If a collegiate team coach performs an intentional tort, battery, against one of his players, is the school responsible and liable for his actions? Why or why not?
5. In what situations are waiver forms usually not upheld by the courts?
6. Describe the differences between the *Tomjanovich* case and the *Averill* case and how the rulings and court rationales differed.
7. What constitutional arguments did the plaintiffs raise in the *Schaill* case?
8. Why was the outcome of the *Hill v. NCAA* case different from the outcome of the *O'Halloran* case?
9. What argument(s) are used in a sex discrimination case to bar a male from competing on a female team? What argument(s) are used in a sex discrimination case to allow a male to compete on a female team?
10. What argument is used in a criminal law case to defend an athlete accused of performing a violent act during a sporting event?
11. What theory did the Supreme Court use in affirming baseball's exemption from antitrust laws in the case *Flood v. Kuhn?*
12. Discuss the importance of the *McNally–Messersmith* arbitration decision.

REFERENCES

Cozzillio, M. (1989). The athletic scholarship and the college national letter of intent: a contract by any other name, 35 *Wayne Law Review* 1275.

DiNicola, R., and Mendeloff, S. (1983). Controlling violence in professional sports: rule reform and the federal professional sports violence commission, 21 *Duquesne Law Review* 843.

Graves, J., (1986). Coaches in the courtroom: recovery in actions for breach of employment contracts, 12 *Journal of College and University Law* 545.

Herbert, D., Herbert, W., and Berger, S. (1988). A trial lawyer's guide to the legal implications of recreational, preventive, and rehabilitative exercise program standards of care, 11 *American Journal of Trial Advocacy* 433.

Hetzel, J. (1987). Gender-based discrimination in high school athletics, 10 *Seton Hall Legislative Journal* 275.

Houser, D., Ashworth, J., and Clark, R. (1987). Product liability in the sports industry, 23 *Torts and Insurance Law Journal* 44.

Johnson, A. (1989). The argument for self-help specific performance: opportunistic renegotiation of player contracts, 22 *Connecticut Law Review* 61.

Karns, J. (1986). Negligence and secondary school sports injuries in North Dakota: who bears the legal liability?, 62 *North Dakota Law Review* 455.

Kovach, K. (1990). Labor relations in the National Football League: illegal procedure, delay of game, and unsportsmanlike conduct. 41 *Labor Law Journal* 249.

Lock, E. (1987). The legality under the National Labor Relations Act of Attempts by National Football League owners to unilaterally implement drug testing programs, 39 *University of Florida Law Review* 1.

Lock, E., and Jennings, M. (1986). The constitutionality of mandatory student-athlete drug testing programs: the bounds of privacy, 38 *University of Florida Law Review* 581.

Notes. (1990). Constitutional law—due process—National Collegiate Athletic Association is not considered a state actor under the Fourteenth Amendment, 21 *Rutgers Law Journal* 519.

Notes. (1990). The Federal Mail Fraud Statute: The government's colt 45 renders Norby Walters and Lloyd Bloom agents of misfortune, 10 *Loyola L.A. Entertainment Law Journal* 315.

Notes. (1986). Sports violence in criminal assault: development of the doctrine by Canadian courts, 1986 *Duke Law Journal* 1030.

Roberts, G. (1986). The single entity status of sports leagues under Section 1 of the Sherman Act: an alternative view, 60 *Tulane Law Review* 562.

Ross, S. (1990). An antitrust analysis of sports league contracts with cable networks, 39 *Emory Law Journal* 463.

Russel, C. (1987). Legal and ethical conflicts arising from the team physician's duel obligation to the athlete and management, 10 *Seton Hall Legislative Journal* 299.

Scanlan, J. (1985). Antitrust issues in amateur sports. Introduction: antitrust—the emerging legal issues, 61 *Indiana Law Journal* 1.

Scanlan, J. (1986-87). Playing the drug-testing game: college athletes, regulatory institutions, and the structure of constitutional argument, 62 *Indiana Law Review* 863.

Stoner, E., and Nogay, A. (1989). The model university coaching contract ("MCC"): a better starting point for your next negotiation, 16 *Journal of College and University Law* 43.

Tagliabue, P. (1985). Antitrust developments in sports and entertainment, 56 *Antitrust Law Journal* 341.

Wong, G. (1985). Of franchise relocation, expansion, and competition in professional team sports: the ultimate political football?, 9 *Seton Hall Legislative Journal* 7.

Wong, G. (1987). Major League Baseball's grievance arbitration system: a comparison with nonsports industry, 12 *Employee Relations Law Journal* 464.

Wong, G. (1985-86). Sex discrimination in athletics: a review of two decades of accomplishments and defeats, 21 *Gonzaga Law Review* 345.

Wong, G. (1986). A survey of grievance arbitration cases in Major League Baseball, 41 *The Arbitration Journal* 42.

Wong, G., and Ensor, R. (1987). Major League Baseball and drugs: fight the problem or the player?, 11 *Nova Law Review* 779.

CHAPTER 14

Sports Law: Product Liability and Employment Relations

Annie Clement

In this chapter, you will become familiar with the following terms:

Equitable hiring practices	Agency relationship
Contract agreement	Independent contractor
Job description	Worker's compensation
Risk management	Product liability
Evaluation	Strict liability in tort
Procedural due process	Manufacturer's defect
Vicarious liability	Warranties
Respondeat superior	Merchantability
Regular employee	Fitness

Overview

In Chapter 7, management's legal concerns as those of employer, employee, equitable hiring, safe work conditions, competent evaluation, and vicarious liability were identified. Also, the standard employment relationships of employer–employee, independent contractor, and leased employee were examined. Product liability, a legal theory that affects not only product manufacturers and retailers, but also those who purchase and oversee product use, was reviewed. This chapter will focus on the practical application of the theories discussed earlier. The reader may wish to review the earlier chapter before applying the theories.

EMPLOYER–EMPLOYEE RELATIONSHIPS
Equitable hiring process

Employment systems are designed to rapidly locate the best talent available for a particular job. Attracting skilled and competent talent is a high priority for any business. Most employers are equally interested in being equitable in their hiring practices. The system was devised with guidance from the decisions in *Griggs v. Duke Power Company*, 401 U.S. 424 (1971); *Equal Employment Opportunity Commission v. Atlas Paper Box Company*, 868 F. 2d 1487 (1989); rehearing denied (April 4, 1989); and *Ward Cove Packing Company v. Atonio*, 104 L.E. 2d 733 (1989). The system is designed to guide the administrator in promoting **equitable hiring practices**.

Preparation

1. Visit with members of the personnel office to learn the standards and expectations of the employer.
2. Become familiar with labor union and other **contract agreements** that affect the job.
3. Determine the status of the agency's or corporation's affirmative action program. Does the organization have such a program? If so, is it voluntary or mandatory? (Note requirements specifically related to job advertising.)

Job description

1. Create a **job description** giving a cross-section of the significant tasks. The description is to be accurate and comprehensive.
2. List qualifications that will be essential to the successful candidates' ability to carry out the tasks mentioned in the job description. Avoid listing degrees or special work experiences that are unrelated to the job.
3. Keep qualifications in line with job requirements. Maintain evidence that documents why candidates were not suitable. Such information would be essential if the selection process were challenged.
4. Advertise the job in publications read by potential candidates. Give adequate time for interested parties to apply. All people, including minorities, who are qualified for the job are to know of the job and be allowed adequate time to make their intentions known.

Pool of candidates

1. Advertise so as to obtain the best pool of candidates for the position.
2. Application information must be easy to understand. All information that will be essential to preliminary screening must be requested in the public announcement.
3. Deadlines are to be published and enforced.

Screening of candidates

1. Preliminary screening is conducted to verify that candidates meet objective published criteria. This type of screening may be conducted by a few people rather than a large group. A small group can make decisions using objective criteria. As the screening becomes more subjective, the size of the committee doing the screening increases.
2. Check sheets covering job criteria are constructed and used in evaluating applications.
3. Second and third level screening follows, if demanded by a heavy volume of candidates. Each screening level involves the use of a new and more detailed check sheet. Check sheets need not be forced choice. When narrative is employed, agreement on the meaning of terms is reached before the use of the screening tool.
4. Screening continues until the interview pool is selected.
5. The screening instruments to be used, the use of recommendations in decision making, and the number of candidates that will constitute the interview pool all are to be determined before beginning screening.

Interviewing and selecting

1. Candidates selected to be interviewed may be ranked or merely listed. The decision to rank or to list is made before screening.
2. Interview procedures should ensure an in-depth assessment while keeping the process civil enough that the candidate retains an interest in the position.
3. When necessary, interviewers should be trained to ensure that they do not ask discriminatory questions. Questions such as age, marital status, the likelihood that a spouse will move to the city, and plans for child care are prohibited.
4. All finalists should understand the employment relationship under which the job will be classified, whether "at will," union, contract, or other. (See Chapter 7 for detailed discussion of these relationships.) When the relationship is an employment contract, the employee should understand the contract and the items that the contract will contain.

5. Interviewers are to submit evaluations for each candidate. Candidates are listed or ranked.
6. The final selection is made.

Documentation

1. The entire process and steps within the process are outlined before beginning the search.
2. This outline is reviewed to ensure that the needs of the job have been clearly defined and that the process is equitable.
3. All screening and interviewing check sheets and reports are dated and signed.
4. Applicants are told their status at certain stages in the process. Those eliminated in the initial review should be informed at once. Some search committees also choose to inform applicants who are eliminated before the interviews. The only requirement is that all eliminated candidates be informed at the completion of the search.
5. Documentation must be sufficient that, in the event that a claim questions either the search and screen process or the content of the job description, evidence would enable the persons directly involved to explain their actions.

Establish a coherent plan, follow the plan, and document each step of the process.

Safe work environment

The organization should institute a **risk management** program that will ensure a safe work environment. Whether or not the employees participate in the creation of the program, they should understand its value and help execute and monitor the system. A comprehensive educational program will enable the employer and employee to become aware of risks and hazards in the work environment. Workers should know the steps the industry has taken to eliminate the hazards and risks. Further, workers should be told about the risks that the industry has not been able to remove. The dangers should be clearly identified. Employees are to be warned of all hazards they face in the work environment.

Although there has not been a great deal of litigation involving physical activity personnel, a recent case is gaining considerable attention. Greg Byrd (*Byrd v. Bossier Parish School Board*, 543 So. 2d 35 [La. App. 2 Cir. 1989]; rehearing granted [February 16, 1989] rehearing denied [June 1, 1989]) a ninth grade student and basketball team manager at Airline High School in Louisiana, was using an extractor (a combination washer-dryer) while washing the basketball uniforms for a tournament. Signs had been posted and students had been warned against opening the extractor while it was spinning; however, when the extractor failed to stop in the normal time, Greg opened the lid. To open the lid he had to jump onto the machine. As he opened the lid his leg became caught. The injury resulted in the amputation of his leg above the knee.

Suit was brought against the coach, the principal, the director of maintainence, and the manufacturer of the extractor. Before the end of the trial the manufacturer settled with Byrd, admitting that the machine, contrary to applicable safety standards, could be opened while it was spinning. The trial court found the student contributorily negligent and denied recovery from the other defendants. The court of appeals affirmed the decision. On rehearing, the court of appeals reversed the decision.

The reversal was based on the fact that the student was 14 years old and should not have been operating a power-driven machine under Louisiana law until the age of 16, and that Greg had not been properly instructed in the use of the machinery.

Another case concerning safety in the work environment was *Wertheim v. USTA*, 540 N.Y.S. 2d 443 (A.D. 1 Dept. 1989). Richard Wertheim, aged 61, was an umpire responsible for calling whether a serve was within the center line at the United States Tennis Open in Flushing, New York, in 1983. He had a history of arteriosclerotic cardiovascular disease. An ace or perfect serve struck Wertheim, and he fell backward, striking his head on the court. He died 4 days later.

The theory of the plaintiff's case was that the "defendant, the United States Tennis Association, Inc., had unreasonably enhanced plaintiff's risk of injury by requiring line umpires to stand in the 'ready position' until the ball was in play. Previously linesmen, as such umpires are called, either sat in elevated chairs or stood at full height. The ready position required the linesman to lean forward with his or her hands placed on or above the knees. The purpose of the ready position was to make the linesmen look more professional and more a part of the game" (p. 444). This request caused the plaintiff's representative to say that the USTA had created an unsafe work environment.

The Supreme Court, New York County, denied the USTA's motion for an order setting aside a jury finding that the USTA was 25% liable. The USTA appealed. The Supreme Court, Appellate Division, reversed and dismissed the complaint, holding that the decedent assumed the risk, the ready position did not increase the risk, and, even if the USTA had breached a duty of care, the breach was not the proximate cause of the death. The death was thought to have been caused by a heart problem or a stroke.

Evaluation

Evaluation of personnel is based on the position description and the day-to-day responsibilities of the job. Even though the industry may use a system of evaluation like management by objectives, the industry is expected to evaluate performance based on the elements identified in *Griggs v. Duke Power Company*, 401 U.S. 424 (1971); *Brunet v. City of Columbus*, 642 F. Supp. 1214 (1986); *Ward Cove Packing Co. v. Atonio*, 104 L.E. 2d 733 (1989); and the procedural due process system of the 14th Amendment to the United States Constitution. Under *Griggs, Brunet, Ward Cove*, and procedural due process, the basis for employee evaluation and hiring in state and federal agencies is the skills and knowledge that are directly related to the job specifications and the day-to-day tasks of the work environment. Some private-sector organizations are not required to adhere to the following system.

A fair evaluation system is based on the job description and tasks the job demands. The employee and employer must have the opportunity to assess the employee's performance of those tasks. When they disagree over the employee's performance, a process is available for resolving the dispute.

A **procedural due process** system is available for use at any time. In particular, it is available to employees who receive negative evaluations or who are to be suspended or terminated. The procedural due process system is in writing and appears in the employee handbook or related documents. Procedural due process is an appeal process that contains but is not limited to the following steps:
1. Written notice of all charges against the employee including dates, times, and details of the

specific charges that, if proven, would justify a penalty.
2. Establishment of a time and date for a hearing. The employee must be given adequate time to prepare for the hearing.
3. Representation, including legal representation, may or may not be permitted in the hearing. This decision is made when the guidelines are established, not shortly before a hearing. Also, the decision to allow legal counsel and the technique of cross-examination is made when the system is created.
4. The hearing is to give all sides the opportunity to present their case. All versions of the problem are to be presented.
5. The presentation is to be heard by an impartial panel. The status and authority of the panel and its leader are to be known to all parties.
6. Effort should be made to negotiate a viable settlement.
7. A decision is made. A written report of the rationale is to accompany the decision.
8. The proceedings are to be recorded and are to be available to the employee.
9. In most employment environments, the next level of appeal is a court of law. When discrimination is alleged, the appeal may be to an administrative agency.

Tarkanian v. NCAA, 741 p. 2d 1345 (Nev. 1987), and *NCAA v. Tarkanian*, 102 L.Ed. 2d 469 (1988), involve several legal theories, including due process. The NCAA began investigating the University of Nevada at Las Vegas shortly after Jerry Tarkanian became head basketball coach in 1973. In 1976, after a 2½-year investigation, the NCAA Committee on Infractions confronted the university with a report alleging that 72 violations occurred between 1970 and 1976. Six more allegations were added later. The Nevada State Attorney General's office investigated the allegations, interviewing the people accused. UNLV submitted responses, including many affidavits, sworn statements, and documents supporting the university's denial of specific rule violations.

The NCAA held a hearing and found 38 violations of NCAA rules, naming Tarkanian in 10 of them. Further, they "directed UNLV to show cause why additional penalties should not be imposed against it if it did not suspend Tarkanian from involvement with the University's Intercollegiate

Athletic Program for two years" (*Tarkanian v. NCAA*, 1987; p. 1347).

In September 1977, UNLV, after conducting a hearing on the matter, suspended Tarkanian. Tarkanian brought suit against UNLV and obtained an injunction. An injunction is a court order that directs a party to refrain from, or to do, a specific act. In this case the court directed UNLV to stop the suspension of Tarkanian and to let him return to his coaching position. The court then reversed the injunction for Tarkanian's failure to name a necessary party in the suit, the NCAA. (*University of Nevada v. Tarkanian*, 594 P. 2d 1159 [Nev. 1979]). The court said, in essence, that Tarkanian had to sue the NCAA in addition to UNLV.

In July 1979, Tarkanian sued again, this time naming UNLV and the NCAA, and received another injunction, thus stopping his suspension. Tarkanian argued that he had not been given formal procedural due process. NCAA rulings do not allow procedural due process for people accused of violations.

In August 1987, the Supreme Court of Nevada held that the NCAA, as an actor in a state agency, was required to use a procedural due process and that Tarkanian had a right to due process. The NCAA petitioned the Supreme Court of the United States (*NCAA v. Tarkanian*, 1988). The Supreme Court reversed its decision, stating that NCAA actions were not state actions and therefore the NCAA did not have to give Tarkanian an opportunity for procedural due process. This decision held, contrary to an earlier decision about television contracts, that the NCAA was a private organization that the university had the freedom to join or not to join. The Supreme Court further remanded the case back to the Nevada Supreme Court, saying that UNLV was in charge of disciplining faculty members and that UNLV, as a state agency, was required to adhere to procedural due process. As of June 1990 the university had made no public statement about its decision.

The Tarkanian Supreme Court decision places the responsibility for evaluating, reprimanding, and terminating state employees in the hands of the state agency and prohibits state agencies from carrying out third-party orders. This case prohibited UNLV from carrying out the NCAA's request that Jerry Tarkanian be suspended without a procedural due process opportunity.

CONCEPT CHECK

Successful employer–employee relationships begin in the employment process. To create positive relationships, the employer must prepare a comprehensive job description, attract qualified candidates, screen carefully, and interview and select candidates.

These successful relationships are maintained when the employer provides a safe work environment and an equitable evaluation system. If an employee's performance is unsatisfactory, a carefully constructed procedural due process system is used first to counsel the employee in an attempt to improve performance and, if performance does not improve sufficiently, to give the employee full legal rights in the termination process.

VICARIOUS LIABILITY

Vicarious liability means that a manager is responsible for the torts of the manager's employees as part of the management role. The tort must have occurred while the employee was carrying out the job responsibilities.

Plaintiffs, in intentional tort injuries among professional athletes, have tried to hold managers liable for those torts under vicarious liability. An example follows.

A fight broke out after an intense play involving Kevin Kunnert of the Houston Rockets and Kermit Washington of the Los Angeles Lakers. Members of both teams, including Rudy Tomjanovich, rushed onto the court. In the ensuing brawl, Washington punched Tomjanovich, fracturing his nose, jaw, and skull, and causing lacerations to his face, a concussion, and leakage of spinal fluid.

Rudy Tomjanovich sued Washington's employer, California Sports, Inc., for failure to control Washington's dangerous tendencies, amounting to vicarious liability (*Tomjanovich v. California Sports Inc.*, No. H-78-243 [S.D. Texas 1979]). A jury award of $3.3 million dollars was appealed and settled out of court.

In *Simmons v. Baltimore Orioles, Inc.*, 712 F. Supp. 79 (W.D. Va. 1989), a fan brought suit against the Baltimore Orioles and the security agency the Orioles employed for crowd control for injuries he received from two Orioles players, Champ and

Hicks. These injuries resulted from a fight in the parking lot after a game in Bluefield, Virginia. Simmons allegedly had been heckling the players during the game. He told the court that after the game he "was punched and kicked by Champ and then hit in the jaw by a baseball bat wielded by Hicks, causing his jaw to be broken in two places" (p. 80).

Simmons argued that the players assaulted him in the course of their employment. The court noted that once the players had left the locker room they were no longer in the course of their employment. The plaintiff's next argument was that the Orioles engaged in negligent hiring, a tort recognized in Virginia. Were Champ and Hicks unfit employees for a baseball team? No previous tendency toward violence was found in either man's background.

The United States District, Western District of Virginia, held that the Orioles were not liable for the actions of Champ and Hicks under **respondeat superior**, negligent hiring, or failure to instruct the athletes on how to handle a heckler, and that the security agency had no duty to patrol the parking lot at the time of the incident.

A student sued Wabash College under the theory of respondeat superior for an injury suffered while participating in a practice baseball program under the direction of a volunteer. The Dean of Student Affairs had paid in part for the equipment. The plaintiff's complaint noted that the college baseball coach knew of the team's practice and had agreed to accept promising players onto the official team. The coach had also said that he did not have time to manage the practice program.

The Court of Appeals of Indiana, First District, held that the college had no duty to supervise practice, because the participants were not children and were old enough to assume the risk of sports play and competition, and that the volunteer student who organized the practice was not an employee of the college; therefore the college was not liable or responsible under the theory of respondeat superior (*Swanson v. Wabash College*, 504 N.E. 2d 327 [Ind. App. 1 Dist. 1987]).

A court also failed to find vicarious liability for a university in the case *Nelson v. Ronquillo*, 517 S. 2d 454 (La. App. 1 Cir. 1987). Mary Ronquillo was driving fellow scholarship basketball players to a team meal in a borrowed van. She stopped for a stop sign and then proceeded into an intersection, hitting a truck driven by Nelson. Plaintiff Nelson sued the Board of Trustees of Southeastern Louisiana University under the theories of respondeat superior and negligence in selecting Mary as the driver of the van. Two factors considered by the court in determining the master–servant relationship in this case were "the degree of control exercised over the alleged employee and the existence of compensation" (p. 455).

The Court of Appeals of Louisiana, First Circuit, ruled for the university, saying that Mary Ronquillo was not an employee of the university, because she received no compensation for playing, nor was she required to eat at the hotel. The university was not involved in her selection as a driver of the van. The university did not own the van, and the athletes had made their own decision in agreeing to ride with Mary.

CONCEPT CHECK

Vicarious liability is the responsibility that management has for the torts of its employees. The legal theory is respondeat superior. The tort must occur while the employee is carrying out job responsibilities.

Colleges and universities have been involved in unique cases in which vicarious liability has been difficult to ascertain. Degree of control and compensation are key factors in determining vicarious liability.

EMPLOYMENT RELATIONSHIP

A **regular employee** is a person who works directly for the employer. He or she answers to the employer or to someone in the employer's chain of command. The employer has the legal right to control the employee and to actively direct the employee's work. The employer dictates the specific duties and how the work will be performed. The employer is also responsible for the actions of the employee. For a regular employer–employee relationship or an **agency relationship,** the employee knows that he or she is acting on behalf of the employer, and the employer assumes a fiduciary duty to pay the employee. The employer maintains records, pays unemployment insurance and worker's compensation, and provides benefits. In a regular employee relationship, the employer is vicariously liable for the work-related tort of the employee.

An **independent contractor** has an employment relationship in which the employer has a contract right to the result to be achieved. The employer has no right to control the employee or how the employee is to accomplish the work. The employer is not vicariously liable for the torts of the independent contractor.

Test to distinguish regular employment relationship from independent contractor relationship

To distinguish a regular employment relationship (courts call this relationship a master–servant relationship) from an independent contractor relationship, the courts will ask a number of questions. The decision will be based upon the responses to the questions. These questions also will guide the reader in establishing a relationship or analyzing an existing relationship.

1. *Extent of control.* Who hires, fires, and evaluates? Who establishes work schedules and methods for carrying out tasks? If the independent contractor controls these tasks, the independent contractor status will be retained.
2. *Distinctiveness of occupation or business.* Is the employee so specialized that he or she must retain control? Exercise specialists in health clubs and stadium concessionaires often fit this category.
3. *Custom in industry.* Are relationships in the particular industry customarily those of regular employment or independent contractor?
4. *Unique skills.* What is the level and rarity of the skills? A company claiming independent contractor status should avoid all but the minimal orientation and training for contractors. For example, requiring that a specific system be followed or uniform be worn will virtually guarantee regular employee status.
5. *Provision of tools and supplies.* Usually regular employment is distinguished from independent contractor status by the fact that independent contractors own the tools. The effect of ownership of athletic equipment has not been litigated by the courts, and it appears that one may be able to retain independent contractor status even though one does not own the equipment.
6. *Duration of employment.* Duration is specified and is not forever for independent contractor status.
7. *Method of compensation.* Payment by job suggests independent contractor; payment by hour suggests regular employee.

These questions will guide a professional in assessing the status of an employee or independent contractor. Independent contractor status is usually established when professionals are asked to sign a contract declaring their status as an independent contractor. If the employer becomes involved in the day-to-day work of the independent contractor, assumes responsibility for hiring and firing, or demands a specific approach or methodology, the courts will terminate the independent contractor status. Termination of independent contractor status creates vicarious liability of the employer for the employee.

WORKER'S COMPENSATION

Worker's compensation is a program that provides benefits and medical care automatically when an employee is injured, and it does not require that liability be established before assisting the injured victim. State governments provide insurance for carrying out the plans. Employers provide the money. Nearly everyone in the sport industry, with the exception of college athletes, is covered by worker's compensation.

CASES INVOLVING EMPLOYMENT RELATIONSHIPS AND WORKER'S COMPENSATION

An example of the court's examination of the issues of the independent contractor relationship, the regular employee relationship, and worker's compensation in sport is *Bryant v. Fox*, 515 N.E. 2d 775 (Ill App. 1 Dist. 1987). Waymond Bryant and Cid Edwards, professional football players, brought action against the Chicago Bears and Dr. Theodore A. Fox, an orthopedic surgeon retained by the Bears. The complaint's legal theory was respondeat superior, that Dr. Fox was an employee of the Bears. Dr. Fox and the Bears filed a motion to dismiss "on the grounds that the plaintiffs' claims were barred by the exclusive-remedy provision of the Workers' Compensation Act. . . . This provision protects employers covered by the Act by limiting an employee to his statutory remedy and prohibiting common law actions against the employer or coemployee" (p. 776).

The trial court granted the motion to dismiss, and the plaintiffs appealed, saying that both the professional players and the surgeon were independent contractors and not covered by the Workers' Compensation Act. The Appellate Court of Illinois, First District, Fourth Division, ruled that the players were employees and the surgeon was an independent contractor.

The employment status (regular employee or independent contractor) is important in determining who covers worker's compensation and whether liability must be determined to ascertain the party responsible for paying the cost of an injury.

When an employee injures another employee, the injured employee's injury is covered by worker's compensation, and thus the injured employee agrees not to sue the business or the employee who caused the injury. When the person who causes the injury is an independent contractor, the injured employee can sue the independent contractor and may not be covered by worker's compensation. These situations require individual analysis by a lawyer competent in the area.

College athletes have sued to gain worker's compensation; however, in most cases they have not been successful. *Rensing v. Indiana State University*, Ind., 444 N.E. 2d 1170 (1983); rehearing denied (May 10, 1983), and *Coleman v. Western Michigan University*, 336 N.W. 2d 224 (1983), are examples. Rensing sustained a fractured dislocation of the cervical spine in a punting drill. He was rendered 95% to 100% disabled. He filed for compensation under the Workers' Compensation Act saying that the athletic scholarship he had received for more than 2 years was an employment contract. When denied, he brought suit. The Supreme Court of Indiana, affirming the lower court, ruled that the "appellant shall be considered only as a student athlete and not as an employee within the meaning of the Workman's Compensation Act" (p. 1175).

Coleman, also injured in football, filed a claim for worker's compensation. The Court of Appeals of Michigan held that an athletic scholarship was a wage but that the athlete was not an employee according to the meaning of the Worker's Compensation Act.

CONCEPT CHECK

Most litigation in employment relationships involves establishing status, whether regular employee or in-

dependent contractor. Primary components of the test to determine status are the extent of control, distinctiveness of the occupation or business, custom in the industry, uniqueness of skills, ownership of tools, duration of employment, and method of compensation.

PRODUCT LIABILITY

Product liability affects manufacturers, retailers, wholesalers, and users. Legal actions alleging product liability may fall under strict liability in tort, negligence, misrepresentation, warranty, and violation of consumer product safety standards.

Strict liability in tort

Strict liability in tort may be based on a manufacturer's defect, faulty design, or lack of proper instruction or warnings.

Manufacturer's defects. A **manufacturer's defect** exists when a defect in the construction process results in an unsafe product. As a result, the product does not perform or was not built according to the original plan. An exercise machine was alleged to be defective in *Diversified Products Corporation v. Faxon*, 514 So. 2d 1161 (Fla. App. 1 Dist. 1987). Faxon purchased the machine and assembled it as instructed in the manual. A few days later Faxon, the plaintiff, sustained serious back injuries while performing a standing curl according to the manufacturer's instruction manual. The eye bolt on the curl bar broke. The equipment was not misused, and the design was not altered. Faxon sued the manufacturer and won in the circuit court. The manufacturer appealed. The First District Court of Appeals of Florida reversed and remanded, holding that there was a genuine issue of material fact whether the eye bolt was defective when it left the factory. No results of further litigation are available.

An alleged defective ski binding was the issue in *Opera v. Hyva*, App. Div., 450 N.Y.S. 2d 615 (1982). An adult male, skiing on a beginners' slope, fell and fractured his leg. He attributed the fracture to the failure of a ski binding to release. The other foot's ski binding released in the fall. Opera sued the manufacturer, saying that the instruction manual recommended a binding setting that was unsafe for the plaintiff. The court examined the issues of the validity of the binding-setting manual contents and the failure to inspect and use the product (skis) as the manufacturer intended. Erie Supreme Court entered judgment for the plaintiff on strict liability. The defendant appealed. The Supreme Court, Appellate Division of New York, reversed and granted a new trial. Again, no additional information is available at this time.

Football cases (Fiske, 1983; Byrns, 1976; Gentile, 1985; and Rawlings, 1981) tend to blur the lines between manufacturing defect and design defect. All four victims were high school athletes either practicing for or engaged in a competitive event. In *Gentile v. MacGregor Manufacturing Co.*, 493 A. 2d 647 (N.J. Super. L. 1985), the reconditioner of the helmet was held strictly liable for the defect created by the original manufacturer. The court noted that the school relied on the report of the reconditioner for the safety of its helmets. In *Fiske v. MacGregor Division of Brunswick*, 464 A. 2d 719 (R.I. 1983); *Byrns v. Riddell*, 550 P. 2d 1065 (1976); and *Rawlings v. Daniels*, Tex. Civ. App., 619 S.W. 2d 435 (1981), the athletes won their cases based on defective helmets.

A defective football helmet was alleged to be the cause of a cervical spine injury in *Hemphill v. Sayers*, 552 F. Supp. 685 (1982). Mark Hemphill, a university football player, brought suit against Southern Illinois University for a football injury, claiming that a helmet was defective and that he had not been warned of the dangers of the helmet. He succeeded in the failure-to-warn claim, although most of the other claims were dismissed. Football helmet litigation does not seem to occur in professional and collegiate football as much as it does in high schools.

Managers in sport need to understand the results of football helmet cases and to use their expertise and join legal professionals in an effort to better protect manufacturers of sport equipment in the future. Participants need to understand the extent of protection that a particular product offers; manufacturers need to commit to meeting that level; participants should be told of the amount of protection they can expect in using the equipment and the risks against which the product does not protect; and manufacturers need legal support and insurance to protect them from consumers who attempt to hold them accountable for injuries the product was not designed to prevent.

Faulty design. *O'Brien v. Muskin Corporation*, 463 A. 2d 298 (N.J. 1983), is a manufacturer's defect case in which a 23-year-old man was severely injured when he dove into an above-ground pool. The court failed to establish whether he dove from

the pool platform or the roof of an adjacent 8-foot-high garage. He sued in strict liability, saying that the pool manufacturer had marketed a defectively designed product and that there had been a failure to warn of the risk of using the pool for diving.

The court used a "risk-utility analysis" in exploring the issues. "Risk utility analysis is appropriate when the product may function satisfactorily under one set of circumstances, yet because of its design present undue risk of injury to the user in another situation" (O'Brien, 1983; p. 304). A second system employed by the court was a consumer expectation test, that is, the reasonable expectation of the consumer. The court stated that "the pool fulfilled its function as a place to swim. The alleged defect manifested itself when the pool was used for diving" (O'Brien, 1983; p. 304).

After examining the risk, the court focused on the reasonableness of placing the product on the market. The court pointed out that risks the manufacturer knew or should have known, and the need for warning about those risks, are balanced against the need for the product and the available alternatives. Was there a safer design that could have been used? A case-by-case analysis is applied. The court also noted that a luxury item should not be viewed the same way as a product that fulfills a need.

The trial court granted judgment in favor of the defendant (Muskin Corp.). The plaintiff appealed. The Superior Court, Appellate Division, reversed and remanded. The Supreme Court of New Jersey held that the jury in the lower court might have made a different decision if it had looked at both issues of failure to warn and defective design. They affirmed the decision of the Appellate Division, reversing and remanding for a new trial.

Faulty design was the issue in *South Dakota Building Authority v. Geiger-Berger Associates*, 414 N.W. 2d 15 (S.D. 1987). The case involved the failure of an air-support dome system at the University of South Dakota. The State Building Authority, on behalf of the university, brought suit against the architect and engineer for faulty design. The court held the architect responsible for the design and noted that the university had not been properly advised in the most efficient way to remove ice and snow from the structure.

Instruction and/or warnings. The duty to warn includes the duty to warn of risks and the duty to provide instruction sufficient to enable the average person to ascertain the need for experience or the fact that the equipment is beyond the person's skill level. *Prince v. Parachutes, Inc.*, 685 P. 2d 435 (Alaska, 1984), and *Pavlides v. Galveston Yacht Basin, Inc.*, 727 F.2d 330 (1984), are cases involving those duties.

Clay C. Prince had learned to parachute jump and had made 29 jumps using a standard military round-canopy chute before attempting to use the Paradactyl Chute, the product that resulted in his injury. He was told he needed permission of the U.S. Parachute Association area safety officer to use the more advanced parachute. He obtained the permission. He jumped using the Paradactyl five times before the accident; however, he had landing problems each time. On the day of the accident he was jumping with three other people. On his second jump he failed to watch the other jumpers and was hit in the shoulder and hip by one of his fellow jumpers. As a result, he lost the air in his chute, fell 30 feet, and broke his neck, becoming a quadriplegic.

Prince admitted that he knew the speed of his chute and failed to recognize its greater speed compared to the chutes of the others, that the person who hit him had the right of way, and that there was nothing wrong with his chute. His problem was his inability to handle the more advanced chute. Prince sued the manufacturer, saying a warning should have been sewn into the parachute. The manufacturer presented a detailed manual on the use of the chute.

The Superior Court granted summary judgment for the manufacturer. Prince appealed. The Supreme Court of Alaska reversed and remanded for a new trial, saying that there was "sufficient evidence in the record from which reasonable minds could conclude that Prince would not have used the Paradactyl had he been adequately warned about the experience level required to properly manage the Paradactyl and that he became inattentive to his surroundings and made misjudgments because he was overtasked by the overwhelming demands of landing the Paradactyl" (p. 89-90).

This case is not just a warning case but one in which the warning needs to be tailored to the specific skill level of the user. The failure here was not just the failure to warn, but the failure to adequately instruct or direct the plaintiff on the use of the equipment. This is a case in which

the manufacturer published a printed warning that accompanied the product when it was purchased.

A decedent's estate brought an action against a boat manufacturer and others to recover for the death of the plaintiff, which occurred when the bilge drain plug fell out of a boat (*Pavlides v. Galveston Yacht Basin, Inc.*, 1984). The drain plug fell out, and the boat took on water and eventually sank. An important element in this case was that the boat that sank, manufactured by AMF, was a blend of two other boats. One of these boats carried a highly respected name. People purchasing sport equipment often rely on brand names. When the quality of the brand-name product changes, purchasers need to be warned. In this case, the very popular Robalo 236, previously manufactured by a Florida concern and acquired by AMF in the early 1970s, had a reputation for "safety arising from the boats' fully-foamed construction, meaning that all of the void spaces in the hull were filled with foam floatation materials so that the boats had no void bilge space" (p. 334). The Robalo also had drain holes in the cockpit. At the same time AMF had purchased a boat design from Slickcraft, a small Michigan manufacturer. The Slickcraft line was not fully-foamed; in these boats the bilge space was wholly or partly empty. AMF merged the boat models, using the Slickcraft construction yet marketing the boat under the Robalo and Slickcraft names.

The United States District Court for the Southern District of Texas found for the manufacturer. The plaintiff appealed. The United States Court of Appeals, Fifth Circuit, reversed and remanded, saying, "The manual does not describe the design of the R-236, unique among Robalos; nor does it mention that the R-236 has a void bilge space, a bilge drain and a bilge drain plug. It does not indicate that the bilge drain plug could come off accidentally; it does not say how an operator is supposed to be aware of the bilge filling with water; it does not state that when water appears on deck in the rear of the cockpit it could well mean that the bilge is flooded and that in consequence the electrical system, including the bilge pump, is in immediate danger of failing and that the engines may shortly fail as well. Nor does it note that replacing the bilge drain plug when the bilge is full of water is a very difficult and hazardous procedure. The only reference in the manual to 'drain plugs' or through-hull openings occurs in Pre-Launch Procedure C" (p. 335).

Instruction manuals are to be comprehensive and understood by the average person who would be inclined to purchase the product. Warnings and instructions are to be strong, clear, accurate, and easy to find. They must be placed in a readily accessible place so that anyone using the product will be able to find the warning and/or the instructions.

Negligence

For negligence to be found in product liability, the same four elements must be found as are required in all forms of negligence: a duty of care, a breach of the duty, the breach directly related to the injury, and substantial damage. *Ryan v. Mill River Country Club, Inc.*, 510 A. 2d 462 (Conn. App. 1986), and *Brown v. Yamaha Motor Corp.*, 691 P. 2d 577 (Wash. App. 1984), are examples of product liability negligence. Gina Ryan was driving a three-wheeled golf cart on a paved cart path when it turned sharply, throwing Ryan's passenger off, and overturned, causing the passenger to sustain injuries. The passenger sued Ryan for careless handling of the cart; Ryan, the plaintiff, sued the manufacturer for negligence.

The Superior Court held for the plaintiff, finding that "the cart path had been maintained in a defective manner and that the defect was the proximate cause of the injury" (p. 463). The golf course owner appealed. The Appellate Court of Connecticut agreed with the lower court in finding that the golf club's negligence was the proximate cause of the plaintiff's injuries.

An action in negligence and strict liability was brought against a motorcycle manufacturer for failing to install a "kill switch" in *Brown v. Yamaha Motor Corp.* A "kill switch" is a device that enables the rider to shut off the engine without letting go of the handlebars. The plaintiff was riding a borrowed motorcycle, it accelerated as it climbed a steep grade and leaped at the top, tossing the rider into the air, rendering him a quadriplegic. The Superior Court entered judgment on verdict for plaintiff for negligence. The manufacturer appealed. The Court of Appeals of Washington affirmed on the negligence theory; the court reversed on the strict liability theory, stating that the facts of defective design should be considered. No further record of the case is available.

Warranties

Warranties may be express or implied. Liability in warranty holds without regard to fault. Express warranties are written statements about the product; implied warranties are warranties that are assumed. Implied warranties will be considered under **merchantability** and **fitness**.

Anthony Pools, a division of Anthony Industries, Inc. v. Sheehan and *Sheehan v. Anthony Pools, a division of Anthony Industries Inc.*, are cases that serve as examples of warranty of merchantability. Merchantability means the product is suitable for its intended purpose. Sheehan sustained injuries when he fell from the side of the diving board of his new swimming pool. He said that the skid-resistant materials built into the diving board stopped 1 inch from the edge of the board. This condition was claimed to be a breach of implied warranty of merchantability. The Circuit Court entered judgment for Anthony, the pool manufacturer. The Court of Special Appeals reversed and remanded. The Court of Appeals affirmed the lower court, stating that the pool manufacturer had not breached the Uniform Commercial Code's implied warranty of merchantability.

A warranty of fitness means the product has been made for a specific purpose and that the product meets the purpose. Cornelius Hurley, in *Hurley v. Larry's Water Ski School*, 762 F. 2d 925 (1985), injured his leg while taking a water ski lesson. As he was trying to stand up, the rope snapped out of his hand and hit his leg, causing a 4-inch cut. He sued on the legal theory of implied warranty for fitness, that is, that the equipment was not suited for a beginning user. The United States District Court for the Southern District of Florida directed a verdict in favor of the water ski school. The student appealed. The Court of Appeals, Eleventh Circuit, held in part, reversed in part, and remanded. The court held that there was "an implied warranty that the equipment supplied by Larry's was fit for the purpose of teaching an individual to ski" (p. 929).

Violation of consumer product safety standards

The Consumer Product Safety Commission researches injuries involving products. On occasion it identifies a product that is hazardous or is hazardous if used by a certain population or in a specific manner. The banning of lawn darts for sale to or use by children is an example of such action.

Ronald Zepik in *Zepik v. Tidewater Midwest, Inc.*, 856 F. 2d 936 (7th Cir. 1988) and 719 F. Supp. 751 (N.D. Ind. 1986); *Zepik v. Pleasure Industries*, 118 F.R.D. 455 (1987); and *Zepik v. Ceeco Pool and Supply, Inc.*, 637 F. Supp. 444 (N.D. Ind. 1986), alleged a violation of the Consumer Product Safety Act, among a number of product liability theories, in suing the excavator and manufacturers of components used in a pool after he sustained injury from diving into an in-ground swimming pool and striking his head on the bottom. The alleged breach was the manufacturer's failure "to inform the Consumer Product Safety Commission of a substantial product hazard, namely that a swimming pool may be defective for failure to warn users that diving into shallow water may result in serious spinal injury" (p. 446). The plaintiff also presented several claims based on strict liability, negligence, willful and wanton misconduct, and breach of express and implied warranties.

The United States District Court for the Northern District of Indiana granted a motion for summary judgment to Pleasure Industries early in the case. Summary judgment means that there was no issue of material fact (Black's Law Dictionary, 1979).

Later, the same court dismissed the Consumer Product Safety complaint against the developer and granted summary judgment in favor of the remaining manufacturers (*Zepik v. Ceeco Pool and Supply, Inc., Zepik v. Pleasure Industries*). The diver appealed. The Court of Appeals held that the excavator and manufacturers were not liable for reporting under the Consumer Product Safety statute and that it was the district court's responsibility to exercise jurisdiction over the state claims. The case was appealed to the United States District Court, Northern District of Indiana, and the case was dismissed.

CONCEPT CHECK

Product liability covers the areas of strict liability in tort, negligence, misrepresentation, warranty, and violations of consumer product safety standards. Strict liability in tort includes manufacturer's defect, faulty design, and lack of proper instructions and warnings.

Negligence requires the same elements essential to all negligence claims, that is, a duty of care, breach of the duty, the breach directly related to the injury, and substantial damage.

Warranties may be express or implied. Express warranties are written and implied warranties are assumed to accompany the purchase. The Consumer Product Safety Commission identifies products that are hazardous to the public. If the commission bans a product, the product is not to be manufactured or used.

SUMMARY

1. Employers use an organized hiring system. The system should recognize labor union and other contracts and state and federal civil rights legislation.
2. Job descriptions are to include the tasks essential to success in the position.
3. Assembling a large pool of qualified candidates is the goal of the search team.
4. Employers are to provide a safe work environment for their employees. When the nature of the work prevents the employer from providing a safe work environment, the employer must warn the employee about hazards.
5. Employee evaluations are to be directly related to the job responsibilities and tasks.
6. An appeal system is to exist and be available to all employees.
7. When state or federal employees are to be terminated, they must be informed of the charges against them, be permitted to obtain advice, be given a hearing in which both sides of the issue are presented, and afforded an impartial decision. The entire process is to be recorded in writing.
8. Vicarious liability is the manager's automatic responsibility for the torts of his or her employees. Professional teams occasionally are held responsible for the torts of their players. Colleges and universities seldom are found liable for the torts of their students.
9. The following areas are examined to determine employment status: extent of control, distinctiveness of occupation or business, custom in industry, uniqueness of skills, ownership of tools and supplies, duration of employment, and method of compensation.

10. Worker's compensation is a program that provides benefits to injured workers without requiring that liability be determined.
11. Product liability areas include strict or automatic liability in tort, negligence, misrepresentation, warranty, and violation of consumer product safety standards.
12. When an unsafe product is created in the construction process, the product has a manufacturer's defect; faulty design occurs when the product is made according to specifications but the specifications are faulty.
13. Warranties may be express or implied. Liability in warranty holds without regard to fault.

REVIEW QUESTIONS AND ISSUES

1. Prepare a job description for a job of your choice. Use the job description to write criteria to be used in advertising for candidates and in assessing candidates' qualifications.
2. Define equitable hiring. List precautions that will help ensure that hiring is equitable.
3. Identify a job and describe a safe work environment for that job.
4. Identify the key components of a procedural due process system. When is such a system used?
5. Find the cases mentioned under vicarious liability and read them in detail.
6. Outline the differences and similarities of a regular employment relationship and an independent contractor relationship.

REFERENCES

Anthony Pools, a division of Anthony Industries, Inc. v. Sheehan, 455 A. 2d 434 (Md. 1983).

Black's law dictionary (5th Edition). (1977). St Paul, Minnesota: West Publishing Co.

Brown v. Yamaha Motor Corporation, 691 P. 2d 577 (Wash. App. 1984).

Brunet v. City of Columbus, 642 F. Supp. 1214 (1986), Appeal dismissed, 826 F. 2d 1062 (1987), Cert denied, 108 S. Ct. 1593 (1988).

Bryant v. Fox, 515 N. E. 2d 775, (Ill. App. 1 Dist. 1987).

Byrd v. Bossier Parish School Board, 543 So. 2d 35 (La. App. 2 Cir. 1989), rehearing granted February 16, 1989; rehearing denied June 1, 1989.

Byrns v. Riddell, 113 Ariz. 264, 550 P. 2d 1065 (1976).

Clement, A. (1988). *Law in sport and physical activity*. Indianapolis, Indiana: Benchmark.

Clement, A. (1989). Employment: how to approach today's risks, *Journal of the National Intramural, Recreation and Sports Association*, p. 18.

Coben, L. (1989). Sports helmets, more harm than protection? *Trial*, p. 74-82.

Coleman v. Western Michigan University, 336 N. W. 2d 224 (1983).

Consumer Product Safety Commission, 16 CFR Parts 1306 and 1500.

Federal Register, Vol 53, No. 223, November 18, 1988.

Diversified Products Corporation v. Faxon, 514 So. 2d 1161 (Fla. App. 1 Dist. 1987).

Equal Employment Opportunity Commission v. Atlas Paper Box Company, 868 F. 2d 1487 (1989), rehearing denied April 4, 1989.

Fiske v. MacGregor Division of Brunswick, 464 A. 2d 719 (R.I. 1983).

Gentile v. MacGregor Manufacturing Co., 493 A. 2d 647 (N.J. Super L. 1985).

Griggs v. Duke Power Company, 401 U. S. 424 (1971).

Hemphill v. Sayers, 552 F. Supp. 685 (1982).

Hurley v. Larry's Water Ski School, 762 F. 2d 925 (1985).

NCAA v. Tarkanian, 102 L. Ed. 2d 469 (1988).

Nelson v. Ronquillo, 517 S. 2d 454.

O'Brien v. Muskin Corporation, 463 A. 2d 298 (N.J. 1983).

Opera v. Hyva, App. Div., 450 N.Y. S. 2d 615 (1982).

Pavlides v. Galveston Yacht Basin, Inc., 727 F. 2d 330, (1984).

Prince v. Parachutes, Inc., 685 P. 2d 83 (Alaska 1984).

Rawlings v. Daniels, Tex. Civ. App., 619 S. W. 2d 435 (1981).

Rensing v. Indiana State University, 444 N. E. 2d 1170 (1983), Rehearing denied May 10, 1983.

Riffer, J. (1985). *Sports and recreational injuries*. Colorado Springs, Colorado: Shepard's/McGraw-Hill Book Co.

Ryan v. Mill River Country Club Inc., 510 A. 2d 462 (Conn. App. 1986).

Sheehan v. Anthony Pools, a division of Anthony Industries, Inc. 440 A. 2d 1085 (1982).

Simmons v. Baltimore Orioles, Inc., 712 F. Supp. 79 (W.D. Va. 1989).

South Dakota Building Authority v. Geiger-Berger Associates, 414 N. W. 2d 15 (S.D. 1987).

Swanson v. Wabash College. 504 N. E. 2d 327 (Ind. App. 1 Dist. 1987).

Swartz, V. (1980). The uniform product liability act: a brief overview. *Vanderbilt Law Review*, 33, 579-592.

Tarkanian v. NCAA, 741 P. 2d 1345 (Nev. 1987).

Tomjanovich v. California Sports, Inc., No. H-78-243 (S. D. Texas, 1979).

University of Nevada v. Tarkanian, 594 P. 2d 1159 (1979).

Ward Cove Packing Co. v. Atonio, 104 L. E. 2d 733 (1989).

Wertheim v. USTA, 540 N. Y. S. 2d 443, (A. D. 1 Dept. 1989).

Wittenberg, J. (1989). *Product liability: recreation and sports equipment*. New York: Law Journal Seminars Press.

Zepik v. Ceeco Pool and Supply, Inc., 637 F. Supp. 444 (N.D. Ind. 1986).

Zepik v. Pleasure Industries, 118 F. R. D. 455 (1987).

Zepik v. Tidewater Midwest, Inc., 856 F. 2d 936 (7th Cir. 1988).

Zepik v. Tidewater Midwest, Inc., 719 F. Supp. 751 (N.D. Ind. 1986).

SUGGESTED READINGS

Appenzeller, H. (Ed.). (1985). *Sports and law: contemporary issues.* Charlottesville, Virginia: The Michie Co.

Duffola, D. (1987). Worker's compensation: student athlete as "employee" of college or university providing scholarship or similar financial assistance. In *American Law Reports* (4th Edition). Rochester, New York: The Lawyers Cooperative Publishing Co., 58:1259-1266.

Ellmore, K. (1987). Baseball player's right to recover for baseball-related personal injuries from nonplayer. In *American Law Reports* (4th Edition). Rochester, New York: The Lawyers Cooperative Publishing Co., 55:664-706.

Fotiades, J. (1989). *You're the judge! How to understand sports, torts and courts.* Worcester, Massachusetts: Edgeworth and North Books.

Graves, J. (1986). Coaches in the courtroom: recovery in actions for breach of employment contract. *Journal of College and University Law,* 12(4):545-559.

Goldberger, A. (1984). *Sports officiating: a legal guide.* New York: Leisure Press.

Maloy, B. (1988). *Law in sport liability cases in management and administration.* Indianapolis, Indiana: Benchmark.

Maloy, B. (1990), *Legal risks in sport and recreational facilities management.* Indianapolis, Indiana: Benchmark.

McGuire, E. (1988). Foreseeable misuse of products. *Trial,* 24(11), 43-45.

Zupanic, D. (1977). Liability of participant in team athletic competition for injury to or death of another participant. In *American Law Reports* (3rd Edition). Rochester, New York: The Lawyers Cooperative Publishing Co., 77:1300-1309.

CHAPTER 15

Collegiate Trademark Licensing

William R. Battle III
Barbara Botsch Bailey
Bruce B. Siegal

In this chapter, you will become familiar with the following terms:*

Licensing	Trademark
Indicia	Service mark
Labeling	Collective mark
Licensors	Mark
Licensees	Registered mark
Consortium	Related company
Retail licensing	Secondary meaning
Promotional licensing	Abandonment
Royalties	Laches
Premium	

OVERVIEW

If one owns a T-shirt, sweatshirt, mug, or key chain bearing the logo of one's favorite university, chances are it was put through a rigorous approval process. Not only was it checked for quality and design, but a portion of the selling price was sent back to the university for deposit in designated funds. This is known as trademark **licensing,** and it has become one of the fastest growing businesses on college campuses.

Licensing is important to a university, because it enables the university to control the way its name and **indicia †** are portrayed on merchandise. Every

---

*See the box on p. 262 for a glossary of some of the basic licensing terms.

†*Indicia* defined in box on p. 262.

licensed collegiate design is approved by someone at the university. Products of inferior quality are rejected. Strict **labeling** requirements are enforced so the consumer can identify the merchandise as authentic. The product manufacturer is required to carry product liability insurance, which protects the university if a legal action is filed against the university because of an incident involving that collegiate product. Finally, companies must sign a contract that holds the companies that produce collegiate merchandise responsible for following the university guidelines. There is a great deal more to licensing than meets the eye!

Licensing is not uncommon. Corporate licensing includes Coca-Cola and Hard Rock Cafe; character licensing includes Mickey Mouse and The Simpsons; professional sports licensing includes the National Football League (NFL), the National Basketball Association (NBA), and Major League Baseball (MLB); movie licensing includes such hits as Star Wars and Batman; and Olympic licensing includes a variety of products. These groups provide licensing for the same reasons as colleges—quality control, market expansion, and royalty revenue.

The licensing division at a university may be housed in one of several locations. The most common location is under the direction of the vice-president of business or finance. It is not uncommon, however, to find the licensing department located in the bookstore, the athletic department, or an auxiliary services office. It is very important that the athletic department, bookstore, and alumni office understand the value of licensing and how it can benefit the entire university.

A BRIEF HISTORY OF TRADEMARK LICENSING
The industry
According to the Licensing Industry Merchandisers' Association (LIMA), a trademark association of **licensors, licensees,** and support groups, licensing has been around for more than 200 years. Of course, licensing as it is known today is much different and more sophisticated than it was 200 years ago. In fact, most of the growth of licensing as an industry has occurred in the last 20 years.

The first forms of licensing were recorded as far back as 1770. "Saintsbury Chemical Fluid for the Obliteration of Marks of the Skin" (the official name of "Saintsbury Soap") gained popularity and in-

creased sales with the endorsement of the Right Honorable Countess Dowagers of Spencer and Jersey.

It was not until the early 1930s, however, that licensing came into its own. New forms of entertainment such as radio, movies, and comics reached more people than ever before. These new forms of entertainment were less expensive and much more impressive than entertainment Americans enjoyed in the past. Mickey Mouse, Shirley Temple, Superman, and Bugs Bunny were among the "hot" stars of the time. It was soon discovered that applying names and likenesses of these lovable characters to merchandise boosted sales tremendously. People enjoyed identifying with these characters. A whole new line of licensed properties was born, and a new market was created (Altchuler, 1989).

The sale of licensed products grew dramatically during the 1970s from almost nothing to 17.6 billion dollars in retail sales by 1979. By 1988, retail sales of all licensed products in the United States surpassed 60 billion dollars.

Today, licensing crosses the entire spectrum of the U.S. economy. Licensors offer characters, personalities, corporate logos and identities, professional sports teams, colleges and universities, and many other properties to licensees who take licensed products and promotions into virtually every market niche.

The rapid growth of the licensing industry has spawned many related businesses and organizations. Licensing publications keep interested parties informed of industry trends. Licensing trade shows provide a forum for vendors to sell and retailers and consumers to purchase licensed products. Licensing consultants advise businesses on how to capture the spirit and emotion associated with licensed properties to increase sales and distinguish that company's products from competing products. Licensing agencies advise and manage the properties of licensors to help them meet all legal requirements, as well as to generate the maximum exposure and revenues from the property. Professional associations have been formed to educate and inform all segments of the licensing industry. Computer software experts, auditors, artists, designers, retail specialists, and many other technicians have found a place in the licensing industry. See the box on p. 247 for a list of licensing organizations.

Professional licensing organizations and related organizations

The Collegiate Licensing Company
320 Interstate North
Suite 102
Atlanta, GA 30339
(404) 956-0520

P.O. Box 5014
Carpinteria, CA 93013
(805) 566-1466

Licensing Industry Merchandiser's Association (LIMA)
350 Fifth Avenue, Suite 6210
New York, NY 10118
(212) 244-1962

NFL Properties
410 Park Avenue
New York, NY 10022
(212) 838-0660

MLB Properties
350 Park Avenue
New York, NY 10022
(212) 371-7800

NBA Properties
654 Fifth Avenue
New York, NY 10022
(212) 826-7000

NHL Properties
650 Fifth Avenue
New York, NY 10019
(212) 398-1100

Licensing Corporation of America
75 Rockefeller Plaza
New York, NY 10019
(212) 484-8807

Association of Collegiate Licensing Administrators (ACLA)
Michigan State University
216 MSU Union
East Lansing, MI 48824
(517) 355-3434

National Association of College Stores (NACS)
P.O. Box 58
Oberlin, OH 44074
(216) 775-7777

National Collegiate Athletic Association (NCAA)
P.O. Box 1906
Mission, KS 66201
(913) 384-3220

United States Trademark Association (USTA)
6 East 45th St.
New York, NY 10017
(212) 986-5880

Professional sports licensing

National Football League (NFL). The first forms of organized sports licensing came in the early 1960s when the National Football League (NFL) took steps to protect its marks. In 1963, all of the NFL member clubs except the Los Angeles Raiders named NFL Properties as their exclusive licensing agent. The primary goals of NFL Properties were to protect the trademarks and to promote and enhance the image of the National Football League and its member clubs.

NFL Properties is the sole source of funding for NFL Charities. All licensing profits are distributed to charities selected by the NFL. Since 1979, NFL Properties has increased its revenue sevenfold. Retail sales of licensed NFL merchandise from 1988 to 1989 were estimated at 750 million dollars. NFL Properties created a model that other professional teams and collegiate licensing programs have tried to duplicate. The NFL paid its dues in both marketing and enforcement in the 1960s and 1970s and paved the way for the successes all sports licensors enjoy today (Flood, 1989).

Major League Baseball (MLB). Major League Baseball (MLB) began its licensing program in 1969. Up until 1985, MLB licensing was very fragmented. National licensees were managed by a prominent New York licensing agency. The agency had its hands tied by an MLB policy that allowed each team to conduct its own local licensing. Enforcement was difficult at best, and an organized marketing approach was virtually impossible. In 1987, Major League Baseball consolidated its licensing efforts for all 26 teams into one company, Major League Baseball Properties. With centralized management, licensing revenues quintupled in 3 years. Retail sales were announced at 1 billion dollars in 1989. Major League Baseball is living proof of the power that a **consortium** can have when licensing activities have a centralized management (White, 1989).

National Basketball Association (NBA). Although the NFL started its licensing program in 1963, the National Basketball Association (NBA) took much longer. From 1980 to 1981, the NBA created a marketing arm dedicated to retail licensing. NBA Properties, Inc. is staffed with more than 20 professionals who coordinate the **retail** and **promotional licensing*** functions for the 27 teams of the NBA.

The Boston Jordan Marsh department stores were the first to recognize the potential of carrying a line of NBA-licensed merchandise. Larry Bird had just signed with the Celtics, and the Jordan Marsh stores noticed the hoopla surrounding this valuable acquisition. A company was commissioned to produce T-shirts featuring Larry Bird, and the shirts sold out in astonishing time. Seeing the profitability of such merchandise, a "Celtics Shop" was formed. Today, there are several such NBA shops throughout the country.

NBA Properties, which recorded retail sales at only 44 million dollars from 1983 to 1984, produced an impressive 500 million dollars in gross retail sales from 1988 to 1989 (Silvan, 1989).

Collegiate licensing

Four factors led to the development of organized collegiate licensing. These are discussed in the following four sections.

Increased popularity of collegiate athletics and the resulting media coverage. The United States has had public and private institutions of higher learning for more than 200 years. In addition to a proud heritage of academic excellence, many of these institutions have developed strong traditions of athletic success.

Successful athletic teams, especially in football and basketball, became a rallying point for students, faculty, alumni, and the public. Esprit de corps and camaraderie were fostered as collegiate teams competed with their counterparts at other institutions.

Intense rivalries developed over the years, and collegiate athletics evolved into one of the most popular spectator attractions in this country. Its popularity has increased steadily from the 1950s through the present.

Increased popularity led to increased attendance at games, leading to increased media coverage; this in turn led to more popularity, more attendance, and even more media coverage. Stadiums and coliseums were enlarged. Front pages of major newspapers carried the outcomes of collegiate contests. Television magnified collegiate athletics and multiplied its popularity. Today, collegiate athletics get headline coverage virtually year round.

The NCAA basketball tournament developed into one of the most successful media spectacles in American sports. Postseason football bowl games dominate holiday conversations and activities. New Year's Day for many years has been filled with college bowl games.

Development of imprinting technology. During the 1970s the technology in "screenprinting" or "silk-screening" rapidly developed. By the end of the 1970s, the equipment was relatively inexpensive and easy to operate. For a few hundred dollars, an individual literally could set up a printing operation in a basement or garage. Screens could be created in hours with virtually any logo, slogan, or catchy phrase. Blank garments were easily acquired from a number of mills and could be printed to meet any demands.

Printed T-shirts became a communications medium during the 1970s. Adults, as well as students and children, were part of a market that grew dramatically throughout the 1980s. Comic book he-

---

*Retail and *promotional licensing* defined in the box on p. 262.

roes, cartoons, schools, professional teams, clubs, causes, characters, and many other subjects became featured designs on clothing. Consumers identified with these designs and enjoyed the association.

Football fans gathering at college stadia in numbers from 50,000 to 103,000 became a nice target for entrepreneurs, who printed college logos on T-shirts, caps, and other garments. Fans developed pride and a sense of loyalty and support by wearing team colors and designs.

Development of trademark licensing as an industry. Although trademark licensing may be traced back hundreds of years, its dramatic growth occurred in the 1970s and 1980s. The development of imprinting technology greatly expanded the licensing industry.

Manufacturers could sell almost anything that they could produce after World War II, during the 1940s and 1950s. "Sales" became the winning edge during the 1960s and most of the 1970s. "Marketing" became the key to business success in the late 1970s and early 1980s.

Marketers learned that associating a generic product with a celebrity, cartoon character, institution, or sports team could set their product apart from their competitors' product. The objective of adding a name or logo to a product was to capture the emotions created by the fans of that property.

"Strawberry Shortcake" and the "Smurfs" became such popular cartoons that children throughout the country persuaded their parents to buy licensed shoes, clothes, toys, lunch boxes, and many other products during the 1980s. "Pierre Cardin," "Izod," "Polo," "Spuds McKenzie," and "Panama Jack" became very popular as licensed names on products geared toward teen-agers and adults. The "Star Wars" and "Rocky" movies spawned tremendous licensing/merchandising success.

Anyone who has attended big-time college football or basketball games knows the emotions fans generate in support of their teams. The collegiate market transcends all demographic boundaries. People of both sexes, varying degrees of wealth, and all ages, races, creeds, and colors find themselves extremely attracted to their school, alma mater, or favorite team.

As the market for imprinted collegiate products expanded, so too did the abuses. T-shirts, banners, and other products began to appear with vulgar and obscene statements used in conjunction with university marks. Merchandise of poor quality or with poor design began to surface. Of even greater significance, products that exposed universities to serious liability risks began to surface. In the early 1980s, handguns and condoms, among other unapproved products, were found emblazoned with college logos and offered for sale in the marketplace.

Financial problems facing universities. The academic community seemed to consider most commercialism distasteful throughout the 1960s and well into the 1970s. The sale of collegiate imprinted merchandise helped build spirit, however, and appeared to cause no problems as long as it was tastefully produced. When the abuses became more frequent, college administrators quickly decided that they needed greater control over the use of their marks to prevent the obnoxious designs, poor quality merchandise, and product liability risks that they were beginning to face.

In addition, the 1970s and early 1980s saw unprecedented high interest rates and inflation hit the U.S. economy. Federal and state governments cut back funding for collegiate programs, faculty, and staff. Many schools struggled for survival. New sources of revenue were needed.

Reacting to the increases in logo abuse and the need for new sources of revenue, universities took the logical step of establishing formal licensing programs. The universities that pioneered collegiate licensing did so primarily to protect and control the use of their marks and the quality of the merchandise associated with those marks. They hoped to generate some revenues, but most did not believe that licensing would ever generate substantial income. As licensing developed, however, universities realized that the income could help ease the monetary problems they faced. By 1990, some schools generated more than 1 million dollars a year in **royalties.**

Licensing revenues are handled differently at different institutions. This money is allocated to several areas. Most schools use the money for academic and athletic scholarships. Others have set up funds for special projects, construction, and other positive university functions. In most situations the school divides the royalties so that several departments benefit from the licensing program.

The beginning. There is some debate as to which university started the first collegiate licensing program. A few universities established internal policies to govern the use of their marks and even signed a few license agreements in the early 1970s. The University of Houston appears to have been the first school to obtain federal registration of a trademark, the university seal, in 1971. Figure 15-1 offers some examples of other university trademarks. Ohio State University filed an application to register its name and related indicia in 1973 with the U.S. Patent and Trademark Office. By 1975 UCLA and the University of Southern California followed suit with the registration of various marks and the implementation of formal, though embryonic, licensing programs (Burshtein, 1988).

These programs set forth a formal process requiring companies producing merchandise bearing university marks to sign a license agreement. Very little organized licensing activity, however, occurred in the college market during the 1970s. Manufacturers were accustomed to using the marks without approval and without paying royalties. Those that were willing to secure rights and pay royalties found this very difficult to do, because most universities did not have organized licensing

FIGURE 15-1   Trademarks of **A,** Georgetown University, **B,** University of Michigan, and **C,** University of Kentucky.

programs. The schools that did have licensing programs were not consistent and, in many cases, not supported by all departments of the university. The schools greatly needed a coordinating entity to bring direction, continuity, and consistency to this fragmented scene.

In August 1983, a company called The Collegiate Licensing Company was developed to do just that—add continuity and consistency to the fragmented area of collegiate licensing. This company was developed as a joint venture of Collegiate Concepts, Inc. of Atlanta, Georgia, and International Collegiate Enterprises, Inc. of Carpinteria, California.

The two presidents, Bill Battle, former head football coach at the University of Tennessee, and Steve Crossland, former bookstore manager at the University of Southern California, believed that centralized management of a consortium of universities was the only way that collegiate licensing could ever reach its potential. The universities of Alabama, North Carolina, Michigan, Illinois, Clemson, and Duke were early members and have played a major role in the development of the consortium concept of licensing. At the same time, other universities (UCLA, Florida, Iowa, and Michigan State) decided to set up and manage their programs separately and independently. In 1990 The Collegiate Licensing Company represented more than 120 universities, bowls, and athletic conferences for retail and promotional licensing. All have helped develop the consortium to its current status. Without the pioneers, collegiate licensing would have remained in a quagmire of uncertainty and fragmentation.

CONCEPT CHECK

In collegiate licensing, a university grants a manufacturer the right to use the university's indicia in producing and selling merchandise. The licensee is required to sign a contract, pay royalties, and adhere to strict licensing regulations. Four factors led to the organization of collegiate licensing: (1) the increased popularity of collegiate athletics and the resulting media coverage, (2) advances in the screenprinting industry, (3) the development of licensing as an industry, and (4) the financial needs many colleges and universities faced.

THE CONSORTIUM APPROACH TO COLLEGIATE LICENSING

Certain universities have chosen to set up, manage, and administer their own licensing programs. They believe that the advantages are the following: (1) they totally control all aspects of their programs, (2) they do not have to share revenues with a third party, (3) they can make every decision based on what is best for their institution without regard for other institutions, and (4) service comes directly from the university.

At the same time, collegiate licensing is becoming more complex every day. Many believe that only through sophisticated and centralized management can collegiate licensing successfully navigate the minefields of the marketplace during the coming decade. The question is not "*Can* an institution effectively manage its own program?" but "*How* can a public or private institution *most* effectively manage its licensing program?" The Collegiate Licensing Company has developed the consortium approach to licensing under the premise that there is strength in numbers and value in centralized management.

Advantages of centralized management

The size and diversification of staff and services are increased. If 20 universities were running their own programs each would need a licensing director and administrative assistant at least. Say that each university could fill those two jobs for 40,000 dollars. That adds up to 40 people, who all perform the same basic functions and get paid 800,000 dollars per year. They must be reasonably skilled in many different areas. They all require computer hardware and software, and their data is limited strictly to their own university's activities.

Through centralized management, one person acting as licensing director, several administrative assistants, an attorney, a paralegal, an accountant, auditors, marketing personnel, and field representatives could be hired for a fraction of 800,000 dollars. One computer system can handle the data base, which becomes more valuable with each university added. As revenues increase, staff members, skills, and services can be added to take advantage of promising areas.

Economies of scale reduce the overall effect of costs, not only in staff and computers, but in virtually every area of activity. Office space, telephone costs, travel expenses, contract compliance audits, enforcement activities, and marketing activities all become very economical when coordinated by one company on behalf of multiple clients.

There is strength in numbers. A group of 20 universities, or 120 universities, carries a great deal of clout in the marketplace, especially if the members have common goals. Licensees, retailers, and consumers pay more attention to a large group of universities than they do to one or two. Being part of a group of universities is an advantage when dealing with infringers.*

Through in-house counsel, as well as outside professional trademark counsel, the Collegiate Licensing Company has developed a pattern of pursuing trademark violations nationwide. Enforcement is consistent across the board rather than isolated or unorchestrated. Priorities are established and litigation cases are carefully selected to have the widest effect. Furthermore, universities appreciate having a third party serving as a buffer in dealing with the unpleasant aspects of trademark licensing.

One of the greatest benefits of centralized management is the data base that it generates. The data base enables management to analyze global data for licensees, infringers, and royalties. Comparing university to university, licensee to licensee, and market to market enables management to identify and solve problems, as well as take advantage of opportunities.

Consistency and continuity are essential to reaching potential. Centralized management enables a large number of universities to develop common policies and procedures. They may vary slightly from university to university but fit within parameters that licensees find acceptable.

Dealing with one office enables licensees to reduce their administrative burden, since they do not have to worry about the intricacies of several different contracts. The bulk of their time can be spent producing and selling licensed products, which helps expand their market.

Licensee and retail support systems, such as the "Officially Licensed Collegiate Products" label, retail signage, consumer awareness programs, and retailer awareness programs become consistent and continuous through centralized coordination.

Consistency and continuity are key factors in maximizing the effect of these programs in the marketplace.

New programs may be leveraged throughout the consortium. The Collegiate Licensing Company staff is involved in virtually all new products and programs that hit the collegiate market. Understanding what is acceptable to universities, the company can guide licensees through a process that will save them time and effort. A company working on behalf of several schools can see the entire picture from an objective viewpoint and help ensure that each project produces the maximum revenue per university and that the greatest possible number of universities participate in the project.

For example, a small company that comes up with a successful new product in a single university market may lack the knowledge, expertise, or capital to take that product to other university markets. The consortium can help leverage that successful product throughout the country.

New programs may apply to licensees, retailers, consumers, or the universities themselves. Auditing licensees for contract compliance has been the greatest single factor in the growth and maturation of collegiate licensing. The Collegiate Licensing Company conducts more audits than any other licensor in the United States.

Contracts provide incentives to ensure progress. If The Collegiate Licensing Company is to endure, it must operate with a benefit-to-cost ratio that is better than the university could achieve independently. The consortium must use its resources to continue to develop innovative and synergistic concepts to keep the collegiate market thriving.

The Collegiate Licensing Company can more effectively budget to increase its staff and improve its services if it has long-term contracts with universities. As incentive, each university is offered percentages of royalty income on an increasing scale. That is, the higher the gross revenue generated, the greater are the percentages of revenue that are paid to the university. Long-term contracts enable The Collegiate Licensing Company to make stronger long-term budgetary commitments and in turn provide greater services to universities, licensees, retailers, and consumers. The system is a good one.

Infringers defined in the box on p. 262.

Individual universities retain control of their programs even as part of the consortium. The biggest disadvantage of centralized management is that individual universities may lose control of their programs and the programs may lose their identity. The Collegiate Licensing Company has worked hard to turn this one disadvantage into perhaps its biggest advantage. Each university is encouraged to set its own policies and procedures and establish annual goals and objectives. The company offers its resources to universities to help accomplish their goals and objectives.

Through an organized product-approval process, each university controls its licensees and the products and designs that those licensees are authorized to produce and sell. Furthermore, all reports and programs are tailored to each university's marketplace. The members of the consortium have as much control over their programs as desired.

Goals, objectives, and strategies

The major objectives of any licensing program are threefold: (1) to protect the trademarks of the institutions, (2) to create a favorable image and positive exposure for the institution, and (3) to maximize revenues.

Realizing that these objectives are a journey and not a destination, The Collegiate Licensing Company developed seven basic goals with short-term and long-term strategies. The consortium not only affects its members, it also directly and indirectly affects nonmember schools. Many independent schools have also developed internal goals and objectives that meet their licensing needs. Many of the goals are similar to the following; others, such as goal 1, pertain only to the consortium.

Goal 1: to attract, maintain, and strengthen a prestigious base of universities, bowls, and athletic conferences. In 1990, The Collegiate Licensing Company represented 116 universities, 8 bowl games, and 3 athletic conferences, and paid its members almost 33 million dollars in royalty revenue between July 1983 and June 1990. Almost 65% of that amount was paid in the 1988 to 1989 and 1989 to 1990 fiscal years. Top independent and consortium schools each generated more than 1 million dollars annually.

Goal 2: to attract and maintain a base of licensees sufficiently large to cover all potential market segments with all marketable products. The con-

sortium's initial goal was to license the manufacturers who were already producing and selling merchandise bearing collegiate indicia. Many manufacturers had been producing collegiate merchandise for years without paying licensing fees or royalties. The universities and The Collegiate Licensing Company faced the task of explaining the newly formed licensing programs. Licensees now needed formal license agreements and were required to pay royalties on all sales.

Invariably their responses were the same: "Now let me get this straight. You want me to pay you 200 dollars and 6.5% of my sales, and you have to approve my product before I can sell it?"

"Yes sir, that is correct."

"Now what are you going to do for me? Are you going to sell my product?"

"No sir, we are going to grant you the right to use the university trademarks on your merchandise."

"Well I've been doing that for years. I don't need you for that."

"Sir, you do now!"

The conversation quickly shifted to the benefits that licensees would receive with a well-managed, consistent licensing program. Most licensees did not understand it, and many did not believe it, but over time, most gave it a try. Those who were skeptics in the early years have become great supporters as the collegiate market, and their sales, grew dramatically.

Goal 3: to identify retailers that are current or potential carriers of collegiate merchandise and show them the requirements and opportunities of collegiate licensing. The Collegiate Licensing Company distributes a Licensee Directory and Buyers Guide each year to nearly 30,000 retailers. The directory lists all licensed vendors of consortium university products. Independent universities distribute lists of licensed vendors to retailers on request. The goal is the same: to educate the retailers and let them know (1) who is licensed to produce particular collegiate merchandise and (2) what type of merchandise is available. Retailers face the same penalties as licensees if they knowingly purchase unlicensed merchandise. Such illegal merchandise may be seized. If the retailers are educated about the licensing program at each university, they are more likely to carry "officially licensed" goods and promote the fact that these goods are authentic.

Retail signage is also provided to retailers. "College Shop" signs, developed by The Collegiate Licensing Company, are offered to encourage merchants to organize specific areas of their stores to display licensed collegiate goods.

Goal 4: to identify consumers of collegiate products and encourage them to buy licensed products. The "Officially Licensed Collegiate Products" label (Figure 15-2) has become the symbol of authenticity that enables consumers to learn whether their university has approved the product and receives royalty income. Some independent universities also require a label for their individual schools. Recognizing that requiring individual labels places a burden on licensees (for example, licensees must carefully ensure that the correct label is matched with a university's products), several independent universities also have adopted a common label (Figure 15-3). Labeling is a very visible sign of collegiate licensing to the consumer.

The Collegiate Licensing Company is committed to conducting consumer awareness campaigns on college campuses. These campaigns are designed to use no-cost or low-cost methods to spread the word about the collegiate licensing to all university constituents (Figure 15-4). Each university has incredible media vehicles in its own publications, radio and television programs, and sports information and public relations departments. Innovative and creative licensing directors have gained access to these vehicles. Think about the effect 100 universities could have if they used in the marketplace only 50% of the media resources available to them. The exposure would equal millions of dollars of advertising and would give licensees and retailers a tremendous boost. Educating retailers and consumers is the greatest deterrent and best long-term solution to infringement.

Goal 5: to improve the effectiveness of current methods of enforcement and to develop new methods. Enforcement efforts are essential in two areas: (1) identifying and handling companies that infringe on protected marks and (2) handling licensees who do not comply with a contract. No licensing program can be successful if it does not effectively handle these issues.

Goal 6: to establish marketing programs that can expand the market for "Officially Licensed Collegiate Products" and take advantage of synergistic marketing, advertising, and promotional programs. As goals 1 through 5 are approached, marketing programs can be structured to help reach each goal, as well as expand the market for licensed products. One area with strong potential is promotional licensing.

Promotional licensing enables a company to offer a licensed product as a **premium,** to give away or sell at cost to induce consumers to buy that company's products. An oil company might give away a logoed glass with a tankful of super unleaded gasoline, or a fast food chain might offer a logoed cap for $1.99 with a purchase. The cap would have a much higher perceived value. In these cases, consumers are encouraged to buy gasoline or fast food to get their favorite team glass or cap.

Substantial local, regional, and national programs have been developed with companies such as Procter and Gamble, Ralston-Purina, McDonalds, Colgate Palmolive, Coca-Cola, Pepsico, Shell, Texaco, Domino's, and many more.

FIGURE 15-2 The "Officially Licensed Collegiate Products" label.

The new "Collegiate Licensed Product" label of the Independent Labeling Group

FIGURE 15-3 The new "Collegiate Licensed Product" label of the Independent Labeling Group.

SUPPORT THE BRYANT MUSEUM AND GRADUATE EDUCATION THROUGH OFFICIALLY LICENSED ALABAMA SOUVENIRS

Your purchase of University of Alabama souvenirs — from your nephew's fuzzy Bama elephant to your daughter's Roll Tide T-shirt to your Crimson Tide cap — can help support the new Paul W. Bryant Museum and graduate education at UA. But only if you buy officially licensed souvenirs that carry a hangtag or label like the one at the bottom of this page.

Officially licensed souvenirs return royalties to The University of Alabama.

Every time you buy an officially licensed souvenir, a portion of the money you spend comes to the University for the use of the names and symbols that identify The University of Alabama. These royalty monies have been earmarked for the new Paul W. Bryant Museum and for the Presidential Graduate Fellowship Support Fund. So before you buy, look for the official label. Make sure the souvenir you buy is as authentic as your support of the Tide.

ALABAMA® **ROLL TIDE**® **BAMA**™ **CRIMSON TIDE**®

Tide ■ *78*

FIGURE 15-4 A consumer awareness campaign developed for the University of Alabama.

Promotional licensing revenues made up about 50% of NFL licensing revenues from 1988 to 1989. They accounted for only 3% to 5% of collegiate licensing. By 1995, promotional licensing should account for 25% of the collegiate market.

Goal 7: to provide unparalleled services to member institutions and licensees* and to develop a data base and reports to give management the information needed to analyze, evaluate, and manage progress toward the goals previously listed. Current information is kept on all potential licensees, royalties, infringers, active licensees, and universities. Reports are generated monthly to allow for comparative analysis. The consortium constantly works to simplify the licensing and reporting process for licensees and to give universities more timely and useful information.

The consortium has made tremendous progress each year toward each goal. Collegiate licensing has come a long way in a short time. This progress may be attributed to synergy. Synergy results when a group of people or institutions join forces and work toward a common goal, and the resulting whole is greater than the sum of its parts. One plus one adds up to more than two.

CONCEPT CHECK

A licensing program may be administered internally or by contract through a third party who has expertise in managing a trademark licensing program. Advantages of the consortium approach include the strength that emerges from working as a group; economies of scale, consistency, and continuity; and ease of administration. Advantages of remaining independent include direct control over all licensing activities, undivided royalties, and the ability to offer service directly from the university. The main reasons for developing a licensing program are to protect trademarks, create a positive image for the university, and maximize revenues. Contracts in the collegiate market are nonexclusive, which increases competition among vendors. Competition spurs increased quality, diversified product lines, and market niches.

---

*Licensees defined in the box on p. 262.

THE LEGAL BASIS FOR COLLEGIATE TRADEMARK LICENSING

The case law governing collegiate licensing is sparse but is developing rapidly. Colleges and universities have a firm legal basis for requiring that users of their trademarks obtain permission to use the trademarks, and for requiring that the users pay royalties for the privilege. This section sets forth general trademark principles, definitions, and concepts, and then surveys important cases involving college and university marks.

Trademark principles, definitions, and concepts

The Federal Trademark Statute, known as the Lanham Act (15 U.S.C. 1051 et seq.), defines terms associated with trademarks and governs the registration of trademarks and remedies for infringement of trademarks. The Trademark Law Revision Act, which went into effect November 16, 1989, is Congress' first overall revision of the Lanham Act since the statute was passed in 1946. The revised Lanham Act codifies the common law of trademark infringement and unfair competition, and provides a national system of trademark protection.

Some of the more commonly used trademark definitions are paraphrased as follows.

Trademark. Any word, name, symbol, or device, or any combination thereof used to identify and distinguish the goods of one person from those manufactured or sold by others (see 15 U.S.C. 1127.)

Service mark. Any word, name, symbol, or device, or any combination thereof used to identify and distinguish the services of one person from the services of others (see 15 U.S.C. 1127.)

A **trademark** identifies and distinguishes the source and quality of a *tangible product*. A **service mark** identifies and distinguishes the source and quality of an *intangible service* (Wong, 1986).

Collective mark. A trademark or service mark used by members of a cooperative, association, or other collective group or organization (see 15 U.S.C. 1127).

Mark. A shorthand reference to any type of mark, including trademarks, service marks, and collective marks (see 15 U.S.C. 1127).

Each of these types of marks is protected equally under the Lanham Act. University names, team names, and logos may be described as trademarks, service marks or collective marks (Wong, 1986).

University marks used on items such as clothing and novelties as well as services, are entitled to protection. Although these rights begin to develop automatically under common law, federal registration of the marks is also available, as will be seen.

Registered mark. A mark registered in the United States Patent and Trademark Office, as provided under the Act (see 15 U.S.C. 1127).

The most fundamental change the Trademark Law Revision Act made is that trademark applicants may file for federal registration based on their *intent to use* the mark in commerce within a reasonable time. Before this change, applicants could file only based on *actual use* of the mark before application.

Although registration is not necessary for trademark protection, federal registration carries certain important legal advantages. Federal registration is denoted by the placement of a ® adjacent to the registered mark. A ™ may be placed by unregistered marks to show a claim of ownership. A registration may be renewed indefinitely as long as the registered mark remains in use and identifies the goods or services to which it relates.

A mark owner may obtain state registration in any state in which the product or service is used. In general, state registration does not give the scope of protection given by federal registration.

Related company. Any company whose use of the mark, and nature and quality of the products or services on or in connection with which the mark is used, are controlled by the owner of the mark (see 15 U.S.C. 1127).

The related company doctrine forms the basis for trademark licensing. A trademark licensee whose use of the mark is controlled by the trademark owner is a related company (McCarthy, 1984). For a trademark owner or licensor to validly license his or her mark, he or she must maintain adequate control over the quality of products or services sold under the mark by the licensee or related company (McCarthy, 1984). If, however, the licensor does not maintain quality control, then the license is invalid, and any registration for the mark may be cancelled (McCarthy, 1984).

Infringement of a registered trademark. This occurs when a person uses in commerce a registered mark (or an imitation) in connection with the sale, offering for sale, distribution, or advertising of any products or services, that is likely to cause confusion, or to cause mistake, or to deceive without consent of the registrant (see 15 U.S.C. 1114).

Infringement of an unregistered trademark. This occurs when a person uses in commerce any mark or any false designation of origin, in connection with any products or services, that is likely to cause confusion, or to cause mistake, or to deceive as to the origin, sponsorship, or approval of his or her products, services, or commercial activities by another person (see 15 U.S.C. 1125).

The likelihood-of-confusion standard is the main standard in determining infringement in trademark cases, including sport trademark cases.

Remedies for infringement may include monetary relief, injunctive relief, seizure of the infringing items, and destruction of the infringing items.

Secondary meaning. Certain terms that are selected or invented for the express purpose of functioning as trademarks may be classified as "inherently distinctive." Such marks are protectable and registrable immediately on use (McCarthy, 1984). Examples include "Kodak," "Polaroid," "Exxon," and "Apple" computers (McCarthy, 1984). However, some potential marks describe products or services, geographic designations, or personal surnames. To qualify for protection as a mark, the courts require evidence that such a term has acquired secondary meaning; that is, consumers associate the products or services under the term with one particular source (McCarthy, 1984).

Abandonment. A mark is abandoned if either of the following occurs:

1. The use of the mark has been discontinued with intent not to resume such use. Nonuse for 2 consecutive years is evidence of abandonment.
2. The mark becomes the generic name for the products or services on or in connection with which it is used or otherwise loses its significance as a mark (see 15 U.S.C. 1127).

Generic terms represent the type of product or service, rather than the source, and thus do not qualify for trademark protection (McCarthy, 1984). Examples of terms that were held to have become generic are "aspirin," "cellophane," "escalator," and "yo-yo."

Laches. Laches may operate to bar a legal claim when a party fails to assert a right or claim within a reasonable time, and the other party relies on this inaction to the other party's detriment.

Legal precedents

Developments in the law have made it possible for colleges and universities to protect their names, team names, logos, slogans, seals, and other marks. The institution can protect those marks by preventing unauthorized uses or licensing acceptable uses. As this section will illustrate, colleges and universities are entitled to use state and federal law relating to trademarks and unfair competition to protect themselves from unauthorized uses of their marks.

Early cases. Several early cases illustrate that the courts have recognized that colleges and universities have a protectable proprietary interest in their names and insignia. For example, in *Trustees of Columbia University v. Axenfeld*, 241 N.Y.S. 4 (N.Y. Sup. Ct. 1930), the court, to protect Columbia University's name and reputation, enjoined another educational institution from using the name "Columbia Educational Institute."

The courts have also prevented the unauthorized commercial use of university marks. In *Cornell University v. Messing Bakeries*, 138 N.Y.S.2d 280 (N.Y. App. Div.), aff'd 128 N.E.2d 421 (1955), the court held that a bakery could not use the "Cornell" name on a loaf of bread without the university's permission.

The case of *John Roberts Manufacturing Co. v. University of Notre Dame du Lac*, 152 F. Supp. 269 (N.D. Ind. 1957), aff'd 258 F.2d 256 (7th Cir. 1958), also strongly protects a university name from commercial use. In that case, Notre Dame had authorized a manufacturer to produce official class rings for sale to only qualified students and alumni. John Roberts Manufacturing Company produced unauthorized imitations of the ring. The court enjoined John Roberts on the grounds that Notre Dame possessed protectable property rights to its name and seal, that John Roberts' use of those marks constituted unfair competition in the form of "palming off," and that the virtual identity of rings led to the likelihood of confusion.

Those early cases established the important rule that a college or university may prevent the unauthorized use of its marks when that use is likely to result in confusion about the source or sponsorship of the products or services (Kintner and Fleischaker, 1984). That confusion can be either about the "source" of the products or services, or about whether the products or services were "sponsored" or "authorized" by the university or college (Kintner and Fleischaker, 1984).

The case of *University of Pittsburgh v. Champion Products, Inc.*, 529 F. Supp. 464 (W.D. Pa.), aff'd in part and rev'd in part, 686 F.2d 1040 (3d Cir. 1982), cert. denied, 459 U.S. 1087 (1982), on remand, 566 F. Supp. 711 (W.D. Pa. 1983), resulted in the first major legal challenge to collegiate licensing.

The University of Pittsburgh had purchased athletic uniforms and other apparel containing Pittsburgh marks from Champion Products since 1936. Champion sold Pittsburgh-logoed items mainly to the campus bookstore. When Pittsburgh played in the Sugar Bowl in 1977, university officials noticed that Pittsburgh-logoed garments and novelties were available in large quantities through sources other than the bookstore.

This prompted Pittsburgh to request that Champion obtain a royalty-bearing license. When Champion refused to become licensed, Pittsburgh brought an infringement claim against Champion.

The District Court denied Pittsburgh's request to bar Champion from manufacturing goods bearing the Pittsburgh marks, based upon **laches.** The District Court concluded that the University of Pittsburgh was guilty of laches, because it failed to object to Champion's use of the marks for an extended period, and that Champion relied on this inaction by spending substantial money in establishing a market for Pittsburgh-logoed items.

On appeal, the Circuit Court ruled that Pittsburgh could obtain "prospective injunctive relief," which meant that Pittsburgh could stop future infringing use of the marks. The ruling said that before the 1977 Sugar Bowl game, Pittsburgh officials were unaware of the volume of sales outside of the university, so Pittsburgh's delay in bringing action was excused. Thus delay alone did not preclude Pittsburgh's claim for injunctive relief, since the scope of the alleged infringement changed substantially over the years.

The ruling also stated that Pittsburgh's delay in bringing action had not resulted in detriment to Champion, because demand for Pittsburgh-logoed products was due to the success of the athletic program and loyalty, and not Champion's efforts to establish a market for Pittsburgh-logoed products. Then the Circuit Court said that Champion's investment was made to establish a market for all Champion products, not specifically Pittsburgh-logoed products.

The next thing to determine was whether consumers would be likely to confuse Pittsburgh's products with Champion's line of soft goods containing the Pittsburgh marks.

On the "likelihood of confusion" issue, the Circuit Court, in dictum, opined that confusion should be recognized since Champion was merely "exploiting" Pittsburgh's popularity and consumers' desire to identify with Pittsburgh by purchasing Pittsburgh-logoed products. The case was then sent back to the District Court to decide the confusion issue.

The District Court ruled that Pittsburgh failed to provide sufficient evidence to prove consumer confusion. According to the court, Pittsburgh had not successfully demonstrated that its indicia had acquired *secondary meaning*, that is, that consumers identified the University of Pittsburgh as the exclusive source for Pittsburgh-logoed products.

Pittsburgh was preparing to appeal the decision when the two parties settled the case, and Champion accepted a license agreement with Pittsburgh. The District Court's judgment was "vacated," or cancelled, by consent of the parties.

Settlement was prompted by Champion's mounting legal fees, a victory by National Football League Properties against another manufacturer to restrain similar activities (Burshtein, 1988), and the damage to Champion's other university business (the company supplied uniforms to many universities) (Wong, 1986). A Champion vice-president said, "You can't do business if you're in the courts with your customers" (Schinner, 1989).

In 1990, Champion is licensed with virtually all major universities and serves as licensing agent for Notre Dame.

Recent cases. In *Texas A&M University System v. University Book Store, Inc.,* 683 S.W. 2d 140 (Tex. App. 1984), a Texas Appeals Court dismissed a lawsuit in which several off-campus bookstores sued Texas A&M to cancel the university's mark registrations and to enjoin the university from licensing and collecting royalties for the use of the marks.

The case was dismissed under the doctrine of sovereign immunity, that is, that a state agency cannot be sued without the state's consent. The court, however, took the opportunity to express its opinion that the university owned its marks.

The Eleventh Circuit Court, in *University of Geor-*

gia Athletic Association v. Laite, 756 F. 2d 1535 (11th Cir. 1985), affirmed a permanent injunction ordered by the District Court against a beer manufacturer who marketed beer cans containing a picture of the university bulldog mascot.

In that case, a novelty beer wholesaler began marketing "Battlin' Bulldog Beer" in cans that were red and black, the university colors, and that featured a bloodshot-eyed bulldog wearing the letter "G" on its sweater, carrying a football with one hand and a beer mug with the other.

The court found likelihood of confusion based on similarity of the mark on the can to the university's bulldog mark and on the infringer's intent to capitalize on the popularity of the University of Georgia football program. In the words of the judge,

"The 'Battlin Bulldog's' football career thus comes to an abrupt end. Laite (defendant) devised a clever entrepreneurial 'game plan,' but failed to take into account the strength of UGAA's mark and the tenacity with which UGAA was willing to defend that mark. Like the University of Georgia's famed 'Junkyard Dog' defense, UGAA was able to hold its opponent to little or no gain."

The University of Alabama cancelled a German boot company's registration for the "Bama" mark in *The Board of Trustees of the University of Alabama v. BAMA-Werke Curt Baumann,* 231 U.S.P.Q. 408 (TTAB 1986). The court said that evidence demonstrated that the "Bama" mark "uniquely identified the University of Alabama, largely as a result of the national reputation achieved by the University's football team, as reflected by the testimony and numerous exhibits of record," and thus the boot company's use of the 'Bama' mark "falsely suggested a connection with the University."

The University of California's trademark rights were upheld against a company that printed apparel with the "UCLA" mark and school seal without authorization and sold it through its retail outlets. The defendant agreed to a settlement order, which permanently enjoined it from using the marks. The order also provided that the defendant pay damages and costs. See *Regents of the University of California v. Just Sweats, Inc.* unreported (S.D. Ohio 1988).

Many other suits have been brought and later settled, including a suit by the University of Alabama against J.C. Penney (Burshtein, 1988). In addition, Michigan State University enjoined Panther

Productions, Inc., from producing calendars showing the "Unauthorized Women of MSU." See *Panther Productions, Inc. v. Michigan State University*, unreported, c.c. Mich, 1988, 88-60463-NZ.

In *Board of Governors of the University of North Carolina v. Helpingstine*, 714 F. Supp. 167 (M.D.N.C. 1989), the court, ruling on summary judgment motions made by each side, upheld UNC's right to license its marks, ruling that UNC has valid trademarks and registrations. The court ruled that the university had not abandoned its mark ownership rights for failure either to prosecute infringers in the past or to develop a licensing program before 1982.

The court ruled, however, that the infringement claim would be tried on the issue of whether there was likelihood of confusion about whether the university was the source or sponsor of the goods. At trial, the university would be required to prove that purchasers of university-logoed merchandise were confused about the source or sponsor of the merchandise. However, before the trial, the case was settled on terms favorable to the university. In accordance with a consent order and judgment mutually agreed to by the parties, the court permanently enjoined the defendant from producing or selling products bearing the UNC marks except under the terms of license agreement between the defendant and UNC's licensing agent—The Collegiate Licensing Company.

In *Temple University v. Michael Tsokas, et al.*, Slip. Op Case No. 88-1106 (E.D. Pa. Sept. 11, 1989), a Pennsylvania district court permanently enjoined the defendant from using the "Temple" marks as part of his dental laboratory and real estate businesses. The court found that the word "Temple" alone, without the word "University," is a trade name for the services and activities of Temple University. Both Temple University and the defendant (who used the names Temple Dental Laboratories and Temple Development Corporation) offered the same services in the same geographical area. The court ruled that there was a likelihood that consumers would be confused about whether the defendant's businesses were associated with Temple University.

Game day seizures. The Collegiate Licensing Company, along with colleges, universities, and bowls that it represents, has sought and obtained from the courts several "John Doe" temporary restraining and seizure orders against vendors selling unlicensed college-logoed and bowl-logoed merchandise at bowl events. The courts are generally reluctant to issue ex parte orders (orders granted at the instance, or plea, of one party only) against unnamed parties. However, such can be obtained against "John Doe" defendants where the plaintiff can show the inherent impracticality of obtaining the names of the defendants in advance, and where it is likely that the defendants will disappear after being served with papers.

These orders have been obtained by The Collegiate Licensing Company and the collegiate entities that it represents, including the Orange Bowl, Mazda Gator Bowl, and Peach Bowl. Cases in which courts have granted restraining and seizure orders include the following: *Gator Bowl Association, Inc. et al. v. Various John Does et al.*, Case No. 89-990-CIV-J-12 (M.D. Fla. 1989); *Orange Bowl Committee, Inc. et al. v. Various John Does et al.*, Case No. 89-2817-CIV-SCOTT (S.D. Fla. 1989); *Peach Bowl, Inc. et al. v. John Does et al.*, Civil Action File No. D-73638 (Ga. Super. Ct., Fulton Cty. 1989); *Gator Bowl Association, Inc., et al. v. Various John Does et al.*, Case No. 88-1059-CIV-J-14 (M.D. Fla. 1988); *Collegiate Concepts, Inc. v. John Doe et al.*, Case No. 87-5444 CA 19 (Fla. Cir. Ct., 11th Cir. 1987) (Orange Bowl); *Pennsylvania State University, et al., v. John Doe et al.*, Case No. 85-52783 CA 06 (Fla. Cir. Ct., 11th Cir. 1985) (Orange Bowl); *Gator Bowl Association, Inc., et al. v. John Doe et al.*, Case No. 85-17461 CA (Fla. Cir. Ct., 11th Cir. 1985); *Peach Bowl, Inc. et al. v. John Does et al.*, Civil Action No. D62338 Q16-569 (Ga. Super. Ct., Fulton Cty. 1988).

CONCEPT CHECK

Developments in the law have made it possible for colleges and universities to protect their indicia. Courts have enjoined companies from producing merchandise or using the name of a university for profit without an authorized license agreement with the university. University of Pittsburgh v. Champion Products was the first important legal case between a university and a manufacturer. Later trademark cases reflect the increasing profitability of university trademarks.

A LOOK TO THE FUTURE

The future of collegiate licensing appears very bright. Collegiate licensing is on solid legal ground. The foundation is in place. The present billion-dollar market easily could evolve into a multi-billion-dollar industry.

The reasons that collegiate licensing has flourished are simple. In a well-managed licensing program, everyone in the chain wins. *Universities* benefit by having their marks protected and by receiving a portion of all sales. *Licensees* benefit by being able to use licensed trademarks on their products, which makes those products more attractive to retailers and consumers. *Retailers* benefit from the large variety of licensees, which results in improved quality, greater product variety, increased geographical coverage, and competitive pricing. *Consumers* benefit from the same things that benefit retailers but to a greater extent because there is additional competition at the retail level. Retailers want to please the consumer and must offer collegiate products that move. Offering high quality products, unique product lines, and depth of selection are some of the ways that retailers set themselves apart. The cycle encompasses all parties, and each affects the others. The consumer, however, is the ultimate judge of any licensing program.

Although education and enforcement were the main activities of the early years of collegiate licensing, marketing and management are the keys to the future. If universities can combine their efforts in the collegiate market, the potential will be limitless. If the independent nature of universities leads to fragmentation, progress will slow and will come by accident rather than by plan.

The market should continue to grow in volume. New products will continue to enter the marketplace. New marketing techniques will also flourish. The trend toward higher fashion and upscale products will continue. This trend means collegiate merchandise will continue to be sold in Bloomingdale's and Saks as well as in K-mart and Wal-Mart.

Every market niche will eventually carry licensed products. NFL Properties is plowing new ground in opening many new markets. NFL-licensed products for golf, skiing, bowling, tennis, pets, and automobiles are just a few markets currently being developed. Major League Baseball has opened retail stores as a laboratory to test merchandising concepts. Techniques used to market professional licensed products seem to trickle down into the collegiate market.

The licensing of university trademarks developed from base zero into a multi-million-dollar industry for universities in the 1980s. Licensing will lead to other related commercial opportunities. Universities must develop policies and guidelines to deal with these opportunities and to ensure that all departments understand the legal and business ramifications. If major universities can develop common goals and pool their resources, the collegiate market will enjoy unprecedented growth and success in the sports marketing industry.

CONCEPT CHECK

More than 1 billion dollars worth of collegiate merchandise was sold in the retail marketplace in 1989. Successful management of a licensing program benefits universities, retailers, licensees, and consumers. If colleges take a fragmented approach, collegiate licensing will not be able to reach its potential.

SUMMARY

1. Collegiate licensing began to organize in the early 1980s. Some schools decided to run their programs internally. Others chose to form a consortium and use the services of a professional licensing agency for management.
2. Collegiate licensing grew because of four basic factors: (1) the increased popularity and media exposure of college athletics, (2) the new and improved technology of the custom imprinting business, (3) the growth of the licensing industry, and (4) the need for universities to find alternative sources of revenue.
3. The consortium approach to licensing is popular with many institutions because of its many advantages. Economies of scale reduce the numbers on the cost side of the ledger, and the leverage and clout that come with having a group of participants boost the numbers on the revenue side of the ledger. The diverse skills and expertise, and the wide range of services that come with centralized management are very expensive for individuals to duplicate.

4. The primary goals of licensing are to protect and control the university's names and logos, to increase the positive exposure of the university through merchandise sold on a local, regional, and national basis, and to generate revenue.
5. Legal precedence has been set upholding a university's right to its trademarks, even after years without any formal licensing program.
6. Athletic administrators should become involved with licensing, since much of the merchandise popularity comes from athletic success. Other university affiliates such as the bookstore, alumni association, and office of business affairs also should become involved and support the licensing program.

REVIEW QUESTIONS AND ISSUES

1. What four factors led to the development of collegiate licensing?
2. What were the key elements that caused university administrators to establish licensing programs at their universities?

3. What are the advantages of centralized management or the "consortium" approach to licensing?
4. What professional sports league recently proved the value of centralized management? How did its sales grow in the first 3 years after the league went to centralized management?
5. What is the difference between retail and promotional licensing?
6. What are the advantages to universities of participating in a trademark licensing program? To licensees? To retailers? To consumers?
7. What do the "Officially Licensed Collegiate Products" and "Collegiate Licensed Product" labels represent?

CASE STUDIES AND ACTIVITIES

1. Go into stores that carry collegiate merchandise. Does the merchandise have an "Officially Licensed Collegiate Products" or "Collegiate Licensed Products" label or hangtag? Is it of high

---

GLOSSARY

Licensing—Granting to a licensee the right to use a property (trademark, name, title, design, symbol, character, or personality image) in connection with that licensee's products or services

Licensee—Manufacturer of products who enters into a licensing agreement with a licensor in hopes that the goodwill associated with the licensor's property will generate consumer demand and spur greater sales

Licensor—The owner of the property who gives or grants the license

Indicia—The designs, tradenames, trademarks, service marks, logographics, and/or symbols that have come to be associated with a licensor

Retail licensing—Granting to others the right to use a licensor's indicia on products sold through traditional retail channels

Promotional licensing—Granting to others the right to use a licensor's indicia on products to be used as premiums, or in promotions, games, sweepstakes, or advertising designed to help sell other products and services

Infringer—One who uses the trademarks of another without permission.

Consortium—*General:* A group of people or institutions who join forces to accomplish common goals and objectives; *Specific:* The Collegiate Licensing Company and its member institutions

Royalty—Compensation reserved for licensor for permitting another to use the property (licensees pay the licensor a royalty of a percentage of net sales)

Label—*General:* A symbol required on all licensed merchandise signifying that a product is authorized by the licensor; *Specific:* The red, white, and blue "Officially Licensed Collegiate Products" symbol and the "Collegiate Licensed Product" label required on all licensed merchandise

Premium—An item given away or sold at less than the usual selling price for the purposes of increasing the sale of, promoting, or publicizing any other product or service

quality? Does it represent the university properly?

2. Compare the licensing program of a school that administers its program internally to one that uses a professional licensing agency. What are the differences and similarities? Which program is more efficient and cost effective? Is there a difference in the quality of merchandise? If so, what advice would you give to the school represented by lesser-quality merchandise?

REFERENCES

Altchuler, M. (1989). Licensing Industry Merchandisers' Association, New York.

Burshtein, S. (1988) Collegiate licensing in Canada and the statutory advantage, *1 Education Law Journal, 277,* 287.

Flood, J. (1989). National Football League Properties, New York.

Kintner, E., and Fleischaker, M. (1984). Licensing: legal perspective. *The College Store Journal,* August/September, 38.

McCarthy, J. (1984). *Trademarks and unfair competition, 18*(16).

Schinner, M. (1989). Establishing a collegiate trademark licensing program: to what extent does an institution have an exclusive right to its name? *15 Journal of College and University Law, 405,* 425.

Silvan, S. (1989). National Basketball League Properties, New York.

White, R. (1989). Major League Baseball Properties, New York.

Wong, G. (1986). Recent trademark law cases involving professional and intercollegiate sports. *1 Detroit College of Law Review, 87,* 89.

CHAPTER 16

Communications

Bruce Watkins

In this chapter, you will become familiar with the following terms:

Clarity of purpose	Communication distortions	Sports information
Empathy	due to:	Media guide
Listening	Size	Trust
Immediate feedback	Diverse goals (compartmen-	Broadcast rights fees
HEAR formula	talization and space)	Copyright Royalty Tribunal
Informational groups	Organizational status and power	Antisiphoning rules
Decision-oriented groups	Sports journalism:	Rating
Task roles	Quality	Share
Relationship roles	Objectivity	Cost per thousand (CPM)
Self-centered roles	Rigor	

Overview

In Chapter 8 some of the theoretical underpinnings of communication were explored. Some of these concepts will now be applied to various sport management issues. First, interpersonal communication will be addressed, with an emphasis on the various means of communicating in sport management organizations. In particular, communication in small groups and in the overall organization will be the focus. In the second half of the chapter, some applications to the mass media, especially those dealing with advertising, sport programming, sport information and public relations, and sport journalism, will be examined.

COMMUNICATION SKILLS IN THE SPORT ORGANIZATION
Communicating clearly: writing

A conservative estimate is that at least half of a professional's working day is spent communicating (Andrews and Baird, 1989). Sometimes the communication is clear and successful, but at other times it is distorted or entirely lost. Often more than factual information is communicated. Information about one's attitude or level of attention to detail, or perhaps one's rank in the corporate hierarchy, may also be communicated.

A good part of organizational communication is written: memoranda, new or changed instructions, policies and procedures. Written communication is successful to the extent that it is clear in purpose, structure, and order. This is important whether the document is a memo from an arena manager to concessionaires, a set of instructions on how to implement a new sport marketing program, or a management position paper on the importance of personal staff attention to health club members. Space limitations prevent a more complete analysis of clear writing in sport management contexts. However, a number of excellent works have detailed the writing process in business and management, and the reader is referred to them (for example, Andrews and Baird, 1989; Munter, 1987; Robbins, 1985; and Zinsser, 1983, 1985). Strunk and White (1984) is also an excellent guide for all types of writing. These works emphasize the importance of written communication to smooth organizational functioning. Each is useful in presenting specific ways to enhance clear writing. The following are among the most frequent suggestions*:

- Order ideas or important points according to a hierarchy, based on chronology (beneficial when detailing steps of a procedure), discrete elements (a report on a university athletic department dealing with the swimming, wrestling, hockey, baseball, football, basketball, and gymnastics programs), or importance (items are dealt with from highest to lowest priority).
- Write brief sentences. Avoid impersonal openings (such as "There was" or "This is"), overused prepositions (such as "because of" or "in regard to"), compound prepositions (such as "despite the fact that" or "previous to"), and repetitious phrasing (such as "end result," "future plan," or "past history").
- Write vigorous sentences. Avoid the use of elongated verbs (for example, use "analyze" rather than "perform an analysis of" and "decide" instead of "make a decision regarding"). Also avoid overused passive verbs (for example, use "No one told them" instead of "They were not told by anyone").

- Avoid overly compound sentences that present too many ideas. Avoid overly complex sentences that use too many phrases, parenthetical ideas, and qualifiers.
- Use transitions (First, . . . Second, . . .); internal enumeration, such as (1) for the first point, (2) for the second point, (3) and so on; and bullet points, as used for these paragraphs.
- Write with simplicity. Use short, familiar words rather than long, pretentious ones ("about" instead of "pursuant to" or "affect" instead of "impact on").
- Write at least one preliminary draft, read and edit it, take time to think it over, then rewrite it.[†]
- Proofread your final draft, then proofread it again, and again.

Communicating clearly: speaking

Oral communication is as important for sharing information within the sport organization as for transmitting information between the organization and the public. There are many opportunities in sport organizations for oral communication. Perhaps the university's popular women's softball coach is in demand for speaking engagements to alumni associations. The local high school's director of athletics must argue budget needs in front of the school board. The manager of an ice arena wishes to keep in touch with employees, letting them know about new plans and listening to their concerns. University sport management faculty use meetings to persuade colleagues to adopt new course proposals, to present new research directions or to argue for a change in departmental policies.

Clarity of structure and presentation are even more important in oral than in written communication. Recipients of a written presentation may read at their own pace, and may re-read sections that are unclear or confusing. Oral communication, especially a presentation or a speech, is delivered at the pace of the speaker, and is not available for "re-reading." Therefore clarity is imperative. The

---

*Munter's (1987) work, from which several of these suggestions are adapted, is valuable in its analysis of writing for business.

†First drafts, as well as subsequent ones, should be written at the keyboard of a word processor (not in longhand on paper). Although it might initially require more time to learn writing in this way, this skill will be valuable in professional life. If one does not have word processing ability, now is the time to learn it.

Oral communication skills are important at all levels of a sport organization. Here former Michigan head football coach and current Detroit Tigers president Bo Schembechler addresses the Michigan State Legislature.

purpose of the presentation must be explicit, the ideas must be arranged coherently, and the speaking style must be understandable. This is important whether the occasion is an informal meeting, a formal presentation, a discussion with colleagues, or a job interview.

Most texts dealing with communication divide oral presentations into three categories: those that inform, those that persuade, and those intended to interest or entertain. As each has a separate purpose, there are separate guidelines for preparation and delivery. There are several excellent sources for preparing oral presentations. Particularly valuable are Andrews and Baird (1989), Knapp (1980), Monroe and Ehninger (1980), O'Keefe (1990), and Richards (1988). The interested reader should consult these for more detailed information.

Effective written and oral communications are the responsibility of each member in a sport organization and will usually enhance intraorganizational functioning. For many sport organizations (such as university athletic departments, professional sports teams, governing bodies of amateur and professional sports) communication with the public is also important. These organizations have created specific departments to handle public communications. The departments go by different names; universities typcially refer to them as sport information departments; professional organizations call them public relations divisions. A more complete description of the role of these departments will be presented later in this chapter.

INTERPERSONAL COMMUNICATION IN THE SPORT ORGANIZATION

Interpersonal communication in organizations occurs at three levels—face-to-face, in small groups, and in the overall organization. In this section theoretical foundations to organizational practice will be applied. First, good communication practices in interview settings will be examined. Next, some prescriptions for effective communication in small groups that are usually found in organizations (for example, department meetings, task forces, committees and subcommittees) will be discussed. Attention will also be devoted to the application of leadership principles. Finally, effective and ineffective principles of communication in larger organizations will be analyzed.

Communicating clearly: interviews

One practical site for the application of interpersonal communication processes is the interview. There are a number of occasions for interviewing in business and management contexts: employment interviews, information-seeking and -sharing interviews (for example, orientation), performance appraisal interviews, problem-solving interviews, counseling interviews, grievance interviews, disciplinary interviews, and exit interviews (Andrews and Baird, 1989). Each has a separate purpose and a slightly different structure, although the skills necessary for successful communication in each are similar.

Because many sport organizations involve frequent interpersonal interactions between staff members and between staff members and clients, success often depends on the employee's interpersonal skills. For example, good health and fitness clubs are usually characterized by friendly staff at the entrance desk (who know the names of the members); helpful, courteous, and attentive staff in the weight training and aerobics areas; and so forth. Recruiting and selecting appropriate staff is important, and the interview is the best setting for a manager to determine whether potential staff members have skills appropriate to the organization. A recent article on selecting staff for a club's youth fitness program detailed seven desirable qualities sought in potential instructors (Yacenda, 1990). The author wanted instructors who demonstrated patience, resourcefulness, consistency, tact, integrity, skill, and enthusiasm. Imagine attempting to identify these characteristics in an interview that lasts only 45 to 60 minutes! Clearly the interview must be organized, thorough, and rich with exchanges of information so that (1) the interviewer might determine whether potential staff have these qualities and (2) the interviewee might understand what the job expectations are.

The sport manager will enhance the usefulness of an interview, whether it be preemployment, information-seeking, or performance appraisal, by seeking and supporting honest and open communication. A climate should be created where the interviewee feels free to speak honestly, as well as to ask questions and contribute his or her own ideas. The following contribute substantially to good communication in an interview: (1) **clarity of purpose,** expectations, and instructions, (2) **empathy** and understanding, (3) **listening** (instead of simply hearing), (4) honest and **immediate feedback.** These four elements are important in other face-to-face interpersonal interactions as well.

As with any oral presentation, clear structure in the interview will enhance the communication. Interviewees come to the session with a number of preconceptions about what is expected of them, how they will be perceived by the interviewer, how the interview will proceed, and especially, what the outcome of the interview will be. To the extent that the interviewer is able to clarify these and relieve any anxieties associated with the process, both participants will be able to focus on the substance of the interview itself.

Empathy and understanding on the part of the interviewer will encourage both self-disclosure and upward communication. Recall from Chapter 8 that communication occurs on both content and relational levels and that upward communication, from lower organizational status to higher, is most often positively biased. This means that the interviewee is not likely to give negative information, even if it is accurate, unless the interview climate is supportive. The author once observed a focus group organized to solicit members' perceptions about services at a local tennis and fitness club. Although there had been considerable grumbling about the club's inattention to its better tennis players, this was never directly addressed in the focus group, which was led by the head of the tennis programs. Instead, group members spent much time on upward communication, discussing the new services that they liked, the pool, the lunchtime aerobics classes, and child care. Because the focus group leader was not aware of the potential bias, he failed to elicit negative as well as positive feedback, and consequently did not receive information that would have been helpful. Afterwards, members continued complaining among themselves about the club management's inattention to the tennis programs.

Listening is perhaps the most underrated communication skill. Most persons in business and management hear, but how many really listen? There are many barriers to good listening. One person may not be interested in what another has to say. This person may believe that he or she already knows what the other will say. He or she may be distracted by intruding thoughts or other factors in the environment that compete for attention. He or she may let disagreement with another's position prevent him or her from fully hearing and understanding positions and arguments other than his or her own. Nature gave humans two ears but only one tongue, a gentle hint that we should listen more than we talk! Whatever the barriers, people will waste their time and that of others if they devote less than full attention to another in a communication setting. There are several techniques to enhance listening ability: maintaining eye contact, encouraging the respondent to elaborate, paraphrasing and summarizing what is being said, asking questions. However, there is no technique that replaces an active desire to understand what another person is saying.

Andrews and Baird (1989) recommend that in a business environment, management employ the **HEAR formula.** In the case of interviews, this involves being **H**elpful (minimize the time spent waiting, don't hurry the interaction, eliminate distractions), being **E**mpathic (understand others' feelings, demonstrate interest and care, listen actively), being **A**ttentive (suspend immediate reactions, understand before disagreeing, paraphrase and summarize), and being **R**esponsive (maintain eye contact, ask questions, allow the other to talk).

Finally, honest and informative feedback should be given to the interviewee as soon as possible. This is particularly important in interviews that are related to employee status: preemployment, disciplinary, performance appraisal, and exit. Feedback indicates the extent to which the interviewer understood, accepted, or learned from the information presented in the interview. Feedback should always serve to benefit the recipient (in this case, the interviewee), and should be given in such time that the recipient will be able to act on it. This also means that feedback should be given in a way that minimizes rejection or defensiveness.

An acquaintance of the author once applied for jobs in sport management departments at two universities. He turned out to be the second choice at both schools. He knew this because Department A contacted him soon after the interview, explained that a job offer had been made to another candidate, and told him why (although his research presentation had been well received, the competing candidate's teaching expertise was better suited to the needs of the department). He heard "through the grapevine" that Department B had made an offer to another candidate as well, although no one from Department B had contacted him. He was left wondering whether his interview had gone well or poorly; he didn't know whether or when Department B was going to make a decision. When the preferred candidates for both departments took jobs elsewhere, he was offered positions at Departments A and B. Which offer do you think he accepted?

CONCEPT CHECK

Interviews are an important setting for interpersonal communication in the sport organization. There are interviews associated with job seeking, orientation, performance appraisal, problem solving, counseling, grievances, discipline, and employment exiting. The sport manager will enhance the usefulness of an interview by making its purpose and expectations clear, showing empathy, listening well, and providing immediate and honest feedback.

Small groups within the organization

There are many functions for small groups within larger organizations. Some are primarily **informational,** an important method to keep colleagues current on organizational change and innovation. For example, a college sport management department might have a computer committee to inform colleagues about the new advances in computer software within the university and the field of sport management. Other groups are task and **decision oriented.** These groups are charged with evaluating policies and procedures, making appropriate recommendations and changes, or accomplishing an organizational goal. For example, a school board might appoint a committee to recommend that the district raise the minimum grade point average from 1.5 to 2.0 for its high school students participating in extracurricular athletic activities. Some groups are social and informal, such as members of the fitness staff from a local health club who socialize on Friday after work, or the local ice arena staff who participate in a Tuesday bowling league.

Management may orchestrate the makeup of small groups to a certain extent but is limited by the number (and personalities) of persons within the organization. Once formed, small groups take on "personalities" of their own. Small group communication, like face-to-face communication, involves messages at the content level and the relational level. Often in groups, the content of what is said is lost because of the way in which it is presented. Indeed, poor relational communication

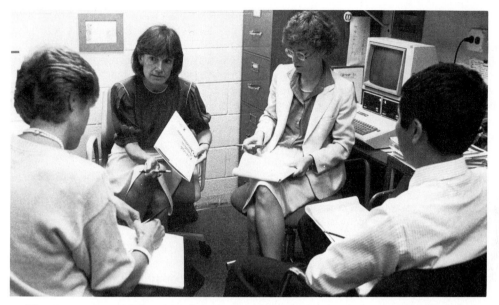

There are many opportunities for group communication in sport organizations: members of a fitness research group plan a study, and members of a women's field hockey team execute a play.

in groups may result in a disruption of content communication and lead to task failure.

Roles in small groups. How do small groups take on personalities? The theory of small group communication, as presented in Chapter 8, addresses the kinds of roles that people assume in groups. Bales (1976) contends that some people are more likely to ask questions, whereas others are more likely to give information. He also indicates that some leaders facilitate the task processes (for example, reaching goals) and others facilitate the socioemotional processes (for example, interpersonal interactions, members' feelings about their efforts and accomplishments). Of course, not all communication processes that occur in groups are intended to facilitate. An apocryphal small-group story shared by many people in the corporate world is of senior managers who, in mid-meeting, direct junior level executives to perform some menial task (retrieve files, photocopy papers), primarily to demonstrate the organizational hierarchy in the presence of clients.

Andrews and Baird (1989) summarized three types of roles in small groups. First, there are **task roles.** These include the initiator—who proposes new ideas or solutions, the information giver and seeker, the opinion giver and seeker, the elaborator—who expands on points that are raised, and the integrator—who synthesizes the evidence or discussion. Second, there are **relationship roles,** including the supporter, the harmonizer, the tension reliever, and the gatekeeper, who provides balance by encouraging quiet members and discouraging monopolizers. Third, there are **self-centered roles,** which appear to be negative relational roles. The blocker—who constantly objects, the aggressor—who criticizes and insults, the dominator, and the recognition seeker are examples of this third category. Managers who are concerned with smooth group functioning should attend to what roles are being played by which group members and encourage group analysis at both the content and relational levels.

The following example demonstrates the way in which group roles hinder group achievement. A current issue in urban school and community recreation divisions is whether to provide same-sex or coeducational sport teams, and whether different options should be available at different ages. Group discussions about these options are often

lively. One eight-member task force was charged with investigating the options and suggesting a policy for schools in surrounding communities. The task force consisted of a school superintendent, a sixth-grade teacher, two members of the community recreation department, a recent university graduate in education (who was looking for a teaching position), and three members of the district's parent-teacher association.

- The new graduate spent most of his time attempting to impress the school superintendent rather than addressing the issues. He was a recognition seeker.
- The sixth-grade teacher was convinced that boys and girls did not play well together. She based this on her years of playground observations. Each new idea or proposal was met by an objection or criticism from her. She refused to recognize that others might have relevant expertise as well. She saw only her opinions as valid. She was a blocker. Eventually, other group members became angry or ignored her. Thus, even when she did have good ideas or observations to contribute, the rest of the group discounted them.
- The superintendent was convinced that he should lead the group toward a solution, although he was not skilled at small group leadership. He tried to reach conclusions when other members wanted a more thorough discussion of the issues. He began to dominate the group.

Ultimately, the task force disbanded without reaching a consensus or recommendation on this important issue. Had the leader been more sensitive to group roles and group processes, failure might have been avoided.

Leadership in groups. This raises a second area of communication-related concern: leadership. What are the most important principles of leadership that will ensure successful group communication and subsequent task completion? Not surprisingly, several of the recommended leadership communication principles are the same as those recommended for speaking and interviewing.

First, a good leader must provide clear structure and focus. The focus will increase productivity of group members and decrease the amount of wasted time. Ultimately it will also make the leadership role easier.

Next, a good leader should move the group toward a goal or sub-goal without rushing the process. The leader should seek consensus without subjecting members to pressure for conformity. With most groups, the leader should encourage participatory decision making by participating but avoiding domination. Mature or high-functioning groups may be given more autonomy to set a pace than immature groups, which may need more direction and control (Hersey and Blanchard, 1988). A newly-formed community group exploring whether a new multipurpose facility and ice arena should be built will require considerable control and direction. Members are likely to be unfamiliar with each other, or at least with each other in a small-group context. They will not necessarily know all the relevant questions that should be asked. They may not know how much authority they have to make decisions or to sign contracts and may be wary about financial commitments made on behalf of the community. In contrast, an ongoing community facilities group considering renovation of an existing multipurpose facility will have had experience with each other and with the issues. This group will probably demand much more autonomy than will the former.

A leader should recognize that there will usually be pressure toward consensus. This is what Janis (1983) found in his studies on groupthink. Factors that increase this pressure include ambiguous group goals, difficult tasks, the need for a quick solution, and a setting in which most members hold a single opinion. A perceptive leader will look for signs that pressure is being directed at members who hold divergent opinions. These signs include majority members directing their communication at those with varying opinions. If this is not persuasive, the majority increasingly will criticize and ridicule the opinions, ultimately rejecting them. As this process occurs, the holders of the divergent opinions become less reasonable and are likely to react more emotionally. This happened to the blocker in the earlier community recreation example. Clearly this behavior prevents successful achievement of goals, and will not contribute to member satisfaction.

Third, a good leader should recognize the value of divergent opinions and ensure that each perspective is thoroughly examined. The leader should therefore encourage communication from each member and discourage evaluative judgments of member input. An athletic director who, in the midst of a heated meeting, calls a coach's suggestion "ridiculous" (even if it is), discourages not only the coach, but others who wish to avoid ridicule. There is nothing wrong with conflict in group meetings, if it is constructive and managed properly. Indeed, conflict can be an important and productive part of organizational functioning and change (Andrews and Baird, 1989).

To encourage quiet or reticent members, a leader might direct questions their way or ask for their ideas and opinions, and he or she should differentiate between those who talk more because they are best informed and those who talk simply because they are garrulous. He or she should also tactfully ensure that some individuals do not monopolize group discussion. Cooperative interpersonal relationships should be encouraged so that personality conflicts do not impede group progress. A good leader facilitates communication at both the content and socioemotional levels.

CONCEPT CHECK

Small groups within the sport organization might be informational, decision oriented, or informal. Small groups assume personalities of their own, often based on roles and communication patterns of individuals within the group. Task roles in small groups—such as initiator, information giver, and elaborator—are those relevant to achieving objectives. Relationship roles—such as harmonizer, supporter, and gatekeeper—are those focused on relational activities in the group. Self-centered roles—such as blocker and dominator—usually function to impede group progress. Group achievement is facilitated by a good leader, who provides a clear structure, moves the group toward its goals, and ensures that all perspectives are examined and that each member is allowed to contribute.

Communication and its barriers at the organizational level

In one way an analysis of organizational communication seems quite simple; after all, organizations are composed of people interacting face-to-face and in small groups. However, there are some differences that affect communication patterns:

1. **Size**—organizations are large; it is difficult to establish and change communication patterns,

and it is easy for communications to be distorted as they travel through multiple receivers.

2. **Diverse goals**—whereas a small problem-solving group may focus on one or two specific problems and goals, there are many goals within large organizations, some of which act in opposition.

3. **Power** and **status**—organizations are characterized by status hierarchies that affect the flow and accuracy of upward, downward, and horizontal communication.

There are predictable barriers to organizational communication, some of which result in complete communication failure, but most of which result in **distorted communications.**

A communication failure occurs when one organizational member refuses to communicate with another. This is often a symptom of Likert's System 1 organization, detailed in Chapter 8. For example, a headstrong college athletic director may decide not to talk to his equally headstrong basketball coach, whom he dislikes and with whom he disagrees on most policy issues. Although this may offer a temporary solution to these disagreements, ultimately it will spell serious trouble for the athletic department. The other coaches, as well as the student–athletes, eventually will be forced to "take sides." The director may become less effective in his ability to set or enforce policies on academic performance or recruiting practices. This lack of communication will negatively affect the student–athletes, the other coaches, the athletic department and possibly the university and its public image.

Some failures or distortions in organizational communication may be caused by inadequate information. We have only pity for the poor sport information director who is not kept informed about the philosophies or activities of team owners and management. Many rumors often surround teams in which this situation occurs. The ill-informed or poorly-informed sport information professional cannot legitimately confirm or deny them; he is never sure. Reporters are unsure about believing him even when he is informed.

Some distortions in communication may be traced to expectations about the communication that overshadow the information; these lead persons to see and hear selectively what they expect to see or to hear. If a young tennis instructor has a poor experience with her first group of students,

she may approach a second group expecting another bad experience. Innocent comments by them, her colleagues, or her supervisors might easily be misinterpreted.

Size and organizational hierarchy will also distort communications. At one time or another, every student has taken part in a class exercise where a message is whispered to one person, who then whispers it to the next person, and so on until each person hears the "message." By the time it reaches the final person, the message has been garbled beyond recognition. Information is similarly distorted when it passes through a number of people in an organization. Without open and functioning channels of communication in an organization, communication is liable to be garbled and distorted. Minimizing the intermediate steps through which information travels, from source to receiver, will diminish the effect of organizational size on communication distortion. A good manager should make it a practice, if possible, to speak with each employee every few weeks, cutting down on the communication distance, and letting each know that he or she is a valuable and contributing member of the organization.

Specialization and **compartmentalization** that result from hierarchical structure also contribute to communication difficulties. Artificial barriers are constructed because, to the extent that each unit is autonomous, the need to share information has become unimportant. In a large corporation, members of the sport marketing department are charged with finding appropriate sporting events to run or to sponsor. Members of the sport advertising department are charged with identifying appropriate print outlets or radio and television sport broadcasts in which to advertise the corporation's products. In slightly different ways, the concerns of both departments are with the demographics of the people who take part in various sports, attend events, or follow them in newspapers or on television. However, because of differences in responsibilities or constituencies, individuals in the two departments may seldom interact with each other. If the lack of communication becomes serious, it could result—at best—in duplication of effort, and—at worst—in internal bickering and struggling for organizational power, recognition, and resources.*

Space might also be a barrier. If people do not

come into contact with each other in the organization, their opportunities to communicate are diminished. A university athletic department that maintains administration offices in one building, coaching offices in another, academic support offices in another, and player training and conditioning rooms in another will find it difficult to maintain smooth communication and functioning. Again, duplication of effort is likely to occur, as is confusion, disorder, and jockeying for power and authority.[†]

In many organizations, information represents power. Control of communication channels and of information that passes along these channels affords power to the controllers. In these situations, constraints will be placed on both upward and downward communication. Not only is information distorted in these organizations, it is lost. Members of the organization find it difficult to share information or find it tempting to adopt someone else's ideas and pass them along as their own.

Among the largest contributors to communication failure in organizations are the differences in **status** at each organizational level. By their nature these differences affect the amount and the tenor of upward and downward communication. Management may be unconcerned about employee input, as in Likert's System 1 organization where management makes policies and decisions without adequate employee input. In such a climate, without feedback and reinforcement for communication, employees soon stop communicating. For example, often new health club employees are able to suggest novel ways to remotivate or to better serve the club's clients. Alternately, staff members who have been around longer know which services might be changed with minimal client discomfort, and which must be maintained at all costs. Should management choose not to consult these rich sources of information, or worse yet, consult them superficially but ignore their advice, employees will eventually stop offering suggestions. Management will find itself well removed from client concerns.

Management may also be defensive about input from below, believing that useful information is generated only at top levels. Employees may also feel threatened about honest and accurate upward communication. Their egos, their positions, their influence in the organization, and perhaps their jobs, may be in jeopardy. Management behaviors that encourage these defensive feelings include[‡]:

- Use of fear to ensure compliance
- Hierarchical pressure to motivate performance
- Attaching value judgments to the motives of the employee, or to the information communicated
- Controlling the attitudes or behaviors of the employees by restricting access to information or to communication channels
- Showing lack of concern or not responding to communications
- Showing superiority in status or using status to indicate that employee input is not needed or useful

Clearly many organizational difficulties may be traced to inadequate communication. It is in management's best interests to ensure that channels of communication are open and functioning. Wanting good communication and achieving it are different, however, and a good manager will actively seek to improve organizational communication. The following are some of the strategies:

- Understand not only the hierarchy of organizational responsibility, but the pattern of communication networks as well. Know who are isolates, bridges, and liaisons (as discussed in Chapter 8), and make sure that the relevant persons are kept informed.

---

[*]A marketing director for a corporation involved in sport sponsorship has suggested that when all sport marketing activities are handled by a single division, there is little competition for human or financial resources, and consequently communication and functioning are smooth. However, when advertising handles some sport marketing business, marketing handles some others, and public relations handles even others, competition for money and staff is a necessary, albeit undesirable, outcome (William Mergler, director of corporate marketing for Volvo North America, in a presentation to the University of Michigan's Sport Marketing Club, March 1990).

[†]Although recent advances in microcomputer conferencing and electronic mail have alleviated the space and compartmentalization problems somewhat, there are few substitutes for face-to-face interaction. A manager who does most of his employee communications at a computer terminal will lose the spontaneously generated information, ideas, and challenges that are part of any good and active discussion on issues.

[‡]From Lewis (1987), Likert (1967), and various other sources.

- Use this information to improve upward communication channels, as well as to improve horizontal communication within and between groups.
- Ensure that management interacts in face-to-face settings with employees to strengthen both upward and downward communication. An office-bound manager is more intimidating than one who interacts with employees in their arena.

Lewis (1987) also has recommended:

- Clarifying objectives, needs, and responsibilities of each organizational division
- Structuring (or restructuring) the organization to decrease the number of message links
- Not bypassing individuals in the organizational hierarchy who should have access to information
- Providing an open and supportive organizational climate that emphasizes understanding each employee

---

CONCEPT CHECK

There are a number of challenges to good communication in an organization. Because of their size, accommodation of diverse goals, and hierarchies based on differences in power and status, organizations often experience failure or distortion in communication. Distortions may be due to inadequate information, expectations, organizational hierarchy and status, specialization and compartmentalization, space, and power-seeking control of communication channels. Analysis of communication macronetworks and special attention to bridges and liaisons will serve to enhance organizational communication.

APPLICATIONS OF MASS COMMUNICATION TO SPORT ORGANIZATIONS

There are several important mass media concepts and processes that are relevant to sport management. The most relevant are those dealing with programming decisions in television, audience identification and advertising decisions in both print and broadcasting, sport information and public relations, and sport journalism. These issues will be addressed in the remainder of the chapter.

Audience identification and advertising decisions: the print media

Defining and attracting an audience, and concerns for advertising income, drive decisions in the print media. As noted in Chapter 8, there are a variety of sport-oriented newspapers and magazines that appeal to either mass or specialized interests. For example, the weekly magazine *Sports Illustrated* has a large circulation base—almost 3 million. If four readers per issue are estimated, this means it is read by about 12 million people weekly. In addition, *The Sporting News,* a weekly sport-oriented newspaper (especially baseball), has circulation figures over 700,000. In 1982 the daily paper *USA Today* began publication; one of its strengths is its comprehensive, multi-colored, multi-article sport section. Indeed, some have called *USA Today* a great 50-cent sport paper surrounded by a few news stories: "Many customers eagerly [seize] the paper's statistics-laden sport section and [chuck] the rest into the trash" (A new daily for sports nuts, 1990). Others, however, have criticized the superficial nature of the stories and the writing, believing that quality and in-depth reporting has been sacrificed for the sheer number of stories. Nonetheless, *USA Today* confounded its critics by identifying a need among an audience of readers and became a circulation success. Publishers of a new daily sports paper, *The National,* believe there is another audience of readers interested in a daily sport paper. Differing from those attracted to *USA Today's* coverage, this audience is seen as literate, young, college-graduated with moderate to higher incomes, interested in more feature- and issue-oriented writing, as well as in statistics and up-to-date results. The paper began publishing in January 1990 in New York, Chicago, and Los Angeles. Ultimately separate editions are envisioned for each city with major league baseball, basketball, football, and hockey franchises.

Publishers of *The National* appear to be following a solid plan of expansion and development. In the publication business, it is very important for editors and publishers to analyze their readership base and potential advertising support in making publication decisions (for example, number of pages per issue, and weekly or monthly publication frequency). Many well-conceived and well-received publications have failed because of poor management in these areas.

TUESDAY, MAY 1, 1990   50¢

THE NATIONAL

Copyright 1990 THE NATIONAL   VOLUME 1, NUMBER 77

WHAT DO YOU SAY, JOSE?

From pride to prejudice, A's Canseco touches all the bases

PAGE 10

(PHOTO BY FRANK BECERRA OF THE NATIONAL.)

PEREZ ON DL, WINFIELD BENCHED; ATHLETICS SLUG YANKEES 6-0

PAGE 14

WHILE CONE BURNS, BRAVES RUN AWAY TO 7-4 WIN OVER METS

PAGE 18

Publishers of the daily sport paper *The National* have attempted to follow a clear plan of readership identification and advertiser appeal to successfully compete in the sport periodicals market.

(Photo courtesy of *The National*.)

For example, in 1989 *Sports Inc.*, a weekly sport business-oriented magazine, ceased publication. Its readers found it informative and useful, but its management never seemed to settle on who the target readers were. Instead of defining its market, the magazine attempted to appeal to sporting companies, media companies, agents, business entrepreneurs, team managers, relevant academics, and so on. By so doing, the magazine was made less-than-necessary to any single group. For example, professionals interested in sport and media issues might read *Sports Inc.* in the library but will purchase or subscribe to *Broadcasting*, which has a better-defined readership and focus. Consequently, the publishers of *Sports, Inc.* overestimated the potential advertiser appeal of the magazine. Companies to which the business content appealed (for example, sport sponsors and marketers) failed to see the magazine itself as a useful advertising vehicle. The advertising representatives sold fewer ads than expected, and therefore advertising income was inadequate to support a weekly business magazine (Applegate, 1989; Jefferson, 1989). Other publishers have considered plans to reach the sport business market, perhaps on a monthly basis, but no replacement has yet appeared.

In Chapter 8, the importance to periodical advertisers of evaluating the number of readers and the type of reader was addressed. For example, it makes sense for a company such as Nike to advertise in a mass-appeal magazine such as *Sports Illustrated*. Why? First, it has a large number of readers. Second, most of its readers are potential users and buyers of shoes, shirts, and other sportswear. However, makers of industrial sport and exercise equipment may not choose to advertise in *Sports Illustrated*. Why? Although the audience is composed of a number of people interested in sport, only a small percentage are potential purchasers of industrial equipment, and the cost to reach those few would be extravagant. *Sports Illustrated* charges $59,345 for a full-page black and white ad and $92,580 for a four-color page.* Alternately, an ad in *Fitness Management* (circulation 21,400; a cost of $2,195 for black and white and $2,840 for color) or *Club Industry Magazine* (circulation 30,000; $2,725 for black and white and $3,525 for color) would cost less and would reach a better-specified, although smaller, market of potential buyers.

Issues in sports journalism

The print media section cannot be left without a discussion of the role of the sports journalist. American newspapers recognized the appeal of sport content to readers very early in their history. The *American Turf Register* (founded in 1829) and *Spirit of the Times* (1831) cultivated educated and literate readers through stories on breeding and racing horses, pastimes of educated and literate people at that time. The *New York Clipper* (1853), through its famous sportswriter Henry Chadwick, contributed substantially to popularizing sports, especially the game of baseball. Subsequently, larger newspapers capitalized on this interest and served a dual role of creating and satisfying readers' needs for information about baseball, football, boxing, and other sports. Often a city's paper unabashedly sought to create community support for its local sports teams as part of its perceived civic duties. Editors also knew that success in sport was tied to its popularity, and print coverage of popular sports was tied to ever-increasing newspaper sales.

Similarly, radio and television coverage of sport is seen as popular entertainment. Attempts to apply the same principles that guide news and investigative journalism—quality, objectivity, and rigor—are generally viewed as inappropriate. This approach to sport by journalists and broadcasters has contributed to criticism about the quality of sport coverage and the journalistic rigor associated with such coverage.

Quality of writing. Despite the success of sport-oriented periodicals and the popularity of broadcast sports, there are several criticisms about **sports journalism** that surface repeatedly. The first is the notion that the **quality** of sports writing and broadcasting is poor. Former *Sports Illustrated* writer and now editor of *The National*, Frank Deford, identified this print bias clearly: "Any well-written article . . . about sports is invariably praised by serious, patronizing critics as 'not really about sports' . . . Sportswriting is assumed to be second-rate, and, therefore, if any sportswriting is not second-rate, then, ergo, it must not be sportswriting" (Deford, 1987; p. 3).

Like other sweeping generalizations, this is not

---

*Printing efforts, and therefore costs, are usually more when multiple colors are used on each page. Cost figures are from *Gale Directory of Publications, 1989*.

Sports Illustrated has been a very successful magazine devoted to covering a wide variety of sports. Its writers have done much to enhance the image of sports writing and sports journalism.
(Photo courtesy of *Sports Illustrated*.)

entirely accurate; Ring Lardner, Grantland Rice ("Outlined against a blue-gray October sky, the Four Horsemen rode again"), Red Smith, Thomas Boswell, even Frank Deford himself, are examples of lucid, expressive, and engaging sports writers. However, it is probably true that promising young writers are not directed into sports journalism.

Objectivity and journalistic rigor. A second, related criticism deals with the journalistic rigor required by and of sports journalists. Journalists pride themselves on their investigative **rigor, objectivity,** honesty, and ability to distance themselves from the subjects they cover. Sports writers and broadcasters are seen primarily as fans, too involved with the athletes, teams, and managers,

or too dependent on their cooperation, to risk alienating them. In such an environment, objectivity, distance, and honesty do not thrive. Professionals in sport often encourage this approach. For example, early in the 1990 college basketball season, Duke coach Mike Krzyzewski chastised the sports writers of the college newspaper "in a profanity-laced diatribe" for their less-than-flattering coverage of the university's basketball team (Kent, 1990).

Early sports writers and broadcasters seldom addressed the issues of drinking, gambling, and racial disharmony, or the sexual peccadillos of athletes whom they covered; it was considered a breach of faith. Only recently have the shortcomings of heroes such as baseball's Babe Ruth and Ty Cobb or tennis' Bill Tilden surfaced. In the past, a "cozy relationship" existed between journalists and athletes: "[Journalists] traveled with the teams, frequently on the team's payroll. Expenses were covered, meals and lodging provided, and a host of other courtesies extended to the journalists, who saw themselves . . . as extensions of the team itself" (Klatell and Marcus, 1988; p. 212).

It is probable that broadcast journalists are under more pressure than those in print to ignore controversy or negative aspects in sport. Most professional leagues or teams have either total or shared power to choose the games' broadcast announcers. Television and radio may be powerful public relations tools. The more popular sports and games become and the better viewers perceive the sport and its participants, the more valuable the broadcast rights become. The roles of the broadcaster are often seen by management as simple ones: reporting the progress of games, providing "human interest" angles on positive aspects of sport, and advancing the prestige of the sport or the team. The journalist is not expected to examine related social issues, to criticize management or athletes, or to dwell on any negative aspects of the games or the performers. Reporting on issues such as drug use or gambling, especially during sports broadcast times, is seen as inappropriate.

Advertisers and corporate sponsors often bank on pairing their image with the performance of an athlete or a team. As long as athletes or teams are perceived positively, all is well; however, when controversy occurs, or teams, leagues, or players receive negative publicity, advertisers perceive themselves at risk as well. For example, before the 1988 Olympics, many companies sought to sign Canadian sprinter Ben Johnson to an endorsement contract. His agent predicted his post–gold medal endorsement income would be from 10 to 15 million dollars. After his disqualification for steroid use, however, most companies withdrew their advertising spots featuring Johnson. Advertisers want nothing to occur, in word or deed, that might reflect negatively on themselves, even if it is honest commentary on player performance or management decisions. Thus broadcast journalists face additional pressures from unwritten rules of performance.

Further information on sports writing and reporting may be found in works by The Missouri Group (1988) and Anderson (1985).

CONCEPT CHECK

Many decisions in print media are driven by the need to define and attract an audience of readers and a pool of potential advertisers. Readers are grouped according to various demographics and lifestyle categories. A well-defined audience of readers (and potential consumers of advertised products) is important to newspaper and magazine success. Sport-oriented writing and journalism has been subjected to criticisms about its overall literary quality, as well as its journalistic rigor and objectivity. This situation is slowly changing; currently broadcast journalists are under more pressure than are print journalists to ignore the more negative aspects of sport.

Sports information and public relations departments

Public perceptions and beliefs about many sport organizations are often crucial to their success. This is particularly true for those organizations involved in spectator sports (for example, Olympic organizations; university teams; professional football, basketball, baseball, and hockey; race car driving, rodeo performing, tennis, and golf). Public information keeps names and sports in the public eye and helps build loyal followers and spectators. However, other sport organizations (ski resorts, health clubs, community recreation programs, and sporting goods manufacturers) may also have a need for liaisons between themselves and the public to increase membership or facility usage or to develop links with the sport consumer.

The **sports information** or public relations department (SID or PRD) is a crucial interface between a sport organization and the media. The role of this department varies somewhat depending on individual organizational needs, but in general it functions to (1) enhance communication between the organization and the outside world, especially through mass media channels and (2) manage impressions about the organization. This impression management is achieved by selective (but, it is hoped, always accurate and honest) release of favorable information and control of unfavorable information.

For many smaller sport organizations and societies these departments function primarily to create informational materials on an organization for use by the media and the public. For example, brochures that describe activity programs provided by local YMCAs, Jewish Community Centers, and community recreation departments are often the responsibility of a public relations office. Some PR departments are responsible for monthly or bimonthly magazines or newsletters that inform members and increase spectator interest. For example, The Amateur Softball Association publishes *Balls & Strikes*, the American Arm Wrestling Association prints *The Arm Bender*, the American Bowling Congress is responsible for *Bowling Magazine*, and the International Pro Rodeo Association publishes *Rodeo News*.

Some PR or SI departments also produce a yearly **media guide** with information about the particular sport organization and its members or competitors. Major universities have annual football and basketball guides that contain information about the school, the academic and athletic departments, and team and individual histories and records. Good guides also provide a mixture of interesting stories that can be fashioned into feature or background stories by print and broadcast reporters. Professional sport teams also produce annual media guides. Many sporting societies (such as the American Bowling Congress, Association of Tennis Professionals, International Pro Rodeo Association, National Association for Stock Car Auto Racing, U.S. Tennis Association, World Professional Squash Association) produce similar guides for a season or for a specific competition (for example, a major tournament).

Sports information and public relations departments are necessary to university athletic departments and professional sport teams. The demands placed on these sport organizations by media reporters and broadcasters, advertisers, corporate sponsors and marketers, and others needing information, requires the services of a full-time staff. Some of the responsibilities entrusted to these departments include:

- Making complete arrangements for print and broadcast media covering athletic contests, including arranging support for the press table (print media) and radio and television broadcasting facilities during each contest*
- Providing player and team statistics to the media for each contest and providing updates and halftime summaries during the contests
- Arranging and managing precontest and postcontest opportunities for media to interview players, coaches, or others (such as team owners, university athletic directors, or university presidents)
- Arranging and conducting press conferences at important occasions (announcing coaching changes, player suspensions, Rose Bowl or National Collegiate Athletic Association [NCAA] basketball tournament games).
- Maintaining daily contact with media reporters, alerting them to important upcoming stories, providing them with updates on continuing stories, and confirming or denying the rumors that surround college and professional sports
- Preparing annual media guides or game-by-game press kits with histories, biographies, and interesting stories for use by print, radio, and television reporters

Some organizations also rely on these SID/PR departments to handle itineraries for local media who travel with the team. Other organizations have also relied on professionals in these areas to provide training for the coaches and players on how to deal with the media (for example, giving interviews or talking with reporters and broadcasters). Recently some university and professional PR departments have assumed responsibility for dealing with corporate sponsors who wish to advertise in or underwrite various promotional endeavors.

Work in this area involves serving a number of different constituencies: owners, athletic directors, coaches, players, universities, the public, and print and broadcast reporters. Public relations professionals must be sensitive to all the media in their markets, making sure not to play favorites with reporters, competing stations and papers, or with

---

*This responsibility also includes more mundane tasks, such as arranging sufficient electrical power for remote broadcast facilities, making sure that adequate parking facilities are available for production and satellite trucks, providing a space for a pregame interview, and sometimes recruiting a reluctant coach, player, or other notable for an interview.

competing media (television vs. print). Although players and coaches might feel that coverage on statewide or national television is more glamorous and important, a wise PR person knows that it is constant coverage by print media that generates and sustains local and national interest in many sports. The sports reporter for the small local newspaper is as important as broadcasters and reporters for the national television networks.

Public relations professionals must be sensitive to timing; indeed, many professionals will assert that the three keys to good public relations are timing, timing, and timing. A good PR director makes sure that news is released in time for various newspaper and broadcast deadlines. He or she also searches for opportune times to release both good information (that is, when it will get the most coverage) and bad information (that is, when it will get the least coverage or will be overshadowed by bigger news events). A PR director for one NFL team has likened the job to keeping a roomful of balloons in the air, moving quickly from balloon to balloon to keep each from hitting the floor. In a recent interview with PR directors of Chicago's four professional sports teams, each director indicated that the primary skills necessary for the job were organization and an ability to remain calm under pressure (Hamrin, 1988).

Good PR people must be sensitive to reporters' needs for facts and information but equally sensitive to the organization's need for privacy. They must know when to speak "on the record," when to speak "on background,"* and when to simply say "no comment." Professionals in PR also emphasize the importance of cultivating **trust** among the print and broadcast reporters. Reporters are more likely to believe those who they think are trusted by, and have access to—players, coaches, and owners or athletic directors. Many organizations soon discover that there is a relationship between poorly-informed PR personnel and poor images in the media. One way to encourage fair and responsible treatment in the media is to make sure that the liaison between the sport organization and

the media is constantly, fully informed about organizational goals and endeavors. A somewhat more detailed description of sport information as a career may be found in Hitchcock (1989), a book that also provides useful information on careers in sport journalism and sport broadcasting. An interesting and more generic approach to the field of public relations is taken by Rein, Kotler, and Stoller (1987).

CONCEPT CHECK

Sports information and public relations departments are interfaces between sport organizations and the public, especially the public media. These departments enhance communication between the organization and the outside world and manage impressions about the organization. Roles of professionals in sports information departments might include producing newsletters and media guides, providing services for media at various competitive contests, maintaining frequent contact with media reporters, and cultivating their trust and cooperation. It is a career serving multiple constituencies.

Programming sports: radio

At one time radio was a popular source of sports coverage in this country. Radio sportscasters covered collegiate competitions (football, basketball, and hockey), amateur sports (tennis and golf), and professional events (boxing, wrestling, football, and baseball). Although radio is not as important to sports as it once was (see Barber, 1985, or McChesney, 1989, for histories of radio sports), it remains an important source of information about and coverage of local sports events.† Even smaller radio stations have at least a part-time sport staff for both sport reporting and event coverage. Each weekend during autumn the evening airwaves are still filled with the sounds of high school, small college, and university sports.

Professional teams in such major sports as baseball, basketball, football, and hockey each have contracts with flagship stations. These are stations

---

*Speaking on the record means that one may be quoted exactly and the quotes may be attributed. Speaking on background means that the substance of what is said may not be reported but is simply for the reporters' information. In addition, it means that information may not be attributed to any identified source.

---

†There is still some network radio coverage of national sports. For example, CBS Radio carries a number of MLB games and many NFL contests (such as Monday night games, playoffs, the Super Bowl). It also carries NCAA basketball.

that serve as the originators for game telecasts. The radio stations and their advertisers have found these sports in particular to be effective in drawing desirable audiences. A broadcast by the flagship station may be sent out to a handful—or to hundreds—of stations in the state or surrounding states. In most cases the stations have purchased the broadcast rights to the games, the fees charged by teams to carry their games. The station will be responsible for producing and airing the game and for selling advertising spots during games. In a few cases the teams retain the rights, produce their own games, broker their own advertising, and buy air time from radio stations.

Collegiate sports teams, particularly those in football and basketball, also have local flagship stations. In some areas of the country where interest is high, radio coverage might include several of the non–revenue-producing sports (such as hockey or baseball) as well. In most cases, collegiate radio rights are bought by radio stations that do the production and ad selling.

Programming sports: television

Sport programming is a valuable commodity to local and national commercial and cable television, even in this era of escalating rights fees (see Eastman and Meyer, 1989). Major sports provide hours of programming for a station or a network and cost considerably less than it would to develop and produce programming with comparable longevity and appeal. Most important, sports programs attract a large and economically desirable audience. The primary appeal is to males aged 18 to 49, but significant inroads have been made in attracting females, especially to tennis and professional football.

Networks. Networks often seek to establish a programming identity that sets them apart from the others. The network strategy of identification is ultimately aimed at attracting a solid and loyal audience. The ad departments at both the network and affiliate levels will use this information during advertising negotiations to garner higher rates. Sports programming is particularly valuable for identification. It involves human interest, drama, physical risks, and thrilling spectacles. Furthermore, it is immediate and live, and the viewer often senses the risk of the unanticipated. This immediacy also means that, in contrast to other programming, reruns of major sports events are almost never broadcast, or if they are, are seldom watched.

Programming decisions at the network level are even more complex than those at the local level. Much of this complexity is due to the risks involved; whereas the local stations are able to readily judge the popularity of local sports teams, network programmers are required to take chances on the future popularity of programs. In the case of sports programs, Klatell and Marcus (1988) have eloquently described the situation:

"We ask network decision-makers to anticipate, years in advance, the participants in major public events, the tenor and tone of the actual contests, and the composition and purchasing power of the audience which will watch them. We then expect these network executives to mortgage a healthy chunk of their company's future on these assumptions, without even knowing the state of the economy, the advertising business, or the public mood during those crucial years. In addition, they have no way of predicting how the television business may have changed by the time the events take place" (pp. 6-7).

Beginning in 1960, ABC—which was a poor third in the network ratings race—made a concerted effort to acquire a variety of sports programming and to identify itself as the "leader in television sports" (see Klattel and Marcus, 1988; Rader, 1984). Throughout the 1960s and 1970s ABC was indeed the leader in sports programming, pioneering programs such as *Wide World of Sports, Monday Night Football,* and Howard Cosell's *Sportsbeat. Wide World of Sports,* in particular, changed the public perception of attractive and interesting sports, covering track and field, swimming and diving, boxing, skiing, cliff diving, wrist wrestling, gymnastics, and a host of winter sports. The program served to stimulate interest in these diverse sports, making them interesting and attractive by virtue of the television coverage itself (see Gunther and Carter, 1988; O'Neill, 1989; and Spence and Diles, 1988 for interesting histories of those glory years).

In the late 1980s, CBS adopted a corporate strategy that completely usurped ABC's sports throne. Compare, for example, CBS's offerings in 1970 with its 1990 schedule. In 1970, CBS's sports commitment was limited to National Football League (NFL) games. ABC and NBC held rights to most other sports. However, because of an aggressive strategy of pursuing rights to major sporting events, CBS has rights to the 1990 Winter Olympics (as well as those for 1994), professional baseball regular and postseason games, NCAA basketball and the NCAA tournament, National Basketball Association games, NCAA football, NFL football (NFC conference), the Daytona 500, golf's Masters tournament, and the U.S. Open Tennis tournament.

Acquisition of all these events by CBS was costly. In fact, the network will probably lose money on some sports. For example, it will be almost impossible to make enough money from national advertisers to compensate for the $1.1 billion CBS will pay Major League Baseball (MLB) during 1990 to 1993. Why, then, would the network make such a move? First, a strong sports lineup during prime time will attract viewers who might stay with subsequent prime time programming, if it is sufficient. Also, playoff time comes in the autumn, just a few weeks before the November sweeps, an excellent time to announce and promote new network prime time programming. Second, in the television industry there are concerns for profit at the network and station levels. CBS's strong moves to acquire a sport identity shows its affiliates that the network is committed to their successful competition at the local level. Even if some money is lost at the network level, affiliates stand to profit at the local level. And in the broadcast industry, networks strive to keep affiliates happy.

Owned-and-operated (OAO) and affiliated stations. Clearly, it is not inexpensive to provide sport programs. Costs have escalated in recent years. The large increase in fees charged for broadcast rights to collegiate and professional sports, as well as in costs associated with productions that sophisticated viewers have come to expect (multiple cameras, special effects, replay machines, even blimp shots), have accounted for much of this increase. Therefore sports programs on network affiliates and OAOs are often restricted to those events that are aired nationally by their respective networks (such as major tennis and golf championships; collegiate basketball and football games, bowls, or playoffs; professional baseball, basketball, and football games and championships).

Some OAOs and affiliates are also flagship stations for their local professional baseball and basketball teams.* As a rule it is financially rewarding to be identified as the station that brings its audi-

ence Twins baseball or Celtics basketball. Programmers count on the good image or positive feelings associated with a winning team to create a similar positive feeling for the radio or TV flagship. Of course, this strategy could backfire if the team is beset with problems (such as drugs or alcohol, contract disputes, questionable behavior) or consistently having a losing record.

There are not collegiate sport flagships in the same sense. The rights to football and basketball games of many of the larger schools are negotiated either by their respective conferences, such as the Big Ten or the Pac Ten, or associations, such as the College Football Association (CFA). These negotiations are generally with the commercial networks, cable channels (for example, ESPN or Turner Network Television), or superstations (for example, WTBS) rather than with individual local stations. There is seldom coverage of the non–revenue-producing collegiate sports on commercial stations, because viewer demand is not adequate to attract advertiser support.

A number of factors affect the amount that teams, leagues, or collegiate conferences and associations charge for broadcast rights and the amount stations and networks are willing to pay for these rights. Space considerations make a detailed examination of these negotiations impossible. However, for the interested reader, there are several excellent sources for further information: Berry and Wong (1986), Eastman and Meyer (1989), and Wong (1988).

Independents. Independent stations usually buy their sports programs from specialized networks (for example, Hughes Television Network or Mutual Broadcasting System) or from independent sports production companies (for example, Mizlou, Raycom, Jefferson-Pilot, Video West Net-

---

*Flagships for professional football teams only negotiate to carry preseason games. Each year, *Broadcasting* magazine publishes special reports on the state of broadcasting contracts with baseball, basketball, and football. The football issue, which appears in early- or mid-August, describes radio and television contracts with both collegiate and professional teams. It details the contracts with the national networks (ABC, CBS, NBC, ESPN) and describes the local scenario on a city-by-city (NFL) and conference-by-conference (collegiate) basis. The basketball issue appears in mid-October, and the baseball issue appears in early March. Each also presents the state of rights for national broadcasters, as well as detailing local radio and TV flagship rights on a city-by-city basis.

work). An independent station may also be a flag-ship for a local professional team if it bids competitively for broadcast rights. In the past the sports offerings available to independent stations were somewhat limited, but recently the availability of events, especially collegiate contests, has increased somewhat. Escalating rights fees have resulted in spirited bidding not only between networks, but between stations within communities.

An important 1984 Supreme Court decision opened up bidding for collegiate football games. Until that year, televising of college football games was under control of the NCAA, which maintained a strict set of requirements. Each school could appear no more than four times in nationally-televised games in any 2-year period, and each was limited to a total of six appearances. The televising networks (ABC, which had exclusive rights from 1966 through 1981, was joined by CBS in 1982) were required to schedule appearances by at least 82 different schools, representing all NCAA divisions, over the same 2-year period. At the urging of several schools with large football programs—Oklahoma and Georgia in particular—the Supreme Court ruled that the NCAA's exclusive hold on college football rights was anticompetitive.*

As a result, schools were "freed" from the "monopolistic" control of the NCAA, and more games became available for television. Ostensibly any broadcast station, network, or production company that could strike a deal could televise a game. Similarly, universities and colleges were free to negotiate directly with broadcasters, although many have allowed the conference (such as Big Ten and Pac Ten schools) or the CFA to negotiate the national television contracts. A university still may sell the rights for games that are not covered under the conference's or CFA's contract. In this way, smaller production companies, independent sta-

tions, and regional cable channels now have access to more collegiate contests.

As the number of games available has increased, the value of each contest has diminished. An unforeseen drawback is that some of the rights fees for college games, especially those of smaller schools, have plummeted. Although the larger (Division I) institutions now have more football games telecast, per-game revenue is significantly less than it was before 1984. Greenspan (1988) noted that in 1982 there were 93 television games for which broadcasters paid a total of 66.8 million dollars. In 1986 there were 99 televised games, but the total rights fees were only 52.7 million dollars. Even major universities found that they needed to increase the number of games televised to earn the same amount of money. Without the NCAA's requirement that smaller schools receive network television coverage, games from these universities are seldom televised on commercial TV. Thus broadcast revenue to these schools has fallen and in some cases disappeared altogether. Finally, overexposure or abundance of games from larger schools seems to pose a risk to live attendance, especially, again, at games played by smaller schools. Indeed, since the court decision, attendance at these games has decreased (Greenspan, 1988).

Superstations. The major superstations have one element in common that has led to their appeal and success: a significant amount of sports programming. WGN has the Chicago Cubs (and announcer Harry Caray), WWOR has the New York Mets, and TBS has Atlanta's Braves and Hawks, as well as selected NCAA contests.

A few of the superstations are willing stations. That is, they wish to have their signal delivered nationally because they are then able to carry national advertising and charge national rates. However some superstations are unwilling or passive stations, generally because they do not wish to be charged at a national rate by program syndicators.

Compensation for rights to superstation telecasts—sports contests as well as movies and syndicated programs—is somewhat complex. Consider that a baseball team or the holder of rights to a film has already been compensated under terms of the contract signed with the broadcast station. Yet, neither the company that picks up and retransmits the signal, nor any of the cable fran-

---

*National Collegiate Athletic Association v. the Board of Regents of the University of Oklahoma, 468 U.S. 85, 104 S.Ct. 2948 (1984). Oklahoma and Georgia essentially represented all schools in the CFA, which included universities from the Big Eight, Southeastern, Southwestern, Atlantic Coast Conference, and Western Athletic Conference, as well as major independents such as Notre Dame, Penn State, Syracuse, Pittsburgh, Army, and Navy. Early in 1990 Notre Dame, displeased with the small number of "national exposures" it would receive under the broadcast agreement between ABC, ESPN, and the CFA, withdrew and sold rights to NBC for 30 of its home games between 1991 and 1995.

chises that receive the transmission, compensate the team for carrying games or the holder of the movie rights for showing the film. To redress this, the federal **Copyright Royalty Tribunal** (CRT) was created in 1976. Cable franchises pay a small percentage of their gross income to the CRT as royalties for copyrighted materials (such as movies, syndicated programs, or sporting events) that they "rebroadcast." The CRT then distributes this money to rights holders. About 75% goes to the Motion Picture Association of America for films and syndicated programs. Only approximately 15% is distributed to joint sport claimants: baseball, hockey, basketball, soccer, plus the NCAA (Cryan and Crane, 1986). Several scholars (Cryan and Crane, 1986; Klatell and Marcus, 1988) have argued that the latter amount is symbolic rather than compensatory.

Superstations are unique as independent broadcasters, because they broadcast into multiple time zones. They may repeat broadcasts several times during each 24-hour period. Although a point made earlier indicated that reruns of sporting events were seldom desirable, superstations represent an exception to this rule. Why? Consider: A baseball game originally is broadcast at 7:30 PM Eastern time. On the West coast it is only 4:30 PM, a time when most people are still working. However, when the game is aired again, perhaps at 1 AM Eastern time, it is only 10 PM in the Pacific time zone, still a "prime time" to watch the Giants play the Mets. This scheduling represents an opportunity for many sport fans who work an evening or night shift to view events that they otherwise would miss.

Cable channels. A national cable network, the Entertainment and Sports Programming Network (ESPN), devoted primarily to sports premiered in September 1979. Initially, because no one was sure that sports could provide adequate content, other entertainment fare was programmed as well. The majority of the sports content was to be the non–revenue-producing NCAA sports. In 1980 ESPN began telecasting 24 hours per day, and with few exceptions its programming is totally sport related. ESPN covers professional tennis and golf, colle-

Developments in cable technology and regulation have significantly increased the availability of sports on television. ESPN, shown here on NFL draft day, provides 24-hour-a-day coverage of a wide variety of sports and sport-related events. (Photo courtesy of ESPN.)

giate basketball and football, and professional basketball and football; it recently signed a contract to carry around 170 MLB games per year from 1990 to 1994.* ESPN also carries sport talk shows and a more diverse set of sports than typically found on commercial television, such as women's basketball, college and Little League baseball, bodybuilding, powerboat racing, and monster truck competitions.

ESPN requires that cable franchises carry it on the basic tier. This minimizes costs to the viewers and maximizes ESPN's cable audience. ESPN also recognizes its national scope and often broadcasts programs several times daily. One of its major effects has been to increase the number of outlets for amateur and professional sporting events. ESPN has also popularized smaller collegiate sports (baseball, volleyball, women's basketball) and some smaller professional sports including beach volleyball. In addition, by bidding with the major networks for professional events, the channel has contributed to the rapid escalation in rights fees charged by professional sports teams and leagues.

For a short time, ESPN's cable competition for broadcast sports was limited to a few offerings by Home Box Office (HBO) and the USA Network. Increasingly, regional cable sports channels have provided additional outlets for sports programs. By early 1990 there were about three dozen regional sports channels around the country (32 Regional Sports Span U.S., 1989).

Regionals are able to carry sport events from local professional or collegiate teams (especially home games) that are not included in teams' contracts with other cable or commercial broadcasters. Many teams now negotiate separate cable and broadcast packages. Some regionals also have carried non-local but popular "national" teams (for example, Notre Dame football and New York Yankees baseball). Regionals also provide outlets for many other sporting events, some of which have been aired earlier by other broadcasters, some of which (high school football and basketball contests) would never be telecast were it not for the existence of regionals. For example, the Midwest's Pro-Am Sports System (PASS) telecasts matches from the Canadian Open Tennis Tournament.

PASS also carries other small tennis and golf tournaments that are not attractive to other broadcasters. To improve their access to diverse sports programs and to share programming with others, sets of regionals have banded together to form regional networks. This strategy has also enhanced their ability to bid competitively for the broadcast rights for several sports, including NHL hockey. The first such network was SportsChannel America, which now includes SportsChannels Chicago, Florida, Los Angeles, New England, New York, Ohio, and Philadelphia, as well as Pennsylvania's PRISM. NBC is part-owner of SportsChannel America, just as ABC is majority owner of ESPN.

Regional channels typically telecast only during selected parts of the day, primarily afternoon, prime time, and late-evening. A few regionals are provided on the basic tier by cable franchises when viewer demand is low, but most are sold as premium services that require an additional cost.

Sport content also has been a central offering of pay-per-view services since its earliest days in the 1940s and 1950s. From 1968 to 1977 the FCC maintained a set of stringent rules about what kinds of sporting events could be shown on pay-per-view broadcast TV and later cable. These "antisiphoning" rules were designed to prevent sports programs (and films) from being siphoned from commercial television. At the urging of HBO, a federal court declared the rules unconstitutional in 1977.[†] This ruling, combined with advances in satellite communications and the easing of several FCC restrictions (in 1976 the Commission reduced size requirements of receive-only dishes and revoked the limit on number of distant signals a cable franchise might import), has resulted in cable now providing significantly more sports programming than does commercial television (Watkins and Brand, 1990).

However, because of the multiple outlets for sports programs in both broadcast and basic and premium cable channels, there are few major sporting events left to air on pay-per-view. Important boxing bouts, or extravaganzas such as professional wrestling matches, basketball one-on-one, and dunk contests are events that have found pay-

---

*This figure may be contrasted with CBS's broadcasting of 14 national games during the 1990 season.

[†]*HBO Inc. v. F.C.C.*, 567 F.2d 9 (185 U.S. App. D.C.). 142 cert. denied (98 S.Ct. 111, 1977).

per-view to be a lucrative outlet. Around the clock Olympic coverage may be the next pay-per-view phenomenon. Currently NBC, which owns the broadcast rights to the 1992 Summer Olympics, is attempting to create three pay-per-view channels to carry up to 600 supplemental hours of its broadcast Olympic coverage. A few MLB teams have pay-per-view contracts to air selected games, but the penetration rate of this service (29% of U.S. households) has not made this a popular strategy in most markets yet.

CONCEPT CHECK

In general, sports programs on radio and television are highly cost efficient, even in an era of escalating fees for rights to broadcast sports events. Radio coverage of sports has declined since the 1930s and 1940s but still remains an important source of information about local sports. Television networks purchase rights to various events to provide themselves with an identity and to help their affiliates compete for viewers and advertising income at the local level. Some network OAOs and affiliates, as well as independent stations, are flagships for various professional and university sports teams. National cable channels, such as ESPN; regional cable channels, (such as various SportsChannels); and pay-per-view channels have provided additional outlets for television coverage of both major and minor sports.

Advertising decisions: the electronic media

Decision making about programming occurs at both the national level (with the networks and major cable channels) and the local level (individual television stations and cable franchises). Similarly, some advertising is solicited and sold nationally, whereas some is sold at the local level. In-house research (for example, focus groups), Arbitron and Nielsen figures, and specialized reports from organizations such as Simmons Market Research Bureau are used to determine what types of viewers are attracted to what types of programming. This information is used by advertisers to make choices about what programs should carry their advertising.

Corporate sponsors use similar information to decide what sporting events to underwrite. For example, it was an almost serendipitous discovery

by Volvo that the demographics of its car owners matched the demographics of viewers and followers of tennis that led it into corporate sponsorship of tennis events. Because of considerable interest and research in both the corporate and academic worlds over the past few years, the demographics of the audiences for most sporting events are among the best known (Schlosberg, 1987).

Ratings. Television ratings and shares are used in several ways by sports programmers. They provide information on what people want to watch and which sports are popular and will attract viewers. Second, ratings provide a rough approximation of when to program particular sports. For example, a Monday Night Football (MNF) game that begins at 8 PM attracts a smaller audience than MNF beginning at 9 PM (especially in the Pacific time zone). Third, as noted earlier, complete ratings information indicates what kinds of viewers are attracted to what kinds of sports. A rating of 3.5 might be more desirable than one of 8, if the 3.5 represents an audience of young viewers (aged 24 to 39) with a higher-than-average disposable income. Ratings are also used to assess how well sports programs do against competing broadcasters and competing types of programs. Finally, ratings and shares are used to determine advertising rates. The reader interested in more complete treatments of viewership ratings and shares should consult Eastman, Head, and Klein (1985) and Beville (1988).

The discussion now turns to the process by which ratings, shares, and advertiser costs are determined.

Calculation of ratings and shares. A program **rating** represents the percent of all households in the area of dominant influence (ADI) or designated market area (DMA) that is tuned to a particular program during a specified time. It is calculated by dividing the estimated number of households viewing a program by the total number of households with television in the market. For example, if there are 400 television homes in Garrison Keillor's mythical Lake Wobegon, and 100 of these homes are tuned to a game featuring their beloved Minnesota Twins, the rating for the station carrying the game is 100 divided by 400, or 25%. A rating indicates how many households are actually watching a program in proportion to all the households that could be watching.

A program **share** represents the percentage of

all households currently viewing television that are tuned to a particular program. It is calculated by dividing the estimated number of homes viewing a program by the estimated number of homes using the television. A share indicates how many households are watching a program in proportion to all households in which something is being viewed. Using the Lake Wobegon example, although there are a total of 400 television homes, in only 200 of these homes are people viewing television. Therefore the share for the station broadcasting the Twins game is the number of households viewing the Twins (100) divided by the number of households viewing anything (200), which leads to the answer of 50%.

A combination of information from viewing diaries, audimeters, and people meters allows ratings services to provide ratings and shares not only for households, but for various demographic categories of people within these households. For example, ratings and shares information about working women, men aged 18 to 34, women aged 18 to 49, children 2 to 11 or 2 to 17, and many other categories, is also available.

The highest-rated program ever broadcast was the final episode of M*A*S*H; watched by over 50 million TV households, its rating was over 50. Interestingly, about half of the 25 highest-rated programs have been sports programs, especially Super Bowls. Super Bowl XXIII reached 39.3 million households, achieving a 43.5 rating and a share of 68—which is why advertisers pay upwards of 1.3 million dollars for a 60-second commercial spot during the Super Bowl.

Buying program advertising time. Strategies for purchasing broadcast-advertising time are important whether the buyer is a local golf and tennis club seeking to attract new members or a large corporation seeking national exposure. To decide which program is the best advertising buy, several pieces of information must be known. First, what is the targeted audience? For example, assume that a computer company's research department has indicated that the majority of those who buy its products are male, college graduates, aged 45 to 54, with an income exceeding 50,000 dollars annually. These individuals compose the target audience for the company's advertising.

Second, what type of television program attracts an audience that is similar to the desired or target audience? Market research indicates that both ten-nis and college football have a strong appeal to males, aged 45 to 54, who are college graduates with a 50,000 dollar + income (see Schlosberg, 1987).

Assume that competing stations are televising tennis and collegiate football. Third, then, one needs to know how many viewers from this target audience are projected to be viewing the various competing television programs. How many viewers are targeted to watch the tennis match? How many are projected to view the football game?

Fourth, one must know what each station is charging in terms of advertising rates; how much will it cost to reach these viewers? Perhaps one station promises more viewers, but sets higher advertising rates.

In this situation, the buyer needs a standardized index to determine which is the better deal. The **"cost per thousand"** (CPM) figure is this index. The index represents how much it will cost the advertiser to reach 1,000 members of the targeted audience. This CPM figure is computed by dividing the advertising cost by the number of projected viewers, in thousands (cost of advertisement/number of viewers, in thousands).

If the number of projected target viewers is the same for both televised tennis and football, the station with the lowest advertising rate should be selected. However, if the number of projected viewers differs, the advertiser must balance this difference with any difference in advertising rates.

The following is an example of how an advertising decision is made at the local level. Assume that an urban health club in a large city wishes to place a 60-second TV ad highlighting its women's aerobic, fitness, weight training, and tennis programs. The club wants the ad to run sometime during Saturday afternoon sports programming. Station A will be showing an important baseball game, and station B will be showing final rounds of a major women's tennis tournament. Ads on station A cost 3,000 dollars per minute, and those on station B cost 4,000 dollars. Each station projects a total audience of 2,000,000 viewers.

At first glance it seems as if station A is the best buy; the ads cost less (3,000 vs. 4,000 dollars) even though the projected audience is the same. However, the target audience for the club is women aged 25 to 49. Perhaps station A's projections estimate that about one quarter of its audience (500,000) will be women aged 25 to 49. Station B's projections estimate that about half its audience (1,000,000) will be women aged 25 to 49. The CPM to reach the target audience on station A is 3,000 dollars divided by 500, or 6 dollars to reach 1,000 women aged 25 to 49 during the baseball game. Station B's CPM is 4,000 dollars divided by 1,000, or 4 dollars to reach one thousand women watching the tennis tournament. Clearly ads on station B are the better buy.

CONCEPT CHECK

Television advertising time during sports coverage is sold at both the national (network) and local (station) levels. Rating and share information from Arbitron and Nielsen shape these advertising decisions, as well as decisions about program placement by providing information about viewer demographics. A program rating represents the number of households viewing a particular program divided by the total number of possible viewing households. A share represents the total number of households viewing divided by the number of households in which television is being viewed. Several pieces of information must be known in order to make an informed advertising buy. What is the target audience? For a particular program, how many projected viewers are from the target audience? What is the cost of an advertisement? From this information, an index that represents the cost to reach 1,000 targeted viewers (CPM) may be calculated.

SUMMARY

1. At least half of a professional's working day is spent communicating orally or through writing. Skills in written and oral communication are consequently important for the sport manager. Written and oral communication that is most successful has a clear purpose and is well structured and organized.

2. Interviews represent a major setting for interpersonal communication between managers and employees. There are employment interviews, information-seeking and information-sharing interviews, counseling interviews, disciplinary interviews, grievance interviews, and exit interviews. Clarity of purpose, empathy, good listening, and immediate feedback contribute to good communication in an interview.

3. Success or failure in small groups is often dependent on the amount and kind of communication that takes place during group work. Persons within small groups may assume a variety of task roles, relationship roles, and self-centered roles that may enhance or hinder communication and subsequent success. A leader who is sensitive to these various roles, provides a clear focus and structure for the group, moves the group toward its goals, and ensures that all perspectives are heard will facilitate group success.

4. Communication in organizations faces a number of hindrances: organizational size and consequent multiple communicators, diversity in individual and group goals, and power and status hierarchies that affect communication flow and accuracy. These may cause either failure or distortion in communication within the organization. To ensure smooth organizational functioning, management should be sensitive to communication patterns within the organization and should work to improve upward, downward, and horizontal communication pathways.

5. Sport information and public relations departments are interfaces between an organization and the public. Most deal primarily with the mass media. These departments enhance communication between the organization and the outside world and work to manage public impressions about the organization. PR and SID professionals are required to serve multiple constituencies and must develop and cultivate the trust of persons with whom they deal.

6. Decisions in both print and broadcast media are often driven by (1) a search to define and attract an audience (readers, viewers) and (2) the subsequent use of that audience to attract advertising support. Newspapers, magazines, and radio and television broadcasters have found sport content to be useful in accomplishing these goals.

7. At one time radio was a popular source of sports coverage. Although coverage is less comprehensive now, radio continues to cover many high school, collegiate, and professional sports. Sports programs are valuable commodities to local and national commercial television and cable broadcasters because they attract a large,

loyal, and economically desirable audience. Network OAOs and affiliates carry major sports fed to them by their network; these stations, as well as independent broadcasters, also carry available sports of various local university and professional teams. Networks view sports as a way to establish a corporate identity and to provide affiliates with programming that enables them to compete locally for viewers and advertisers.

8. The advent of superstations and national and regional sports cable channels has increased the number of sports options available to viewers and driven up the cost for rights to broadcast major collegiate and professional sports. Although sports on commercial television has not increased appreciably in the recent past, many more options are available on cable. ESPN cablecasts sports nationally 24 hours per day, and around three dozen regional cable sports channels provide programming during the day. Groups of regionals have banded together to share programming and to bid competitively for rights to major sports. Pay-per-view technology has long been heralded as a potential source of sport programming, but it is not likely to be so until its penetration rate is significantly higher.

9. Ratings and shares information are used by sports programmers to make decisions about program popularity and placement. They are used by advertisers and sales personnel to help determine advertisement placement and cost. Many major decisions in sports programming and advertising are made based on ratings and shares data obtained from Arbitron, Inc. and A.C. Nielsen.

CASE STUDIES AND ACTIVITIES

1. Create a fictitious sport organization structured like that in Figure 8-3, p. 118. Perhaps it might be a sport marketing firm, an athletic department, a national sport governing body (such as the U.S. Olympic Committee or the U.S. Tennis Association) or a community recreation program. Describe each department and provide each with a set of organizational responsibilities. Then explain the communication networks in this organization. Where is good communication most likely? What are likely to be major communication problems? Discuss ways to alleviate these problems.

2. You are the community recreation director in a moderately sized city. The mayor and city council have asked you to lead a group of community leaders in the task of reorganizing community and public school athletic services. How would you do it? What communication-related steps would you take to enhance the chance for successful task completion?

3. Sport management represents an important new area of business. There is a need for a business-oriented sport magazine, national in scope, to serve professionals in this area. Assume that you are in charge of reviving a magazine similar to *Sports Inc.* on a monthly basis. Who would you target as your intended audience? How would you identify potential sponsors? What magazines would be your competition? (HINT: You may want to examine several early issues of *Sports Inc.* at your university or public library before you begin your solution. The magazine was published between November 1987 and March 1989.)

4. You have accepted a job as the sports information director of a large public university. The previous director has left the entire department in disarray. Neither the athletic director nor any of the university's coaches were able to maintain a working relationship with this director, so communication between the sports information department and the athletic department is poor. There are no plans to produce media guides or press kits for the upcoming year for any of the school's sports. In addition, relations between university athletics and print and broadcast reporters have been strained. Finally, the NCAA is investigating several of the men's sports for various infractions. What activities would you undertake during your first week, month, and year in your new job?

5. Assume that you are a sport programmer for a regional cable channel. You wish to specialize in programming smaller sports from high school, collegiate, and professional sources. Plan your schedule for the upcoming year. What sports will you identify as desirable to air? From whom will you purchase the rights fees? How much is your overall budget, and how much are you able to afford for (1) rights fees, (2) taping and production equipment for coverage of local and remote contests? Who are your projected

viewers for the various sports? What advertisers do you imagine will be attracted to these viewers? (HINT: Schlosberg [1987] is a useful source on viewer demographics. An entire section on sports directing and producing in Bode [1987] may be useful in answering the production part of this question.)

REFERENCES

Anderson, D. (1985). *Contemporary sports reporting*, Chicago: Nelson-Hall Publishers.

Andrews, P., and Baird, J. (1989). *Communication for business and the professions*, Dubuque, Iowa: William C. Brown Co.

A new daily for sports nuts. (1990). *Time*, *135*(6): 66 (February 5).

Applegate, J. (1989). Sports Inc. to fold: low ad sales cited. *Los Angeles Times*, IV:3 (March 15).

Bales, R. (1976). *Interaction process analysis: a method for the study of small groups*, Reading, Massachusetts: Addison-Wesley Publishing Co., Inc.

Barber, R. (1985). *The broadcasters*, New York: Da Capo Press, Inc.

Berry, R., and Wong, G. (1986). *Law and business of the sports industries*. Volume II. Dover, Massachusetts: Auburn House Publishing Co.

Beville, H. (1988). *Audience ratings: radio, television, and cable*, Hillsdale, New Jersey: Lawrence Erlbaum Associates, Inc.

Bode, W. (1987). *Live TV: an inside look at directing and producing*, Boston: Focal Press.

Cryan, T., and Crane, J. (1986). Sports on the superstations: the legal and economic effects. *Entertainment and Sports Law Journal*, 3:35-56.

Deford, F. (1987). *The world's tallest midget: the best of Frank Deford*. Boston: Little, Brown & Co.

Eastman, S., Head, S., and Klein, L. (1985). *Broadcast/cable programming: strategies and practices* (2nd Edition). Belmont, California: Wadsworth, Inc.

Eastman, S., and Meyer, T. (1989). Sports programming: scheduling, costs, and competition. In L. Wenner (Ed.), *Media, sports, & society*, Newbury Park, California: Sage Publications, Inc., 97-119.

Greenspan, D. (1988). College football's biggest fumble: the economic impact of the Supreme Court's decision in *National Collegiate Athletic Association v. Board of Regents of the University of Oklahoma*. *The Antitrust Bulletin*, 33:1-65.

Gunther, M., and Carter, B. (1988). *Monday night mayhem: the inside story of ABC's Monday Night Football*, New York: William Morrow & Co., Inc.

Hamrin, J. (1988). Sports PR: all work, no play (Or, if you like to watch the game, don't go to work in the front office). *IABC Communication World*, (July/August): 36-39.

Hersey, P., and Blanchard, K. (1988). *Management of organizational behavior: utilizing human resources* (5th Edition). Englewood Cliffs, New Jersey: Prentice Hall.

Hitchcock, J. (1989). *Sports & media*. Vincennes, Indiana: The Original Co.

Janis, I. (1983). *Groupthink: Psychological studies of policy decisions and fiascoes*. Boston: Houghton Mifflin Co.

Jefferson, D. (1989). Times Mirror Co. blows final whistle on its *Sports Inc.*, citing lack of ads. *Wall Street Journal* (March 15), 86.

Kent, M. (1990). Krzyzewski jabs stun students, *Ann Arbor News* (January 28), D13. (Reprint of article originally printed in *The Baltimore Sun*.)

Klatell, D., and Marcus, N. (1988). *Sports for sale: television, money, and the fans*. New York: Oxford University Press.

Knapp, M. (1980). *Essentials of nonverbal communication*. New York: Holt, Rinehart & Winston, Inc.

Lewis, P. (1987). *Organizational communication: the essence of effective management*. New York: John Wiley & Sons.

Likert, R. (1967). *The human organization: its management and value*. New York: McGraw-Hill Book Co.

McChesney, R. (1989). Media made sport: a history of sports coverage in the United States. In L. Wenner (Ed.), *Media, sports, & society*. Newbury Park, California: Sage Publications, Inc., 49-69.

The Missouri Group (1988). *News reporting and writing*. New York: St. Martin's Press.

Monroe, A., and Ehninger, D. (1980). *Principles of speech communication* (8th Edition). Glenview, Illinois: Scott, Foresman & Co.

Munter, M. (1987). *Guide to managerial communication* (2nd Edition). Englewood Cliffs, New Jersey: Prentice Hall.

O'Keefe, D. (1990). *Persuasion: theory and practice*. Newbury Park, Calfornia: Sage Publications, Inc.

O'Neill, T. (1989). *The game behind the game: high stakes, high pressure in television sports*. New York: Harper & Row Publishers, Inc.

Rader, B. (1984). *In its own image: how television has transformed sports*. New York: Free Press.

Rein, I., Kotler, P., and Stoller, M. (1987). *High visibility*. New York: Dodd, Mead & Co., Inc.

Richards, I. (1988). *How to give a successful presentation: a concise guide for every manager*. Boston: Graham & Trotman.

Robbins, L. (1985). *The business of writing and speaking*. New York: McGraw-Hill Book Co.

Schlosberg, J. (1987). Who watches television sports? *American Demographics 9*(2): 45-49, 59.

Spence, J., and Diles, D. (1988). *Up close & personal: the inside story of network television sports*. New York: Atheneum Publishers.

Strunk, W., and White, E. (1984). *The elements of style* (3rd Edition). New York: Macmillan Publishing Co.

32 regional sports networks span U.S. (1989). *Cable/Television Sports* (October 13) 7(21):1,7-8.

Watkins, B., and Brand J. (1990). Sports programming on pay television and cable: a history and prognosis. Unpublished manuscript, Department of Sports Management and Communication, The University of Michigan.

Wong, G. (1988). *Essentials of amateur sports law*. Dover, Massachusetts: Auburn House Publishing Co.

Yacenda, J. (1990). Staffing youth exercise. *Fitness Management* 6(2):31-33.

Zinsser, W. (1983). *Writing with a word processor*. New York: Harper & Row Publishers, Inc.

Zinsser, W. (1985). *On writing well* (3rd Edition). New York: Harper & Row Publishers, Inc.

CHAPTER 17

Personnel Issues

Jed Friend

In this chapter, you will become familiar with the following terms:

Personnel	Affirmative action
Systems approach	Screening
Job analysis	Selection
Job descriptions	Interview
Job specifications	Placement
Personnel inventories	Training
Needs assessment	Feedback
Management information system	Performance appraisal
Strategic planning	Rating errors
Recruiting	

Overview

Sport organizations and their administrators are constantly challenged to choose a human resources alternative from several options. Each decision incurs a cost to the organization. Therefore sport administrators need a set of policies or rules, or in short, a system of ideas that will enable them to reduce this expense effectively.

Organizations are said to be open systems, that is, they have inputs, throughputs, and outputs. The elements in a personnel system—which should include job analysis, needs assessment, management information systems, strategic planning, selection, training, and performance appraisal—can have a tremendous effect on the sport administrator. This effect, in the form of a cost to the franchise, federation, club, or institution, can be estimated and implemented into the organization. When this is done, the sport administrator can more carefully evaluate his or her options.

The idea of **personnel** management for sport administrators is not new. Yet, the processes for executing this overall function are not consistent among sport organizations, and consistent procedures seem to have remained somewhat elusive. More often than not, personnel issues have been buried or absent in sport management or athletic administrative textbooks, curricula, and perhaps even worksites. The fact that an applied personnel chapter is included in this text as a separate management discipline departs from convention and is a sign of a broad-minded approach to sport administration. The purpose of this chapter is to provide an overview of personnel functions and their role in sport, whether professional, Olympic, collegiate, or amateur. In no way is this intended to be a comprehensive report of personnel policies or activities. Before discussing what personnel is, a glance of why it is important, in relation to other areas of management, is in order.

Personnel is critical to every area of sport administration. The reason is quite clear. The one common thread in all phases of sport management is people, regardless of whether one is employed in marketing, public relations, sales, advertising, communications, finance, facility operations, concessions, or any other area. An organization cannot operate without people. Having the right person on the job is imperative for increasing productivity, improving morale, and ensuring job satisfaction. The institution must limit absenteeism and turnover and simultaneously give the employee an opportunity to earn satisfaction, and not just a paycheck! Organizations will waste countless thousands of dollars if they must continually replace employees. These are the fundamental reasons for having a strong human resources division. An organization simply cannot afford to waste money through an inefficient personnel program. Take a quick look at why this is true from two perspectives.

When an individual investigates a job, he or she might become overwhelmed by the variety of duties in the job and the variety of ways the employee might perform the duties. For instance, this person may know that the assistant director of a health club plays many roles, such as responsibility for sales, public relations, membership services, facility topics, finance, and more. Following the rule of matching the person to the job, the human resources department must identify an individual with the correct attitudes, values, motivation, interests, and abilities to handle the many requirements of the job.

Moreover, people differ in how they perform their jobs. Some are simply more proficient than others. This is due to differences in skills, abilities, motivation, satisfaction with the job, personality, and other factors. Consequently the organization invests time and money in people, through the recruiting, hiring, and training processes. The return on this investment should be an employee who performs well in all aspects of his or her job and is motivated and satisfied with the job.

Obviously, organizations have many economic concerns. The National Basketball Association Players Association (NBAPA) has a contract that pays them 53% of the revenue that the individual franchises generate (Steve Patterson, general manager, Houston Rockets, personal communication, 1990). In short, the NBA is very labor intensive. The Major League Baseball Players Association (MLBPA) is paid 48% of the revenue generated by the baseball clubs. In other words, a large part of the owners' revenue is paid out as compensation for work. These costs are a strong economic incentive for effective human resources in sport.

Achieving results from human resource efforts is much more difficult when negotiating with a union; however, organizations have tremendous opportunities for employing human resource activities with such persons as athletes. The same applies for all other sport and fitness organizations. Errors in the scouting and player development systems cost thousands, if not millions, of dollars when a player does not produce. Likewise, a health club that must hire a new director of operations every year wastes several thousand dollars.

Other economic costs are incurred when a front office employee or another employee quits and is later hired by another organization, especially one that competes with the first organization. At the collegiate level, a head coach may resign and take a position as head coach and athletic director with another school in the same conference. Occasionally, the two universities are archrivals. Additionally, if the organization declines to hire or draft an athlete or front office worker, and that individual eventually becomes successful, then that organization suffers an indirect cost for failing to hire that individual.

Consequently, organizations suffer noticeable

economic loss when they have a poor or nonexistent personnel policy. Now that the importance of personnel management has been delineated, specific personnel activities will be discussed.

DEFINITION

Personnel can be considered the procedures in an organization that focus on the identification, recruitment, screening, selection, training, and evaluation of its employees. As one baseball team owner so eloquently said, it is "the hiring and firing of people." Obviously, it is much more than this. Sport executives frequently seem to underestimate the money their institutions lose because of employee behaviors such as absenteeism, turnover, and low productivity and motivation, which were mentioned previously. In addition, sport administrators may not see the savings in an efficient personnel program. Such a program can save money by lowering payroll costs, reducing staff, and increasing employee production. Clearly, the success of an organization depends on the production of its people. By increasing the probability of having the right person on the job, management can properly address morale, output, and employee performance. This is the objective of a well-planned personnel management program.

HUMAN RESOURCES

The term *human resources* has recently evolved. Most people use the terms *personnel* and *human resources* interchangeably. Although this has become accepted, there really are vast differences between them. The label of human resources includes personnel, but covers much more than personnel activities. For instance, the issues of motivation, leadership, organizational structure, communication, and group dynamics all fall under the category of human resources. Certainly these issues play an important role in the prosperity of the organization, yet they do not fall under the responsibilities of personnel as previously described.

In some companies, personnel is structured as a single department, with training or training and development as another. The newer trend is to combine these two divisions and create a human resources department. Within sport, the issue is much simpler. Many sport agencies, franchises, or companies are so small that separate divisions are not necessary. Moreover, the personnel duties re-

quire the sport manager to be a generalist in the sense that the sport manager must be able to handle other administrative tasks. With this perspective in mind, the personnel process as a complete system will now be described.

THE SYSTEMS APPROACH

What is a system or a **systems approach?** How does it relate to staffing an organization? For us to understand the systems approach, the term must be defined by an explanation of what a system is and how the system works. When working with a system, the sport administrator should learn how the elements are arranged and how they fit and work together. There are many definitions of a system, yet the common factor is that the system must consist of a collection of interrelated parts with the one purpose of achieving a specific goal or objective (Kroenke, 1989).

In this instance, the purpose of the systems approach is to aid the sport executive in the personnel decision-making and problem-solving process. The procedure is designed to compile information on all the factors that may affect the decision. Sport executives and administrators, for the most part, have ignored or been unaware of personnel advances using the systems approach.

The box below delineates a systems approach for personnel management in sport organizations. The system is composed of different subsystems

---

Components of a systems approach for sport organizations

1. Job analysis, including job descriptions, specifications, and personnel inventories
2. Needs assessment
3. Management information systems (MIS)
4. Strategic planning
5. Selection
   A. Recruitment
   B. Affirmative action
   C. Screening
   D. Decisions
   E. Interviews
   F. Placement
6. Training through the systems approach
7. Performance appraisal

that play roles in the entire personnel function. These seven areas are the core components for a sport organization and represent a systems approach that can be used in identifying, describing, analyzing, measuring, and evaluating performance. The systems approach discussed in this chapter and shown in the box is only a template. An administrator may wish to include or exclude some components for his or her specific application. Next each component in this model along with its subsystems will be examined.

CONCEPT CHECK

Personnel management, sometimes called human resources, is the acquisition, "training," and evaluation of employees. Sport institution employees include front office employees and athletes. Individuals differ in their performance and how they meet the many requirements of the job. It makes economic sense to implement personnel policies. The systems approach to personnel consists of a set of interrelated parts that must work together to produce a positive result.

Job analysis

Job analysis, as used in personnel management, is defined by Cascio (1987) as obtaining all relevant information about jobs. From this analysis, **job descriptions** and **job specifications** are written, and **personnel inventories** are created. Job analysis consists of identifying and describing the knowledge, abilities, skills, and behaviors required of the individual. Using job analysis enables management to integrate different employees with different roles so they can work together. As the first component in the system, job analysis is a data-gathering step. It is also considered an input into the system.

Job analysis has a wide range of uses. In fact, the information obtained can and should be used for all personnel decisions. The type of analysis used (there are several) depends on the needs of the organization. Regardless of the type used, job analysis is a vital part of a solid personnel policy.

In actual practice, Libkuman, Love, and Donn (1989) have used job analysis as a tool for building a computer model for predicting quarterback success. The Houston Astros baseball club used job analysis data to select a new director of commu-

nications for its marketing division. YMCAs across the country also use job analysis, as do U.S. Swim and Fitness health clubs. Obviously formal job analysis has been used in sport, and its use is growing.

Job analysis yields several advantages. First, it separates the organization or department into smaller elements, giving management a micro view of the behavioral components of the organization. By splitting the institution into its finer components, the components become much easier to manage. Second, job analysis enables the manager to identify the behaviors and skills needed to perform specific activities. The tasks that the individual must accomplish and the abilities that the individual must possess become clear. Third, position analysis can be used as the point of departure for prediction of employee or athlete success, as well as for selection, placement, and training purposes. Fourth, the analysis can enable management to evaluate an employee's pay. Finally, job analysis helps in performance appraisal. For instance, by describing the specific behaviors or duties required to perform the job of sports information director, management can tailor a detailed performance appraisal system, yielding a more reliable measure for this position. In contrast, a generic performance appraisal system for the athletic department or company may not provide enough details for a difficult decision. As previously discussed, job analysis is the cornerstone of the systems approach and should be the basis for any sport personnel decision.

Job descriptions, specifications, and personnel inventories. A job description contains information about the tasks that must be performed to accomplish the job. For instance, suppose a health club has a vacancy for a fitness manager. The job description covers the position's duties (see the box on p. 296). It may include such things as the job title, working conditions, and even conditions of employment, that is, the salary, fringe benefits, and so on (Cascio, 1987).

Job specifications are the individual attributes that are needed to perform the job. Education, special training, or experiences are outlined. For the position of director of promotions within a marketing department, the individual may need a degree in sport management and an internship experience in marketing or sales.

A typical job description for use in a health club position

Position title: Program director
Reports to: Fitness Director
Responsible for: 1. Testing and assessing current fitness levels of members
                         2. Designing a specific exercise program for members based on fitness assessments
                         3. Scheduling first workouts for members
                         4. Supervising members and guests while in weight room and cardiovascular
                            equipment room for safety and accuracy of movement
                         5. Enforcing club rules and regulations
                         6. Cleaning weight room and cardiovascular equipment room
                         7. Assisting with club special events and promotions
                         8. Other special duties, as needed
Qualifications: Previous experience in a gymnasium weight room or health club atmosphere
Compensation: $6 to $8 per hour, depending on experience
Benefits: Free use of club during off hours
Hours: To be arranged (TBA)

Personnel inventories are reports of an individual employee's talents. It lists all the employee's previous experiences and education that might be useful in either the current job or a future position. For example, if a swimming coach also has had experience as a track coach, this information is listed in an inventory. Therefore, if a new job were created, the administrator would have a source of information or an individual with whom to consult, or perhaps even a candidate for the position. Consequently personnel inventories can help management when predicting personnel requirements.

Needs assessment

Needs assessment is a method of diagnosing the organization, in much the same way a dentist conducts a check-up. In actual practice, needs assessment is seen as a way of evaluating the organization with respect to human resources. It helps determine the elements in the network that either weaken or encourage attempts to achieve the goals of the institution. In addition, needs assessment is also a goal-setting procedure used in managing the direction of the organization, or in this instance, the personnel department. It is the second component in the systems approach, and it is an input into the system.

Needs assessment must be considered closely related to the planning of the systems approach

that was previously discussed. Moreover, for an institution to benefit from the systems approach, personnel needs must be estimated. The needs assessment is one way an organization's or department's needs can, in essence, be measured.

An organization must set specific goals to integrate the entire personnel department or portions of the personnel policy. Goals should be planned and written for specific portions of the personnel program, such as player development. For example, suppose the front-office employees of the local sports foundation have low morale. A needs assessment could help the foundation learn whether employees had conflicts of interest, unsatisfactory job duties, or personality differences. Such an evaluation could help determine whether foundation employees should be relocated, retrained, or released from the organization. When used this way, the needs assessment also becomes valuable documentation for the personnel department to support the decision made about an employee. Indeed, the needs assessment has the potential to be an effective tool in sport—not only in human resources, but in many other ways.

Conducting a needs assessment. Sport administrators have two basic methods of conducting a useful needs assessment. First, the administrator can seek out knowledgeable people (either inside or outside the organization) and interview them about important issues. These experts can be an excellent source of information about the organization's operations or the service it provides. For example, one might seek out the advice of an organization's general manager or executive director, either past or present, or someone who holds a similar position. His or her expertise may be an excellent resource. Another useful technique may be to learn what similar organizations have done.

Second, and the more popular method, is to survey the appropriate population. Conceiving, designing, conducting, and evaluating a survey is an intricate process. Yet the feedback of the respondents may be a guideline for change.

CONCEPT CHECK

Job analysis, the process of gathering all information relevant to a job, is the first step in making any personnel management decision. The job analysis produces job descriptions and specifications, and enables management to create personnel inventories. The needs assessment is an organizational tool that helps identify areas of strength and weakness. It helps management evaluate current operations and set goals. These two elements, job analysis and needs assessment, are the first two elements in the systems approach. They are the inputs of the systems approach.

Management information systems (MIS)

A **management information system** is an organized method of gathering information on past, present, and future internal operations and external conditions (Kroenke, 1989). It helps management plan, control, and operate the organization by producing uniform information on a proper schedule. Most large management information systems are kept on a computer system. The MIS, which is the third element in the systems approach, begins the *throughput* process. Throughput is the action; that is, the information has been gathered and will now be manipulated, such as being pared down to a more useful or meaningful set of data or information. After the basic data has been gathered, MIS serves as a vehicle for the system, holding and delivering the information on demand.

Most sport organizations have some sort of MIS. An MIS can be as simple as an index card with basic statistics on it that is kept in a file cabinet, or

it can be a complete and detailed record of performance kept on a large computer (called a mainframe). If kept on a computer, the data must be managed; this is called data-base management.

Data bases and the entire MIS are useful in making personnel decisions. How the administrator uses the MIS for problem solving and decision making is key. MIS has two essential personnel applications that sport managers should consider. First, the MIS is an assessment device. Since the system should contain quantified employee performance measures, it enables management to compare, analyze, and evaluate performance. Second, the numerical data that the MIS contains can help management devise recruitment or training changes during employee evaluations or decision making. More uses for computers for sport administrators are discussed in Chapter 20, Computer Applications.

Strategic planning

Strategic planning in the systems approach is a procedure for predicting an organization's personnel needs. It is the long-term planning for an organization. Strategic planning is used to eliminate any uncertainty about the future personnel needs of the organization (Cascio, 1987). Both needs assessments and personnel inventories play a part in strategic planning. This component of the system also is considered a throughput, because it involves the processing of data to aid in decision making.

The heart and soul of a strategic planning system is the management information system (MIS) discussed previously. The data from the MIS enables management to make predictions. To predict needs and to aid recruitment, the MIS must furnish enough data to enable the sport executive to create personnel inventories of employees. The personnel inventory is derived from the job analysis, needs evaluation, goals and objectives of the organization, performance appraisal, and other information about the employee and the program.

Managers sometimes use a needs forecasting model to predict personnel requirements. There are several different models for predicting needs. The most popular procedure is the collective opinion, which is a consensus judgment made by a group of experts. For instance, when a professional baseball team decides to draft an athlete, the scouting director, scouts, and sometimes the director of player development and/or general manager discuss the athlete's potential and then make a group decision on not only whether to draft the athlete, but also on the individual's value to baseball and the franchise. In short, this group of experts puts a dollar value on the athlete. In effect, the team is conducting strategic planning, although the validity of the process in this example remains questionable by today's standards (Friend and LeUnes, 1990). In addition, one could argue that the collective opinion process used in strategic planning is in fact, a performance appraisal. That idea will be explored later.

Strategic planning typically is conducted at the highest levels of management. Strategic planning is not performed by one person, but by groups. The groups could contain any number of people. For example, in a professional franchise, the president, chief executive officer (CEO), chief operating officer (COO), and senior vice-presidents or vice presidents meet to discuss long-term objectives. Given the different structures of franchises, one person could hold several titles. In amateur and Olympic sport, a board of directors establishes policy and an executive director implements those plans. The executive director is comparable to the COO or CEO in a franchise. In other organizations, such as health clubs or private gymnasiums, an athletic director or other high-level administrator may establish goals and implement them. Finally, collegiate conferences have a commissioner who acts as the chief administrative officer.

So far, the factors in the systems approach that lead to decision making have been explored. The single most important step in the procedure is the actual decision to select an employee. Without a doubt, selection is one of the most difficult aspects of human resources.

Selection

The selection process is the nucleus of the systems approach; all other components are designed to ease the procedure. The idea of selection resembles the throughput process of the system in that it takes the inputs and begins to initiate actions regarding the collected information. The selection process is made up of four basic procedures, not all of which must be used by the sport manager. These four sub-elements, recruiting (including affirmative action), screening, selection, and placement, are each explored in detail.

Recruiting. The objective of **recruiting** is to create a pool of candidates who are able to perform the job. The reason is to create competition for a position, which usually produces a group of finalists who are the best people for the job. There are many ways to recruit for jobs. To illustrate, suppose a high school needs to hire a volleyball coach. The school would advertise in appropriate media, such as the *NCAA News* or coaching magazines. Employment agencies or executive search firms could be used. Another technique is to mail job announcements to prospective candidates or their institutions, through the alumni office or career placement office, or directly to the program's director. A third way is to recruit at professional conferences, conventions (which often have job placement services), and seminars. This may need to be done at both the regional and national level. Finally, one may advertise a position vacancy by networking (through word of mouth). Having contacts with one's colleagues at other organizations is imperative. Employee, coach, or athlete referrals may also help.

During the recruiting process, job applications are gathered by mail or in person. Other information about the candidate is often obtained through a résumé or vita, physical examination, recommendations, or perhaps even a quick interview via telephone or in person. In some cases, candidates are asked to take some sort of psychological test. Regardless of which of these sources are used, the same objective is served, which is to paint a more accurate or complete picture of the potential candidate.

Clearly, the recruitment process must be managed in some way. Cascio (1987) outlines four essential records that must be maintained in recruitment operations. First, all applications, résumés, and such must be kept at a central location. Presumably, these records would be at the disposal of the individual who makes the decision or those who play a part in the process. Second, and also to be recorded at this central office, is the decision about the candidate. Such facts as whether a candidate is invited in for an interview and whether that person is offered or accepts a position also are recorded at this central office. Third, all related correspondence should be added to the individual's file. Fourth, records of individuals no longer considered for the position should be retained for a reasonable amount of time.

Affirmative action. During the recruiting process, **affirmative action** issues must be considered. The Equal Employment Opportunity Commission (EEOC) defines affirmative action as actions designed to reduce past or future effects of obstacles that stifle equal employment opportunity (EEOC, 1979). The purpose is to establish an atmosphere of equal employment opportunity. An in-depth review of affirmative action for sport executives has been presented by Friend and LeUnes (1989). However, because of its importance, several points will be noted here. Affirmative action is a policy of fair decision making in selection decisions.

From a group of individuals, the best person is chosen, regardless of race, color, country of natural origin, sex, or religious beliefs. Affirmative action policies are useful only during the selection process. Furthermore, the type of affirmative action policy to be followed is an organizational issue.

Affirmative action goals may include any or all of the following ideals. First, the organization should try to recruit individuals from groups that are not fairly represented by the organization's workforce. For example, if a health club has a staff of 15 but no women among its workers, then it should try to recruit women. Second, discriminatory attitudes among top management must be exposed. Intentional and unintentional bias of executives and managers should be reduced, if not eradicated, so that unfairly represented groups have a fair chance for employment. Third, management must establish fair practices that eliminate bias in employee selection, training, and appraisal. Fourth, underrepresented groups can be given preferential treatment.

Finally, affirmative action has been strongly encouraged by the legal system for all institutions, in and out of sport. Without question, there have been gross violations of these policies, especially at the professional level of sport. Indeed, Friend and LeUnes (1989) strike directly at the problem. They conclude that, as in other industries, only the legal system will correct the outright denial of management opportunities to minorities and women.

The next step is to begin screening applicants to determine who will become a candidate for the position.

Screening. The **screening** process begins the moment an individual submits an application for the job. The purpose of screening is to reduce the pool of applicants to a short list of several plausible candidates ranked according to the collected information. All the individuals on a short list may be invited to interviews; however, if the short list has five or more names, then usually the first three are called. This depends on the time, effort, and expense that the process incurs to both the manager and the institution. The goal is to offer the job to the top candidate, and, if the candidate accepts, to negotiate a fair compensation package. If the top candidate is not interested or an agreement cannot be arranged, the job is offered to the second candidate.

Typically, an administrator reviews a candidate's application and immediately decides whether the individual is a legitimate contender for the position. Several sources provide information that helps determine whether the individual can compete with other applicants. One such source is the personal reference or recommendation. A reference or recommendation typically gives information about the applicant's employment and educational background, human or interpersonal skills, and ability to perform the job. The most critical factor in the reference is whether the individual giving it has observed the applicant in a position similar to the one for which the candidate is being considered.

Another important piece of information used in the screening process is the reference check. Agencies are available to investigate an applicant's background. These checks usually produce a summary of the applicant's driving record, criminal activity (if any), bankruptcy record, court proceedings, and other history. The applicant also can report his or her employment. Biographical information sheets or weighted application forms actually can assign a numerical value to items such as values, attitudes, interests, and opinions. From this data, applicants are screened according to a predetermined numerical criterion. For occupations in which money is handled, polygraph tests are used. These are physiological recordings used in attempts to determine one's honesty. Their validity remains in dispute at this time, since there is data both supporting and refuting the validity of these devices. Drug testing has become a frequent tool for exposing the use of illegal, banned, or restricted substances. Urinalysis is the most common test, and it is administered with the physical if the position requires one. The purpose is either to ensure the safety of employees on jobs that may be hazardous (such as operating field maintenance equipment) or to ensure fair competition among athletes. The validity of drug screening has increased recently.

Most administrators should have a list, produced from the job analysis, of the minimum qualifications needed to perform the job adequately. A quick review of the basic job application and other information may enable the administrator to decide the applicant's status. For more detailed or higher-level positions, the applicant may need a minimum score on a number of the previously mentioned indices before he or she can be interviewed. Moreover, a search committee or headhunting firm may be used.

Decisions. After the candidates for a position have been screened, the administrator must decide whom to hire. Countless articles have been written on selection and decision strategies, and many of these are overbearing. Sometimes an administrator has an easy choice, at other times, he or she faces a very difficult decision. There are decision strategies that sport administrators can use that are based on factors such as level of decision difficulty, amount of information collected on candidates, the cost to the organization of inadvertently hiring an unproductive or incompetent employee, the number of individuals needed, and the size of the organization.

Friend (1991) analyzes a variety of **selection** tactics for sport executives, and explores the field of human resources in sport. It is well beyond the scope of this chapter to discuss these detailed selection tactics (because of their statistical and psychometrical complexity); however, a brief description of these procedures is in order. The reader should remember two points. First, selecting managers differs substantially from selecting nonmanagers, because it is difficult to define exactly what managers do and therefore difficult to predict those activities. Second, as previously discussed, the selection process consists of collecting and measuring applicant qualifications that may affect job performance and using this information to make the best possible decision. Few sport organizations understand this concept or have advanced selection strategies. Some of these misunderstandings are explained on pp. 301-303, where reasons that some of the following selection devices are not used are also explored. For the purpose of this discussion, a starting point will be the selection ideas for non-

managers, which consist of classical validity and decision models.

Classical validity models include procedures known as multiple regression, the multiple cutoff technique, and the multiple hurdle process. Briefly, the multiple regression (MR) model posits that predictors (past evaluations, test scores, interview information) can be weighted by giving each of them a numerical value. That value then contributes to the overall effort to achieve a minimum cutoff score. The MR model has only a minimum total cutoff score, and it makes no difference if the candidate does poorly on one measure and outstandingly on another, as long as that minimum score is met. This is called a compensatory system, since a candidate can compensate for a poor score by doing well in other categories used in the selection process.

For example, suppose a hockey franchise wants to draft a goalie. The general manager (GM) decides to look at (1) performance in college, (2) his (the GM's) coach's recommendation, and (3) a motivation inventory. All three measures must be on the same scale. Let's say that performance in the first criterion above is rated on a scale of one to seven with one being very poor and seven the best goalie that the scouting director has ever seen play the game. The coach's recommendation also needs to be a number on this one to seven scale, as does the motivation measure. Given this scenario, the candidate can score a maximum of 21. Combining all three predictors, the GM decides that a minimum score of 16 must be met to be drafted. The goalie in question must meet or exceed that score. It makes no difference whether the hockey player scores low on the coach's recommendation; as long as he reaches the minimum cutoff score of 16 when the three instruments are added, he will be drafted.

The multiple cutoff approach (MC), however, does not allow one to do poorly on a measure. The candidate not only must meet a minimum total cutoff score when the three values are added, but also has to meet a minimum cutoff score for each predictor. This is a noncompensatory system. Continuing with the above example, the athlete not only must achieve a total score of 16, he must, for instance, achieve a minimum score of five on each of the indices.

Finally, the multiple hurdle (MH) is a sequentially based model in which a minimum must be met on a number of predictors, but failure to achieve a minimum score on a predictor does not necessarily eliminate the candidate. Generally, it means that one may be accepted on a provisional basis or be given a temporary job so his or her performance may be observed.

To wrap up the above example, suppose the individual predictor minimums are met, but the total score is only 15, instead of the required 16. The individual might be drafted and placed in the minor league system or invited to try out for the team. He then would be evaluated further after officials get a chance to see him perform against other members of the team. All three of these models, although applicable to business, are not widely used in sport.

Next we will consider decision models. The decision models are complex, as are the previously discussed classical validity models. The decision models include the Taylor-Russell (1939) approach, the Naylor-Shine (1965) strategy, and the Brogden-Cronbach-Gleser equation (Brogden, 1949; Brogden and Taylor, 1950; Cronbach and Gleser, 1965). The best to use depends on the context. These models assume that the job and previous selection data have been validated. That is, the minimum criteria to qualify for the job have been determined. In brief, the Taylor-Russell model is a table that categorizes candidates as either successful or unsuccessful, based on past performance. There is equal work performance by all candidates.

The Naylor-Shine table assumes that as job performance increases, so does the probability of being selected, based on doing a better job. In other words, the utility of the table is measured. This explains how the table increases the probability of a correct selection.

Last, the Brogden-Cronbach-Gleser model incorporates the same data as the Naylor-Shine, but goes two steps further by looking at the job criteria in a dollar amount, and by attaching a dollar figure to the selection process. Again, these models probably have no use for a sport organization at this time. As do the classical validity techniques, these decision models require one to have training in specialized fields, such as personnel management, psychometrics, or applied psychology.

In addition, the concepts and applications that these models represent have not been accepted by sport administrators for several reasons. First, the field of sport administration has not inspected all the components of the discipline, much less those of conventional personnel management. Second, personnel management is not a core topic in sport management programs. Third, the sophistication of these models is beyond the undergraduate level where a significant number of sport management programs are offered. Fourth, many sport executives have little or no training in either sport administration or personnel management and have not been exposed to these tactics. Their training is solely from the job experience or other partially related fields.

Fifth, since these models are fairly complex, a special type of management expert is required to use them. Consequently it may be some time before these strategies can be used in sport. Finally, these models are for larger organizations that employ hundreds of people with similar jobs. Such is not always the case with sport institutions. However, marketing departments in professional baseball continue to grow to a large size (Bernie Mullin, former senior vice-president, Pittsburgh Pirates, personal communication, 1989). In addition, several national governing bodies (the organizations that oversee a sport) and the United States Olympic Committee (USOC) have many employees. One of these models may become usable in the near future in such settings.

Managerial and executive selection. The hiring of managers, administrators, or executives deserves separate mention because of its idiosyncrasies. Various tools, as well as past performance indicators, can be used to help predict how a candidate will perform.

Instruments provide clues about a candidate's managerial ability. First, cognitive measures can be used to determine intellectual and perceptual ability and other psychological knowledge; data from leadership questionnaires can help, but only if the criteria for performing the job is known. The criteria are derived from the job analysis, descriptions, and specifications mentioned previously.

Second, potential managers can be requested to give a sample of their work. This is done with what is called an in-basket process. Most executives have an in-basket and an out-basket on their desks. Issues needing attention are put into the in-basket, and the candidate is observed. Tasks given to the candidate should accurately reflect duties of the job. Third, peer assessment can be used. If the candidate has previously worked in the department or within the company, the candidate's peer group often can predict how that person will perform as an administrator.

Fourth is the leaderless group technique. Candidates are placed in a small group of four to six people and are given a problem to solve or are asked to hold a discussion. Nobody in the group is appointed to be a group spokesperson. After resolving the conflict, the group must be represented by one member. Raters observe the groups to learn who emerges as a leader and then evaluate that person based on predetermined criteria. Fifth are business games. These are actual live scenarios requiring candidates to think on their feet. There is little or no time for deep thought on how to resolve an issue.

Last is a technique called assessment centers. Assessment centers can include any or all of the techniques mentioned previously. They can last for several days, have several observers evaluating candidates' performance, and are in-depth. The purpose is to look closely at an individual. Usually, but not always, assessment centers are used for upper-level executive positions. In addition, they are expensive to operate, and are used for evaluating large numbers of people.

Clearly these selection procedures are different from those used for nonmanagement positions. The one selection device that remains controversial but is the most often used is the interview. It is often used for both managerial and nonmanagerial positions.

Interviews. Most individuals have had face-to-face **interviews** for employment or for other reasons. Interviews are widely used on personnel for screening, selection, and placement. They are used most frequently in the selection process, primarily because organizations are reluctant to hire individuals they have not met. Since interviews are tests, they must meet the same criteria for validity and reliability as the paper and pencil instruments that an organization might use. The Equal Employment Opportunity Commission subjects interviews to the same scrutiny as other tests.

Stewart and Cash (1988) strongly urge the use of structured interviews. This position has been supported by Schraibman (1989) for cases in which

coaches and other sport officials are hired. Structured interviews are designed with a set of questions so that all candidates are asked for the same information. In contrast, unstructured interviews have no template and tend to wander. When this happens, often the candidate does not have the opportunity to disclose important information. Or, the interviewer may make a decision quickly, before the individual has the chance to reveal more data. The same information must be gathered from all candidates when an employment decision is made. The only consistent information obtained with the unstructured approach is background data. Clearly, the structured approach is superior.

Stewart and Cash (1988) suggest that information should be uncovered in eight areas when conducting the selection interview. Questions should cover the following topics: (1) interest in the organization, (2) general work attitude and knowledge, (3) specific work attitude and knowledge, (4) education and training, (5) career plans, (6) job performance, (7) salary and benefits, and (8) career field ideas.

Candidates should be evaluated immediately after the interview. Interviews and interviewer evaluation sheets must be job related and should be based on information from job descriptions, specifications, and realistic expectations for employees. Some organizations have standardized interviewer forms, which would give structure to the interview. Regardless, the evaluation usually asks how the candidate performed against other candidates and his or her strengths and weaknesses.

The single most important step in a selection interview is preparing. As previously mentioned, the interview needs structure, not only in the questions to be asked, but also in any meetings or presentations that may be required of the candidate. In short, there should be an itinerary or agenda for all candidates. Moreover, the person or people (group interviews) conducting the interviews should have the authority either to make an offer or to make a recommendation to the appropriate authority. Once the decision to hire an individual has been made, and that person has agreed to take the position, the organization may need to consider the **placement** of the individual within the organization.

Placement. Large companies frequently hire generically. They need several employees in a division, but the jobs vary within the division. Matching individuals to jobs within a department can be somewhat tricky. The notion of considering placement a formal component of selection has recently been explored. The purpose simply is to try to put an employee in a job that he or she desires, if there is more than one job and the jobs are similar. For example, suppose a sporting goods retail store needed both retail and commercial salespeople. Inserting a newly hired employee into a commercial market without experience or knowledge may not be wise. Furthermore, the employee should have some say in the job chosen for him or her. The key to successful job placement seems to be the flexibility of the institution and the individual. Only when both are flexible can an agreement be reached. Once these issues have been resolved, the organization moves to the next major component in the system, training the employee.

CONCEPT CHECK

The management information system (MIS) is generally a computer system that provides numerical information on personnel to the administrator. Strategic planning, conducted by top management, is the long-range planning of the organization. It depends heavily on the MIS. The selection process consists of recruiting, affirmative action, screening, the selection decision, and placement within the institution. Organizations with many employees can use the classical validity models or the decision models, whichever are more appropriate. Using these devices requires a qualified individual. There also are several methods for selection of managerial or executive positions. The interview is the most commonly used selection tool. These elements, the MIS, strategic planning, and selection are the throughputs of the systems approach.

Training

Personnel, organizational, and other management consultants are often employed in the design, implementation, and evaluation of **training** programs for almost every nonsport industry. In sport, coaches or administrators seem to be entirely responsible or completely knowledgeable about all of training. It would be presumptuous to think that this is true all the time. Player development and training programs can be very complex. To expect a person or a couple of coaches to know everything is unreasonable. Yet sport organizations continue to think along these lines. The training of employees, the sixth element in the systems approach, is the final phase of the throughput process.

There are four basic types of training: (1) orientation training, (2) preliminary training, (3) specialty training, and (4) upgrade training. These usually are independent groups, but are not necessarily mutually exclusive. In fact, an overall upgrade training system may include one or more of the other types. Orientation training is exactly what the name implies. It consists of teaching the newly arrived employee the rules, policies, and structure of the organization. The employee learns, for example, the managerial hierarchy and location of coaching or other administrative offices and the role the employee will be expected to fulfill.

Preliminary training is a prerequisite to more in-depth types of training. Specialized training programs are specially constructed for certain groups. An example might be a seminar for athletic directors that focuses on contract negotiations. Another example would be a special lecture or presentation on nutrition for directors of corporate wellness programs. Once the employees complete these initial training programs, they can go on to more in-depth types of training.

Finally, upgrade or improvement training is the prototypical form of training that is associated with the learning process.

A training plan cannot operate effectively in a vacuum, however. The training phase must be orchestrated with the other aspects of the personnel process, such as recruiting. Consequently, training is a crucial subsystem of the overall systems approach to sport.

Systems approach to training. The idea of establishing an overall training program as a subsystem of the systems approach has sparked interest among sport scientists (Gould and Landers, 1986). Goldstein (1986) says that a successful training program requires (1) planning, (2) implementation, and (3) evaluation. This philosophy and technique transform training into a smaller subsystem of the systems approach, which has three elements in common with the overall system. Figure 17-1 is a training flowchart by Goldstein (1986) that has been altered to represent a systematic approach to training sports personnel. When an or-

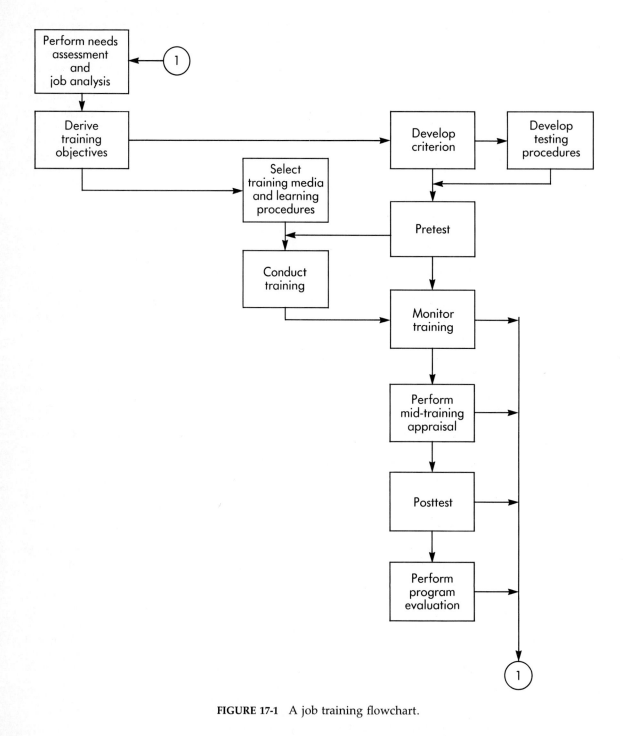

FIGURE 17-1   A job training flowchart.

ganization establishes a training program, the larger systems approach is applied, albeit on a smaller scale. First, the organization analyzes its training systems. This includes data from a job analysis, needs assessment, and any other source of information that proves useful (Friend and LeUnes, 1987). This analysis is specifically conducted to determine instructional needs. In addition, the organization should determine whether attitude or behavioral modification training is needed, since changes in attitude do not reflect changes in behavior. Second, training objectives must be identified and defined. Training objectives are the behavioral goals for observable and measurable actions and skills (Cascio, 1987). Third, training objectives and tests are firmly established.

Fourth is the development and implementation of training plans. Fifth, participants must be tested to establish their degree of learning, if any. Testing the program participants or graduates is often neglected. This type of feedback is critical because it gives the instructor or coach information about course difficulty, course format (such as whether visual aids are needed), and the employees' learning and retention abilities. Sixth, the instructors and the athlete development system are evaluated and appraised, respectively.

Feedback or knowledge of results is critical to the learning process and should be built into the system. The employee or athlete should be told why he or she made a mistake and how the procedure should be performed. Research shows that feedback, especially positive reinforcement, will increase performance (Cascio, 1987). The importance of the way feedback is given to the employee cannot be overemphasized. Unfortunately, administrators may overlook or may not know how the employee perceived the feedback.

One of the most effective methods of training (one often used by administrators) is to attend conferences and seminars in one's area of expertise. Seminars attract professionals from the same field who come together to share their experiences. Conventions are usually, if not exclusively, research oriented. Convention meetings and conferences are designed to encourage the sharing of information related to the area of expertise. Moreover, they provide opportunities to network for future employment and research projects. In essence, they enable professionals to become acquainted with other authorities in sport.

Three final points about training merit a mention. First, the instructor, coach, or manager should realize that individuals differ in their ability to learn. Some employees will require more patience to reach their full potential. Individualized training will give a higher success rate and is a method that should be used. Although it will not give all employees equal abilities, it will teach each employee how to do his or her job.

Second, when done properly, training should increase commitment and motivation. If the training is meaningful for the employee, then the employee will be intrinsically motivated. If the employee views the program as a means to an end, such as a higher salary or advancement in the company, then the employee will be extrinsically motivated.

Third, the employee should understand and see the logic of the program. The instructors should provide a thorough orientation and a set of ultimate objectives. Although no training program will be 100% successful, without doubt using some of the aforementioned elements can produce a more fertile environment for learning.

Performance appraisal

The evaluation of an individual's work behavior is called **performance appraisal**, evaluation, or review. From an administrator's perspective, these judgments are usually limited to the employee's performance, but they can include interpersonal skills and personality (Cascio, 1987). The appraisal can be used to evaluate potential; it can be a basis for other personnel decisions, such as promotion, transfer, or assignment to additional training; and it can be used to predict employee or athlete performance or to act as a measuring tool for personnel research and applications. Appraisal simply is the yardstick by which employees are judged.

The performance review is also a type of formal feedback that can help management set goals for training programs, organizational design, and assessment. A sport institution also can improve morale and stimulate performance, and employees can grow personally if the appraisal is performed in a positive manner (Friend and LeUnes, 1987). The evaluation should distinguish marginal performances and exceptional ones. Performance appraisal, the seventh ingredient of the systems approach, is the output stage.

Performance evaluation measures can be objec-

OUTFIELD SKILLS
(Please rate left, center, and right fielders only)

The outfielder should assume a semi-crouched ready position before each play. He should drift or sprint with the path of the fly ball into the outfield as appropriate to gain position to make the catch. The outfielder should sight the ball in the air and follow the ball into his glove before attempting to return the ball to the infield. When the ball is still in play, the outfielder should be able to complete the long, hard, accurate throw from his outfield position to any of the three bases or home plate.

Using this scale as a reference—

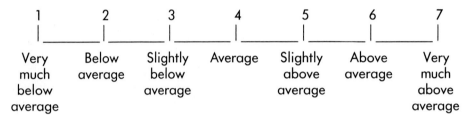

Complete the following statement for each player by indicating the number of the response that is most descriptive of that player.

Relative to other players that I have coached at this level, the <u>specific outfield skills</u> of this player are _____ .

FIGURE 17-2 A performance appraisal for an outfielder.

tive (such as number of runs batted in) or subjective (on a motivation scale of one to seven, this employee has a 6.4 rating). Figure 17-2 gives an example of a baseball player's (outfielder's) performance review. Although numerical scales are by definition objective, the ratings chosen are subject to an evaluator's arbitrary or subjective decision. Moreover, psychological constructs such as motivation or attitude are extremely difficult to measure, yet they play integral parts in the overall success and satisfaction of both the employee and the organization. Undoubtedly, subjective measures are more prone to error than objective criteria.

Subjective appraisal measures include absolute

methods, essay reports, behavioral checklists, and graphic rating scales. Absolute methods are processes in which the employee is compared to a predetermined criterion. The best understood example is the exam system so often used in higher education. To make an *A* in a class, a student must achieve a 90 score or above on an examination. If no student met or exceeded this score, then no student would make an *A* in the course.

Essay reports are reports written by the employee of what he or she has done over a specified time. They explain in detail what the employee has done to perform the job. Behavioral checklists are lists of all the behaviors that are required to perform the job. The evaluator checks off those that the employee exhibits, usually without regard to the frequency the employee exhibits the behavior. It is checked only if it has been observed.

Graphic rating scales (see Figure 17-2) are numerical values assigned to a sentence or phrase that describes how well (if at all) the employee performs the work behavior. Graphic rating scales are the most commonly used type of performance rating system.

Relative methods are ranking and paired comparison. Ranking is a method in which candidates are listed in the preferred order for a position. It is often used after other screening devices and selection procedures have been used. Paired comparison is the technique of comparing employees to one another. Usually they must have the same jobs, but occasionally their jobs are different but have similar duties that make a comparison of employees fair. Both subjective and objective methods are used quite frequently, and on occasion they are used together to provide a better "snapshot" of the employee's work performance.

Some specific types of performance rating systems are the critical incidents technique and organization-specific measures, such as the group evaluation or multiple group review. Critical incidents is a process in which the employee keeps a record of the job's incidents over a month or quarter. He or she records the highs and the lows of the job, that is, the most important components of the job, be they excellent or poor.

Group evaluations and multiple reviews have received mixed reports from organizations. Group reviews save time but give the employee little useful feedback. Multiple reviews, although time consuming, give the employee several types of feedback from the raters.

The purpose of the performance review and the individual who conducts it will affect the choice of the type to use. People commonly consider evaluations only as steps toward greater monetary rewards. This may be true, but the performance appraisal also can be used for research, or for determining who needs training or may be promoted or transferred.

The choice of the type of review system should be made collectively by management. The rater or evaluator may be a general manager, athletic director, coach, assistant coach, or other employee in the organization. Indeed, an appraisal from all the raters would give an overall estimate of how an employee, team, coach, or manager is performing; yet such an approach may not be practical. Furthermore, there are problems with the validity and reliability of the ratings when any type of subjective rating system is used.

Rating errors or bias can appear in the performance evaluation system. Coaches or managers may inadvertently commit halo, leniency, or severity errors, or any combination of these errors. Halo error occurs when a rater gives an employee a high or low rating on one dimension and therefore gives a similar rating on other unrelated dimensions. For example, if a basketball player dribbles the ball well, the rater may incorrectly presume that he or she must also be a good outside shooter.

Leniency and severity bias enter an evaluation through the rater's own assumptions. For instance, a coach of an Olympic team may believe that none of the team members are poor players because they would not have been selected if they were not good players. Consequently, the coach may be lenient in his or her ratings. Severity bias, on the other hand, occurs when a coach or rater is too harsh.

There are several theories about performance appraisal. First, personnel specialists have become interested in the idea of training the raters, to reduce rater error. Research on rater training suggests that the most effective training encourages accurate observations of the employee (Cascio, 1987).

Second, performance evaluation itself can motivate the employee, and it helps guide the employee toward his or her goals, if goals have been plotted. In this way, it improves the goal-setting and achieving process.

Third, the information obtained through the performance review is invaluable as a tool for the selection system. Adding it to other relevant data in the management information system (MIS) adds depth to the entire personnel operation.

Fourth, and certainly an important point, is that the performance evaluation should be a frequent procedure, not a periodic one. Organizations rarely adhere to this.

Ideally, a manager should evaluate the employee every 3 or 4 months. When this is done, decisions are not based on a one-time appraisal.

When observing the employee or athlete, the rater should ask the employee questions, if the rater has any uncertainty about how the job should be or is being performed. After the evaluation has been completed, an interview should be held to give the employee feedback. The manager should thoroughly prepare the content of this interview. Will the feedback attempt to increase performance, or will it be about salary and benefits? Addressing both of these matters simultaneously would be difficult. When giving feedback to the athlete or employee, the rater must decide why he or she is giving the feedback ahead of time. If the feedback is only related to performance, then issues about salary should not be discussed at this time. Feedback with respect to salary should be administered at another time.

The thought of conducting performance reviews or being evaluated often causes anxiety for administrators and employees. It is true that the decisions made affect people's lives. Culkin and Kirsch (1986) make a good suggestion about the process of conducting reviews. They urge administrators to have a positive and open relationship with their employees. With trust, the appraisal feedback process flows much more smoothly.

CONCEPT CHECK

Training, whether for an athlete or an employee is a process of teaching the individual what one must know to perform the job adequately. Training programs require planning, implementation, and evaluation. Most programs are upgrade, that is, they focus on increasing abilities beyond the basic skills needed to do the job. Performance appraisal is the evaluation of the employee's work performance. This appraisal may be used in determining continued employment, salary increases, promotions, or further training. It can also be used to motivate individuals to achieve goals. Rating errors are the unfair biases that can enter a rater's evaluation of a person's work performance. Training and peformance appraisal are the outputs of the systems approach. They then feed back into the system for further processing.

This chapter has presented an overview of the systems approach to personnel issues for sport managers. The components of the overall personnel system (see the box on p. 294) when combined into a single process, become effective for a sport organization. The components of the approach must interact, which creates the necessary loop between the components. The systems approach offers a concise method of reducing decision-making errors.

Some sport organizations have a sophisticated personnel system. However, professional baseball certainly does not, and it has no systematic procedure for drafting players (Dan O'Brien, Houston Astros scouting director, personal communication, 1990). This appears to be the case for other professional sports as well. It is the sport administrator's job to introduce the systems approach to the sport organization. With exposure and training through sport management and related academic programs, sport industries will eventually begin accepting personnel systems.

SUMMARY

1. The field of personnel management, sometimes called human resources, has recently begun to develop within sport management. The systems approach, shown in the box on p. 294, shows the components as inputs (job analysis and needs assessment), throughputs (MIS, strategic planning, selection, and training), and outputs (performance appraisal).
2. Generating a job analysis, including descriptions and specifications, is the first step in the systems approach. Personnel inventories, derived from the job analysis, are used exclusively for determining personnel requirements of the organization.
3. Organizations can benefit from a needs assessment, which is a method for evaluating the organization. It can be used not only in human resources but also in other areas. This diagnostic device is a check and balance system. Most needs assessments are conducted via interviews, surveys, or questionnaires.
4. Organizations require a management information system (MIS) to provide uniform data to administrators. They are frequently used for financial, accounting, and other purposes; however, almost no sport organization uses MIS in personnel matters.
5. Strategic planning is the long-term planning for an organization and relies heavily on management information systems. It sets goals and estimates the human resource requirements of the

institution. In addition, operational (day to day) planning often is a smaller element of strategic planning.

6. All of these components assist the selection effort, which is made up of recruiting, affirmative action, screening, hiring, and perhaps placement. Affirmative action policies are designed to produce equal employment opportunity for all qualified individuals. Psychological tests, personal background, letters of reference, and other similar data help in the screening process. Several selection methods can be used to help employers hire employees, but they are rarely used in sport, primarily because of their complexity. Interviews are often used in these procedures. The structured interview is preferred over the unstructured interview, because it is more complete.

7. Training is the learning process by which employees or athletes increase their skills. In most organizations, the most common type is upgrade training. There are different types of training policies, but all require planning, implementation, and evaluation. Feedback helps the administrator make personnel decisions, such as selecting individuals for hiring, training, or performance appraisal.

8. The performance review procedure can be subjective or objective. Management may choose from several types of performance review procedures and employee rating systems. In many cases, both objective and subjective types are used. Graphic rating scales are the most commonly used rating system. Raters must be taught how to evaluate employees if the rating system is to be meaningful. Employees should be rated frequently rather than after long intervals.

CASE STUDIES AND ACTIVITIES

1. As the executive director at Sportstown Health Club, you have the responsibility of hiring a new swimming instructor. How might you go about this process? What issues are of concern?

2. The U.S. Pogostick Association has appointed you to a committee on training athletes for the upcoming Olympics. What kinds of training policies would you design and implement?

3. You have just assumed the position of general manager and vice-president of football operations for the Georgia Gunslingers. You are considering firing the head coach, because of a low winning percentage over the past year. What other factors will you consider? How can you evaluate this person's effectiveness as head coach?

4. As the assistant commissioner of a conference, you are responsible for meeting the human resources needs of the office for the next 3 years. The office has a staff of 45 people in five departments: marketing, finance, operations, legal, and executive. What needs must be met? How will you proceed? Make your answer a systems approach (that is, discuss the components that will play a role).

5. Students should form groups of two. One is to assume the role of marketing director for a "big-time sports" equipment company. The other is to be the prospective employee. The marketing director conducts an interview. What differences can you see between a structured interview and a short, quick interview? Would you make a decision about hiring this person based on the short interview alone?

6. Form groups of two again. One student is the director of membership services for an amateur sport organization. The other is an employee in the office who has not performed in his or her job adequately. The director must discuss possible disciplinary action with the employee. How will you approach this sensitive subject? Can you motivate your employee? How can you do this without hurting the employee's feelings?

REFERENCES

Brogden, H. (1949). When testing pays off. *Personnel Psychology, 2,* 171-183.

Brogden, H. and Taylor, E. (1950). The dollar criterion—applying the cost accounting concept to criterion construction. *Personnel Psychology, 3,* 133-154.

Cascio, W. (1987). *Applied psychology in personnel management* (Third Edition). Reston, Virginia: Prentice Hall.

Cronbach, L. and Gleser, G. (1965). *Psychological tests and personnel decisions* (Second Edition). Urbana, Illinois: University of Illinois Press.

Culkin, D and Kirsch, S. (1986). *Managing human resources in recreation, parks, and leisure services.* New York: Macmillan Publishing Co.

Equal Employment Opportunity Commission (1979, October). *Affirmative action guidelines,* 44 FR 4421.

Friend, J. (1991). *Human resources in sport.* Chicago, Illinois: Nelson-Hall Book Publishers (in production).

Friend, J., and LeUnes, A. (1987). *The systems approach: a paradigm for sports personnel management.* Paper presented at the second annual conference of the North American Society for Sport Management (NASSM), Windsor, Ontario.

Friend, J., and LeUnes, A. (1989). Overcoming discrimination in sport management: a systematic approach to affirmative action. *Journal of Sport Management, 2,* 151-157.

Friend, J., and LeUnes, A. (1990). Predicting baseball player performance. *Journal of Sport Behavior, 13,* 73-86.

Goldstein, I. (1986). *Training in organizations: needs assessment, development, and evaluation* (Second Edition). Monterey, California: Wadsworth, Inc.

Gould, D., and Landers, D. (1986). *Panel discussion on sport psychology programs for developing junior elite athletes.* United States Olympic Committee Sport Psychology Workshop, June, Phoenix, Arizona.

Libkuman, T., Love, K., and Donn, P. (1989). *Validation of predictors of quarterback success: a computer based model.* Paper presented at the International Sports Business Conference, University of South Carolina, Columbia, South Carolina.

Kroenke, D. (1989). *Management information systems.* New York: McGraw-Hill Book Co.

Naylor, J., and Shine, L. (1965). A table for determining the increase in mean criterion score obtained by using a selection device. *Journal of Industrial Psychology, 3,* 33-42.

Schraibman, C. (1989). *The structured interview: a selection and developmental tool.* Paper presented at the International Sports Business Conference, University of South Carolina, Columbia, South Carolina.

Stewart, C., and Cash, W., Jr. (1988). *Interviewing: principles and practices.* Dubuque, Iowa: Wm. C. Brown Group.

Taylor, H., and Russell, J. (1939). The relationship of validity coefficients to the practical effectiveness of tests in selection. *Journal of Applied Psychology, 23,* 565-578.

CHAPTER 18

Sport Marketing

Dianna P. Gray

In this chapter, you will become familiar with the following terms:

Strategic decision	Niche	Discount pricing
Final consumer	Product	Promotional mix
Demographics	Service	AIDA formula
Incentive	Product benefits	Personal selling
Lifestyle	Core product	Public relations
Psychographics	Product extensions	Publicity
AIOs	Concept testing	Sales promotion
Product usage	Barter	Distribution
Mass marketing	Trade-out	Channels of distribution
Market segmentation	Skim pricing	Marketing plan
Multiple segmentation	Penetration pricing	

Overview

A thorough understanding of sport marketing theory and its application is a requirement for success in the sport industry. Whether the sport administrator works in an upper-level management position as an athletic director, general manager, or club manager, or in an entry-level position as an assistant to senior management, marketing is integral to the successful operation of the organization. In Chapter 10 the theoretical basis for sport marketing was introduced. Some of these concepts will now be applied to various sport marketing situations. The first section of this chapter deals with identifying and targeting the sport consumer. Strategies for defining a target market and planning a strategy to reach the target market will also be covered. The second half of the chapter explores the elements of the marketing mix and identifies ways to develop a marketing plan. Readers may wish to review Chapter 10 before working with the applications that follow.

STRATEGIC MARKET MANAGEMENT

Strategic market management is a system designed to help management make strategic decisions. A **strategic decision** is the creation, change, or retention of a strategy (Aaker, 1988). Philip Kotler (1987) defines the strategic market planning process as the managerial process of developing and maintaining a strategic fit between the organization's goals and resources and its changing market opportunities. The tangible result of this planning process is a marketing plan. Later in the chapter, the development of a marketing plan will be covered in detail. In Chapter 10 the concept of strategic planning was introduced, and the research phases necessary to segment the market were presented. The sport marketer uses research techniques to identify and then classify market segments. Once the segments are identified, the sport marketer then targets the appropriate market segment(s) and develops the core marketing strategy. This includes the selection of target market(s), the choice of a competitive position, and the development of an effective marketing mix to reach and serve the chosen consumers (Kotler, 1987).

MARKET AWARENESS
Identifying and targeting sport consumers

The focus of marketing begins and ends with the consumer. To be successful in the highly competitive sport and entertainment business, the sport marketer must know something about the people who will be the ultimate consumers. This learning process consists of examining the characteristics and needs of the target market, including the consumer's lifestyle and purchase decisions, so that product, distribution (place), promotion, and pricing decisions are made accordingly. By knowing as much as possible about the consumer, the sport marketer can satisfy the target markets, keep consumer dissatisfaction to a minimum, and remain competitive by maintaining or increasing market share.

Before beginning to plan ways of marketing a sport product or service, the sport marketer should answer some general questions about the consumer. First, who is the consumer of the product or service? Here the marketer is trying to obtain information about the **final consumer,** the person who actually decides to purchase the product or service. Where does the consumer live? How does the consumer learn about the available sport and entertainment opportunities? To what forms of media is the consumer exposed? How far in advance of the event does the consumer decide to attend or participate? When does the consumer purchase the ticket to the event? What does the consumer do before the game (pre-event) and after the game (post-event)?

After getting general information about the sport consumer, the marketer seeks answers to more specific questions. At this stage the marketer begins to compose a profile of the sport consumer by examining demographic and lifestyle information. Consumer **demographics** are the statistical descriptions of the attributes or characteristics of the population. By looking at demographic information, both individual characteristics and overall descriptions, the sport marketer can develop consumer profiles that may pinpoint both attractive and declining market opportunities. Figure 18-1 illustrates some of the common factors that are used to determine a demographic profile.

One of the best ways to obtain demographic information is to conduct primary research, usually by means of a survey. This is not always feasible because of financial or time limits; however, there are several secondary sources of information. These sources give the sport marketer not only information about the general population, but also specific information about sport consumers. The *Census of Population* is a publication of the federal government, and it provides a wealth of demographic data. Census data are gathered only once every 10 years, so current data may be lacking. However, population statistics from other sources such as chambers of commerce, public utility companies, and marketing firms can supplement the census data. Sport-specific demographic data can be obtained from individual sport franchises, the national offices of the major sport leagues, sport marketing firms, institutions and private corporations that have commissioned studies (such as Miller Brewing Company's 1983 study of sport participation), or university libraries.

The Simmons Market Research Bureau, Inc. annually conducts personal interviews with more than 19,000 subjects on many consumer issues, in-

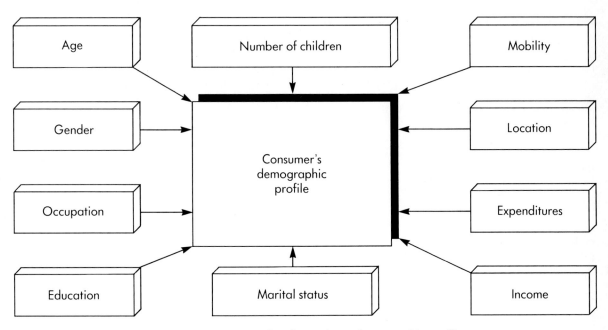

FIGURE 18-1 Factors that determine a demographic profile.

cluding sport participation and live and televised sport viewing. Most university libraries have the results of this study, one volume of which is devoted entirely to sport and leisure.

There are also a variety of serial publications that offer the marketer demographic information. *American Demographics* is a monthly magazine that specializes in demographic information, including trends and predictions. *Sports Inc.*, although no longer in publication, had a number of articles presenting demographic data on specific sports. *Sporting News* has a section devoted to sport business. Other secondary sources of demographic information include The Women's Sport Foundation, *Athletic Business, Club Business* (publication of the International Racket Sports Association), USA Today, and local newspapers.

Developing a demographic profile

Although the information gathered from secondary sources can help the sport marketer identify potential consumers, it is at best general information. Specific information about current consumers should be collected directly if possible. The most feasible way of gathering information on cur-

rent consumers is to conduct an in-arena or club member survey.

In-arena survey. When preparing to survey current consumers or members, the sport marketer, with the organization's management, should determine the objectives for the survey. What information does the organization need? How is this information to be gathered? How much will it cost? How will the information be used after it has been collected? These and other questions must be answered before actually starting the data collection phase of the project. Although the following steps are not offered as a comprehensive guide to conducting survey research, they have been used successfully by many sport marketers to obtain primary data on the final sport consumer.

1. *Preparation:* Determine the objectives of the research project in cooperation with management.
2. *Questionnaire development:* Prepare a questionnaire that integrates the objectives of the project and that will elicit answers to questions about the sport consumer. The box on p. 314 lists typical variables that may be used to generate questions for the questionnaire. After developing the questionnaire, give a draft copy to the athletic

---

Bases of segmentation

Market segments can be based on personal and
geographic demographics, and lifestyles.

Personal demographic segmentation measurements:

Gender: Male or female
Age: Child, teenager, adult, senior
Education: High school, college, beyond college
Income: Low, middle, or high
Marital status: Single, married, divorced, or widowed

Geographic/demographic segmentation measurements:

Population: location, size, and density
Climate: Warm or cold
Media present: Local, regional, and/or national
Commerce: Tourist, local worker, resident

Lifestyle segmentation

This segment includes, among other measurements, **product usage,** a key dimension for
sport marketers. Other examples of lifestyle
measurements include the following:

Social class: Lower-lower to upper-upper
Family life cycle: Bachelor to solitary survivor
Brand loyalty: None, some, complete
Attitudes: Neutral, positive, negative

---

director or general manager and other colleagues for their feedback. Figure 18-2 is an example of a questionnaire developed by the author and used by the Youngstown Pride of the World Basketball League to gather information about its fans.

3. *Distribution:* Obtain a copy of the arena or stadium floor plan to help determine how the questionnaire will be distributed to the consumers. It is also important to plan how to collect the completed questionnaires. The following strategy has consistently resulted in a return rate of 85% to 90%:

a. Assign each section of the stadium or arena a number. Using a table of random numbers (or a computer program that generates random numbers) select the sections that will be targeted, *as well as the seat numbers from each row,* in the identified sections.

b. After the consumers are comfortably seated, give the targeted consumers a copy of the questionnaire and a pencil. Giving fans a questionnaire when they enter the arena through the turnstiles *will not* result in a good return rate. Many of the questionnaires distributed this way end up on the floor or in the trash receptacles.

c. Announce periodically that a survey is being distributed and encourage the consumers to cooperate. One of the most successful tactics to get consumers to fill out the questionnaire completely is to offer an **incentive.** This may take many forms, including a bumper sticker, a key chain, or the chance to be in a lottery for an attractive prize. The incentive should be discussed with management during the preparation phase.

d. Ushers or other facility personnel should collect the questionnaires before the contest begins. Fans are at the event because they are interested in the game, not because they want to fill out a questionnaire. Having ushers or other personnel* collect the questionnaires shortly after the fans have completed them is preferable to asking the fans to drop the questionnaires into a collection box as they exit the arena or stadium.

4. *Analysis:* After the questionnaires are collected, the data must be coded and analyzed. This is usually done by a research firm or the computer systems department at a nearby university.

After analyzing the questionnaires and examining each of the demographic variables individually, the sport marketer develops a profile of the consumer, which is a composite picture of the typical fan. Table 18-1 summarizes the demographic characteristics of attendees of women's basketball games from a national study sponsored by the Women's Basketball Coaches Association (WBCA).

---

*It is the author's opinion that it is best to have personnel other than the ushers collect the completed questionnaires. The ushers, although usually cooperative, must attend to crowd control, and their primary responsibility is the seating of stadium or coliseum guests. Students from nearby institutions, preferably from sport management programs, can assist by collecting them.

THE Youngstown PRIDE™

In order to better serve you and because you are a Youngstown PRIDE fan, we are interested in your opinions. If you wish to be eligible for tonight's special half-time drawing for a Pride sweater and two tickets to the game of your choice, please complete this fan survey and return it to one of the Pride Ushers.

1. NAME _____
   ADDRESS _____
   CITY _____
   STATE _____ ZIP _____
   TELEPHONE NO.   (   ) _____

2. Approximately how many Youngstown PRIDE home
   games have you attended so far this season?
   [   ] 1-3   [   ] 4-6   [   ] 7 or more

3. How did you become aware of tonight's Youngstown Pride game?
   [   ] Newspaper   [   ] Billboard
   [   ] Television   [   ] Radio
   [   ] Word-of-Mouth   [   ] Store display/poster
   [   ] Flyer   [   ] Magazine

4. When did you decide to attend tonight's game? _____
5. How many people are in your party tonight?
   [   ] Just Myself   [   ] Three others
   [   ] One other   [   ] More than three others
   [   ] Two others

6. With whom did you attend tonight's game?
   [   ] Alone   [   ] Business Associates
   [   ] Friends   [   ] Date
   [   ] Family   [   ] Community, Civic or Company Group

FIGURE 18-2 The first page of a questionnaire used by the Youngstown Pride to gather information about its fans.

TABLE 18-1 *Women's college basketball attendees*

	Total	Percentage
Males	772	44.9
Females	949	55.1
17 & under	137	7.6
18-24	262	14.5
25-34	284	15.8
35-44	370	20.5
45-54	312	17.3
55-64	256	14.2
65 & older	180	10.0
High school	342	19.9
Attended college	592	34.5
College graduate	442	25.7
Graduate degree	341	19.9
Single	645	36.3
Married	976	54.9
Widowed	64	3.6
Divorced/Separated	93	5.2
$14,999 − Household income	259	15.2
$15,000 + Household income	105	6.2
$20,000 + Household income	327	19.2
$30,000 + Household income	494	29.0
$50,000 + Household income	516	30.3
1 Person household	296	16.4
2 Person household	662	36.8
3 Person household	326	18.1
4+ Person household	516	28.7
No children	792	44.3
Children	995	55.7
Own residence	1115	73.2
Rent	408	26.8

Average games attended 1987-88: 7.5
Average women's games watched
on television: 2.6

From Gray, D. (1989), *Demographic profile of women's basketball attendees.* Kent, Ohio: Women's Basketball Coaches Association Report.

Lifestyle marketing

Although demographics are valuable in giving the marketer descriptive information about the consumer, the data do not reflect the psychological or social factors that influence consumers. The sport marketer also needs to know why consumers make particular decisions. One solution to this dilemma is to use demographic data in conjunction with consumer **lifestyle** analysis.

The technique marketers use to measure lifestyles is **psychographics.** Consumers' activities, interests, and opinions **(AIOs)** are inventoried by asking respondents various questions about their work, sport activities, family, social life, education, and political preferences—in other words, their lifestyles. Psychographic analysis is important to sport marketers, because it presents a more detailed and accurate picture of the consumer. Table 18-2 lists some of the variables explored in the activities, interests, and opinions categories.

Lifestyle marketing provides a platform for the delivery of products and services. By knowing the consumer's lifestyle, the marketer can develop a relationship with the consumer and create the best match between the consumer and the sport product or service. Lifestyle segmentation includes, among other segments, **product usage**, a key dimension for sport marketers. The product usage dimension of lifestyle marketing has great value for sport marketers. Product usage is traditionally divided into light, medium, and heavy users. As shown in Table 18-3, Mullin (1983), identifies four more sport-specific categories.

College, professional, and private sport and leisure organizations pay most attention to the heavy user, that is, the season ticketholder or the club participant who has a yearly rather than a 3-month membership. The percentage of consumers who are heavy users varies from sport to sport, fran-

TABLE 18-2 *Typical psychographic variables*

Activities	Interests	Opinions
Work	Family	Themselves
Hobbies	Home	Social issues
Social events	Job	Politics
Vacation	Community	Business
Entertainment	Recreation	Economics
Club membership	Fashion	Education
Community	Food	Products
Shopping	Media	Future
Sports	Achievements	Culture

From Plumber, J. (1974). The concept and application of lifestyle segmentation. *Journal of Marketing, 38*(1), 33-37.

TABLE 18-3 *Consumption rate groupings*

Usage segment	Identification Pattern
Heavy user	Season ticket holders
	Club members and/or contract-time holders
Medium user	Mini-season plan users
	Heavy single game/event ticket purchasers
	Purchasers of one-season-only membership
Light user	Infrequent single game/event ticket purchasers
	Infrequent facility users/guests or members
Defector*	Individuals who have used the sport product in the last 12 months but who have not made a repeat purchase since that time
Media consumer	Individuals who do not go to the stadium or coliseum, but rather "follow" the team or sport via the media
Unaware consumer	Individuals who are unaware of the sport product and its benefits
Uninterested consumer	Individuals who are aware of the sport product, but choose not to try it.

From Mullin, B. (1983), *Sport marketing, promotion and public relations.* Amherst, Massachusetts: National Sport Management, Inc.
*Levine defines defectors as people who have attended an organization's event at least once but have not returned within the last 12 months. In many cases, disenchanted heavy users become defectors; in other cases, defectors are individuals who did not gain sufficient satisfaction on the initial purchase or trial.

chise to franchise, and club to club. Some baseball organizations rely heavily on the light user, the person who purchases a ticket 1 hour before the game. Other baseball organizations rely more on season ticket sales. Some football organizations sell out stadia every week and have long waiting lists of loyal fans who want to purchase season tickets, whereas others have difficulty selling out one game. In a similar fashion, fitness and health clubs put a great deal of effort into the renewal of annual memberships, usually at the end of the "indoor" season, since the late spring and summer months are low usage months, even among heavy users, at most clubs.

Sport marketers should realize the importance of classifying consumers by product usage rate. The differing needs of light, medium, and heavy consumers must be satisfied as much as possible. Furthermore, the marketer should consider the light consumer's needs as much as the heavy user's, since today's light consumer could be tomorrow's medium or heavy consumer. An overdependence on the heavy or medium consumer at the expense of the light user could be shortsighted. For example, in the mid-1980s, the men's basketball program of Cleveland State University enjoyed great success. The team played in a small gymnasium to capacity crowds. Students, faculty, and the community alike had to stand in line for the opportunity to purchase single tickets the day of the game. Had they wanted, the Cleveland State Athletic Department could have pre-sold the entire season. However, the administration did not want to alienate the light and medium users, knowing that in the next 5 years a new and much larger home arena would be built. If these consumers had been denied the opportunity to watch the team play occasionally they might have lost interest in the team in the future. Knowing that selling out the new arena would be more difficult and that future financial success would depend on some of the light and medium consumers becoming season ticketholders (heavy users), the marketing staff maintained opportunities for all three consumer levels to enjoy the games.

Even though measuring and analyzing the consumer's lifestyle can benefit marketing, the sport marketer should be aware that the consumer's subjectivity and tendency to report the desired behavior rather than the actual behavior can make psychographic qualities difficult to measure.

CONCEPT CHECK

Strategic planning is a systematic process by which managers evaluate the sport organization's strengths and weaknesses, measure the competition and external environment, and then develop a marketing strategy that matches the team's goals with the opportunities in the marketplace. Steps in this process include the selection of target market(s), the choice of competitive position, and the development of an effective marketing mix to satisfy sport consumers. Developing a profile of current consumers, including demographic and psychographic information, is an important component of the strategic plan.

DEVELOPING A TARGET MARKET STRATEGY

Once the demographic and lifestyle characteristics of the consumer have been determined, the sport marketer is ready to segment and select the target market(s) to which an appeal will be made. Theodore Levitt, in his book *Marketing Imagination* (1986), said that if marketers were not thinking about market segmentation, then they were not thinking. The strategy of target marketing is based on the concept that it is more profitable to zero in on a specific and often narrow market using a focused approach than it is to use the shotgun approach of attempting to appeal to every consumer.

Defining the target market

There are three proven methods of defining and satisfying a target market: (1) mass marketing (undifferentiated), (2) marketing segmentation (concentrated), and (3) multiple segmentation (differentiated).

In **mass marketing,** a single, undifferentiated marketing strategy is used to appeal to a broad range of consumers. In **market segmentation,** the marketing plan is designed to appeal to one well-defined market segment or group of consumers. In **multiple segmentation,** a marketing plan is designed to appeal to two or more market segments, with specialized approaches developed for each well-defined consumer group. Table 18-4 and Figure 18-3 compare the three methods for defining a target market.

Mass marketing. In the past, millions of dollars were spent marketing a product to some "typical"

or "average" consumer. However, no company or organization can survive in today's competitive marketplace by selling to a mythical average customer. The mass-marketing or undifferentiated approach does not recognize different market segments; the focus of this marketing strategy is on the common needs of consumers, rather than on their differences. Within a mass-marketing approach, different consumer groups are not identified or sought.

Although a mass marketing approach is not the sport marketer's principal method of reaching consumers, it does have a place in the marketing of the sport product. Bruce Burge, director of marketing for the World Basketball League and assistant general manager of The Youngstown Pride, uses mass mailings as a low-cost way of getting ticket and game information to Youngstown area residents. The Pride, working with local banks and credit unions, uses statement stuffers* as its primary mass marketing approach. Any entity that mails retail bills or statements, such as banks, utility companies, and department stores, can be approached for this cooperative venture.

Market segmentation. Market segmentation is gaining growing acceptance for its benefits. Nearly all businesses and organizations serve a multitude of market segments, and future market share will be won by the sport organizations that do a better job of identifying and targeting different market segments. A market segmentation or concentrated approach identifies and approaches a specific consumer group through one ideal marketing mix that caters to the specific needs of the chosen segment. Market segmentation is an efficient way to achieve a strong following in a particular market segment.

One caution should be noted. After identifying two or more potential market segments, the segment with the greatest opportunity should be selected as the target market, not necessarily the segment with the most consumers. The largest seg-

---

*Statement stuffers are coupons or advertisements that are sent to consumers with a bill or invoice. The company sending the bill absorbs the mailing costs, which usually does not entail cost beyond what was already involved in mailing the bill or invoice. The sport organization assumes the cost of developing and printing the coupon or advertisement. In addition to the obvious publicity for the sport organization, the company sending the bill or invoice engages in positive public relations, as well as association with a sport franchise.

TABLE 18-4 *Methods for developing a target market*

Marketing approach	Mass marketing	Market segmentation	Multiple segmentation
Target market	Broad range of consumers	One well-defined consumer group	Two or more well-defined consumer groups
Product	Limited number of products under one brand for many types of consumers	One brand tailored to one consumer group	Distinct brand for each consumer group
Price	One "popular" price range	One price range tailored to the consumer group	Distinct price range for each consumer group
Distribution	All possible outlets	All suitable outlets	All suitable outlets—differs by segment
Promotion	Mass media	All suitable media	All suitable media—differs by segment
Strategy emphasis	Appeal to many types of consumers through a uniform, broad-based marketing program	Appeal to one specific consumer group through a highly specialized, but uniform, marketing program	Appeal to two or more distinct market segments through different marketing plans catering to each segment

From Evans, J., and Berman, B. (1988). *Principles of marketing,* New York: Macmillan Publishing Co.

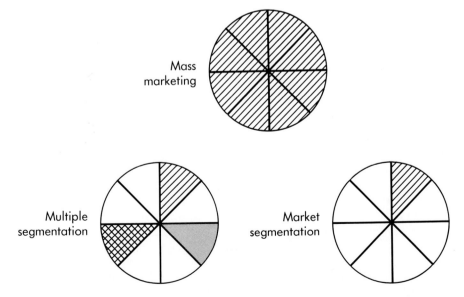

FIGURE 18-3 Three approaches to market segmentation.

ment may not provide the greatest opportunity because of heavy competition or high consumer satisfaction with a competitor. Finding a **niche*** is a key to successful market segmentation.

Multiple segmentation. A multiple-segmentation approach combines the best aspects of the mass-marketing and segmented-marketing approaches. It is similar to the segmented-marketing approach except that the sport organization markets to two or more distinct segments of the market with a specialized plan for each segment. Sometimes a sport organization will market to consumers through a mass marketing strategy to reach a very broad audience and also use a segmented approach geared to specific segments. The more unique segments there are, the better a multiple-segmentation approach will be.

For example, The Youngstown Pride uses an approach segmented by age-groups. Youngsters between the ages of 6 and 15 are targeted and invited to join the Pizza Hut Fan Club, a benefit of which is a free season ticket. Students (aged 16 to 22) are another segment and are targeted for a student season ticket, available for $75, which is $125 less than the regular season ticket price. Finally, consumers aged 24 and above are targeted with an offer of the regular season ticket, costing $200, because a reduced price is usually not necessary to attract these people to games. Brochures describing the appropriate offer are sent to these segments, followed by individual telephone calls.

Steps in planning a segmentation strategy

Figure 18-4 depicts the six steps in developing a segmentation strategy. First, the sport marketer should determine the characteristics of consumers and their need for the product or service. In this step, demographic and psychographic data are collected. Next, the consumers' similarities and differences are analyzed and third, a consumer profile is developed. These profiles help to define the market segments by combining consumers with similar characteristics and wants into distinct groups.

At this point the sport marketer must make some decisions. The segment(s) that offer the greatest opportunity must be selected. The mar-

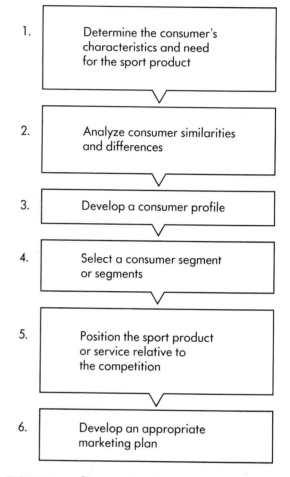

FIGURE 18-4 Six steps in planning a segmentation strategy.

keter must decide how many segments to pursue. The sport organization's financial and human resources must be evaluated and compared with the cost of developing this segment. The timing of the marketing efforts must be decided. Fifth, once a market segment has been selected, the organization must look at its competitors and, considering this competition, select a niche. Finally, a marketing mix is developed for each target market.

CONCEPT CHECK

For best results, the sport marketer should develop a campaign that is highly focused and directed to a spe-

---

*Sport marketers attempt to find a unique position in the marketplace by distinguishing their sport product from competing products. This unique position is called a niche.

cific group of people. This practice is target marketing. The three methods of reaching the target market(s) are mass marketing, market segmentation, and multiple segmentation. The sport marketer must identify and target different market segments to succeed in today's changing marketplace.

THE SPORT PRODUCT
Product vs. service

A **product** is any item that can be offered for sale or barter to satisfy the needs of customers. **Services,** which are also marketed by sport and fitness organizations, are activities or benefits that are offered for sale or barter to consumers. **Product benefits** are the aspects of the product that satisfy the consumers' needs.

Core product and product extensions. The sport product has characteristics of both a tangible product and an intangible service. Moreover, the sports team is different from other traditional products or services that can be purchased at the local department or convenience store. This is both a blessing and a curse for the sport marketer. The very characteristics of sport that endear it to the public, including player characteristics, pomp and pageantry, ritual, uncertain outcome, emotion, public consumption, and opportunity for socializing, also make sport difficult to market. The sport team, although composed of the same players, will not perform exactly the same way twice, and whether the home or favorite team wins usually affects the consumer's satisfaction in the outcome. In addition, the sport marketer has no voice in the makeup of the team, league schedule, weather, and player injuries. All of these factors reduce the locus of control of the marketer and either contribute to or detract from customer satisfaction with the sport product. For these reasons, the sport marketer should market both the **core product**—the game, program, or event—and the **product extensions**—such as the concessions; well-lighted, convenient, and safe parking facilities; half-time entertainment; picnic and tailgate party areas; family atmosphere; child care facilities; and other ancillary facets of the sport product.

Product planning

Before an individual or organization introduces a sport product to the marketplace—whether a new game, such as arena football or MSL (Major Soccer League) soccer, or a variation of an existing product, such as the cross-trainer athletic shoe—they must determine how that product will fit into the marketing and management objectives of the company. The objective might be to introduce a product that will enable the company to break into a market, increase market share, or develop a reputation for being the first to introduce unique sports footwear and apparel. When the company's goals are determined, the next step is to proceed through the phases of the product development process.

Product development process

The product development process has five stages. Stages one through three compose **concept testing.** During these first three stages the sport product or idea is tested before it is actually manufactured or marketed (Seglin, 1990). Although this process applies more to an individual or company wishing to develop a tangible product, such as a new baseball training aid, the process is useful as a guide for developing a new league or sports event. The five stages are as follows:

1. *Generating new product ideas.* One must read widely, including business, sport, and entertainment trade publications, to discover the characteristics of the marketplace and what consumers want. Brainstorm with associates and colleagues to generate creative ways of looking at sport. Do not discard any idea at this stage.

2. *Evaluating new product ideas and analyzing products.* Evaluate the product for its business value. Develop a proposal to predict the market demand, profitability, and start-up costs, and, if necessary, develop a manufacturing program.

3. *Product development.* In this stage the product idea is developed more fully or, in the case of a tangible product such as athletic equipment or footwear, a prototype is made. The product or idea is then analyzed to see whether it is feasible to try to market it to consumers.

4. *Test marketing.* Test the product in one or more target markets to decide whether to proceed and commit large sums of money and human resources to full development. Some products are more easily test marketed and produced than others. The first season for a new league or sport event is a test marketing phase. It is much more difficult for new sport leagues to test market

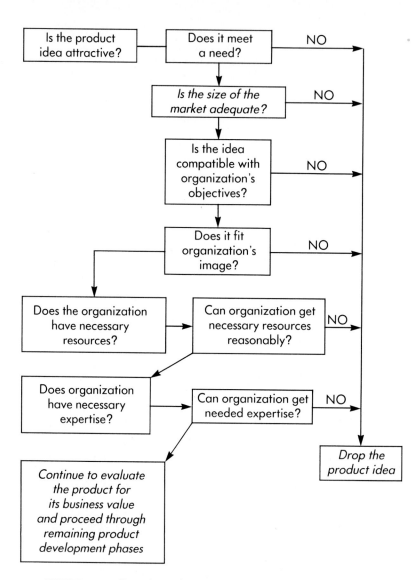

FIGURE 18-5 Overview of a product idea screening procedure.

their ideas than for manufacturers of sport equipment. The degree of acceptance of the product will result in changes in the product. Once all the information and data from this stage of the product development are evaluated, the organization makes the final decision on whether to begin full-scale implementation or production.

5. *Implementation or commercialization.* At this stage the product or idea is produced, and marketing campaigns are developed. When the individual or company arrives at this stage, the decision has definitely been made that the product or idea has merit and is worth marketing.

If, at any stage of the product development process, the company determines that there is no market for the product, the product idea should be dropped. Figure 18-5 presents a product idea screening procedure.

CONCEPT CHECK

The sport product is difficult for the sport marketer to control, since it is intangible, unpredictable, perishable, and consumed as a social event. For these reasons, the product benefits and product extensions must be marketed. New sport products and/or events go through a rigorous screening process, including test marketing, before they reach the marketplace.

PRICE

Price is another of the elements of the marketing mix. As discussed in Chapter 10, price is very visible and intricately related to the other major elements of the marketing mix—product, promotion, and place (distribution). The fan pays a certain price for a ticket to a sports event that has been promoted in various media and distributed through particular channels. If any of the elements of the marketing mix change, the price aspect also must be reevaluated.

Price is most commonly considered as an amount of money; however, it can be more broadly defined as anything of value that is exchanged. **Bartering,** also known as **trading-out,** is a common practice in sport marketing and consists of an exchange that does not involve money. Tickets, program ads, scoreboard space, and arena signage are valuable commodities to some companies. Sport organizations should use these commodities to trade for goods and services that are needed to execute the campaign (Hardekopf, 1989).

Indiana University's director of corporate relations, Mike Wolinsky, uses this strategy to trade women's basketball tickets for radio advertising. The university gives 100 tickets to selected local radio stations in exchange for advertising equal to the face value of the tickets. For example, if the face value of the ticket were $5, the amount of advertising traded would be $500. The radio station gives tickets away in pairs over the air, resulting in a minimum of 50 "mentions." An additional feature of this trade-out agreement is that three additional "mentions" per giveaway are required, resulting in a total of 150 advertising slots in exchange for the 100 tickets (Wolinsky, 1990).

Pricing strategies

Early in the planning process the sport marketer will have to choose a pricing strategy. Some of the more common techniques are skim pricing, penetration pricing, and discount pricing.

Skim pricing. **Skim pricing** is pricing a product at the high end of the price range. This technique is frequently used to maximize profits when a product is introduced to the marketplace, particularly if the demand is inelastic—that is, does not change significantly regardless of price—and there is little competition. As competitors enter the marketplace, the sport marketer may choose to lower the price of the sport product in an attempt to capture market share. During the 1980s, Prince Manufacturing, the maker of the first oversized tennis racket, introduced an oversized graphite racket. The company priced the racket at more than $200, higher than any other racket on the market. When Prince introduced its graphite racket, the demand for high-tech rackets was high, and no other manufacturer had successfully produced an oversized graphite racket. Tennis pro shops could barely meet the demand for the new Prince rackets. However, once competing racket manufacturers successfully developed graphite rackets, Prince reduced the cost of the Prince Graphite to prevent the loss of market share.

Penetration pricing. **Penetration pricing** is the opposite of skim pricing. In this strategy the sport marketer initially sets the price of the product at the low end of the price range to attract the mass market. Penetration pricing is also used at the later stages of the product life cycle, again to reach the mass market. Penetration pricing is an effective strategy when the demand for the sport product is elastic, meaning that lower prices will increase the quantity of the product purchased. A low penetration price may be called a "stay out" price. It discourages competitors from entering the market (McCarthy and Perreault, 1990).

Discount pricing. Often, for a particular game or event, the sport marketer will offer a discount from the regular price of the product or ticket. These discounts usually are offered under certain conditions such as (1) a minimum number of tickets must be purchased, (2) cash transactions only are allowed, or (3) a service, such as a typesetter covering the costs of printing the program, is provided in return for the discount. This strategy is also useful in marketing a single event, to attract community, civic, or church groups to games, or to increase attendance at events that otherwise would not be well attended.

Another benefit of **discount pricing** is that it is a way of lowering the price of the sport product without lowering its value. Discounting solves the dilemma of the sport marketer who wants to attract consumers but not at the expense of reducing the perceived value of the event. This pricing strategy complements the sales promotion strategy that will be discussed more fully in the next section.

CONCEPT CHECK

Price is a very visible element of the marketing mix and, although most often thought of as a dollar amount, can include anything of value that is exchanged. Exchanging tickets for services, especially advertising, is a form of bartering or trading-out, and is a common practice in sport marketing. Pricing strategies include skim and penetration pricing, that is, setting prices at the high or low end of the pricing range, respectively. Discounting tickets for an event is another useful strategy for the sport marketer.

PROMOTION

Promotion, another of the "*P's*" in the marketing mix, is a process in which various techniques are used to *communicate* with consumers. Sport promotions are most successful when the message the marketer wants to convey is directed toward one or more target markets.

The communication process

The communication process in sport marketing is no different from that used by marketers of other products. A knowledge of the communication process is useful in understanding how a message travels from its origin, the sport marketer, to its intended receiver, the fan or consumers. Figure 18-6 shows a communication model and its implications for sport marketers.

Exactly how the communication process works in sport marketing will now be examined more closely.

1. The *source* of the message is the sport marketer or the sport organization. Keeping the sport organization's philosophy and mission in mind, the sport marketer must decide what message will be sent about the product or service (team, club, event, lesson) and to whom (target market) the message will be directed.
2. The sport marketer *encodes* the message by choosing the words, sounds, symbols, or pictures to be used to communicate the intended message.
3. The *channel* is the vehicle the sport marketer uses to get the message to the receiver. This could take any number of forms, from a personal invitation to a commercial on an electronic medium.
4. The *receiver* is the target market that the sport marketer wants to receive the message.
5. The way the message is understood by the receiver or target market is the *decoding* aspect of the communication process.
6. The *response* is how the target market reacts to the message. Are consumers motivated to purchase the product or service, or do they merely acknowledge hearing or seeing the message?
7. *Feedback* or evaluation is a measure of the success in getting the intended message to the target market. Marketing research, ticket sales, and attendance indicators give the sport marketer feedback on how well the message was communicated.

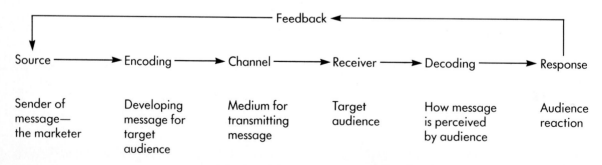

FIGURE 18-6 The communications model.

At any or all points of the communication mechanism there is a possibility that noise* will distort the message. It is important, therefore, to learn how clearly the intended message is being received.

The promotional mix

The communications model (see Figure 18-6) can be useful in planning marketing communications via the **promotional mix,** which, as presented in Chapter 10, includes advertising, personal selling, publicity, and sales promotions. Before implementing any promotion, the sport marketer should map out the goals of the campaign. The following steps can serve as a general outline for planning a promotion:

1. *Define your target market.*
2. *Set measurable objectives.* What do you want to achieve?
3. *Determine the strategy.* How will you motivate the target market(s) to take the desired action?
4. *Research various promotional ideas.* Talk to other sport marketers, at both the professional and institutional (high schools and colleges) levels for ideas. Visit health and fitness clubs in your locale. Other sources for ideas include the library (for books that catalog promotions), marketing organizations, and local businesses.
5. *Select the promotional approach.* Choose one that is the most likely to be successful with your target market(s).
6. *Develop a theme for the promotion.* Devise a short, catchy slogan to attract the attention of the target market.
7. *Create support material.* This material should be in the form of advertising, sales promotions, and publicity.

Keep in mind that the promotional mix used for one product, event, or service may not be appropriate for another. Sometimes the emphasis will be on personal selling, and at other times advertising will be the primary need.

Advertising. Because of the tremendous role of media in sport, advertising is probably the most crucial element of the promotional mix. Advertising, that is, presenting a paid message about the sport organization's product or service, is possibly

the most readily identifiable form of communication in this country. Billions of dollars are spent annually on advertising, involving the following media:

Newspapers	Direct mail
Magazines	Posters
Television	Outdoor advertising
Radio	

As introduced in Chapter 10, the **AIDA formula** shows the stages a prospect undergoes in deciding to purchase a product or service. AIDA stands for Attention, Interest, Desire, and Action. The sport marketer wants the consumer to experience all of these stages in response to advertising communication.

SELECTING THE ADVERTISING MEDIUM is the first step. The key element in selecting the medium to carry the advertising message is determining which medium will best reach the target market. All of the various media, including newspapers, radio and television stations, and magazines, have conducted their own demographic studies to describe the audience they reach. The sport marketer should match the demographics of the sport audience with those of the advertising medium.

Another factor to be considered in selecting the medium is the cost of each. It is much more expensive to advertise on a national network affiliate than on a local cable network. Advertising via television may be the best way to reach the target market, but a limited budget may mean that other outlets, such as radio or outdoor advertising, have to be used. The sport marketer should also consider other creative advertising outlets, such as shopping cart placards, grocery bags, bus posters, banners on street light poles, or electronic messages such as marquees, in an attempt to convey a message to prospective consumers.

CREATING AN ADVERTISING PLAN to ensure continuity in the marketing communications effort is necessary. The following steps can serve as a guide for developing such a plan:

1. *Set objectives for advertising.* What does one want to accomplish? To create an awareness of a product or service? To rouse the consumer to action, that is, to purchase a ticket? To maintain the current consumer's support? To improve an existing image?
2. *Develop an advertising budget.* Research the costs of advertising in each of the media.

---

*Noise is any interference that distorts the message or prevents the receiver from receiving or understanding the message.

If You're Over 55, This Could Be The Fountain Of Youth.

A lot of good things happen when you exercise regularly.

You're stronger. More independent. Less stressed. Have a better self-attitude.

You feel stronger. You're healthier. Which often leads to lower health costs.

Which are several very good reasons to join LifeCenter Plus. The health and fitness center is designed especially for the special requirements of the over-55 adult.

LifeCenter Plus features a fitness center, aerobic rooms, walking track, swimming pool, sauna and whirlpool. Not to mention companionship, camaraderie, and a place where everybody knows and welcomes you.

If you're over 55, join LifeCenter Plus today.

Because it's not how old you are — it's HOW you are old.

This newspaper ad makes excellent use of target marketing, aiming at the 55 and older population. Does this ad prompt the reader to take action and join Life Center Plus?

3. *Create an advertising theme.* Develop a catchy slogan relating to the team, event, or club.
4. *Select the media outlet.* Choose the outlet that provides the "biggest bang for the buck."
5. *Create the advertisement.* This can be done in-house or by a local advertising agency.
6. *Develop a media schedule.* When will each advertisement be run? Will the advertising be spread over the entire season or focus on the pre-season?
7. *Evaluate the effectiveness of the marketing message.* Use marketing research to evaluate the effectiveness of the advertising strategy. Precampaign and postcampaign testing, recall tests, and postcampaign purchase monitoring are common techniques used to measure advertising effectiveness.

Personal selling. **Personal selling** is personal communication with prospective consumers with the goal of persuading them to purchase a product or service (Seglin, 1990). Unlike the other elements of the promotional mix, personal selling is face-to-face or individual communication with a prospective consumer. Like advertising, personal selling uses the AIDA formula to persuade consumers to use a product or service. One advantage personal selling has over advertising is that personal selling is better suited for influencing potential buyers to make the purchase. Advertising may create attention, maintain interest, and arouse desire, but it may not be able to incite action by the consumer since no one from the sport organization is present to close the sale.

Telemarketing is personal selling over the telephone, and it has tremendous potential for sport marketers. One advantage of telemarketing is its low cost and the immediate response it draws from consumers.

THE SELLING PLAN of personal selling, like many of the other techniques of sport marketing, entails a routine that will help the marketer organize the sales process (Evans and Berman, 1988; Seglin, 1990). The following outlines the typical steps in a selling plan:

1. *Determining sales objectives.* How much of the product is one attempting to sell?
2. *Preparing.* Know as much about the product or service as possible. One should try to put himself in the consumer's shoes and think of questions the customer may want answered. Learn about the competition and the marketplace in which one is competing.
3. *Prospecting.* Develop a list of prospective consumers for the product. Avoid blindly calling potential consumers since the odds of success are low. The success rate improves markedly when prospects are referred by current customers.
4. *Approaching.* Learn everything possible about the prospect and decide how to solicit this consumer's business.
5. *Making the sales presentation.* Use the AIDA formula to get the consumer's attention, maintain interest in the product or service, and arouse a desire for the product or service.
6. *Closing the sale.* Persuade the consumer to act and purchase the product or service.
7. *Conducting followup or postsale communication.* To ensure that the consumer is satisfied with the product or service, maintain contact with him or her. This builds a rapport with the consumer and encourages future purchases and consumer referrals.

Publicity and public relations. **Public relations** is a sport organization's overall effort to create a positive image for itself with its target market or markets and the community in which it operates. Chapter 16 presents an excellent discussion on sports information and public relations. Public relations is the overall plan for conveying this positive message, but **publicity,** which is nonpaid and nonpersonal, is the tool that communicates the message (Seglin, 1990). The box on p. 328 lists the avenues that publicity can take.

Sales promotion. **Sales promotion,** another part of the promotional mix, is any activity that cannot be called advertising, personal selling, or publicity. However, like the other aspects of the promotional mix, the goal of sales promotions is to induce the consumer to purchase the sport product or service. Sales promotions include many strategies, such as the following:

Coupons	Gifts or premiums
Free samples	Point-of-purchase displays
Contests	Cash refunds
Giveaways	Sweepstakes

Publicizing your event

News Media	Direct mail
Radio	Personal letters
Television	Brochures
Newspaper	Invitations

Publications	Personal contacts persentations
Professional journals	Service clubs
Magazines	Professional organizations
Periodicals	Chamber of commerce
Tabloids	YMCA/YWCA
Newsletters	Institutional organizations
	Public affairs programs
Printed materials	Conferences
Posters	Festivals
Brochures	Classes
Fliers	Word of mouth
	Other institutions

Special promotions

Advertising

Special promotions	Advertising
Phonathons	News media
Shopping malls	Publications
Lobby displays	Ticket outlets
Bus posters	Miscellaneous
Billboards	
Marquees	
Bulletin boards	

CONCEPT CHECK

Promotion is the process of communicating with the consumer about the sport product. The sport marketer must be aware that interference or noise in the communication process may prevent the consumer from receiving or understanding the intended message. This knowledge is useful in planning and implementing the promotional mix. Elements of the promotional mix are advertising, personal selling, publicity/public relations, and sales promotions. The marketer develops promotional strategies to get the consumer's attention, arouse interest in the product, create a desire, and ultimately, motivate the consumer to purchase.

PLACE

The place element of the marketing mix is the geographic location of the product, such as the stadium, arena, or club, as well as the point of origin for distribution of the product or service. In Chapter 10, the concept of **distribution** as the transfer of products, goods, and services from the producer to the consumer was introduced. Products move from the producer to the consumer through **channels of distribution**—any series of firms or people who participate in the flow of the product or service to the consumer (McCarthy and Perreault, 1990). The length of distribution channel varies. Because the sport product is produced and consumed at the same site, the distribution channel is short, and attention to distribution seems unnecessary. This is not true. Sport marketing does not affect the sport product as much as it affects the *delivery* of the sport product. Place decisions have long-run effects. They are harder to change than product, price, and promotion decisions (McCarthy and Perreault, 1990).

Establishing the distribution network

Given the effect of the media on sport and the fact that most sport products cannot be physically delivered to the consumer, sport marketers use the media to develop their market. Marketing one's event through a wide-broadcast network not only generates widespread interest in and awareness of the product, but it can also have a direct effect on sales by creating "media consumers" who could become light users at a later date (Mullin, 1983). The scope of this chapter does not permit a full treatment of this aspect of sport marketing. More information on setting up a broadcast network can be found in Mullin (1983) and Mason and Paul (1988).

Another way of distributing the product to consumers is via the telephone. The University of Kentucky uses a "900" number and an extensive radio network to get information about the Wildcats basketball team to its alumni and fans. Interested parties throughout the United States can call a 900 number for information about upcoming games, comments from the coaching staff, game statistics, and player profiles. In addition to the 900 system, any restaurant or similar establishment that has closed circuit radio can arrange to broadcast Kentucky games live. Wildcats fans around the country can listen to Kentucky basketball games that they otherwise could not enjoy.

Ticket distribution

The physical distribution of game or event tickets is an important part of the place aspect of the marketing mix. The goal of the ticket distribution system is to encourage consumer purchases by making the system as convenient and accessible as possible. Strategies used by sport organizations include the following three tactics. First, the selling of tickets is franchised to third-party companies such as Ticketron. The advantage of such a contract for the sport marketer is the connection with a well-established, highly visible network of ticket outlets. A consumer can go to any of these ticket outlets, and thanks to the computerized ticket system,

buy the desired seat from the pool of available seats for a particular event. After the consumer selects the seat, the computer prints the event ticket. This system enables the consumer to choose a seat from all the unsold seats rather than having to select from a limited allotment of tickets. However, a disadvantage of this system is the sport marketer's loss of control over the operation and loss of ability to monitor consumer satisfaction. Franchised ticket outlets sell tickets for many organizations and do not promote any game or event. They also charge consumers a service fee, often as much as $2.50 per ticket sold.

Second, establishing ticket outlets in local banks and large department and grocery stores is a popular strategy. This system is especially effective in areas where there are no third-party ticket outlets. The Houston Astros have a creative approach to ticket distribution with their Astros' van. Mike Levy, Astros' director of season ticket services, says that to sell more tickets one must "go to the people rather than expecting them to come to you" (Levy, 1990). In an agreement with a local automobile dealer and cellular telephone company, the Astros are given use of a van, which transports ticket office personnel into the community to sell tickets to upcoming games.

The front office has set an ambitious schedule in which the van goes out every day during the season. On weekdays the van travels to stores of the Astros' supermarket sponsor, and on weekends it tours shopping malls and major department stores. The van's schedule is announced at all home games, over the radio, and in the local print and electronic media. When the team is playing on the road, Orbit, the Astros' mascot, travels with the van.

So popular is this system that people wait at the announced sites, camera in hand, to take pictures of the mascot and to purchase tickets for games. This distribution system and promotion have brought positive results for the Houston team and have brought increased ticket sales, both those tickets bought on impulse as well as those that are renewals.

Finally, improving in-house ticket operations is a necessary tactic. This includes expanding the hours of operation so that consumers can come to the ticket office before or after work as well as during the lunch hour. The ticket office should be open late at least one evening a week. Telephone numbers, including "800" numbers, should be available for the convenience of consumers who wish to charge their tickets to credit cards. Tickets should also be available for pick-up by consumers just before the game at a "will-call" window.

CONCEPT CHECK

The place element of the marketing mix is both the physical sport facility and the physical distribution of the product by means of tickets. The transfer of the product to the consumer is made through channels, that is, ticket outlets. Other ways of distributing the sport product include telemarketing, such as through 800 or 900 numbers, and through a radio network.

MARKETING PLAN

The tangible result of the strategic planning process and development of the marketing mix is the **marketing plan,** a document that becomes the framework for the marketing process of the sport organization. The sport manager's and/or marketer's research becomes most effective when it is incorporated into a systematic and formal marketing plan.

Successful marketing is like a successful team. Both the coach and the team members need to follow a plan. A marketing plan is a game plan for the marketer. It enables a sport organization to establish objectives, priorities, schedules, budgets, strategies, and checkpoints to measure performance.

Marketing plan outline

I.   Background and environmental analysis
  A. Analyze relevant past and current marketing data. Developing a marketing plan begins with a clear understanding of "where we are."
  B. Determine history of the organization, previous target markets, and the sport organization's philosophies (written or unwritten) that may have an impact on marketing programs.
  C. Analyze the external environment by reviewing the economic indicators that may affect your product or service. Governmental agencies, trade associations, libraries, and business publications are excellent sources of data on the economic conditions that affect sport.
    1. Use this information to determine market potential and trends in market behavior.
    2. Assess the political and social trends that affect sport.
  D. Analyze the internal organization. Construct an organizational chart of the organization.
  E. Perform an analysis of competitors. Knowledge of competitors is critical in designing effective marketing strategies. It is important to understand what the competition is doing even if one believes it is wrong.
    1. Most necessary information about competitors can be found in the following sources:
      a. Newspaper articles
      b. Annual reports
      c. Company or department literature
      d. Trade journal articles
    2. Evaluate the strengths and weaknesses of the competition's marketing mix (all components).

II. Consumer analysis and target market(s) identification
  A. Perform consumer analysis.
    1. List consumers that one serves.
    2. Include consumer demographics.
    3. If available, include psychographics, such as purchase frequency, brand or team loyalty, where tickets are purchased or service is enjoyed, and so on.
  B. Determine target market(s).
    1. Select market segments that are the most likely consumers for the product or service.
    2. Develop a consumer profile of target market segments.

III. Specify objectives. The sport organization should set marketing objectives that help the organization achieve its goals.
  A. What is one setting out to do in the plan? Set goals and objectives as specific quantities to be achieved by specific deadlines. Objectives must be stated in measurable terms.
  B. Marketing objectives generally are stated as a percentage of market share for a particular product or service, penetration of

certain market segments, and sales growth for all or selected product lines or tickets.

IV. Determine marketing strategies. How does one plan to achieve his or her objectives?

   A. Strategies are built using a mixture of the "four P's," product, price, promotion (advertising), and place (distribution).

   B. Use the following steps to develop marketing strategies.

      1. Describe the product and the strategy that will be used to accomplish the stated objectives (as determined in section III).

      2. Set prices for each product line or service. Pricing objectives must match objectives for product lines. Describe the pricing objective for each product line or service.

      3. Describe the distribution objectives for each product line or service. Using new distribution channels may offer opportunities to gain a competitive edge. Alternate distribution channels include direct mail, door-to-door sales, electronic shopping, and site flexibility.

V. Specify the advertising and sales promotion program. Before setting an advertising budget, determine the goals of the advertising.

   A. The creative component is the essential core of the approach, what sets one apart; develop a slogan for the campaign.

   B. Increasing sales, gaining market share, and accomplishing marketing objectives all require sales promotions. Promotions include couponing, public relations, trade shows, and specialty advertising. Determine the sales promotion's objectives and strategies for each product line or service.

   C. Identify the advertising strategies and media (print, radio, television, specialty, direct mail, point of purchase, or other), including the approximate cost and frequency of the advertisement.

VI. Set the marketing budget. The budget should reflect the projected costs of the proposed marketing plan.

VII. Set the marketing activities timetable. Prepare a schedule, calendar, or chart showing the events, ads, and so on, that will be used, the person responsible for completing each task, and the month in which the activity should be completed.

SUMMARY

1. The marketing of the sport product should be strategically and systematically planned. The strategic plan gives a framework to the entire marketing process.

2. The focus of sport marketing is on identifying and selecting the target market(s) and then developing a marketing mix that will appeal to the selected target(s). To learn the needs of sport consumers, the marketer must conduct demographic and lifestyle analyses.

3. The three proven methods of defining and satisfying the target market are (1) mass marketing, (2) market segmentation, and (3) multiple segmentation. Mass marketing is often used to appeal to a broad range of consumers or to launch a campaign. Market or multiple segmentation strategies, which have a narrower focus, are preferable to the mass marketing approach; however, they are more expensive and may be beyond the financial ability of the sport organization.

4. Product usage information is crucial to sport marketing. Because product usage varies by strata, the marketer must develop strategies that address the needs of light, medium, and heavy consumers. Overemphasizing strategies targeted to the heavy users, particularly if it means neglecting light and medium users, could cost the sport organization in the future.

5. Because of the unpredictability of the sport product, the sport marketer must market both the core product and the product extensions.

6. The sport marketer must select a pricing strategy early in the marketing planning process. Price is the most visible and flexible component of the marketing mix, and it contributes to the consumer's perception of the value of the sport product. The decision to use skim, penetration, or discount pricing depends on the elasticity of the demand for the sport product.

7. Knowledge of the communication process is essential for the sport marketer and can be useful in planning the promotional mix. The promotional mix includes advertising, personal selling, publicity, and sales promotions. Before launching any promotion, the sport marketer

should set the goals of the promotional campaign.

8. The sport marketer should use the AIDA formula (attention, interest, desire, and action) as a guide to producing marketing communications that motivate consumers to purchase the sport product or service.

9. Personal selling has an advantage over advertising in that it is better suited to persuading prospects to make an actual purchase. Like other aspects of sport marketing, developing and following a specific procedure for selling tickets will help keep the process organized and efficient.

10. The marketing plan is a written document, resulting from the strategic planning process, that guides the sport marketer throughout the season.

REFERENCES

Aaker, D. (1988). *Developing business strategies* (2nd Edition). New York: John Wiley & Sons, Inc.

Broyles, J., and Hay, R. (1979). *Administration of athletic programs: a managerial approach.* Englewood Cliffs, New Jersey: Prentice Hall.

Burge, B. (1990). (Telephone interview), Bloomington, Indiana.

Evans, J., and Berman, R. (1988). *Principles of marketing.* New York: Macmillan Publishing Co.

Evans, J., and Berman, R. (1990). *Marketing* (4th Edition). New York: Macmillan Publishing Co.

Gray, D. (1989). *Demographic profile of women's basketball attendees.* Unpublished manuscript, Kent State University, School of Physical Education, Recreation and Dance, Kent.

Hardekopf, B. (1989). Creating a winning marketing campaign. *College Athletic Management,* January: 35-36.

Kotler, P. (1987). *Strategic marketing for non-profit organizations.* Englewood Cliffs, New Jersey: Prentice Hall.

Levitt, T. (1986). *Marketing imagination.* New York, New York: The Free Press.

Levy, M. (1990). (Telephone interview), Bloomington, Indiana.

Mason, J., and Paul, J. (1988). *Modern sports administration.* Englewood Cliffs, New Jersey: Prentice Hall.

McCarthy, E., and Perreault, W., Jr. (1990). *Basic marketing* (10th Edition). Homewood, Illinois: Richard D. Irwin, Inc.

Mullin, B. (1983). *Sport marketing, promotion and public relations.* Amherst, Massachusetts: National Sport Management, Inc.

Plumber, J. (1974). The concept and application of lifestyle segmentation. *Journal of Marketing,* 38(1), 33-37.

Research and Forecasts, Inc. (1983). *Miller Lite report on American attitudes towards sports.* New York.

Seglin, J. (1990). *The McGraw-Hill 36-hour marketing course.* New York: McGraw-Hill Book Co.

Sutton, W. (1987). Developing an initial marketing plan for intercollegiate athletic programs. *Journal of Sport Management,* 1(2), 146-158.

Wolinsky, M. (1990). (Personal interview), Bloomington, Indiana.

SUGGESTED READINGS

Baker, M. (1986). Marketing women's athletics without money. *Athletic Administration,* 21(3), 15-18.

Fannin, R. (1988). Gold rings or smoke rings? *Marketing & Media Decisions,* 23(9), 64-70.

Hardekopf, B. (1989). Creating a winning marketing campaign. *College Athletic Management,* 1(1), 35-36.

Lapin, J. (1987). How to win with sports. *Public Relations Journal,* 43(2), 31.

Plumber, J. (1974). The concept and application of lifestyle segmentation. *Journal of Marketing,* 38(1), 33-37.

Siegel, L. (1989). Planning for a lifelong logo. *Marketing Communications,* 14(3), 44-47.

Stotler, D., and Johnson, D. (1989). Assessing the impact and effectiveness of stadium advertising on sport spectators at Division I institutions. *Journal of Sport Management,* 3(2), 90-102.

Yiannakis, A. (1989). Some contributions of sport sociology to the marketing of sport and leisure organizations. *Journal of Sport Management,* 3(2), 103-115.

19

Strategic Sport Marketing: Case Analysis

Brenda G. Pitts
Lawrence W. Fielding

In this chapter, you will become familiar with the following terms:

Strategic sport marketing
Case analysis
Case analysis model

Overview

As stated earlier in this book, the growth of the sport industry has been phenomenal. As it continues to grow, competition for the consumer dollar will also increase. The sport organizations that survive will be managed by people with formal training and education in sport management in general and in sport marketing and promotions in particular. A comprehensive understanding of sport as a product and a knowledge of the fundamentals of sport marketing are essential to the sport manager—especially if the manager must also act as the marketing director, as is the case in many small sport businesses.

Businesses succeed, or at least survive, when revenues consistently exceed expenditures. Therefore the bottom line in any business is the profit line. A sport business is no exception. The successful positioning of a sport product requires fundamental marketing techniques: carefully analyzing external market factors, linking these factors to internal organizational forces, employing critical decision-making strategies, and finally developing an appropriate strategic marketing plan.

In the business world, most strategic marketing concepts are modeled after strategic planning concepts. **Strategic sport marketing** is modeled after the fundamental strategic marketing concepts.

Strategic sport marketing may be defined as the process of designing and implementing activities for the promotion and distribution of a sport product from producer to consumer. This process creates exchanges that satisfy both consumer wants and organization objectives (Pitts, 1988). The successful application of this process begins with an understanding of the product: the sport industry.

STRATEGIC SPORT MARKETING APPLICATION: THE CASE ANALYSIS METHOD

The purpose of this chapter is to help the sport management student understand the sport marketing process by applying sport marketing principles to case studies. Students will be able to use basic knowledge about sport marketing gained from chapters 10 and 18, from a sport marketing course, or from a marketing principles course.

Strategic sport marketing is best learned through **case analysis.** The **case analysis model** presented in this chapter was developed from several case analysis models (Aaker, 1984; Bernhardt and Kinnear, 1985; Kotler and Andreasen, 1987; McCarthy and Perreault, 1984; Pitts, 1986). Case analysis, as a teaching method, presents the student with a case: a real or simulated situation with information about the individuals, business, issues involved, and other related material. The student may be given one or more assignments related to the case. These activities may range from answering questions about the data in the case, to analyzing the case to identify problems, to analyzing the problems and developing elaborate solutions. These activities may also range from short in-class discussions to outside written assignments. One or more of the case-analysis steps may be used with the case studies presented here.

Sport industry case studies will be presented, and the student will be asked to assume the role of the sport marketing director. As the sport marketing director, the student must analyze the situation, identify problems, develop solutions, and develop a strategic marketing plan (refer to Chapter 10 for an explanation of this process).

The situations and organizations presented will be real. However, the cases are not designed to provide all the information that one would like to have. First, to present every tidbit of information on the organization would require too much space.

Second, a case with missing information is a more realistic portrayal of the real world. Moreover, because the purpose of case analysis is to help students understand the process of strategic marketing analysis and planning, the authors encourage students to make some realistic assumptions where there are gaps in the data given. In a real situation, certain assumptions are made because some data is unavailable. A good analysis will include assumptions about missing data, whereas a bad analysis will simply state that the data is not given.

The case analysis model

The case analysis model has three phases. Students should study the model to understand the complete process and each of its step before attempting to apply it to the cases.

Phase one: situation analysis and problem identification

The objectives of phase one are (1) to learn how to state the situation based on the facts presented and (2) to analyze the situation according to specific factors to identify problems. The steps of phase one are the following:

Step 1: State the situation. Identify pertinent facts and describe the situation in your own words. This helps to focus on the facts of a situation.

Step 2: Identify area(s) of management. Identify the areas of management within which problems fall. Do the problems fall into organizational, financial, facility, legal, program, and/or other areas of management? This guides one to the resources that may be needed and to the individuals working in those areas on whom one might need to call. For example, if you suspect the problems in a situation may stem from personnel, then personnel policy becomes a resource to be used in developing solutions and strategies.

Step 3: Identify causes. Determine the factors you perceive to be causing the problem. Some factors might be attitude, policy or lack of policy, or environmental, social, or cultural issues. If all the factors causing the problems are not identified, and a solution is not offered for those factors, then the problem is likely to recur.

Step 4: Identify the problems and opportunities. Identify and list the primary problems and opportunities derived from the analysis of the situation. Some marketing problems are opportunities. Do the identified problems require just a remedy, or might they be opportunities for the company?

Phase two: marketing analysis

Some steps from phase one will be repeated in this phase with special emphasis on the marketing aspects of the situation.

Situation analysis. Identify and discuss the following:

a. Nature of demand: Describe the demand for existing products. Answer questions such as, "What are the existing products, when and how is the product purchased, who is purchasing the product, how much are they paying, why are the consumers purchasing the product, and how can the market be segmented?"

b. Extent of demand: Describe the market and estimate potential sales.

c. Nature of competition: Describe and analyze the present and potential competition in this particular product-market. Determine the number of competitors and their market shares, financial resources, and marketing resources.

d. Environmental factors: Describe internal and external factors in the product-market that affect or could affect the organization. Some factors are the political, social, legal, and physical environments. Others are quality control, product prestige, and availability of substitute goods.

e. Stage of product life cycle: Identify the current stage of the product's life cycle. Describe the target stages you have set for the product.

f. Present cost structure and price structure: Describe the current cost-per-unit of the product. Describe the current price to the consumer for the product.

g. Skills of the organization: Describe the current skills of the organization.

h. Financial resources: Describe the financial situation of the organization. Identify financial resources.

Phase three: marketing program development

Developing the complete marketing program is the final phase in the process. Based on the work completed, assumptions, and critical analysis in the first phases, suggest and develop ideas for the marketing program. The steps of phase three follow.

Step 1: Identify marketing objectives. Identify objectives for the marketing program you suggest. Identify target market segments and profit objectives.

Step 2: Identify marketing mix and program decisions. Develop the complete marketing program and marketing mix components: product, price, distribution, and promotion. Include strategies for goal attainment and schedules for your program.

Step 3: Suggest marketing program alternatives. Identify some alternatives to the program you outlined in Step 2.

A NOTE TO THE INSTRUCTOR: SUGGESTIONS FOR ASSIGNMENTS/ ACTIVITIES

Cases one and two were written specifically for use in an undergraduate level course. Cases three and four were written for the advanced or graduate student and are much more complex. Each case is followed by a set of questions. The following are suggested assignments and activities for applying the model and using the cases:

1. Case analysis model: Have the students apply the model to a case as an out-of-class assignment. In addition, have the students present their work to the class.

2. One or more phases: Have the students apply one or more of the phases or just one or more of the steps to a case. This could be done as an in-class discussion or as an out-of-class written assignment.

3. Small group project or competition: Divide the class into teams of five or six. Have the teams apply the full model to a case and develop all materials in a marketing plan, including the logo, the advertising slogan, a sales brochure, a poster, a full-page advertisement, a 60- or 30-second radio spot, and a 60- or 30-second television commercial. Each team presents its marketing plan to the class to be judged by the instructor.

4. In-class discussion: Present the case in class. Use the case questions or the model for discussion.

5. Outside short assignment: Assign the case questions to the students with written answers due on a specific date.

6. Small group analysis: Divide the class into small groups of five or six. Have the groups answer the case questions individually and then present

their answers to the rest of the class for discussion.

STRATEGIC SPORT MARKETING: THE CASES

Study each of the following cases before beginning the case analysis. Each case includes questions for thought or discussion.*

CASE STUDY ONE: THE MIDDLE SIZE UNIVERSITY FOOTBALL PROGRAM

Marketing plans are produced from the interaction of management objectives, management strategies, strategic plans, and marketing strategies. Two important products of this interactive process are the marketing objectives and the target markets. A key element in this process is the use of marketing research. The case of Middle size University's football program demonstrates how this interactive process works.

Middle size University is a commuter, inner-city campus with an enrollment of 20,000 students. Fewer than 1,000 students live in university dormitories. The university is located in a city of about 325,000 people; the metropolitan area has slightly more than 900,000 residents. Management objectives were set by an executive committee of the athletic council made up of local businesspeople (all of whom were men), university administrators, and athletic department administrators. The principal management objective was to increase revenues produced by the football program. More specifically, the executive committee wanted to improve the football program from an average loss of 185,000 dollars a year to an average profit of 250,000 dollars a year. The move was to be completed over 5 years. Management strategy targeted the following revenue producing areas: television and radio, donations, and ticket sales. Management and marketing personnel developed separate strategic plans for each of the three revenue-producing areas. The three separate plans then were combined into an overall marketing strategy with the

principal theme of promotion of football: that is, marketing the extensions as well as the core product. The following analysis deals only with ticket sales and emphasizes the relationship between marketing objectives and the target market.

To determine marketing objectives and target markets, the marketing department used a series of four market research studies. The first study analyzed the product (football team's won/loss record, number of star players, and general drawing power) and the local competition for entertainment dollars. The study made the following points:

1. Even though the football program won 60% of its games over the preceding 5 years and had star players each year, paid attendance averaged only 15,000 for the 5 years. The stadium capacity was 31,500.
2. Season ticketholders accounted for only 12% of total ticket sales.
3. The university football team competed for spectators with 34 local high school football teams. An average of 20 games were played each Friday by local teams. Local teams were spread across three divisions; the top division offered high-quality high school football.
4. The university played its football games on Saturday afternoon or evening. Both of these times competed directly with horseracing, which was a popular spectator sport throughout the state.
5. The university football team competed for attendance with three other Division I football teams within the state. These other schools were within driving distance and had substantial followings within the metropolitan area.
6. The university football program competed directly with local cultural events. A cultural festival designed to highlight local ethnic culture was held on the same day the university football team played at home.

The second market research study gathered demographic data about the metropolitan area and local businesses from the local chamber of commerce. The key points of this report included:

1. Per capita income varied with specific locations within the city and the metropolitan area. These figures were compared with property and housing costs. The result was a grid of the metropolitan area that correlated ZIP codes with personal income ranks.

---

*Information for the case studies was gathered by the authors over 3 years. Research in all cases is still being conducted. Solutions to problems are available on request. Send requests to Dr. Brenda Pitts and Dr. Lawrence Fielding, University of Louisville, Sport Administration Programs, HPER Dept., Louisville, KY 40292.

2. Local businesses were ranked based on five factors: location of corporate headquarters, location of regional headquarters, business type, business size, and business financial strength.

The final two market studies were related. One study surveyed spectators at football games and the other surveyed spectators at basketball games.* The surveys gathered information on demographics (age, sex, occupation, education, salary range, and distance traveled to games), reasons for attendance, frequency of attendance, and whether spectators were season ticketholders or walk-in trade. Results of the two surveys were then compared. This comparison of the two spectator groups resulted in three important discoveries:

1. Basketball and football season ticketholders tended to be in middle- to upper-income brackets.
2. Nearly one third of all basketball season tickets were sold to local corporations and businesses, compared to only 5% for football.
3. More than 60% of basketball fans expressed an interest in football to the extent that they watched two or three football games each week during football season.

Based on the market studies and directed by management's objective to increase revenue, the following marketing plan was proposed:

1. Link the purchase of the best basketball seats with high donations and the purchase of football tickets.

    The seat sections in the football stadium and the basketball arena were graded into best seat sections. To obtain the best seats for basketball games, basketball season ticketholders were required to donate a specific amount of money to the Middle size University athletic fund *and* to purchase football season tickets in addition to basketball season tickets. The target market for this strategy was the business community. Special box seats were set aside for businesses that purchased at least 12 season tickets; purchasers of 6 to 12 season tickets were grouped in special sections; special services were offered with these special group season ticket purchases.[†] Business donors were also listed in the program. Football and basketball were marketed as events that could attract clients or consumers and promote company name recognition and good will.

2. Link lower donations with basketball tickets and football tickets.

    This approach copied the previous approach, except that the size of the required donation was substantially lower and the seats were farther from the action. The target market for this strategy was smaller businesses and higher-income people. Smaller businesses were courted in the same manner as the larger businesses. Higher-income individuals were approached through direct mail, based on the income grid developed in the second marketing research study. Again, the objective was to sell group season tickets.

3. Link basketball season tickets with football season tickets by offering special seats and special prices.

    The idea was to set aside a third level of good seats at basketball and football games for those who purchased season tickets for both football and basketball. As an added inducement, a 20% discount on both football and basketball season tickets was offered to purchasers willing to buy both. The target market for this option was middle- and upper-income individuals. The "special-offer" was marketed through direct mailings that were restricted to the middle- and upper-income sections of the metropolitan area.

4. Establish cheap seat packages to sell to lower-income groups.

    Family plans for football games and special one-game offers were developed to attract spectators. These plans were advertised on radio and through the newspaper, and frequently were linked with the purchase of products at local businesses.

1. *What groups at Middle size University were involved in developing the marketing plan for football?*

---

*Basketball spectators were surveyed because the basketball program was extremely successful. Market researchers wanted to know whether basketball fans were significantly different from football fans and whether basketball spectators had any interest in football.

---

†For example, the company box package included free parking, free programs, television monitors, and a cash bar.

2. *What part does marketing research play in developing marketing plans?*

3. *What effect did the management objective—to increase revenues—have on the development of the marketing plan?*

4. *Who are the direct and the indirect competitors of the Middle size University football program?*

5. *Why did the marketing plan link basketball season tickets with football season tickets?*

6. *What criterion was used to segment the consumer market?*

7. *What are the differences between the marketing approaches for the market segments?*

8. *Even though team quality is an important factor in marketing, the marketing plan developed does not consider this factor. Is this an oversight? Why would team quality not be considered?*

9. *What other activities would you suggest Middle size University use to promote its football program?*

10. *Will the marketing plan developed increase revenues? Why or why not?*

CASE STUDY TWO: HAPPINESS IS WOMEN'S ATHLETICS

Naomi "Nel" Gray was the women's basketball coach at Knoll High School. Nel had mixed emotions about the upcoming 1986 women's basketball season. Despite several good seasons and several outstanding players, women's basketball never had acquired much of a following at Knoll. The men's team played before packed houses; women's basketball drew an average of only 60 spectators a game to an arena that seated 1,200 spectators. Nel's 1986 team would be very talented; they would compete for sectional and state honors. In short, this would be Nel's best team ever, and she wanted this team to play before capacity crowds in the Knoll Gymnasium.

Women's basketball was a second-rate attraction at Knoll High School for several reasons. Knoll High School, a school housing 1,500 students in grades 10 through 12, was located on the outskirts of the city of Knoll. Knoll was a prosperous railroad town in the 1930s and 1940s. During the 1950s the railroad moved away. Many people moved with the railroad; the population dropped from 41,000

in 1950 to 19,000 in 1980. The town had one large industry (Champion Knit Wear) but primarily had small manufacturers and other small businesses. Knoll was surrounded by farms, mostly dairy and beef, with some corn, wheat, and vegetable farms mixed in. In short, Knoll was a small town and a family community dominated by men's interests in both business and leisure. Men's sports ruled the athletic calendar. High school football, basketball, and baseball had a large following. Hunting, fishing, and bowling were the most popular participant sports. In such a community women's basketball, indeed women's sport, fought an uphill battle for recognition and support.

Basketball games were played on Tuesday and Friday evenings. The women's team either played its game before the men's (in which case average attendance increased to about 100) or played away games when the men's team was at home and vice versa. In the latter case the women's basketball team competed directly with the men's team. Knoll High School athletic teams played opponents in a 12-team league. Travel distances ranged from 20 to 85 miles. Followers of men's basketball could reach the team's games, whether at home or away, with relative ease.

The preliminary marketing objective was to increase attendance at women's basketball home games. However, this was quickly changed for two reasons.

The first reason was philosophical. Nel recognized that improving attendance at women's basketball games was a very narrow goal given the problems women faced in the community. She equated increased attendance with program recognition and acceptance. Women's basketball was important, but it was no more important than any other women's sport. Nel decided that the marketing objective should be the promotion of women's sport and female athletes in general.

Nel's second reason was more pragmatic. The potential following for women's athletics was much larger than the potential following for women's basketball by itself. Furthermore, Nel reasoned, if women's athletics could be linked with female students' involvement in all Knoll High School activities, then this potential larger following could be attracted. The best way to promote women's basketball was to promote women's athletics and female students' contributions to Knoll High School in general. The principal target market included high school students and their families. The secondary target market included middle school students and their families.[‡]

Because the marketing objective was to promote women's involvement in all Knoll High School activities, the market plan had to be sufficiently diverse to reach all groups in the high school that included women. This strategy was implemented in two ways. First, Nel organized a school spirit committee. The spirit committee included women from all student clubs.[§] Second, Nel created a unifying theme: "Happiness is School Spirit."

The "Happiness is School Spirit" theme easily could be tailored for several groups. For example, "Happiness is Women's Athletics," "Happiness is Student Council," "Happiness is French Club" all were legitimate theme extensions. To market this theme in all its forms, Nel used T-shirts and buttons. Knoll's largest industry (Champion Knit Wear) contributed the money to purchase these items. The vice-president of the company had three daughters, two of whom were Knoll High School athletes.

All the T-shirts and the buttons had the slogan "Happiness is," but differed according to the club or women's team that they intended to promote. For example, some shirts and buttons contained the slogans "Happiness is Student Council," "Happiness is School Spirit," "Happiness is Women's Athletics," and so on, so that all groups had their special T-shirt or button. All T-shirts and buttons pictured women doing something. For example, the "Happiness is Women's Athletics" shirts and buttons contained a picture of a female athlete kicking a soccer ball, carrying a basketball, or hitting a tennis ball.

"Happiness is School Spirit" shirts and buttons included everyone, whether student or adult; the special shirts or buttons carried the school spirit theme further to market women's involvement in school activities.

The school spirit committee actually functioned as a public relations committee. They met once each week to talk about club and athletic activities and to plan promotions for these events. Although the spirit committee's activities varied, its central focus was activities that featured women students. For example, women who worked on the school newspaper established a column called "Be a Booster." The column covered all high school activities, but nearly 90% of it was devoted to women students and their activities. Women student leaders and women athletes received special attention in the "Be a Booster" column for their contributions toward school spirit.

The spirit committee made women students, women athletes, and women's activities far more visible within the school and the community. Part of this success resulted from networking. Because of the weekly meetings, women students knew about events and joined to make them successful. Promotional efforts also played a part. The spirit committee organized T-shirt days, special assemblies, booster days, and parades. They were able to obtain special seating sections at athletic contests, which they used to recognize the student clubs. They arranged for student clubs and women's teams to be introduced at half time during women's athletic events. Finally, their promotional efforts reached into the middle and elementary schools of the community when they also began to highlight activities and accomplishments of younger female students.

1. Why was women's basketball a second-rate attraction at Knoll High School?
2. What was the marketing objective?
3. What two considerations were involved in developing the marketing objective?
4. Which of the two considerations do you think is more important?
5. How did the marketing plan reflect the considerations listed in question three?
6. What were the key elements in the marketing plan?
7. Who were the target markets?
8. Could Nel or Knoll High School be liable for using the "Happiness is" slogan without permission?
9. Do you think Nel's marketing plan worked? Why or why not?
10. What other promotional activities would you suggest for the spirit committee?

[‡]There were two middle schools in Knoll.
[§]For example, the Student Council, Science Club, and French Club, as well as women's athletic teams.

CASE STUDY THREE: THE J.P. DODD TENNIS CLUB

In July of 1987, J.P. Dodd, the owner and manager of the J.P. Dodd Tennis Club, hired a marketing analyst to review her business and to suggest ways to increase profits from the sale of tennis court time. She reviewed the marketing report and the alternatives for reaching her two specific objectives. First, she wanted to increase her court-fill ratio from 70% to 95%. Second, she wanted to keep her profit margin at its current overall level of 18.8%. J.P. Dodd had been managing tennis courts for 25 years. She had owned her own tennis complex for nearly a decade. She was acutely aware of the pitfalls of trying to increase court usage and at the same time maintain profit margins.

Club description. The J.P. Dodd Tennis Club has eight indoor and four outdoor courts. Although the outdoor courts can be used during most of the year, the climate effectively limits planned program use to only 6 months. The club is open 360 days a year from 8:30 AM to 10:30 PM. Program offerings include group lessons, clinics, private lessons, leagues, instructional leagues, teams, tournaments, tennis parties, junior workshops, a junior starter program, junior leagues, and junior tournaments. Facilities are meager. The club has locker rooms, a vending machine area, a lounge, and a small pro shop. The tennis staff consists of a head pro who is on salary, four full-time pros, two male and two female, who are not on salary, and several part-time pros who work for minimum wage. The club also pays salaries for janitorial services, administration, maintenance, and accounting. Mortgage payments on the club are relatively small but financial resources are limited at best.

Nature of demand. The J.P. Dodd Tennis Club is located in the northwest corner of the Bauer metropolitan area. The city of Bauer has a population of 225,000; the metropolitan area contains nearly 750,000 people. The marketing report emphasized the following information:

1. Between 1980 and 1987 tennis participation in the Bauer metropolitan area increased an average of about 3% each year.
2. The age groups with the greatest increases were 33 to 44 and 45 to 54. This included both male and female participants.
3. The age groups with the most participants (male and female) were 15 to 24 and 24 to 34.

4. Ranked by the number of times an individual played each week, the two leading age groups were 25 to 34 and 35 to 44. The data also revealed that frequent players played at more than one location.
5. For men, the most popular times slots during the week were 5 PM to 9:30 PM. Popular weekend times for men were limited to Saturday mornings and early afternoons (10 AM to 2 PM). Women were more flexible. Popular weekday times for women included 9 AM to 12 PM, 1 PM to 3 PM, and 6 PM to 8:30 PM.
6. The most popular programs for men were leagues, individual matches, teams, clinics, and reserved court time. The most popular programs for women were teams, leagues, clinics, and private lessons.
7. Club location per capita was not a major determinant of club choice. Convenience of road access was more important. Most players surveyed (63%) traveled 5 to 15 miles to reach the courts.

Nature of competition. The J.P. Dodd Tennis Club is one of seven year-round tennis clubs within the city of Bauer. All seven clubs are located within a 10-mile radius of the center of the city. Two clubs are centrally located; the other five are located along compass points—northwest, northeast, southwest, and southeast. The marketing report gave the following profiles of J.P. Dodd and competing clubs:

Club A: Location along major highway provides relatively easy access. Located in high-income area. High initiation fee with monthly membership fees. Caters to upper-middle and upper class with emphasis on corporate memberships. Has a 60% court-fill ratio. Has plush facilities including locker rooms, sauna and tanning rooms, lounges, and seating and viewing areas. Has large, well-equipped pro shop. Has restaurant and bar. Offers aerobic classes, plush fitness facilities, racquetball, and swimming pool. Has 12 indoor hard-surface courts and 12 outdoor clay courts. Offers small number of tennis classes and clinics. Has very small junior program. Hosts some tournaments. Has large amount of open court time, allowing members freedom to reserve their preferred playing time.

Club B: Has the most central location of all the clubs but heavy traffic in the area makes access difficult. Located in middle-income district. Has low membership fee, no initiation fee, and no monthly fees. Attracts primarily middle-class patrons. Has a 70% court-fill ratio. Has locker rooms, small lounge area, and vending machines. Has six indoor hard-surface courts and six outdoor clay courts. Has small pro shop. Offers leagues, group lessons, clinics, teams, and private lessons. Has small junior program. Has small tournament schedule. Offers members open court time.

Club C: Located off main highway with easy access. Located in low-income district. Has low membership fee, no initiation fee, and no monthly fees. Caters to middle and lower-middle-class patrons. Has 65% court-fill ratio. Has locker rooms, two small lounge areas, and vending machines. Has small pro shop. Has six indoor hard-surface courts. Offers tennis classes, clinics, teams, leagues, and private lessons. Has junior program. Has club tournaments and hosts a few city tournaments. Has open court time.

Club D (Dodd): Has relatively easy access. Located in a mixed (middle to upper-income) district. Has low membership fee, no initiation fee, and no monthly fees. Membership is dominated by middle and upper-middle-class patrons. Has 70% court-fill ratio. Has locker rooms, vending machines, and a fair size lounge area. Has eight indoor hard-surface courts and four outdoor hard-surface courts. Offers a wide range of tennis programs.

Club E: Located slightly more than 2 miles from the Dodd Tennis Club. Has relatively easy access and is located in a mixed (middle to upper-income) area. Membership is dominated by middle and upper-middle-class patrons. Has 65% court-fill ratio. Has locker rooms, vending machines, and a large lounge and viewing area. Has small pro shop. Offers racquetball and has well-equipped fitness facility. Has 12 indoor hard-surface courts and 12 outdoor clay courts. Offers a wide range of tennis programs comparable to Dodd Tennis Club. Has some open court time.

Club F: Located just off a main highway with excellent access. Located in a middle-income district. Has membership fee, no initiation fee, and no monthly fees. Has 85% court-fill ratio. Has small locker room facilities, small lounge area, snack bar and beer license. Has small pro shop. Has four indoor hard-surface courts. Offers limited tennis program. Offers indoor soccer.

Club G: Access is difficult. Located in large business area. Clientele is middle and upper-middle class. Has 65% court-fill ratio. Has small locker room facilities, small pro shop, and small fitness center. Has six indoor hard-surface courts. Offers group and private lessons, leagues, and teams. Has open court time.

In addition to these full-time courts, the Bauer metropolitan area has six spring-through-fall tennis complexes connected to country clubs. These tennis facilities were omitted from the marketing report. In addition, there are slightly more than 300 tennis courts in the metropolitan area that offer open court time on a first-come–first-served basis. These courts were not included in the marketing report.

With the exception of club A (which advertises four times a year), all tennis clubs advertise twice a year through a newsletter and a brochure. Club programs, times, and costs are listed; club professionals are highlighted; successful players and teams are applauded; and announcements are included. Each tennis club uses a mailing list of its current and past members. The advertising campaigns do not use local radio, television, or newspapers. All clubs recruit through tennis professionals, team members, and league members.

Product life cycle. The product life cycle depends on the specific part of the tennis program. In the case of adult lessons, whether group or private, most clients (nearly 70%) stayed with one professional teacher for only two or three years and then changed to another professional. Nearly 50% of these clients changed clubs when they changed teachers. The percentages for league membership were nearly the same. Team membership, however, tended to be more stable. However, the individual and team ranking system and the new Volvo system, because they give players and teams a universally recognizable rank, make it easier for clients to change teams and possibly clubs. Individual skill level, sex, and age all influenced the length of time a client remained with a particular club. Less skilled players tended to stay with a particular coach and club for longer times. This meant that 2.5, 3.0, and 3.5-level players had longer affiliations. Players above these levels were more mobile. Male tennis players moved to a new club an average of once every 1.6 years. The most stable group was female players over 30 years of age who had ranks of 2.5 to 3.5.

Cost structure analysis. The marketing report provided the following listing of specific tennis program offerings at the Dodd Tennis Club during the period from July 1, 1986, to July 1, 1987. Each part of the program is listed and the net gain in profit per court per hour of court time is provided.

Adult program

1.	Instructional league	$13.13
2.	Clinics	10.48
3.	Leagues	8.56
4.	Teams	7.28
5.	Reserved court time	6.80
6.	Group lessons	4.08
7.	Private lessons	2.08

Junior program

1. Workshops $23.00
2. Starter program   22.00
3. Leagues   17.23

Skills of tennis club. During the period of the marketing study, the Dodd Tennis Club had a fill ratio of 70% and a profit margin of 18.8%. The report attributed the club's success in these two areas to the organizational skills and popularity of two club professionals. Any attempt to improve fill ratios and profit margin would have to be based on combining these organizational skills with the club's cost structure.

1. Are J.P. Dodd's objectives (attain a fill ratio of 95% while maintaining profit margin at 18.8%) attainable? If so, why? If not, what would you recommend?
2. What does the "nature of demand" section of the report tell us about segmentation possibilities? Target markets?
3. According to the "nature of competition" section of the report: Who are Dodd's primary competitors? What do the court-fill ratios tell us about Dodd's competitors?
4. What information does the "product life cycle" section of the report give about the target market?
5. What market mix would you recommend to J.P. Dodd?
6. How does the market mix you recommend reflect information in the section "tennis club skills"?
7. Given the data, do you think the advertising approach has been effective? How would you change the club's advertising?
8. J.P. Dodd's underlying objective is to make more money. What other alternatives (besides increasing the court-fill ratio and maintaining the profit margin) are open to her?
9. Pick one of the alternative objectives you listed in answer to question number eight and develop a marketing plan to attain it. Explain why you think the plan you develop will be successful.

CASE STUDY FOUR: HILLERICH & BRADSBY, INC.

Hillerich and Bradsby began manufacturing baseball bats in 1880. The company prospered over the next 40 years as baseball bat sales increased annually. The company's "Louisville Slugger" was a handcrafted bat endorsed by popular professional baseball players. This bat soon became synonymous with baseball excellence. Sandlot enthusiasts were eager to purchase an autographed replica of the bat used by favorite professional players. By 1921 Hillerich and Bradsby had become the leading baseball bat manufacturer. Hillerich and Bradsby launched a second line of sporting goods in 1918. The company's "XLR" golf clubs did not capture the market as successfully as did its baseball bats. In fact, in 1921 the golf club sales began to fall. The company's board of directors urged management to consider ways to ameliorate sales.

In early January of 1922, Frank Bradsby, secretary, treasurer, plant manager, and sales manager of Hillerich and Bradsby, Inc., began contemplating corporate strategies that might impove the company's marketing plan. Before 1922 Bradsby had employed cost accountants and efficiency experts to increase baseball bat production and sales. Bradsby believed that these efforts were responsible for the improvement of Hillerich and Bradsby's market position in baseball bat sales from number three in 1919 to number one in 1921.

Bradsby's objective was to improve the company's ratio of net profit to sales. The 1921 figure of 5.8% was significantly worse than the 1920 figure of 14.9%:

1920

Total sales	$293,479
Cost of goods sold	163,468
Overhead cost	86,311
Profit	43,700

Ratio of net gain to cost of goods sold = 26.7%
Ratio of net gain to sales = 14.9%

1921

Total sales	$576,086
Cost of goods sold	396,923
Overhead cost	145,671
Profit	33,492

Ratio of net gain to cost of goods sold = 8.4%
Ratio of net gain to sales = 5.8%

Nature of the problem. In further analyzing the problem, Bradsby discovered several factors that were not directly noted in the accounting report.

1. Increased labor costs (89%) contributed significantly to the increase in the cost of goods sold (143%). Ironically, the labor cost of producing

baseball bats had decreased 11% during the same time.

2. Baseball bat sales produced slightly more than 85% of total sales in 1920 and constituted nearly 94% of total sales in 1921.

3. Baseball bat sales increased 70% in 1921 over 1920.

Bradsby further discovered that 54% of the increase in the cost of goods sold could be attributed to two interrelated factors:

1. Production efficiency had declined tremendously during the late spring and summer months of 1921.

2. Sales had fallen during this same time and had continued to plummet until late November of 1921.

The production increase throughout September, October, and November, combined with smaller sales, resulted in large inventories requiring additional storage. Bradsby concluded that the drop in sales was caused by a lower demand.

Nature of the demand. The year 1921 had been a mixed year for sporting good sales in general and for baseball bats and golf clubs in particular. There were reasons for this. First, food prices had dropped significantly below 1920 prices. This caused farmers severe difficulties. Credit was tight. These factors contributed to a general business depression during the last four months of 1921. In addition, the U.S. government imposed a 10% sales tax on sporting good sales. The sales tax increased prices and angered customers. In response to the increase in prices, sporting goods dealers kept inventories low and purchased only what was sure to sell. Jobbers* and wholesalers were expected to deliver prompt and efficient service when a dealer's stock became depleted.

During the early months of 1921, jobbers and wholesalers were able to maintain abundant inventories and give sporting goods dealers the prompt and efficient service they demanded. To continue this high level of service, jobbers and wholesalers needed to carry large inventories. They did this by placing large orders with sporting goods manufacturers. However, as the year progressed, dealers submitted smaller orders. In turn, jobbers and wholesalers accumulated excess in-

ventories. They, in turn, stopped ordering from the manufacturer. Nearly 70% of the Hillerich and Bradsby business was sales to wholesalers and jobbers. When these middlemen stopped buying, Hillerich and Bradsby were forced to cut back production and let inventories grow. Because golf club production at Hillerich and Bradsby was far less efficient than baseball bat production, shutdowns and inventory increases hurt profits much more.

The marketing report for 1922 was encouraging. Most dealers, jobbers, and manufacturers anticipated a very profitable year. Baseball popularity and the demand for baseball equipment were expected to hit an all-time high. The predictions for golf were similarly optimistic. However, these optimistic predictions assumed that sporting goods manufacturers would cut prices significantly during 1922. Jobbers and dealers believed that increased sales required lower prices. Sporting goods manufacturers were asked to cut prices well below those of 1921. Jobbers demanded price cuts to make or maintain their profit margins. Jobbers blamed manufacturers for the drop in sporting goods sales during the last months of 1921. They believed manufacturers' prices had been much too high. Jobbers argued that they had been hit hard during 1921 because the stiff competition had required them to maintain large inventories to fill last-minute orders from sporting goods dealers. Sporting goods dealers wanted lower prices because they believed that consumers were most concerned with prices and most attracted by lower prices. In addition, dealers wanted more advertising and promotional aid from manufacturers. Successful dealers in 1921 reported that they had spent significant amounts of time and money on promotion and advertising. These same dealers believed that 1922 would be a successful year for dealers who went after business. They wanted manufacturers to help by sponsoring national advertising campaigns. Most dealers reported that they would continue to maintain small inventories and would be reluctant to buy in large quantities even if prices dropped significantly.

Nature of the competition. Bradsby divided the competition into two areas: baseball bats and golf clubs. In the area of baseball bats, Hillerich and Bradsby had four major competitors: (1) Thos. E. Wilson Company, (2) Spalding Brothers, (3) Wright & Ditson-Victor, and (4) Hilton Collins Company. Wilson, Spalding, and Wright & Ditson-Victor manufactured several lines of sport-

---

*A jobber is a person who starts in retail and moves to wholesale.

ing goods; baseball bats were an important but secondary interest to them. Wright & Ditson-Victor appeared to be moving out of the baseball bat business.

Before 1921 Wilson and Spalding had been Hillerich and Bradsby's biggest competitors in the baseball bat business. Improved production efficiency and national marketing had moved Hillerich and Bradsby ahead of Wilson and Spalding during 1921. Bradsby wondered whether Wilson or Spalding would try to regain the lead. Both companies had announced major price cuts. Wilson was cutting prices 15% on all its lines, and Spalding had advertised cuts of 20% to 40% on its major lines. Bradsby knew that price cuts on baseball bats would be necessary, but he doubted Hillerich and Bradsby could match even Wilson's 15% cut. Bradsby also knew that both Wilson and Spalding would give the cuts to jobbers and wholesalers. Both companies also intended to sell directly to dealers. Wilson had three major distribution centers and Spalding had 20.

The Hilton Collins Company was the newest and most dangerous competitor that Hillerich and Bradsby faced in 1922. Hilton Collins was located in Louisville, Kentucky less than a mile from the Hillerich and Bradsby plant. Hilton Collins manufactured only baseball bats. Their "Louisville Mascot" bat competed directly with the Louisville Slugger. Hilton Collins also competed directly with Hillerich and Bradsby for professional baseball players' endorsements on autograph model bats. Bradsby believed, for example, that the new Roger Hornsby autograph model Louisville Mascot bat would be an important challenge to Louisville Slugger sales. Bradsby knew that Hilton Collins was an aggressive competitor with a large sales force bolstered by national advertising.

In the business of manufacturing golf clubs, Hillerich and Bradsby had 12 major competitors. Nine of these competitors produced a wide variety of sporting equipment. Three companies concentrated solely on golf equipment. Unlike Hillerich and Bradsby, all 12 competitors manufactured golf balls and golf bags in addition to golf clubs. Three companies produced steel-shaft golf clubs. Seven of Bradsby's competitors had large distribution systems that enabled them to sell directly to dealers. Hillerich and Bradsby did not have a large distribution system and was forced to rely on jobbers and wholesalers. Hillerich and Bradsby's market

share in golf clubs was comparable to any of its competitors, and no golf club dominated the market. Bradsby believed that the company that could manufacture inexpensive, high-quality golf clubs could capture a large share of the golf club market.

Trend analysis. The marketing report said that there were the following trends in sporting goods sales.

1. Sporting goods sales had increased every year since 1918.
2. All sporting goods dealers, jobbers, and manufacturers believed that 1922 would be a banner year for sporting goods sales provided prices were cut and significant promotional efforts were made.
3. Most sporting goods, 70%, were purchased by youths 18 years of age or younger.
4. The year 1922 was predicted to be excellent for baseball bat sales.
5. The year 1922 was predicted to be excellent for golf club sales.

Additional trends shown in Hillerich and Bradsby Company records are found in the following table:

Golf club sales

Year	Sets	Percentage increase (decrease)
1918	166	0%*
1919	645	289%
1920	1229	90%
1921	1144	(7%)

Baseball bat sales

Year	Dozens	Percentage increase (decrease)
1918	26,000	29%
1919	33,000	27%
1920	44,000	33%
1921	70,000	59%

Cost structure analysis

	Sales	Cost of goods sold	Overhead	Profit
1921				
Total	$576,086	$396,923	$145,671	$33,492
Bats	$536,049	$360,049	$135,474	$40,526
Golf	$ 40,037	$ 36,874	$ 10,197	($7,034)

*No golf club sales in 1917.

Golf clubs. Hillerich and Bradsby sold their golf clubs exclusively through jobbers and wholesalers. They sold their XLR brand golf clubs for $35 a set. Competitors sold golf clubs for an average price of $20 a set. In 1920 Hillerich and Bradsby relied on jobbers and wholesalers to sell clubs and used no national advertising. This differed from Hillerich and Bradsby's competitors, who used national advertising, sold the vast majority of their golf equipment directly to dealers, and gave large distributors significant discounts.

Baseball bats. Hillerich and Bradsby manufactured several lines of baseball bats. The lines could be divided into two general categories: machine-made bats and handcrafted bats. Machine-made bats accounted for 64% of total bat sales by volume but only 32% of profits from bats. The top three sellers in each category for 1921 are as follows:

Bat name	Profit per bat	Gross profit per dozen*	Gross profit*
Machine made:			
Junior	$ .11	$1.32	$20,304
Amateur	.25	3.00	28,295
League	.34	4.13	11,956
Handcrafted:			
Slugger special	$1.15	$13.80	$52,357
Ruth autograph	1.15	13.80	37,495
Cobb autograph	1.15	13.80	36,253

---

*Does not include overhead costs.

In 1921 Hillerich and Bradsby launched a national advertising campaign for baseball bats. The central feature of this campaign was a booklet, "Famous Sluggers," that was given free to jobbers and dealers to be passed on to customers. The advertising campaign focused on autograph model bats, primarily the Ruth autograph model and the Cobb autograph model.

Hillerich and Bradsby sold nearly 70% of their baseball bats to jobbers and wholesalers. The jobbers and wholesalers benefited from a rapid bat turnover at a markup exceeding 15%. Although Hillerich and Bradsby recommended specific store prices for machine-made bats, jobbers and sporting goods dealers were able to sell the bat for much more. For example, Hillerich and Bradsby recommended that the Junior Bat be priced at $.60. Sporting goods dealers frequently sold the bat for $1 or as much as $1.20. An autographed model sold for $6 in the store. This price included a 15% markup by the jobber and another 15% by the dealer.

Strengths and weaknesses
STRENGTHS

1. The production process Bradsby used to manufacture both machine and handcrafted baseball bats was far more efficient than the process competitors used. Bradsby was applying this same process to the manufacture of golf clubs. In January of 1922 machines for manufacturing golf clubs were nearly ready to start production.
2. The national advertising campaign of 1921 and the Famous Slugger booklet had been extremely successful. Hillerich and Bradsby had become the number one manufacturer of baseball bats. Bradsby thought that this same approach might be applied to golf club sales to produce similar results.
3. The Louisville Slugger name was well known throughout the United States.
4. Hillerich and Bradsby had signed nearly all the most famous professional baseball players to contracts for autograph model bats.

WEAKNESSES

1. The company lacked a national advertising campaign for golf clubs.
2. The company lacked an efficient production system for the manufacture of golf clubs.
3. The company lacked a sufficient sales force to sell directly to sporting goods dealers.
4. The company lacked a distribution system that would enable the company to sell directly to the sporting goods dealer.

Financial resources

Year	Capitalization	Debt limit	Net worth
1918	$125,000	$75,000	$225,240
1919	$125,000	$75,000	$254,221
1920	$250,000	$100,000	$337,806
1921	$250,000	$175,000	$363,783

1. *What does the financial report for 1920 and 1921 tell us about Hillerich and Bradsby's business?*
2. *Bradsby's analysis of the "nature of the problem" has five important additions to the financial report and two interpretations of*

cause and effect. What exactly is Bradsby's problem? What actions would you suggest to correct the problem?

3. Does the "nature of demand" section support Bradsby's explanation of the nature of the problem?

4. What does the marketing report tell us about the prospects for 1922?

5. Who are Hillerich and Bradsby's competitors, and what are they doing that is different from Hillerich and Bradsby?

6. Does this difference give Hillerich and Bradsby's competitors an advantage? If it does, what would you recommend to Hillerich and Bradsby to solve the problem?

7. What do the Hillerich and Bradsby records reveal about the trends in baseball bat sales and golf club sales?

8. Does the "Cost structure analysis" section support the conclusions in the "Nature of the problem" and "Nature of the demand" sections?

9. If you were Frank Bradsby, what options would you consider for meeting the target objective (net gain in sales of 14.9%)?

10. Consider the sections on Hillerich and Bradsby's "Strengths and weaknesses" and "Financial resources." Choose one of the options you gave for question nine and explain why you believe it will be successful.

REFERENCES

Aaker, D. (1984). *Strategic market management*. New York: John Wiley & Sons, Inc.

Bernhardt, K. and Kinnear, T. (1985). *Cases in marketing management*. Plano, Texas: Business Publications, Inc.

Kotler, P., and Andreasen, A. (1987). *Strategic marketing for nonprofit organizations*. Englewood Cliffs, New Jersey: Prentice Hall.

McCarthy, E., and Perreault, W. (1984). *Basic marketing: a managerial approach*. Homewood, Illinois: Richard D. Irwin, Inc.

Pitts, B. (1986). *The case analysis model in sport administration*. Unpublished manuscript. Sport Administration Programs, Louisville: University of Louisville.

Pitts, B. (1988). *The sport industry as product: product-markets within the sport industry*. Unpublished manuscript. Sport Administration Programs, Louisville: University of Louisville.

CHAPTER 20

Computer Applications

Terry R. Haggerty

In this chapter, you will become familiar with the following terms:

Data	Scanner	EGA
Information	CD-ROM	VGA
Information overload	LAN	LCD
Information anxiety	FAX	ROM
Channel	DOS	WORM
System	MS-DOS	WYSIWYG
Mainframe	MH	Relational database
Minicomputer	K	Project management
Workstation	MB	CPM
Microcomputer	Laser printer	PERT
Personal computer	VDT	Expert systems
Modem	CGA	Data encryption
Mouse		

Overview

The thesis of this chapter is that computers, when used properly, can play a major role in helping the sport manager compile information. The first half of the chapter presents an overview of the typical hardware and software used by many sport and exercise organizations, as well as examples of computer use by sport-related organizations. The second half discusses managerial concerns that need to be addressed, such as: (1) the selection of software and hardware, (2) staff resistance to technological change, (3) ergonomics, (4) possible detrimental effects on the health of users, (5) training programs, (6) the tendency to computerize trivial tasks that can be handled adequately without the computer, (7) data safety and security, and (8) the effect computerization has on the role of a manager.

MANAGING INFORMATION

Managers need information. The principal management functions of planning, organizing, leading, deciding, and evaluating are dependent on information. Many managers consider information to be a prime resource. Accordingly, an increasing number of workers are classified as knowledge workers and work with information technology devices such as computers.

Before a discussion of the computer as an information tool, the terms *data* and *information* should be distinguished. **Data** are simply facts. **Information** is data placed in context so that they change people—perceptions, attitudes, beliefs, or knowledge base. For example, the numbers 8145550355 are data for most readers. Once the data are placed in context, such as with the explanation that the numbers represent the author's area code and phone number, then they become information. The distinction between these two terms is important, because managers require information, not data. However, the needed information is usually embedded in myriad data, and much of the data are meaningless. Today more than ever, the environment is both data-rich and information-poor.

The focus on information and information technology has resulted in a situation wherein administrators often feel that not only should the data that cross their desks be assimilated or at least read, but also that more data are needed on various other concerns. The task of staying informed can be overwhelming. For example, more information has been produced in the last 30 years than in the previous 5,000. Currently, the amount of data doubles every 5 years, and about 1,000 books are published each day (Wurman, 1989). No wonder many administrators are overwhelmed with data and are hard pressed to filter out the essential information needed to operate their sport organizations.

USING COMPUTERS TO HELP MANAGE INFORMATION

Many authors have advocated using computers to help manage this overload of information. However, an important and often overlooked caveat is that their use must be carefully designed or they will make matters worse. Naisbitt (1982) pointed

out that the net effect of the introduction of increasingly sophisticated information technology is a faster flow of information through the **channels**, bringing sender and receiver closer together and decreasing the amount of time information spends in the channel. This means that running out of information is not a problem, but drowning in it is. Penzias (1989) noted that on a typical working day, computers produce over 600 million sheets of printout in the United States alone. This is estimated to be 30 times the document output of the human work force. In a similar vein, Klapp (1986) noted that better information processing can speed the flow of data, but it is of little help in reading the printout, deciding what to do about it, or finding a higher meaning. Meaning, he noted, requires time-consuming thought, and the pace of modern life works against affording us the time to think. Wurman (1989) concluded that the problem now faced is to realize that understanding lags behind the production of data. He feels that too much attention has been focused on computers and hardware and too little on the people who actually use the information to make sense of the world and do useful things. The main problem is "much of what we assume to be information is actually just data or worse. . . . The great information age is really an explosion of non-information; it is an explosion of data" (Wurman, 1989; p. 38).

The preceding statements highlight the problem that many sport managers face—**information overload.** Information overload occurs when the information inputs are so great that they exceed the capabilities of the human information processing system (Snowball, 1979). Wurman (1989) has coined the term **information anxiety** to describe the state in which individuals are apprehensive about the nature of the information they receive and feel self-doubt about their capacity to cope with it. Managers must realize that it is impossible for them to know all the details about their organization—its budget, purchasing records, policies and procedures, and so on. Wurman concludes, "You don't have to know everything, you just need to know how to find it" (1989; p. 52).

CONCEPT CHECK

Managers face information demands in excess of their processing capabilities, which can lead to a state of information anxiety. Computers, if properly used, can assist managers to cope with the demands by increasing their capacity to store, retrieve, and selectively manipulate data.

COMPUTER SYSTEMS: AN OVERVIEW

A **system** can be defined as a purposeful set of interacting and interrelated elements. A computer system includes interrelated elements such as a microprocessor, keyboard, disk drives, monitor, printer, and software (instructions). In recent years, the technology in all these areas has undergone rapid changes. It is becoming increasingly difficult to keep up to date with new hardware and software items. The weekly television show *The Computer Chronicles,* and the biweekly magazine *PC Magazine* are filled with new developments. Although the next section is as up to date as possible, students and managers should consult with knowledgeable users before making decisions regarding hardware and software.

Hardware

Microcomputers. Computers are typically classified as **mainframe, minicomputer, workstation,** and **microcomputer** or **personal computers.** The distinctions are becoming blurred, since microcomputers are increasingly more powerful and can handle many tasks previously assigned to minicomputers. The focus of this chapter is on microcomputers. A typical microcomputer system consists of the following items:

1. The computer (microprocessor, memory)
2. A keyboard
3. A video display terminal (monochrome or color monitor)
4. One or more floppy disk drives for storage
5. A hard (or fixed) disk for storage
6. A printer
7. A **modem** (an electronic <u>mo</u>dulator-<u>dem</u>odulator for communicating between computers using telephone lines or communication satellites)
8. Additional input items such as a **mouse, scanner, CD-ROM** disk, local area network **(LAN)** connections, and barcode reader may be used. Output devices include sound synthesizers, facsimile **(FAX)** boards, and storage devices such as CD-ROM optical disks.

North American sport managers have a wide selection of vendors and machines from which to select. However, buyers must be careful in selecting a computer system because some competing machines are not software compatible. For example, Apple, Atari, and IBM computers are based on different microprocessor chips and have different disk operating systems **(DOS)**. This means that a program purchased for the Apple II family will not work in an IBM, Atari, or Tandy computer. (It is possible to purchase additional hardware options that will allow an IBM to operate Apple programs and vice versa. Also, many popular programs such as WordPerfect have versions for most machines.) Because of this lack of compatibility, an important consideration in selecting a computer is to determine which software it can run. Computer pundits recommend that first one should decide what software will perform the desired tasks, and then select a computer to run it.

For most management purposes, the main machines to consider are IBM, IBM compatibles, and Apple (Macintosh, SE) computers. IBM computers and IBM compatibles (for example, Commodore, Compaq, Dell, Swan, and Tandy) represent the largest base of computers for business use. Microsoft Corporation designed the main set of instructions—the disk operating system (DOS)—that control the general operation of both IBM and the compatibles. As a result, most computers that use the Microsoft disk operating system **(MS-DOS)** can operate the same programs. (Hereafter, both IBM and IBM-compatible computers will be referred to as MS-DOS computers.) Apple computers have made some inroads—especially in text editing; however, most business and sport organizations now use MS-DOS–based computers.

Within the MS-DOS family of computers there are several models that have very different levels of power. The main differences relate to the actual processor (chip) in the computer. Microprocessor chips are identified by manufacturers using a series of numbers such as Intel 80286 and 80386. As processors have evolved from the 8088 chip to the 8086, and then to the 80286, 80386, and 80486, they have become much faster and are able to access larger amounts of memory. Speed is typically measured in megahertz **(MH)**, the number of thousands of operations that can be performed in 1 second. Memory is measured in kilobytes **(K)**. Approximately 1,000 characters or numerals can be stored in 1K of memory. In 1982 the original IBM-PC operated with an Intel 8088 chip at a speed of 4.77 MH with total memory of 64K, and the Apple II operated with a 6502 processor at approximately 1 MH and with a memory of 48K. This chapter is being written on a machine with an Intel 80286 chip operating at 16 MH with a memory of 1,000K—a megabyte **(MB)**. Recently, 80386 and 80486 machines capable of speeds greater than 30 MH and the ability to access more than 16 MB of memory have been introduced.

The office trend is to network (hook up) many computers to share data and expensive hardware devices. A local area network (LAN) generally connects computers located within several hundred feet of one another. Most LANs select a powerful computer (for example, a 80386 machine) as a host and link numerous less powerful computers or "dumb terminals" to this host. The host machine stores the appropriate network version of the software and permits the other computers to legally use the software and share information or update a common database. A LAN can also share common peripherals such as a laser printer or plotter.

Printers. In addition to the array of computers to select from, there are various types of printers that have varying degrees of quality, speed, and cost. The main printer types are dot matrix printers, daisy wheel printers, thermal type printers (for example, IBM Quietwriter), ink jet printers, and high-quality **laser printers.**

Video display terminals. There are several options for viewing information. Most computers have video display terminals **(VDT)** with either a green, yellow, or white display (monochrome), or a color screen available with varying levels of clarity and cost. At present, the four main color display options are based on either a color graphic adapter **(CGA)**, an enhanced graphic adapter **(EGA)**, a vertical graphics array **(VGA)**, or a noninterlaced color image. Most users would consider the CGA display as barely adequate, the EGA as adequate, the VGA as very good, and the noninterlaced monitors as stunning. Portable computers can have liquid crystal displays **(LCD)**, backlit LCD, or gas plasma displays. Again, the quality of the image depends on the type of display used.

Software

Computers can do very little without software. Software is the set of instructions that operate the computer's hardware to permit a person to make use of it. DOS (usually it is software but it can be resident on a chip—firmware) handles all of the basic operating tasks. For example, when the "e" key is pressed, the screen will show an "e." DOS will allow the user to change the color of the screen, copy files, and delete files.

To do other things, like calculate a budget total or store and retrieve the names of all athletes who meet certain requirements, the operator has two main options:

1. Have a computer programmer write the necessary instruction to control the computer instructions using a computer language such as BASIC, Pascal, Forth, Cobol, Fortran, C, or ADA.
2. Buy an applications program (such as Lotus 1-2-3, dBASE IV, Clarion, R:Base) that allows a non-programmer to control the computer with a set of English-like commands, which is generally easier than programming in a more traditional language. (In most cases, these programs will also permit knowledgeable programmers to create powerful programs that can interact with other computer languages if needed.)

The main software application areas for management purposes are (1) word processing, (2) database, (3) spreadsheets, (4) graphics, (5) communications, (6) personal information managers, and (7) expert systems. In addition to the main commercial software options, there are many good "public domain" programs that are usually free or available for a nominal charge. (For a list of public domain programs, users could consult their local computer users group.)

There are many books that explain the details of many of the commercial software packages. The next few sections will provide a brief overview of the general capabilities of software in the main management application categories.

Word processing

There are many software programs designed for writing. At present, the most popular word processing program is WordPerfect. However, many writers use other programs such as Wordstar, Microsoft Word, or XY Write. Word processing programs allow the user to enter text, change it, save it, print the text, or communicate it to other computers. Powerful editing functions will cut and paste blocks of text, integrate pictures with the text, check the spelling electronically, and search an electronic thesaurus for alternate words.

In addition, electronic editors such as Right Writer, and Grammatix will even check the style of the document and offer suggestions to improve grammar. For users with a compact disk read-only memory disk (CD-ROM disk) capabilities, the information retrieval capabilities of the computer are increased considerably. Special CD-ROM players attach to computers and are similar to compact disk (CD) players that play music; however, a music CD player will not access the information stored on a CD-ROM disk. The main advantage of having a CD-ROM is sheer capacity. A single disk can hold 660MB of data. This is equivalent to 17 40-megabyte hard disks, or 270,000 pages of text. These storage devices are designed for information that needs to be accessed but not changed, hence it is "read-only memory" **(ROM)**. However, Sony has introduced a "write-once read-mostly" device **(WORM)** that permits the user to store information for archival purposes. Although the access is slower than a hard disk, the capacity makes it useful for some applications.

In early 1986, Grolier Electronic Publishing introduced the first mass-market CD-ROM disk when it introduced "The Electronic Encyclopedia." The disk includes the text of all 21 volumes of the encyclopedia plus cross-references to all 30,690 articles, bibliographies, and summaries. Microsoft Corporation introduced "Microsoft Bookshelf," a CD-ROM disk for writers. Currently, it contains the following features: (1) *The American Heritage Dictionary*, (2) *Houghton Mifflin Spelling Verifier and Corrector*, (3) *Roget's II: Electronic Thesaurus*, (4) a world almanac, (5) the U.S. ZIP code directory, (6) *Bartlett's Familiar Quotations*, (7) *The Chicago Manual of Style*, (8) *Houghton Mifflin Usage Alert*, and (9) *Business Information Sources*. The user can search for information faster than with the printed reference works and then paste the information into a document.

A main business application uses the word processor to create and print form letters. A form letter is a standard letter that has personalized information about the recipient so that the letter appears to be written specifically for the recipient, although it is sent to many individuals. A symbol such as "&" is embedded in a form letter wherever the computer should insert a name or address from a list (database) at the appropriate location in the letter. A sample form letter and the database that supplies the data are presented in Figure 20-1.

Sport-specific applications of word processing. Word processing programs are essential tools for producing error-free documents such as year-end reports for commercial health and fitness clubs, personalized form letters to athletic season ticket holders, policy and procedure manuals for intramural sport departments, and news releases for professional sport teams. Also, information produced by database and spreadsheet programs can be further processed with a word processor to produce high-quality, attractive documents suitable for public distribution.

Desktop publishing

These programs function similarly to word processors, but their editing capabilities are not as complete as a full-featured word processor. Their main purpose is to permit more complex integration of text with graphic images and provide a more accurate "what you see is what you get" **(WYSIWYG)** image on the screen. The distinction between desktop publishing programs and word processing software is becoming increasingly blurred. Many high-end word processing programs have many features that rival desktop publishing programs. With a powerful microcomputer, laser printer, and software such as Ventura Publisher, Aldus PageMaker, Legend, or GEM Desktop Publisher, users can create documents comparable to those of a publishing firm.

Sport-specific applications of desktop publishing. Exercise and sport organizations frequently need to announce events using flyers, posters, and letters that include graphic images. For example, an announcement for an aerobics class schedule could include graphics showing people exercising, intramural sport schedules could include a graphic layout of the facilities to be used, and a letter to prospective season ticket holders could highlight a box with a comment on the upcoming season. With effort and the right software, small organizations can produce impressive flyers to improve promotion and public relations ventures.

Database programs

One of the most useful programs for any organization is a **relational database** program (for example, dBASE IV, R:Base, or Clarion). A database

(FIELD)1″   (FIELD)2″   (FIELD)3″,
(FIELD)4″,
(FIELD)5″,
(FIELD)6″,

Dear (FIELD)1″   (FIELD)3″,

Your (FIELD)7″ season tickets in section (FIELD)8″ are available if you reserve within
the next 30 days. This season promises to be one of the best ever as the Lions defend their
A   national title.

We appreciate your support of the Lions since (FIELD)9″. If you need tickets for away
games, contact the ticket office soon.

Sincerely,

S. Smith,
Ticket Manager

Dr.(END FIELD)
Sally(END FIELD)
Forth(END FIELD)
123 Main St.(END FIELD)
Buffalo(END FIELD)
NY 16801(END FIELD)
2(END FIELD)
WA(END FIELD)
1973(END FIELD)
(END RECORD)
B

Prof.(END FIELD)
Cliff(END FIELD)
Hanger(END FIELD)
731 South St.(END FIELD)
Philadelphia(END FIELD)
PA 16234(END FIELD)
4(END FIELD)
NC(END FIELD)
1947(END FIELD)
(END RECORD)

FIGURE 20-1 **A,** A sample form letter and **B,** the data file to be inserted. Note that in
the actual use of WordPerfect 5.1, the parentheses in this illustration are replaced by
brackets and the quotation marks by the tidle key.

Structure for database: C:pro.dbf
Number of data records: 110
Date of last update   : 06/26/90

Field	Field Name	Type	Width
1	TEAM	Character	26
2	ADDR1	Character	26
3	ADDR2	Character	30
4	CITY	Character	20
5	STATE	Character	2
6	COUNTRY	Character	16
7	ZIP	Character	12
8	SPORT	Character	15
9	WINS	Numeric	4
10	LOSSES	Numeric	4
11	SEATS	Numeric	6

FIGURE 20-2 A sample database structure.

is considered relational if it can access data in several databases at once. This can be done as long as they are all related by identical information in each—such as a student number. A database permits the user to define categories (fields) that the organization wishes to access, such as name, address, phone, age, and 40-yard speed. Once the user creates the fields that are needed, the program will accept data that is keyed into each field. For all practical purposes, the powerful databases have sufficient capacity to store all the information any sport organization can enter. Once entered, the data can be organized (indexed) on various fields or combinations of fields and then retrieved as needed. A sample database structure from dBASE III⁺ is presented in Figure 20-2.

The user could enter basic information on all professional basketball, baseball, hockey, and football teams in North America into this database. Using simple commands, the user could then find all records that meet a certain set of criteria and display the results on the screen or have them sent to a printer. For example, to display all professional baseball, football, and hockey teams in the states of Pennsylvania and New York, ordered alphabetically by state, the user would enter the following database commands:

- Index on state to statendx
- Set index to statendx
- List state, team, city for state = "PA" .or. state = "NY"

In addition to this simple example, a relational database such as dBASE IV, FoxBase, or R:Base can link several databases to combine information from them into one report. For example, this powerful feature could link an alumni database with a season ticket database to identify the seat location and alumni status of all individuals. Once the individuals who relate to these two areas are identified, they can be "filtered" out of the main database and sent a personalized form letter such as the one in Figure 20-1.

A form letter could be generated entirely by the database program, or the data could be sent to a file that could then be used by a word processing program to create the personalized form letters.

In addition to the ability to allow users to find and display data, the more advanced programs also have their own applications language that permits an experienced user to write programs that automate many of the features that would otherwise require keyboard input.

By using an applications language, an experienced user can create a series of programs to permit an inexperienced user to complete various tasks. (For an explanation of how to program in dBASE IV the reader should consult one of the many textbooks on this topic.) A good database program is probably the most useful software program for sport managers. Students and managers are encouraged to enroll in a local course that focuses on a popular database program such as dBASE IV or R:Base.

Sport-specific applications of database programs. Databases are useful for any management task that requires storage and retrieval or large amounts of data in a combination of ways. For example, a database would be helpful in maintaining the following: equipment inventories for clubs and sport teams, consumer information for commercial health and fitness clubs, season ticket holder information in professional and college sport, injury records in the training room, athlete participation records, and awards won in intramural and athletic departments. Further, if a health and fitness club could not find a commercial program to meet its needs in keeping track of clients' training scores, one could be designed using a powerful database program such as dBASE III⁺. Raw data from various tests could be entered for preestablished formulas to calculate desired results and produce summary statistics about the clients' progress over time. Database programs are very versatile and can be used to develop customized accounting, inventory, and sport statistic applications.

A special type of database software, called **project management,** is essential for the planning and control of large, complex projects such as building a new facility or conducting a major marketing or fundraising campaign. Programs like Timeline can calculate the necessary statistics and show graphic images needed by network analysis techniques such as the critical path method **(CPM)**, and the program evaluation and review technique **(PERT)**.

Communications

An increasingly important function that microcomputers perform in today's information society is to communicate with other computers to share information. Computers can send and receive information via telephone wires, coaxial cables, satellite communication technology, and cellular phone systems. This next section will provide a brief overview of this aspect of information technology.

Microcomputers require a communication link such as cable, phone line, or radio wave link to communicate with other microcomputers or mainframe computers. When the distances are greater than about 1 mile, a device is used that converts the digital data that computers understand to a sound signal that can be carried by phone lines. An electronic device linked to a computer called a modem (modulator-demodulator) serves this purpose. A modem can be either a card that fits into a slot in a computer (internal modem) or a separate electronic box that attaches to the computer by a short cable (external modem). Once this device is connected to a computer and a normal telephone line jack, the appropriate software (for example, PROCOMM, Kermit, BITCOM, or PCTalk) can dial the phone number of another computer and then send and receive files. Also, such software as Carbon Copy Plus permits a user to remain at home and connect the computer there with an office computer and operate the office computer almost as if the user were actually using the office machine.

Computer communication provides tremendous power to the user. For example, some organizations have electronic bulletin boards that can be accessed by a computer dialing the bulletin board's phone number. Once the user has logged onto the bulletin board, an amazing variety of services are available. A typical session in which the author used a computer to access an electronic bulletin board is outlined in Figure 20-3. Entries by the user are underlined. This information can be saved on the user's disk or output on a printer.

An additional communication link available at some universities permits access to the library's holdings. For example, the Library Information Access System (LIAS) is an online library catalog that contains basic bibliographic information about books, journals, magazines, music scores, and theses that are available. Figure 20-3 illustrates only a few of the many possibilities available from one university. Many major universities are connected to an electronic mail system that allows members of the university community to communicate electronically with colleagues at other universities throughout the world. Memos, manuscripts, and files can be sent to almost any mainframe computer destination in minutes.

A similar communication procedure that uses one of the commercial online information services such as Dialog or Compuserve can provide access to most national and international publications. Dialog has 150 million records for written works available in books, newspapers, journals, magazines, and so on. For a reasonable fee, this information can be accessed from an office or home. These information utilities offer an attractive feature for professionals and students who are overloaded with information. One feature allows a user to identify topics that are of particular interest, and the information service will filter the information it receives and produce daily, weekly, or monthly reports that include only those references which fit the user's area of interest. By using the newspaper service, users can create their own personal newspaper that would include only certain filtered information, such as baseball, Detroit Tigers, Penn State football, college sports, information technology, Florida weather, or opera.

Sport-specific applications of communication software. The use of communication software will be somewhat limited until more people obtain and use computers. On campuses with widespread

ATX2DT865-2424
CONNECT 2400

LOGON AT 18:46:40 EST SUNDAY 03/04/90

EBB (Electronic Bulletin Board)

Title	Description	Title	Description
HELP	Help with EBB	TIP	For 999 entry TIP 999
MAJORS	Academic Majors	HEALTH	Health Services
PROGRAMS	Academic Programs	HOUSING	Housing
ARTS	Arts	LEGAL	Legal & Safety
ATHLETICS	Athletic Sch., Fac., etc.	PINN	Prospective Student Info.
BOOKSTORE	Book Store	RECREATION	Things To Do and See
CAMPUSES	Campuses of Penn State	STUDENTS	Services for Students
COMPUTING	Computing	SPORTS	Sports Information
DIRECTORY	Directories: Staff, etc.	UNIV-LIFE	University Life
FOOD	Eating, On & Off-Campus	TRANSPORT	Transporation

Enter the Title to select an item

—>   **.ATHLETICS**

Athletic Sch., Fac., etc.

Title	Description
FACILITIES	Hours for Buildings & other Facilities
SCHED	Schedules for Intercollegiate Athletic Events

Enter the Title to select an item, enter to quit

—>   **.SCHEDULE**

Schedules for Intercollegiate Athletic Events   (Page 1 of 2)

Title	Description
BASEBALL	Baseball
M-BASKET	Basketball (Men)
W-BASKET	Basketball (Women)
W-CROSS	Cross Country (Women)

...etc....

Enter the Title to select an item

—>   **.W-BASKET**

...etc....

FIGURE 20-3   A sample session at an electronic bulletin board (with user entries in boldface).

availability of computers, the intramural and athletic departments could design a bulletin board system that not only provides information on upcoming events, but could also allow authorized callers to sign up for recreation classes and sport clubs.

Spreadsheets

Software companies have created spreadsheets such as Lotus 1-2-3, Excel, SuperCalc, Lucid 3-D, Quattro, and Multiplan to manipulate numerical data. On a computer monitor, an electronic spreadsheet appears as a grid with thousands of rows and columns. Most monitors can display only about 19 rows and 10 columns at one time, but by using the cursor the user can scan the entire spreadsheet. One spreadsheet claims 32,768 rows and 10,000 columns—with the actual size dependent on the computer's memory. If this spreadsheet was made of paper, it would encompass a rectangle 220 yards by 270 yards! In addition, some spreadsheets, such as Lotus 1-2-3, can also manipulate a stack of 255 smaller spreadsheets so data in different spreadsheets can be related.

The intersection of a spreadsheet row and a column is called a cell. The user can type words, numbers, and financial, statistical, and mathematical formulas in the cells to complete a complex array of calculating tasks. Spreadsheets are especially suited for completing calculations with a large set of numbers. They are popular for budgeting, compiling sport statistics, and accounting. A prime feature is that once a number is changed, the entire spreadsheet can recalculate new figures in seconds. Thus a manager can plan a budget based on data available and then pursue a series of "what if" iterations to see the impact of a change in one or more revenue or expense figures. Spreadsheets also have features similar to those of simple database programs. Some organizations use spreadsheets to manage database functions; however, their capabilities do not match those of a relational database program.

Sport-specific applications of spreadsheet software. These "number crunching" programs are helpful in all types of sport organizations for preparing a budget, compiling team and league statistics, and producing financial reports on such topics as games, athletic scholarships, and meal allowances. Almost any type of numerical data can be stored, manipulated, and retrieved with these pro-grams. In general, they are easy to use and, similar to word processing programs, are found in most sport-related organizations.

Graphics

Graphics refer to the visual effects that computers can create for on-screen display and for printing, such as pictures, graphs, or the style of print used. Basic, easy-to-use programs such as Printshop and Fontesy can produce an interesting array of pictures and typefaces, whereas some of the more specialized programs such as GEM Artline by Digital Research, Inc. can produce high-quality text and original graphics from freehand drawing. The images can be rotated, scaled, colored, and then used by one of the desktop publishing programs mentioned in the word processing section of this chapter.

Business graphics such as bar and pie charts can be produced by spreadsheet programs such as Lotus 1-2-3 and Super-Calc; however, specialized programs such as Harvard Graphics are more effective in integrating pictures into a graph. Micrografx, Inc.'s program Graph Plus was selected by *PC Magazine* as one of the best graphics products. This program allows the user to draw such shapes as rectangles, squares, triangles, circles, ellipses, and parabolas that can be produced in 3-D for any surface and at varying depths. Graphics as large as 8½ × 11-inch pages can be created. When these programs are coupled with a scanner, any picture or photograph can be modified, stored, and printed.

Sport-specific applications of graphic software. In the sport management area, graphics are mainly used to make business presentation graphs and to create attractive flyers and publications. For many people, pictures are more meaningful than words and numbers. With a graphics program, a health and fitness club could provide clients with a series of bar, pie, and line graphs to show their fitness status compared with state or national norms. Managers or their assistants can produce simple desktop publishing documents such as flyers and banners to promote intramural or athletic events, and the managers can then use them to make overhead transparencies more interesting in staff development sessions. Coaches can use these programs to provide players with a series of charts to highlight offensive and defensive statistics. Since many graphic programs can access spreadsheet or database files, the user does not have to type in data that has already been entered. Thus graphs can accompany many spreadsheet documents.

Personal information managers

Personal information management software represents a category of programs that attempt to help managers keep track of the random pieces of information that come across their desks on a daily basis. They are similar to database programs but are usually less structured and more flexible in how data is entered and retrieved. Dozens of programs are available (for example, Lotus Agenda, AskSam, GrandView, The Idea Generator, and PackRat), with varying degrees of success. Rather than scribble ideas, notes, and messages on slips of paper, managers can use these software programs to bring order to these bits of information, which is helpful to the manager and any subsequent user. Typically, these programs can be used as appointment calendars, personal time trackers, outliners, and electronic note pads. Other more specific programs have expert system capabilities and lead managers through a series of steps to help them make decisions or evaluate personal management skills. In due time, these programs will be valuable aids to busy managers.

Sport-specific applications of personal information management software. Certainly, all sport managers could take advantage of the uses previously mentioned. In particular, these database-type programs would help when information arrives from a variety of sources and needs to be stored in loosely organized ways. For example, a coach with a portable computer could use one of these programs to store data on prospective athletes and their coaches. While traveling, the coach can enter data as they become available, schedule appointments, and review the data on certain athletes. Later, if needed, these data could be transferred to a more structured database program.

Expert systems

Expert systems, also referred to as knowledge systems, are computer programs that can advise, analyze, categorize, consult, and diagnose. In designing these programs, engineers interview experts to determine the set of questions, rules, or guidelines that they use to solve a problem (for example, hir-

ing competent staff). The results from the experts are used to generate a program that asks a set of questions and, based on the responses by a non-expert user, allows the user to follow a similar thought process that the experts use. The programs typically ask questions, explain their reasoning, and justify their conclusions in problem situations that normally require the expertise of a human specialist. Expert systems (such as MYCIN and PROSPECTOR) offer solutions to complex problems that are often better than those available from human experts. In addition, some expert systems software can analyze numerous examples of a phenomenon and "infer" relationships that are not obvious to the experts in the field.

The advantages of using these systems are (1) they are unbiased, (2) they can consider many variables, (3) they are reliable, (4) once developed they have a low marginal cost, and (5) if based on a valid model of a problem, they can derive the best possible solution from the available data. Harmon and King (1985) noted that in the 1990s, experts and professionals will routinely use computer knowledge systems to refine and improve their own expertise.

Sport-specific applications of expert system software. Until recently, expert system software programs were very expensive and had limited capabilities. In the near future, these programs may prove to be the most valuable type of software an organization uses. Once experts in an area are willing to share their knowledge, programs will become available. Fitness clubs could use a well-designed expert system program to help in reducing the time and calculations involved in designing individualized exercise prescriptions. Inexperienced sport managers could use these programs to help make decisions that require experience, such as hiring decisions and strategic planning. (NOTE: These programs should only *help* the manager make decisions—not actually make the decisions.)

CONCEPT CHECK

There are thousands of software items that can be used to help manage exercise and sport-related organizations. Although this vast array of options makes for difficult decisions, it provides an opportunity for knowledgeable managers to select the programs that best suit their organization's needs. Inexperienced sport managers are advised to consult with colleagues who are using computers or with computer consultants with a background in sport management to help determine the best configuration of hardware and software to suit their needs.

THE ADMINISTRATIVE USE OF COMPUTERS IN PROFESSIONAL SPORT

A recent study conducted by the author (Haggerty, 1991a) surveyed professional baseball, basketball, football, and hockey teams to determine (1) their use of hardware items such as computers, printers, and networks, (2) the software used for 30 managerial areas, (3) their computer training methods, and (4) the major computer-related problems they face.

Of the 102 professional teams that were mailed a self-administered questionnaire, 51 (50%) responded. Sixty-five percent of the responding teams used a mainframe computer (includes minicomputers and mainframes) for data-intensive administrative functions such as accounting and payroll tasks. Football teams were the greatest mainframe users—92.9% of all responding teams used mainframes. The percentages of baseball, basketball, and hockey teams using mainframes were 53.9%, 62.5%, and 37.5%, respectively.

Except for three football teams relying solely on mainframe computers, all other teams used microcomputers for administrative functions. The teams showed great variability in the number of microcomputers they used. The range ($\underline{R}$), mean ($\underline{M}$), and standard deviation ($\underline{SD}$) for the sports were as follows: (1) baseball ($\underline{R}$ = 6-54, $\underline{M}$ = 22.0, $\underline{SD}$ = 12.9), (2) basketball ($\underline{R}$ = 2-43, $\underline{M}$ = 16.0, $\underline{SD}$ = 11.7), (3) football ($\underline{R}$ = 0-50, $\underline{M}$ = 12.5, $\underline{SD}$ = 15.8), and (4) hockey ($\underline{R}$ = 3-11, $\underline{M}$ = 6.1, $\underline{SD}$ = 2.6). This large within-sport variability resulted in no significant differences among the sports in the mean number of microcomputers used. On average, teams had few of the newer 80386 machines ($\underline{M}$ = 1.6) and nearly equal numbers of AT-style 80286 computers and the older 8088 machines. Only 10 (19.6%) of the teams used Apple Macintosh (MAC) computers. One baseball team had 12 MACs, one football team had 17, and the other eight teams had 5 or fewer MACs per team.

The software programs used most frequently were Lotus 1-2-3 for budgeting (53%), and WordPerfect for word processing (33% of teams).

There was a great variety of software used for most tasks. For example, for database applications the programs noted were dBASE III (N = 3), Foxbase (N = 1), SAS PC (N = 1), Lotus 1-2-3 (N = 4), Paradox (N = 2), R:Base (N = 2), Statman (N = 1), WordPerfect (N = 2), custom programs (N = 3), and mainframe programs (N = 11). Most teams relied on a knowledgeable staff member for training computer users and hardly ever used commercial videos or tutorial programs. The most frequently mentioned problem areas were user training, improving performance, keeping abreast of technological changes—especially networks, and scarce resources.

The findings suggest that professional sport managers need to focus on better user training and consider using consultants to help them with their concerns about networks, compatibility, upgrades, and performance improvement. Because of the variety of software used, there was no clear choice for programs that students should learn. However, based on the areas of concern, knowledge of networks and the most popular MS-DOS business and education programs such as WordPerfect and Lotus 1-2-3 are advisable.

THE ADMINISTRATIVE USE OF COMPUTERS IN COLLEGE SPORT

Walnut (1987) investigated the relationship between the use of computers in the athletic department of Division I football institutions and the inclusion of computer courses in graduate level sport administration programs. He found that computers were not being used as widely as anticipated and that few colleges required their students to take computer courses. This situation has now changed. In a study of a random sample of Division I NCAA athletic departments that compete in basketball, the author (Haggerty, 1991b) found that all departments except one used microcomputers. On average, they had 12.8 microcomputers with a range of 0 to 41 machines. The most popular type was MS-DOS computers ($\underline{M}$ = 10.4). The departments had an average of 2 Apple Macintosh machines and .42 Apple II computers.

As was the case with professional sport organizations, a wide variety of software was used. However, 27% of the departments surveyed used minicomputer-based programs from Paciolan Systems to manage many of their operations, such as tickets, accounting, budgeting, financial reporting, and game reporting. The only other programs that were frequently used were Lotus 1-2-3 for financial aspects (15% of departments), and WordPerfect for word processing (27%). The most frequently mentioned problems were (1) inadequate user training, (2) problems with coordination and compatibility of their computer systems, and (3) scarce resources.

SPORT MANAGEMENT–SPECIFIC COMPUTER SOFTWARE

In addition to the normal management-related applications such as word processing, database, spreadsheet, communications, and graphics applications previously outlined, there are some sport management–specific software items available. The Software Encyclopedia (1989) listed over 55 firms that market sport management software. The programs can be grouped into the following categories: (1) athletic management, (2) sport statistics, (3) event management, and (4) fitness club management. Each of these categories will be briefly described in the next section.

Athletic management

The software package most frequently used by Division I athletic departments is that manufactured by Paciolan Systems. Paciolan offers modules that can help control business office systems, alumni databases, game analysis, training room statistics, recruiting, scheduling, sports camps, and ticketing. Although the system is designed for a minicomputer, some of the smaller modules can be used on microcomputers. Andrus and Lane (1989) have provided a brief summary of software designed for athletic departments. They identified Data Flow, MTD, Renaissance, Select Ticket Systems, and Sports Stats as companies that offer comprehensive microcomputer programs similar to those offered by Paciolan.

Sport statistics

Sport statistic programs are designed to keep track of individual and team statistics in several performance areas. The most elaborate system exists in baseball—a "numbers game". In 1988 IBM and Major League Baseball established the *Baseball Information System* (Waggoner, 1989). It consists of five databases that store information on the following: (1) player statistics, (2) waivers, (3) player con-

tracts, (4) scouting, and (5) league scheduling. An IBM System/38 minicomputer calculates 300 individual reports in 29 categories on a daily basis. A more detailed baseball decision support system is offered by the Baseball Analysis Company (BACball). BACball, at a cost of approximately 50,000 dollars, allows a team to track the characteristics of each pitch thrown (velocity, effect, and type), every batted ball, the position of the fielders, and the results of every play. The system requires two individuals—one to observe the game and another to press the appropriate computer keys—and a microcomputer for data entry.

Several companies (for example, Sports Stats, Midwest Software, and Big G Software) offer microcomputer software to help enter, compile, and report game statistics for most sports. For example, Big G Software has easy-to use, low-cost ($40-$60) sport statistic programs for baseball, baseball pitching, basketball, football, football scouting, and volleyball. The basketball program is comprehensive and records the following player and team statistics: (1) 2-point, 3-point, and free-throw shot attempts, as well as shots made and percentage of shots made, (2) assists, steals, fouls, charges taken, and playing time, (3) offensive and defensive rebounds, total rebounds, bad passes, double dribbles, lane violations, traveling, and other turnovers, and (4) five user-defined statistics. The program is not copy protected and includes a generous site license that permits all teachers on the same campus to copy and use the program. The program is written for MS-DOS and Apple IIe computers and comes with a simple manual.

Event management

Software is available to help managers run tournament-type events such as golf and tennis, road race events, and major multi-sport events such as the Special Olympics. For golf tournaments, companies such as Lake Avenue and Handicomp, Inc. have scoring and handicapping programs that are suitable for professional, as well as amateur, tournaments. The programs record and report data involving low gross, low net, partners or team best ball, and unlimited partner competition. Handicomp also has a comprehensive software package to run all aspects of a golf club operation.

A well-developed software package from Runtime Software is designed to manage races and triathlons. The program can handle up to 10,000 entrants; the user enters finish times by keyboard or by attaching an electronic timer or a push button to the computer. Competitor numbers can be read by a barcode reader for easy event entry. Numerous options are available for reporting race results.

The Special Olympics International organization has been involved in the development of a comprehensive software package that can be used in handling many of the management functions involved in operating a very large sporting event. The program, written in Foxbase Plus (a dBASE III$^+$-type development program), is invaluable for managing a complex event such as the Olympic games. The program permits the manager to perform the following tasks:

1. Register thousands of athletes, coaches, volunteers, families, and media personnel
2. Assign housing
3. Provide medical reports
4. Determine heats and seeding based on user-defined criteria
5. Enter team and individual preliminary and final results
6. Print name tags, labels, and form letters, as well as numerous summary reports about housing
7. Compile final results according to delegation, age, and so on

The above is indispensable for managing a large event.

Fitness club management

Companies such as InterVisions, HealthCheck Software, Computer Outfitters, and ClubRunner have designed software for managing health and fitness clubs. In general, these programs are useful for membership data, front desk operation, and statistical and financial reporting.

Membership management. These programs can usually store information on members, match members with other members with similar interests or schedules, prepare renewal notices, electronically transfer funds from the members' bank accounts via phone lines, and send out notices to selected members.

Front desk management. A computer equipped with a barcode reader at the front desk allows the club to perform a number of the membership features. Personal messages can be relayed by the computer screen, and reservation information can

be displayed or added. If employee data are also added to the system, the computer can keep track of hours and calculate payroll information.

Reports. The following reports on members and employees can be produced from the data entered at the front desk or through the keyboard: attendance analyses by sex, age-group, or days of the week; daily sales analysis; analyses by zip code; accounts receivable reports; employee work logs; employee overtime; and sales commissions.

ADDITIONAL MANAGERIAL CONCERNS

To use computers effectively in an organization, managers should carefully consider the following aspects of computerization:

1. Selection of software and hardware
2. Staff resistance to technological change
3. Ergonomics
4. Possible detrimental effects on the health of users
5. Training programs
6. The tendency to computerize trivial tasks that can be handled adequately without a computer
7. Data safety and security
8. The effect of computerization on the role of a manager

The next section will briefly discuss these issues.

Selection of software and hardware

Depending on the users' levels of expertise, there are several main approaches to the selection of software or hardware. The first approach is to use cost effectiveness analysis (Haggerty, 1985). In this approach the manager would determine the main factors to consider (such as ease of use, power, and training support), weigh the importance of these factors, list the possible alternative products, estimate how effective each alternative would be in meeting needs, and then calculate a weighted effectiveness score for each alternative. The product with the highest weighted effectiveness is the best suited for the task at hand. To take cost into account, divide the effectiveness score by the cost and express the result as a ratio. This is known as the cost: effectiveness ratio. The best choice will have the lowest score. This procedure is appropriate if the manager knows what is needed and has detailed information about the competing products.

A second approach is to select the software and

hardware that similar users have found effective for their needs. This approach is conservative and has the advantage that there is often safety in numbers. For this approach, the survey results presented earlier in this chapter are especially helpful. In addition, *PC Magazine* carries a "Pipeline" section that identifies the top 10 business software sellers. Based on the information available at the time of this writing, managers should select Lotus 1-2-3 for spreadsheet applications, dBASE IV for serious database projects, and WordPerfect for word processing.

However, for each application area there are several quality commercial and public domain products that are less expensive and as effective as those in the top 10 list. In addition, the consumer should be aware that the bestsellers are often the products that are advertised the most. The advantage of selecting one of the popular "heavyweights" is that a large third party aftermarket (such as consultants and user clubs) provides many training aids, books, and other services that can help a manager solve specific problems.

A third approach is to hire a sport software consultant to aid in the purchase decision and implementation. The advantage here is that the consultant can select software that can be modified to suit the unique needs of the specific organization.

Staff resistance to technological change

Many employees resist technological change (McNamara, 1989). This resistance often occurs when the jobs of employees, including managers, are threatened by the four *R*'s: redundancy, redeployment, retraining, and reduced skills (Laver, 1989). The wise manager seeks to ease the undesirable effects of technological change; Laver noted that one way is to accomplish this is by allowing those who will be affected by a new system to participate in setting the specifications for its design and then to plan and oversee its implementation and operation. Laver stresses that the involvement must be genuine, not merely superficial. There must be real possibilities for modification based on user input. In addition, the involvement of employees in the introduction of a new system typically produces a better system.

Ergonomics

Managers should realize that the addition of a computer system to an employee's work area necessitates a consideration of many other physical factors. The following is a brief list of factors to consider.

1. Sufficient grounded electrical outlets
2. Possible change in lighting, or blinds, to cut glare
3. The adequacy of the desk for positioning a computer and printer
4. The additional noise resulting from keyboards and printers
5. The use of antistatic mats
6. Devices to secure (lock) the equipment, if necessary

Because of the numerous factors to consider, an office specialty firm should be consulted before installing computer systems. These additional items may cost more than the computers.

Health-related concerns

Users may experience real or imagined health-related problems with extended use of computers. These concerns range from wrist, forearm, back, and eye problems due to typing (keyboarding) for extended periods, to the possibility of harm to the fetuses of pregnant women due to VDT emissions (McAlister, 1987). In addition, McAlister noted that feelings of powerless and victimization resulting from automation may contribute to users' health complaints, which in turn may be largely psychosomatic. McAlister (1987) noted that one study found significantly more musculoskeletal complaints among clerical VDT operators than among a group of professionals who used VDTs just as heavily. Managers can choose to solve this problem by limiting the amount of time that an employee spends at a computer each day (for example, a maximum of 3 to 4 hours a day). This may require a change in job description to delegate noncomputer tasks (such as filing, sorting mail, dealing with the public, answering the telephone, and so on) among several people.

Training programs

Learning to use effectively one of the powerful application products such as dBASE IV, Lotus 1-2-3, and WordPerfect is not easy. The process is analogous to climbing a mountain—one has to expend much time and effort to "get on top of it." Managers should provide time and the necessary resources for members of their staff to get on top of the software *before* they are expected to use it productively.

What to computerize

Managers should recognize that some tasks should not be computerized. Computer users tend to consider all tasks as suitable for a computer. This tendency fits the "Law of the Hammer." This analogy states that if you give a 2-year-old child a hammer, he or she will soon hammer all things—the floor, toys, walls, fingers, breakable items, and so on. In an analogous way, some computer pundits suggest computerizing appointment books and other data that can be easily located using paper files.

Cheng (1989) noted that too many people seem to regard computers as a magical push-button solution to all their problems. He states that a kind of computer chic prevails, convincing many people that they must computerize or be left behind. Cheng aptly states, "A computer doesn't necessarily mean efficiency and a manual system doesn't necessarily mean inefficiency. There's a time and a place for every kind of system and if you think it through and decide not to computerize, that doesn't mean you are backward. You may very well be justified" (p. 28).

Data safety and security

Data safety. One important consideration that is often overlooked is the safety of the data. Hard disks will undoubtedly fail (crash) at some point, the magnetically stored data on floppy disks can be scrambled by the magnets in telephones, and power failures can render a database useless. Managers should be sure that all staff make frequent back-ups of all data. The frequency depends on the amount of data that is crucial to the organization. For example, a word processing operator may only have to back up files once per week, since a paper copy or audio tape of letters and memos is usually available. However, an online facility or ticket reservation system might require an automatic data back-up each hour.

Users should assume that the hard disk or floppy disk may be destroyed at any minute and take protective back-up measures. Software programs such as Fastback and PC Tools Deluxe are useful in automating the back-up procedure. Three back-ups of essential data are recommended, and one copy should be kept in a different building in case of a catastrophic fire.

Data security. Security measures are necessary to prevent confidential data (such as salary figures and staff and athlete personal data) from being viewed and to discourage computer crime. Computer crime is a relatively new phenomenon, which may occur when a disgruntled staff member attempts to sabotage organizational data or when others—even those outside the organization—infect the data with a computer "virus" that either destroys data or causes the system to crash. Also, financial data may be altered to benefit an individual.

In addition to a back-up procedure, managers should set up data-handling policies to protect the organization. Laver (1989) noted that most computer crimes have been committed by trusted insiders and suggests the procedures outlined below:

1. Establish stringent control over the removal of disks and printed outputs.
2. Check all log-ins and contacts from remote terminals to ensure that the person is authorized to use the system for the purposes specified at the prescribed time of the day. The computer can do this automatically through a series of screenings that include a password and restricted access to files.
3. Ensure that the patterns of users from individual terminals, including their access of individual records and files, are being logged by the computer. Any significant change in use (such as volume or files accessed) will then be automatically reported to the data manager.
4. Use **data encryption** programs for confidential information; these programs can encode the data so only individuals with the encryption key can access the data.
5. Establish regular audits and random security inspections to delay the onset of complacency.

Laver noted that given time, a determined expert can penetrate the security of even the most elaborate system—the important thing is to see that enough time is not available.

Effect of computerization on the role of the manager

Penzias (1989) noted that as automation reduces the number of lower-skilled workers needed to perform a given task, more work is generally required from the managers supervising them. In addition, he noted that as the workforce continues to become more specialized and technically sophisticated, "more managerial effort will go into understanding the work of subordinates to supervise their work. . . . The more knowledge a job demands, the more help and expert supervision it requires" (p. 113). This trend should not only challenge sport managers, but highlight the importance of becoming computer literate in the major software categories covered in this chapter.

CONCEPT CHECK

The purchase of computers and the appropriate software is only the first step in using computers effectively. It is essential to realize that the most important resource of an organization is its staff. Therefore managers must carefully consider the human factors associated with using computers. This is best achieved by including staff in decisions about setting the specifications and in planning and overseeing the implementation and operation. The participation must be genuine, not merely superficial.

SUMMARY

1. Managers need information. The main management functions of planning, organizing, leading, deciding, and evaluating are dependent on information. However, many administrators are overwhelmed with data and are hard pressed to filter out the essential information needed to operate their sport organizations.
2. An important consideration in selecting a computer is to determine what software it can run. First, decide what software will perform the desired tasks, then select a computer to run it.
3. Most business and sport organizations now use MS-DOS–based computers. The office trend is to network many computers to share data and expensive hardware devices.
4. The main software application areas for management purposes are (1) word processing, (2) database, (3) spreadsheets, (4) graphics, (5) communications, (6) personal information managers, and (7) expert systems.
5. Professional sport teams and athletic departments noted that the most frequently mentioned problem areas were (1) inadequate user training, (2) problems in coordination and compatibility of their computer systems, and (3) scarce resources.
6. Sport-specific software is available to help managers operate tournaments, calculate game statistics, manage road races, and control the vast amount of data needed to effectively host a major multi-sport event such as the Olympic games.
7. To use computers effectively in an organization, managers should carefully consider the following (1) selection of software and hardware, (2) staff resistance to technological change, (3) ergonomics, (4) possible detrimental effects on the health of users, (5) training programs, (6) the tendency to computerize trivial tasks that can be handled adequately without the computer, (7) data safety and security, and (8) the effect computerization has on the role of a manager.
8. To improve the effectiveness of computerizations and to reduce staff resistance to change, ensure that those who will be affected by a new system participate in setting the specifications for its design and in planning and overseeing its implementation and operation.
9. The addition of a computer system to an employee's work area necessitates a consideration of many physical factors.
10. Users may experience real or imagined health-related problems with extended use of computers.
11. Managers should provide time and the necessary resources for members of their staff to learn the software *before* they are expected to use it productively.
12. Managers should recognize that some tasks should not be computerized. A computer does not necessarily mean efficiency, and a manual system does not necessarily mean inefficiency.
13. Managers should ensure that staff members make frequent back-ups of all data.
14. Security measures are necessary to prevent confidential data from being viewed and to discourage computer crime.

CASE STUDIES AND ACTIVITIES

1. Naisbitt (1982) concluded, "The more high technology around us, the more need for human touch" (p. 53). Do you agree? If yes, what does this mean for sport managers? If you do not agree with the statement, explain why not.
2. Interview a sport manager. Identify sport management tasks that are computerized (such as

scheduling the use of facilities and compiling game statistics) and ask the manager to comment on the benefits and liabilities of using computers. Report your findings to the class.

3. Select a sport management topic that interests you. Go to a library that offers online database services (such as DIALOG or BRS), and have a librarian perform a computer search for the topic. Be sure to set a dollar limit for the cost of the search before it is begun. (If the library permits users to search on CD-ROM, try the search yourself.)

4. In his article on computers in pro baseball titled *It's A Whole New Ballgame* (1989), Waggoner states that "Fresh-faced computer phenoms are challenging crusty old-timers for the soul of the National Pastime. The winner will decide the future of the game itself." Will computers change sports such as baseball? Discuss.

5. Some people would argue that administrators work mainly with people and do not really need to know how to operate a computer. Discuss.

6. Use the data at the bottom of Figure 20-1 to create a form letter to five individuals. (NOTE: The actual symbols and data structure will depend on the word processor used.)

7. Use a spreadsheet to compile basic game statistics for a game in a sport of your choice. For example, in basketball the spreadsheet might identify for each player (1) field goals, (2) free throws, (3) minutes played, (4) fouls, and (5) assists. Totals, highs, lows, and averages for the team could be computed. In addition, can you create a bar graph to indicate the field goals for the top five players?

8. Contact your local state or provincial Special Olympics chapter to volunteer as an assistant to the computer committee.

9. As a group project, visit vendors, read trade publications, and interview users about designing a complete computer system to manage one of the following: (1) college or high school athletic department, (2) college or high school intramural department, (3) fitness club, (4) retail sport store, or (5) a sport team.

REFERENCES

Andrus, S., and Lane, S. (1989). Athletic software programs. *College Athletic Management, 1*(3):34-36.

Cheng, V. (1989). Computers' best use is in information management. *Athletic Business, 13*(3), 28-31.

Haggerty, T. (1985). *Developing microcomputer literacy: a guide for sport physical education and recreation managers.* Champaign, Illinois: Stipes Publishing Co.

Haggerty, T. (1991a). *The administrative use of computers in professional sport organizations.* Unpublished manuscript. Pennsylvania State University.

Haggerty, T. (1991b). *The administrative use of computers in Canadian and American athletic programs.* Unpublished manuscript. Pennsylvania State University.

Harmon, P. and King, D. (1985). *Expert systems: artificial intelligence in business.* New York: John Wiley & Sons, Inc.

Klapp, O. (1986). *Overload and boredom: essays on the quality of life in the information society.* New York: Greenwood Press, Inc.

Laver, M. (1989). *Information technology: agent of change.* Cambridge: Cambridge University Press.

McAlister, N. (1987). Visual display terminals and operator morbidity. *Canadian Journal of Public Health, 78*(1), 62-65.

McNamara, B. (1989). Relationship between computer resistance and worker characteristics in the sport industry: an exploratory analysis. *Journal of Sport Management, 3*(1), 33-43.

Naisbitt, J. (1982). *Megatrends.* New York: Warner Books, Inc.

Penzias, A. (1989). Managing in a high-tech world. *PC/Computing, 2*(8), 108-115.

The software encyclopedia 1990: system compatability/applications. New York: R.R. Bowker.

Snowball, D. (1979). Information overload in accounting reports: too much, too little, or just right? *Cost and Management, 53*(1):22-28.

Waggoner, G. (1989). It's a whole new ballgame! PCs and baseball. *PC Computing, 2*(6), 61-73.

Walnut, H. (1987). Computers in college and university athletic departments: the case for inclusion of computer courses in graduate sports administration curricula. *Pennsylvania Journal of HPERD, 57*(1):4-5.

Wurman, R. (1989). *Information anxiety.* New York: Doubleday & Co.

Sport software companies mentioned in the chapter

Avenue Software, 650 Sierra Madre Villa, Pasadena, CA 91107-2013

Big G Software, Rt. 2 Box 111, Alleyton, TX 78935

ClubRunner, 1 Devika Drive, Englewood, NJ 07631

Computer Outfitters, 4633 East Broadway, Tucson, AZ 85711

Data Flow, 314 Church Street, Greensboro, NC 27041

HealthCheck Software, 16801 Addison Road, Dallas, TX 75248

InterVisions Inc., 9001 Airport Blvd., Suite 209, Houston, TX 77061

Midwest Software, 22500 Orchard Lake Road, Farmington, MI 48024

MTD, 8050 Seminole Office Center, Suite 300, Seminole, FL 34642

Paciolan, 2875 Temple Avenue, Long Beach, CA 90806

Renaissance, 320 Congress Avenue, Suite 200, Austin, TX 78701

Runtime Software, 3717 Wildwood Drive, Endwell, NY 13760

Select Ticket Systems, P.O. Box 959, Syracuse, NY 13201

Sports Stats, 320 Brookes Drive, Hazelwood, MO 63042

CHAPTER 21

Ethics

Scott Branvold

In this chapter, you will become familiar with the following terms:

Relativism	Ethics
Rationalization	Teleology
Morality	Utilitarianism
Values	Deontology
Moral norms	Theory of justice
Moral principles	Principle of proportionality
	Ethical code

Overview

This chapter provides the foundation for a rational application of the principles of ethics to the ethical problems that confront the sport manager. Such principles, some would argue, are not being applied systematically or with any consistency in matters of moral uncertainty. Many would suggest that the present ethical environment is in an abysmal state in all facets of life. Members of society are regularly exposed to accounts of unethical and illegal activities in many basic social institutions, including government, business, and even religion. Government has certainly had its share of incidents of ethical misconduct. During the Reagan admin-

istration, several of Ronald Reagan's top advisors resigned and some were charged with influence peddling, all of which led to the coining of the phrase "sleaze factor" in reference to many of Reagan's aides. Even the Speaker of the House, James Wright, relinquished his congressional seat after an ethics committee investigation uncovered questionable behavior.

The business world has also been confronted with ethical problems, some of monumental pro-

A debt of gratitude is owed to Dr. R. Scott Kretchmar, whose insightful and substantive comments aided greatly in the preparation of this chapter.

portions. Several recent polls suggest a very basic distrust of American business and businesspeople (Robin and Reidenbach, 1989). Situations such as the insider trading scheme and the junk bond financing scandal in the late 1980s involving Ivan Boesky and Michael Milken (among others) have done nothing to alter this apprehension. Although the "caveat emptor" or "let the buyer beware" ideology may not be as prevalent or acceptable as it once was, many consumers are still skeptical. The many instances of disregard for consumer safety and the environment that frequently plague business organizations simply add to the perception that business operates in an ethical quagmire.

Even religion, which is the foundation for the moral beliefs of many, has had embarrassing ethical problems. Examples include the indiscretions of prominent television evangelists, which received enormous publicity and damaged the credibility of their respective religious efforts.

The business of sport has not been immune to or isolated from the ethical problems so prevalent elsewhere. The belief that sport is a haven for fair play and justice is largely a romanticized ideal. College athletic programs are being investigated with monotonous regularity, and famous professional athletes routinely appear on magazine covers—for their deeds and exploits *off* the field rather than *on* it. Olympic athletes are banned from competition for drug use, and fitness clubs make outlandish advertising claims while using staffs of high-pressure salespeople with little or no fitness training.

Whether the level of ethical behavior in society and business today is significantly different from other eras or generations is probably subject to debate. What is apparent, however, is that behavior in this day and age is likely to be more closely scrutinized and ethical misconduct likely to be more widely publicized. Actions appear to be guided by a sense of **relativism**, a belief that there are no absolutes, and what is right or wrong depends on the situation (Robin and Reidenbach, 1989). One consequence of this relativism is the loss of clear standards and expectations, which increases the latitude for rationalizing one's actions.

Rationalization of actions occurs in a variety of ways. Perhaps the chances of getting caught are slight, or the penalties are minimal. In some circumstances, behavior is justified by saying "Everyone else is doing it!" or "Who's going to be hurt?" Actions may also be rationalized because the stakes are sufficiently high to be worth the risks. For example, the economic incentives of successful college football and basketball programs may be enough to produce recruiting improprieties. This contingent view of what is acceptable may actually create confusion about ethics itself. Individuals charged with ethical misconduct frequently defend their actions by saying "I have broken no laws." Rather than viewing the law as the floor for acceptable behavior, many view the law as the standard for ethical conduct. The result is an increasingly regulated society that relies on the law rather than on ethical standards to achieve fairness and justice. Kristol states, "It is a confession of moral bankruptcy to assert that what the law does not explicitly prohibit is therefore morally permissible" (In Solomon and Hanson, 1983; p. 2). It seems that rules are now viewed as barriers to get around rather than guidelines by which to live. A monument to this perspective is the voluminous NCAA manual, which undergoes frequent revisions to close the loopholes that are continually sought in order to beat the system. If this represents the standard most people and organizations use to guide their actions, then an ethical crisis does indeed exist.

FUNDAMENTAL CONCEPTS

Developing a foundation for ethical analysis first requires an understanding of the fundamental concepts of morality and ethics. These terms are often used interchangeably, and although one must not get bogged down in semantics, a brief discussion of distinctions between the two terms is appropriate.

Morality has been defined as the special set of **values** that frame the absolute limitations on behavior. It may include such basic rules as "Don't steal" **(moral norms),** as well as a more general system of duties and obligations **(moral principles)** (Solomon and Hanson, 1983).

De George (1982) and Beauchamp and Bowie (1988) place emphasis on morality's concern with the "good and bad" or "right and wrong" character of actions within the context of social customs and mores of any particular culture. They also stress the idea that morality is based on impartial considerations and that individuals cannot legitimately create their own personal moral codes.

De George (1982) defines **ethics** as a systematic attempt to make sense of our moral experience to determine what rules should govern conduct. This definition suggests that ethics is the study of morality. Beauchamp and Bowie (1988) and Velasquez (1988) seem to support this idea, while stressing that ethics involves the justification and application of moral standards and principles.

CONCEPT CHECK

Although the terms "morality" and "ethics" are used interchangeably, ethicists do note some semantic differences between them. Morality provides the set of values that limit behavior, whereas ethics involves the application of and justification for moral principles.

PERSONAL MORAL DEVELOPMENT

Often morality is viewed as a matter of personal conscience, with everyone entitled to their own moral opinion. However, morality is much more objective than many perceive. Moral development involves the ability to distinguish right from wrong; this ability to make moral judgments and engage in moral behavior increases with maturity (Cavanaugh, 1984).

Lawrence Kohlberg (1976) has developed perhaps the most widely accepted model of individual moral development, which involves three developmental levels with each level subdivided into two stages.

Level I: *Preconventional.* At this level, a child can respond to rules and social expectations and can apply the labels "good," "bad," "right," and "wrong." These rules, however, are seen as externally imposed (such as by parents) and in terms of pleasant and painful consequences (for example, a spanking for wrongdoing or a piece of candy for desirable behavior). The child does not have the ability to identify with others, so the motivation for action is largely one of self-interest. Stages one and two within level I reflect largely instrumental orientations. The behavior is not motivated by a moral sensitivity but simply by the consequences of an action—at first avoiding punishment and later receiving rewards and praise.

Level II: *Conventional.* At this level the expectations of family and peer groups become primary behavioral influences. The individual exhibits loyalty to the group and its norms and begins to identify with the point of view of others. This level is characterized by conformity and a willingness to subordinate individual needs to those of the group. The first stage within this level (stage three) focuses on a "good boy/nice girl" morality, in which good behavior involves conforming to the expectations of family and friends. Actions are guided by stereotypes of what is normal behavior and are frequently judged by intention. The next stage of this level (stage four) is termed the "law and order" stage. Right and wrong extends to conforming with societal laws, and there is a recognition of socially prescribed duties, responsibilities, and obligations. De George (1982) contends that most adults live at this conformity stage of development and that many never go beyond it.

Level III: *Postconventional or Principled.* At level III, there is an attempt to find a self-chosen set of moral principles that can be justified to any rational individual. Proper laws and values are those to which any reasonable people would want to commit, regardless of social position or status. The first stage (stage five) within this level has a social contract orientation. There is an awareness of conflicting personal views and a sense that the rules should be upheld impartially because they are the social contract. A primary concern in this stage is that laws and duties be based on their overall utility as guided by "the greatest good for the greatest number." Cavanaugh (1984) points out that this stage is the "official" level of moral development of the United States government and the Constitution. The final stage (stage six) is based on the acceptance of universal ethical principles. At this stage, appropriate action is defined by the conscious choice of universal ethical principles that are comprehensive and consistent and deal with justice, equality, and human dignity. The motivation for adherence to these principles is a basic belief in their encompassing validity and a willingness to commit to them (Cavanaugh, 1984; Kohlberg, 1976; Velasquez, 1988).

Kohlberg's model of moral development describes the progression of moral reasoning from the childlike motivations of avoiding a spanking to the mature moral reasoning of taking a principled stand based purely on the "rightness" of the principle. Kohlberg's level III has at its roots the most widely accepted normative ethical theories, which serve as the basis for ethical analysis.

THEORIES OF ETHICS

Normally, references to ethical theories or decision rules take the form of simple ethical maxims, such as the following (Laczniak and Murphy, 1985):

1. *The golden rule*: Act toward others the way you would want them to act toward you.
2. *The utilitarian principle*: Act in a way that results in the greatest good for the greatest number.
3. *Kant's categorical imperative*: Act in such a way that the action taken under the circumstances could be a universal law or rule of behavior.
4. *The professional ethic*: Take only actions that would be viewed as proper by an impartial set of professional colleagues.
5. *The TV test*: Act in such a way that the actions could be defended comfortably in front of a national television audience.

While these maxims may serve as handy "rules of thumb" for ethical conduct, the purpose of this section is to provide a more comprehensive foundation for ethical analysis. Several authors have developed theories for the ethical analysis of actions and decisions. Most of these theories are either teleological, deontological, or some combination of the two.

Theories based on **teleology** (from the Greek meaning "end") assess the morality of actions on the basis of the consequences or results of those actions; the most widely studied of these theories is **utilitarianism**. Jeremy Bentham (1748-1832) and John Stuart Mill (1806-1873) were the most influential developers of utilitarianism, which is predicated on the idea of "creating the greatest good for the greatest number." Actions are evaluated by judging their consequences and weighing the good effects and bad effects. The attempt is to achieve an optimal balance of benefits vs. harms on those affected by the action. Applying utilitarianism to decision making requires selecting the action that will produce the greatest net social benefit. The good of the group supersedes the good of the individual (Beauchamp and Bowie, 1988; De George, 1982; Robin and Reidenbach, 1989). The major criticisms of the utilitarian approach include (1) the difficulty in measuring utilitarian value, (2) the opportunity for unjust net consequences, and (3) the lack of concern for how results are produced (Beauchamp and Bowie, 1988).

The deontological or formalistic approach to ethical analysis was formulated primarily by Immanuel Kant (1734-1804), with more contemporary work done by William D. Ross and John Rawls. **Deontology** (derived from the Greek for "duty") is based on the idea that what makes an action right is not the consequences but the fact that the action conforms to some absolute rules of moral behavior. Kant's categorical imperative statements serve as guidelines for what would be considered moral behavior. Moral action would (1) be universalizable (that is, it would make sense for everyone in a similar situation to take the same action), (2) demonstrate respect for the individual (that is, others are never treated simply as means), and (3) be acceptable to all rational beings (Tuleja, 1985). Kant's vision was one of universal and consistent application of the rules of morality. His critics maintain that the theory is too vague and imprecise. There are also claims that it does not help resolve the issue of balancing conflicting individual rights and has too little regard for consequences (Velasquez, 1988).

Ross put forth a theory that combined certain aspects of utilitarianism with Kantian theory. He postulated that action is bound by the duties of fidelity, gratitude, justice, beneficence, self-improvement, and noninjury. These are seen as universal moral obligations above and beyond the law, but there is a recognition that some exceptions may exist (Laczniak and Murphy, 1985).

John Rawls has also formulated an influential ethical approach called the **theory of justice**. The major premise behind his proposals is that rules and laws of society should be constructed as if we did not know what roles we were to play in that society (what Rawls terms the "veil of ignorance"). This creates an objectivity and fairness to the ethical principles that guide actions (Cavanaugh, 1984).

CONCEPT CHECK

The most widely accepted ethical theories are either teleological or deontological in nature. Utilitarianism is the most prominent teleological theory, and its focus is on consequences of actions and "creating the greatest good for the greatest number." Deontology has a more absolute orientation, suggesting that what makes an action right is not consequences but adherence to basic moral laws.

MODELS FOR ETHICAL ANALYSIS

The ethical theories in the previous section provide the foundation for numerous models that can aid in evaluating moral dilemmas. An approach suggested by Tuleja (1985) has a utilitarian orientation in which actions are evaluated on the basis of their effect on various constituent groups or stakeholders. Owners, employees, customers, the community, and society as a whole are identified as the stakeholder groups that should be of concern to decisionmakers.

Many of the models use a combination of the basic theories to provide a multi-dimensional approach to dealing with ethical questions. Goodpaster (1984) summarized three avenues for ethical analysis, one based on utility (maximal benefits), one based on rights, and one based on duty or obligation. Garrett (1966) developed a theory specifically with the business manager in mind that combines concern for outcomes (utilitarianism) and process (deontology) and adds the dimension of motivation. These three components (means, ends, and intentions) are synthesized into what Garrett calls the **principle of proportionality**, which states that undesirable side effects of an action can be accepted if and only if there is some proportionate reason for doing so (Laczniak and Murphy, 1985).

Cavanaugh (1984) has also suggested a tridimensional approach to ethical decision making that includes characteristics of both teleological and deontological theories. He uses utility, rights, and justice as the ethical evaluation criteria. If conflicts arise among the three criteria, further analysis must be done based on the relative importance of the criteria, the freedom with which the action is taken, and the nature of the undesirable effects. Figure 21-1 provides a flow chart of steps to guide this ethical evaluation process; it is rather simplistic but does provide a system that can be useful in decision making.

CONCEPT CHECK

The models for ethical analysis are built on the foundations of basic ethical theories. They are not designed to provide indisputable answers to every ethical dilemma, but they can provide a systematic methodology for assessing ethical questions and clarifying the alternatives. Cavanaugh's model is but one of many approaches that may be useful in the quest for ethical decisions.

PERSONAL ETHICS AND ORGANIZATIONAL RESPONSIBILITY

The foundation for ethical analysis has a personal orientation. The distinction between personal and professional ethics is a difficult matter to address. Ultimately, organizations are collections of individuals and decisions are made and carried out by individuals. This would seem to indicate that the ultimate responsibility for ethical behavior rests with the individual, thereby demonstrating the importance of personal ethics. If this is the case, however, how is it that people who consider themselves to be basically honest and compassionate can act irresponsibly at times? It seems as if a different set of values are applied on the job than are applied outside the workplace. One author cites a former corporate vice-president who says, "What is right in the corporation is not what is right in a man's home or in his church. What is right in the corporation is what the guy above you wants from you" (Jackall, 1988; p. 6).

Circumstances may arise in which professionally defensible behavior is not always congruent with the guiding principles of ordinary norms. Honesty is a basic virtue; yet, at the personal level the "little white lie" may be a justifiable action for some situations. Are the standards of honesty at the professional level any different?

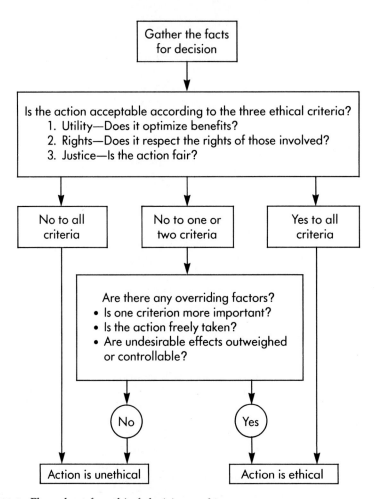

FIGURE 21-1 Flow chart for ethical decision making.
From Cavanaugh, G. (1984). *American business values* (2nd Edition). Englewood Cliffs, New Jersey: Prentice Hall. 2nd ed., 1984.

Advertisers use the "white lie" in many cases; they stretch or bend the truth with inflated claims and exaggerations. Indeed, advertising is often considered one of the most ethically suspect aspects of business operations. An example of advertising that is not dishonest but certainly misleading involves food products advertised as "cholesterol free." In many cases these products never had cholesterol, and consumer advocates claim such advertising is misleading because it implies something has been done to remove cholesterol or that other similar products have it. A recent advertisement for a Continental Basketball Association (CBA) franchise encouraged people to purchase tickets to see a team whose roster was purported to be filled with future National Basketball Association (NBA) stars. Anyone familiar with professional basketball recognizes the extravagance of such a claim, yet many would not question the ethics of such an advertisement.

There are many examples both personally and professionally in which behavior does not adhere to the ideal societal standards of virtue. The frequency of departure from these standards and, perhaps more importantly, the willingness to routinely accept such departures are basic ethical concerns.

Milton Friedman, a prominent American economist, maintains that businesses are amoral entities and the corporate executive's only responsibility is to maximize profit. Yet even this extreme proponent of free market capitalism recognizes that this must be accomplished within the framework of basic societal rules of law and custom. Work values may be developed through conscious organizational effort, or they may evolve without organizational attention. When performance is the primary or perhaps only organizational value supported, the result may be an "anything goes" ethical climate. Indeed, there are likely to be situations in which unethical behavior will produce greater profits, especially in the short run (Robin and Reidenbach, 1989). Organizations that ignore or even reward unethical behavior are likely to have personnel who behave unethically.

The role models of an organization will set the tone for the behavior of the entire organization. Kristol states, "Businessmen have come to think that the conduct of business is a purely "economic" activity to be judged only by economic criteria and that moral and religious traditions exist in a world apart, to be visited on Sunday perhaps" (In Solomon & Hanson, 1983; p. 2).

The leadership of the organization will determine what the dominant perspective is toward ethical behavior. The demands, expectations, and traditions of an organization will be the behavioral guides. The organizational leader must set clear, unambiguous expectations for the ethical conduct of its employees. When this is done, employees must then be given the authority to act and be held accountable for the ethical quality of their actions. It takes integrity and courage to act on one's values, especially when the stakes are high. An organization must work diligently to create a climate in which ethical conduct is a matter of habit rather than one of expedience.

CONCEPT CHECK

The relationship between personal and professional ethics is difficult to determine with great precision. Individuals will bring a personal set of values to the job, but to what extent that set of values will influence job behavior depends on a number of factors, including the strength with which those values are held, the integrity and courage to act upon those values, the ethical environment within the organization, and the role models and leaders that influence the work environment.

ETHICS AND THE PROFESSIONALIZATION OF SPORT MANAGEMENT

Many occupations, including those in sport management, desire recognition as a profession for a variety of reasons. Law and medicine are prime examples of professions that traditionally carry with them prestige, respect, status, and autonomy (De George, 1982). Although the desire for professional status is important and certainly understandable, the purpose of this section is not to debate the merits and demerits of sport management as a profession. (For an articulate discussion of the issue of professionalization, see Chapter 13 in *Business Ethics* by Richard De George.)

As sport management strives to move toward a greater professional status, the aspect of autonomy does have particular relevance with regard to ethics. Professions have traditionally been allowed more control to set their own standards and to be self-regulating and self-disciplining. The standards are frequently expressed in the form of an **ethical code,** often developed and enforced by a professional organization. Many businesses and professional business organizations have also developed ethical codes and creeds. The boxes on pp. 372 and 373 contain examples of advertising ethics and marketing ethics codes. However, many researchers question the impact some of these codes have had, contending that they lack depth or are filled with platitudes that do little to guide behavior (Robin and Reidenbach, 1989). De George (1982) recommends that a code should (1) be regulative, not simply a statement of ideals, (2) protect public interests and not be self-serving, (3) be specific and

American Advertising Federation's Code of Advertising Ethics

1. **Truth**—advertising shall reveal the truth, and shall reveal significant facts, the omission of which would mislead the public.
2. **Substantiation**—advertising claims shall be substantiated by evidence in possession of the advertiser and the advertising agency prior to making such claims.
3. **Comparisons**—advertising shall refrain from making false, misleading, or unsubstantiated statements or claims about a competitor or his products or services.
4. **Bait advertising**—advertising shall not offer products or services for sale unless such offer constitutes a bona fide effort to sell the advertised products or services and is not a device to switch consumers to other goods or services, usually higher priced.
5. **Guarantees and warranties**—advertising of guarantees and warranties shall be explicit, with sufficient information to apprise consumers of their principal terms and limitations or, when space or time restrictions preclude such disclosures, the advertisement shall clearly reveal where the full text of the guarantee or warranty can be examined before purchase.
6. **Price claims**—advertising shall avoid price claims which are false or misleading, or savings claims which do not offer provable savings.
7. **Testimonials**—advertising containing testimonials shall be limited to those of competent witnesses who are reflecting a real and honest opinion or experience.
8. **Taste and decency**—advertising shall be free of statements, illustrations, or implications which are offensive to good taste or public decency.

From American Advertising Federation, 1400 K Street, NW, Suite 100, Washington, DC 20005. Reprinted with permission.

relevant to the specialized concerns of the members, and (4) be enforceable and enforced.

In sport, several coaching organizations have addressed the issue of ethical conduct, including the National High School Athletic Coaches Association in the United States, the Coaching Association of Canada, the American Football Coaches Association, and the National Association of Basketball Coaches. Outside of a few authors (most prominently Zeigler), there is little in the literature of sport management that provides any formal treatment of ethics within the field. Zeigler (1989) has expressed the need for those involved in sport management to develop a sound approach to ethics as it relates to their duties and responsibilities and suggests that a comprehensive code of ethics is urgently required.

Developing a code of ethics for sport managers is a problematical undertaking. The breadth of the field makes it very difficult to create a code that has encompassing relevance. In addition, no organization fully accommodates the tremendous variety of practitioners and academicians in the field. The North American Society for Sport Management (NASSM) has approved an ethical creed for sport managers and has a committee to develop an ethical code for the consideration of its members. This process will require cooperation with a wide range of other professional associations in the field, such as the National Association for Sport and Physical Education (NASPE) and closely related occupational and professional groups.

The following is the ethical creed approved by NASSM at its annual meeting in 1989.

Professional members of the North American Society for Sport Management, living in a free, democratic society, have respect for the worth and dignity of all people in our society. As professionals we honor the preservation and protection of fundamental human rights. We are committed to a high level of professional practice and service, professional conduct that is based on the application of sound management theory developed through a scientific body of knowledge about sport and developmental physical activity's role in the lives of all people. Such professional service shall be made available to clients of all ages and conditions, whether such people are classified as accelerated, normal, or special insofar as their status or condition is concerned.

As NASSM members pursuing our professional service, we will make every effort to protect the welfare of those who seek our assistance. We will use our profes-

---

World Marketing Contact Group Marketing Creed

1. I hereby acknowledge my accountability to the organization for which I work, and to society as a whole, to improve marketing knowledge and practice and to adhere to the highest professional standards in my work and personal relationships.

2. My concept of marketing includes as its basic principle the sovereignty of all consumers in the marketplace and the necessity for mutual benefit to both buyer and seller in all transactions.

3. I shall personally maintain the highest standards of ethical and professional conduct in all business relationships with customers, suppliers, colleagues, competitors, governmental agencies, and the public.

4. I pledge to protect, support, and promote the principles of consumer choice, competition, and innovative enterprise, consistent with relevant legislative and public policy standards.

5. I shall not knowingly participate in actions, agreements, or marketing policies or practices which may be detrimental to customers, competitors, or established community social or economic policies or standards.

6. I shall strive to insure that products and services are distributed through such channels and by such methods as will tend to optimize the distributive process by offering maximum customer value and service at minimum cost while providing fair and equitable compensation for all parties.

7. I shall support efforts to increase productivity or reduce costs of production or marketing through standardization or other methods, provided these methods do not stifle innovation or creativity.

8. I believe prices should reflect true value in use of the product or service to the customer, including the pricing of goods and services transferred among operating organizations worldwide.

9. I acknowledge that providing the best economic and social product value consistent with cost also includes: A. recognizing the customer's right to expect safe products with clear instructions for their proper use and maintenance; B. providing easily accessible channels for customer complaints; C. investigating any customer dissatisfaction objectively and taking prompt and appropriate remedial action; D. recognizing and supporting proven public policy objectives such as conserving energy and protecting the environment.

10. I pledge my efforts to assure that all marketing research, advertising, sales promotion, and sales presentations of products, services, or concepts are done clearly, truthfully, and in good taste so as not to mislead or offend customers. I further pledge to insure that all these activities are conducted in accordance with the highest standards of each profession and generally accepted principles of fair competition.

11. I pledge to cooperate fully in furthering the efforts of all institutions, media, professional associations, and other organizations to publicize this creed as widely as possible throughout the world.

Draft approved by World Marketing Contact Group in Verona, Italy, September 1976.

---

sional skills only for purposes which are consistent with the values, norms, and laws of our society. Although we, as professional practitioners, demand for ourselves maximum freedom of inquiry and communication consistent with societal values, we fully understand that such freedom requires us to be responsible, competent, and objective in the application of our skills. We should always show concern for the best interests of our clients, our colleagues, and the public at large.

This creed is one of the few efforts made in the area of sport management to formally address the issue of professional ethics. Regardless of the status of sport management as a profession, this can serve as a foundation for encouraging sport managers to act professionally.

CONCEPT CHECK

One of the characteristics of professionalization is the autonomy that provides opportunity for self-regulation. This often manifests itself in a formalized approach to ethical standards and conduct. Increasing attention is being paid to ethics in many business fields, as reflected by both ethics training and the development of formal codes of ethics. Various sport and recreation organizations have made modest efforts to deal with pertinent ethical concerns, but only very meager beginnings can be reported regarding efforts at formalizing the treatment of ethics in sport management.

IMPLICATIONS FOR SPORT MANAGEMENT PREPARATION AND PRACTICE

As the twenty-first century approaches, one must examine the relationship of ethics and the future of sport management preparation and practice. With the number of academically prepared practitioners in sport management likely to increase-substantially, the move toward a greater professional status will probably continue. This trend has implications for the preparation of graduate and undergraduate students in sport management programs. Coursework should contain more material dealing with ethically sensitive issues, and more sport ethics and philosophy courses need to bedeveloped. (The American Assembly of Collegiate Schools of Business [AACSB] accredited business schools are required to include instruction on ethics within their curricula [Laczniak and Murphy, 1985; Robin and Reidenbach, 1989].)

There are ethical issues in virtually every area of sport management coursework. Marketing, management, legal issues, and personnel management are but a few of the topical areas that are sources for a variety of ethical predicaments. From the marketing of 150-dollar tennis shoes to children to the baseball owners colluding to control free agent salaries, there is no shortage of relevant material for ethical discussion and analysis.

That there is a wealth of ethical material for the classroom certainly indicates that numerous ethical issues surround the practice of sport management.

Several studies indicate that ethics committees and employee ethics training programs are becoming more prevalent in mainstream business firms (Cavanaugh, 1984; Robin and Reidenbach, 1989). This is likely to occur in sport businesses as well, and two particular reasons stand out. With the attention that many sport enterprises receive, unethical actions result in negative publicity that can be very damaging to public support. A very different concern has to do with the increasingly international nature of the sporting business. The international community may have a very different perspective on what actions are ethical and unethical. Reconciling the different cultural mores will require a far more conscientious effort of ethical preparation.

CONCEPT CHECK

There are ethical implications that will affect both academic preparation of sport managers and the practice of sport management as the next century approaches. It is likely that more concerted efforts will be made to emphasize ethical training in both educational and job settings.

There are numerous examples of ethical misconduct in all segments of society, and certainly sport is no exception. The focus of this chapter is to encourage recognition of the ethical dimensions of decision making and to provide a framework for a logical and reasoned approach for dealing with the moral and ethical choices that are certain to confront the sport management professional.

Professional behavior is grounded in personal values, but professional conduct does not always coincide with those personal values or the ideals of societal norms and virtues. To raise the level of professionalism in sport management, it is essential to take a proactive approach to ethical training. Ethical guidelines need to be carefully developed, and prospective sport managers should be schooled in the use of a systematic and analytical approach to the ethical dilemmas that they will undoubtedly encounter.

There is certainly a need for an increased awareness of and concern for the ethical issues of sport management; this is something that can be accomplished in a variety of ways. Incorporating ethical issues into existing academic coursework and developing courses in the ethics of sport are logical beginnings. The development of a code of ethics has begun to assist in providing a framework for ethical analysis. Beyond the classroom, practitioners must provide an environment in which a high standard of ethical conduct is the norm. Strong role models must be available and high expectations clearly outlined, and practitioners must be willing to accept that ethical behavior will not always bring the short-term, immediate benefits so demanded in this culture. The professionalization of sport management will ultimately be a cooperative venture between the academic community and the practitioner in the field. How each partner in this endeavor deals with the issue(s) of ethics will be important in determining the extent to which sport management moves toward a greater professional status.

SUMMARY

1. Numerous examples of ethical misconduct exist in many of the basic social institutions, and sport is certainly no exception.
2. The relativistic approach to ethics creates a more ambiguous behavioral environment, and action is frequently guided by legal standards rather than ethical standards.
3. Ethics and morality are interrelated concepts that provide guidelines for acceptable conduct.
4. Moral development starts with a very self-centered motivation, progresses to conforming with social norms, and ideally reaches the stage in which there is a reasoned belief in and commitment to universal moral principles.
5. Teleology and deontology are the two primary categories of ethical theory.
6. Maxims such as the golden rule are used as "rules of thumb" for ethical conduct, but more extensive frameworks for ethical analysis have been developed.
7. Many useful models have been developed to systematize the task of ethical decision making. Several of these models incorporate characteristics of both deontology and teleology.
8. Personal ethics must serve as the foundation for professional ethics, but the ethical character of the workplace will influence behavior.
9. Organizational and industry standards of conduct are often not congruent with personal standards, and the differences may be difficult to reconcile at times.
10. Development of a code of ethics is a step that established professions have taken but few sport organizations have as yet.
11. The North American Society for Sport Management (NASSM) has developed an ethical creed for sport managers.
12. One implication of sport management progressing toward professional status is an increasing concern for a formal and systematic approach to ethical training and behavior.
13. Ethics training is becoming more prevalent in the academic, as well as the business, setting.

REVIEW QUESTIONS AND ISSUES

1. Cite examples that depict the ethical climate that exists in society and in sport.
2. How are the concepts of ethics and morality related?
3. Discuss the contention that stage four of Kohlberg's model for moral development is the stage from which most adults tend to function ethically.
4. What are the primary characteristics of teleological and deontological theories of ethics?
5. What are the strengths and weaknesses of Cavanaugh's model for ethical decision making?
6. What is the relationship between personal and professional ethics?
7. Explain why personal ethics and ethics in sport management need to be addressed in an academic setting.
8. What is the responsibility of an organization's leadership with regard to the level of ethical conduct exhibited by its employees?
9. What can an organization do to encourage high standards of ethical conduct?
10. Is all legal behavior ethical? Is all ethical behavior legal? Defend your position.
11. What are the strengths and weaknesses of the ethical creed approved by the North American Society for Sport Management (NASSM)?
12. What role does ethics play in the professionalization of sport management?
13. Discuss what barriers you see that impede the ability of the field of sport management to develop an encompassing ethical code.

ETHICAL SITUATIONS FOR DISCUSSION

The situations presented here are but a few examples of the ethical issues that can arise in sport. One or more of the following suggestions may help to make these situations more useful exercises: (1) Evaluate how each situation might be dealt with at stages four, five and six of Kohlberg's model of moral development, (2) Evaluate each situation from both teleological and deontological points of view, (3) Use one or more of the five maxims on p. 368 to assess the appropriate actions in each situation, and (4) Apply Cavanaugh's model for ethical decision making (or some other model of ethical analysis) to the situations in order to arrive at an ethically reasoned response or decision.

1. What are the ethical considerations to be addressed in the decision to use drug testing as a screening tool for prospective employees? What about the use of lie detector tests? Would you submit to such testing? Why or why not? At what point do these tests become an invasion of privacy or a threat to basic constitutional rights?

2. Are the ethical considerations cited above the same for drug testing college and/or professional athletes? If athletes should be randomly tested, should all students? Professors? Administrators? Should drug testing be concerned only with performance-enhancing substances?

3. The hiring of Bill Frieder, former basketball coach at Michigan and current coach at Arizona State University, was a situation that raises some interesting ethical questions for several of the parties involved. Frieder accepted the coaching job at Arizona State just before the start of the NCAA basketball tournament in 1989. At that point he was relieved of his duties at Michigan, and his assistant took over the team (which went on to win the NCAA title). Without being privy to all the details of the situation, it may be difficult to be overly critical of the parties involved. On the other hand, the situation poses some interesting ethical questions. What are the ethical responsibilities of the coach to his team? The University of Michigan? Arizona State University? What ethical standards should Arizona State University be held to in this circumstance? Given that the letter of intent for signing recruits is shortly after the completion of the NCAA tournament, what does Arizona State have to gain and lose by waiting until after the tournament is completed before publicly consummating the deal?

4. It is relatively common practice now for professional baseball teams to offer to pay for the college education of high school draftees as an enticement to get them to sign a professional contract out of high school. Are there any ethical concerns surrounding this practice if baseball administrators are also aware that this is a benefit that players often will not ever use. Is this simply "good business"?

5. Al Davis, the owner of the Los Angeles Raiders, moved the team from Oakland to Los Angeles in the early 1980s, primarily because of the tremendous financial potential of a major market like Los Angeles. Oakland had supported the team well and the team had been very successful playing there, but from a business perspective Los Angeles was deemed to be a more profitable locale. After numerous lawsuits and appeals, the courts affirmed that Mr. Davis indeed had every right to move the franchise wherever he desired. Do professional franchise owners have any ethical obligations to the communities that support them? If so, what are they? Are they different from those of any other business operation?

6. The difference between serving the public well (social obligations) and serving as the social conscience is sometimes difficult to determine. Several examples involving health and fitness clubs may serve to amplify this issue. Should health clubs serve alcoholic beverages in their lounge area? Should they have cigarette machines? Should they provide tanning beds for those who wish to use them? From a business standpoint, each of these may be a profitable service. From a health standpoint, there are various levels of concern about each of these services. What ethical consideration comes into play in making the decision about the provision of such services? By not providing such services, are you playing the role of social conscience and limiting people's freedom to make their own choices?

7. Organizational image is the primary concern of the public relations effort. In many sport organizations the media are important players in the manipulation of that image, and the ethics of this relationship may bear scrutiny on both sides. Is it appropriate to curry the attention of

the media through providing free tickets, food, transportation, accommodations, and so on? Should these favors be provided only for favorable coverage? Should the media accept such favors? What are the risks to each party and to the general public with such an arrangement?

8. In many circumstances it may be the actions of others that pose a personal ethical quandary. In such situations the question of how you tolerate or deal with such behavior becomes the ethical dilemma. Do you report a fellow employee who is skimming small amounts of money from the cash register? Do you accept an outstanding prospective athlete's transcript that you know has been altered? Do you report a supervisor who is providing inside information to a favored supplier about competitors' bids on athletic equipment? What are the circumstances in which you tolerate these situations? Under what circumstances do you take action?

9. Employee and consumer safety are often cited as ethical problems that occur when organizations attempt to balance economic and safety concerns. For example, many considerations go into the decision on what type of playing surface to install. Are there ethical dimensions to this decision? Should artificial turf be used if the incidence of injury or the severity of injuries is higher than on natural surfaces? How much more dangerous would the surface have to be before the risks outweigh the benefits?

LABORATORY ACTIVITIES

1. Working in small groups, select an organization and develop the framework for an ethical code for the members of that organization. (Keep in mind the characteristics De George outlined for ethical codes.) Perhaps using the nine principles of the American Psychological Association (1977) as an example will help clarify your task. These principles address the following professional concerns: (1) responsibility, (2) competence, (3) moral and legal standards, (4) public statements, (5) confidentiality, (6) welfare of the consumer, (7) professional relationships, (8) utilization of assessment techniques, and (9) pursuit of research activities.

2. Each student or small groups of students should develop a case study that poses some ethical question or problem. These case studies can then be exchanged or used as the basis for further class discussion on ethics in sport. The attempt may be made to analyze these cases using different ethical models.

3. Small groups of students can be assigned the task of bringing in a current ethical issue and presenting their analysis using Cavanaugh's model for ethical decision making to the rest of the class. The presentation should include the following elements: (1) scenario, (2) ethical problems or dilemma, (3) rationale for their analysis, (4) results of their analysis, and (5) probable criticism of the decision.

REFERENCES

American Psychological Association. (1977). *Ethical standards of psychologists*. Washington, DC: The Association.

Beauchamp, T., and Bowie, N. (1988). *Ethical theory and business* (3rd Edition). Englewood Cliffs, New Jersey: Prentice Hall.

Cavanaugh, G. (1984). *American business values* (2nd Edition). Englewood Cliffs, New Jersey: Prentice Hall.

De George, R. (1982). *Business ethics*. New York: Macmillan Publishing Co.

Garrett, T. (1966). *Business ethics*. Englewood Cliffs, New Jersey: Prentice Hall.

Goodpaster, K. (1984). *Ethics in management*. Boston: Harvard Business School.

Jackall, R. (1988). *Moral mazes: the world of corporate managers*. New York: Oxford University Press.

Kohlberg, L. (1976). *Moral development and behavior: theory, research, and social issues*. New York: Holt, Rinehart, & Winston.

Laczniak, G., and Murphy, P. (1985). *Marketing ethics*. Lexington, Massachusetts: D.C. Heath and Co.

Robin, D., and Reidenbach, R. (1989). *Business ethics: where profits meet values systems*. Englewood Cliffs, New Jersey: Prentice Hall.

Solomon, R., and Hanson, K. (1983). *Above the bottom line*. New York: Harcourt Brace Jovanovich, Inc.

Tuleja, T. (1985). *Beyond the bottom line*. New York: Facts on File Publications.

Velasquez, M. (1988). *Business ethics: concepts and cases* (2nd Edition). Englewood Cliffs, New Jersey: Prentice Hall.

Zeigler, E. (1989). Proposed creed and code of professional ethics for the North American Society for Sport Management. *Journal of Sport Management*, 3, 2-4.

SUGGESTED READINGS

Braybrooke, D. (1983). *Ethics in the world of business*. Totowa, New Jersey: Rowman & Allanheld.

Desjardins, J., and McCall, J. (1990). *Contemporary issues in business ethics* (2nd Edition). Belmont, California: Wadsworth, Inc.

Donaldson, J. (1989). *Key issues in business ethics*. San Diego: Academic Press, Inc.

Frankena, W. (1973). *Ethics* (2nd Edition). Englewood Cliffs, New Jersey: Prentice Hall.

Rosen, B. (1990). *Ethics companion*. Englewood Cliffs, New Jersey: Prentice-Hall.

Shea, E. (1978). *Ethical decisions in physical education and sport*. Springfield, Illinois: Charles C. Thomas, Publisher.

Thiroux, J. (1980). *Ethics: theory and practice* (2nd Edition). Encino, California: Glencoe Publishing.

Zeigler, E. (1984). *Ethics and morality in sport and physical education*. Champaign, Illinois: Stipes.

PART IV

Future Directions in Sport Management

CHAPTER 22

Future Directions

Betty van der Smissen

In this chapter, you will become familiar with the following terms:

Environmental scanning
Demographics
Singles population
Discretionary income
Self-worth
Age-appropriate stereotypes
Amenities
Two-tier income classes
Information worker

Information society
Wellness & fitness programs
Global arena of human equality
Pathology of society
Human rights, but with
 responsibilities
Environmental quality
Corporate sponsorship
Facility versatility

Facility flexibility
Experiences
Accreditation
Certification
Licensure
Critical thinking
Operational research
Basic/applied research

Overview

Future directions of sport management are determined by the impact of society itself, the changing mode and role of the programs and services offered by the industry, and the nature of professional leadership.

In the first major part of this chapter, three of the impacting factors of society are briefly discussed: demographic perspectives, the workplace and economics, and social concerns. The demographic perspectives of age, gender, and family life-

style are particularly germane. There appear to be three changing directions as related to children: (1) the decline in the number of children and the increase in the elderly, with the shift of societal resources away from children toward the elderly, (2) the need for child care programs because there are a greater number of women in the workforce, as well as a greater number of single parents who must provide for one or more children, and (3) a concern for the lack of fitness, for drug abuse and chemical dependency, and for violence among youth. The decade of the 1980s seemed to be an era of the young, single adult with changing lifestyles or family styles. The singles population is composed of three types of persons: (a) those young adults who delay first marriage, (b) those middle-aged adults who reenter singleness due to divorce or another situational factor, and (c) those elderly who are experiencing widowhood. Maturing adults' lifestyles will greatly influence sport management services and programs. The elderly are not a sedentary population, but economics and family relations may be influencing factors regarding physically active sport participation. The workforce and economics, the second societal factor, includes the two-tier income class society that seems to be developing, the role of women, and worker benefits, particularly concerning the care of children and the elderly. The third societal factor, social concerns, includes the global arena of human equality, the pathology of society (such as, drug abuse, intoxication, steroid use, violence, gangs, child abuse, sexual and ethnic harassment, and gambling and bribery), human rights as related to individual responsibility, and environmental quality.

The second major part of this chapter focuses on the industry of sport and fitness, setting forth four considerations: economics, facility management, program services, and management aspects. Economics reflects on the amount of money spent for sport and fitness and salaries for professional athletes. Corporate sponsorship as a source of funds has an impact on television coverage of sports, particularly professional sports and intercollegiate athletics; but, because of the poor images of some professional sport celebrities, corporations are having second thoughts about certain types of sponsorship. However, the use of corporate sponsors for special events financing may become more extensive as corporations seek to project good public images. The key to facility management is in the provision of quality services, especially amenities for spectators, as well as participants, and in multiple use of the facility, extending beyond sport events. The provision of program services will be based on primacy of the consumer, what experiences the participant has. As with facility utilization, program services also must be multi-faceted. The fitness boom of the 1980s will turn to broader, more extensive wellness programs with emphasis on a healthful lifestyle. As for management aspects

of the future, these include information management systems, risk management, and government and association controls.

The third part of this chapter discusses sport management as a profession in four aspects: (1) self-disciplining and ethics, (2) professional associations and certifications, (3) professional preparation academic base, including both undergraduate and graduate education, and (4) research, a body of knowledge, distinguishing operational research, so critical to the field, and basic research, the type expected of university faculty.

DETERMINING FUTURE DIRECTIONS

At the turn of the decade into the 1990s, there were many prognosticators regarding the future. No one really knows the future, but it is certain that there is no such thing as status quo. Thus, it is appropriate to look at the trends or direction predictions as the Year 2000 is approached. In what direction is sport management as a career field going, or should it go, or it may be pushed into going, to take its place as a profession in society? The direction has three determinants: (1) society—the impact of society itself, with its sociological, psychological, political, and economic aspects, that is, the environmental context in which the services of the sport and fitness industry are provided, (2) the industry—the changing mode and role of the sport and fitness industry in providing services and products in response to societal needs and desires of people and corporate entities, and (3) the profession—the response of individuals who seek to provide these services and products in terms of willingness to make the field professional. Thus this chapter has three parts, the three determinants of the future: (1) society, (2) the sport and fitness industry, and (3) the profession.

To prognosticate is often an exercise in wishful thinking, rather than a realistic assessment of determinants. In this chapter, a concerted effort has been made to avoid wishful thinking, which so often is done by those who present careers in sport management in "glowing" terms. When making projections or forecasts, one must be cautious and consider whether the "trends" projected are cyclic or structural. Structural trends have the most impact because they embody a change in societal values and economies and are long term forces toward a "true" or enduring directional change.

"One major force that impedes change is basic values and personal priorities. Society is very slow to accept developments that 'violate' its value of life, family, education, spirituality, 'profit', power and control, etc. Another powerful impeding force is fear of the unknown. . . . [Nevertheless], man is an animal of curiosity, and a major force in changing our society is exploration and opportunity. Developments that result from exploration, . . . are likely to change society a great deal as people take advantage of them. The same is true for developments that offer opportunities for taking greater control of one's life. . . . Developments that provide high utility also change our society. With higher utility comes a bigger impact. . . . [This includes transportation, the living environment, and life-enhancing factors of medicine] . . . Society also reacts to demographic and economic forces. When there is a shift in dominance from a group of people with one set of characteristics to a group that is very different, the society reflects that change. . . . In a similar manner, economic change can cause social change, [particularly discretionary income]." (*The Futurist*, Jan/Feb 1990; pp. 24-25)

Some determinants are based in fact, such as the projections on age and gender of the population already born; however, some forecasts of the future are weak because they are simple extrapolations of historical data. The most "correct" forecasts appear to be those which take into account the basic human needs and culturally determined wants of a demographic group, as well as good analysis of economic and utility values, that is, people tend not to exchange money for a product or service unless they perceive it to be a fair exchange.

There have been many predictions for the decade approaching the Year 2000 and the twenty-first century. This chapter is not just a review of these predictions. Many are at variance and sometimes have a real difference of perspective in reading societal indicators. The ideas in this chapter are a composite from statistical data and readings on trends and societal indicators, as well as personal experience and discussion with others. However, the critical key for those who are in sport management is insight—insight to changing societal conditions and how the industry itself is responding to and leading in these changing conditions. This takes skill in the utilization of data and in being proactive. A true professional is one who leads, is dynamic and in the forefront, and makes things happen, or at least influences direction. This chapter seeks to make the student and professional more aware of selected determinants and possible implications for the sport manager, especially for the academic curriculum and career opportunities. Then it is essential that the ramifications be discussed in class, at professional meetings, and in the professional literature. It is important that individuals in the sport management field read widely newspapers and magazines, noting important social, political, and economic trends. This is imperative because so often young people or newcomers to the field are so intent on the operational skills and getting ahead in the job and experienced professionals may become so immersed in the day-to-day operational minutia, that both let the foundation on which the sport management enterprise builds slip into oblivion. Thus both types of professionals lose the effectiveness that they might have. It is exciting to plan for the future and professionally stimulating to be a part of making the plans become reality.

SOCIETY

In considering directions for the future, many organizations have engaged in strategic planning. One of the first steps is to perform "environmental scanning," which means to assess the issues and trends in society, and specifically, to scan the external and internal environments via statistical data and professional expertise. **Environmental scanning** involves a number of areas of change, such as economy/consumerism, education/learning/training, environment/ecology, family/social relationships, health/fitness, lifestyle/values, technology/science, and business/management.

"The United Way of America's Strategic Institute, working with its volunteer Environmental Scan Committee, has identified more than 100 specific trends in society and grouped them into nine major 'changedrivers' for the 1990s. . . . [which] represents the Institute's best collective judgment of the key developments likely to affect American society in the next decade." (*The Futurist*, July/August, 1990; p. 9)

The nine forces reshaping America are (1) the maturing of America, (2) the mosaic society, (3) redefinition of individual and societal roles, (4) the information-based economy, (5) globalization, (6) personal and environmental health, (7) economic restructuring, (8) family and home redefined, and (9) rebirth of social activism. (For the full report, see *What Lies Ahead: Countdown to the 21st Century*, United Way of America's Strategic Institute, 701 North Fairfax Street, Alexandria, Virginia 22314-2045, 1989, 112 pages, paperback, approximately $20.) Only a few areas included in environmental scanning can be presented in this chapter, and these are: (1) demographic perspectives on age, gender, and family lifestyle; (2) the workforce and economics; and (3) social concerns and sport.

Demographic perspectives of age, gender, and family lifestyle

"The demographic perspective will play a key role in helping decision makers in both the public and the private sectors understand and prepare for the future. Over the past decade or so, demographic forces, such as the 'graying' of society and the influx of mothers into the work force, have attracted wide public notice, shaping the contexts that business firms and government agencies encounter. That attention has accorded the demographic *perspective* a new prominence in public affairs. The term **'demographics'** is now entrenched in the national vocabulary . . . The demographic perspective now permeates and influences public discourse." (*The Futurist*, March/April 1990; p. 9)

Demographic segmentation is a common strategy to define markets. The demographics of present participants and identification of those markets not participating are important, but through trend analysis or the projection of demographic changes in society, potential shifts in marketing services can be determined. "Any marketer that hopes to prosper in the challenging decade of the 1990s must be aware of the demographics of that decade. . . . 'You cannot understand the consumer marketplace today without an appreciation of demographic trends. . . . Demographic characteristics help shape preferences, determine attitudes, and mold values.'" (Stanton, W., and Futrell, C., (1987), *Fundamentals of Marketing*, New York: McGraw-Hill Book Co.; p. 91). Closely related to planning, and having gained some popularity in the latter part of the 1980s, is psychographics. Demographics is the statistical study of the human population and its distribution, with variables such as age, gender, income, education, marital status, and number of children; psychographics is a collective synonym for psychological variables and lifestyle values that affect consumer behavior. These include, but are not limited to, such variables as learning experiences, personality, attitudes and beliefs, and self-

concept, all of which have an impact on the formation of a person's perceptions (Stanton and Futrell, 1987). It is projected that by Year 2000 nearly one in three Americans will be a minority and that in the 1990s racial and ethnic diversification will expand the number of cities in which no one group constitutes the "majority." It is essential that there be greater understanding of the changing age structure in society, the changing numbers (quantity), and the roles of children, of young adults, and of mature adults. Only a few aspects as related to age, gender, and family lifestyle are presented in this section. The information may appear disjointed, but it is meant to be a catalyst for individual thinking. Beginning with the following commentary, one should add current readings from the periodicals, journals and newspapers, and then discuss/consider the meaning for the direction of sport management in regard both to providing services and products and to providing a professional opportunity for individuals interested in a career in the field.

Children and family. The era since World War II has been one of children, when everything in society seemed to revolve around the family, and more specifically, the children. Marketing was directed toward children, and certainly much of it will continue to be. The leisure activities focused on the children, and the children dictated the family schedule. There was a permissiveness toward the behavior of children, and the parents sacrificed to reallocate financial resources to accommodate children's wants. In many homes, the children were "king." At the turn of the decade into the 1990s, there appear to be three changing directions as related to children.

First, there is a definite decline in the number of children, and some would say that there is a shift of societal resources away from children toward the elderly, who percentage-wise are increasing greatly in society, and that the children are thus becoming a "forgotten population." (See later discussion on the "mature adult" and the next section on economics and the workforce.)

Second, because of the greater number of women in the workforce and the number of single parents who must provide for one or more children, there is a concern for acquiring and retaining these persons in the workforce. One factor is child care by the employer, either as a fringe benefit or at a nominal cost. Child care programs are also being offered by private enterprise, with the incentive of tax deductions. Related is the desire for child care services or activities by the "older" parent, who as a young adult enjoyed the fitness center, the resort, and other recreational activity. The active, young, single adults of the 1980s, now married, still want to engage actively in sport, but often they cannot unless some provision is made for children. Thus the fitness center or the resort may provide either child care or special children's activities, as bowling alleys have for some time, particularly for daytime use by women in the home. Should the singles fitness clubs of the 1980s become family-oriented in the 1990s? Although programs for children may be an asset as a marketing tool to appeal to a new source of consumers and as an additional profit center, there are two constraining factors. One is the increasing day care licensing requirements, and the other is that liability fear and insurance costs keep many workplaces and entertainment facilities from offering children's services. This latter factor, however, can be overcome with proper risk management practices.

A third changing direction for children and youth is a concern for lack of fitness, drug abuse and chemical dependency, and violence among youth. Although this concern is expressed by many, it seems that "what's everybody's business, is nobody's business!" Parents, the youth agencies, and the schools—not private enterprise—are all charged with the responsibility of doing something about this concern. Many parents certainly have become exasperated with their children and seem either unwilling or unable to manage their behavior. These parents turn to the schools and youth organizations to do it for them. The youth agencies, both private nonprofit and community public recreation, are making an effort to address these areas of concern, and a number of programs are quite effective. Furthermore, many of these programs utilize sport and physical activity. As for the schools, any programs to combat drug abuse and chemical dependence, as well as to deter youth violence, must be supported with tax dollars, similar to any educational program; however, the record of tax levy authorization by voters for even basic education is not good. Furthermore, as related to fitness, the physical education programs have been eroded over time in many schools, os-

tensibly because of lack of funds. Schwarzenegger, chair of the President's Council on Fitness and Sports, in 1990 stated that one of his goals was to institute physical fitness programs where there were none and increase physical education toward fitness in the schools of America. However, there must be parental support, not only in voting for levies, but also in involvement in programs. In a survey sponsored by Wilson Sporting Goods Co. and the Women's Sports Foundation entitled *The Wilson Report: Moms, Dads, Daughters and Sports*, there was strong parental support for participation in sport for both boys and girls. However, there was a reported decline in the number of boys participating in high school sports. Further, with both a greater number of mothers in the workforce and more single parent families, the number of volunteers working with youth sport has declined. Another alleged causative factor in this decline of parental involvement is the fear of liability for injuries to participants by the volunteers; however, more than one half of the states at the turn of the decade had legislation limiting the liability of a nonprofit organization volunteer as an individual. Ten states had legislation specific to sports. Notwithstanding the desirability of school physical education programs, some private entrepreneurs believe that the private sector can provide more effective and more cost efficient programs than can the schools.

Although the primary marketing and service thrusts in private enterprise related to sport in the 1980s focused on adults—single and married—as individuals, a question for the decade of the 1990s is whether services and marketing should be extended to have an emphasis on families. There really are three approaches: (1) to continue to provide services to persons as individuals, with separate activities offered for children and for adults, (2) to continue to provide services to the adults and include the older children, and then to provide child care for the younger children, and (3) to provide services in which the family, whether single parent or both parents, participates as a unit. Of course, there could be a combination, that is, some activities for the family unit and others for children only and others for adults. (See the section on the industry for further discussion.)

Young, single adults. The decade of the 1980s seemed to be an era of the young, single adult, predicating a changing lifestyle, or perhaps better said, family-style—young people were staying single longer, marrying later, having families later. As members of the workforce, these persons had more money to spend on pleasure and entertainment. It became fashionable to be fit and active. Marketing heightened not only the social status, but also the fashion status of each activity. At the beginning of the 1990s, this era has not yet passed. Perhaps it will not; it may only have less visibility and emphasis with the increasing number of mature adults. However, one should not overlook the probability that the young singles of the 1990s will indeed have different characteristics from those of the 1980s.

The singles population 18 years of age and older in 1970 made up 28% of all adults, whereas in 1988 it was 37%. The **singles population** is composed of three types of persons: (1) young adults who delay first marriage, (2) middle-aged adults who reenter singleness due to divorce (some of these may be singles with children, which places them in a different category), and (3) elderly persons who are experiencing widowhood. Although about 90% of people are married at one time during their lives, while they are single they have a set of unique needs for public and private sector services. There can be both social companionship and self-enhancement through sport and fitness activities. It is this singles component of society that has greatly stimulated sport services through private enterprise. As stated in the preceding section on children, should the singles' fitness clubs become family-oriented clubs in the 1990s? There may be certain family needs; however, it appears that the segment of young adults who are single and marry later will remain in the 1990s and must be serviced. One thing is certain, however; there must be variations on services, because participants invariably become bored with sameness. Sport activity participation also has its social cycles. For example, just consider what happened to jogging in the late 1980s; the trend shifted toward more walking, perhaps for health reasons, but certainly with social status overtones. The racquet sports also seem to have cycled over a decade or two, with squash, badminton, tennis, and racquetball each taking their turn at being the sport of social status. The same is true for aquatic activities, especially re-

garding certain types of watercraft and open water activities. Different sports and activities rise and fall in popularity, and an entrepreneur must keep one step ahead of participants, be flexible, and not get locked into one type of service or activity. (See the next section on economics and the major section on the industry.)

What about male- and female-oriented activities? Although there may be a predominance of one gender in certain activities such as aerobic dance, for the most part, both men and women participate in all types of activities. Weight training no longer is primarily for males. In offering services, however, proper provision must be made for the size and physical condition of individuals, but this is true whether male or female. Marketing can affect social stereotypes for participation. This is not to say, however, that there should not be activities in which the participants are all one gender. Individuals should not be forced always to associate with other participants of the opposite gender. (See the next section on the workforce.)

The maturing adult. In 1990 it was estimated that 55% of the U.S. population was under 35 years of age; however, by Year 2000, it is estimated that the median age will be 36—that is, only 50% of the population will be under 36—and by the year 2080 the median age will be 44 years. It is not just a matter of the median age, but, more importantly, the fact that one's life expectancy has been extended, so that the common life expectancy will be 85 to 90 years of age. It is rather disconcerting to think that if people continue to retire at age 60 to 65, approximately one third of one's life would be spent in schooling and initial occupational pursuit, primarily as a single person; one third in productive occupational engagement and family involvement; and one third in being "placed on the shelf" at leisure—one third of one's life "at leisure"?— this seems neither feasible nor functional. The future of this population should not be projected on past performance, but on changing impacting forces. This is a changing world, and the mature adults of the twenty-first century will have different characteristics from those of the 1990s and different roles in society.

First, few people can amass sufficient economic resources in one third of their lives (occupational years) to sustain them for the final one third of life at leisure in a lifestyle of comfort. Someone has said that the three-legged stool of retirement is savings, social security, and pensions, and that a fourth leg may become health insurance, which also requires financial outlay. The U.S. social security system does not have sufficient funds to sustain people for 25 to 30 years on "retirement," and the amount is usually not sufficient for an appropriate income above the poverty level. Furthermore, the social security retirement financing for the increasing mature adults would be placed upon tomorrow's smaller workforce in the 1990s. Payroll taxes may reach 40% for social security, instead of less than 15% in 1990, or else there would have to be scaled-back benefits, benefits that presently are meager. Does the United States want to become a social state? It cannot afford to economically. In addition, most company pension plans also are inadequate, particularly when there continue to be escalating costs that must be met on a fixed income of the elderly. Furthermore, "baby boomer" parents lived in better economic times, but didn't save; why should the "baby boomers"? Because of escalating costs, not only for nursing home care for the elderly, but also for retirement villages or maintaining one's own home/apartment, it is predicted that there will be many more two or more generational families living in one house. Some prognosticators predict that the nuclear family will be replaced by several generations of a family living under the same roof, rendering the child-centered nuclear family obsolete. If not, older persons may find themselves short on family support where it counts most in old age—at home. Of course, the amount of **discretionary income** available—that money not needed for essentials of housing, food, and self-care—has an impact on the type and extent of sport and fitness services and products that can be purchased.

Second, it is suggested that individuals will not retire at age 60 or 65, but rather that their active work years will extend to 70 to 75 years of age. This may be not only an economic necessity, but there are other factors, too. Not only will individuals be needed in the workforce (see workforce perspective in the next section), but also the meaningfulness of life comes from a feeling of self-worth, and society has not yet honored the leisure-person as a status of worth. Leisure can contribute

toward the meaning of life, but not all of it, and the sport manager must respect the role of sport in the life of a person. Sport may seem very important to many individuals and may be one contributor toward self-enhancement, but it is not the most important thing in life, when the basics of life and happiness are at stake. **Self-worth** is rooted in contribution to production of products or services and is defined by work. What is it that women have been fighting for? A meaningful place in the workforce—a measure of self-worth. Generally, only those persons who have something "to retire to," a change of life occupation, (not necessarily a full-time job, but sufficient to keep one's self-esteem and the ability for self-maintenance) should retire; those who do not have something to provide self-esteem and self-worth find "time hangs heavy" and life is not filled with as much happiness as it might be. Usefulness to family, to friends, to community, to profession—that defines self-worth. When one no longer has a meaningful purpose to life, then one does not enjoy living or want to live. Furthermore, to assist in self-maintenance, employment options will greatly expand for older persons who want to work. The trend toward utilizing more experienced retired workers in traditionally entry-level jobs will increase and may ease the burden on employers in a dwindling workforce. (See the next section on workforce.) Many people talk about second careers, taking early retirement and then doing something else. Others have predicted that individuals will change occupations or careers 3 times and positions 10 or more times during their lives. There are plenty of volunteer opportunities, and persons are greatly needed for social causes; however, although much gratification can come from these, such volunteer positions often do not adequately provide the feeling of worth that comes from being economically productive, and certainly they do not bring in the needed income. The nature of the work and the length of time working each year may differ, but many persons will continue or desire to "work" into their 70s. The Hudson Institute suggests that policymakers may want people not to retire, but to take more breaks in their 30s and 40s with families and work until they are 70 or 75. That may be acceptable for professionals, but perhaps not for factory workers who may not be able to work longer physically. However, with an increase in information and service jobs and a greater emphasis on health and fitness, the physical condition of a person may not be as great a factor in work longevity. In 1948, 89% of the men aged 55 to 64 were in the workforce; at the turn of the decade, this has declined to 67%. Early retirements, indeed, have made an impact on the age in the workforce; perhaps this will be reversed. (See the section on workforce.)

Third, the mature population is not a sedentary population. Of course, there always will be those who require nursing home care, but the physical and mental vitality of the elderly will be retained a decade or two longer in the future. Not only greater medical knowledge, but also the active lifestyle itself, will enable individuals to have vigor and vitality as they go through the last one third of their lives. New leisure skills and activities will not present a block to participation. In this age of biology and biotechnology with its elaborate array of information feedback systems, the very structure of the biological organism will result in bigger, stronger, and longer living people. What the long-range impact of inactive and unfit children, the "couch potatoes" of the 1980s, will be, is not known; however, adult concern for health and wellness may be an overriding factor. Whatever, the sport manager is cautioned not to be controlled by **age-appropriate stereotypes** of the 1980s. Most all activities are suitable for any age and both males and females, only constrained by the factors applicable to all participants, such as physical strength and endurance, skill, ability, financial capability, and desire to do the activity. The enterprising sport entrepreneur will find a market for a very broad array of sport activity.

Yes, as consumers of sport and fitness activities, children and young adults will always compose a market, but the expanded market is the active mature adult. Life is to be lived, and to do so, individuals will demand opportunities and services, the essence of sport management. These changing demographics have an impact on the nature of the market and what it requires. Businesses hoping to carry their profits into the 1990s will have to cater to a more mixed demographic population than ever before; that is, the target population no longer can be a single gender or age grouping. The focus must be on the type of experience offered, which appeals to a broad range of people. The question is not

"who are you wanting to target, to serve?" but "what type of experiences are you offering?" (see the section on programming) Sport management personnel will require a knowledge of and the ability to use applied demographic and trend analyses, as well as psychographics. Then, there must be a gradual modification in making transitions within a changing society. There must be understanding of the nature of the services required; there must be **amenities** for the population serviced; adults are less willing to put up with hassles than younger participants; that is, they want and expect the amenities of convenience and courtesy, an aesthetically pleasing environment, and cost effectiveness.

CONCEPT CHECK

Demographic characteristics are one of the most important factors in determining future directions. There is a declining population of children and youth, but an increasing population of older citizens, causing a reallocation of resources. In the 1980s, single adults became a dominant constituency of sport and physical activity. The nature of their continued involvement is to be determined. With a maturing adult population, the stereotypical age-appropriate activities must be dismissed and programs and services focus on the nature of the experience individuals receive.

The workforce and economics

There are a number of aspects related to the workforce and economics that have particular relevance to sport and fitness services and products. Three of these are briefly set forth: (1) the **two-tier income classes** in society, (2) the role of women, and (3) worker benefits.

The two-tier income classes in society. For years there have been lower-, middle-, and upper-income classes in society, but nearly all prognosticators state that, at the turn of the decade into the 1990s, the middle class is disappearing. Most of this class is moving upward due to the income of a working mother in the family, making it a two-income family. In many situations, both mother and father are well-educated professionals, and furthermore, with later marriages both are better established in their occupations before having families. It should be noted that women in the middle and upper classes refer to their working as a "career," whereas the women of the lower class refer to it as a "job." According to a New York Times poll on women's issues in 1989, there is a distinct difference in the roles in the workforce between women in the upper and middle classes and those in the lower class. Also, as ethnic groups' occupational status improves, so do the dollars. Furthermore, the developing information society requires workers to be more educated. At the turn of the decade, of households earning $75,000, two-thirds of the heads of these are college graduates.

The difference in income of two-parent and single-parent families, especially disparity between male and female single parents, is evidenced in the mean income of mother-only families of $11,989; father-only, $23,919; and both-parent, $40,067. The poverty ratio of single-parent families with two or more children has tripled since 1983. Some have stated that poverty results from the failure to create viable two-parent families. On the other end of the life continuum, there is concern regarding the financial (poverty) status of so many of the elderly, with the increasing costs of retirement and low fixed income of the elderly. Furthermore, in the quest for money, according to a Louis Harris & Associates 1987 poll, there has been a decrease of leisure hours from 26.3 hours/week in 1973 to 16.6 in 1987. According to the Bureau of Labor Statistics, 44% of the men executives, administrators, and managers, and 37.4% of the men professionals, worked 49 or more hours a week in 1989.

Although there certainly are still many low-paying jobs, from March 1985 to March 1989, 73% of new jobs created fell into the top three paying Department of Labor categories: professional administrative, sales and technical, and precision crafts; from March 1988 to March 1989, 53.4% of the new jobs were in the category "professional and managerial"—certainly not low-paying jobs. More than 70% of new job growth has been in occupations that average $20,000 per year, as indicated by the Secretary of Labor. This upgrading of jobs is apparently produced by the information economy, which requires education. Those in the lower middle class who do not have the skills and education drop back into the lower class economically. With the information society, the 1990s project to be a decade of high-wage economy and affluence. Skilled information workers will earn the highest wages in history; however, the service

economy will have lower-level paying positions that are permanent, but still low-paying and without many benefits. No welfare program can turn uneducated, low-skilled persons into economically productive people in an information-based economy. The problem in the 1990s will be how to educate people to qualify for the jobs available. It is projected that the gap between the upper- and lower-level economic classes, because of diminishing opportunities for the uneducated and unskilled, will widen, and that there will be polarization between rich and poor before the gap tends to close somewhat in approximately the year 2050.

However, sport management personnel should be aware that most of the information and service society jobs are middle-management level; more educated people with higher expectations for advancement will be competing for limited top managerial positions. Also, there will be less rapid advancement opportunities for professionals as the workforce ages and remains in top positions. It is projected that the criteria for competent workers will be generalist, flexible, creative, computer literate, and a good communicator.

Megatrends 2000 (Naisbitt, J., and Aburdene, P. [1990]. New York: William Morrow and Co.) states that in the decade of the 1990s the world is entering a period of economic prosperity. The world certainly is in an era of global economy, that is, the United States cannot and does not stand alone; it is dependent on other nations. The world economy is indeed interlinked and one marketplace. Economic considerations almost always transcend political consideration in the global economy. Sport is a part of the global economy because of its universality, international competition, developments in telecommunications, and the availability of products to foreign markets. Sport also has been used as a political tool.

A high income and global economy is what sport management needs; it is the climate for thriving. In general, sport management services the affluent, and the affluent expect to be provided the amenities (see the section on the industry), but the services required for the lower-level income group should not be overlooked. However, not all observers of social indicators agree with the strength of the information and service society economics. They do agree, though, on a higher employment rate and the improvement in income of various segments of the population, including a decline in the level and rate of poverty—all evidence of a vigorous economy. But the indicators of tough economic times include the U.S. trade deficit, social decline, violence in the streets, breaking of families through divorce, the homeless in cities, lonely and abandoned elderly in institutions, and increase in stress-induced illnesses at all ages. These social ills cost the public money. (See the section on social concerns.)

The role of women. There are different roles that women play related to the workforce and the economy. As shown in a previous section, when a woman is a single head of the household, the family is apt to be in the poverty level, but when she is the second wage earner in a two-parent family, the family can be in the upper-middle class level or even in the lower-upper class level. What is the role of women in the workforce itself? Is there equity of genders, and what is the impact of women? Is the impact not so much one of gender, but type of job?

Megatrends 2000 states that "If the male was the prototypical industrial worker, the **information worker** is typically a woman. In sheer numbers women dominate the **information society.** Eighty-four percent of working women are part of the information/service sector. Of the people whose job title falls under the category of 'professional'— versus clerical, technical, laborer—the majority are women. Forty-four percent of adult working women (ages 25 to 64) are college-educated, compared with 20 percent in 1965. The jobs of people in the information, service, finance, computer, biotechnology, and health care sectors are not performed on an assembly line and cannot be managed as though they were. It is almost impossible to 'supervise' information work. Mental tasks have replaced mechanical ones [of the industrial worker, who makes products]. 'Work' is what goes on inside people's heads at desks, on airplanes, in meetings, at lunch. . . . Now we are managing people paid for their knowledge" (p. 220). Naisbitt and Aburdene go on to say that:

"Considering the complex tasks of the information era and its elite labor force, the business leader's job is quite a challenge. He or she possesses no authority over people whatsoever. . . . Managing through authority is out of the question. Workaholics simply burn themselves out. Loyalty is a quaint memory of the industrial past, a bone

in the throat of hundreds of thousands of auto and steel-workers who thought it went both ways. . . . If people are not loyal and you have no authority over them anyhow, how do you accomplish anything?" (p. 222).

While "the majority of the information/service sector is female. . . . (women) were barred from the boardroom during the 1970's and 1980's. No wonder so many talented, successful women . . . started their own businesses. The Small Business Association reports that 30 percent of small businesses are owned by women. Each decade the percentage of female-owned small businesses has increased . . . (Women have not reached the top positions, however, in corporations.) For most women that requires a new set of skills. The people skills of middle management, where women may possess a slight advantage over men, are not enough at the top. Those skills must be coupled with extensive knowledge about the external environment in which a business exists. The major themes of the 1990's—technological change, compressed product cycles, and global competition—require a leader to scan the global environment and organize the internal tasks, while remaining market-sensitive" (Naisbitt, J., and Aburdene, P. (1990). *Megatrends 2000.* New York: William Morrow & Co.; pp. 226, 235).

Skill and ability are not enough for women to rise to the top in the business world. Despite some gains for women, a quarter century after the beginning of the women's rights movement and various legislation such as Title VII and the Equal Pay Act, the workplace is still a "man's world," and women must realistically face such fact, although not necessarily accept it. According to a 1990 survey financed by Phillip Morris USA, women have changed, but not men to any extent; that is, women now are in the workforce, but they have had to retain household responsibilities. On the other hand, men have benefited from the second income of the women in the household, but many men have refused to accept greater home responsibilities in return. By entering the labor force, perhaps women have seen a different side of men, and according to a *New York Times* poll on women's issues, this is true. Some women have seen the "mommy track" designation not really a recognition of women's desire to both work and have a home with children, but as a sophisticated guise to restore discrimination against women because of their childbearing.

More specifically, as related to women in sport positions, several studies at the end of the decade of the 1980s have all established that women did not gain in the workplace in the last decade, although certainly female athletic participation in sport increased greatly. For example, in the Acosta and Carpenter study (Brooklyn College), it was reported that in 1989, 47.3% of intercollegiate sport coaching jobs within women's athletics were held by women, compared with 58.2% in 1977 and over 90% before the enactment of Title *IX* in 1972. At the high school level, a 1989 study by Stangl and Kane (Bowling Green State University) found that in Ohio, the number of women coaching high school sports in the 1988-89 school year had dropped by almost two thirds since 1975. In 15 years the number of women coaching girls' sports dropped from 93% to 33%. Over the same span of time, women principals and superintendents rose from less than 1% to 5.6% and 6.2%, respectively. The reasons given for the reduction in the number of women coaches include that with the upgrade of women's sport positions in salary and media visibility, such positions now are sought by men; and that women are not as qualified as men, although some research disputes this statement, where the criteria compared were athletics ability, sports participation, and scholastic aptitude.

Worker benefits. The biggest problem in the decade of the 1990s may not be jobs, but recruiting and retaining qualified and motivated workers. There does not seem to be loyalty to a company, but instead a movement to better oneself financially or for benefits. Worker benefits and incentives may be the key to business and agency recruitment.

In 1990, with the increasing number of women working and single-parent families, there is an increase in the number of companies providing day care. Most do not have on-site facilities but offer some financial help or referral services. Some companies issue vouchers or pay a portion of costs. Even so, in 1990, nearly 90% of establishments with 10 or more employees did not provide direct benefits such as day care or financial assistance. This is not just a way to keep and attract good people; there can be substantial cost savings as well. A 1988 study reported a 31% drop in absenteeism among parents who used day-care centers, and a 10% drop in the employee turnover rate. One need not be a big operation or build an expensive center to pro-

vide leadership in day care. A small enterprise can cooperate with other businesses and with local schools. The need for children's day care extends to women's professional sports, such as golf, where at the turn of the decade not only were more married women on the tour, but also taking their young children with them.

Related to day care is the concern for eldercare. Eldercare affects a wider segment of employees than child care, since almost one third of all working adults are responsible for providing some care for an elderly person. Three quarters of those who care for the elderly in a family are women; many workers involved in eldercare are still raising their own children. One approach of business and industry is to provide a "cafeteria" of benefits in which employees select from a menu of different benefits according to their needs. This would include various "family leaves," such as for maternity leave and family illnesses, as well as alternative work schedules, which may vary with options as flextime, part-time, alternative work sites, and job sharing, that is, two people sharing a full-time job. Such work schedules also help make commuting less time consuming by avoiding rush hours and choosing a closer alternative work site.

Employers are continuing to expand their employee caretaking role to include such new benefits as **wellness and fitness programs,** child care and eldercare—services that the government does not seem able to provide to the levels needed. Will the federal government mandate health care, that is, health insurance benefits for all employees, thereby dictating that basic health care be provided by all employers, rather than just offered to the employee as a fringe benefit? The fitness programs are not so much for economics of fit employees, but as a fringe benefit. Corporate fitness/wellness management companies should do well. Large corporations can afford their own fitness/wellness facilities and staffing, but smaller ones may need to contract services from a private entrepreneur or nonprofit organization for either or both facility and staffing. Furthermore, the number of programs that extend beyond physical fitness and its exercise machines to wellness/health will increase substantially. Programs must be more broad—a health education program requiring teams of specialists. (See the section on program services.)

CONCEPT CHECK

The United States is moving toward a two-tier income class society. Sport and physical activity thrive in an affluent population, thus sport management entrepreneurs should do well with the upper tier, but not with the lower tier. Although women play a vital role in sport management, especially in information/service sector positions, there is question whether women will ever receive true equity.

Social concerns

When considering future directions, one cannot overlook the social concerns of society. This is especially true of sport, for sport is a microcosm of society. Often social concerns are responded to by the legal system embodied in the courts, the legislatures (federal and state), and the executive branch (rules and regulations). Whether private or public enterprise, the sport manager and fitness director must adhere to the law in operating facilities and providing services. To know the law, to live within it, and to utilize it properly is indeed a challenge to the professional. Moreover, it is not only from the legalistic approach, but also from the ethical and humanitarian approach that one must deal with the type of society one has and desires as related to its treatment of people, as persons of dignity and deserving of a quality of living. Four aspects are briefly discussed: (1) the global arena of human equality, (2) the pathology of society, (3) human rights, but with responsibilities, and (4) environmental quality.

The global arena of human equality. Whether as part of the workforce or as a consumer of services and products, equality of persons is not only a part of human dignity owed all, but also enforceable under the U.S. Constitution, although it is recognized that one cannot legislate behaviors of people, their attitudes, and actions. The cornerstone of **human equality** is the Equal Protection Clause of the 14th Amendment of the U.S. Constitution. When one considers equality, not only must race and gender be included, but also age and disabilities. Although Title IX opened many doors for participation of girls and women in sport, especially at the high school and college levels, the same has not been true for women in the workforce, particularly female coaches and administrators (see the preceding section on the workforce). However, the road was a rocky one, with action held in abeyance during the time following a court case that restricted the application of Title IX in athletics until the Civil Rights Restoration Act of 1988 restored the original intent of the law. The impact of tough economic times in schools and community recreation on equality of opportunities in sports for boys/girls and men/women is to be watched into the 1990s. The matter of gender discrimination applies not only to females, but males have also brought legal actions regarding use of services restricted to females, such as certain health clubs. Also to be considered by management are discriminatory practices toward women in golf country clubs and private social clubs where business contacts, particularly at meals, are a primary function.

A second area of human equality is that of racial and ethnic equality. One of the ironies of society is that there are so many black athletes, but few blacks in managerial sport positions and in education positions related to physical education and sport. Northeastern University's Center for the Study of Sport in Society studied professional baseball, football, and basketball as related to progress toward a greater number of managerial jobs for minorities. In its "1990 Racial Report Card" based on this study, the Center gave the NBA an "A," the NFL a "B," Major League Baseball a "C+," and society a "D+" for improvement from the 1988 to the 1989 seasons. The high grades for sport, it was noted, were given because progress was put in perspective of society, which the Center perceived as having done very little in 1988-89 toward placing blacks in managerial positions. The study pointed out that although the U.S. population is 12% black, in the seasons most recently completed (1989), the percentage of black players was 75% in the NBA, 60% in the NFL, and 17% in Major League Baseball. While professional sports are used as a showcase, the study also warned minorities against the irrational pursuit of 10,000 to 1 odds against a high school athlete reaching the pros. However, there should be greater opportunities for minorities in the sport and fitness management career tracks.

The 14th Amendment and the Civil Rights Restoration Act also affect equality as related to age discrimination and disabilities. As for participation in sport, under the American Medical Association (AMA) guidelines, schools and organizations played the role of "protector" of athletes and curtailed their participation; however, the American Academy of Pediatrics guidelines, which replace those of the AMA, reflect both the new protective equipment available for sport and the rights of an individual to make one's own decision regarding participation. The Academy guidelines emphasize that participation is a matter of human rights to the quality of life and the right of self-determination. Accessibility of facilities and services to the disabled also is a management consideration enforceable through the courts. As for age discrimination, it is not just a matter of discrimination against older workers or services for the elderly, but discrimination against youth, especially in the workplace. There also, though, are protective laws relating especially to youth, the child labor laws.

One must constantly be aware of changing laws in respect to equality of human beings. This includes not only legislation, such as the Civil Rights Act of 1990, but also court decisions, which can have far-reaching effects on how an individual is treated, whether in the workforce or as a consumer. In the management of sport, one must abide by the law, as must persons in all enterprises and activities. It is essential that one be informed through reading newspapers and periodicals regularly.

Pathology of society. Yes, sport is a microcosm of society, and the **pathology of society** is the "darker" side of sport—drug abuse, intoxication, steroids, violence, gangs, child abuse, sexual and ethnic harassment, gambling and bribery, violation of NCAA regulations, breaking of contracts, and so on. These reach into all levels of sport from elementary school and community programs through college and the pros, and into coaches and management, as well as participants. While one can say that athletes and those who conduct sport are a cross-section of society, it also is true that these same persons are the "models" for many children and youth, and also some adults. The lifestyle of many well-known sports figures, both intercollegiate and professional, is highlighted in the media when there is an arrest for intoxication, gambling, or drug trafficking. Furthermore, one must question where society is going—and where sport

is going when sport products become objects of violence—when in the mid-1990s youth are attacking, and in some instances killing, other youth over sneakers and other sports apparel promoted by sport celebrities such as Michael Jordon of the Chicago Bulls professional basketball team. Also, social workers and child psychologists have promoted the desirability—especially for boys in a home with a female head—of companionship between a boy and an adult male, which usually includes considerable sport activity, either as participants or spectators. However, several national youth organizations concerned with such boy/adult male relationships have now established strict guidelines to protect their leadership, particularly volunteer leaders, from charges of child physical or sexual abuse. Whatever the future direction of sport and fitness management, one cannot overlook the impact of the pathology of society on sport as a business enterprise and sport as a modality of expression of quality of life. Where do professional ethics and morality fit in? The sport manager in the decade of the 1990s must know not only how to handle disruptive behaviors at sport activities and undesirable behaviors of participants, but also how to foster desirable behaviors through sport and physical activity. A number of sports celebrities have been endeavoring to work with youth, and such work is valuable, but inadequate. Extensive effort must be made by volunteers on the local community and school levels to counter undesirable behaviors with self-enhancement behaviors.

Human rights, but with responsibilities. The era of human rights began in the latter part of the 1950s and continued to accelerate in respect to all types of human rights, not just human equality related to gender, race, age, and disability, as set forth in the first section of social concerns. The human rights were extended to protection of the Constitutional rights of due process, right to just compensation for injuries, and right of privacy, among other rights. Yes, drug testing of athletes and persons in the workplace came within the rights protected. But perhaps the right that had the most impact on society, and particularly sport and recreation, was compensation for injury. Whereas private enterprise always had to pay for injury due to its negligence, public entities such as public schools, state agencies, and municipalities, were protected by governmental/sovereign immunity, although statutory provision was made for carrying insurance. Then this immunity was codified through the state tort claims acts, but still insurance was a "security blanket" for the entities. The method of obtaining financial remuneration through litigation or threat of suit was quickly found by many people, particularly the middle class, who were being pressed financially, and much litigation was instituted. At the same time, the jury awards began to escalate, endeavoring to give "just compensation" over a lifetime and reflecting inflation. In the mid-1980s insurance coverage became very expensive and in some instances not even available, and many sport and recreational activities no longer were offered or were greatly curtailed. Furthermore, one of the underlying social problems was that individuals no longer seemed to take personal responsibility for their actions or be concerned about a safe environment and participation. As one second grade student said to the physical education instructor, who had asked if she knew how to do a skill in order to demonstrate to the class, "Doesn't make any difference if I know or not, if I get hurt, I'll sue you!" Hence the title of this section, **human rights, but with responsibilities.** A 1990 Ohio Supreme Court case spoke to the individual acceptance of responsibility when participating in physical activity (in this situation the game was "kick the can") when it said that:

"We require that before a party may proceed with a cause of action involving injury resulting from a recreational or sports activity, reckless or intentional conduct must exist. We hold that where individuals engage in recreational or sports activities, they assume the ordinary risks of the activity and cannot recover for any injury unless it can be shown the other participant's actions were either reckless or intentional."

Many of the social concerns in the previous section on the pathology of society, too, are rooted in the lack of individuals taking responsibility for their own actions and their own lives. Some would say also that the failure to assume such responsibility is because individuals do not have self-esteem, a quality self-image, or a direction for life. Sport has long prided itself in what it can do for

the physical and emotional development of the person, toward peak experiences, toward fulfillment of self—but how much of this really is only "wishful thinking" as society turns into the decade of the 1990s? By failure of individuals to take responsibility, certain rights of individuals also are being denied, sometimes because of the fear of litigation and large awards and sometimes because those in management just do not want to deal with such behaviors. Have the business-oriented sport enterprises been too busy making money, too busy managing a facility, to be concerned about the quality of human life? A headline in the *New York Times* sports section in June 1990 was "A Time for Everyone to Take Responsibility." Perhaps those going into sport and fitness management need to think more carefully and fully about what it means to have rights without responsibilities in contrast to rights with responsibilities, and how they can have an impact on the morals of society and the quality of life in general.

Environmental quality. **Environmental quality** is one of society's primary concerns, and it has many dimensions, many of which interrelate with sport and fitness. Air pollution has a direct impact on the health of individuals and where one can exercise safely. Jogging on roadways in areas of considerable vehicle and industrial air pollution can, indeed, be hazardous to one's health, rather than beneficial. The disposal of solid waste from sporting events and cities in general is an increasing problem in the decade of the 1990s. The manufacture of sporting and fitness equipment may not only relate to renewable resources, but also to pollution of the environment by release of various gases and particles into the air, and can be international in concern, such as acid rain from the United States falling in Canada. The aesthetics and quality of a facility, especially a large outdoor facility, have an impact on the environment, including large paved parking areas. Population size and distribution also are of concern, that is, the ability of the environment to sustain such. The quantity and quality of water available to service the population is another environmental concern. These are only a few of the environmental quality ramifications; there are many more, and the person in sport and fitness management should be cognizant of and responsive to environmental impacts.

CONCEPT CHECK

Sport is a microcosm of society and as such has its problems. Social concerns include the global arena of human equality and the pathology of society, such as intoxication and drugs. All persons have human rights, but sport should be conducted with individual responsibilities. Environmental quality also is a factor as related to sport events and physical activity.

THE INDUSTRY

The sport and fitness industry is multi-faceted, and no single set of future directions projections can be set forth. In this part, considerations for future directions include four areas of commentary: (1) economics, (2) facility management, (3) program services, and (4) management aspects. Personnel is not specifically a subsection; Chapter 2 deals with careers. There are considerable differences between private-sector establishments, primarily commercial for-profit, such as fitness clubs and health spas, ski resorts, professional sports, and public-sector athletic and sport events, and programs and services of the schools and municipal recreation. It is projected into the 1990s that the public sector will of necessity have to utilize more management and financial strategies of the commercial enterprises and that the private for-profit sector because of societal concerns will have to give more consideration to what is happening to people from a behavioral perspective, as the public sector does. Thus professional preparation will have a more common core, regardless of whether one wishes to be associated with the public or private sector.

Economics

The decade of the 1980s was one of change, growth, and profits. Comparatively within the industry, the dollars have increased dramatically into the billions, with professional athlete salaries and television revenues leading the way in sport. However, in comparison with other industries, the dollars do not seem that great. However, one also can see the potential economic growth. For example, McDonald's, as a single fast food entity, was projected to generate $60 billion in business in 1990,

with a $1 billion marketing budget. The National Sporting Goods Association (NSGA) reported in 1989 that sports equipment, footwear, and apparel expenditures were $36 billion; and, in 1990 the NSGA indicated an increase to $44.3 billion, with much of the increase tied to the sale of athletic footwear. A study done for *The Sporting News* by the WEFA Group research firm stated that sports generated $63.1 billion in output and services in 1988. The largest contributors were participatory sports ($22.7 billion) and sporting goods ($19 billion). In 1988 the Seattle Mariners sold for $78 million, but Busch Entertainment Corporation paid $1.1 billion for HBJ's six theme parks at the end of 1989. CBS paid more than $1 billion for the NCAA basketball tournament rights over 7 years, but Philip Morris alone spent about $1.9 billion in advertising, while General Motors spent about $1.8 billion. The WEFA study also reported that from 1987 to 1988 the overall sports industry growth was 7.5%, whereas growth in the U.S. Gross National Product (GNP) was about 7.9%. As for pro athlete salaries in 1990, such as the approximately $15 million over several years for Jose Canseco of the Oakland Athletics, athletes have been stating that sport constitutes a form of entertainment, and therefore they should receive pay comparable to that of other entertainment celebrities in pop music, television, and movies. It should be noted that boxers for a single fight at the world title level have long been receiving millions, for example, the $15 million and $8 million guarantees in December 1989 to Leonard and Duran, respectively. And, as one projects into the 1990s for both professional sports and intercollegiate athletics, one must not forget cable television and the $1 billion television contract of the NCAA with CBS over 7 years for its basketball tournament.

But, for all the big dollars in professional and intercollegiate sports, it almost is like the "haves" and "have nots." The coffers of the school athletic programs and the community/amateur sports programs are, indeed, meager, notwithstanding the NCAA's efforts in distributing its television revenues to include in its plan an allocation to schools in lower-echelon conferences that traditionally fare poorly in the national playoff tournaments, and the 1984 Olympic Games (Los Angeles), which provided funds generously to youth sports in Southern California and the amateur sport associations from the profits of the Games. And, furthermore, it must be realized by personnel in sport management, whatever type of position is held, these big dollars do not normally translate into high salaries for them. In fact, although there is a surplus of entry-level jobs, with attendant low salaries, the career-ladder of sport management is not lucrative. (See Chapter 2 on careers.)

Corporate sponsorship is a facet of financing that may have a considerable impact on the future directions of sport and fitness. One must distinguish between corporate sponsorship and advertising, that is, providing support dollars to an event or program in contrast to taking advertising airtime during a sporting event. The per minute advertising rates are very high for national sport events, and the image of sport is a factor in determining who advertises. For example, seldom is a beer, liquor, or tobacco ad seen during these events, notwithstanding the Virginia Slims sponsorship of women's tennis. In 1990 several advertisers, including IBM, American Honda Company, and Toyota Motor Corporation, withdrew their ads from the Professional Golf Association (PGA) Championship at Shoal Creek Country Club because of the Club's exclusionary membership policy. There is some evidence that in the 1990s there will be a great deal more corporate sponsorship of events or programs. There already are the television/media events, such as golf and tennis tournaments and the intercollegiate football bowl games, that at the turn of the decade have incorporated the name of the corporate sponsor in the name of the event, such as the Mazda Championship, Buick Open, and Lipton's International Players Championship in golf; Thriftway ATP and GTE Hardcourt tennis tournaments; the Poulan-Weed Eater Independence Bowl, Sunkist Fiesta Bowl, Mobil Cotton Bowl, and John Hancock Bowl in football; and the Danskin Women's Triathlon Series. The "official Olympic sponsor" concept first introduced in the 1984 Olympic Games in Los Angeles has been used considerably not only for such Olympic activities but also for sponsorship of local community events. In 1990 it was estimated that $2 billion was spent by corporations to have their names associated with athletic events. When a corporation attaches its name to an event, it usually also buys one third to one fourth of the advertising time; also,

corporations contribute generously to the prize money, such as most of the $50 million in prize money for the PGA Tour, Senior PGA Tour, and Ladies PGA Tour. Special Events Report listed the largest corporate budgets for sports in 1990 as Phillip Morris Companies ($78 million), Anheuser-Busch ($60 million), RJR Nabisco ($48 million), General Motors ($25 million), Procter & Gamble ($20 million), Coca-Cola ($20 million), Eastman Kodak ($16 million), AT&T ($16 million), Chrysler Motors ($15 million), and Visa ($15 million). The "bottom line" is corporate image; how the corporation and its products can be positively perceived by the public via sports. However, there are those who project that sport has reached a plateau in corporate sponsorship, and that corporate sponsorship dollars will turn to the cultural arts. This is partly because of the image of sports, that is, the association of athletes with drug use, sexual misconduct and violence. Corporate support of the arts in the late 1980s did indeed increase greatly; for example, in 1985 the National Gallery of Art received $2.7 million from corporations, but in 1988 it received $6.3 million. Similarly, in 1978-1979 corporate support for the Lincoln Center was $4.5 million, and 10 years later it was $12.2 million. *Megatrends 2000* reported that in the last 3 years of the decade of the 1980s, expenditures for attending arts events was greater than sports attendance expenditures, with $3.7 billion and $2.8 billion spent, respectively, in 1988. In the 5 years between 1983 and 1987, arts spending increased 21%, while sports expenditures decreased 2%. This is a reversal; 20 years ago people spent twice as much on sports as on the arts. Megabucks paid by corporations for national and international sporting events, especially those on television in the 1990s could well depend on the ability of professional and intercollegiate sports to again depict a wholesome image; however, corporate sponsorship of local and regional special sport events may not have such a problem, and such events could well be attractive to corporations. (See special events management in the following section on facility management.)

Facility management

Facility management, in its broadest sense, is one of the growth areas in sport management careers in the 1990s. (See Chapter 2 on careers.) However, the focus of this chapter is on future directions, that is, some considerations related to the nature of facility management as part of the sport and fitness industry in the decade of the 1990s. There will be even greater emphasis on public and private cooperative financing, of which the City of Indianapolis is one of the best examples on a large scale, and on quality, maintenance-free construction materials. However, future directions of the management of facilities projects more than business operations and maintenance. The focus appears to be directed toward **facility versatility** in terms of drawing new markets. This includes both provision of amenities and **facility flexibility** to accommodate diverse special events. According to Roper, the pollster, the 1990s will bring a "culture of convenience." Sport and facility management tends to cater to the affluent because of economic expediency. People want time-saving and convenient services that are accessible from the parking lot and for the physically disabled or frail; aesthetically pleasing in decor, interior design, and furnishings; comfortable with plentiful and well-designed restrooms; and without "hassles" to obtain food, tickets, or care for children or persons that take extra consideration. Although traditional foods at sporting events continue to be provided, the additional availability of health foods and gourmet fare will enhance attendance. It will be common practice to make available certain amenities with the consumer paying for services received. However, accommodating the less affluent sport enthusiast should not be overlooked. In other words, there must be services on a financial scale to provide for individuals of many different economic levels. For people to return, the participants must have had a good experience related to the accommodations or amenities provided by the facility, in addition to the activity in which they were engaged, whether participatory or spectator.

The facility of the 1990s must be flexible; the one-purpose arena may have a very difficult time financially. Multiple use must extend beyond sport events and might include concerts, the circus, and trade shows or exhibits. Management must work with the city in which the facility is located and corporations to enhance the image of both through special events. Special events management is a specialized aspect of management and one that takes a great deal of "entrepreneurship," whether the facility is publicly or privately owned. Special events management involves a singular event usually with corporate sponsorship and special promotion to the general public.

Program services

The decade of the 1990s will be not only a "culture of convenience," as indicated in the last section, but also an era of "primacy of the consumer." Sport and fitness participation is not a matter of time, but lifestyle, fashion, and social status. There will be intense and high-pressure marketing in the competition for time among the many opportunities available to individuals, whether in sport and fitness, the cultural arts, volunteer activities, or environmentally-related involvements. Hence, there will need to be more customized marketing of products and services. Individuals will be purchasing *experiences,* rather than products or services per se. The experience comprises the entire environmental milieu—the interrelationships among people involved, including participants and service personnel, the nature of the services, products, and amenities being provided, and the physical environment in which the experience takes place. The activity is important, but will no longer be the determinant of return visits or retention of membership. There will be a more integrated mind-body approach. Although there are at the turn of the decade sport psychologists, and the Association for Advancement of Applied Sport Psychology (AAASP) has set forth criteria for "certified consultant," this is not primarily what is meant. The integrated mind-body approach is more the interrelationship of mind and body as related to physical and psychological well-being. This is an area of expertise with which most managers of sport and fitness enterprises are not familiar; yet, it is projected that in the 1990s mind-body integration will be a most important element in programming, including an educational component for participants. This developing emphasis related to services is partially in response to the high-pressure, stressful society in which people live, but perhaps more because of the need of people to have a higher quality personal life. People must feel "good" about themselves and the experience they are having, both physically and emotionally. Each person must feel comfortable within oneself. The concept of "well-being" is one that extends throughout life. To "sell" this concept of experience, the "communication" to individuals will be more intensive and invasive through television, VCRs, and computers. Further, in marketing, one must distinguish sport, the entertainment industry, and sport and fitness for individual participation and enhancement, although both come within the concept of "experiences." Similarly, whether the target population is the local community or the external community, or both, must be determined; that is, whether one seeks participants primarily from the immediate local area or whether one desires to market to the greater regional area, or even the state or nation. Marketing strategy also must consider whether the target population is to one of expansion from present constituency; that is, seek additional constituent groups, or whether there is to be penetration into the present constituency, that is, luring a higher percentage into participation. The nature of potential consumers has been discussed in a previous section on demographic characteristics.

There must be a multi-service emphasis, particulary in fitness and racquet clubs—the single-purpose clubs are losing out. To standardize programs and services is going backwards—clubs must keep changing because participants become bored with the same old routine, whether it is a fitness routine or a sport. There must be both variations and diversification. For example, to maintain only traditional fitness equipment will not retain club members; there must be variation with continual updating with new types of equipment and different forms of activity through which fitness can be obtained, such as outing pursuits (for example, bicycling, hiking, and water sports). Outing pursuits are "excursions" away from the fitness building/room and give variety both through the activity being away from a building or a running track or jogging path and through the form of activity. Yes, there always will be some basic pieces of equipment and running tracks and jogging paths, but in the 1990s there will be greater expectation by participants to feel that they are being serviced with the newest in technological developments and fitness training methods. This is the age of biotechnology and medical advances, as well as the age of information systems, and not only must personnel keep-up-to-date but also the educational program within a club must communi-

cate new health information. The communication of information should utilize the latest in technology, including computers, VCRs, and television. The importance of this educational thrust requires clubs to have someone on staff who is knowledgeable about adult education. There also will be greater career opportunities with companies who develop such educational materials and processes. These will be with both private non-profit and commercial enterprises and public entities.

To survive the decade of the 1990s, the fitness club or health spa of the 1980s must become much broader in its approach, not just fitness through exercise. In many ways, the "fitness boom" of the 1980s seemed driven by a compulsiveness toward fitness, which was often social-status controlled. Already at the turn of the decade, one sees clubs responding to some of the "ills" of the fitness "craze" through extending services into sport medicine, and also there are private sports medicine clinics. However, sports medicine tends to deal more in treatment and rehabilitation than in prevention of injury. In the 1990s there will be even greater career opportunities in sport medicine, both in the community sports programs and local school system athletic programs, as well as with intercollegiate and professional sports. Particularly, opportunities will be developing in the professional individual sports, such as tennis and golf. At the turn of the decade, there already are limited "fitness vans" on the pro golf tour, providing a physical therapist and athletic trainer services, as well as making available to the athlete certain types of fitness equipment. The financial requirements will limit certain services to community participants, but in general it will be considered good management to provide sport medicine services. Fitness will be subsumed as only a facet of a larger focus on human wellness and well-being in the decade of the 1990s, with the overriding concern for the quality of life and with pride in "being" and "doing" for the intrinsic values therein. This direction already is seen, especially in some corporate fitness programs, which have included nutrition, stress management, and smoking cessation. Employees should be given an opportunity to change their lifestyles and improve their overall health.

The importance of exercise, however, should not be minimized. A 1990 report from the Centers for Disease Control points out the vital role of exercise as related to heart disease, in contrast to the usually listed "risk factors." There are contradictions in the data regarding the effectiveness of corporate fitness programs in reducing health care costs to the corporation; however, there is little question as to the viability of a wellness program as a fringe benefit to employees. Large corporations can provide their own programs and services; however, small companies have neither the financial resources nor the facility space to provide a special wellness program for their employees. Thus there is and will continue to be considerable opportunity for those persons interested in providing such services to smaller businesses and industries. These services might be through a private club, the schools, or a non-profit organization, such as the YMCA. Although the foregoing has focused upon the fitness club, similar projections are made for racquet clubs—they must become more all purpose with variations and diversification of services to survivie in the 1990s. Furthermore, all clubs must consider participant comments regarding desired amenities.

Just as wellness programs will be an important fringe benefit in companies, so will sport and fitness (wellness) services be an important adjunct in leisure retirement communities, day care for children and the elderly (see the section on society for the need for such day care), and hospitality settings (motels/hotels, resorts), as a contributor toward enhanced quality living. The essentialness of such services should be obvious as related to leisure retirement communities. The utilization of hospitality settings for meetings with diverse purposes has given rise to the career opportunity of "meeting planner." An occupational title, "meeting and convention manager," appears in the government directory of occupational titles. And, there is a national organization, *Meeting Planners Int'l*, which at the turn of the decade had nearly 10,000 members, and a plan for "certified meeting professional." There are a number of approaches to providing sport and fitness services as hospitality settings, in addition to offering such to the regular transient clientele. There is the "working vacation" promoting business and pleasure, alleging that there is more productivity in meetings when in an atmosphere that challenges and invigorates the participants through sport and other fitness-related ac-

tivities. Golf and outdoor activities, especially, are an integral element. These are individual "sports" in a "team" atmosphere. Hospitality facilities, of course, must be expanded to accommodate small group sessions along with expedited and quality services. People do not like to be hassled or wait when it is time to "recreate"! Some people have referred to these working vacations as "executive leisure," but one should not overlook organization conferences and special working meetings for task forces. Usually very good combination rates can be given for food and lodging when in the "off-season," both during the week and on the weekend, and the sport and fitness services can be utilized more efficiently when these groups come in for meetings. Another approach is that of special occasion packages or special event promotion.

Management aspects

There are several aspects to management that must be addressed when one is talking about future directions, including information management systems, risk management, and government and association controls. As indicated in the section on society, as society moves toward the twenty-first century, it is, indeed, the age of information. No, not just or primarily computers—computers are only a tool, a technological technique to facilitate the management of information systems. In addition to the storing and retrieving of information, one must have capability of utilizing information. It is not too difficult to employ someone with "computer skills," but the premium characteristic is the capability of processing and utilizing the information, both in office records and general operations and in servicing the clientele. (See chapter on computer applications.)

At the turn of the decade, the term "risk management" has become popular, and in the decade of the 1990s it will become essential to operations of sport and fitness enterprises. Risk management encompasses more than legal liability for personal bodily injury. It is both a system for financial risk management and operational management to reduce both the severity and frequency of potential loss. Risk management touches every aspect of an operation. One particular concern, which probably will escalate in the 1990s before management can cope (and it may not be able to cope until societal behaviors change), is that of crime and vandalism.

Such not only destroys physical assets of buildings and areas, but also, and more important, disturb the peace of mind of potential and current participants. This deters many from engaging in activity, whether participatory or spectator (for example, jogging alone in a wooded area, along a roadway, or in a park).

The third management aspect is that of external controls for sport and fitness enterprises by both government and controlling associations. As the dollars get bigger and the "stakes" higher, human behaviors also have a tendency to lose ethical control or discipline. With the projection of sport, especially, being big business in the decade of the 1990s, (as indicated in the section on economics), it also is projected that there will be more and more governmental and association controls, and the attendant enforcement cadre of people. Furthermore, society as a whole has certain characteristics regarding social behavior (see section on society), which also will mean greater legal constraints in the 1990s. Although there are indications that sport organizations are endeavoring to "reform" certain practices, the internal reform movement will not satisfy the public in general and the legislators will respond, but probably not adequately. The courts also will be a factor in "molding" human behaviors.

CONCEPT CHECK

The sport and fitness industry is multi-faceted. On the one hand, there is considerable funding available for professional and some intercollegiate sports. On the other hand, meager funding is available for most schools and nonprofit organizations. Corporate sponsorship will be a factor in obtaining funding both to support sport at the megabucks level of television and to underwrite local sport events. Both facility management and program services must become more flexible and multi-purpose, if each is to be financially profitable and to maintain constituency.

THE PROFESSION

The success of any profession is related not only to the needs of society, but also, and perhaps more important, the perception of society. That is, the degree to which that particular service requires the *special* expertise needed to meet these needs. This is partially dependent on the excellence of those who serve the field who consider themselves ed-

ucated in the field of sport management and part of the profession, in contrast to others who are not. Those who are concerned with quality of service through excellence of educational preparation seek to professionalize the field. There are criteria for an occupation to be considered a profession. Those considered herein are (1) self-disciplining and ethics, (2) professional associations and certification, (3) professional preparation, and (4) research. A profession should have uniqueness. Sport management has a real problem—because it came out of physical education in many academic institutions and was borne from necessity of falling enrollments in physical education. It became a non-teaching option (no teaching certificate) within physical education, but often the courses were not appropriately changed to meet the needs of non-teaching careers in sport management. However, there is another consideration as related to uniqueness—a good number of curriculums—in endeavoring to distinguish themselves from physical education—have swung far toward business, so that one must question whether the curriculums really are diluted business programs with some sport, or perhaps sport with a good number of business courses. As a unique profession, the criteria for an educational program should meet the specific needs of the profession. (See subsequent section on professional preparation.)

Self-disciplining and ethics

Most professions have their own self-disciplining of members via a code of ethics. Sport management does not have this aspect of a profession well established, although at the turn of the decade, the North American Society for Sport Management (NASSM) has developed a code. Ethical considerations is an important element for all who are in the field of sport management. All sport managers are faced with decisions that may lead to uncertain consequences—the consequences may be favorable to some persons and unfavorable to others. Responsible managers at all stages of their careers need to be equipped to think about and resolve those dilemmas in an ethical way (see Chapter 21 for further discussion of ethics).

Professional associations and certification

A mark of a profession is the formal organization of members into an association. The North American Society for Sport Management (NASSM) and the National Association for Sport and Physical Education's (NASPE) Task Force on Sport Management were organized by educators to service primarily the academicians in the profession, especially those who are affiliated with university and college sport management programs. (See Chapter 1 for further discussion of these associations.) The sport management field is diverse, as indicated in Chapter 2 on careers, and each of the different types of career opportunities has its own organization, for example, the various fitness and aerobic dance organizations, public relations, athletic directors, sport information, marketing, personnel. There is, however, no organization that endeavors to encompass the entire field of sport management for practitioners.

Although active membership in a professional association is an important indicator of professionalism, accreditation of academic programs and certification and licensure of professionals are usual approaches by which the quality of the profession is controlled and enhanced.

Accreditation. **Accreditation** is directed toward college and university programs of study, and is a process whereby the various elements of the program, including the curriculum, faculty, facilities, support resources, admission standards, and placement are evaluated against standards set forth by the profession. Those institutions that meet the required standard then are said to have an "accredited program."

There are more then 100 accrediting agencies for the many professions. To control the proliferation of such agencies and give greater credibility to accrediting agencies, especially on college and university campuses, the Council on Postsecondary Accreditation (COPA) was organized in 1975, essentially by college and university presidents. There are two accrediting bodies for fields related to sport management recognized by COPA— physical education through the National Council for Accreditation of Teacher Education (NCATE) and recreation through the National Council on Accreditation (NCA) established jointly by the American Alliance for Health, Physical Education, Recreation, and Dance (AAHPERD) and the National Recreation and Park Association (NRPA).

To become a COPA-approved accredited body is a long and difficult process. The first step is for the profession to develop its own guidelines for programs of study, and then conduct its own in-

stitutional evaluations, giving recognition to those institutions that meet the stated standards. Sport management is in the first phase of this process at the turn into the 1990s. NASPE and NASSM are working cooperatively in developing professional accreditation standards for sport management. This work is particularly important because of the proliferation of sport management programs in colleges and universities, many of which are of very poor quality. A student should be aware of whether one's program of study meets standards set forth by the profession.

Certification and licensure. **Whereas** accreditation is focused on the program of study at a college or university, certification and licensure are credentials related to the individual professional. Certification usually is a function of a professional organization, and licensure is a governmental function of the state.

There are many, many different certifications related to the sport management field. An organization or professional association will set forth minimum competencies that must be met to obtain the certificate. The two best known certifications in the general sport management field are granted by the American College of Sports Medicine (ACSM) for the health and fitness professional and by the National Athletic Trainers' Association (NATA) for athletic trainers. ACSM has two separate tracks, one in preventive health and fitness and one in rehabilitative health and fitness. Each track has three levels of certification, with competencies at each level. In the preventive health and fitness track, the three levels are exercise leader/aerobics, health/fitness instructor, and health/fitness director. In the rehabilitative track, competencies have been developed for the exercise test technologist, the exercise specialist, and the program director levels. The certifications of both organizations frequently are required for positions in related programs.

There are many other certifications, especially for aerobics, and one must ascertain the quality of the organization offering the certification as well as the nature of the competencies required. Many are lacking in substance, and one should beware of them.

Licensure is a method by which government controls persons authorized to practice a given profession or trade and is granted to an individual. Licensure is usually established in field where the consumer is "at risk" if the service rendered is not done at a high level. For example, medical doctors, dentists, lawyers, beauticians, barbers, and many other professions and trades are licensed by the state. Usually a person has to take an examination in order to be licensed, and the license is valid to practice only in the state issuing the license.

There are few states that require licenses for any of the sport management fields. A few states do require licensing of athletic trainers. This should be distinguished from certification by NATA. NATA certification is valid nationally.

The terminology related to teachers is confusing. They must be authorized by the state, however the teachers' authorization is referred to as a teacher's certificate, rather than a teacher's license, although criteria are set by the state and the program is administered by the state.

Licenses, of course, are required in order to practice in a state; however, in cases in which there is professional certification it is very desirable to obtain such certification and for administrators to require it as a protection in regard to hiring competent personnel.

Professional preparation—academic base

A defined program of study, usually accredited, is the basis of a profession. However, there are several dimensions to the academic base. Social and industrial directions suggest that sport managers need to know something about the following:

1. Societal values—of life, family, education, spirituality, profit, power and control
2. The changing world—the ability to understand and project the consequences of changes in the world occurring at the turn of the decade; the intellectual challenge involved in defining culture, sovereignty, democracy, human rights, capitalistic system, and political economics; cultural diversity and bilingual capability; insights and critical analysis of the changing society and industry.
3. Demographic analysis and trend analysis; psychographics—understanding needs and wants of particular groups, economic and utility values, discretionary income, influence of distribution of demographic characteristics.
4. Critical thinking—key to educational reform with focus of education shifting from learning to thinking; thinking skills are those mental op-

erations that are used to solve problems, the process; also logical reasoning or rationale thinking as a tool for making moral and ethical decisions; integrated thinking.

Second, there are certain principles related to professional educational preparation that are essential for quality programs. Programs must not be only applied; there must be a theoretical base and such theory then must be applied. (See Chapter 3 for further discussion.) Such a base will help educate students as scholars in the body of knowledge unique to sport management. Although sport management may draw from a number of disciplines, the uniqueness is in the organization and approach used. It is essential that one remembers that an institution cannot graduate a completely prepared professional; however, a basic education that provides the foundation for further professional skill development can be provided. The educational base must not be too narrow, because most persons change occupations two or three times in their lives, and change positions seven, eight, or more times. The educational program must provide a foundation that gives flexibility in the future. As part of this foundation, the basic skills of reading, written and oral communication, and ability to use math can not be overemphasized.

There are two additional educational dimensions that are factors in professional success. There is considerable evidence that there is a competitive edge in the clear thinking of executives who have a personal wellness priority. Professional education should include some background related to healthy lifestyle and understanding of the human body. The other dimension of success is that of "tough-minded optimism." Individuals need to believe in themselves and their future, but not to believe that life is easy. One must work to create the future. There should be high expectation for oneself and a respect for excellence within a moral framework. With the foregoing foundation, a professional can build the operational skills through in-service education and on-the-job training. All professionals should be involved in "lifelong learning" and continuing education.

Third, essential to professional preparation is quality faculty. A real concern at the turn of the decade is the critical shortage of faculty holding a doctorate qualified to teach in the sport management curriculum. Those persons who are in the industry usually do not hold a doctorate, and if they do, they often either are making so much money that academe cannot lure them to an educational institution or they do not desire the academic environment and its demands, particularly research required for tenure. Although it is desirable for individuals to have experience in the industry before returning for graduate work (masters or doctorate), it is not believed essential that established persons in the field are required for instruction. It is instead thought that there should be a partnership between the field and academe in terms of guest lecturers, symposia, workshops, research projects, field trips, and especially practica and internships. Often, from a quality teaching perspective, it is better to obtain a familiarity with a variety of operations through this partnership than for faculty members to have only one or two personal experiences in limited settings to which they continually refer or place their teaching in reference. Further, the nature of the position in academe is quite different from the industry itself, and so an excellent practitioner may not make a good faculty member, and vice versa.

Fourth is the formal curriculum for educational preparation of sport management personnel at both the undergraduate and graduate levels. (See Chapter 1 for further discussion.)

Research

Research is one of the essential criteria for a profession. There must be contributions to the body of knowledge of the field. The *Journal of Sport Management* sponsored by NASSM, is the only journal specific to sport management research; however, there are many other periodicals that accept articles on research in sport management for publication. Most of these relate to the diverse fields mentioned in the section on professional associations.

Two types of research should be distinguished—**operational** and **basic/applied.** The basic tools and techniques of operational research, including statistics and interpretation of data, are essential for all students to obtain at the undergraduate level, because they will be used immediately in any position obtained in sport management. The basics in marketing require such ability, as do many other operational tasks. Operational research should be more than the gathering of demographic and other statistics; it also should encompass aspects of psychographics as related to

attitudes and psychological variables. However, in most higher education institutions, operational research does not bring academic recognition as being scholarly and in some institutions might not be considered very highly for tenure. However, faculty not only must know operational research and work with the field on applications and projects, but also must engage in basic/applied research to contribute toward the basic knowledge of the sport management field. For example, faculty might research different types of techniques to conduct operational research, the most effective procedures and methods for obtaining data, or different methods of analysis in order to assess more accurately the meaning of data. Sport management faculty must do more than surveys of the status of the field—they must contribute to the theoretical aspects of this profession. (See Chapter 3 for further discussion.)

CONCEPT CHECK

Accreditation, certification, and licensure are three different approaches by which a profession monitors and exerts influence on those institutions that prepare professionals. A defined program of study (usually accredited) is the basis of a profession. Since it is imperative that there is continuous contribution to the body of knowledge of a field, research is an essential criterion for a profession.

What is the future direction of the profession?

The society in which sport management functions is indeed complex in its impact on sport management, and the industry itself is very diverse in nature and scope; therefore the future of the profession rests not in unity, but in affiliation with the respective fields of the particular career orientation. For example, a person in the career orientation of marketing would affiliate with the professional associations and journals related to marketing. There will be no time of greater unity in sport management than in undergraduate and graduate programs within universities. The quality of these programs will determine whether students will be hired on graduation. Only those students of high quality will survive. In considering future directions, one should separate those opportunities in the commercial enterprise field and those in schools, municipalities, and nonprofit private organizations. The future of the first is, indeed, bright for the enterprising entrepreneur; there always seems to be room for innovative businesses. The future for middle-level management is good for those who have quality performance, but when difficult economic times come, often these persons are expendable. Further, the lower-level positions are certainly low paying and in many ways filled with "expendable" personnel, that is, young people seeking a job in the field who will take low pay to get an opportunity. Unfortunately, these types of positions have no career ladder but are plentiful. The future of those persons interested in public and private nonprofit entities is solely dependent on the funding available and the priorities given to sport and physical activity not only by these organizations, but also by the public constituency. For the sake of a quality society, these positions should be available, but what is best for society is not always what is done! As for the future in universities and colleges, unless faculty can be obtained who have the interest and capability to produce basic research, sport management curricula in research universities will not survive but will be centered in non-research institutions. Although criteria for a profession have not been met to date, this does not mean that those in the field and in academic institutions cannot perform as professionals of excellence.

REVIEW QUESTIONS AND ISSUES

1. What is a trend? What are the determinants? Distinguish structural and cyclic trends.
2. What are the demographic forces that influence directions? Illustrate such influence in several aspects of sport management.
3. In the workplace, what is the nature of positions in the information and service sectors? What is the role of women? What does this mean regarding sport management?
4. Watch the papers carefully regarding areas of social concern related to sport management. What are the current trends? Discuss.
5. What are the types of corporate sponsorship of sport? Discuss the nature and potential of these types.
6. In what way is facility management changing? Discuss such areas of change as flexibility in facility utilization, multi-programming, and requirement of amenities.
7. Discuss the concept of "experiences for participants" in contrast to providing activities or services.
8. What makes a profession? Does sport management meet the criteria? Why?

SUGGESTED READINGS

Because of the nature of this chapter, no references are given for further readings on the topic, that is, readings that would give additional depth information specifically related to sport management. A number of the professional periodicals within the industry published special articles at the turn of the decade (December 1989 and January 1990); these would be interesting retrospective discussion as to what various individuals foresaw for the specific aspects of the field and what seems to be happening.

However, for one to do what is suggested in this chapter, be aware of the changing society in its various dimensions, it is essential that current sources be utilized. There are two primary sources—newspapers, such as the *New York Times* and the *Wall Street Journal,* and weekly/monthly magazines, such as news, business, and political magazines. It is important to get a variety of perspectives or views, because most publications represent a particular belief or approach, such as conservative or liberal. In addition, *The Futurist,* the periodical of the World Future Society, has articles regarding future directions; also the Society issues an annotated bibliographical publication regarding publications or articles focusing on the future in a wide variety of fields. Seldom will sport management itself ever be referenced; however one must be very alert to happenings in all dimensions of society.

As a class assignment it is recommended that *at the beginning of the term* a brief discussion be held on important factors in society and that students be divided to read pertinent newspapers and magazines. Throughout the term, then, there could be a reporting on what items had been found. After more thorough discussion of Chapter 22, the students could write a brief essay regarding the interrelationship of sport management and society.

Index